# Sisson's
# WORD and
# EXPRESSION
# LOCATER

### Second Edition

## A.F. Sisson
### revised by Barbara Ann Kipfer, Ph.D.

**PRENTICE HALL**
Englewood Cliffs, New Jersey 07632

Prentice-Hall International (UK) Limited, *London*
Prentice-Hall of Australia Pty. Limited, *Sydney*
Prentice-Hall Canada, Inc., *Toronto*
Prentice-Hall Hispanoamericana, S.A., *Mexico*
Prentice-Hall of India Private Limited, *New Delhi*
Prentice-Hall of Japan, Inc., *Tokyo*
Simon & Schuster Asia Pte., Ltd., *Singapore*
Editora Prentice-Hall do Brasil, Ltda., *Rio de Janeiro*

© 1994 *by*
PRENTICE-HALL, Inc.
Englewood Cliffs, N.J.

10  9  8  7  6  5  4  3  2  1

**Library of Congress Cataloging-in-Publication Data**

Sisson, A. F. (Albert Franklin)
  Sisson's word and expression locater / by A. F. Sisson—2nd ed.
  revised by Barbara Ann Kipfer.
    p.  cm.
  Includes index.
  ISBN 0–13–814088–X   ISBN 0–13–814096–0 (pbk.)
  1. English language—Glossaries, vocabularies, etc.   2. English
language—Terms and phrases.   3. Figures of speech.   4. Vocabulary.
I. Kipfer, Barbara Ann.  II. Title.
PE1689.S5   1994
423'.1—dc20                                          94–12091
                                                         CIP

ISBN 0-13-814088-X (Case)
ISBN 0-13-814096-0 (Paper)

**PRENTICE HALL**
**BUSINESS & PROFESSIONAL DIVISION**
A division of Simon & Schuster
Englewood Cliffs, NJ 07632

**Printed in the United States of America**

# Contents

# Acknowledgments

The editor believes that the strength of Dr. Sisson's original manuscript has been greatly enhanced in this revision. His basic entries were a great starting point and much has been done to make them even fuller and more interesting.

Highest respect and admiration must be expressed for Dr. A.F. Sisson, who toiled for eight years to compile a remarkable reference book. Dr. Sisson held many degrees and was an attorney with the United States federal government for more than 25 years. He published many other works, including *Sisson's Synonyms* (An Unabridged Synonym and Related-Terms Locater) and *The Unabridged Crossword Puzzle Dictionary*. His thoroughness and scholarship made it a joy to work with his material in preparing this new edition.

The editor would like to thank Ellen Schneid Coleman of Paramount Publishing, who sought to make this great reference book "come alive" again.

Thanks also to Dr. Frank W. Tompa, head of the University of Waterloo (Canada) computer science department, for his programming assistance in preparing the manuscript.

The editor would also like to express deep gratitude to her family—Paul Kyle, and Keir—for their support and loving kindness.

# Introduction

*Sisson's Word and Expression Locater* was the first attempt to provide the public with a book that takes them from a concept or "meaning" to a word or expression. This valuable reference has inspired other "reverse" dictionaries and books that help users find the words they need to describe what they want to say.

*Sisson's Word and Expression Locater* is an essential companion to every general dictionary, offering a single manageable source for words we've somehow lost or those that are sitting on the tips of our tongues and, occasionally, to those we never knew.

The addition of an index to *Sisson's Word and Expression Locater* serves a twofold purpose. First, its inclusion helped eliminate the interruption created by cross-references that once dotted the text and, second, it added another mode of access to the vocabulary. But the index is not *required* for lookups—because the entry words are logical and clear—merely an enhancement that offers the user another avenue to seek out probable choices.

There are other major and minor improvements that accompany this change, but none obscure the impressive accomplishment of Dr. Sisson's eight years of toil. His conception of a "dictionary in reverse" nearly 30 years ago was ahead of its time.

In the new *Sisson's Word and Expression Locater*, users will find a world of language from which they can expand their vocabulary and become more accurate and articulate speakers, readers, writers, and word puzzle/game players.

*Sisson's Word and Expression Locater* is a type of thesaurus, containing a complete list of entry words with useful inflections and derivatives for each entry and the more important synonyms or related words for each.

Dr. Sisson described the first edition as, "in some respects, a dictionary in reverse. Instead of supplying the meaning of a word, it furnishes the word from its meaning." The book's comprehensiveness is easily seen by flipping through the pages.

The original *Sisson's Word and Expression Locater* was intended as "an index to the unabridged dictionary and to other sources of the more obscure and unusual words and phrases" which Dr. Sisson believed were still useful in English construction. Dr. Sisson's "dictionary in reverse," however, is so well-conceived that it would be a shame not to keep it up to date with words and expressions that are current and useful, combined with various other words that are slightly more unusual.

The book was and is intended for the person who may need to locate a

**v**

word or expression simply from an idea. For example, you may wish to know a word meaning "lack of ability," but you would be unlikely to find it just by looking in a dictionary. These words (incapacitation, incompetence) cannot be found under **ABILITY** in any other word book, but they can in this volume. Perhaps you would like to locate the word for figuring time by tree rings. In this book, under **TREE** is the subheading *time,* under which you will find the answer "dendrochronology." That word can also be found under **TIME** and its subheading *tree ring.*

*Sisson's Word and Expression Locater* enables you not only to locate, from the thought involved, a word or expression (usual or unusual), but also helps call to mind a word or phrase that may have been temporarily forgotten. It is thus a locater, an aid to memory, and an aid to vocabulary enhancement.

One of the greatest, and, we believe, most helpful changes effected in this new edition of *Sisson's Word and Expression Locater* is a combining of separate entries like *injurious* and *injury; cook, cooked,* and *cooking;* and *produce, produced, product,* and *productive* into single, complete entries. Besides making *Sisson's Word and Expression Locater* easier to consult and to browse through, this unification has made it possible to correct inconsistencies and duplications and allow more room for new, updated words and expressions.

A second major change in *Sisson's Word and Expression Locater* is the incorporation of new material and the deletion of the more obscure words and expressions under the entries. The subheadings have been simplified and modernized. In the previous edition, many subheadings were multi-word descriptions. In this edition we sought to reduce the subheadings to one- or two-word descriptors, both to make them more user-friendly and to allow more room for the words and expressions themselves.

The addition of an index is another major change; one that provides a second mode of access to the body of text. It could be considered the biggest step toward making this renowned reference book even more useful. Divided among 10 broad categories, the main entry words fall within a simple-to-use hierarchy. This hierarchy of the vocabulary is included to allow the users to search for words and expressions in more than one fashion. The groupings are offered to stimulate the path of thought into expression by mirroring the way humans group ideas and concepts in their minds.

Other changes are less obvious. The earlier edition placed semicolons between the words within an entry. The semicolons have been replaced with less obtrusive commas.

Also, the previous edition generously used cross-references which are distracting to the eye and to readability. In this revision, the cross-references are included as synonyms or related words within the entries. For example, instead of ATTRIBUTE: (see "characteristic") as in the first edition, the current book includes "characteristic" as one of the words under the entry for ATTRIBUTE. Many of the words that received only cross-references in the earlier book, now have a full list of words and expressions. The purpose of all these changes is to make it easier to find the right word or expression for one's idea.

# What This Book Will Do for You

*Sisson's Word and Expression Locater* has been prepared for those who seek to express their thoughts precisely and effectively, and who desire a resource that will help them in their work, studies, or leisure activities. Business executives, advertising copywriters, authors, journalists, teachers, editors, critics, linguists, and others who prepare literature and texts will find among the synonyms and related terms a wellspring of variable choices to overcome the bromidic and stereotypical words and expressions so often encountered. Their writing and speaking may become more exciting, meaningful, and original.

This volume will be of invaluable assistance to college and high-school students in the preparation of term papers, theses, and other writings, or as a vocabulary builder. Any educated person who wishes to enhance his or her vocabulary, or to locate a word or expression that has escaped memory, will find this book useful.

Many ordinary synonyms and related words and expressions are not included, nor is the book loaded with scientific or technical terms. Only those scientific and technical terms with some general application are listed. In this way, as in many other respects, *Sisson's Word and Expression Locater* differs from all other and previous thesauri, word finders, and other books dealing with vocabulary.

Students and businesspeople today face extremely fierce competition in their quests to excel. Communication—the ability to convey facts and ideas—has become an increasingly important component of success in the information age. Words are the most important tool available. *Sisson's Word and Expression Locater* provides an arsenal of such tools, removing barriers to full comprehension and effective expression. Supplementing the book's value as a word finder and a vocabulary builder is its entertainment value: some of the more obscure terms in the text are included for pure fun.

Although *Sisson's Word and Expression Locater* contains scores of bizarre, amusing, and startling words and phrases, it is much more than an entertaining compendium of peculiarities. It is a practical reference filled with concepts and ideas that people have trouble naming—mainly elegant and precise, yet less frequently used, words. It is a revision of a book which for decades has helped users resolve the "tip of the tongue" syndrome.

For those who have an idea, concept, or definition but do not know, cannot remember, or are uncertain of the word—*Sisson's Word and Expression Locater* is a creativity and idea generator, entertainment, inspiration, a vocabulary builder, word puzzle and game help, and a word/name/place finder. It is a writing and speaking aid for browsers, businesspeople, consumers, crossword puzzlers and word-game players, students, trivia buffs, and wordsmiths.

*Sisson's Word and Expression Locater* is set up the way most people think, speak, and write, and, therefore, not only provides synonyms—it offers subheadings of related words, an index by categories, and emphasizes words of foreign derivation by italicizing them. You cannot locate a word or expression in a dictionary unless you have a reasonable idea of the spelling of the word—which is extremely unlikely if you are not certain exactly which word you are looking for to begin with. That's where this amazing reference helps—because it is a "dictionary in reverse." You supply the meaning or idea, and *Sisson's Word and Expression Locater* furnishes the words and expressions that fit that meaning.

# How to Use Sisson's Word and Expression Locater

In *Sisson's Word and Expression Locater*, you will find the entry words arranged in traditional alphabetical or "dictionary" style. Sample entry words are ABANDON, ABASH, ABBREVIATE, ABDOMEN, ABERRATION, ABET, ABHORRENCE, ABILITY, ABJECT, and ABNORMAL.

But you are not restricted to this one method of lookup. The index contains a hierarchy of ten broad categories under which the entry words are grouped.

The list of categories used to group the entry words is: (1) actions and events; (2) business; (3) feelings and communication; (4) ideas, ideals, and values; (5) measurements; (6) people and the social world; (7) space, form, and placement; (8) structures, materials, and parts; (9) the living world; and (10) transport, movement, and transfer.

So, the entry words mentioned above would be in the index under these categories:

Actions and Events
abbreviate
abet

Feelings and Communication
abash
aberration
abhorrence
abject

Ideas, Ideals, and Values
ability
abnormal

Living World
abdomen

People and the Social World
abandon

*Sisson's Word and Expression Locater* is enriched by directing users to the broad categories in the index, which appear in alphabetical order, as do the entry words under them. By offering this way of both gathering and classifying the entry words, *Sisson's Word and Expression Locater* organizes the entry-words in a way that mirrors the way we "classify" and "connect" vocabulary in our brains. The index allows users to enhance their prose from another perspective and to think more about the relationships between the words and expressions.

When an initial alphabetical search does not yield adequate results, the index provides users with an alternative point of entry. By restricting the index to ten broad categories, the editor attempted to reduce the possibility of misunderstanding the classification scheme. The index is intended as a research and creative tool.

The alphabetical format works very well in most instances, but the index greatly enhances the book's value by offering a second mode of access—another way to get to the word or expression you want. Users can peruse all the entries under People and the Social World to get started in a search or use it as a spur to inspiration. The index of *Sisson's Word and Expression Locater* is as simple to use as the book itself.

*Barbara Ann Kipfer, Ph.D.*

# Abbreviations and Symbols

Each entry word is divided by parts of speech: (a) adjectives (and adverbs), (n) nouns, and (v) verbs. Subheadings of the entry words appear in italics. For example, *great* and *lack* are subheadings indexed under ABILITY, with words and expressions provided for each.

INDEX GROUPINGS

*actions and events*
*business*
*feelings and communication*
*ideas, ideals, and values*
*the living world*
*measurements*
*people and the social world*
*space, form, and placement*
*structures, materials, and parts*
*transport, movement, and transfer*

## ABANDON

**a:** abandoned, alone, apostate, apostatic, bereft, comfortless, derelict, renunciative, renunciatory

**n:** abandonment, abdication, abjuration, apostasy, defection, recantation, relinquishment, renunciation, waiver

**v:** abdicate, abjure, abscond, apostatize, defect, desert, forgo, forsake, jettison, recant, reject, relinquish, renounce, repudiate, surcease, surrender

*child:* foundling

## ABASH

**n:** abashment, discomposure, embarrassment, humiliation, mortification, shame

**v:** awe, chagrin, confound, confuse, cow, daunt, discomfit, discompose, disconcert, humble, humiliate, mortify, shame

## ABBREVIATE

**a:** abridged, brief, condensed, contracted, cryptic, cut, diminished, short, shortened, simplified, truncated

**n:** abbreviation, abridgement, abstract, acronym, condensation, initialism, letterword, logogram, logograph, *precis*, reduction, *schema*, shortening, summary, synopsis

**v:** abridge, clip, compress, concentrate, condense, curtail, diminish, elide, epitomize, pack, reduce, shorten, shrink, simplify, slash, squeeze, syncopate, synopsize, truncate

## ABDOMEN

**a:** abdominous, alvine, celiac, coeliac, intestinal, splanchnic, ventral, ventripotent, visceral

**n:** belly, breadbasket, middle, paunch, pleon, tharm, venter

*contents:* viscera, viscus

*pain:* colic, gastralgia

## ABERRATION

**a:** aberrant, erratic

**n:** anomaly, change, deviation, error, failure, hallucination, lapse, mania, phobia, warpage

## ABET

**a:** adjuvant, aiding, ancillary, contributory, subsidiary

**n:** abetment, adjuvancy, assistance, boost, encouragement, endorsement, fostering, furtherance, help, incitement, promotion, sanction, support

**v:** advance, advocate, aid, assist, back, boost, countenance, egg on, encourage, espouse, foment, foster, further, hasten, incite, instigate, promote, sanction, subscribe, subsidize, succor, uphold

## ABHORRENCE

**a:** abhorrent, abject, contemptible, contemptuous, disgusting, dislikable, execrable, foul, loathsome, nasty, nauseating, odious, offensive, reprehensible, repulsive, revolting, vile

**n:** abomination, antagonism, antipathy, *bete noire*, execration, hate, hatred, horror, odium, repulsion

**v:** abhor, condemn, curse, damn, denounce, disapprove, execrate, hate, loathe, reject, revile, spurn

## ABILITY

**a:** able, adept, adroit, capable, clever, competent, dextrous, dynamic, endowed, expert, ingenious, knowledgeable, practiced, proficient, qualified, skillful, smart, tested, trained, versatile, versed

1

**n:** adroitness, ambidexterity, aptitude, attainment, caliber, capability, capacity, competence, dexterity, *dynamis*, dynamism, endowment, faculty, ingenuity, panurgy, proficiency, talent, versatility

> *great:* acumen, endowment, expertise, gift, virtuosity

> *lack:* incapacitation, incompetence

## ABJECT

**a:** base, contemptible, degraded, despicable, dispirited, downtrodden, groveling, helpless, hopeless, ignoble, low, mean, miserable, sad, vile, wretched

## ABNORMAL

**a:** aberrant, adventitious, anomalistic, anomalous, atypical, bizarre, eccentric, exceptional, extraordinary, heteroclite, heterodox, idiosyncratic, pathological, phenomenal, preternatural, unconventional

**n:** aberration, abnormality, anomalism, anomaly, atypical, deviant, deviate, foible, heterodox(y), idiosyncrasy, imperfection, macula, mutation, phenomenality, phenomenon, prodigy, *rara avis*, stigma

> *combining forms:* dys-, -osis, para-, terat-, terato-

## ABODE

**a:** domiciliary

**n:** address, aerie, caravansary, castle, domicile, dwelling, estate, habitat, habitation, hearth, hearthstone, house, igloo, ingleside, inn, location, lodging, nest, quarters, residence, xenodochium

## ABOLISH

**n:** abolishment, annihilation, cancellation, countermand, disestablishment, murder, obliteration, ostracism, overthrow, recision, repeal, supersedence, termination, undoing

**v:** abrogate, annihilate, deracinate, destroy, disestablish, dissolve, eliminate, eradicate, expunge, exterminate, extirpate, get rid of, invalidate, ostracize, revoke, scratch, terminate, vitiate, void

## ABOMINABLE

**a:** accursed, detestable, distasteful, Godawful, hateful, loathsome

**n:** abhorrence, abomination, antipathy, aversion, detestation, disgust, distaste, execration, hate, hatred, horror, iniquity, loathing, snowman, wickedness

**v:** abhor, abominate, detest, hate, loathe

## ABOUT

**n:** *volte-face*

> *prep:* abroad, almost, anent, approximate, apropos, apropos of, around, circa, circiter, close, concerning, encircling, *in re*, near, nearly, *re*, round, some, throughout

## ABOVE

**a:** aloft, atop, celestial, exalted, heavenly, high, higher, overhead, skyward, superadjacent, superior, supernal, *supra*, surmounting, surpassing, *ubi supra*, ultra, up, upon, *ut supra*

**n:** *par excellence*, paramount

## ABRADE

**a:** abradant, abraded, abrasive, chafed, eaten, eroded, filed, flat, frayed, grazed, irritate, raw, roughened, rubbed, scraped, scratched, skinned, smooth, worn

**n:** abrasion, abrasive, attrition, chafing, corundum, emery, erosion, friction, gnawing, grinding, pumice, roughness, rub, sandpaper, scrape, scratch, sore, weakening, wear

**v:** anger, annoy, chafe, eat, irritate, revile, rub, scrape, scratch, skin, wear

## ABREAST

**a:** knowing, tied, up-to-date

## ABRUPT

**a:** brusque, curt, gruff, impetuous, instantaneous, precipitant, precipitate, precipitous, rude, sharp, staccato, subitaneous, terse, tumultuous, unceremonious, violent

**n:** abruptness, brusqueness, brusquerie, expedition, gruffness, haste, impetuosity, impulsivity, instantaneity, precipitancy, quickness, rapidness, suddenness, swiftness

## ABSENCE

**a:** absentaneous, abstracted, AWOL, distrait, distraught, *durante absentia,* elsewhere, gone, *in absentia,* inattentive, left, missing, nonexistent, oblivious, off, preoccupied, vacant, void, withdrawn

**n:** abiosis, *absence d'esprit,* absent-mindedness, absentee, abstraction, anarchy, awol, dream, French leave, heedlessness, leave, negation, preoccupation, privation, reverie, truant, vacancy, vacuum, void

## ABSOLUTE

**a:** arbitrary, arrant, authentic, authoritative, autocratic, categorical, despotic, exhaustive, imprescriptible, inalienable, inclusive, indubitable, invincible, out-and-out, plenary, plenipotentiary, *pur et simple,* rank, sweeping, thoroughgoing, tyrannic, tyrannical, unadulterated, unalienable, unequivocal, unmitigated, unqualified, unquestionable, wholehearted

**n:** concretum, positiveness, positivity, totality, unconditionality

> *rule:* autarchy, autocracy, benevolent control, despot, despotism, monopolization, possession, totalitarianism, *tyrannis,* tyranny

## ABSORB

**a:** absorbent, assimilative, assimilatory, bibulous, imbibitional, monopolistic, osmotic, porous

**n:** absorption, assimilation, bibulosity, consumption, inhibition, incorporation, metabolism, monopolization, osmosis

**v:** assimilate, consume, engulf, imbibe, incorporate, ingest, metabolize, monopolize, osmose

> *opposite:* adsorption

## ABSTRACT

**a:** abstruse, acroamatic, esoteric, figurative, hermetical, *in abstracta,* inconcrete, incorporeal, metaphysical, nebulous, nomothetic, recondite, stratospherical,

supernatural, theoretical, transcendental

**n:** abbreviature, abridgement, abstraction, abstractum, abstrusity, architectronic, capsulation, compendium, conspectus, epitome, immateriality, incorporeality, incorporeity, nebulosity, precis, resume, subsistent, summary, syllabus, synopsis, transcendentality

**v:** abbreviate, abridge, condense, epitomize, extract, purloin, remove

> *mental:* brown study, cogitation, dream, lucubration, preoccupation, reverie, trance, withdrawal

## ABSTRUSE

**a:** abstract, arcane, cabalistic, complex, cryptical, dark, deep, difficult, epoptic, esoteric, hard, inaccessible, inscrutable, intricate, involved, metaphysical, mysterious, mystic, nebulous, obscure, profound, remote, secret, stratospheric, subtle, tangled, unknown

**n:** abstrusity, immateriality, incorporeality, incorporeity, nebulosity, profundity

## ABSURD

**a:** *ad absurdo, ad absurdum,* apagogical, asinine, baroque, bizarre, chimerical, daedalic, egregious, fantastic, fatuous, funny, grotesque, impracticable, inane, infeasible, insuperable, laputan, ludicrous, macaronic, paradox, preposterous, *reductio ad absurdum,* ridiculous, unbelievable, unrealistic

**n:** absurdity, apagoge, asininity, betise, caricature, charade, coquecigrue, farce, inanity, incredibility, irrationality, maggotry, *non sequitur,* ridiculosity, travesty

## ABUNDANCE

**a:** abounding, abundant, affluent, ample, copious, cornucopian, feracious, inexhaustible, lavish, lush, luxuriant, opulent, plenteous, plentitudinous, plethoric, profuse, prolific, replete, teeming

**n:** affluence, amplitude, copiosity, copiousness, cornucopia, excess, luxuriance, magnitude, opulence, plentitude, plenty, pleonasm, plethora, prodigality, profusion, repletion, satiety, sumptuosity

> *combining form:* -ulent

## ABUSE

**a:** abusive, captious, castigatory, censorious, clamorous, condemnatory, contemptuous, contumelious, cuatic, defamatory, despicable, disparaging, malign, opprobrious, reproachful, sarcastic, sardonic

**n:** abusiveness, calumny, castigation, condemnation, contumely, defamation, excoriation, execration, humiliation, infamy, maltreatment, objurgation, obloquy, sassiness, villification, vituperation

**v:** blaspheme, censure, damage, defame, derogate, desecrate, disparage, ill-use, impute, injure, malign, maltreat, oppress, persecute, punish, rail, revile, scathe, scold, traduce, victimize, vituperate

> *loud and abusive:* scurrilous, thersitical

## ACADEMIC

**a:** collegiate, conjectural, didactic, doctrinaire, hypothetical, interdisciplinary, learned, lettered, literary, pedantic, Platonic, postulatory, professorial, scholarly, scholastic, speculative, suppositional, theoretical

**n:** academe, academia, academician, academy, colloquium, ivory tower, scholasm, school, seminar, teacher

## ACCENT

**a:** guttural, tonic

**n:** brogue, cadence, dialect, emphasis, ictus, inflection, intensification, intonation, mark, oxytone, pulsation, rhythm, sound, stress, tempo, tone

**v:** accentuate, emphasize, enhance, highlight, increase, insist, intensify, intone, mark, press, sharpen, stress, underscore

> *marks:* acute, circumflex, dieresis, grave, tilde, umlaut

## ACCEPT

**a:** acceptable, accepted, according to Hoyle, canonical, *comme il faut*, conformable, conventional, ethical, orthodox, palatable, prevalent, sanctioned, traditional, valid

**n:** acceptance, acceptation, accession, canonicity, canons, convenances, conventions, credence, endorsement, Hobson's choice, norm, nostrification, orthodoxy, proprieties, sanction, standards

**v:** abide by, acede to, acquiesce in, comply with, nostrificate, pass muster, reconcile

## ACCESS

**a:** accessible, available, open, ready

**n:** approach, avenue, channel, corridor, entree, entry, freedom, liberty, pass, passage, passageway, path, postern, road, route, street, use, way

## ACCESSORY

**a:** additional, auxiliary, complementary, incidental, subsidiary, succenturiate

**n:** accomplice, addendum, adjunct, appurtenance, auxiliary, buddy, coadjutor, collaborator, colleague, complementary, confederate, confrere, crony, incidental, parergon, satellite, subordinate, tool

## ACCIDENT

**a:** accidental, adventitious, aleatory, contingent, extraneous, fortuitous, haphazard, inadvertent, incidental, involuntary, serendipitous, unintentional, unpremeditated, unwitting

**n:** accidentality, act of God, calamity, casualty, *casus fortuitus*, catastrophe, contingency, contretemps, crash, curse, *damnum fatale*, disaster, extraneity, fatality, *force majeure*, fortuity, hazard, hitch, holocaust, inadvertence, inadvertency, incident, misadventure, mischance, mishap, serendipity, sorrow, tribulation, trouble, unluck, vicissitudes, *vis major*

## ACCLAIM

**a:** applaud, approve, cheer, clap, extol, glorify, hail, honor, laud, plaudit, praise, revere, root, shout

**n:** acclamation, approval, cheer, cry, eclat, fame, glory, homage, honor, kudos, laudation, plaudit, praise, reverence, shout

**ACCLIMINATE**

**n:** acclimatization, adaptation

**v:** acclimatize, accustom, acquaint, adjust, conform, discipline, enure, familiarize, habituate, indoctrinate, inure, prepare, season, steel, tolerate, toughen, train

**ACCOMPANIMENT**

**a:** *a capella*, accompanied, accompanying, adventitious, associated, at same time, attended, circumstantial, concomitant, incidental, secondary

**n:** agreement, background, chaperon, circumstantiality, collaboration, complement, concomitance, concomitant, convoy, corollary, guard, melody, obligato, protection, support

**v:** add, associate, attend, chaperon, collaborate, concur, convey, convoy, escort, foster, guard, guide, heed, join, lead, pilot, protect, shepherd, squire, steer, support, tend, usher

**ACCOMPLISH**

**a:** attained, discharged, done, efficient, established, executive, expert, finished, fulfilled, gained, implementary, implemented, managed, mastered, performed, produced, reached, realized, successful

**n:** accomplishment, achievement, actuality, actualization, consummation, effectuation, entelechy, *fait accompli*, fulfullment, implementation, metier, realization, talent, *tour de force*

**v:** actualize, complete, conclude, consummate, dispatch, effectuate, enact, end, execute, finish, fulfill, implement, invoke, make, master, perpetrate, realize, satisfy, secure, succeed, win

**ACCORD**

**a:** agreeing, concordant, consentaneous, consentient, consonant, en rapport, harmonious, unanimous

**n:** affinity, agreement, assonance, balance, coherence, compatibility, concert, concord, concordance, congruity, consentience, consonance, coordination, correspondence, euphony, harmony, unanimity, unity

**v:** accede, adapt, adjust, agree, allow, approve, bestow, conform, coordinate, correspond, give, grant, harmonize, prepare, reconcile, render, tolerate, unite

**ACCORDING**

> *to custom: ad usum, comme il faut, ex more*
>
> *to rule:* ad amussim, ad usum, consuetudinary, conventional, *de regle, de rigueur, en regle, selon les regles*, traditional

**ACCUMULATE**

**a:** accumulatable, accumulated, accumulative, acquired, augmentative, cumulative, pyramidal

**n:** accrescence, accretion, accrual, accumulation, acervation, acquirement, agglutination, aggregation, assemblage, cache, congeries, conglomeration, gain, harvest, increase, pool, pyramid, superfetation

**v:** accresce, accrete, accrue, acquire, add, agglomerate, agglutinate, amass, attain, cache, cluster, collect, conglomerate, gain, garner, gather, get, harvest, hoard, increase, lay up, mass, muster, pyramid, reap, stack, stock, store, win

**ACCURATE**

**a:** authentic, authoritative, authorized, correct, *de rigueur*, definitive, indisputable, orthodox, precise, reliable, sincere, true, trustworthy, unquestionable, veracious, verified, word-for-word

**n:** accuracy, authenticity, correctness, decorum, definitude, exactitude, fidelity, literality, meticulousness, precision, rigor, stickler, strictness, truth, truthfulness, validity, veracity

**ACCURSED**

**a:** abominable, bad, deplorable, detestable, execrable, inimical, loathsome, maledictive, maledictory, malefic, revolting, unbearable, vile, wicked, wretched

## ACCUSE

**a:** accusatory, accused, blameworthy, censurable, guilty, imputable, incriminative, inculpative, inculpatory, peccable, recriminative, recriminatory, reprehensible, reprovable

**n:** accusant, accusation, accuser, aspersion, betrayer, calumny, denunciator, imputation, incriminator, indictor, informer, plaintiff, prosecutor, recrimination, *touche*, traitor, traitoress

**v:** accost, arraign, challenge, criminate, denounce, impeach, indict, invoke, point, repudiate, reveal, tax, tell

## ACCUSTOM

**a:** acclimatized, accustomed, attuned, customary, habituated, inured, wont

**n:** acclimation, acclimatization, habituation, inurement, orientation

**v:** acclimate, acclimatize, acquaint, adapt, adjust, adopt, conform, discipline, educate, familiarize, habituate, harden, indoctrinate, inure, naturalize, orientate, prepare, season, teach, train

## ACID

**a:** acescent, acidiferous, acidulated, acidulent, acidulous, acrimonious, amphiprotic, astringent, caustic, corrosive, penetrating, photeric, trenchant, vinegary

**n:** acerbity, acidification, acidity, acor, acrimony, alkahest, causticity, corrosive, litmus paper, mordant, pH test, phenolphthalein

**v:** acidify

> *types:* acetic, amino, ascorbic, bile, carbolic, citric, conjugate, deoxyribonucleic, fatty, folic, formic, hydrochloric, hydrocyanic, lactic, linoleic, malic, metenoic, mineral, monobasic, nitric, nitrohydrochloric, pangamic, para-aminobenzoic, polyunsaturated fatty, prussic, ribonucleic, salicyclic, sulfuric, tannic, tartaric, uric

## ACME

**a:** climacteric, climactic, greatest

**n:** apex, apogee, cap, capstone, climacteric, climacterium, climax, consummation, culmination, end, epi, excellence, heyday, meridian, *nec plus ultra*, pinnacle, sublimity, ultimate, vertex, zenith

## ACQUAINTED

**a:** *au courant, au fait,* cognizant, conversant, familiar, familiarized, informed, known, related, schooled, versant, versed

**n:** acquaintance, associate, awareness, cognizance, conversance, conversancy, experience, familiarity, friend, intimacy, personal knowledge, relationship

**v:** acquaint, apprise, educate, familiarize, inform, introduce, notify, school, teach, tell, train

## ACQUITTAL

**a:** absolutory, justificatory, vindicatory

**n:** absolution, amnesty, clearance, conciliation, deliverance, discharge, emancipation, exculpation, excuse, exoneration, forgiveness, freedom, justification, pardon, release, vindication

**v:** absolve, acquit, annul, clear, condone, defend, discharge, disregard, emancipate, exculpate, excuse, exempt, exonerate, forget, forgive, free, pardon, release, sanction, vindicate

## ACRIMONY

**n:** acerbity, acridity, asperity, causticity, irascibility, malevolence, virulence

## ACT

**a:** *in actu, in flagrante delicto,* in the act, red-handed

**n:** action, adventure, amenity, *casus fortuitus,* civility, convenance, course, effort, exploit, *force majeure,* geste, gyration, mien, move, performance, play, propriety, step, urbanity, *vis major,* work

**v:** comport, conduct, do, drive, execute, function, labor, move, officiate, operate, play, produce, toil, try, wield, work

> *illegal:* crime, felony, malefaction, malfeasance, misdemeanor, murder

## ACTING

**a:** affected, dramatic, histrionic, melodramatic, operatic, pretending, showy, substitutionary, surrogate, theatrical, thespian, tragicomic, ultracrepidarian, vicarious

**n:** cabotinage, footlights, histrionic, *locum tenems*, theatricality

> *combining forms:* -fax, -fex, -ician, -ist, -or, pro-, -trix

## ACTION

**n:** accomplishment, achievement, actification, activity, advancement, *alarums and excursions*, charade, *coup*, deportment, discipline, execution, hyperkinesia, incentive, inducement, initiative, labor, liveliness, maneuver, mechanics, motivation, play, plot, power, practice, proceeding, process, production, sprightliness, stimulus, suit, tempest, thrust, vivacity, vortex, work

> *out of action:* emerited, emeritus, inactive, retired, superannuated

## ACTIVE

**a:** agile, animated, athletic, bold, busy, diligent, driving, dynamic, employed, energetic, engage, engrossed, enterprising, enthusiastic, expeditious, flourishing, hardworking, impetuous, indefatigable, industrious, intense, intent, keen, kinetic, lively, mobile, nimble, operose, peppy, perky, persevering, ready, sedulous, spirited, sprite, vigilant, vivacious

> *inactive:* dormant, extinct, latent, passive

> *very:* frenetic, hectic, hyperactive, hyperkinetic, manic

## ACTOR/ACTRESS

**n:** barnstormer, deuteragonist, *dramatis persona*, extra, facient, ham, histrion, ingenue, mime, mummer, participant, premiere, protagonist, soubrette, supernumerary, thespian, tragedian, tragedienne, tritagonist, trouper, understudy

> *related words:* catchword, curtain call, debut, monologue, soliloquy, typecast

## ACTUAL

**a:** authentic, concrete, *de facto*, definitive, existent, indisputable, legitimate, literal, material, objective, official, positive, present, real, right, substantial, sure, true, unadulterated, veritable

**n:** actuality, authenticity, being, certainty, certitude, circumstance, concretum, data, datum, entelechy, entity, essence, evidence, existence, *factum est, fait accompli*, grounds, manifestation, materiality, objectivity, occurrence, proof, reality, status, substantivity, truth, validity, veritability, verity, way

**v:** hypostatize

## ACUTE

**a:** critical, crucial, discerning, exigent, extreme, immediate, lancinating, penetrating, penetrative, piercing, poignant, pointed, sensitive, severe, sharp, shrill, trenchant, trying, urgent, weighty

**n:** acumen, acuteness, criticality, cruciality, danger, exigency, extremity, urgency

## ADAGE

**a:** aphoristic, apothegmatical, bromidic

**n:** aphorism, apothegm, axiom, *bon mot*, bromide, byword, catchword, dictum, epithet, maxim, moto, phrase, precept, proverb, saw, saying, truism, wisecrack, witticism

## ADAPT

**a:** adaptable, adjusting, amenable, flexible, labile, malleable, plastic, pliable, teachable, tractable, variable, versatile

**n:** adaptation, adjustment, conformation, habituation, inurement, lability, orientation, *rifacimento*, temporization

**v:** acclimate, acclimatize, accommodate, accustom, arrange, assimilate, conform, familiarize, habituate, harmonize, naturalize, orientate, reconcile, temporize, transcribe

## ADD

**a:** added, additional, adjunct, adscititious, adventitious, cumulative, extraneous, extrinsic, incidental, incremental, supplementary

**n:** accessory, accrescence, accretion, addendum, additional, adjunct, afterthought, agglutination, annex, appendage, appendix, *au reste*, augmentation, codicil, pleonasm, postscript, rider, superimposition, supplement, tautology

**v:** add, addend, affix, aggrandize, annex, augment, boost, complement, compound, elaborate, enhance, extend, grow, inflate, intensify, introduce, magnify, protract, subjoin, suffix, superimpose, widen

## ADDICT

**a:** addicted, captive, hooked

**n:** buff, dependence, devotee, enthusiast, fan, fiend, habituate, habitue, house, user, zealot

**v:** crave, habituate, incline, indulge, surrender, use

## ADDRESS

**a:** addressable, addressing, apostrophic, salutational, salutatory

**n:** adroitness, bearing, deportment, dexterity, ingenuity

**v:** apostrophize, dedicate

*mail:* general delivery, *poste restante*

*speech or writing:* allocution, apostrophe, dedication, salutation

## ADEQUATE

**a:** commensurate, competent, condign, equivalent, mediocre, modest, sufficient

**n:** abundance, adequacy, adequation, amplitude, competence, competency, copiosity, copiousness, equivalence, modestness, modesty, plentitude, sufficiency, suitability, worthiness

## ADHERE

**a:** adhering, adhesive, agglutinative, cohesive, glutinous, mucillaginous, osculant, tenacious, viscid, viscous

**n:** accretion, adherent, agglutination, clinginess, follower, glue, gum, paste, stickiness, tenacity, viscosity

**v:** agglutinate, cohere, combine, glue, glutinate, hold, join, paste, persevere, remain, stick, unite

## ADJACENT

**a:** abutting, adjoining, beside, close, contiguous, coterminous, intermediate, juxtaposed, juxtapositional, limitrophe, nearby, neighboring, next, nigh, satellite, tangent, touching

**n:** adjacency, contiguity, contiguousness, immediacy, juxtaposition, tangency

**v:** abut, append, border, impinge, join, juxtapose, meet, touch

## ADJUNCT

**a:** accompanying, added, attached, joined, secondary, subsidiary, tangent

**n:** accessory, accompaniment, addendum, addition, additive, adjective, appanage, appendage, appurtenance, attachment, auxiliary, endowment, help, ornament, part, perquisite, subsidiary, tangency

## ADJUST

**a:** adaptable, adjustable, adjustmental, amenable, fictile, malleable, modificatory, modulatory, plastic, pliable

**n:** acclimation, acclimatization, accommodation, adaptability, adjustability, collimation, concinnity, harmonization, modulability, orientation, remedy, synchronization, voice

**v:** accommodate, acculturate, align, assimilate, collimate, concinnate, equalize, harmonize, modify, orientate, rectify, redress, regulate, remedy, resolve, synchronize, systematize, voice

## ADMIRE

**a:** admired, admiring, adulatory, commendable, complimentary, encomiastic, estimable, eulogistic, idolatric, idolatrous, laudable, laudatory, panegyrical

**n:** adoration, approbation, canonization, cynosure, deification, high esteem, idolatry, idolization, regard, veneration

**v:** adulate, apotheosize, canonize, deify, eulogize, hold in high esteem, idolize, panegyrize, revere, venerate

> *person who:* admirer, adorer, adulator, devotee, disciple, fan, follower, worshiper

## ADMIT

**n:** acceptance, acknowledgment, acquiescence, admission, allowance, concession, embracement, entree, entry, initiation, intromission, matriculation, *mea culpa, peccavi*, reception, ticket

**v:** accept, acknowledge, acquiesce, adhibit, affirm, allow, assent, cede, certify, concede, divulge, embrace, intromit, permit, surrender, take in, trust, yield

## ADO

**n:** agitation, bother, brouhaha, coil, commotion, difficulty, disturbance, excitement, fanfare, flourish, flurry, fuss, hubbub, hullabaloo, imbroglio, stir, storm, to-do, turbulence, turmoil, unrest

## ADORN

**n:** adornment, bedizenment, caparison, decoration, *drap d'or*, dress, embellishment, enrichment, fancification, garnishment, ornamentation, splendor

**v:** add, beautify, bedizen, caparison, clothe, deck, decorate, dress, embellish, endow, enrich, furbish, garnish, gild, invest, lard, ornament, refurbish, suit, trim

## ADROIT

**a:** adept, clever, dexterous, expert, finished, good, polished, ready, resourceful, shrewd, skilled, skillful, slick, smart, suave, urbane, witty

**n:** address, adroitness, artfulness, cleverness, cunning, dexterity, expertise, finesse, knack, magic, resourcefulness, *savoir-faire*, skillfulness

## ADULT/ADULTHOOD

**a:** developed, grown up, manlike, mannish, mature, matured, maturescent, of age, postpubertal, ripened, womanish

**n:** homeostasis, majority, maturation, maturescence, maturity

*rite:* bar mitzvah, bas mitzvah

## ADULTERY

**a:** extramarital

**n:** connivance, corespondent, criminal conversation, cuckold, infidelity, unfaithfulness, wittol

## ADVANCE

**a:** accelerated, advanced, deep, metastatic, precocious, progressed, senior, superior, tramontane, ultramontane, upward

**n:** advancement, aggrandizement, anabasis, ante, augmentation, breakthrough, development, encroachment, enhancement, escalation, evolution, exacerbation, gradation, graduation, incursion, infringement, inroad, overture, preferment, progression, quantum jump, quantum leap, tender, trespass

**v:** aggrandize, aggravate, augment, enhance, escalate, exacerbate, graduate, progress

> *person:* announcer, bellwether, forerunner, harbinger, herald, outrider, precursor, predecessor, reconnoiterer, scout

## ADVANTAGE

**a:** advantageous, auspicious, avail, beneficial, benignant, expedient, favorable, healthy, opportune, opportunistic, preferential, profitable, propitious, remunerative, strategic, tactical

**n:** benefit, boon, favor, head start, opportuneness, opportunity, precedence, preference, preferment, privilege, start, superiority, surplus, toehold, upper hand, whip hand, windfall

**v:** capitalize, exploit, leech, take advantage, utilize

> *one who takes advantage:* leech, opportunist, parasite, spooner

> *taken advantage of:* cat's-paw, fool, mark, patsy, stooge, stoop

## ADVENTURE

**a:** adventuresome, adventurous, bold, brash, cavalier, daring, incautious, picaresque, precarious, precipitate, quixotic, rash, risky, speculative, swashbuckling, temerarious, uncalculating, venturesome

**n:** caper, chance, *conte*, *dido*, escapade, exploit, frolic, gambade, gambado, *geste*, harlequinade, indiscretion, peccadillo, peril, ploy, prank, quest, risk, vagary

*adventurer:* picaro, picaroon, rogue

## ADVERSARY

**a:** adversarial

**n:** antagonist, competitor, disputant, doe, enemy, foil, opponent, unfriend

## ADVERSE

**a:** adversative, antagonistic, antipathetical, antipathic, antithetical, calamitous, catastrophic, counter, counteractive, critical, deplorable, derogatory, detrimental, disparaging, inimical, malevolent, mean, ominous, portentous, prejudicial, repellant, repugnant, repulsive, sinister, stubborn, tragic, unfriendly, unpropitious, untoward

**n:** adversity

## ADVERTISE

**a:** advertised, exploitative, promotional, propagandistic

**n:** advertising, ballyhoo, bill, circular, dissemination, exploitation, flier, handbill, hype, jingle, leaflet, notice, promotion, promulgation, propaganda, publicity, razzle-dazzle, razzmatazz, slogan

**v:** advocate, air, announce, bark, broadcast, bulletinize, circulate, communicate, convey, disclose, divulge, endorse, exploit, pitch, plug, proclaim, propagandize, publicize, publish, puff, sell, tout

*related:* agate line, billboard, copywriter, hard sell, Madison Avenue, subliminal advertising

## ADVICE

**a:** admonitory, advisable, advisory, consultative, consultatory, exhortative, expedient, judicious, opportune, politic, provident, prudent, recommended, salutary, seemly

**n:** adhortation, admonition, advisory, consultation, counsel, exhortation, expostulation, intelligence, monition, recommendation

**v:** admonish, advise, advocate, charge, counsel, direct, exhort, give opinion, guide, inform, instruct, notify, recommend, teach, tell, urge, warn

*adviser:* advocate, aid, aide, *amicus curiae*, attorney, counselor, doctor, Egeria, instructor, kibitzer, lawyer, leader, mentor, Nestor, preacher, preceptor, priest, professor, referee, teacher

## ADVOCATE

**n:** advocate, *advocatus diaboli*, agent, barrister, champion, counselor, exemplifier, exponent, hierophant, lawyer, paladin, paraclete, paranymph, partisan, protagonist

**v:** advertise, back, beg, champion, commend, defend, desiderate, endorse, espouse, favor, plead, plug, promote, support, urge

*advocacy:* commendation, desiration, espousal, patronage, pleading, subscription

## AFFABLE

**a:** agreeable, benign, charming, complacent, complaisant, conversable, cordial, friendly, gallant, genial, gracious, hospitable, ingratiating, kind, likable, merry, nice, open, pleasant, sociable, urbane

## AFFECTED

**a:** affectational, artificial, aureate, chichi, dainty, disposed, distingue, *effete*, genteel, high-falutin, histrionic, hypocritical, la-di-da, melodramatic, mincing, niminy-piminy, over-refined, overelegant, pedantic, pietistic, pompous, *precieuse*, *precieux*, precious, pretended, pretentious, puritanical, *recherche*, staged, susceptible, theatrical

**n:** affectation, air, artificiality, display, euphuism, grandiloquence, hypocrisy, mannerism, minauderie, pietism, pose, preciosity, pretense, pretension, sham, simulation

*combining form:* -otic

*person: poseur, poseuse, precieuse*

## AFFIRM

**a:** affirmative, affirmed, approved, certified, declarative, established, position

**n:** affirmation, asseveration, declaration, predication, ratification, validation

**v:** approve, asseverate, attest, avow, back, certify, check, claim, confirm, corroborate, declare, endorse, evidence, guarantee, justify, notarize, predicate, profess, ratify, reassure, sanction, seal, second, stamp, support, swear, testify, validate, vow, witness

## AFFLICTION

**a:** afflicted, diseased, hurt, ill, stricken

**n:** abuse, ailment, anguish, annoyance, botheration, calamity, curse, disease, disorder, epidemic, grief, handicap, hurt, illness, incapacitation, infestation, infliction, injury, nuisance, pain, plague, scourge, sickness, torment, tribulation, trouble, vexation, visitation, worry

**v:** abuse, ail, beset, bother, burden, curse, damage, gall, gnaw, grieve, hamper, handicap, harass, hurt, incapacitate, infect, infest, inflict, injure, overrun, pain, persecute, pester, plague, rack

## AFFRONT

**n:** assault, displeasure, humiliation, indignity, *infra dignitatem*, irritation, offense, provocation, slap, slight, taunt, wound

**v:** annoy, displease, humiliate, insult, irritate, offend, peeve, provoke, shame, slight, taunt, tease, vex

## AFRAID

**a:** alarmed, apprehensive, awestricken, awestruck, concerned, cowardly, dismayed, fearful, frightened, gun-shy, jittery, nervous, reluctant, scared, terrified, timid, timorous

*combining forms:* -phobe, -phobia, -phobic

## AFRESH

**a:** anew, anon, *bis, de integro, de novo,* new, newly, renewed, repeated

## AFTER

**a:** *apres,* astern, behind, below, beyond, *ex post facto,* later, next, past, *post hoc, postmortem,* posteriad, posterior, posthumous, postliminiary, residual, succeeding, subsequent, succedent

*combining forms:* epi-, post-

## AFTERNOON

**a:** *post meridiem,* postmeridian

**n:** matinee, siesta

## AGE

**a:** advanced, aet, aetat, aged, anile, antediluvian, antiquated, decrepit, distressed, gerontophilic, Nestorian, patriarchal, senescent, senior, superannuated, venerable, veteran, yellowed

**n:** aeon, anecdotage, caducity, century, dotage, eon, epoch, era, lifetime, longevity, oldness, patina, period, senectude, siecle, stage, superannuation, time, years

**v:** antiquate, develop, grow, mature, mellow, ripen, season, senesce

*50+:* quinquagenarian

*60+:* sexagenarian

*70+:* septuagenarian

*80+:* octogenarian

*90+:* nonagenarian

*100+:* centenarian

*study of:* geriatrics, gerontology, nostology

## AGENT

**a:** by proxy, *per procurantionem, per procuration*

**n:** advocate, *agent provocateur,* ambassador, assignee, bailiff, broker, coefficient, delegate, dragoman, dummy, eminence grise, emissary, facient, factor, *factotum,* fiduciary, front, intermediary, minister, ombudsman, panderer, plenipotentiary, proctor, procurer, proxy, representative, steward, syndic, trustee, vicar, vicegerent

**v:** depute

*earning:* commission

## AGGRAVATE

**a:** aggravating, annoying, exacerbating

**n:** aggravation, alarm, anger, arousal, exacerbation, exacerbescence, excitement, fever, frenzy, heat, inflammation, infuriation, provocation, stimulation, stir, vexation, worry

**v:** aggrandize, anger, annoy, arouse, enhance, exacerbate, exaggerate, exasperate, feed, heat, infuriate, intensify, irritate, madden, magnify, *pique*, provoke, raise, rankle, stimulate, stir, vex, worsen

## AGGRESSIVE

**a:** assertive, bellicose, belligerent, combative, contentious, enterprising, gladiatorial, hostile, martial, militant, provocative, pugilistic, pugnacious, self-asserting, taurine, truculent, warlike

**n:** aggrandizement, aggressiveness, belicosity, belligerency, combativeness, hostility, pugnacity, truculency

*person:* psychopath, sociopath

## AGILE

**a:** acrobatic, active, adroit, athletic, brisk, fast, graceful, light, lissome, lithe, nimble, speedy, volant

**n:** address, adeptness, adroitness, agility, athleticism, dexterity, flexibility, legerity, lissomeness, nimbleness

## AGITATED

**a:** activated, cyclonic, demoniacal, distracted, febrile, fervid, feverish, foaming, fuming, maniacal, overwrought, perturbed, seething, tumultuary

**n:** ado, agitation, chemistry, hatemongering, instigation, jacitation, jactation, perturbation, tumult, turmoil

**v:** afflict, agitate, brew, commove, disconcert, disturb, drive, evoke, excite, incite, kindle, liven, prompt, provoke, trouble, vex

*agitator:* agent provocateur, firebrand, hatemonger, hothead, hotspur, incendiary, instigator, prompter, stimulator

## AGONY

**a:** agonized, agonizing, painful

**n:** ache, angoisse, anguish, distress, excruciation, Gethsemane, grief, heartache, hell, hurt, misery, misfortune, pain, purgatory, travail, tribulation, unhappiness

**v:** agonize

## AGREE

**a:** acquiescent, affirmative, agreeable, amenable, apolaustic, appetizing, assentatious, compatible, complaisant, concordant, congruent, congruous, consentaneous, consentient, consonant, *d'accord*, dulcet, *en rapport*, halcyon, harmonious, in concert, in unison, palatable, plausible, pleasing, pursuant to, receptive, sapid, sardonic, savory, synchronous, *una voce*, unanimous

**n:** agreeability, agreeableness, amenity, compatibility, complaisance, congeniality, delectation, docility, synchronicity, synchronism, tractability, unanimity

**v:** accede, accord, acquiesce, assent, chime, coincide, comport, concur, consent, equate, harmonize, quadrate, square, subscribe, synchronize, tally, yield

## AGREEMENT

**n:** accession, accord, analogy, arbitration, assentation, assonance, communion, compact, compatibility, composition, concilliation, concord, concordance, conformity, congruity, consensus, consistency, coordination, correspondence, covenant, *entente*, *entente cordiale*, harmony, mediation, pact, rapport, treaty, unanimity

**v:** negotiate, stipulate

*related words: aide-memoire*, bilateral, bipartite, signatory, tacit

## AGRICULTURE

**a:** agrarian, agrestic, agricultural, agronomical, farming, horticultural

**n:** agronomics, agronomy, farming, geoponics, horticulture, husbandry, tillage

## AHEAD

**a:** above, accelerated, advanced, afore, ante, antecedent, anterior, avant, avant-garde, before, *ci-devant*, earlier, early, ere, former, forward, initial, leading, precedent, preceding, premature

**n:** *avant-garde*, avant-gardism, vanguard, vanguardism

## AID/AIDE

**a:** accessory, adjuvant, adminicular, aiding, approbatory, benevolent, contributory, helping, inspirational, ministrant, persuasive, propitious, serving, subsidiary, supplemental, supporting, upholding

**n:** abettor, accessory, adjuvant, adminicle, ancillary, assistant, blessing, coadjutor, cohort, contributor, facilitation, facilities, handmaid, helper, indulgence, partner, provisions, secours

**v:** abet, add, advance, assist, benefit, bolster, boost, collaborate, fortify, harbor, nourish, nurse, nurture, plug, promote, prompt, provide, serve, supplement, support

> *financial:* appurtenance, benefit, endowment, gift, goodwill, grant, indulgence, *largesse*, patronage, pledge, raise, subvention, welfare

## AIM

**a:** tendentious

**n:** ambition, aspiration, bent, cause, course, design, destination, direction, drify, end, fate, goal, grounds, ideal, incentive, intendment, philosophy, plot, purpose, significance, will, wish

**v:** aspire, desire, determine, dream, hope, intend, long, pine, plot, purpose, seek, thirst, wish, yearn

> *aimless:* capricious, chaotic, desultory, fickle, haphazard, hit-or-miss, indirect, indiscriminate, random, stray, tumultuary, unintentional, unpremeditated, unpurposed, vagrant, wandering, wild

> *aimlessness:* idleness, idling, indirection

## AIR

**a:** *a la belle etoile*, aeriferous, *al fresco*, ambient, atmogenic, hypaethral, miasmic, pneumatic, rarefied, *sub Jove*, upaithric

**n:** atmosphere, aura, breeze, demeanor, deportment, exhalation, expiration, *flatus*, heaven, miasma, mien, nimbus, minauderie, ozone, wind

> *airtight:* hermetic, hermetical, impenetrable, impervious

> *combining forms:* aer-, aero-, atmo-, pneum-, pneumato-, pneumo-

## AIRY

**a:** aerial, animated, atmospheric, blithesome, buoyant, debonair, ethereal, frolicsome, riant, sprightly, unrealistic, visionary, vivacious, zephyrean, zephyrous

**n:** aeriality, airiness, attenuation, buoyancy, ethereality, etherealness, incorporeality, sprightliness, superficiality, vivacity

## AKIN

**a:** affiliated, agnate, cognate, collateral, compatible, congeneric, consanguineous, fraternal, germane, like, near, propinquitous, related, similar, synonymic, synonymous, synpathetic

**n:** agnation, consanguinity, propinquity

## ALARM

**a:** alarming, fearful, frightful

**n:** apprehension, awe, *bete noir*, consternation, disturbance, dread, fear, fearfulness, fright, horror, misgiving, panic, peril, petrification, scare, SOS, terror, threat, tocsin, trepidation, wonder

**v:** arouse, daunt, disquiet, disturb, excite, horrify, intimidate, panic, perturb, petrify, rattle, rouse, scare, shock, startle, surprise, terrorize, threaten, unnerve, upset, warn

## ALCOHOL

**a:** abstaining, alcoholic, bacchanalian, bibulous, dipsomaniacal, drunk, drunken, intoxicating, liquorish, liquory, spiritous, vinic, vinous

**n:** *aqua vitae,* ardent spirits, ethanol, ethyl alcohol, ethyl hydroxide, gin, hard liquor, intoxicant, jigger, libation, liquor, methanol, rum, spirits, spirituosity, stimulant, vodka, whiskey

**v:** bootleg, drink, imbibe, indulge, lace, spike, tipple

*abstinence:* nephalism, nephalist, teetotaler, teetotalism, teetotalist

*alcoholic:* bacchanalian, bacchante, dipsomaniac, drunkard, oenophilist, winebibber

*alcoholism:* bibacity, bibation, bibulosity, crapulence, dependence, dipsomania, dipsophobia, ebriosity, inebriation, inebriety, insobriety, intemperance, oenophlygia, temulence, winebibbing

*related words:* breathalizer, cirrhosis, delirium tremens, prohibition, shebeen, speakeasy, tincture, victualer

**ALERT**

**a:** active, agog, Argus-eyed, aroused, attentive, conscious, eager, heads-up, heedful, keen, observant, on the lookout, on the *qui vive*, percipient, preceptive, prompt, roused, vigilant, wary, watchful

**n:** alacrity, alarm, alertness, heedfulness

**v:** arouse, scramble, waken, warn

**ALIEN**

**a:** adventitious, adverse, contradictory, estranged, external, extraneous, extrinsic, forane, foreign, impertinent, inappropriate, inconsistent, irrelevant, nonnative, unfamiliar, unsympathetic

**n:** auslander, emigre, foreigner, immigrant, invader, nonnative, nonresident, outlander, peregrine, Philistine, stranger, tramontane, ultramontane

**v:** alienate, divide

**ALIGN**

**a:** aligned, true

**n:** adjustment, alignment, arrangement, array, collimation, coordination, focus, hierarchization, plan, positioning, range, regimentation, view

**v:** adjust, allineate, arrange, array, collimate, coordinate, fix, focus, hierarchize, line, position, range, regiment, rig, set, square, straighten

**ALIKE**

**a:** akin, analogical, analogous, comparable, concordant, congruent, equal, equivalent, homogeneous, homologous, homomorphic, homonymous, parallel, similar, synonymous, uniform, unisonant, unisonous

**n:** alikeness, uniformity

**ALIVE**

**a:** active, alert, animated, awake, aware, cognizant, living, pullulant, spirited, teeming, unperished, vibrant, vital, vivacious

**ALL**

**a:** aggregate, any, complete, each, entire, every, greatest, gross, plenary, quite, sum, thorough, together, total, *toto,* unabridged, uncut, undivided, unexpurgated, whole, wholly

**n:** allness, completeness, comprehensibility, comprehensiveness, entireness, entirety, monopolization, monopoly, mutuality, omneity, omnificence, omnipotence, omnipresence, omniscience, omnitude, totality, *tout le monde,* ubiquity, unanimity, universality, wholeness

*all right:* hunky-dory, kosher, ok, okey-doke

*comprehensive:* encyclopedic, omnigenous, unabridged, universal

*creating:* omnific, omnificent

*devouring:* omniverous

*inclusive:* catholic, encyclopedic, panoptic, universal, wide-ranging

*knowing:* omniscient, pansophic

*powerful:* almighty, multipotent, omnipotent

*present:* omnipresent, ubiquitous

*seeing:* panoptic

*the more: a fortiori*

**together:** *en bloc, en masse,* unanimous

## ALLEGORY

**a:** allegorical, parabolic(al)

**n:** allegorization, apologue, emblem, fable, legend, metaphor, myth, parable, simile, similitude, symbolization, tale

**v:** allegorize

## ALLIANCE

**a:** agnate, akin, allied, analogous, ancillary, associated, coalesced, cognate, collateral, concomitant, confederated, connected, federated, grouped, inherent, joined, kindred, leagued, linked, one, parallel, related, secondary, similar, subordinated, subsidiary, tangential, united

**n:** accord, affinity, agreement, association, axis, body, coalition, confederation, consociation, consortion, consortium, *entente,* league, monopolization, monopoly, pact, treaty, understanding, union

## ALLOT

**n:** allocation, allotment, distribution

**v:** allocate, apportion, appropriate, assign, authorize, award, bestow, deal, dispose, distribute, divide, dole, earmark, give, grant, impart, mete, ordain, parcel, ration, share, slice, split

## ALLOW

**a:** allowable, allowed, authorize, *cum grano salis,* dispensable, empowered, franchised, legitimate, licensed, licit, permissive, sanctioned, stipendiary

**n:** allowance, authorization, emolument, *honorarium,* indulgence, mileage, *per diem,* permission, perquisite, sanction, *solatium,* stipend, subsistence, tolerance

**v:** accredit, acknowledge, acquiesce, authorize, certify, concede, condescend, countenance, deign, discount, empower, enable, franchise, indulge, legislate for, license, permit, sanction, suffer, tolerate, warrant

## ALLURE

**a:** *aguichant(e),* alluring, arresting, beguiling, bewitching, captivating, catching, charming, Circean, contagious, enticing, fascinating, infectious, influential, inviting, magnetic, mesmeric, persuasive, provocative, seductive, sirenic, stimulating, tantalizing, tempting

**n:** allurement, appeal, attraction, bait, beauty, blandishment, cajolement, cajolery, captivation, charm, diversion, enticement, influence, lure, magic, persuasion, power, provocation, spell, temptation

**v:** beckon, beguile, cajole, captivate, enamor, enthral, entice, fascinate, instigate, inveigle, lead, lure, mesmerize, prompt, provoke, seduce, stimulate, tantalize, tempt, thrill, transfix, win, woo

## ALLUSION

**n:** connotation, denotation, hint, indication, inference, inkling, innuendo, insinuation, intimation, reference

**v:** allude, cite, connote, denote, hint, imply, impute, indicate, insinuate, intimate, mention, point, refer, signify, suggest, touch

## ALMIGHTY

**a:** all-powerful, authoritarian, autocrat, great, heroic, multipotent, omnipotent, powerful, puissant, strong, tyrannical, tyrannous

**n:** almightiness, God, omnipotence, Pantocrator, puissance, ruler

## ALMOST

**a:** about, apparently, approaching, approximate(ly), *circa,* close, near, nearly, nigh, nominal, quasi, roughly, semi

## ALONE

**a:** aloof, cloistered, detached, exclusive, immanent, incommunicado, incomparable, individual, insulated, isolated, lonely, lorn, odd, only, *per se,* secluded, segregated, separated, sequestered, single, solitary, solo, *solus,* stag, *tout seul, toute seule,* unaccompanied, unattended, unique

**n:** autophobia, hermit, monophobia, recluse, solitudinarian *combining forms:* mon-, mono-, soli-, solo-, uni-

## ALONGSIDE

**a:** abutting, accompanied, adjacent, attingent, contiguous, juxtaposed, juxtapositioned, next to, tangent, tangential

**n:** collocation, juxtaposition

**v:** appose, collocate, juxtapose

## ALOOF

**a:** alone, cautious, circumspect, cold, cool, delitescent, detached, haughty, icy, indifferent, remote, reserved, secluded, sequestered, unapproachable, unemotional, unfriendly, unsociable, withdrawn

**n:** aloofness, delitescence, delitescency, detachment, indifference, remoteness

## ALOUD

**a:** *a haute voix*, audible, distinct, heard, oral, vocal

## ALPHABET

**a:** abecedarian, alphabetarian, alphabetical, alphabetiform, alphabetiquement, ordered, *par ordre alphabetique*, phonetic, rudimentary

**n:** abecedarius, boustrophedon, cuneiform, Cyrillic, demotics, Devanagari, futhark, Glagolitic, Greek, hieroglyphics, ideography, International Phonetic Alphabet, IPA, kana, kanji, Kufic, Linear A, Linear B, ogham, orthography, pictography, Pinyin, romaji, Roman, Rosetta stone, rudiments, runes, script, syllabary, typeface, Wade-Giles, writing system

**v:** transliterate

## ALTER

**a:** alterative, altered, emendatory, varied

**n:** alteration, conversion, deformation, deviation, diversion, emendation, metastasis, modulation, mutation, permutation, reciprocity, transfiguration, transformation, transmogrification, transmutation

**v:** castrate, change, commute, diversify, falsify, metamorphose, metastasize, modulate, spay, swerve, tamper, transfigure, transform, transmogrify, transmute

## ALTERNATIVE

**a:** alternant, oscillative, reciprocative, synalagmatic

**n:** alternant, choice, dilemma, option, preference, quandary

## ALTITUDE

**a:** altitudinous, culminant

**n:** acme, elevation, loftiness, stature

## ALTOGETHER

**a:** all, collectively, *en banc, en bloc, en masse, en toto,* entire, entirely, point-blank, quite, thorough, *tout ensemble,* unanimous, unanimously, wholly

## ALWAYS

**a:** *ab aeterno, ad infinitum,* constant, constantly, everlasting, habitually, *in adfinitum, in aeternum,* in perpetuity, *in perpetuum,* invariably, lasting, permanent, perpetually, unceasingly, uniformly

## AMATEUR

**a:** amateurish, crude, dabbling, dilettanish, elementary, green, incomplete, nonprofessional, primitive, rookie, rudimentary, undeveloped, unprofessional

**n:** apprentice, beginner, *catechumen,* dabbler, devotee, dilettante, disciple, ham, initiate, layman, learner, neophyte, novice, novitiate, proselyte, pupil, trainee, tyro, votary

## AMATIVE

**a:** affectionate, amatory, amorous, anacreontic, ardent, brotherly, doting, enamored, erotic, fervent, fervid, impassioned, indulgent, loving, overindulgent, sisterly, tender, warm

**n:** amorosity, amorousness, love

## AMAZE

**a:** alarming, amazing, astonishing, astounding, exciting, impressive, incredible, ineffable, monstrous, portentous, preposterous, prodigious, spectacular, strange, stunning, stupendous, unspeakable

n: amazement, astonishment, awe, bewilderment, confusion, consternation, dismay, paralysis, perplexity, perturbation, petrifaction, stupefaction, surprise, terror, wonder

v: affect, alarm, astonish, astound, awe, bewilder, confound, confuse, daze, dazzle, dumbfound, excite, flabbergast, frighten, impress, overwhelm, paralyze, perplex, petrify, rock, shock, surprise

## AMBIGUITY

a: ambiguous, amphibolic, amphibological, amphibolous, cabalistic, Delphic, dubious, enigmatic, equivocal, evasive, homonymous, indeterminate, obscure, paradoxical, sibylline, unintelligible, vague

n: ambivalence, amphibology, contradiction, *double entendre, double entente*, doubt, dubiosity, enigma, equivocation, paradox, polysemy, prevarication, temporizing, tergiversation, uncertainty, vagueness

phrase: amphibologism, amphibology, verbal fallacy

remove: disambiguate

## AMBITION

a: ambitious, ardent, aspirant, aspiring, bold, desirous, elaborate, emulous, extensive, fervent, impetuous, keen, overactive, overweening, pretentious, rapacious, sedulous, solicitous, workaholic

n: aspiration, desire, *folie de grandeur*, initiation, initiative, intendment, midnight oil, purpose, striving, thirst, workaholicism

## AMENDS

a:, compensative, compensatory, expiatory, reparative

n: apology, atonement, expiation, indemnity, penance, quittance, recompense, reconciliation, redress, reparation, repatriation, retribution, reward

v: adjust, better, compensate, correct, doctor, edit, expiate, fix, improve, mend, mitigate, modify, patch, recompense, recoup, rectify, redress, reform, reimburse, repair, repay, requite, revise

## AMIABLE

a: affable, agreeable, amicable, amical, civil, civilized, complaisant, cordial, gentle, good-humored, gracious, hospitable, indulgent, kind, loving, neighborly, obliging, sweet, unctuous, winsome

n: amiableness, amity, friendliness

## AMONG

a: *entre nous, inter alia, inter alios, inter nous*

combining forms: epi-, inter-

## AMOUNT

n: aggregate, allotment, · allowance, amplitude, capacity, extent, magnitude, number, portion, purse, quanta, quantity, quantum, share, split, stipend, sum, total, totality, volume, worth, yield

## AMPLE

a: big, boundless, capacious, commodious, copious, expansive, fat, full, generous, great, hefty, huge, liberal, much, plentiful, profuse, prolific, prolix, replete, spacious, vast, verbose, voluminous

n: abundance, amplitude, plenty, riches

## AMUSE

a: amusing, comic, comical, diverting, divertive, entertaining, facetious, farcical, funny, humorous, jocose, jocular, laughable, ludicrous, merry, recreative, risible, whimsical, zany

n: amusement, charm, cheer, delight, distraction, diversion, *divertissement*, enjoyment, entertainment, festival, frolic, fun, gaiety, merriment, picnic, play, sport, treat

v: beguile, cheer, disport, divert, entertain, gratify, occupy, play, please, recreate, regale, sport, titivate, toy

amusement park: barker, bumper car, geek, roller coaster, whip

**ANAL**

**n:** breech, hemorrhoids, perineum, podex, pudendum

**ANALOGOUS**

**a:** alike, cognate, commensurate, comparable, corresponding, equivalent, homeopathic, homogeneous, homologous, like, proportionate, related, same, similar, synonymous, uniform

**n:** analogy, collation, commensurability, correspondence, equivalence, homogeniety, likeness, similarity, *simulacra*

**ANALYSIS**

**a:** analytic(al), clinical, collative, determinative, dialytic, exegetic(al), expositive, expository, hermeneutic, interpretative, investigative, metaphorical, relative, tautological

**n:** anatomy, assay, critical-path, critique, dialysis, exegesis, explication, exposition, hermeneutics, interpretation, postmortem, reductionism, synopsis, synthesis, titration

**v:** anatomize, ascertain, break down, clarify, decipher, diagnose, dissect, divide, evaluate, examine, explore, inquire, parse, probe, pry, question, quiz, scan, scrutinize, sift, study, winnow

**ANATOMY**

**a:** anatomical

**n:** analysis, anthropotomy, body, bones, cadre, frame, framework, outline, phytotomy, plan, remains, skeleton, structure, *substantia*, support

**ANCESTOR**

**a:** agnate, ancestorial, ancestral, atavic, atavistic, cognate, consanguineous, genealogical, hereditary, monophyletic, more majorum, polyphyletic, primogenitive, progenitive, progenitorial

**n:** ancestry, antecedent, ascendant, atavism, clade, cult, derivation, extraction, forebear, forefather, forerunner, genealogy, lineage, monophyletic, paternity, pedigree, polyphyletic, precursor, primogenitor, procreator, progenitor, prototype, stemma

**ANCHOR**

**n:** crown, drogue, grapnel, hawse, hawsehold, hawser, hook, kedge, killick, support

**v:** secure, trip, weigh

   *anchorage:* dock, harbor, haven, inlet, marina, moorage, port, seaport

   *of hope: anchora spei*

   *of salvation: anchora salutis*

**ANCIENT**

**a:** aged, ancestral, antediluvial, antediluvian, antemundane, antiquated, antique, archaic, classical, cuneiform, dated, immemorial, obsolete, old, old-fashioned, outmoded, paleolithic, paleozoic, passe, preadamite, prehistoric, primeval, primitive, pristine, protohistoric, venerable

**n:** ancientness, ancientry, antiquarian, antiquity, antiquities, archaicism, cuneiform, hieroglyphics, oldness, relic, venerability

**AND**

**a:** coordinating conjunction, *et al, et alii, et cetera, et sequens, et sequentia, und so weiter*

**n:** ampersand, plus, polysyndeton

   *sign:* &, +

**ANEMIA**

**a:** anemic, ashen, bloodless, etiolated, faint, feeble, languid, lifeless, listless, livid, low, lusterless, pale, pallid, sickly, wan

**n:** aplastic anemia, bloodlessness, chlorosis, emptiness, *ischemia*, lifelessness

**ANEW**

**a:** afresh, *de integro, de novo*

**ANGEL**

**a:** angelic, beatific, blessed, celestial, cherubic, deific, godlike, godly, heavenly, pietistic, pious, religious, saintly, seraphic, sublime, transcendental, unearthly

**n:** amoretto, archangel, celestial, cherub, cherubim, domination, dominion, *dulia*, guardian, harbinger, messenger, power, principality, *putto*, saint, seraph, seraphim, spirit, throne, virtue, visitation

*study:* angeology

## ANGER

**a:** acrimonious, angered, angry, apoplectic, bilious, cantankerous, choleric, curmudgeonly, disgruntled, dyspeptic, fractious, hostile, ignescent, incendiary, indignant, inflammatory, irascible, irate, ireful, livid, mad, petulant, phlogistic, piqued, provocative, provoked, querulous, rampageous, rancorous, riled, seditious, splenetic, tetchy, wrathful

**n:** acrimony, animosity, *animus*, asperity, chagrin, choler, conniption, dudgeon, ebullition, exasperation, fit, fulminations, fury, grievance, hackles, hoity-toity, incensement, indignation, invective, irascibility, irritability, malice, paroxysm, petulance, pique, rancor, resentment, tantrum, turbulence, umbrage, vexation, virulence, vituperation

**v:** alienate, antagonize, envenom, exacerbate, inflame, irk, irritate, pique, provoke, rankle, vex

## ANGLE(S)

**a:** equiangular, isagonal, isagonic, multiangular, salient

**n:** axil, azimuth, bevel, cant, complement, critical angle, crotch, dihedral angle, inclination, rake

**v:** subtend

*combining forms:* -clin, clino-, -gon

*instrument:* protractor, sextant

## ANGUISH

**n:** ache, affliction, agony, *angoisse*, angst, anxiety, bereavement, consternation, distress, dolor, excruciation, Gethsemane, pain, pang, regret, remorse, sorrow, suffering, travail, worry

## ANIMAL

**a:** animalic, animalistic, biological, carnal, ethological, gross, mammalian, mammality, mammalogical, philotherian, theriomorphic, zoic, zoogenic, zoogenous, zoological, zoomorphic, zoophilic

**n:** animalcule, *animalculum, animalia,* animality, *biota,* bird, denizen, fauna, hybrid, mammal, mammalian, mammality, migrant, predator, protozoan, quadruped, theriomorph, vertebrate, zoomorphism

**v:** domesticate, propagate

*characteristic:* animalistic, animate, mammalian, theriomorphic, zoic, zoological, zoomorphic

*combining forms:* theri-, therio-, -zo, -zoa, zoo-

*related words:* aquatic, arboreal, bestiary, besticulture, carcass, diurnal, domestication, flash, marine, muzzle, nocturnal, pelt, philotherianism, terrestrial, vermin, veterinary, zoonosis, zoophyte

*study:* biogeography, biology, ethology, zoology

*stuffing:* taxidermy

## ANIMATE

**a:** activated, animated, enlivened, enthusiastic, excited, fired, lively, organic, prompted, spunky, stimulated, vitalized, vivacious, zealous

**n:** animation, ardor, ebullience, effervescence, exhilaration, exuberance, happiness, headiness, intoxication, invigoration, liveliness, spirit, sprightliness, vivaciousness, vivacity, zeal, zest

**v:** actuate, drive, energize, ensoul, importune, incite, invigorate, motivate, prompt, push, quicken, stimulate, stir, urge, vitalize, vivificate, vivify, waken

*suspended:* anabiosis, catalepsy, hibernation

## ANNIHILATE

**n:** annihilation, cancellation, destruction, eradication, finish, killing, murder, slaying, wrecking

**v:** abolish, abrogate, decimate, demolish, deracinate, eradicate, execute, expunge, exterminate, extinguish, extirpate, kill, neutralize, nullify, obliterate, overrun, pulverize, quell, slay, vanquish

**ANNOTATION**

**a:** scholiast

**n:** addition, clarification, marginalia, postil, scholia, scholium

**v:** define, elucidate, explain, gloss, illustrate

> *annotator:* definer, glossarist, scholiast

**ANNOUNCEMENT**

**a:** announcing, annunciatory, declamatory, declaratory, enunciative, proclamatory, pronunciative

**n:** annunciation, communique, declamation, manifesto, proclamation, pronunciation

**v:** announce, articulate, assert, broadcast, disclose, divulge, exclaim, explain, herald, intimate, make known, proclaim, promulgate, propound, publicize, reveal, spill, squeal, unveil, utter, vocalize

**ANNOY**

**a:** abhorrent, aggravating, annoying, calamitous, discommodious, disconcerting, excruciating, execrable, galling, invidious, irksome, mortifying, nettlesome, pestiferous, pestilent, pestilential, provocative, repellant, repulsive, vexatious

**n:** anger, annoyance, discomfiture, harassment, irritation, molestation, nuisance, pique, provocation, umbrage, vexation

**v:** abrade, anger, bedevil, bother, chafe, discomfit, discommode, disconcert, distress, disturb, eat, egg, gall, harass, importune, irk, molest, pique, provoke, rag, trouble, unnerve, wear, worry

**ANNUAL**

**a:** etesian, yearly

**n:** almanac, annuity, annularity

**ANNUL**

**a:** alienating, annulling, recissory, revocative, revocatory

**n:** abrogation, annulment, cancellation, cassation, defeasance, destruction, disaffirmance, disaffirmation, disclaimer, divorce, erasure, nullification, obliteration, recision, recission, revocation

**v:** abolish, abrogate, countermand, disaffirm, disclaim, divorce, end, neutralize, nullify, obliterate, overrule, quash, recant, repeal, rescind, retract, revoke, supersede, undo, withdraw

**ANOINTING**

**n:** baptism, chrism, unction

**ANOTHER**

**a:** alias, different, fresh, further, new, second

**n:** alter ego

**ANSWER**

**a:** evasive

**n:** antiphon, confirmation, counterstatement, *esprit d'escalier,* monosyllable, negation, prolepsis, rebuttal, rejoinder, repartee, replication, replique, reply, response, responsion, retort, riposte

**v:** act, do, explain, react, rejoin, replicate, reply, resound, respond, retaliate, retort, return, solve, speak, write

**ANTAGONISM**

**a:** adverse, ambivalent, antagonistic, averse, combative, conflicting, contrary, discordant, dissident, dissonant, hostile, incompatible, inimical, militant, oppositional, schizoid, unfriendly, warring

**n:** anger, antipathy, competition, conflict, contrariety, dissonance, enmity, friction, hostility, oppostion, rivalry, unfriendliness, war, warfare

> *antagonist:* adversary, agonist, archenemy, assailant, attacker, challenger, combatant, contender, disputant, enemy, fighter, foe, foil, invader, opponent, opposer, protagonist, rival, Satan

**ANTICIPATION**

**a:** anticipatory, awaiting, expectant, hopeful, inchoate, inchoative, intuitive, possible, potential, prevenient, prospective, suspicious, wished

**n:** assumption, belief, design, envisionment, expectation, future, guess, hope, intuition, postulation, presumption, prolepsis, reasoning, speculation, supposition, suspicion, trust, wish

**v:** ascertain, assume, diagnose, estimate, excogitate, figure, forecast, hypothesize, obviate, plan, postulate, predict, preempt, premise, presume, speculate, surmise, suspect, theorize, think, wish

## ANTICLIMAX

**a:** anticlimactical, bathetic

**n:** *bathos*, damp squib, disappointment, failure

## ANT(S)

**a:** formic, formicivorous, myrmecophagous

**n:** formicidae, termite

**v:** formicate

*combining forms:* myrmec-, myrmeco-
*related words:* anthill, dulosis, formicary, formicologist, helotism, myrmecologist, myrmecology, termitarium

## ANXIETY

**a:** anxious, apprehensive, concerned, distraught, expectant, fraught, fretful, impatient, in suspense, nervous, on tenterhooks, overwrought, perturbed, rattled, solicitous, solicitudinous, tense, uneasy

**n:** angst, anxiousness, apprehension, burden, disquiet(ude), dyspathy, dysphoria, foreboding, inquietude, malaise, millstone, panophobia, premonition, solicitude, trepidation, uneasiness, worry

**v:** burden

## APATHY

**a:** adiaphoristic, adiaphorous, apathetic, blase, casual, degage, detached, dispirited, hebetudinous, impassive, imperturbable, impervious, indifferent, insipid, lackadaisical, languid, languorous, Laodicean, lethargic, phlegmatic, spiritless, stoical, supine, torpid, unenthusiastic, unfeeling

**n:** acedia, adiaphoria, detachment, doldrums, hebetude, immobility, impassiveness, impassivity, inaction, inappetency, indifference, inertia, inertness, languor, lassitude, lethargy, listlessness, minauderie, nonchalance, phlegm, stoicism, supinity, torpor

## APE

**a:** anthropoidal, pithecomorphic, pongid, simian, simious

**n:** anthropoid, pongid, primate, shrewdness, simian, troglodyte, troop

*study:* pithecology

## APERTURE

**a:** patulous

**n:** chasm, cleft, crack, fenestration, gap, hiatus, hole, mouth, opening, orifice, os, ostiole, pore, slit, window

## APEX

**n:** acme, apogee, cacumen, cap, capstone, climax, crest, culmination, grand finale, head, meridian, peak, *perihelion*, pinnacle, point, sublimity, summit, tip, top, turning point, vertex, zenith

## APOLOGY

**a:** abject, apologetic, contrite, deprecating, deprecatory, excusatory, expiatory, justifiable, penitent, regretful, remorseful, rueful, self-reproaching

**n:** acknowledgment, alibi, *amende honorable*, amends, apologetic, *apologia*, atonement, defense, exoneration, explanation, justification, makeshift, pardon, plea, pretext, regret(s), vindication

**v:** apologize

*person:* apologete, apologist

## APOSTLE

**n:** *aficionada*, *aficionado*, apprentice, disciple, fan, follower, harbinger, ist, learner, messenger, proselyte, scholar, student, supporter, votary

## APPARATUS

**n:** accoutrements, appliance, appurtenances, armamentarium, baggage, belongings, device, equipment, fixture, gadget, goods, implement, instrument, invention, junk, knickknack, machination, machine, machinery, materiel, means, mechanism, notion, paraphernalia, project, rig, stratagem, tool, trappings, utensil, utility

## APPARENT

**a:** conspicuous, demonstrable, discernible, evident, exoteric, explicit, illusory, indubitable, manifest, obvious, ostensible, ostensive, palpable, patent, perceptible, presumptive, *prima facie*, real, seeming, self-evident, superficial, unconcealed

**n:** parallax, purport

> *apparently:* almost, quasi, reputedly, specious, supposedly

## APPEAL

**a:** *ad hominem, ad populum,* alluring, appealing, Circean, cogent, compelling, convincing, invocative, invocatory, provocative, supplicative

**n:** allure, appellant, attraction, attractiveness, aura, charisma, cogency, *cri de coeur,* enchantment, entreaty, fascination, imploration, invocation, mystique, popularity, siren song, supplication

**v:** adjure, apply, beseech, entreat, exhort, implore, invoke, plead, solicit, supplicate, urge

## APPEAR

**a:** apparent, appearing, seeming

**n:** appearance, aspect, attendance, aura, color, countenance, debut, development, expression, facade, facies, feature, guise, *habitus,* manifestation, manner, mien, ostent, patina, perspective, physiognomy, physique, profile, semblance, superficies, visage

**v:** gloss, mimic, simulate, veneer

> *combining form:* –phany

## APPEASE

**a:** appeased, appeasing, assuageable, expiatory, flexible, mitigable, mitigatory, peaceful, piacular, propitiative, propritiatory, tamable, yielding

**n:** appeasement, atonement, conciliation, expiation, mitigation, pacification, propitiation, reconciliation

**v:** allay, alleviate, assuage, conciliate, dulcify, lenify, mitigate, moderate, mollify, propitiate, reassure, satisfy, settle, smooth, soothe, tame, temper, tranquilize

## APPETITE

**a:** anorexic, appetible, appetitive, appetizing, bulimic, epicurean, epithumetic, hedonistic, insatiable, orectic, polyphagous, ravenous, Sybaritic, voracious

**n:** acoria, *appetit,* appetition, craving, desire, edacity, glutton, gluttony, hunger, hungering, liking, obsession, *orexis,* passion, predilection, preference, proclivity, taste, thirst, urge, voracity

> *person: bon vivant,* epicure, gastronome(r), gourmet, hedonist, sybarite

> *related words:* allotriogeustia, anorexia, bulimia, hyperorexia, inappetence, phagomania, polyphagia

## APPETIZER

**n:** antipasto, aperitif, apertive, canape, *hors d'oeuvre,* relish, salad

## APPETIZING

**a:** ambrosial, appetible, appetitious, appetitive, delectable, gustable, gustatory, luscious, nectareous, orexigenic, palatable, piquant, sapid, saporous, savory, succulent, tantalizing, toothsome

**n:** piquance, piquancy, sapidity, sapor, saporosity

## APPLAUSE

**a:** commendatory, laudatory, plauditory

**n:** acclaim, acclamation, accolade, approval, captation, commendation, curtain call, eclat, encomium, esurience, eulogy, laudation, ovation, plaudit, praise

  *people:* claque, claqueur, crowd

**APPLE**

**a:** pomaceous

**n:** codling, pomace, pome

**APPLICABLE**

**a:** adaptable, apposite, appropriate, apt, commensurate, congruent, expert, germane, pertinent, proper, proportional, qualified, relevant, suitable, suited, useful

**APPOINTMENT**

**n:** accoutrements, assignation, consultation, designation, enactment, engagement, meeting, rendezvous, schedule, station, time, tryst

**APPORTION**

**n:** allotment, apportionment, appropriation, assignment, award, budget, disposition, distribution, division, grant, part, portion, provision, ration, share, slice, split, supply

**v:** admeasure, allocate, appropriate, bestow, budget, consign, direct, dispense, grant, lend, mete, parcel, portion, prorate, provide, ration, release, share, split, supply

**APPRECIABLE**

**a:** cognizable, determinable, discernable, evident, measurable, objective, obvious, palpable, perceivable, perceptible, ponderable, recognizable, seeing, tangible

**APPREHENSION**

**a:** anticipative, apprehended, apprehensive, conscious, discerning, impalpable, intuitional, intuitive, knowing, premonitory, presentient

**n:** cognition, cognizance, cold feet, disquiet(ude), fear, foreboding, forewarning, inquietude, intuition, misgiving, pang, perception, prehension, premonition, presentiment, understanding, worry

**v:** anticipate, ascertain, detect, dread, fear, feel, foreknow, foresee, imagine, intuit, know, perceive, sense, take, understand

**APPROPRIATE**

**a:** apposite, apropos, *comme il faut*, concordant, condign, decorous, felicitous, germane, idoneous, opportune, pertinent, relevant, seemly, suitable, well-chosen

**n:** appropriateness, aproposity, decorousness, decorum, fitness, ideality, idoneity, relativity

**v:** accroach, add, apportion, arrogate, award, claim, commandeer, confiscate, formulate, grab, help, impound, preempt, sequester, take

**APPROVAL**

**a:** *a la bonne heure,* acclamatory, adulatory, affirmatory, approbatory, authorized, commendable, commendatory, laudable, laudatory, plauditory, sanctionative

**n:** acclaim, acclamation, accolade, accreditation, approbation, *bravissimo,* bravo, cachet, commendation, eclat, endorsement, imprimatur, kudos, plaudit, ratification, sanction, subscription, unanimity

**v:** accredit, agree, allow, approbate, approve, assent, commend, compliment, countenance, endorse, homologate, permit, ratify, sanctify, sanction, subscribe, validate

**APPROXIMATION**

**a:** about, almost, approaching, approximately, *circa,* close, near, nearly, nominal, quasi, roughly

**n:** *circa,* nearness

**v:** accost, advance, approximate, estimate, face, meet

**APT**

**a:** acute, apposite, appropriate, apropos, competent, decorous, fit, fitting, knowing, ok, pertinent, poignant, proper, qualified, relevant, seemly, suitable, useful

**n:** appropriateness, aproposity, aptness,

*bijouterie, bon mot,* epigram, penchant, poignancy, predilection, preparation, qualification, readiness, towardliness

### ARBITRARY

**a:** absolutist, arrogant, authoritarian, bigoted, capricious, captious, despotic, determinate, dictatorial, dogmatic, imperious, inexorable, positive, preferential, thetical, totalitarian, tyrannical

**n:** *dicta, dictum,* dogmatism, *ipse dixit,* ipsedixism

### ARCH

**a:** arcate, arched, arcuate, bowed, bulging, cambered, chamfered, circular, concamerated, concave, convex, coped, curved, domed, gibbous, rampant, relieving, rounded, rounding, surbased, vaulted

**n:** arc, arcade, arcuation, bend, bow, bridge, camber, concameration, crown, curvature, curve, fornix, hance, incurvation, ogive, proscenium, sky, span, support, trellis, trumeau, tympanum, vault

### ARCHERY

**a:** toxophilite, toxophilitic

**n:** clout, main, sagittarius, sagittary, toxophilite, toxophily

### ARCHITECTURE

**a:** architectonic, Baroque, Brutalism, Byzantine, Classical, Colonial, Decorated, Early English, Flamboyant, Gothic, Neoclassical, Norman, Palladian, Perpendicular, Regency, Renaissance, Rococo, Romanesque, tectonic, Transitional, vernacular

**n:** anntic, architectonics, caratid, draftsman, draftsperson, telamon

> *related words:* arcade, *arc-boutant,* ashlar, bargeboard, bay, boss, buttress, campanile, cartouche, caryatid, coffer, coffering, cruck, cupola, dado, engaged, entasis, exedra, facade, fan vaulting, finial, flying buttress, gable, gargoyle, groin, hammerbeam, lantern, lierne, loggia, molding, ogive, piano nobile, pilaster, podium, qua-

trefoil, quoin, rustication, saucer dome, stoa, strapwork, string course, stucco, stylobate, swag, trabeated, tracery, transom, vault

### ARDENT

**a:** crusading, devoted, dithyrambic, eager, ebullient, enraptured, enthusiastic, evangelical, evangelistic, fervent, fervid, glowing, igneus, impassioned, passionate, perfervid, plutonic, rapturous

**n:** animation, ardor, burning, compassion, dedication, desire, devotion, diligence, drive, eagerness, eclat, energy, enthusiasm, fever, flame, gusto, love, loyalty, pep, rapture, spirit, verve, zeal

### ARDUOUS

**a:** difficult, exacting, hard, laborious, lofty, onerous, rigorous, steep, strenuous, trying, uphill

### AREA

**a:** sympatric, regional

**n:** acre, arena, bailiwick, commonwealth, demesne, domain, dominion, enclave, environment, environs, expanse, farm, fiefdom, ground, habitat, landscape, locale, lot, milieu, *mise-en-scene,* neighborhood, parish, penumbra, range, reach, realm, region, scope, spread, surroundings, tract, venue, way, zone

### ARGUE

**a:** *a posteriori, a priori,* agonistic, analytical, argumentative, belligerent, carping, casuistic, circuitous, cogent, contentious, controversial, debatable, deductive, dialectic, disagreeable, discursory, disputatious, disputative, embroiled, empirical, eristic, factional, forensic, incisive, incontrovertible, inductive, insidious, iron-clad, irrefutable, misopolemical, pedagogical, polemic, presumptive, quodlibetic, sophistical, specious, tenable, trenchant, turbulent, unassailable, unruly, warring, watertight, wrangling

**n:** *ad hominem argument,* altercation, appeal, argumentation, argumentum, casuistry, choplogic, contretemps, devil's advocate, dialectic, discursive, disputation, enthymeme, expostulation, forensics, hypothesis, induction, lemma, man of straw, paralogism, Parthian shot, philosophism, pilpul, polemic, posit, postulate, predicate, premise, prolepsis, quodlibet, reasoning, ruction, sophism, sophistry, sorites, special pleading, speciosity, submission, syllogism, touche, ultimo ratio

**v:** accommodate, adduce, bicker, cavil, clinch, compose, contend, controvert, ergotize, expostulate, gainsay, invalidate, maintain, nullify, oppugn, posit, quibble, rebut, reconcile, refute, remonstrate, repudiate, retort, vitiate, void

## ARID

**a:** adust, anhydrous, bare, barren, desiccated, dry, jejune, monotonous, parched, seared, shriveled, sterile, thirsty, torrid, unproductive, withered

**n:** aridity, barrenness, desiccation, dryness, dullness, jejunity, monotony, sterility, unproductiveness

## ARISING

**a:** abiogenic, ascendant, assurgent, emergent, escalating, idiogenetic, idiopathic, issuing, originating, proceeding, rising, soaring, springing, stemming

**n:** arise, arrive, ascend, derive, educe, emanate, emerge, evolve, happen, issue, loom, materialize, rise, spring, stem

## ARISTOCRAT

**a:** aristocratic, elite, exclusive, genteel, hierarchical, high-hat, noble, patrician, powerful, privileged, royal, snobbish, superior, thoroughbred

**n:** *aristoi, bas bleu,* blue blood, bluestocking, Brahmin, elite, *grand signeur,* grandee, nobility, parvenu, patrician, patriciate, royalty

## ARISTOTLE

**a:** Aristotelian, Peripatetic

**n:** Aristotelian, *dictum de omni et nullo,* eudemonia, Peripatetic, Peripateticism

## ARM

**a:** akimbo, alar, axillary, brachial, brachiate, tentacular, tentaculate

**n:** armpit, axilla, brachium, oxter, tentacle

## ARMOR

**n:** agraffe, armiger, breastplate, chamfron, panoply, shield, tabard

## ARMS

**a:** tentacular, *vi et armis*

**n:** accouterment, armament, armamentaria, armamentarium, arsenal, materiel, ordnance, tentacles, weapon, weaponry

## AROUND

**a:** about, almost, approximate, approximately, circa, circiter, close, near, nearly

*combining forms:* amph-, amphi-, cir-, cum-, epi-, peri-

## AROUSE

**a:** arousing, galvanic, hair-trigger, inflammatory, piqued, provocative, stimulating, titillating

**v:** agitate, discompose, egg, elicit, evoke, fillip, goad, incite, interest, liven, pique, precipitate, prevail, provoke, rile, rouse, spur, stimulate, stir, summon, tempt, titillate, urge, waken, whet

## ARRANGE

**a:** alphabetized, arbitrary, arranged, categorized, compartmentalized, concinnate, haphazard, orchestrated, random, schematic, stratified, stratose, synthesized, systematized, tabulated, under the aegis of, under the auspices of

**n:** alphabetization, arrangement, array, categorization, collation, collocation, combination, compartmentalization, concinnity, configuration, conformation, contrivance, disposition, hierarchization, hierarchy, improvisation, logistics, *lucidus ordo, modus vivendi,* orchestration, ordonnance, permutation, plan, posture, *schema, schemata,* stratification, subordination

**v:** alphabetize, catalog, catalogue, categorize, classify, codify, collate, collocate, compartmentalize, concinnate, coordinate, correlate, dispose, improvise, marshal, methodize, mobilize, orchestrate, predetermine, synthesize, systematize, tabulate

*combining forms:* tax-, -taxis, taxo-, -taxy

## ARRAY

**n:** arrayment, battalion, battery, crowd, display, gamut, group, horde, host, legion, multitude, number, panoply, rainbow, series, show, spectrum, supply, troops

**v:** adorn, apparel, arrange, assemble, bedeck, clothe, dress, garb, marshal, robe

## ARREST

**n:** apprehension, arrestation, arrestment, *capias*, capture, containment, custody, delay, detention, restriction, sanctuary, securement, seizure, stay, warrant

**v:** apprehend, attach, bust, capture, catch, collar, defer, grab, hook, jail, nail, net, pinch, protract, restrain, retard, seize, snag, snare, stop, take, thwart, trap

## ARROGANCE

**a:** arrogant, audacious, autocratic, boastful, bold, bumptious, cavalier, commanding, compelling, dictatorial, disdainful, dogmatic, domineering, fastuous, forward, haughty, high-handed, hubristic, imperative, imperious, impudent, masterful, narrow-minded, opinionated, overbearing, overweening, preemptory, priggish, pushy, self-satisfied, supercilious, vainglorious

**n:** audacity, effrontery, haughtiness, *hauteur, hubris,* insolence, *nouveau riche, parvenu,* presumption, superbity, upstart

## ARROW

**a:** sagitatte, sagittal

**n:** arrowhead, bolt, butt shaft, dart, fletcher, flight, fluke, indicator, mark, marker, missile, nock, pointer, quarrel, quiver, reed, vane, weapon

**v:** fledge, fletch, volley

## ART(S)

**a:** aesthetic, *ars gratia artis,* artistic, *avant-garde,* Bohemian, esthetic

**n:** aesthetics, atelier, *beaux arts, chef d'oeuvre,* clique, collage, composition, coterie, decorative arts, dexterity, expertise, finesse, genre, graphics, incunabulum, interpretation, juvenilia, kitsch, maestro, *magnum opus,* masterpiece, *meisterwerk, objet d'art, objet trouve,* painting, *piece de resistance,* renascence, salon, sculpture, skill, techne, troupe, vanguard, virtuosity

*movements:* Art Deco, Art Nouveau, Barbizon school, Baroque, Bauhaus, Constructivism, Cubism, Dada, de Stijl, Expressionism, Fauvism, Futurism, Impressionism, Mannerism, Neoclassicism, Op Art, Pointillism, Pop Art, Postimpressionism, Pre-Raphaelitism, Quattrocento, Realism, Romanticism, Surrealism, Vorticism

*person:* aesthete, artist, Athena, connoisseur, curator, custodian, dabbler, Dadist, dilettante, esthete, Muse, virtuoso

## ARTERY

**a:** arteriosclerotic

**n:** aorta, arteriosclerosis, atheroma, carotid, sclerosis, subclavian

## ARTIFICIAL

**a:** affected, artifactitious, contrived, counterfeit, ersatz, fabricated, factitious, false, feigned, fictitious, histrionic, *in vitro,* mannered, melodramatic, not natural, postiche, prosthetic, *pseudo,* simulated, spurious, strained, studied, stylized, substitute, supposititious, synthetic, theatrical

**n:** affectation, android, artifact, artifice, artificiality, astrucity, automaton, contrivance, deception, *deus ex machina,* finesse, fructus industriales, gambit, golem, humanoid, imposture, ingenuity, intrigue, inventiveness, machination, maneuver, pretentiousness, prosthesis, saccharin, simulation, strategem, subterfuge, theatricality, trick

**v:** artificialize

**ARTLESS**

**a:** candid, ignorant, inartistic, ingenue, ingenuous, naive, unaffected, unauspicious, uncultured, unskillful, unsophisticated

**n:** artlessness, naivete, simplicity, unsophistication

**AS**

**prep:** *a l'ordinaire, comme a l'ordinaire, comme d'ordinaire, comme il faut, pro re nata, qua, quasi, quod hoc, ut intra, ut supra*

**ASCENDENCY**

**n:** domination, dominion, elevation, glory, leadership, mastery, paramountcy, precedence, prevalence, sovereignty, success, supremacy, sway

**ASCETIC**

**a:** austere, drastic, Essenian, Essenic, exacting, firm, fixed, harsh, precise, rigorous, self-denying, self-disciplined, self-mortifying, severe, strict, unbending

**n:** anchoret, anchorite, ascesis, asceticism, austerity, Cathari, Essene, hermit, nun, perfecti, recluse, sabbatarian, self-denial, self-discipline, self-mortification, solitudinarian, yogi

**ASCRIBE**

**a:** ascribable, due

**v:** accredit, arrogate, assign, attribute, certify, commission, credit, impute, place, refer, sanction, vouch, warrant

**ASEXUAL**

**a:** abiogenetic, agamic, agamogenetic, agamous, parthenogenetic

**n:** abiogenesis, agamogenesis, parthenogenesis

**ASH**

**a:** cineraceous, cinerous

**n:** breeze, cinders, cinerarium, clinker, columbarium, embers, urn

**ASLEEP**

**a:** abed, comatose, dormant, hibernating, hypnotic, inactive, latent, lethargic, motionless, quiescent, quiet, somniferous, somnolent, torpescent, torpid, unawake

**n:** hibernation, obdormition

**ASPECT**

**a:** faceted, heterogeneous, multifarious, multiphasic, multivarious, omnifarious

**n:** angle, appearance, color, component, countenance, effect, facade, facet, facies, feature, habit, habitus, idiosyncrasy, look, mien, ostent, part, physique, property, semblance, state, superficies

**ASPIRIN**

**n:** acetylsalicylic acid, salicylism

*alternative:* acetaminophen, codeine, paracetamol

**ASSAIL**

**n:** accusation, aspersion, assailment, attack, castigation, criticism, harassment, oppugnation

**v:** accuse, assault, berate, castigate, censure, charge, confront, criticize, harass, libel, malign, offend, strike

**ASSEMBLE**

**n:** agglomeration, aggregation, agora, assemblage, assembly, conglomeration, constituent, convocation, ensemble, gathering, synod

**v:** categorize, collimate, conglomerate, congregate, convene, convoke, correlate, muster, rendezvous, synthesize

**ASSENT**

**a:** acquiescent, approbative, assentatious, compliant

**n:** acquiescence, approbation, assentation, concurrence, sanction

**v:** accede, accord, acquiesce, admit, agree, cooperate, grant, receive, sanction

**ASSERTIVE**

**a:** affirmative, articulate, declaratory,

insistent, peremptory, positive, pronunciative, pushy, strident

**n:** announcement, assertion, declaration, *dictum, dogma, ipse dixit,* postulation, proclamation, say-so, statement

## ASSIGN

**n:** allotment, appointment, appropriation, assignation, assignee, assignment, cessionary, designation

**v:** affix, allocate, allot, apportion, ascribe, attribute, delegate, depute, designate, distribute, impute, predicate, refer

## ASSIST

**a:** ancillary, assisting, auxiliary, secondary, subsidiary, supplementing

**n:** abetment, aid, aide, assistance, coadjuvancy, cooperation, encouragement, furtherance, help, patronage, secours, subvention, succor

**v:** abet, assist, attend, feed, further, guide, help, minister, prod, prompt, support

> *assistant:* accessory, accomplice, acolyte, ADC, adjutant, adjuvant, affiliation, aide, aide-de-camp, ancillary, associate, coadjutant, coadjutor, coadjutress, coadjutrix, cohort, collaborateur, collaborator, colleague, companion, confederate, confrere, consort, deputy, *factotum,* handmaiden, partner, socius, subalternate, subordinate, subsidiary, supporter

## ASSOCIATE

**a:** affiliated, appendant, associated, concomitant, corollary

**n:** affiliation, alliance, association, brotherhood, comity, companionship, concomitance, concomitancy, congress, conjunction, connotation, consortium, fraternity, group, partnership, symbiosis

## ASSORTED

**a:** disparate, diverse, diversified, heterogeneous, miscellaneous, mixed, motley, multiform, varied, variegated

**n:** assortment, collection, farrago, hash, heterogeneity, hodgepodge, lot, miscellanea, miscellaneity, miscellany, mixture, multiformity, *olla-podrida,* set, suite, variegation, variety

## ASSUME

**a:** academic, appropriated, assumed, assumptious, assumptive, conjectural, counterfeit, factitious, feigned, fictitious, gratuitous, hypothesized, hypothetical, inferred, postulated, postulatory, putative, simulated, *soi-disant,* speculated, speculative, spurious, *sub silentio,* supposed, supposititious, theoretical, usurped

**n:** adoption, appropriation, arrogance, assumption, constantation, hypothesis, incorporation, postulata, postulate, postulation, premise, presumption, supposition, susception

**v:** appropriate, arrogate, ascribe, attribute, conjecture, hypothecate, hypothesize, posit, postulate, premise, presume, theorize, undertake

## ASSURE

**a:** assured, assuredly, certes, confident, indubitably, verily

**n:** aplomb, arrogance, assurance, audacity, certitude, confidence, effrontery, guarantee, impudence, infallibility, *savoir faire,* self-possession, self-reliance, surety, warrant, warranty

**v:** affirm, attest to, certify, convince, ensure, guarantee, insure, pledge, promise, prove, secure, substantiate, swear, vouch, vouch for, vow, warrant

## ASTONISH

**a:** astonishing

**n:** amazement, astonishment, *coupe de foudre,* petrifaction, petrification, surprise

**v:** affright, amaze, astound, flabbergast, paralyze, petrify

## ASTRONOMY

**n:** aberration, aphelion, apogee, armillary sphere, asteroid, azimuth, big-bang theory, binary, black hole, celestial sphere, conjunction, Copernican theory, corona, cosmology, declination, double star, ecliptic, equinox, geocentric theory, heliocentric theory, magnitude, meteorite, nadir, nebula, nova, nutation, orrery, perigee, perihelion, Ptolemaic theory, pulsar, quasar, red shift, singularity, solstice, steady-state theory, super nova, syzygy, Urania, zenith

**ATHLETICS**
n: athleticism, athletics, decathlon, gladiator, proselyte

**ATMOSPHERE**
a: ambient, amiable, atmogenic, congenial, convivial, evocative, gemutlich, miasmal, miasmatic, noxious, rarefied

n: ambiance, ambience, aura, barometer, decor, environment, fascination, glamour, greenhouse effect, isobar, miasma, millibar, mystique, nimbus, ornamentation, pall, stratosphere, vibes, wavelength

**ATOMIC**
a: Democritean, infinitesimal, minute, molecular

n: accelerator, atom, betatron, cesium clock, corpuscle, dot, fragment, granule, ion, iota, jot, minim, mite, molecule, monad, mote, particle, speck

**ATONE**
a: expiatory, inexpiable, piacular, propitiative, propitiatory

n: amends, atonement, compensation, expiation, propitiation, purgatory, reconciliation, redemption, redress, reparation, satisfaction

v: amend, appease, expiate, harmonize, pay, propitiate, reconcile, redeem, satisfy

**ATTACK**
a: blistering, denunciatory, *en garde*, expugnatory, invective, paroxysmal, scathing, vituperative, withering

n: access, ambuscade, assailment, *coup*, *coup de main*, denunciation, diatribe, enfilade, foray, fusillade, incursion, invective, irruption, offensive, onslaught, oppugnation, paroxysm, philippic,

polemic, reprisal, retaliation, sally, salvo, seizure, sortie, strafe, tirade, vituperation

v: aggress, ambush, assail, assault, battle, beleaguer, beset, besiege, bombard, castigate, clash, combat, contend, criticize, demolish, insult, inveigh, maim, oppugn, smash, trouble, war

*combining form:* -lepsy

**ATTEMPT**
a: conative

n: assay, conation, conatus, *coup d'essai*, effort, endeavor, essay, go, shot, stab, start, test, trial, try, undertaking, venture

v: assay, endeavor, entreat, essay, explore, fish, hunt, probe, pursue, search, seek, solicit, start, strive, try, undertake, venture

**ATTENDANT**
n: accompaniment, appendant, auxiliary, chaperone, *chasseur*, concomitant, corollary, cortege, entourage, famulus, guardian, guide, hireling, mercenary, minion, myrmidon, retinue, servant, server

v: associate, attend, escort, frequent, guide, haunt, help, maintain, protect, shepherd, squire, tend, usher

**ATTENTION**
a: advertent, alert, assiduous, attentive, circumspect, diligent, heedful, inspective, on the *qui vive*, perceptive, sedulous, solicitous, vigilant, watchful

n: advertence, advertency, application, assiduity, attentiveness, circumspection, complaisance, concentration, consideration, diligence, fixation, intendence, limelight, notice, perception, prevenience

**ATTIRE**
n: accoutrements, array, caparison, clothes, dress, equipage, garb, guise, habiliment, habit, investment, livery, outfit, pontificalibus, regalia, robes, toilette, uniform, vestment, vesture

## ATTITUDE

**a:** attitudinal, cavalier, disposed, orientated, oriented, *volte-face*

**n:** attitudinarianism, attitudinization, bearing, behavior, carriage, deportment, disposition, mood, philosophy, point of view, posture, slant, spirit, stance, stand, standpoint, viewpoint

**v:** attitudinize

## ATTORNEY

**a:** *in propria persona*

**n:** barrister, counselor, lawyer, solicitor

## ATTRACT

**a:** alluring, arresting, attractive, beguiling, bewitching, bonny, captivating, Circean, comely, decorative, decorous, enticing, fascinating, intriguing, magnetic, mesmeric, personable, seductive

**n:** affinity, appeal, attraction, attractiveness, charm, encouragement, lure, magnetism, minion, provocation, seduction, stimulation, stimulus

**v:** allure, captivate, capture, charm, draw, enchant, entice, gravitate, influence, interest, lure, magnetize, seduce, solicit, tempt

    *combining forms:* phil-, -philia

## ATTRIBUTE

**n:** accessory, appanage, appendage, cachet, characteristic, endowment, essence, idiosyncrasy, perquisite, property, proprium, quality, sign, symbol, token

**v:** assign

## AUCTION

**n:** Dutch auction, job lot, licitation, sale, vendue, venture

## AUDACITY

**a:** audacious, bold, brave, cheeky, fresh, imprudent, impudent, insulting, nervy, presumptuous, rude, sassy, shameless, unrestrained, wild

**n:** arrogance, boldness, cheekiness, effrontery, gall, guts, *hubris*, impertinence, impetuosity, intrepidity, mettle, nerve, temerity

## AUDIENCE

**n:** assembly, cabotinage, ratings, Sardoodledom, theatricality

## AUGMENT

**n:** addition, augmentation

**v:** add, aggrandize, beef up, enhance, enlarge, exacerbate, expand, feed, increase, intensify, magnify, multiply, swell

## AUGUR

**a:** auspicatory

**n:** augury, divination, handsel, indication, omen, portent, sign, signal, token

**v:** auspicate, foretell, portend, prophesy

## AUSPICES

**a:** apt, auspicious, benignant, *bonis avibus*, fair, favorable, fortitudinous, fortunate, good, happy, hopeful, likely, lucky, *melioribus auspiciis*, opportune, promising, propitious

**n:** aegis, aid, care, favor, guidance, influence, omen, patronage, portent, protection, sign, token, tutelage

## AUSTERE

**a:** acrimonious, ascetic, disciplined, extortionate, imperative, inexorable, inflexible, inquisitorial, obdurate, procrustean, rigorous, ruthless, Spartan, stringent, uncompromising, unrelenting

**n:** ascesis, austerity, desolation, disciplinarian, hardship, inflexibility, lugubriosity, rigidity, Spartanism, strictness, stringency, vicissitude

## AUTHENTIC

**a:** approved, authoritative, authorized, *bona fide*, confirmed, credible, kosher, legal, legitimate, official, original, reliable, sanctioned, trustworthy, valid(ated), verified, veritable, worthy

**v:** authenticate, confirm, verify

## AUTHOR

**a:** anonymous, apocryphal, auctorial, authorial, holographic, onomastic, polygraphic, pseudonymous

**n:** ancestor, anonym, authorship, compiler, composer, correspondent, creator, editor, intigation, inventor, maker, *opera omnia*, origin, origination, originator, paternity, penman, procreator, producer, pseudonym, pseudonymity, scribe, sire, source, writer, writing

## AUTHORITY

**a:** absolute, accredited, apostolic, areophagitic, attributive, authentic, authoritarian, authoritative, authorized, autocratic, canonical, *carte blanche*, certified, classic, commanding, conclusive, controlling, convincing, definitive, dictatorial, documented, dogmatic, *ex cathedra*, hierarchic(al), magisterial, multipotent, official, omnipotent, orthodox, peremptory, plenipotentiary, *pleno jure*, reliable, totalitarian

**n:** absolutism, *ancien regime*, apostolicity, autarchy, authorization, autocracy, bailiwick, *carte blanche*, control, despot, despotism, devolution, *dictum, dogma*, domain, dominion, fiat, fiefdom, hegemony, *ipse dixit*, jurisdiction rule, mandate, martinet, officiality, orthodoxy, parish, paternalism, permission, power, realm, sovereignty, supremacy, totalitarianism, tyrant, ukase

**v:** allow, approve, authorize, empower, permit, pontificate, sanction, warrant

## AUTOBIOGRAPHY

**n:** *anamnesis*, biography, *curriculum vitae*, history, life, memoirs, *personalia*, profile, recollections, reminiscences, resume, *vita*

## AUTOMATIC

**a:** accidental, automatous, kneejerk, mechanical, Pavlovian, predictable, reflex, self-regulating, spontaneous, unintentional, unthinking

**n:** android, automation, automatism, automaton, golem, kneejerk reaction, mechanization, robot, spontaneity

**v:** automate, automatize, mechanize, robotize

## AUXILIARY

**a:** adminicular, assistant, subsidiary, supplementary, syncategorematic, synsemantic

**n:** adjunct, adjunctive, adminicle, appendix, assistant, help, incidental, satellite, subordinate, subsidiary, supplement, tributary

*combining form:* para-

## AVAILABLE

**a:** accessible, attainable, dispensable, disposable, easy, expendable, facile, obtainable, open, ready, receptive, remittable, utilizable, voluntary

## AVARICE

**n:** covetousness, cupidity, greed, greediness, parsimony, rapaciousness, rapacity, stinginess, venality

## AVENGER

**n:** Nemesis, retaliator, *vindex injuriae*, vindicator

## AVERSION

**a:** anthropohobic, antipathetic, antipathic, apanthropic, averse, aversive, grudging, hesistant, indisposed, obnoxious, recalcitrant, reluctant, remiss, repugnant, repulsive, unresponsive, unwilling

**n:** abhorrence, animosity, antipathy, *bete noire*, disgust, disinclination, dislike, distaste, nausea, opposition, opprobrium, recalcitrance, reluctation, repugnance, revulsion, unwillingness

## AVOID

**a:** inconspicuous, low-profile, unobtrusive, unostentatious

**n:** abjuration, annulment, avoidance, avoiding, bypass, digression, eschewal, evasion, fencing, obviation, prevention, rejection, renunciation, sidestep, tack

**v:** abjure, avert, bypass, circumvent, delude, depart, detour, disregard, elude, eschew, evade, fence, flee, foil, hedge, ignore, mislead, outwit, refuse, scorn, screen, shuffle, sidestep, ward off

## AVOWED

**a:** accepted, acknowledged, admitted, affirmed, avowedly, *ex professo*, professed, sworn

## AWAKENING

**a:** aroused, attentive, awake, aware, cognizant, conscious, keen, mindful, observant, ready, roused, sharp, stirring, unsleeping, watchful

**n:** acuteness, alertness, burgeoning, disenchantment, disillusionment, enlightenment, quickening, realization, recognition, revival, vigilance

**v:** awaken, waken

## AWARD

**n:** accolade, bestowal, bounty, certificate, citation, commendation, cordon bleu, crown, cup, garland, gift, grand prix, guerdon, honor, keepsake, largess, laurel(s), medal, pin, plaque, ribbon, trophy

**v:** adjudge, apportion, bequeath, bestow, confer, crown, designate, earmark, give, grant, nominate, present, reward

## AWARE

**a:** apprised, cognizable, cognizant, cognoscible, cognoscitative, conscious, informed, knowledgeable, mindful, observant, perspicacious, responsive, sensible, sensitive, sentient, vigilant, watchful

**n:** apprehension, awareness, cognition, cognizance, consciousness, discernment, insight, intuition, knowledge, observa-tion, orientation, perception, percipience, sentience, sentiency, vigilance

## AWE-INSPIRING

**a:** august, awesome, doughty, exalted, fell, formidable, illustrious, numinous, redoubtable, reverent, sinister, sublime

**n:** abasement, awe, devotion, fear, regard, respect, reverence, veneration, wonder

## AWFUL

**a:** appalling, awe-inspiring, awesome, dangerous, disagreeable, ghastly, horrendous, horrible, horrific, indescribable, ineffable, morbid, ominous, outrageous, portentous, redoubtable, unpleasant

## AWKWARD

**a:** bumbling, bungling, clumsy, cumbersome, difficult, elephantine, gauche, gawky, ham-handed, ill-at-ease, inapt, inept, inexpert, infelicitous, inopportune, loutish, lubberly, lumbering, maladroit, ponderous, uncoordinated, uncouth, ungainly, unwieldy

**n:** awkwardness, clumsiness, contretemps, discomposure, embarrassment, gaucherie, hobbledehoy, inaptitude, inelegance, ineptitude, maladroitness, ponderosity, rusticity, uneasiness

## AXIOM

**a:** aphoristic, axiomatic, hypothetical, hypothetico-deductive, postulational, primitive, self-evident, witty

**n:** byword, canon, convention, law, maxim, motto, postulate, principle, proverb, rule, saw, standard, theorem, theorum, truism, truth, witticism

# B

**BABBLE**

**a:** stultiloquent

**n:** babblement, bavardage, galimatias, gibberish, harangue, jargon, palaver, stultiloquence, stultiloquy, talk, twaddle

**v:** blah, blather, blurt, chat, chatter, gibber, gossip, jabber, palaver, prate, prattle, rave, say, speak, tattle

**BABY**

**a:** hypocoristic, neonatal, prolific

**n:** bambina, bambino, changeling, embryo, fetus, foundling, hypocorism, papoose, suckling

**v:** caress, coddle, comfort, cosset, dandle, fondle, indulge, love, mollycoddle, nurse, pamper, placate, please, satisfy, spoil, swaddle, wean

*combining form:* -ling

*related words:* day care, pacifier, stroller, walker

**BACHELOR**

**a:** agamous, celibatarian, eligible

**n:** agamist, bachelorhood, bachelorism, Benedict, celibacy, celibate, coelebs, misogynist

**BACK**

**a:** abaft, aft, ago, arear, astern, dorsal, posterior, posteriormost, rear, rearward, recessive, regressive, retroactive, retrograde, retroverse, supine, tergal

**n:** dorsum, nape, nucha, occiput, posteriority, postern, recession, reclination, regression, retrogression, reversion, supinity, support, tergum

**v:** blench, flinch, recede, recoil, wince

*back again combining form:* palin-, re-

*combining forms:* ana-, dors-, dorsi-, dorso-, not-, noto-, retr-, retro-

**BACKER**

**n:** abettor, angel, cohort, collaborator, colleague, constituent, corroborator, exponent, follower, insurer, proponent, subscriber, supporter, underwriter

**BACKGROUND**

**a:** ambient, antecedent, circumstantial, employmental, environmental, incidental, inconspicuous, low-profile, situational, unobtrusive, unostentatious

**n:** accompaniment, antecedents, atmosphere, circumstances, conditions, context, experience, family, heredity, history, lineage, milieu, *mise-en-scene*, music, Muzak, past, pedigree, precedence, setting

**BACKSLIDE**

**n:** recidivation, recidivism, retrogression

**v:** degenerate, ebb, fade, fail, fall, falter, fizzle, flag, flop, lessen, recidivate, regress, relapse, renege, retrogress, revert, sink, slump, wane, weaken, worsen

*backslider:* apostate, recidivant, recidivist, renegade, turncoat

**BACKWARD**

**a:** *a reculons,* astern, behindhand, diffident, reactionary, recessive, regressive, reluctant, remedial, retarded, retrograde, retrogressive, unprogressive

**n:** ananym, backwardness, backwash, palindrome, regression, retrocession, retrogradation, retrogression, retrospective

*combining forms:* palin-, retr-, retro-

**BACTERIA**

**a:** antibiotic, antiseptic, biodegradable

**n:** aerobe, anaerobe, antibiotic, antiseptic, bacillus, coccus, culture, nidus, spirillum, spirochete, staphylococcus, streptococcus, zooglea

**BAD**

**a:** abject, abominable, abysmal, adverse, atrocious, base, bitter, blameworthy, damnable, deficient, delinquent, delitescent, demeritorious, deplorable, despicable, detestable, diabolic, dilapidated, disagreeable, discreditable, diseased, disobedient, displeasing, egregious, excruciating, execrable, feeble, flagitious, harmful, heinous, ignominious, improper, inappropriate, infelicitous, iniquitous, lamentable, malignant, mean, nefarious, obnoxious, odious, pernicious, putrid, rancid, reprehensible, rotten, seedy, shady, sinister, sordid, squalid, stinking, undesirable, unredeemable, unsavory, untimely, untoward, vile, viperous, weak, wicked

**n:** abomination, badness, cacoethes, caitiff, charlatan, curmudgeon, delinquency, depravity, enfant terrible, hoodoo, jinx, jonah, malaise, malevolence, malignancy, malum prohibitum, mauvais, misadventure, mischance, misconduct, miscreant, misdemeanor, mishap, pas, plight, rapscallion, reprobate, scallywag, sinisterity, villain, virulence, wretch

    *combining forms:* caco-, dys-, mal-, mis-

**BAFFLE**

**a:** baffled, baffling, bewildering, disconcerting, enigmatic, inexplicable, intriguing, mysterious, nonplussed, obfuscatory, obscure, odd, perplexed, perplexing, puzzling

**n:** bafflement, confusion, obfuscation, perplexity

**v:** astonish, checkmate, circumvent, confound, counteract, disconcert, euchre, foil, frustrate, muddle, neutralize, nonplus, obfuscate, obscure, outfox, puzzle, rattle, stultify, thwart, unsettle, upset

**BAGGAGE**

**n:** appurtenances, backpack, belongings, case, ditty bag, equipage, equipment, furnishings, gear, handbag, haversack, impedimenta, luggage, paraphernalia, purse, rucksack, satchel, suitcase, valise

**BALANCE**

**a:** *aequo animo*, Apollonian, balanced, balancing, compensative, compensatory, equalized, equanimous, equilibrant, equipollent, equiponderant, harmonious, isonomic, libratory, neutralized, stabilized

**n:** compensation, composure, equanimity, equilibrium, equipoise, equipollence, harmony, homeostasis, libration, poise, proportion, serenity, stability, stasis, symmetry

**v:** average, compensate, countervail, equalize, equate, equilibrize, equiponderate, equilibrate, librate, neutralize, poise, redress, stabilize

    *combining form:* -stasis

**BALD**

**a:** alopecic, epilated, glabrate, glabrescent, glabrous, outright, palpable, patent, receding, unadorned, undisguised

**n:** acomia, alopecia, anaphalantiasis, atrichia, atrichosis, baldness, calvities, phalacrosis, pilgarlic

**BALK**

**a:** balky, contrary, mulish, recalcitrant, restive, shy, stubborn

**n:** demur, hindrance, shyness

**v:** baffle, beat, block, check, defeat, delay, demur, disappoint, frustrate, hesitate, hinder, impede, refuse, stop, thwart

**BALL**

**a:** conglobate, conglomerate, globular, orbicular, spheroid(al)

**n:** caltrop, conglomeration, crowfoot, globe, globule, marble, mass, orb, pill, sphere, spheroid

**v:** conglobe

**BALLET**

**a:** balletic, choreographic

**n:** ballerina, balletomane, choreographer, choreography, coryphee

*related words:* arabesque, attitude, ballon, barre, battement, batterie, battu, bourree, brise, cabriole, capriole, chasse, ciseaux, corps de ballet, coryphee, divertissement, ecarte, elevation, entrechat, fish dive, fouette, glissade, jete, pas de deux, pas de seul, pirouette, plie, pointes, regisseur, repetiteur, splits, stulchak, tutu

**BALMY**

**a:** anodyne, anodynous, aromatic, balsamic, dreamy, favonian, gentle, lenitive, mild, mitigative, quiet, soothing, sunny, temperate, tranquil, warm

**BAN**

**a:** banished, banned, barred, blocked, canceled, censured, disallowed, forbidden, interdictive, interdictory, outlawed, prevented, prohibited, proscribed, proscriptive, restrained, unpermitted

**n:** anathema, armistice, banishment, block, censure, condemnation, curse, edict, enjoinder, execration, injunction, interdiction, moratorium, prohibition, proscription, taboo, veto

**v:** anathematize, banish, bar, blackball, block, debar, enjoin, exclude, excommunicate, execrate, exile, expatriate, interdict, ostracize, prevent, prohibit, proscribe, reject, restrain, shun, suppress

**BANAL**

**a:** asinine, average, commonplace, corny, drab, everyday, familiar, humdrum, inane, insipid, low-class, ordinary, pedestrian, plain, platitudinous, silly, stale, stock, tedious, trite, unimportant, worn

**n:** banality, pedestrianism

**BANISH**

**a:** banished, exiled, expatriate

**n:** banishment, expatriation, expulsion, extradition, ostracism, relegation

**v:** deport, dispossess, eject, exile, expatriate, extradite, ostracize, proscribe, relegate

**BANKRUPT**

**a:** barren, broke, depleted, deprived, destitute, destroyed, exhausted, impecunious, impoverished, indebted, insolvent, penniless, poor, ruined, stripped

**n:** bankruptcy, composition, depletion, destitution, divestation, failure, foreclosure, impoverishment, insolvency, receiver, ruin

**v:** break, deplete, dispossess, divest, empty, fail, fold, impoverish, liquidate, ruin, spoil

**BANNER**

**n:** badge, bunting, color, emblem, flag, gonfalon, jack, labrum, legend, motto, oriflame, oriflamme, pennant, pennon, signal, standard, streamer, symbol

**BANQUET**

**a:** convivial, epulary, festive

**n:** banqueter, convivium, feast, feed, food, junket, lucullan, meal, spread, symposiarch, symposiast, symposium, toastmaster

**v:** dine, eat, feast, feed, regale, sup, wine

**BANTER**

**n:** asteism, badinage, caricature, contumely, derision, disdain, irony, jest, joking, mockery, mocking, persiflage, raillery, ridicule, sarcasm, sardonicism, satire, scorn, scurrility, slight, slur

**v:** belittle, contemn, deride, disdain, jeer, jibe, josh, kid, lampoon, mock, persiflate, rag, rail, rib, ridicule, scorn, slight, slur, sneer, taunt, trick

**BAPTISM**

**n:** affusion, aspersion, baptistry, catechumen, chrism, consolamentum, Eucharist, immersion, sacrament

**BARBARIC**

**a:** atrocious, barbaresque, barbarous, cruel, feral, ferocious, gross, harsh, inhuman, inhumane, philistinic, procrustean, rough, savage, tramontane, tyrannical, tyrannous, uncivilized, wild

**n:** barbarism, barbarity, barbarousness, brutality, ferity, ferocity, inhumanity, philistinism, savagery, unrestraint, wildness

**BARE**

**a:** barefooted, denudate, denudative, discalced, exposed, manifest, minimum, naked

**n:** modicum, semblance, trace

**v:** denudate, denude

*combining form:* nudi-

**BARGAIN**

**a:** *a bon marche, a vil prix,* cheap, dirt cheap

**n:** agreement, buy, compact, contract, deal, pact, steal

**v:** barter, cavil, chaffer, clinch, dicker, haggle, hawk, horsetrade, huckster, negotiate, palter, secure, sell, trade, traffic, truck

**BARK**

**a:** corticolous

**n:** cortex, covering, decortication, hull, husk, rind, skin, warp

**v:** decorticate, girdle, peel, ringbark

**BARREL**

**a:** doliform

**n:** bilge, cask, chime, chock, firkin, gantry, hogshead, kilderkin, pin, pipe, puncheon, spigot, spile, stave, tun

**v:** broach, draft

**BARREN**

**a:** acarpous, divested, effete, fruitless, hardscrabble, immature, infecund, infertile, jejune, nonparous, nulliparous, sterile, unfructuous, unfruitful, unprofitable, vacant, void, worthless

**n:** barrenness, desert, desolation, destitution, infecundity, infertility, sterility, waste, wasteland

**BARTER**

**n:** commerce, commutation, deal, exchange, *quid pro quo,* sale, swap, trade, traffic, transaction

**v:** auction, bandy, bargain, commute, dicker, exchange, haggle, hawk, interchange, parley, reciprocate, sell, settle, substitute, trade, traffic, truck, vend

**BASE**

**a:** contemptible, counterfeit, degenerate, degraded, degrading, despicable, dishonorable, ignoble, inferior, low, mean, menial, plebian, proletarian, substratal, unworthy, wicked

**n:** baseness, degeneration, degradation, turpitude, wickedness

**BASIC**

**a:** abecedarian, basal, canonical, constitutional, elementary, essential, fundamental, indispensable, inherent, innate, intrinsic, irreducible, orthodox, primary, primeval, primitive, sessile, substrate

**n:** alpha and omega, anlage, assumption, authority, axiom, basicness, bedrock, canon, constitution, decalogue, elixir, essentiality, foundation, frame of reference, fundament, fundamentality, hypostasis, infrastructure, magna carta, nature, philosophy, *point d'appui,* postulate, *pou sto,* premise, primality, principium, quintessence, rationale, reason, rudiment, substratum, superstructure, tenet, theory, ultimacy

**BASK**

**n:** aprication

**v:** apricate, delight, luxuriate, revel, sun, wallow, warm

**BASTARD**

**a:** counterfeit, debased, illegitimate, misbegotten, natural, sinister, spurious, supposititious

**n:** bar sinister, *filius nullis, filius populi,* hybrid, illegitimate, mongrel

**BAT**

**a:** chiropteran, vespertilian, vesptertine

**n:** chiropter, chiropteran, fledermaus, patagium, pipistrelle, Vespertilio

## BATH

**a:** ablutionary, balneal, balneary

**n:** ablution, balneation, balneology, bathing, caldarium, hipbath, hydrotherapy, Jacuzzi, sauna, sitz bath

**v:** bask, cleanse, immerse, indulge, languish, lave, luxuriate, moisten, revel, shower, suffuse, swim, wallow, wash, wet

## BATTLE

**a:** internecine

**n:** Armageddon, collision, conflict, encounter, engagement, phalanx, prowess, skirmish, wager of battle

> *field:* aceldama, Armageddon, battlefield, battleground, battlement

> *flag:* oriflamme, standard

## BEAK

**a:** aduncous, aquiline

**n:** lorum, mandible, mouth, neb, nib, nose, point, proboscis, projection, promontory, rostrum, snout, tip

## BEAN

**a:** fabaceous, fabiform

**n:** flageolet, frijol, haricot, legume, mung bean, sprouts, tofu

## BEAR

**a:** arctoid, ursine

**n:** arctoid, bruin, sloth

## BEARD

**a:** aristate, awned, barbate, bearded, pogoniate

**n:** beaver, dundrearies, goatee, Louis Napoleon, muttonchops, peak, pogonology, pogonotomy, pogonotrophy, sideboards, sideburns, Van dyke, whiskers, ziff

## BEARING

**a:** multiparous, oviparous, ovoviviparous, proligerous, viviparous

**n:** address, application, behavior, carriage, comportment, *demarche, demarche noble,* demeanor, deportment, direction, gait, manner, mien, poise, posture, prestance, purport, relation, significance

## BEARINGS

**n:** orientation

> *lost:* disorientated, disorientation, disoriented

## BEAST

**a:** animal, bestial

**n:** behemoth, quadruped

> *combining forms:* theri-, therio-

## BEAT

**a:** palpitant

**n:** arsis, bastinado, ictus, intonation, palpitation, percussion, pulsation, tachycardia, thesis

**v:** baste, bludgeon, castigate, cudgel, defeat, drub, flagellate, flail, flay, flog, fustigate, hit, lambaste, palpitate, pommel, pulsate, pummel, scourge, smite

## BEAUTY

**a:** aesthetic, artistic, attractive, beauteous, beautiful, captivating, comely, delectable, excellent, exquisite, gorgeous, philocalic, pulchritudinous, ravishing, statuesque, tempean, voluptuous

**n:** Adonis, aesthete, aesthetics, Aphrodite, Apollo, *beau ideal,* beauteousness, comeliness, demigod, esthete, excellence, glory, magnificence, philocaly, phoenix, pulchritude, radiance, splendor, symmetry, Venus

## BED

**n:** charpoy, cot, couch, cubiculum, foundation, framework, futon, hammock, lair, matrix, pallet, palliasse, stratum, trundle

## BEDECK

**v:** adorn, caparison, decorate, lard, ornament

## BEFORE

**a:** antecedent, antenatal, anterior, awaiting, confronting, precedent, preceding, prelatory, preliminary, premundane, prenatal, preparatory, prevenient, previous

**n:** antecedence, anteriority, *deja vu*, forerunner, harbinger, herald, paramnesia, precedence, precursor, predecessor, prolepsis

**v:** foreshadow, portend, presage

*combining forms:* ante-, fore-, pre-, pro-

## BEG

**a:** beggarly, beseeching, contemptible, importunate, mendicant, precative, precatory, soliciting, solicitous, sordid, supplicatory, tatterdemalion

**n:** beggar, cadger, freeloader, gaberlunzie, leech, mendicancy, mendicant, mendicity, pariah, *petitio principii*, petitioner, scrounger, sponger

**v:** adjure, apply, beseech, entreat, exhort, importune, intercede, petition, pray, request, solicit, sue, supplicate

## BEGIN

**a:** *ab initio, ab initium, ab ovo,* aborning, alpha, catechumenical, elementary, embryonic, genetic, germinal, *in principio,* inchoate, incipient, inconabular, initiatory, nascent, parturient, primitive, primordial, rudimentary

**n:** actuation, beginning, commencement, conception, debut, exordium, foundation, genesis, impulsion, inauguration, inception, incipience, incipiency, inconabulum, initiation, innovation, onset, origin, outset, *premier pas,* primordium, principium

**v:** actuate, broach, commence, embark, engender, generate, germinate, inaugurate, initiate, innovate, institute, introduce, launch, motivate, originate, pioneer, trigger, usher in

*beginner:* abecedarian, actuator, amateur, apprentice, catalyst, catechumen, fledgling, founder, greenhorn, learner, neophyte, novice, novitiate, originator, postulate, rookie, tenderfoot

*combining form:* -escent

## BEHAVIOR

**a:** artificial, depressive, ethological, exhibitionistic, improper, infantile, infantilistic, manic, rampageous, riotous, sociopathic, theatrical

**n:** affectation, attitude, bearing, behaviorism, benignity, civility, compensation, comportment, conditioned response, conditioning, conduct, congeniality, cordiality, demeanor, deportment, discipline, eccentricity, ergasia, ethics, ethology, foible, idiosyncrasy, manner, mannerism, mien, norm, protocol, psychology, quirk, trait, whim

*bad behavior:* beastliness, bestiality, buffoonery, exhibitionism, immaturity, infantility, misconduct, pretentiousness, puerilism, puerility, sociopathy, theatrics

## BEHEAD

**n:** guillotine

**v:** decapitate, guillotine, obtruncate

## BEHIND

**a:** *a tergo,* astern, *en arriere,* posterior

**n:** derriere, gluteus, podex, posterior

*combining form:* meta-, post-, retr-, retro-

## BEING

**a:** *ad hoc, in esse,* ontic, ontological, *pro tem(pore)*

**n:** actuality, *animalcule,* beast, bios, creation, creature, earthing, ens, Ens Entium, entity, *esse,* existence, existent, flesh, human, individual, life, living, man, mankind, men, mortal, person, reality

*combining form:* onto-

*study:* metaphysics, ontography, ontology

## BELIEF

**a:** believable, credible, creditable, credulous, doxastic, gullible, incredulous, plausible, skeptical, syncretic, syncretistic, trustworthy

**n:** acceptation, adherent apologia, apostasy, apostate, article of faith, conviction, credence, creed, delusion, doctrine, dogma, fundamentalism, heterodoxy, *idee fixe*, ideology, materialism, mythos, persuasion, philosophy, plausibility, positivism, principle, profession, sentiment, tenet, testament, warrant, work ethic

**v:** apostatize, assent, declare, espouse, justify, profess, recognize, subscribe, syncretize

## BELITTLE

**a:** belittling, denigratory, depreciatory, derogative, derogatory, minimizing, villipending

**n:** belittlement, denigration, derogation, disparagement, minimization, stigmatization

**v:** debase, decry, defame, denigrate, deprecate, depreciate, deride, disparage, minimize, stigmatize, vilify, villipend

## BELL

**a:** campaniform, campanular, campanulate, cloche, tintinnabular

**n:** Angelus, belfry, campanile, campanology, carillon, clapper, curfew, knell, peal, tintinnabulation, tintinnabulum, tocsin, tolling

## BELLIGERENT

**a:** aggressive, argumentative, assertive, bellicose, furious, hostile, irate, mad, pugnacious, quarrelsome, umbrageous

**n:** aggressor, *bashi-bazouk*, belligerence, combatant, competitor, militancy, pugnacity, quarrelsomeness, truculency, warrior

## BELLOW

**a:** bellowing, mugient, vociferating, vociferous

**v:** bawl, cy, howl, roar, weep

## BELLY

**n:** abdomen, solar plexus, venter

## BELONG

**a:** appurtenant, inherent, integral, intrinsic

**n:** appurtenance, appurtenant

**v:** appertain, apply, bear, conform, fit, go, inhere, own, pertain, relate

## BELOW

**a:** ancillary, auxiliary, beneath, descending, inferior, *infra*, low(er), nether, servile, subalternate, subjacent, subliminal, suboptimal, subordinate, substrative, under, underlying, *ut infra*

*combining forms:* hypo-, infra-, sub-

## BEND

**a:** arcuate, bent, circumflex, contorted, flexible, flexuous, geniculate, incurvate, limber, lissom, lithe, malleable, pliable, pliant, pronate, sinuous, supple, twisted, wry

**n:** affectation, arcuation, circumflexion, curvature, flexion, flexuosity, flexure, inclination, incurvation, incurvature, meander, oxbow, penchant, retroflexion, sinuosity, spring, tendency, tortuosity

**v:** arcuate, circumflex, deflect, genuflect, incurve, negotiate, replicate

## BENEATH

**n:** *infra dig, infra dignitatem,* infraposition

**v:** infrapose

*combining forms:* hypo-, infra-, sub-

## BENEFACTOR

**n:** donor, grantor, Maecenas, patron, philanthropist, Prometheus, Samaritan, sponsor

*beneficiary:* cestui, donee, legatee

## BENEFIT

**a:** advantageous, benefic, beneficial, beneficient, benevolent, charitable, munificent, opportune, rewarding, salubrious, salutary, sanative

**n:** advantage, benefaction, benefice, beneficience, benevolence, blessing, bonus, dividend, fringe benefit, perk, perquisite, privilege

## BERATE

**a:** castigatory, execratory, objurgatory

**n:** execration, objurgation, vituperation

**v:** abuse, attack, blame, castigate, charge, chew out, chide, condemn, correct, denigrate, denounce, dig, discredit, execrate, lambaste, rake, rebuke, reprove, scold, slam, vilify, vituperate

**BESEECH**

**a:** beeseeching, imploratory, importunate, precative, precatory, solicitous

**n:** beseeching, imploration, obtestation, solicitation

**v:** appeal, ask, entreat, impetrate, implore, importune, obsecrate, obtest, pray, press, pressure, solicit, sue, summon, supplicate

**BESIEGE**

**v:** assail, beleaguer, crowd, hem, importune, pester, plague, press, solicit, surround

**BEST**

**a:** A-one, choice, elite, first-rate, foremost, good, grand, nonpareil, *nulli secundus*, optimal, optimum, Panglossian, *par excellence*, paramount, peerless, preeminent, prime, richest, supereminent, superior, superordinary, superordinate, supreme, tops, ultimate, unsurpassed

**n:** choice, chosen, cream, *creme de la creme*, elite, highlight, *ne plus supra, ne plus ultra*, preeminence, tops, ultimacy, vintage

**BET**

**n:** croupier, gamble, gambling, hedge, horse racing, martingale, pari-mutuel, pledge, punter, totalizator, tote, wager

**v:** ante, chance, gamble, hazard, hedge, lay, parlay, play, plunge, risk, speculate, stake, wager

**BETRAY**

**a:** perfidious, treacherous

**n:** apostasy, betrayal, duplicity, perfidy, prodition, seduction, slander, treachery, treason, triplicity

**v:** deceive, delude, double-cross, dupe, entrap, hoax, inveigle, slander, snare, tell, traduce, trick

*betrayer:* apostate, recreant, traitor

**BETROTH**

**a:** betrothed

**n:** affiance, betrothal, engagement, espousal, sponsalia, troth

**v:** affiance, engage, espouse, pledge, plight, promise, troth

**BETTER**

**a:** improved, meliorative, optimum, superordinary, superordinate, *tant mieux*

**n:** betterment, *faute de mieux*, Hobson's choice, improvement, melioration, meliorism, meliority

**v:** ameliorate, convalesce, correct, doctor, exceed, excel, meliorate, mend, optimalize, outdo, recuperate, renew, restore, revise, surpass

**BETWEEN**

**a:** average, *entre nous, inter nous*, interjacent, intermediary, intermediate, intervenient, intervening, mean, medial, medium, middle-of-the-road, middling, moderate, parenthetical, separating

*combining form:* inter-

**BEVERAGE**

**n:** cocktail, draught, juice, libation, liquid, nectar, potable, potation, water

**BEWAIL**

**a:** deprecable, lamentable, moaning, plangorous

**n:** bewailment, deploration, deprecation, lamentation

**v:** bemoan, cry, deplore, lament, rue, wail, weep

**BEWILDER**

**a:** astonished, bemused, bewildered, confused, dazed, disoriented, distraught, dumbfounded, *eperdu*, puzzled, rattled, stunned, surprised, thunderstruck, uncertain

**n:** bewilderment, confusion, disorientation, embranglement, obfuscation, perplexity

**v:** addle, astonish, astound, bemuse, circumvent, disconcert, electrify, flabbergast, foil, frustrate, metagrobolize, muddle, obfuscate, perplex, puzzle, rattle, stagger, surprise, tease

## BEWITCH

**a:** attractive, bewitching, charming, circean

**n:** bewitchment, charm, hex, hoodoo, jinx, sorcery, spell, voodoo

**v:** beguile, captivate, capture, charm, enchant, ensorcel, fascinate, hex, hoodoo, hoodwink, jinx, jonah, magnetize, mesmerize, take, thrill

## BIAS

**a:** biased, bigoted, diagonal, favoring, oblique, one-sided, opinionated, partial, partisan, prejudiced, prejudicial, slanting, tendentious

**n:** inclination, *parti pris,* partiality, preconception, predilection, predisposition, preference, preformed judgment, prejudice, prepossession, tendency

## BIBLE

**a:** biblical, ocanonical, scriptural, synoptic

**n:** anagignoskomena, anagogy, apocrypha, Authorized Version, biblicality, Biblicism, Biblicist, Bibliolatry, Biblist, canon, covenant, Douay, exegesis, fundamentalism, Gideon, hermeneutics, homologoumena, polyglot, revelation, scripturality, Vulgate

   *books:* Acts, Amos, 1 Chronicles, 2 Chronicles, Colossians, 1 Corinthians, 2 Corinthians, Daniel, Deuteronomy, Ecclesiastes, Ephesians, Esther, Exodus, Ezekiel, Ezra, Galatians, Genesis, Habukkuk, Haggai, Hebrews, Hosea, Isaiah, James, Jeremiah, Job, Joel, 1 John, 2 John, 3 John, Jonah, Joshua, Jude, Judges, 1 Kings, 2 Kings, Lamentations, Leviticus, Luke, Malachi, Mark, Matthew, Micah, Nahum, Nehemiah, Numbers, Obadiah, 1 Peter, 2 Peter, Philemon, Philippians, Proverbs, Psalms, Revelation, Romans, Ruth, 1 Samuel, 2 Samuel, Song of Songs, 1 Thessalonians, 2 Thessalonians, 1 Timothy, 2 Timothy, Titus, Zechariah, Zephaniah

## BIG

**a:** full, huge, large, preeminent, pregnant, pretentious, prominent, teeming

**n:** bigwig, celebrity, cynosure, luminary, magnate, magnifico, notability, panjandrum, personage, royal

## BIGOTED

**a:** biased, blind, inegalitarian, intolerant, narrow-minded, prejudicial, sectarian, stubborn, zealous

**n:** bigot, bigotry, fanatic, fanaticism, fiend, intolerance, lunatic, maniac, narrow-mindedness, provincialism, racist, sectarian, sectarianism, sectionalism, visionary, zealot

## BILATERAL

**a:** binary, bipartisan, double, dual, duplicate, reciprocal, synallagamatic, twin, twofold

**n:** bilaterality, bipartisanship, duality

## BILK

**v:** cheat, check, deceive, disappoint, foot, frustrate, swindle

## BIND

**a:** astrictive, astringent, cohesive, constraining, imperative, indissoluble, obligatory, sacramental, stringent

**n:** astriction, astrictive, colligation, contraction, gathering, ligation, ligature, linchpin, objurgation, signature, stringency

**v:** bandage, colligate, constrain, contract, fasten, join, ligate, pinion, restrain, restrict, shackle, swaddle, swathe, whip, wrap

## BIOGRAPHY

**a:** biographical

**n:** anemnesis, article, autobiography, *curriculum vitae, entwicklungsroman,* essay, history, memoir(s), *personalia*, potted biography, profile, prosopography, reminiscence(s), *vita*

**BIOLOGICAL**

a: ontological

n: classification, genetics, heredity, isomorphism, ontology, taxonomy

**BIRD**

a: altricial, avian, callow, crepuscular, cursorial, ornithic, ornithoid, ornithophilous, passerine, sedentary, unfledged

n: aviculture, avifauna, fledgling, nestling, oology, ornithofauna, ornithology, ornithoscopy, phoenix

*combining form:* ornitho-

*groups:* bitterns, choughs, coots, cranes, crows, doves, ducks, eagles, falcons, finches, geese, goldfinches, grouse, gulls, hawks, herons, hummingbirds, jays, lapwings, larks, magpies, mallards, nightingales, owls, partridges, peafowl, penguins, pheasants, pigeons, plovers, quails, ravens, rooks, snipe, sparrows, starlings, swans, teal, thrushes, turkeys, wigeon, woodcock

**BIRTH**

a: aborning, antenatal, congenital, connatal, connate, familial, genetous, hereditary, *in statu nascendi, in utero,* inherent, innate, natal, native, neonatal, oviparous, ovoviviparous, parturient, perinatal, postnatal, postpartum, prenatal, primeval, proligerous, viviparous

n: accouchement, ancestry, childbirth, confinement, debut, embarcation, extraction, genesis, geniture, gentility, inauguration, inchoation, insipience, lineage, nativity, procreation

v: drop, slink, slip, spawn, yean

*combining forms:* -gen, -genesis, -genous, -parous

**BISEXUAL**

a: androgynous, hermaphrodite, hermaphroditic(al)

n: androgymy, androgyne, androgyneity, bisexuality, hermaphrodite, hermaphroditism

**BIT**

n: driblet, granule, hair, iota, minimum, minum, modicum, moiety, morceau, morsel, pittance, quanta, scintilla, scrap, sland, sliver, smack, smidgen, snippet, soupcon, speck, tincture, tinge, vestige

**BITTER**

a: acerbic, acetous, acidulous, acrid, acrimonious, aggrieved, astringent, biting, caustic, censorious, corrosive, cynical, distasteful, harsh, incisive, jaundiced, mordacious, mordant, pessimistic, piquant, piqued, poignant, rancorous, resentful, sarcastic, sardonic, scathing, sour-tasting, tart, unpalatable, vehement, vinegary, virulent, vitriolic, vituperative

n: acerbity, acridity, acrimony, bitterness, causticity, gall and wormwood, mordacity, poignancy, recrimination, spinosity, wormwood

**BIZARRE**

a: atypical, baroque, chimerical, daedalic, eccentric, fantastic, freakish, grotesque, odd, oddish, ridiculous, rococo, unconventional, weird

n: bizarrerie, oddity, whimsy

**BLACK**

a: achromatic, atramental, atramentous, blackish, discreditable, monochrome, nigrescent, nigricant, piceous, swart

n: *bete noir,* blackness, negritude, nigrescence, nigritude

v: blacken, nigrify, sully

*combining forms:* melan-, melano-

**BLAME**

a: blamable, blameworthy, censurable, condemnatory, culpable, demeritorious, discreditable, guilty, heinous, peccable, reprehensible, reprovable

n: animadversion, culpability, obloquy,

onus, reprehension, scapegoat, whipping boy

**v:** accuse, animadvert, censure, condemn, criticize, extenuate, impute, incriminate, inculpate, reprehend, reprimand, reproach, reprove, scold, upbraid

 *blameless:* beyond doubt, exculpable, exculpatory, impeccable, inculpable, innocent, irreproachable, unimpeachable

## BLAND

**a:** affable, anodyne, anodynic, anodynous, benign, complaisant, favonian, halcyon, ingratiating, lenient, soothing, suave, tasteless, unconcerned, unperturbed, urbane

## BLEACH

**a:** achromatized, alabaster, ashen, blanches, bleached, blond(e), decolorized, etiolated, lightened, purified, whitened

**n:** etiolation, Javelle water, ozone

**v:** achromatize, albify, blanch, decolorize, etiolate, fade, lighten, pale, whiten

## BLEMISH

**n:** cloud, imperfection, maculation, stigma

## BLEND

**n:** amalgamation, coalescence, conflation, harmonization, merger, mix, mixture, montage, pool, portmanteau, tincture, union, unit

**v:** amalgamate, coalesce, combine, fuse, harmonize, inosculate, join, meld, merge, mingle, mix, rectify, unify, unite

## BLESS

**a:** benedictory, blessing, invocatory, macarian

**n:** approval, beatitude, benedicite, benediction, benefit, benison, blessedness, blessing, boon, felicitation, gesundheit, grace, invocation, nirvana

**v:** consecrate, deify, exalt, gesundheit, hallow, laud, macarize, pray, sacralize, sanctify, thank, venerate

## BLIND

**a:** amaurotic, blindly, covered, dim, doctrinaire, ignorant, purblind, unseeing

**n:** ablepsia, ablepsy, amaurosis, anopsia, ate, blindness, Braille, cecity, hemianopsia, ignorance, impasse, nyctalopia, obscurity, sightlessness, typhlology

**v:** conceal, cover, fool, hide, hood, mask, secrete, shade, veil

## BLINK

**n:** flicker, fulguration, nictitation, twinkle, wink, winking

**v:** nictitate, palpebrate, twinkle, wink

## BLISS

**a:** beatific, beatified, blissful, connubial, delightful, ecstatic, Edenic, elysian, enchanted, felicific, felicitous, halcyon, paradisiacal, rapturous, transported

**n:** beatitude, ecstasy, elysium, felicity, happiness, nirvana, paradise, transport

## BLOCK

**a:** blocked, clogged, congested, impedimental, occlusive, overful

**n:** hindrance, impediment, occlusion, oppilation, repression, suppression

**v:** impede, obstruct, occlude, oppilate, parry, prevent, scotch, ward off, wedge

## BLOOD

**a:** arterial, bloody, deferent, efferent, engorged, hemal, hematic, hemic, incardine, ischemic, plethoric, sanguine, sanguinolent, sanguinous, venous

**n:** aneurysm, capillary, consanguinity, embolism, embolus, gore, hematology, hemophilia, hemophiliac, hemorrhage, hyperglycemia, hypertension, hypoglycemia, hypotension, lineage, thrombus

**v:** coagulate, welter

 *blood vessel combining forms:* angio-, vas-, vaso-

 *combining forms:* em-, hem-, hemato-, hemo-

 *stopping:* astringent, nemostatic, pressure point, styptic

## BLOOM

**a:** blooming, burgeoning, efflorescent, effloriferous, prosperous, recrudescent, remontant

**n:** anthesis, burgeoning, efflorescence, heyday, maturescence

**v:** burgeon, effloresce, flourish

## BLOTCH

**a:** macular, maculate

**n:** imperfection, macula, maculation

## BLOW

**a:** blown, traumatic, winnowed

**n:** assault, calamity, concussion, contrecoup, coup, impact, knockdown, recumbentibus, trauma

**v:** bluster, fulminate, parry, squander, traumatize, ward off

## BLUE

**a:** aqua, azure, bluish, cerulean, cobalt, cyanotic, depressed, eton, indigo, livid, melancholy, perse, puritanical, teal, turquoise, unpromising, violet

**n:** blues, boredom, cordon bleu, cyanosis, despondency, doldrums, dumps, gloom, lislessness, megrim, melancholy, navy, sadness, slump

## BLUNDER

**a:** solecistic(al)

**n:** blundering, boner, bungling, *faux pas*, gaffe, howler, *lapsus linguae*, mistake, muddle, parapraxia, parapraxis, solecism, stumble, stupidity

**v:** botch, bungle, err, flounder, mismanage, misstep, muddle, slip

## BLUNT

**a:** brusque, callous, frank, hebetate, insensible, insensitive, lackluster, lifeless, monotonous, obtund, obtuse, pointless, rude, unceremonious, unfeeling, untactful

**n:** bluntness, brusquerie, dullness, hebetude, insensibility, obtusity

**v:** anesthetize, hebetate, narcotize

## BLUSH

**a:** blushing, erubescent, reddened

**n:** bloom, color, erubescence, flush, glow, redness, rubedo, tinge

**v:** bloom, color, flush, glow, mantle, redden

## BOAST

**a:** boastful, bombastic, braggadocian, grandiloquent, grandiose, magniloquent, ostentatious, pompous, rodomontade, sonorous, swashbuckling, thrasonial, vainglorious, vaporing, vaunting

**n:** boasting, bombast, bravado, cockalorum, fanfaronade, gasconade, jactitation, pomposity, rodomontade, vainglory

**v:** bluster, brag, congratulate, emblazon, flaunt, flourish, gasconade, plume, preen, rodomontade, swagger, swashbuckle

> *boaster:* blusterer, braggadocio, braggart, bravado, cockalorum, fanfaron, gasconade, hector, jackanapes, megalomaniac, rodomont, roisterer, Scaramouche, swashbuckler

## BOAT

**a:** marine, naval, navicular, navigable

**n:** bumboat, caique, catamaran, coble, coracle, currach, cutter, dhow, dinghy, dory, drifter, felucca, gig, gondola, hoy, hydrofoil, hydroplane, junk, kayak, lugger, nuggar, pedalo, pink, pinnace, pirague, pirogue, proa, punt, randan, sampan, scull, shallop, shell, ship, skiff, sloop, smack, tanker, tender, trawler, trimaran, umiak, vaporetto, vedette, wherry

## BODY

**a:** autogenic, autogenous, bodily, constitutional, corporal, corporeal, corporeity, endogenous, eumorphic, gestic, homologous, incarnate, materiality, mesomorphic, physical, somatic

**n:** cadaver, carcass, constitution, corpse, *corpus, corpus et ame*, ectomorph, endomorph, habitus, mesomorph, physique, quantum, substance, tenement, torso

**v:** corporify, embody, incarnate

*combining forms:* -ome, somat-, somato-, -some

*heavy:* endomorphic, pyknic

*muscular:* mesomorphic

*thin and weak:* ectomorphic, leptosomic

**BOG**

**a:** quaggy

**n:** marsh, mire, morass, quagmire, slough, swamp

**BOGUS**

**a:** artificial, counterfeit, factitious, fake, faked, false, fraudulent, phony, pretended, pseudo, sham, spurious, supposititious

**BOIL**

**a:** furuncular

**n:** anthrax, eruption, furuncule, furunculosis, lesion, pimple, sinus, sore

**v:** blanch, infuse, parboil, recoct, reflux

**BOISTEROUS**

**a:** brawling, disorderly, noisy, raucous, robustious, robustuous, roisterous, termagant, truculent, tumultuous

**n:** boisterousness, disorder, horseplay, raucousness, rowdiness

**BOLD**

**a:** adventuresome, adventurous, audacious, brave, cheeky, chivalrous, *con bravura*, courageous, doughty, enterprising, impudent, intrepid, presumptuous, resolute, vainglorious, valiant

**n:** assumption, audacity, boldness, bravado, bravura, doughtiness, effrontery, impudence, intrepidity, presumption, temerity

**BOMBAST**

**a:** boastful, bombastic, declamatory, fustian, grandiloquent, grandiose, inflated, magniloquent, pompous, rhetorical, stilted, tumescent, tumid, turgescent, turgid, vainglorious

**n:** balderdash, braggadocio, fustian, gasconade, grandiloquence, grandiosity, magniloquence, pomposity, rhapsody, rodomontade, tumidity, turgidity, tympany

**BOND**

**a:** Gordian

**n:** agreement, collateral, covenant, debenture, glue, Gordian knot, hold, liaison, ligation, ligature, mortgage, nexus, note, obligation, recognizance, security, shackle, vinculum, vow

**v:** bind, cement, glue, hold, link, tie, unite

**BONE**

**a:** ankylotic, osseous, osteal

**n:** ankylosis, cartilage, diaphysis, lamella, lamina, os, ossification, osteogenesis, synostosis

*bone marrow combining forms:* myel-, myelo-

*combining forms:* oste-, osteo-

**BOOK**

**a:** bibliognostic, bibliolatrous, bibliopegistical, bibliophilic, bibliotaphic, casebound, cased, clothbound, hardcover, paperback, softcover

**n:** almagest, almanac, annals, anthology, appendix, armorial, backlist, Baedeker, bestiary, bibliolater, bibliology, bibliomania, bibliomaniac, bibliophage, bibliophile, bibliopole, bibliotheca, breviary, cambist, catechism, chapbook, concordance, dispensatory, faction, festschrift, formulary, herbal, holograph, hornbook, incunabulum, lectionary, ledger, lexicon, manual, missal, monograph, omnibus, pharmacopoeia, potboiler, prequel, primer, princeps, promptuary, psalter, pulp, remainder, sequel, sleeper, *succes d'estime*, thesaurus, tome, *vade mecum*, variorum

*combining form:* biblio-

*related words:* addenda, addendum, bibliography, bibliolatry, blurb, call number, corrigenda, critical apparatus, errata, excerpt, extract, fascicle, fascicule, fasciculus, flyleaf, format, frontispiece, gut, imprimatur, ISBN, lectern, *nihil obstat*, pendantry, recto, thumb index

## BOOKISH

**a:** academic, bibliognostic, erudite, knowing, learning, lettered, pedantic, philomathic, scholarly, scholastic, studious, thoughtful

**n:** literati, scholar

## BOOKLET

**n:** brochure, manual, monograph, pamphlet

## BOON

**a:** bountiful, convivial, intimate, jovial, merry, salutary

**n:** *alter ego*, benefit, benevolence, blessing, *bon camarade*, gain, gift, help, patronage, profit

## BOOR

**a:** boorish, churlish, clownish, disagreeable, dull, gauche, loutish, oafish, philistinic, rude, savage, uncouth, unpolished, unsophisticated, vulgar

**n:** boorishness, bromide, bumpkin, churl, clodhopper, cornball, dullard, fool, gaucherie, grobian, idiot, rudeness, rusticity, yokel

## BORDER

**a:** abutting, adjacent, adjoining, bordering, contiguous, discrete, juxtaposed, limbate, limitrophe, peripheral, tangential, trimming

**n:** boundary, confine, edge, extremity, margin, periphery, precinct, purlieus, selvage, terminus, trimming, verge

## BORDERLINE

**a:** controversial, debatable, dubious, intermediate, liminal, limitrophe, marginal, peripheral, problematic, questionable, skeptical, suspicious, unsure, vague

**n:** boundary

## BORE

**a:** *ad nauseam*, annoying, apathetic, arid, blase, boring, colorless, commonplace, desiccated, dull, ennuye, everyday, humdrum, irksome, jaded, monotonous, stultifying, stupefying, tedious, tiresome

**n:** boredom, depression, doldrums, ennui, inactivity, listlessness, pall, *taedium vitae*, tedium, wearisomeness

**v:** eat, grind, labor, pall, penetrate, push

## BORN

**a:** aborning, illegitimate, *in statu nascendi*, legitimate, misbegotten, nascent, native, natural, parturient, spurious, supposititious

**n:** nascency, parturition

## BOUNCE

**a:** resilient

**n:** buoyancy, elastic, hop, lifeliness, repercussion, resilience, resiliency, ricochet, spirit, zest

**v:** carom, dap, glance, jump, react, rebound, recoil, resile, richochet, skip, volley

## BOUND

**a:** circumferential, circumscribed, conterminal, conterminous, contiguous, coterminous, finite, limited, peripheral, *sevare modum*

**n:** ambit, border, circumference, circumscription, compass, confines, contiguity, edge, environs, finitude, parameter, perimeter, periphery, precinct, purlieu, terminal, terminus, threshold, trimming

**v:** circumscribe, confine, delimit, delineate, demarcate, embosom, encompass, leap, restrain, scope

## BOUNDLESS

**a:** eternal, illimitable, immeasurable, impenetrable, inexhaustible, infinite, limitless, measureless, unbounded, uncircumscribed, unfathomable

**n:** boundlessness, illimitability, infinitude, infinity

**BOW**

**a:** arcate, arched, arcuate, bent, bowed, inclined, kyphotic, semierect, stooped

**n:** curtain call, curtsy, genuflection, kiss, kowtow, namaste, obeisance, salaam, salutation

**v:** bend, genuflect, go to Canossa, incline, prostrate, salute, stoop, yield

**BOWELS**

**a:** borborygmic, cathartic, laxative, purgative, softening

**n:** borborygmus, cacation, crepitation, defecation, excretion, feces, flatus

**v:** disembowel, eviscerate, exenterate

**BOXING**

**a:** pugilant, pugilistic

**n:** fistiana, Marquis of Queensberry, pugilism, Queensberry rules

*boxer:* bantamweight, featherweight, flyweight, heavyweight, light heavyweight, middleweight, palooka, pugilist, southpaw, stumblebum, welterweight

**BOY**

**a:** boyish, ephebic, immature, juvenile, puerile, youthful

**n:** adolescent, beau, boyfriend, boyhood, boyishness, bub, bud, catamite, chap, ephebus, fellow, gamin, guttersnipe, juvenility, lad, lover, male, manikin, nipper, paramour, puerilism, puerility, ragamuffin, scapegoat, shaver, son, spalpeen, stripling, sweetheart, tad, urchin, waif, whipping boy, youth

**BRACELET**

**a:** armillary

**BRACING**

**a:** brisk, fresh, healthful, invigorating, quick, refreshing, reinforcing, roborant, salubrious, stimulating, strengthening, tonic, vigorating, vigorous, zestful, zesty

**BRAG**

**a:** boasting, bragging

**n:** boaster, braggadocio, braggart, bragger, fanfaron, loudmouth, puffer, rodomontade, Scaramouche, swashbuckler

**v:** gasconade

**BRAIN**

**a:** brainy, cerebral, clever, ingenious, intellectual, intelligent, knowing, learned, smart

**n:** beta wave, cerebration, cerebrum, cognition, cognoscenti, convolution, encephalon, faculty, genius, gyrus, hemisphere, intellect, intelligence, mahat, meninges, noesis, psyche, reason, sensorium

*combining forms:* cerebr-, cerebro-, encephal-, encephalo-, phren-, phreno-

*parts:* cerebellum, cerebrum, corpus callosum, cortex, frontal lobe, hypothalamus, mantle, medulla oblongata, occipital lobe, pallium, parietal lobe, pineal body, pituitary gland, pons, spinal cord, temporal lobe, thalamus, ventricle

*related words:* alpha rhythm, apoplexy, cerebral hemorrhage, concussion, EEG, electroencephalograph, encephalitis, endorphin, epilepsy, lobotomy, neurosurgeon, prefrontal leucotomy

**BRAN**

**a:** furfuraceous

**n:** fiber, roughage

**BRANCH**

**a:** bifurcated, biramose, biramous, brachiate, cladose, dichotomous, divergent, forked, furcate, patent, patulous, polychotomous, radial, radiating, ramate, ramifying, ramose, ramous, ramulose, sarmentose, sarmentous, tentacular

**n:** arborization, axil, bifurcation, discipline, divarication, divergence, fascicle, fascicule, node, ramification, ramus, snag

**v:** arborize, bifurcate, deliquesce, divaricate, diverge, furcate, ramify, subdivide

**BRANDY**

**n:** *aqua vitae,* Armagnac, cognac, *eau de vie,* marc, spirits, whiskey

**BRASS**

**a:** brazen, forward, resolute, shameless

**n:** audacity, effrontery, hubris, impertinence, impudence, insolence, presumption, temerity

> *alloy:* aerugo, bronze, metal, patina, *verd antique,* verdigris

**BRAVADO**

**n:** bombast, flamboyance, nerve, ostentation, panache, pomposity, pride, swagger, verve

**BRAVE**

**a:** audacious, bold, cavalier, chivalrous, courageous, dauntless, doughty, fortitudinous, gallant, heroic, intrepid, martial, resolute, stalwart, undaunted, valiant, valorous, venturesome

**n:** audacity, award, bluster, braggadocio, bravado, bravery, bravura, chivalry, commendation, dauntlessness, derring-do, emprise, fortitude, gallantry, gumption, honor, intrepidity, intrepidness, nerve, panache, prowess, skill, strength, swagger, temerity, valiancy, valor, verve

**BRAWL**

**n:** altercation, argument, brannigan, brouhaha, contention, controversy, din, disputation, dissention, donnybrook, doscord, fracas, melee, quarrel, squabble, to-do, tumult, wrangle

**BRAZEN**

**a:** arrogant, audacious, brassy, clangorous, crass, daring, defying, extreme, forward, gaudy, hard, hubristic, impudent, insolent, intense, nervy, presumptuous, resolute, shameless, unscrupulous

**n:** audacity, boldness, brazenness

**BREACH**

**a:** dissentious, indecorous, schismatical, solecistic

**n:** abruption, abscission, barbarism, crevasse, crevice, desuetude, discord, dissension, *faux pas,* gap, hiatus, impropriety, infraction, infringement, interruption, nonfulfillment, nonobservance, rupture, schism, solecism, split, suspension, tear, transgression, violation

**BREAD**

**a:** cheese, egg, French, granary, oatmeal, poppy-seed, potato, raisin, rye, soda, unleavened, Vienna, wheat, white

**n:** bagel, bannock, brewis, brioche, challah, chapatti, croissant, flatbread, gluten, grissini, hardtack, heel, host, matzo, nan, paneity, paratha, pita, pumpernickel, puri, roll, roti, sippet, sop, sourdough, stollen

**v:** leaven

**BREAK**

**a:** hiatal, perfidious, traitorous

**n:** abruption, abscission, apostasy, caesura, catabolism, cataclasm, cessation, comminution, decomposition, discontinuity, disintegration, disruption, dissolution, fragmentation, hiatus, infringement, intermission, interregnum, interruption, lacuna, liquidation, malfeasance, malversation, pause, perfidy, prostration, recess, respite, schism, scission, transgression, trituration, violation

**v:** atomize, bankrupt, comminute, decompose, disintegrate, disjoin, divaricate, fractionalize, fracture, fragment, liquidate, pulverize, reave, rend, rift, rupture, scarify, schismatize, secede, spall, stave, sunder, transgress, triturate, vaporize, violate

> *breakable:* brittle, crumbly, fracturable, fragile, frangible, friable
> *combining form:* fissi-
> *unbreakable:* immarcescible, imperishable, indestructible, irrefrangable

**BREAST**

**a:** bathycolpian, bimastic, mammary, mammiferous, pectoral, pneumatic

**n:** areola, bimasticism, bimasty, cleavage, dug, mammae, pectorals, teat, udder

**v:** lactate

**BR EATH**

**a:** aspiratory, dyspneic, labored, respiratory, stertorous, suspirious

**n:** animation, apnea, asphyxiation, *elan vital*, emanation, exhalation, flatus, halitus, hypernea, hyperventilation, hypopnea, inhalation, inspiration, pneuma, polypnea, prana, suspiration, utterance

**v:** exhale, expire, inhale, suspire

*combining forms:* pneum-, pneumato-, pneumo-, spiro-

**BREED**

**n:** eugenics, genetic engineering, hybrid, mestizo, metis, mongrel, mulatto, pedigree, pullulation

**v:** multiply, procreate, propagate, pullulate

**BREVITY**

**a:** breviloquent, brief, cryptic, laconic, monosyllabic, *paucis verbis*, succinct

**n:** abbreviation, abridgement, aphorism, breviloquence, compactness, conciseness, ephemerality, laconism, monosyllabicity, pithiness, shortness, succinctness, terseness

**BREW**

**n:** brewing, concoction, decoction, mash, pulp, zymurgy

**v:** concoct, contrive, decoct

**BRIEF**

**a:** abrupt, briefly, brusque, compendiary, compendious, concise, cryptic, cursory, *en abrege*, ephemeral, epigrammatic, evanescent, fugacious, laconic, monosyllabic, *paucis verbis*, perfunctory, pithy, short-lived, succinct, summary, superficial, transient, transitory, vanishing

**n:** abstract, brevity, cameo, compendium, epitome, inventory, monosyllabicity, short shrift, shortness, summarization, summary, syllabus

**BRIGHT**

**a:** auroral, auspicious, brilliant, burnished, coruscating, effulgent, emblazoned, flamboyant, fresh, furbished, garish, gaudy, glittering, glossy, illustrious, incandescent, irradiant, luminous, lurid, lustrous, meteoric, nitid, opalescent, pyrotechnic, radiant, refulgent, resplendent, scintillating, shiny, showy, spiritual, undimmed, vivid

**n:** brightness, brilliance, brilliancy, eclat, effulgence, fluorescence, fulgor, incandescence, iridescence, lambency, luminance, luminescence, luminosity, luster, nitidity, opalescence, prodigy, pyrotechnics, refulgence, refulgency, resplendence, scintillation, *tour de force*, virtuosity, vivacity, *wunderkind*

**v:** brighten, effulge, illuminate, scintillate

**BRING**

**a:** aborning, parturient

**n:** bringing, correlation, parturition

**v:** advance, assemble, bear, beget, correlate, deliver, elicit, institute, pilot, reanimate, regenerate, resurrect, resuscitate, revitalize, revivify, shepherd, transport

**BRINK**

**n:** bank, bluff, border, boundary, brim, circumference, crest, edge, end, extremity, frontier, limit, line, lip, margin, periphery, precipice, ridge, rim, threshold, tip, top, verge

**BRISK**

**a:** alacritous, *allegro, con brio*, ebullient, effervescent, energetic, galvanic, lively, snappy, spirited, stimulating, zestful

**n:** alacrity, briskness, ebullience, effervescence, rapidity, spiritedness, swiftness, vivacity, zip

**BRISTLES**

**a:** aristate, barbellate, bristly, chaetigerous, chaetophorous, exhinate, hispid, setaceous, setarious, setiferous, setigerose, setose, spiny

**n:** horripilation, piloerection

*combining form:* echino-

**BRITTLE**

**a:** crumbly, delicate, evanescent, fragile, frangible, friable, perishable, pulvurulent, tenuous, transitory, weak

**n:** brittleness, delicacy, fragility, frangibility, friability, tenuity, tenuousness, weakness

**BROKEN**

**a:** contrite, decrepit, dilapidated, disconnected, discrete, disreputable, disunited, fractional, fractured, fragmental, fragmentary, humbled, interrupted, kaput, ruptured, spasmodic, subdued, tatterdemalion

**n:** bit, debris, fragment, shard, smithereens, splinter

**BROTHEL**

**n:** bagnio, bawdyhouse, bordello, cat house, disorderly house, lupanar, *maison de tolerance,* seraglio

**BROTHER**

**a:** affectionate, amicable, brotherly, fraternal, sibling

**n:** alliance, brotherhood, companionship, confraternalization, confraternity, confrerie, fellowship, fraternity, sibling, sodality

**BROWBEAT**

**a:** dictatorial, domineering, swashbuckling, tyrannical, tyrannous

**v:** bludgeon, bulldoze, bully, cow, dictate, domineer, dragoon, frighten, hector, intimidate, overawe, scare, subdue, swashbuckle

**BROWN**

**a:** beige, bruneous, brunescent, brunette, cafe au lait, coffee, cordovan, fulvous, khaki

**BRUISE**

**a:** black-and-blue, livid

**n:** black eye, black-and-blue mark, contusion, ecchymosis, laceration, lividity, petechia, trauma

**v:** contuse, disable, traumatize

**BRUTAL**

**a:** barbous, bestial, brutish, Caliban, draconian, feral, harsh, inhuman, insensate, insensible, Procrustean, repressive, sadistic, severe, troglodytic, vindictive

**n:** barbarity, brutalitarian, brutality, brutishness, ferity, inhumanity, sadist

**BUBBLING**

**a:** carbonated, ebullient, effervescent, effusive, exuberant, fizzy, yeasty

**n:** ebulliency, effervescence, effusiveness, exuberance, yeastiness

**BUD**

**a:** budding, burgeoning, emanating, emergent, pullulant, viviparous

**n:** burgeoning, efflorescence, plumule, pullulation

**v:** burgeon, germinate, pullulate

*combining form:* blasto-

**BUFFOON**

**n:** clown, comedian, comic, fool, grobian, harlequin, humorist, jester, joker, merryandrew, mime, mimic, stooge, wit, zany

*buffoonery:* clownage, foolishness, harlequinade, humor, jest, nonsense

**BUGBEAR**

**n:** apprehension, *bete noire,* bogey, boogeyman, dread, fear, ghost, goblin, gremlin, hobgoblin, *loup-garou,* problem, scare, specter, terror, threat, wraith

**BUILD**

**a:** architectonic, architectural, constructional, custom-built, jerry-built, prefabricated, tectonic

**n:** annex, building, composition, development, edifice, fabric, fabrication, folly, foundation, house, landmark, makeup, module, pantheon, pavilion, physique, pile, pueblo, real estate, roof, stature, structure, tenement

**v:** chisel, compose, contrive, fabricate, fashion, manufacture, renovate

*combining forms:* -arium, -orium

**BULGE**

**a:** bulging, convex, exophthalmic, gibbous, obtrusive, protrudent, protrusive, protuberant, swelling, swollen, tuberous, tumescent, tumid, turgid

**n:** convexity, gibbosity, protrusion, protuberance

**v:** beetle, protrude, protuberate

**BULK**

**a:** bulky, corpulent, magnitudinous, massive, ponderous, unwieldy, voluminous

**n:** aggregate, bulkiness, corpulency, dimension, fiber, largeness, magnitude, majority, massivity, ponderosity, quanta, quantum, roughage, voluminosity

**BULLY**

**a:** bullying, despotic, domineering, imperious, overbearing

**n:** blusterer, hector, martinet

**v:** bluster, browbeat, coerce, dragoon, frighten, hector, intimidate, punish, tyrannize, victimize

**BUNGLING**

**a:** amateurish, awkward, gauche, inept, inexpert, maladroit, unskillful

**n:** blac-bec, bungler

**v:** botch, bungle, butcher, confuse, fail, flounder, flub, fluff, fumble, garble, goof, hack, jumble, miscue, misdo, mishandle, misstep, mistake, mix up, muddle, muss, slip, stumble

**BURDEN**

**a:** burdened, burdensome, cumbersome, cumbrous, encumbered, formidable, grievous, impedimental, impeditive, impregnated, obstructive, onerous, oppressed, oppressive, overpowering, ponderous

**n:** albatross, duty, encumbrance, handicap, hindrance, impediment, imposition, incubus, infliction, millstone, obligation, obstacle, *onus*, *onus probandi*, perplexity, responsibility, task

**v:** encumber, freight, handicap, hinder

**BUREAUCRAT**

**n:** apparatchik, mandarin, official

*jargon:* gobbledygook, officialese

**BURIAL**

**a:** cemeterial, cinerary, funebrial, funereal, mortuary, sepulchral

**n:** barrow, catacomb, chamber, charnel nouse, cromlech, crypt, deposition, dolmen, exequy, hypogeum, inhumation, interment, mausoleum, mound, necropolis, obsequy, repository, sepulcher, tomb, vault

**v:** entomb

*clothes:* cerecloth, cerement, shroud, winding sheet

**BURN**

**a:** burnable, caustic, combustible, conflagrant, conflagratory, corrosive, flammable, ignescent, inflammable, inflammatory

**n:** arson, *auto-da-fe*, brazier, burning, cinder, cineration, combustion, cremation, effigy, incineration, kindling, tinder

**v:** brand, braze, cauterize, char, cremate, deflagrate, fire, gutter, ignite, inflame, kindle, light, roast, scald, scorch, singe, sizzle, sterilize

**BURST**

**a:** burgeoning, bursting, dehiscent, dissilient, efflorescent

**n:** barrage, blossom, dehiscence, dissilience, efflorescence, fusillade, proruption, rupture, salvo, volley

**v:** barrage, blossom, burgeon, dehisce, effloresce, explode, irrupt, rupture, volley

**BUSINESS**

**a:** Babbitical, incorporated, intangible, practical, pragmatic, subsidiary

**n:** articles of association, asset, cartel, clientele, commerce, commercialism, company, conglomerate, consolidation, consortium, employment, establishment, factor, flagship, flotation, industrialism, industry, labor, *les affaires*, line, mercantilism, metier, patronage, proprietorship, province, pursuit, racket, route, subsidiary, syndic, syndicate, trade, traffic, work

**v:** diversify

    *people:* Babbitt, businessman, businesswoman, entrepreneur, *homme d'affaires*, magnate, tycoon

**BUSY**

**a:** assiduous, diligent, dynamic, engaged, engrossed, frantic, hectic, industrious, occupied, operose, persevering, sedulous, vibrant

**n:** assiduity, engagement, operosity, sedulity

**BUSYBODY**

**n:** gadfly, gossip, intermeddler, meddler, polypragmatist, pragmatic, quidnunc, zealot

**BUTTER**

**a:** butyraceous, rancid

**n:** shortening

**v:** clarify

**BUTTERFLY**

**a:** lepidopterological, lepidopterous

**n:** caterpillar, chrysalis, lepidopteran, metamorphosis, moth, pupa

**BUTTOCKS**

**a:** callipygian, callipygous, pygal, steatopygic, steatopygous

**n:** breech, derriere, fundament, gluteus maximus, haunches, hunkers, keister, nates, podex, posterior, rump, steatopygia

**BUYER**

**a:** monopsonistic

**n:** *caveat emptor*, consumer, *emptor*, monopsonist, oniomaniac, purchaser, vendee

    *buying:* arbitrage, simony, speculation

**BUZZ**

**n:** bombilation, bombination, buzzing, kazoo, tinnitus

**v:** bombinate, whizz

**BYGONE**

**a:** antiquated, elapsed, extinct, out-of-date, outmoded, *passe*, past, quondam, *whilom*, yore

**n:** *ancien regime*, antiquity

**BYPASS**

**n:** circumnavigation, circumvention, detour

**v:** circumnavigate, circumvent, detour, dodge, eschew, evade, ignore, neglect, short-circuit, shunt, sidestep

## CALAMITY

**a:** calamitous, cataclysmal, cataclysmic, catastrophic, dangerous, desperate, disastrous, harmful, holocaustic, precipitous, sad, terrible, tragic, unfortunate, unlucky, woeful

**n:** Armageddon, atrocity, blow, cataclysm, catastrophe, debacle, difficulty, disaster, doom, fiasco, holocaust, loss, misfortune, reverse, strife, tragedy, tribulation, woe

## CALCULATE

**a:** algorismic, calculating

**n:** abacus, accumulator, algorism, algorithm, calculator, dead reckoning, microchip, ready reckoner

**v:** appraise, assay, assess, cipher, compute, determine, estimate, examine, figure, forecast, gauge, infer, measure, predict, prognosticate, project, reason, score, tally, theorize, value, weigh

## CALENDAR

**a:** intercalary

**n:** agenda, almanac, calends, chart, diary, docket, Gregorian, intercalation, Julian, list, log, menology, record, table

**v:** intercalate

## CALF

**a:** gastrocnemial, sural

**n:** gastrocnemius
   *animal:* cade, dogie, freemartin, slink, stirk

## CALL

**a:** convocational, evocative, evocatory

**n:** appeal, beckoning, clarion, command, convocation, demand, draft, evocation, muster, notice, notification, request, scream, shriek, signal, subpoena, summons, yell

**v:** address, convocate, denominate, designate, dub, entitle, evocate, invoke, muster, nominate, style

## CALLOUS

**a:** adamant, anesthetic, cold-blooded, cruel, dedolent, emotionless, hardened, impertinent, impiteous, indifferent, indurative, inexorable, insensible, insensitive, obdurate, stubborn, unfeeling

**n:** callousness, hardness, inflexibility, insensitivity, stubbornness, toughness

## CALM

**a:** anodynic, apathetic, assuasive, calmant, calmative, composed, dispassionate, dispassive, equanimous, fatalistic, grave, halcyon, hermetic, hesychastic, impartial, impassive, imperturbed, impervious, indifferent, insensate, insouciant, lackadaisical, nepenthean, nonchalant, oasitic, pacific, peaceful, philosophical, phlegmatic, placative, placatory, placid, pococurante, quiescent, sedate, sedative, self-possessed, serene, sober, staid, stoic, stolid, subdued, temperate, tranquil, tranquilizing, unagitated, undisturbed, unruffled, untroubled

**n:** apathy, assuagement, ataraxia, calmness, composure, detente, dispassion, equability, equanimity, forbearance, impassivity, imperturbation, insouciance, lackadaisy, lassitude, *nepenthe*, nonchalance, passivity, phlegm, placation, pococurantism, propitiation, quietude, repose, *sang-froid*, sedation, sedative, serenity, solemnity, tranquility, tranquilization, tranquilizer

**v:** abate, allay, appease, assuage, conciliate, dispel, mollify, pacify, placate, propitiate, quell, quiesce, reconcile, sedate, simmer, slacken, soothe, subside, tranquilize

## CAMP

**a:** castrensian

**n:** bivouac, cantonment, castrametation, laager, outspan, *pied-a-terre*, transit camp

**v:** bivouac

## CANCEL

**a:** abrogative, cancellable, recissory, revocable, revocatory, revokable

**n:** abrogation, cancellation, cessation, deletion, disaffirmance, disaffirmation, expunction, invalidation, nullification, recision, reduction

**v:** abjure, abolish, abrogate, annul, countermand, delete, disavow, efface, erase, expunge, invalidate, neutralize, nullify, obliterate, quash, recant, remit, renounce, repeal, repudiate, rescind, retract, revoke, vacate, viviate

> *uncancellable:* inalienable, indefeasible, unbreakable

## CANCER

**a:** benign, cancerous, cancroid, carcinogenic, carcinomatous, malignant, sarcomatous, terminal

**n:** carcinogen, carcinoma, malignancy, malignant neoplasm, metastasis, sarcoma

combining form: -oma

> *related words:* chemotherapy, interferon, Laetrile, Pap test, radiotherapy, remission

## CANDID

**a:** artless, forthright, forward, frank, guileless, honest, impartial, implicit, incorruptible, ingenuous, naive, pure, serious, straightforward, unprejudiced, unsophisticated, unsubtle, wholehearted

**n:** candidness, candor, honesty

## CANDIDATE

**n:** aspirant, choice, hopeful, nominee, office seeker, postulance, postulancy, postulant, seeker, striver

## CANE

**a:** arundinaceous

**n:** bamboo, cylinder, ferule, malacca, rattan, rod, sorghum, staff, stem, stick, swagger stick, walking stick

## CANNIBAL

**a:** anthropophagous, cannibalistic

**n:** anthropophagi, anthropophaginian, anthropophagite, anthropophagus, cannibalism, cannibality, exophagy, long pig

## CAPABLE

**a:** able, accomplished, adequate, competent, consummate, efficient, expert, fit, licensed, potential, qualified, responsible, sciential, virtuosic

**n:** ability, capability, capacity, competency, expertise, power, qualification, resourcefulness, resources, skill

## CAPACITY

**a:** ample, broad, capacious, copious, expansive, extensive, large, magnitudi-*nous*, unlimited, virtuosic, voluminous, wide

**n:** amplitude, attainment, capability, content, endowment, faculty, genius, intellect, intelligence, latitude, magnitude, measure, potentiality, *puissance*, qualification, talent, virtuosity, volume

## CAPER

**n:** *capriccio, capriole, caracole, curvet,* frolic, *gambade, gambado,* gambol, marlock, prank, romp, saltation, trick, turn

**v:** cavort, frisk, gambol, play, romp

## CAPITAL

**a:** *majuscule*

**n:** *factotum, majuscule,* uppercase

> *opposite:* lowercase, minuscule

## CAPTIVATE

**a:** alluring, attractive, captivating, charming, enchanting, seductive, winning

**n:** bondage, captivity, chains, dependency, domination, enslavement, oppression, restraint, thrall, thralldom

**v:** allure, amuse, attract, bewitch, capture, charm, elate, enamor, enrapture, enslave, ensorcel, enthral, entrance, excite, fascinate, influence, please, satisfy, seduce, take, transport, win, woo

## CARAVAN

**n:** campaign, cavalcade, convoy, excursion, expedition, group, odyssey, peregrination, pilgrimage, reconnaissance, safari, tour, travel, trek, trip

## CARD

**a:** *a la carte*

**n:** bridge, card, cartomancy, court, flashcard, honors, poker, singleton, stock, talon, tarot, thaumatrope

**v:** *abattre son jeu*, riffle, ruff, stack

    *person:* croupier, kibitzer

## CARE

**a:** custodial, pastoral, solicitous, solicitudinous, supervisory, tutelary, tutorial

**n:** attention, attentiveness, circumspection, consideration, custody, guardianship, management, maternalism, paternalism, precaution, prudence, solicitude, supervision, tutelage, vigilance, ward

**v:** commend, commit, consign, entrust, *gardez bien*, minister

    *carefree:* degage, incautious, insouciant, irresponsible, *san souci, sine cura*

## CAREFUL

**a:** analytical, assiduous, attentive, calculating, cautious, circumspect, conscientious, diligent, discreet, discriminating, discriminatory, fastidious, finical, gingerly, heedful, hypercritical, judicious, meticulous, noncommital, observant, particularistic, pedantic, politic, precise, provident, prudent, punctilious, punctual, rabbinic, regardful, scrupulous, sedulous, solicitous, tactful, timid, vigilant

**n:** carefulness, caution, circumspection, fastidiousness, meticulosity, particularity, prudence, punctiliousness, scrupulosity, scrupulousness, solicitude

## CARELESS

**a:** apathetic, casual, clumsy, cursory, feckless, harum-scarum, heedless, impetuous, improvident, imprudent, inadvertent, inattentive, incautious, incurious, indifferent, indiscreet, injudicious, neglectful, negligent, oblivious, *per incuriam*, perfunctory, pococurante, precipitate, promiscuous, random, remiss, slipshod, slovenly, superficial, unconcerned, unmindful, unsolicitous

**n:** carelessness, improvidence, imprudence, inattention, incaution, incuriosity, indifference, indiscretion, neglect, negligence, nonchalance, perfunctoriness, pococurantism, promiscuity, superficiality

## CARESS

**a:** affectionate, amative, caressive, endearing

**v:** baby, coddle, cuddle, dandle, embrace, fondle, hug, indulge, kiss, love, pamper, pat, pet, stroke

## CARETAKER

**n:** concierge, conservator, curator, custodian, doorman, janitor, keeper, ostiary, porter, super, superintendent

## CARNIVAL

**a:** carnivalesque, festive

**n:** celebration, feast, fiesta, holiday, jamboree, Mardi Gras

## CAROUSE

**a:** bacchanal(ian), bacchanalic, carousing, roystering, roysterous

**n:** bacchanal, bacchant(e), binge, bout, carousal, carouser, debauchery, excess, festivity, merrymaking, orgy, rampage, revel, revelry, saturnalia, spree, wassail

**v:** binge, debauch, drink, feast, frolic, revel, roister, royster, spree

## CARP

**a:** captious, carping, hypercritical

**n:** carping, cavil, pettifoggery

**v:** bicker, cavil, censure, complain, criticize, disparage, dissent, nag, pettifog, quibble

## CARRIAGE

**n:** bearing, deportment, front, gait, manner, mien, port, posture

   *vehicle:* buggy, bus, conveyance, dickey box, outrider, passage, perambulator, *porte cochere*, rumble seat, surry, transport(ation), trolley, waftage, wagon

## CARRY

**a:** ablative, afferent, deferent, efferent

**n:** ablation, portage

**v:** bear, cart, convey, deliver, execute, impart, implement, move, port, portage, remove, shift, take, tote, transact, transfer, transmit, transport, waft

   *combining forms:* -fer-, -phore, -phorous

## CAST

**a:** desquamative, desquamatory, exuvial

**n:** casting, conjunction, desquamation, exuviation, incantation, invocation, matrix

**v:** desquamate, exfoliate, exorcise, exuviate, slough

## CASTE

**n:** Brahmin, harijan, kshatriya, pariah, sudra

## CASTRATE

**n:** asexualization, castration, demasculinization, emasculation, eunuchism, eviration, gonadectomy, mutilation, orchidectomy, ruination

**v:** asexualize, desexualize, emasculate, eunuchize, geld, neuter, remove, ruin, spay, weaken

   *animals:* barrow, capon, eunuch, gelding, stag, wether

## CASUAL

**a:** accidental, adventitious, contingent, cursory, debonair, degage, desultory, dishabille, disorganized, fortuitous, haphazard, impromptu, incidental, indiscriminate, informal, insouciant, lackadaisical, nonchalant, offhand, perfunctory, precarious, random, superficial, uncertain, unexpected, unimportant, unpremeditated, unstructured, unstudied

**n:** serendipity

## CAT

**a:** aeluropodous, ailuropodous, cheliferous, feliform, feline

**n:** aelurophile, ailurophile, ailurophilia, civet, felinity, galeophilia, grimalkin, kitten, kitty, moggy, Siamese, tabby, zibet

**v:** caterwaul

   *hate:* aelurophobe, ailurophobe, ailurophobia, galeophobia, gatophobia

## CATALOG(UE)

**a:** catalogical

**n:** book, compendium, index, invoice, list, prospectus, record, register, repertorium, repertory, roll, series, table

## CATASTROPHE

**n:** Armageddon, battle, catastasis, conflict, destruction, *gotterdammerung*, holocaust

## CATEGORY

**n:** class, classification, concept, genre, idea, lexicon, rubric, title

## CATER

**v:** bend, bow, condescend, defer, deign, favor, humor, kowtow, lower, oblige, pander, patronize, purvey, salute, serve, stoop, supply, yield

## CAUGHT

**a:** *(in) flagrante delicto, in actu,* redhanded

## CAUSE

**a:** aprioristic, conducive, endogenous, etiological, evangelistic, exogenous, spontaneous, teleological

**n:** *a priori,* apriority, *casus belli, causa finalis,* causality, determinant, determinism, etiology, fountainhead, genesis, mainspring, origin, provenance, teleology

**v:** bring about, devise, effectuate, encompass, engender, espouse, foment, give rise to, instigate, occasion, precipitate, produce, promote, prompt, provoke, stir up

*causing combining forms:* -facient, -fic, -otic

*combining forms:* -gen-, -genesis, -genous

**CAUSTIC**

**a:** acidulous, acrimonious, biting, corrosive, incisive, keen, malevolent, mordant, pyrotic, sarcastic, satirical, scathing, trenchant, virulent, vitriolic

**n:** alkali, causticity, corrosive, lime, lye, malevolence, mordacity, phenol, spinosity, virulence

**CAUTION**

**a:** admonitory, Argus-eyed, attentive, calculating, careful, cautious, circumspect, discreet, expectant, *festina lente*, judicious, meticulous, provident, prudent(ial), scrupulous

**n:** admonishment, admonition, alarm, alert, calculation, cautiousness, *caveat*, circumspection, concern, cunctation, discretion, observance, portent, prudence, vigilance, wariness, watchfulness

**v:** admonish, advise, alert, apprise, awaken, counsel, flag, notify, sermonize, signal, warn

**CAVE**

**a:** speleological, troglodytic(al)

**n:** antra, antrum, caveman, cavern, cavity, cellar, cove, crypt, den, grotto, hole, hollow, lair, opening, sinus, speleologist, speleology, spelunker, stalactite, stalagmite, troglodyte, tunnel

**CELEBRATE**

**a:** *cause celebre*, celebrated, commemoratory

**n:** bacchanal, carousal, celebration, commemoration, exultation, festivity, jubilation, jubilee, junket, orgy, outing, ovation, party, potlatch, revelry, saturnalia, shindig, solemnization, wassail

**v:** commemorate, emblazon, lionize, maffick, revel, roister, solemnize

*celebrity:* big-wig, dignitary, luminary, personage

**CELESTIAL**

**a:** divine, empyrean, ethereal, etheric, heavenly, otherworldly, spiritual, supernal, supernatural, transcendental, unearthly

**n:** *arcana caelestia*

**CELL**

**n:** cleavage, cytology, egg, epithelium, fission, gamete, isomorphism, matrix, meiosis, mitosis, *oubliette*, ovum, protoplasm, segmentation, sperm, spermatozoon, zygote

*combining forms:* -blast, cyt-, -cyte, cyto-, kary-, karyo-, -plasm, -plast

**CEMETERY**

**n:** boneyard, burial, burying ground, campo santo, catacomb, city of the dead, Golgotha, graveyard, necropolis, ossuary, polyandrium

**CENSOR**

**a:** calumnious, castigative, censorial, censorious, condemnatory, defamatory, excoriative, faultfinding, slanderous, stigmatic, vituperative

**n:** Cato, *censor morum*, critic, detractor

**v:** ban, blue-pencil, bowdlerize, edit out, expurgate, interdict, muzzle, prohibit, proscribe, remove, suppress

*censorship:* censureship, exclusion, *imprimatur*, *nihil obstat*

**CENSURE**

**a:** blameworthy, censurable, condemnatory, reprehensible

**n:** animadversion, calumniation, censureship, excoriation, reprehension, reprobation, reproof, stricture v: abuse, animadvert, berate, calumniate, castigate, chastise, chew out, condemn, damn, excoriate, lambaste, opprobriate, rebuke, reprobate, revile, scarify, stigmatize, traduce, vilify, vituperate

## CENTER

a: afferent, amalgamative, basic, centralizing, centripetal, centrogenic, concentric, dominant, equidistant, essential, integrative, middlemost, pivotal, principal, umbilical, unicentric

n: axis, centrality, centricity, centripetalism, centripetence, concentricity, cynosure, epicenter, focus, ganglion, hub, linchpin, Mecca, *nidus*, nucleus, *omphalos*, pivot, polestar, umbilicus

v: concentrate, converge, direct toward, focus

> *away from:* acentric, centrifugal, decentralized, decentralizing, efferent, excentric, excentrical, polycentric
>
> *combining forms:* mes-, meso-

## CENTURY

a: centenary, centennial, centurial, fin-de-siecle

n: centenary, centennial, siecle

## CEREMONY

a: ceremonial, ceremonious, conventional, formal, punctilious, ritualistic, solemn

n: accolade, cavalcade, commemoration, commencement, custom, decorum, dedication, etiquette, formality, graduation, inauguration, induction, initiation, investiture, observance, ostentation, panjandrum, panoply, pomp, procession, propriety, protocol, rite, rite of passage, ritual, service, trooping the color, unveiling, wedding

v: celebrate, solemnize

> *master of:* ceremoniarius, compere, MC, officiator

## CERTAIN

a: absolute, acataleptic, adamant, apodictic, categorical, conclusive, explicit, incontestable, incontrovertible, indisputable, indubitable, inevitable, infallible, irrefrangible, irrefutable, probabilistic, proved, undeniable, unequivocal, unerring, unmistakable

n: accuracy, assurance, certainty, certitude, foregone conclusion, incontrovertibility, indisputability, indubitability, ineluctability, infallibility, open sesame, positivism, reality, securement

> *certainly:* absolutely, *bien entendu*, ineluctably, inevitably, *sans doute*, undoubtedly, unquestionably

## CHAIN

n: catenation, chain, *chatelaine*, concatenation, crosspiece, fetters, guy, manacles, peg, rope, shackles, toggle, vinculum

v: catenate, fetter

## CHAIR

a: *ex cathedra*

n: *antimacassar*, bench, cucking stool, rocker, seat, sedan, stool, support, throne

> *parts:* caster, *saltire*, slat, splat, stave, stile, stretcher, upholstery

## CHAMBER

n: area, berth, bin, camera, cameration, cell, compartment, concameration, container, cubbyhole, cubicule, cubiculum, division, hollow, kiva, receptacle, space, vault

## CHANCE

a: accidental, adventitious, aleatory, arbitrary, casual, contingent, fortuitous, haphazard, inadvertent, incidental, *par hasard, per accidens*, random, unexpected, unplanned, unpremeditated

n: accidentality, casualism, *casus fortuitus*, contingency, fortuitiveness, fortuity, haphazardry, on spec, opportunity, peradventure, serendipity, speculation, tychism, vicissitudes

v: hazard, venture

## CHANGE

a: adaptable, alchemic, alterable, ambivalent, amenable, amphibolic, *autre temps*, capricious, chameleonic, changeable, changing, chatoyant, climacteric, digressive, erratic, evolutionary, fickle, fluctuating, inconstant, involutional, iridescent, itinerant, kaleidoscopic, labile, mercurial, metamorphic, metamorphous, metastatic, mutable, *mutatis mutandis*, nomadic, penitent, pliable, protean, quicksilver, shifting, shot, tangential, temperamental, tractable, transitional, turbulent, unstable, vagrant, variable, variational, versatile, vertiginous, whimsical

**n:** (per)mutation, (r)evolution, alternance, alternation, cavalcade, chameleon, climacteric, heterization, kaleidoscope, lability, levity, metamorphosis, metastasis, modification, modulation, mutability, penitence, proteus, repentance, saltation, substitution, transfiguration, transformation, transition, transmogrification, transmutation, transubstantiation, variation, vicissitude

**v:** acclimatize, alchemize, alternate, apostasize, commute, diversify, evolve, fluctuate, graduate, inflect, metamorphose, metastasize, modify, modulate, mutate, orient, orientate, oscillate, permutate, regulate, substitute, tergiversate, transfigure, transform, transmogrify, transmute, transplant, transpose, transubstantiate, vacilate, variegate

*combining forms:* -plasia, -plasy, trans-, trop-, -tropic, tropo-

## CHANNEL

**a:** canalicular, canaliculate, cannellated, chamfered, channeled, grooved, vascular

**n:** aqueduct, bay, *canaliculus*, cavity, chase, conduit, culvert, ditch, duct, estuary, fiord, firth, flume, groove, gully, hollow, *meatus*, pipe, race, sinus, spillway, strait, trench, *vas*, vessel

## CHAPERON(E)

**n:** attendant, convoy, *duenna*, escort, *gouvernante*, governess, guard, guardian, guide, monitor, protector, scout, surveillant, usher

**v:** attend, escort, guard, monitor, protect, usher

## CHAPTER

**a:** capitulary

**n:** assembly, body, branch, capitulary, clan, contingent, division, lodge, organization, post, section, unit

## CHARACTER

**a:** characteristic, characterological, diacritical, distinguishing, ethological, individual, pathognomonic, peculiar, quintessential, symbolic, symptomatic, typical

**n:** accoutrement, attribute, caliber, constitution, disposition, *dramatis personae*, eccentricity, *ethos*, humor, idiosyncrasy, individuality, lineaments, mitigating factor, oddity, peculiarity, persona, personae, personality, protagonist, redeeming feature, reputation, savor, singularity, spirit, symptom, temperament, texture, trait, vagary, values

*study:* characterology, ctetology, ethology, psychology

## CHARGE

**a:** accusable, ascribable, attributive, charging, imputable, imputative, mandatory

**n:** accusation, ascription, behest, gravamen, imposition, imputation, indictment, injunction, management, mandate, objuration, supervision

**v:** arraign, enjoin, indict, prefer, undercut

*clear:* exculpate, exonerate

## CHARITY

**a:** beneficent, benevolent, charitable, eleemosynary, generous, gracious, humanitarian, lenient, philanthropic

**n:** agape, baksheesh, benefaction, beneficence, benevolence, covenant, donation, generosity, *largesse*, lenity, liberality, love, mercy, philanthropy, widow's mite

**v:** subscribe

*person:* almoner, charitarian, eleemosynar, humanitarian, philanthropist, Samaritan, sponsor

## CHARM

**a:** alluring, arresting, beguiling, bewitching, captivating, charming, disarming, enchanting, fascinating, felicitous, ingratiating, irresistible, magnetic, mesmeric, naive, personable, phylacteric, pleasing, unctuous, winsome

**n:** abracadabra, abraxis, allure, amulet, animal magnetism, blandishment, charisma, enchantment, enticement, fetish, geegree, idyll, incantation, juju, madstone, *obeah, obi, paternoster, periapt,* phylactery, scarab, seduction, talisman, voodoo, witchery

**v:** bewitch, captivate, disarm, enchant, enrapture, ensorcel, enthrall, entice, entrance, fascinate, ravish, transport

## CHARTER

**n:** canon, commission, constitution, decalogue, deed, franchise, grant, guarantee, instrument, license, Magna Carta, permit, warrant, warranty

**v:** commission, constitute, empower, license

## CHASTITY

**n:** abstention, continence, innocence, modesty, pucelage, pudicity, purity, virginity, virtue, *votum castitatis*

## CHAT

**a:** chatty, discursive, garrulous, loquacious

**n:** bavardage, causerie, chatter, confabulation, conversation, small talk

**v:** confabulate, gibber, maunder, prattle, talk

## CHEAP

**a:** *a bon marche,* bedizened, Brummagem, chintzy, gimcrack, inexpensive, meretricious, picayune, pinchbeck, tawdry, wholesale

**n:** bedizenment, cheapness, flummery, worthlessness

## CHEAT

**a:** cheating

**n:** charlatan, cheating, chicanery, circumvention, cozenage, defraudation, duplicity, imposture, jiggery-pokery, mountebank, scheming

**v:** bamboozle, beguile, bilk, chicane, circumvent, cozen, deceive, defraud, delude, double-cross, dupe, finagle, fleece, flimflam, foist, gammon, gull, hoodwink, mulet, swindle, trick, victimize

## CHECK

**a:** abortive, checking, inhibitory

**n:** abortifacient, bar, discouragement, inhibition, lock, occlusion, rebuke, wedge

**v:** abort, acclude, authenticate, checkmate, counteract, counterbalance, counterpoise, inhibit, monitor, obstruct, rebuff, repress, restrain, slacken, stanch, staunch, stymie, validate, verify

> *pattern:* checkered, hound's-tooth, tattersall, variegated

## CHEEK

**a:** buccal, haggard

**n:** jaws, jowls, jugal, malar, zygoma, zygomatic bone

## CHEER

**a:** allegro, blithe, buoyant, cheerful, congenial, ebullient, eupeptic, euphoric, exhilarative, friendly, *gemutlich,* genial, jocular, jocund, optimistic, Pollyannish, sanguine, vivacious

**n:** acclamation, applause, cheerfulness, ebullience, eclat, euphoria, exhilaration, geniality, jocularity, jocundity, joviality, merriment, Pollyana, sanguinity, vivacity

**v:** alleviate, comfort, delight, gladden, help, inspirit, invigorate, raise, solace, soothe, succor

## CHEF

**n:** *chef de cuisine, cordon bleu,* cuisinier(e), culinarian

## CHERISH

**a:** cherished, precious

**v:** covet, embosom, enshrine, foster,

idolize, indulge, nurture, pet, prize, spiritualize, venerate, worship

**CHEST**

**a:** pectoral, thoracic

**n:** pectorals, thorax

**CHEW**

**a:** *al dente*, chewy, manducatory, masticatory

**n:** bite, manducation, mastication, nibble, quid, rumination

**v:** bite, champ, chaw, chomp, consume, crush, gnaw, insalivate, manducate, masticate, munch, nibble, ruminate

**CHIEF**

**a:** capital, cardinal, eminent, foremost, leading, main, paramount, predominant, preeminent, preponderant, principal, sovereign, superior, supreme

**n:** *chef d'oeuvre*, director, hierarch, imperator, leader, *magnum opus*, *meisterwerk*, pendragon, *piece de resistance*, provost, sachem, sagamore, sovereign, superior

*combining form:* arch-

**CHILD**

**a:** childish, dutiful, filial, juvenile, pedologic, philoprogenitive, precocious, prolific, pubescent

**n:** bambino, changeling, children, descendant, enfant gate, *enfant terrible*, foundling, infant, issue, juvenile, nestling, nipper, offspring, posterity, prodigy, progeny, ragamuffin, scion, shaver, sprog, suckling, tyke, urchin, waif, ward, *wunderkind*, youngster

**v:** conceive, procreate

*combining forms:* paed-, paedo-, ped-, pedo-

*illegitimate:* bar sinister, *filius nullius, filius populi,* mongrel

**CHILDBIRTH**

**a:** obstetric, parturient, perinatal, puerperal

**n:** *accouchement*, birth, confinement, couvade, delivery, labor, lying-in, parturition, *puerperium*, travail

*after:* postnatal, postpartum

*before:* antenatal, antepartum, prenatal, prepartum

*combining forms:* -para, -parous

*related words:* afterbirth, contraction, eclampsia, induce, lochia, oxytocic, secundines

**CHILDHOOD**

**a:** *ab incunabilis*, childish, immature, infantile, infantine, infantive, jejune, juvenile, pediatric, puerile

**n:** childishness, descendants, dotage, formative years, immaturity, infantility, *jeune age*, juniority, juvenilia, juvenility, pediatrics, posterity, progeny, puerilism, puerility, scions

**CHILL**

**a:** chilly, cold, frigid, frosty, gelid, glacial, icy, nippy, raw

**n:** ague, *frisson*, frost, gelidity, ice, refrigeration, rigor

**v:** cool, freeze, frost, ice, infrigidate, nip, refrigerate

**CHIN**

**a:** genial, mental, orthognathous, prognathous

**n:** cleft, lantern jaw, mental prominence, mental protuberance, *pogonion*

**CHINESE**

**a:** mandarin, Oriental

**n:** Celestial Empire, sinophile

*combining form:* Sino-

**CHINK**

**a:** rimose, rimous, rimulose

**n:** aperture, cranny, interstice, *lacuna*

**CHIVALRY**

**a:** brave, chivalresque, chivalrous, courageous, heroic, noble, quixotic, valiant, valorous

**n:** boldness, bravery, *chevalier*, courage,

courageousness, grit, honor, nerve, nobility, pluck, valiancy, valor

**CHOICE**

**a:** careful, choosing, choosy, discretional, discriminative, eclectic, elective, fastidious, optional, preferential, voluntary

**n:** alternant, alternate, alternative, alternativity, best, candidate, discretion, election, Hobson's choice, opinion, option, triage

**v:** choose, cull, differentiate, discriminate, distinguish, elect, favor, pick out, plump for, single out

**CHORUS**

**a:** choreutic, choric

**n:** burden, refrain

> *leader:* choirmaster, chorypheus, maestro, *maestro de cappella*

**CHRONIC**

**a:** confirmed, deep-seated, habitual, ingrained, intractable, inveterate, irradicable, lingering, obstinate, persistent, prolonged, routine

**CHRONOLOGICAL**

**a:** anachronistic, anachronous, proleptic

**n:** anachronism, prochronism, prolepsis

**CHURCH**

**a:** apostolic, ecclesiastic(al), ecclesiologic(al), ecumenical, encyclic(al), episcopal, hierarchical, sacerdotal

**n:** apostolicity, communion, confession, consistory, conventicle, convocation, denomination, diocese, dispensation, ecclesiasticism, ecclesiolatry, episcopate, hierarchy, precinct, synod, vestry

> *leader:* archimandrite, churchwarden, hegumen, hierophant, minister, officer, pope, priest, sidesman, sinecure

**CIRCLE**

**a:** annular, circular, circumferential, concentric, cyclic, cyclical, cycloid, cylindrical, elliptic, elliptical, nummiform, nummular, orbicular, peripheral, rotund, spherical, spheroid

**n:** ambit, circuit, circularity, circumduction, circumference, circumlocution, disk, epicycle, girth, globe, group, gyre, henge, hoop, itineration, loop, orb, orbit, perimeter, periplus, revolution, rotary, rotundity, round, sphere, spheroidicity, vortex

**v:** circumduct, circumgyrate, circumscribe, describe, gyrate

> *combining forms:* circ-, cycl-, cyclo-, orb-

**CIRCUMSTANCE(S)**

**a:** adventitious, circumstantial, contingent, expedient, extenuating, inadvertent, incidental, mitigating, opportune, opportunistic, perforce, politic, precarious

**n:** concomitant, condition, contingency, episode, eventuality, expediency, inadvertency, incident, occurrence, opportunism, particularity, posture

**v:** temporize

**CITIZEN**

**a:** cosmopolitan

**n:** burgher, citoyen, constituency, constituent, cosmopolitan, cosmopolite, denizen, habitue, national, oppidian

**v:** enfranchise, naturalize

> *citizenship:* civics, initiative, *jus sanguinis*

**CITY**

**a:** civic, cosmopolitan, metropolitan, municipal, urban

**n:** conurbation, ghetto, mall, megalopolis, metropolis, municipality, precinct, ward

**CIVIL**

**a:** civilian, civilized, communal, courteous, cultured, debarbarized, educated, genteel, libertarian, metropolitan, municipal, nonclerical, parliamentary, refined, secular, sophistical, urban

**n:** amenities, debarbarization, laity, polity, proprieties, temporality, urbanities

**v:** debarbarize

**CLAIM**

**a:** alleged, assertive, claimed

**n:** arrogation, postulate, premise, pretension

**v:** affirm, allege, appropriate, arrogate, assert, *asseverate*, aver, avouch, avow, invalidate, maintain, postulate, predicate, profess, purport, repudiate, supersede, underlie

### CLAMOR

**a:** blatant, boisterous, clamorous, clangorous, demonstrative, importunate, pressing, strepitant, strepitous, vociferant, vociferous

**n:** alarum, brouhaha, din, hubbub, noise, outcry, racket, tumult, uproar

**v:** cry, howl, rage, yell

### CLARIFICATION

**a:** clarifying, elucidative, elucidatory, epexegetic(al), exegetic, explanatory

**n:** *eclaircissement*, elucidation, enlightenment, *epexegesis*, *exegesis*, interpretation

**v:** amplify, clarify, depurate, elucidate, elutriate, enlighten, explicate, illume, interpret, resolve, subtilize, unscramble

### CLASH

**n:** conflict

**v:** brawl, conflict, contravene, differ, disagree, dispute, encroach, fight, impinge, knock, oppose, quarrel, skirmish, wrangle

### CLASS

**a:** categorical, classificatory, generic, hierarchic(al), multipartite, phyletic, polychotomous, polytomous, proletarian, stratified, *sui generis*, taxonomic(al)

**n:** caste, categorization, category, classification, clique, compartmentalization, coterie, denomination, departmentalization, designation, distribution, genera, genre, genus, gradation, hierarchization, hierarchy, individualization, nomenclature, phyla, phylum, polychotomy, rubric, stratification, stratum, subordination, taxonomy

**v:** alphabetize, catalog, categorize, classify, codify, collimate, compartmentalize, departmentalize, digest, hierarchize, individualize, pigeonhole, subsume, synthesize

> *living things:* breed, class, division, family, genus, individual, kingdom, order, phylum, race, species, stirps, stock, strain, subspecies, superfamily, variety

> *low: canaille, petite bourgeoisie,* rabble, riffraff

> *middle:* Babbit, Babbitry, *bourgeois(ie),* Philistine, proletariat

> *upper:* aristocracy, aristocrat, gentry, nobility, patrician, superordinate

### CLASSICAL

**a:** Augustan, elegant

**n:** classicality

### CLAW

**a:** cheliferous, unguiferate

**n:** chela, hook, nail, paw, pincer, pounce, talon, unce, uncus, unguis

### CLAY

**a:** argillaceous, ceramic, porcelain, terracotta

**n:** adobe, argil, bole, ceramic, fuller's earth, kaolin, porcelain, sienna, silt, slip, *terra alba, terra cotta,* umber

### CLEAN

**a:** abstergent, abstersive, abstrusive, antiseptic, cathartic, cleansing, detergent, disinfected, expiatory, hygienic, immaculate, kosher, pristine, purgatorial, sanitary, sanitized, sterile, unblemished, undefiled, unspoiled, unstained, unsullied, untainted

**n:** ablution, abstersion, balneation, cleanliness, depuration, detergent, elutriation, expiation, immaculacy, lavage, lavation, lustration, maundy, purgation, purification, sterility, *tabula rasa*

**v:** absterge, depurate, deterge, elutriate, expiate, expurgate, mundify, refurbish

### CLEAR

**a:** accessible, articulate, cogent, conspicuously, crystal(line), decisive, definitive, demonstrable, diaphanous, evident, exoteric, explicatory, explicit, graphic, hyaline, incisive, limpid, lucent, lucid, luculent, luminous, manifest, obvious, orotund, palpable, patent, pellucid, perspicacious, perspicuous, plain, resonant, signally, sonorous, translucent, transparent, transpicuous, trenchant, unambiguous, unequivocal, unimpeded, unmistakable, unquestionable

**n:** clarity, clearness, comprehensibility, diaphaneity, explication, limpidity, lucidity, luminosity, orotundity, pellucidity, perspicacity, perspicuity, sonority, translucence, transparency

**v:** absolve, acquit, clarify, disambiguate, elucidate, exculpate, exonerate, explicate, manifest, subtilize, vindicate

**CLEFT**

**a:** bipartient, bipartite, bisulcate, cloven, cracked, dichotomous, divided, forked, schismatic(al), separated, split

**n:** breach, break, chasm, cleavage, crack, crevasse, crevice, division, fissure, fracture, gap, incision, indentation, interstice, parting, rift, rima, seam, split

**v:** adhere, cleave, divide, separate, split

**CLERGY**

**a:** clerical, ecclesiastical, incumbent, ministerial, parsonic(al), prelatical, pulpitarian, sacerdotal, sacerdotical

**n:** archdeacon, canon, chancellor, chaplain, clergyman, cleric, clericature, curate, deacon, dean, ecclesiastic, ecclesiasticism, *gens d'eglise*, hierophant, incumbent, *locum, locum tenens,* man of the cloth, metropolitan, ordinary, padre, prebendary, precentor, prelate, primate, prior, proctor, provost, pulpitarian, rural dean, spiritualities, suffragan

**v:** collate, frock, ordain

**CLERK**

**a:** clerical

**n:** amanuensis, clericality, clericature, notary, scribe, secretary

**CLEVER**

**a:** adept, adroit, apt, astute, canny, dexterous, discerning, habile, heady, ingenious, judicious, penetrating, perceptive, percipient, perspicacious, politic, precocious, prudent, receptive, resourceful, sagacious, sapient, skillful, sophisticated

**n:** acumen, adroitness, astucity, *bel esprit, bon mot,* child prodigy, cleverness, dexterity, discernment, *esprit,* gumption, hability, ingeniosity, ingenuity, inventiveness, resourcefulness, whiz kid, *wunderkind*

**CLIMATE**

**a:** equable, *fin de siecle,* maritime, salubrious, temperate

**n:** clime, environment, milieu

**v:** acclimatize

**CLIMAX**

**n:** acme, alp, apex, *climacterium,* consummation, culmination, *denouement,* grand finale, meridian, orgasm, peak, perihelion, pinnacle, piton, sublimity, summit, turning point, ultimate, vertex, zenith

**v:** come, crest, crown, culminate, surmount, top

**CLINGING**

**a:** adhamant, adherent, adherescent, agglutinant, coherent, persistent, tenacious, viscid, viscous

**n:** burr, leech, limpet

**v:** adhere, agglutinate, clinch, cling, cohere, grasp, hold, hug, persevere, persist, stick, vine

**CLOAKED**

**a:** arcane, cabalistic, clandestine, disguised, esoteric, larvated, mystic, occult, screened, secret, stealthy, surreptitious, veiled

**v:** blind, camouflage, clothe, conceal, cover, deceive, hide, mantle, screen, secrete, shade, veil

**CLOG**

**n:** block, hindrance, impediment, jam, occlusion, oppilation, stoppage

**v:** bar, block, congest, hinder, impede, jam, obstruct, occlude, oppilate, overload, pack, plug, stop, stuff

**CLOISTER**

**n:** abbey, aisle, ambulatory, claustration, convent, friary, isolation, monastery, nunnery, quarantine, sequestration, veil

**CLOSE**

**a:** abutting, adjacent, adjoining, apposed, cheek by jowl, contiguous, imminent, intimate, juxtaposed, juxtapositional, near

**n:** adjacency, closeness, contiguity, imminence, juxtaposition, nearness, next of kin, propinquity, proximity, vicinity

**v:** juxtapose

*combining form close to:* epi-

*end or closure:* atresia, cloture, denouement, discontinuation, epilogue, obturation, occlusion, peroration, stenosis, stop

**CLOT**

**n:** coagulation, thrombosis

**v:** agglutinate, clump, coagulate, congeal, curdle, fix, gel, harden, jell, lump, mass, solidify, stiffen, thicken, thrombose

**CLOTHING**

**a:** dowdy, epicene, frumpy, sartorial, unisex

**n:** accessory, accouterments, adornment, anorak, apparel, array, attire, Bermuda shorts, blouse, bolero, cagoule, camisole, canonicals, caparison, capote, *chaparejos*, chaps, chemise, chesterfield, civvies, cloak, clothes, coat, coordinates, corset, culottes, *dirndl*, dolman, domino, drapery, dress, duds, duffle coat, dungarees, ensemble, Eton jacket, fallal, finery, frippery, *froufrou*, garb, garments, gilet, guernsey, guimpe, haberdashery, habiliments, habit, hacking jacket, halter, *haute couture*, Inverness, investiture, jeans, jerkin, jodhpurs, khakis, layette, *lederhosen*, leotard, livery, mantle, mufti, muumuu, negligee, Norfolk jacket, pants, paraphernalia, parka, *peignoir*, *pelerine*,

*pelisse*, petersham, plus fours, poncho, raiment, regalia, shift, shirt, skirt, sloppy joe, spencer, toggery, togs, trousers, ulster, vestments, vesture, wardrobe, weeds, zoot suit

**v:** doff, don, dress

**CLOUD**

**a:** clouded, cloudy, flocculent, fuliginous, *in nubibus*, murky, nebular, nebulated, nebulose, nebulous, nimbose, nubilous, obscure, overcast, roily, turbid

**n:** altocumulus, altostratus, cirrocumulus, cirrostratus, cirrus, cloudiness, cumulonimbus, cumulus, nebula, nimbostratus, nimbus, rack, scud, stigma, stratocumulus, stratus, woolpack

**v:** obfuscate, obnubilate, seed, tarnish

*study of:* nephelognosy, nephology

**CLOWN**

**a:** baboonish, buffoonish, farded

**n:** buffoon, clownery, clowning, *gracioso*, *grobian*, Harlequin, jester, lubber, merryandrew, Pantaloon, *Pierrot*, Punchinello, *scaramouche*, zany

**CLUB**

**n:** association, athenaeum, chapter, consortium, coterie, fraternity, fratority, sodality, sorority

**v:** blackball

**CLUE**

**n:** characteristic, clew, criterion, giveaway, implication, indication, innuendo, key, landmark, lead, sign, signal, suspicion, symptom, tip, tip-off

**CLUMSY**

**a:** awkward, bumbling, cumbersome, cumbrous, elephantine, *gauche*, gawky, graceless, ham-fisted, ham-handed, inelegant, inept, jerky, loutish, lumbering, maladroit, ponderous, uncoordinated, uncouth, ungainly, unwieldy

**n:** clodhopper, clumsiness, galoot, klutz, lubber, lummox, palooka, *schlemiel*, stumblebum

**CLUSTER**

**a:** acervate, acervuline, aciniform, agglomerated, aggregatory, caespitose, clustered, conglomerated, fascicular

**n:** agglomeration, aggregation, conglomerate, fascicle, mass, nucleation, pile, truss

**v:** agglomerate, aggregate, nucleate

**COARSE**

**a:** artless, barbarous, brutish, earthy, *gauche*, immature, incondite, indelicate, inelegant, inurbane, plebeian, ribald, rude, scurrilous, squalid, *tramontane*, troglodytic, uncouth, unpolished, unrefined

**n:** barbarism, barbarity, buffoonery, coarseness, *gaucherie, grossierete*, indelicacy, inurbanity, rascality, scurrility, vulgarity

**v:** coarsen, vulgarize

**COAST**

**a:** littoral

**n:** corniche, littoral

**COATING**

**n:** bloom, *carapae*, cladding, facing, incrustation, insulation, integument, laminate, layer, mantle, patina, pelage, pellicle, size, veneer

**v:** cover, daub, dredge, parget, render

**COAX**

**n:** cajolement, cajolery

**v:** beg, cajole, charm, entice, influence, lure, manipulate, persuade, seduce, solicit, tempt, urge, wheedle

**COCKTAIL**

**n:** aperitif, beverage, drink

**CODE**

**n:** cipher, cryptanalysis, cryptogram, cryptography, cryptology, *en clair*, pandects, phonetic alphabet, pig Latin, semaphore

**v:** decipher, decrypt, encipher

**COERCE**

**a:** coercive, compelling, compulsatory, compulsory, obligatory, oppressive

**n:** coercion, duress, pressure, puissance

**v:** blackmail, compel, dictate, discipline, dominate, dragoon, hound, influence, intimidate, menace, necessitate, prod, push, ride, rule, steamroller, terrorize, tyrranize

**COEXIST**

**a:** coexisting, compossible, living, symbiotic

**n:** compossibility, symbiosis

**COFFEE**

**a:** decaffeinated, percolated

**n:** *cafe au lait, cafe creme, cafe noir*, caffeine, cappuccino, chicory, demitasse, espresso, grouts, mocha, stimulant

**COFFIN**

**n:** *bier catafalque*, box, sarcophagus

**COHERE**

**a:** conglutinate

**n:** coherence, conglutination, union

**v:** adhere, agglutinate, cement, cleave, cling, conglutinate, glue, glutinize, hold, solidify, stick, unify, unite

**COIL**

**a:** circinate, coiled, convolute(d), gyrate, meandrine, spiral, tortile, volute

**n:** convolution, entanglement, hank, perplexity, skein, solenoid, volution, whorl

**COIN**

**a:** numismatic(al), nummiform, nummular

**n:** circumscription, denomination, die, dime, engrailing, fluting, legend, milling, nickel, numismatics, obverse, penny, picayune, quarter, reeding, reverse, *rouleau, seigniorage*, specie, verso

**COINCIDE**

**a:** coextensive, congruent, congruous, coterminous, identical, simultaneous

**n:** coincidence, conjunction, synchronicity

**v:** agree, concur

**COLD**

**a:** algid, arctic, boreal, frigid, frigorific, glacial, hyperborean, indurate, marmoreal, poikilothermal, poikilothermic, saturnine

**n:** frigidity, gelidity, glaciation, hypothermia, *sang-froid*, windchill factor

**v:** infrigidate

**COLLAPSE**

**n:** cataclysm, dissolution, failure, holocaust, prostration

**v:** break, break down, cave in, concertina, crumple, fail, fall, founder, implode, subside, telescope

**COLLECT**

**a:** collective

**n:** agglomeration, aggregation, aglutination, anthology, assemblage, *collectanea*, collection, collectivity, colluvies, compendium, conflation, congeries, conglomeration, congregation, corpus, crowd, exotica, fascicle, group, heterogeneity, hodgepodge, ingathering, job lot, miscellaneity, miscellany, motley, nucleation, *oeuvre*, offertory, omnibus, potpourri, repertory, stockpile, sylloge, *virtu*

**v:** accumulate, agglutinate, conflate, conglomerate, congregate, convoke, muster

 *book:* bibliophile

 *coin:* numismatics, numismatist

 *combining forms:* -ana, -iana

 *curio:* antiquary, curioso

 *matchbox:* phillumenist

 *postcard:* deltiologist

 *shell:* conchologist, conchology

 *stamp:* philatelist, philately

**COLLEGE**

**a:** extramural, intramural, parietal

**n:** academe, academia, hall, professordom, professoriate, tertiary education, university

**COLLISION**

**a:** colliding, encroaching, impingent

**n:** clash, encounter, encroachment, impingement, infringement, renitency, retroactionsmash, wreck

**v:** bump, clash, collide, crash, encounter, hit, impact, impinge, meet, strike, wreck

**COLONY**

**n:** habituation, installation, palatinate, protectorate, settlement

 *colonist:* colonizer, oecist, planter, representative, resident

**COLOR**

**a:** allochromatic, apatetic, aposematic, chameleon, chatoyant, chromatic, complementary, garish, gaudy, heterochromatic, heterochromous, incarnadine, iridescent, kaleidoscopic, motley, mottled, multicolored, opalescent, particolored, pastel, piebald, pied, pinto, polychromatic, polychromatous, polychrome, primary, prismatic, shot, suffuse, taffeta, technicolor, varicolored, variegated, versicolor(ed)

**n:** cast, chromatics, coloring, fascia, hue, kaleidoscope, melanin, nuance, palette, pigment, rainbow, shade, spectrum, tincture, tint

**v:** achromatize, colorize, decolorize, dye, etiolate, imbue, infuse, paint, shade, stain, tinge, tint, tone

 *colorless:* achlorophyllaceous, achromatic, achromatous, achromous, diatonic, neutral

 *colorless combining forms:* leuc-, leuco-, leuko-

 *combining forms:* chrom-, chromo-

 *one:* homochromatic, monochromatic, unicolorous

 *two:* bichromatic, bichrome, bicolored, bicolorous, dichromatic

**COMA**

**a:** comatose, lethargic, sleeping, stuporous, torpid, torporific, unconscious

**n:** anesthesia, *carus*, hypnosis, lethargy,

seizure, sleep, stupor, torpidity, torpor, unconsciousness

**COMBAT**

**a:** agonistic, armigerous, bellicose, belligerent, combative, disputatious, hostile, martial, militant, oppugnant, pugnacious, taurine, unpacific

**n:** joust, *rencontre*, sciamachy, *tilgint match*, wager of battle

**v:** attack, battle, contend, defy, duel, face, fight, joust, oppose, struggle

*combatant:* enemy, gladiator, *retiarius*

**COMBINE**

**a:** *biune*, biunial, combined, concerted, coordinated, *portmanteau*, synergetic, synergical, synergistical

**n:** agglutination, amalgamation, coalescence, coalition, collection, combination, conjoinment, conjugation, conjunction, conjuncture, consolidation, consortium, gestalt, group, homogeneity, lamination, merger, mixture, permutation, polysynthesis, syncretism, syndicate, synergism, synthesis, valence

**v:** amalgamate, arrange, blend, coalesce, collocate, combine, conjoin, consolidate, incorporate, join, laminate, meld, syncretize, synergize, synthesize

**COME BETWEEN**

**n:** intermediation, interposition, intervention

**v:** intermediate, interpose, intervene

*come together:* converge, rencounter

**COMEDOWN**

**a:** anticlimactic, bathetic, denigratory

**n:** anticlimax, bathos, comeuppance, denigration, disappointment, setback

**COMEDY**

**a:** Aristophanic, burlesk, comic, comical, Falstaffian, farcical, harlequin, ludicrous, Rabelaisian, risible

**n:** burlesque, harlequin, harlequinade, joke, satire, slapstick, *vis comica*

*comedian:* buffoon, *farceur*, stooge, straight man

**COMFORT**

**a:** anodyne, comfortable, comforting, commodious, consolatory, cozy, cushy, *gemutlich*, habitable, nepenthean, spacious, tranquilizing

**n:** amenities, comforter, consolation, ease, intercessor, nepenthe, paraclete, solace, tranquilizer

**v:** allay, alleviate, assuage, palliate

**COMMAND**

**a:** august, authoritative, autocratic, commanding, exalted, grandiose, imperative, imperial, imperious, imposing, magisterial, mandatory, peremptory, predominant

**n:** adjuration, *bravura, caveat, fiat*, imperative, mandament, mandate, mastery, precept

**v:** imperate, order, rule

*commander:* imperator

**COMMEMORATE**

**n:** commemoration

**v:** award, celebrate, cite, elegize, fete, honor, memorialize, observe, signalize, solemnize

**COMMEND**

**a:** admirable, approbatory, commendable, commendatory, complimentary, creditable, encomiastical, estimable, eulogistic, exemplary, honorific, laudable, laudative, laudatory, meritorious, panegyric

**n:** approbation, commendation, compliment, encomium, laudation, panegyric, praise

**v:** applaud, approve, cite, compliment, congratulate, extol, honor, laud, laureate, panegyrize, praise, recommend

**COMMENTATOR**

**a:** barbed, cogent, cutting, incisive, mordant, penetrating, to the point, trenchant

**n:** annotator, exegete, exegetist, expositor, glossator, scholiast

**v:** comment, descant, discourse, expound, interject, interpose, interrupt, remark

*comment:* animadversion, commentary, *obiter dictum*

## COMMERCIAL

**a:** business, economic, mercantile, mercenary, trade

## COMMODIOUS

**a:** baronial, broad, capacious, cavernous, expansive, extensive, large, roomy, spacious, voluminous, wide

## COMMON

**a:** communal, customary, demotic, endemic, epidemic, generic, habitual, hackneyed, joint, lumpen, monogenic, mutual, pagan, plebian, predominant, prevailing, prevalent, proletariat, reciprocal, regnant, rife, scurrile, scurrilous, shared, standard, undistinguished, universal, unrefined, vernacular, vulgate

**n:** *canaille,* commonality, commonness, consensus, *hoi polloi,* mode, prevalence, proletariat, rabble, riffraff, staple, unrefinement

**v:** heathenize, paganize, vulgarize

*combining forms:* coen-, coeno-

*commoner:* bourgeois, lowest common denominator, pleb, plebian, roturier

*commonplace:* banal, bourgeois, bromidic, cliche, dull, hackneyed, pedestrian, platitudinal, plebian, prosaic, stereotyped, stereotypical, trite, uneventful

*commonplaceness:* bathos, topos, triteness

*sense: bon sens,* gumption, nous, rationalism, shrewdness, *sophrosyne*

## COMMOTION

**a:** perturbational, turbulent

**n:** ado, agitation, *bouleversement,* brouhaha, clamor, convulsion, flourish, flurry, hubbub, hurly-burly, pandemonium, perturbation, racket, storm, tempest in a teapot, tumult, turbulence, turmoil

## COMMUNICATION

**a:** paralinguistic, phatic

**n:** call, contact, fax, impartment, kinesics, letter, liaison, telepathy, telephone, telex, transmission, wavelength, wire

*non:* incommunicado

## COMMUNITY

**a:** environmental, microcosmic, neighborhood, neighboring, pragmatic, sectarian

**n:** affinity, body politic, brotherhood, city, district, environment, environs, fellowship, fraternity, microcosm, milieu, municipality, neighborhood, people, public, region, settlement, society, sodality

## COMPACT

**a:** brief, compendious, compressed, concentrated, concrete, condensed, consolidated, crammed, crowded, dense, firm, full, massed, packed, solidified, succinct, terse, thick, tight

**n:** alliance, compendium, covenant

## COMPANION

**a:** brotherly, commensal, comradely, convivial, festive, friendly, jovial, sisterly, sociable

**n:** accessory, *alter ego, bon camarade,* boon companion, camaraderie, chaperone, cohort, commensal, commensality, compeer, consort, counterpart, *duenna,* escort, *esprit de corps,* friend, sibling

## COMPARE

**a:** analogical, analogous, approximate, commensurate, comparable, comparative, corresponding, equiponderant, equivalent, homogeneous, homologous, metaphorical, positive, proportionate, similar, superlative, *vis-a-vis*

**n:** analogy, benchmark, collation, commensuration, comparability, comparison, conceit, control, equivalence, homogeneity, metaphor, parable, simile, similitude, yardstick

**v:** collate, contrast, equate, estimate, evaluate, relate

## COMPASSION

**a:** compassionate, humane, humanitarian, kind, merciful, soft, sympathetic, tender, understanding

**n:** benevolence, charity, clemency, commiseration, grace, kindness, leniency, mercy, pathos, pity, ruth, sympathy, tenderness, understanding

> *person:* almoner, charitarian, eleemosynar, humanitarian, philanthropist, Samaritan

## COMPATIBLE

**a:** agreeable, congenial, congruent, consentaneous, consonant, fitting, friendly, harmonious, homogenous, proper, suitable, synonymous, uniform

**n:** compatibility, congeniality, congruity, consentaneousness, homogeneity

**v:** reconcile

## COMPEL

**a:** cogent, compelling, convincing, demanding, impelling, imperious, obligatory, urgent

**n:** cogency

**v:** coerce, commandeer, discipline, dragoon, drive, make, necessitate, require, shanghai, thrust

## COMPENDIUM

**n:** abridgement, abstract, *apercu*, condensation, digest, distillation, epitome, lexicon, outline, *precis*, sketch, summary, survey, syllabus, sylloge, synopsis

## COMPENSATE

**a:** compensated

**n:** amends, compensation, honorarium, perk, perquisite, recompense, redemption, redress, remuneration, reparations, requital, restitution, *solatium*

**v:** atone, counterbalance, countervail, couterpoise, indemnify, offset, recompense, reimburse, remunerate, requite

## COMPETE

**a:** agonistic, competitive, rivalrous

**n:** competition, *concours*, contest, race, rivalry, round robin, sweepstakes

**v:** contend, emulate, face, fight, grapple, oppose, pit, rival, strive, struggle, vie, war, wrestle

> *competitor:* adversary, candidate, combatant, enemy, entrant, foe, opponent, protagonist, rival

## COMPETENT

**a:** able, adequate, ambidextrous, *capax*, ingenious, panurgic, proficient, *puissant*, versatile

**n:** ability, ambidexterity, competence, *compos mentis*, effectiveness, ingeniosity, panurgy, success, versatility, worthiness

## COMPLAIN

**a:** clamorous, complaining, complaintive, querimonious, querulent, querulous, vociferous

**n:** allegation, complaint, criticism, *demarche*, expostulation, gravamen, jeremiad, lamentation, objection, protest-(ation), querulity, remonstrance, remonstration

**v:** bewail, carp, cavil, expostulate, fret, grumble, inveigh, kvetch, lament, lodge, object, protest, regret, remonstrate, repine, yammer

## COMPLETE

**a:** accomplished, circumstantial, completed, completely, completing, concluded, concluding, consummate, consummated, consummative, consummatory, definitive, diametrically, done, ending, established, exhaustive, finalized, *in toto*, integral, outright, plenary, rank, realized, replete, saturative, unabridged, unconditional, unexpurgated, unmitigated, utterly

**n:** accomplishment, actuality, actualization, complement, completion, consummation, *coup de grace*, end, entelechy, *fait accompli*, finality, integrality, integrity, panoply, plenitude, plenum, realization, stop, turnaround, wholeness

**v:** accomplish, complement, conclude, consummate, do, end, finalize, finish, get done, realize, stop, terminate

*combining forms:* hol-, holo-, tel-, telo-

**COMPLEX**

**a:** abstract, Byzantine, complicated, *daedalic*, devious, heterogeneous, intricate, involuted, labyrinthian, labyrinthine, reticular, sinuous, sophisticated

**n:** complexity, complexus, complicacy, compositeness, entanglement, intricacy, involvement, labyrinth, maelstrom, maze, sinuosity

**COMPLIANCE**

**a:** accommodating, amenable, assentatious, assiduous, complaisant, compliant, docile, ductile, facile, malleable, obsequious, pliable, sequacious, servile, submissive, subservient, tractable, yielding

**n:** assiduity, concord, conformance, facilitation, facility, harmony, obsequence, obsequency, obsequity, sequacity

**v:** adapt, assent, comply, endure, obey, respect, submit, surrender, yield

**COMPLICATED**

**a:** abstruse, complex, difficult, Gordian, intricate, involuted, labyrinthine, *prolix*, recondite, reticular

**n:** aftereffect, aggregation, complexity, complexus, complicacy, complication, convolution, entanglement, intricacy, involution, involvement, ramification, *sequella*, sinuosity

**v:** complicate, confuse, obfuscate, obscure

**COMPOSED**

**a:** calm, collected, prepared, tranquilized

**n:** composure, countenance, equability, equanimity, phlegm, placidity, poise, posture, repose, *sang-froid*, self-possession, serenity, stability, temperament

**COMPREHEND**

**a:** cognitive, discernable, interpretable, learnable, noetic, perceivable, understandable

**n:** cognition, comprehension, connotation, inclusion, intuition, knowledge, *noesis*, panorama, understanding

**v:** understand

*comprehensive:* all-inclusive, catholic, connotative, consolidated, ecumenical, encyclic, encyclopedic, inclusive, intensive, synoptic, transcendental, universal, wide-ranging

**COMPROMISE**

**n:** abatement, arbitration, concession, conciliation, embarrassment, humiliation, jeopardy, *modus vivendi*, understanding

**v:** adapt, adjust, arbitrate, embarrass, endanger, expose, humiliate, jeopardize, submit, temporize

**COMPUNCTION**

**a:** compassionate, compunctious, contrite, grievous, penitent(ial), qualimish, regretful, remorseful, sorry

**n:** compassion, conscience, contrition, misgiving, penitence, qualm, reluctance, remorse, scruple, sorrow, uneasiness, woe, worry

**COMRADE**

**a:** comradely, trusting

**n:** *alter ego*, associate, *bon camarade*, colleague, compeer, *confrere*

*comradeship:* camaraderie, *esprit de corps*, geniality, rapport

**CONCEAL**

**a:** abeyant, clandestine, concealed, covert, delitescent, dormant, hidden, larvate, latent, potential, quiescent, surreptitious, veiled

**n:** abscondence, clandestinity, concealment, delitescence, dissimulation, eclipse, fraud, *misprision*, obscuration, occultation, smoke screen, subreption, *suppressio veri*

**v:** cache, camouflage, cover up, dissemble, ensconce, obscure, secrete, sequester, whitewash

## CONCEDE

**a:** conceded, undeniable

**n:** acknowledgement, admission, capitulation, concession, condescendence, indulgence

**v:** acknowledge, acquiesce, allow, capitulate, give, own up, surrender, waive, yield

## CONCEIT

**a:** arrogant, bumptious, conceited, egomaniac, egomaniacal, egotistical, haughty, hubristic, opinionated, pragmatic, presumptuous, priggish

**n:** *amour-propre*, bumptiousness, caprice, egocentricity, egoism, egomania, egotism, *hauteur*, *hubris*, pomposity, presumption, presumptuousness, self-esteem

## CONCEIVE

**a:** ideational

**n:** category, concept, conception, envisagement, hypothesis, idea, ideation, postulate, presupposition, prochronism, prolepsis, rubric

**v:** apprehend, coin, comprehend, concoct, contrive, create, fabricate, formulate, give birth, ideate, think up

## CONCENTRATE

**a:** concentrated, engrossed, inspissated, intent

**n:** agglutination, centralization, concentrate, concentration, essence, *idee fixe*, inspissation, monomania, *nidus*, nucleation, nucleus, polarization, quintessence

**v:** agglutinate, assemble, centralize, condense, conglomerate, consolidate, epitomize, nucleate, thicken

## CONCERN

**a:** *anent*, apprehensive, concerned, concerning, distressed, disturbed, *in re*, interested, regarding, respecting, solicitous, solicitudinous, versant

**n:** altruism, anxiety, apprehension, concernment, solicitude

**v:** bother, distress, disturb, engross, hold, interest, involve, matter, occupy, pertain, refer, relate, trouble

## CONCILIATE

**a:** conciliatory, mollifying, pacific, placatory, propitiatory, propitious

**n:** appeasement, conciliation, mollification, olive branch, pacification, propitiation, tranquilization

**v:** appease, mollify, pacify, placate, propitiate, reconcile, tranquilize

## CONCISE

**a:** aphoristic, brief, compendious, comprehensive, cryptic, elliptical, epigrammatic, gnomic, laconic, lapidary, pithy, pregnant, sententious, succinct, summary, telegraphic, terse, trenchant

**n:** brachylogy, brevity, conciseness, summary, terseness

## CONCLUSION

**a:** conclusive, consummative, consummatory, decisive, definitive, desitive, determinative, ending, final, illative, irrefutable, legitimate, logical, reasonable, terminal, unanswerable, unequivocal

**n:** cessation, *coda*, consequence, consummation, deduction, ending, *envoi*, epilogue, finality, finalization, generalization, gradation, illation, inference, liquidation, *non sequitur*, premise, settlement, termination, *terminus ad quem*

## CONCORD

**a:** harmonious

**n:** agreement, congeniality, harmony, rapprochement, simultaneity, synchroneity, unanimity

## CONCRETE

**a:** idiographic, materialistic, pragmatic

**n:** aggregate, cement, concreta, concretum, raft, screed

## CONCURRENCE

**a:** synchronistic, synchronous

**n:** simultaneity, synchromism, synchroneity, unanimity

**v:** agree, concur

## CONDEMN

**a:** condemnatory, condemning, damnatory

**v:** censure, criticize

## CONDENSE

**a:** condensed

**n:** aphorism, brachylogy, condenser, maxim, paraleipsis, rectifier

**v:** abbreviate, abridge, compress, concentrate, consolidate, epitomize, inspissate

## CONDESCENDING

**a:** hoity-toity, patronizing

**n:** paternalism

**v:** patronize

## CONDITION

**a:** apodosis, circumstantial, conditional, consequent, contingent, limitative, provisional, provisory, tentative

**n:** antecedent, circumstance, conditionality, contingency, difficulty, dilemma, disease, distress, eventuality, facet, obstacle, plight, predicament, prerequisite, presupposition, protasis, provision, proviso, quandary, reservation, restriction, status, *status quo*, stipulation, tentativeness

**v:** stipulate

*combining forms:* -osis, -tude

## CONDOLE

**a:** compassionate, condolent

**n:** commiseration, compassion, condolence

**v:** commiserate, lamet

## CONDUCT

**a:** casuistic

**n:** behavior, casuistry, comport, comportment, correctitude, demeanor, deportment, heroics, management, meticulosity, mien, praxiology, praxis, *punctilio*, rectitude, theatrics

**v:** behave, escort, manage, negotiate

## CONFERENCE

**n:** caucus, colloquium, colloquy, confabulation, consultation, deliberation, dialogue, discussion, palaver, parley, *pourparler*, seminar, summit, symposium

**v:** bestow, confabulate, confer, consult, delegate, deliberate, endow

*record:* proceedings, transactions

## CONFESSION

**n:** *confessarius, mea culpa, peccavi,* penance, penitent, shrift

**v:** acknowledge, admit, avow, concede, confess, hear, shrive

## CONFIDENCE

**a:** assured, cheerful, confident, optimistic, peremptory, prepossessing, presumptuous, sanguine, unabashed

**n:** aplomb, assurance, *bravura,* certainty, certitude, credence, doughtiness, morale, poise, positivism, presumption, presumptuousness, *tour de force*

**v:** bolster

## CONFIDENTIAL

**a:** classified, confidentially, covert, covertly, *entre nous,* esoteric, secret, *sub rosa,* trustworthy

## CONFINE

**a:** bound, caged, captive, captured, confined, confining, held, immured, restrained, restricted, trapped

**n:** *accouchement,* circumscription, confinement, immurement, incarceration, limbo

**v:** circumscribe, demarcate, encompass, immure, impale, impound, imprison, incarcerate, pinion, secure, shackle

## CONFIRM

**a:** confirmative, confirmatory, corroborative, corroboratory

**n:** affirmation, authentication, confirmation, corroboration, investiture, substantiation, validation

**v:** attest, authenticate, confirm, corroborate, establish, ratify, sanction, satisfy, strengthen, substantiate, sustain, validate, verify, vouch for

## CONFLICT

**a:** antagonistic, antithetical, at loggerheads, at variance, conflicting, contending, contradictory, crosscurrent, hostile, incompatible, incongruous, inconsistent, inharmonious, irreconcilable

**n:** antagonism, antimony, argument, Armageddon, collision, confliction, contrariety, crossfire, deadlock, discord, discrepancy, disharmony, disparity, dispute, dissension, dissonance, encroachment, faction, fight, friction, impingement, incompatibility, incongruity, internecine, irreconcilability, skirmish, stalemate, strife

**v:** dispute, fight

## CONFORM

**a:** accepted, canonical, comformable, conforming, conventional, *en regle*, ethical, procrustean

**n:** canonicity, conventionalism, conventionality, propriety, ritual, rituality, rule, standards

**v:** adapt

## CONFUSE

**a:** anarchic, baffling, befuddled, bemused, bewildered, chaotic, confused, confusing, dazed, discombobulated, disconcerted, disordered, disorientated, disoriented, distraught, dizzy, embroiled, entangled, flummoxed, flustered, frantic, haywire, helter-skelter, incoherent, indiscriminate, muddle, mystified, nonplussed, obfuscated, obfuscatory, perplexed, promiscuous, puzzled, stunned, stupefied, topsy-turvy, turbid, woozy

**n:** anarchy, *ataxia,* babel, Babelism, bear garden, Bedlam, bewilderment, chaos, commotion, confusion, delirium, disarrangement, disarray, discomfiture, dis-

order, disorientation, ferment, furor, havoc, hubbub, hullabaloo, imbroglio, incoherence, maelstrom, malapropism, mayhem, morass, obfuscation, obnubilation, pandemonium, perplexity, predicament, quagmire, rigmarole, shambles, snafu, tumult, turbidity, turbulence, turmoil, upheaval, vertigo, warren, welter

**v:** Babelize, bemuse, bewilder, complicate, confound, discomfit, disconcert, discountenance, disorient, embarass, embrangle, fluster, mistake, obfuscate, obscure, perplex, perturb

## CONGRATULATE

**a:** congratulatory, gratulant

**n:** commendation, congratulation, felicitation, praise

**v:** commend, compliment, felicitate, laud, macarize, *pique*, praise, preen, sympathize

## CONJECTURE

**a:** conjectural, hypothetical, imaginary, stochastic, suppositional, suppositious, theoretical

**n:** belief, fancy, hypothesis, opinion, postulation, presumption, speculation, supposition, surmise, theorem, theory, thought

**v:** assume, believe, conceive, devine, fancy, guess, hypothesize, imagine, infer, opinionate, postulate, presuppose, speculate, suppose, surmise, suspect, theorize, think

## CONJUNCTION

**a:** coordinating, correlative, polysyndetic, subordinating, suppositive, syndetic

**n:** association, hypotaxis, parataxis, subordinator

   *omission:* asyndetic

## CONNECTION

**a:** affined, anastomotic, articulate, coadunate, coadunative, conjunctive, connected, connecting, contiguous, osculant, synaptic, syndetic

**n:** affinity, alliance, apparentation, causality, colligation, conjunction, consanguinity, contiguity, continuity, liaison, ligament, ligature, *nexus*, relationship, *symphysis*

**v:** apparent, appertain, catenate, communicate, concatenate, dovetail, fit, join

## CONQUER

**a:** conquerable, conquered, domitable, expugnable, surmountable, vincible, vulnerable

**n:** acquisition, conquerability, conquest, debellation, domitability, expugnability, reduction, subjection, subjugation, surmountability, triumph, vincibility

**v:** annex, defeat, overthrow, subdue, subjugate, surmount, vanquish

> *conqueror:* conquistador

> *unconquerable:* impregnable, inconquerable, insurmountable, invulnerable

## CONSCIOUS

**a:** aware, cognizable, cognizant, lucid, qualmish, responsive, scrupulous, sensible, sentient, subliminal

**n:** automatism, awareness, cognizance, compunction, consciousness, percipience, percipiency, qualm, scruple, scrupulosity, sentience, sentiency

## CONSECUTIVE

**a:** alphabetical, back to back, categorical, chronological, following, orderly, running, sequel, sequential, serial, successional, successive

## CONSENT

**a:** consensual, consentaneous, consentient, unanimous

**n:** accord, approbation, assent, concurrence, consension, consensus, corroboration, permission, ratification, sufferance, unanimity

## CONSEQUENCE

**a:** consequential, corollary, rational, residual, self-important, sequential

**n:** consecution, *contrecoup*, corollary, emanation, importance, ramification, residual, residue, residuum, result, sequela, weight

## CONSERVATIVE

**a:** antiprogressive, conventional, diehard, lethargic, old-fashioned, Old-Guard, reactionary, sustentative, traditionalistic, unenterprising

**n:** conservation, conservatism, conventionality, diehard, economy, establishment, fundamentalism, husbandry, perpetuation, preservation, sustentation, sustention, traditionalism, traditionality

**v:** conserve, manage

## CONSIDERATION

**a:** considerate

**n:** advisement, attention, cogitation, contemplation, deliberation, estimation, excogitation, *honorarium, quid pro quo*, reward

**v:** *ad referendum*, cogitate, consider, contemplate, deliberate, excogitate, perpend, ponder, reflect, take under advisement, think

## CONSISTENT

**a:** chronic, commensurate, compatible, comportable, concordant, congenial, congruous, consentaneous, consonant, constant, coordinated, harmonious, invariable, inveterate, isogenous, steadfast, unchanging, undeviating, unfaltering, uniform, unregenerate, unswerving, unwavering

**n:** compatibility, concord, concurrence, consistency, correspondence, harmony, homogeneity, isogeny, persistency

**v:** reconcile

## CONSPICUOUS

**a:** egregious, eminent, flagrant, glaring, manifest, noticeable, outstanding, prominent, striking, supereminent

**n:** supereminence

## CONSPIRE

**a:** cabalistic, collusive, collusory, conniving, conspirative, conspiratorial

**n:** association, cabal, cahoots, collusion, confederacy, conjuration, connivance, conspiracy, covin, intrigue, *junta,* machination, plot

**v:** collude, connive, conspire, contrive, machinate

## CONSTANT

**a:** abiding, chronic, continent, continual, continuous, durable, immutable, incessant, invariable, inveterate, perennial, permanent, persevering, persistent, resolute, steadfast, steady, unceasing, undeviating, unfading, unfailing, unfaltering, unflagging, uniform, uninterrupted, unregenerate, unremitting, unswerving, untiring, unwavering

**n:** parameter

## CONSTITUTION

**n:** character, charter, *crasis,* decalogue, disposition, lustihood, Magna Carta, ordinance, physique, stamina, temperament, virility

## CONSTRICTION

**a:** constricted, constringent, restrained

**n:** choking, coarctation, coercion, compression, hindrance, inhibition, knot, obstruction, oppression, stenosis, strain, strangulation, stricture, tightening

**v:** bind, choke, constrain, cramp, gag, hamper, hamsring, restrain, restrict, strangle, tie, tighten

## CONSTRUCT

**a:** architectonic, constructional

**n:** architectonics, construction, tectonics

**v:** build, compose, confect, fabricate, improvisate, improvise, manufacture

> **constructive:** affirmative, definitive, inferred

## CONSUME

**a:** consuming, devouring, edacious, voracious

**n:** consumption, edacity, voracity

**v:** expend, use up

## CONTACT

**a:** abutting, bordering, communicable, contacting, contagious, contiguous, edging, joining, juxtapositional, tangential, touching

**n:** apposition, contiguity, contingence, juxtaposition, tangency, touching

**v:** border

## CONTAGIOUS

**a:** catching, communicable, contaminating, contractable, corrupt, corruptive, epidemic, infectious, infective, noxious, pathological, pestilential, septic, vitiating

**n:** contagion, contamination, disease, infection, influence, pathology, purulence, spread, virus

## CONTAMINATE

**a:** contaminated, defiled, insanitary, polluted, scrofulous, septic, unsanitary

**n:** scrofulosis

**v:** defile

## CONTEMPLATE

**a:** comtemplative, meditative, ruminant, thoughtful

**n:** anticipation, cogitation, contemplation, excogitation, expectation, meditation, orison

**v:** anticipate, cogitate, comprehend, determine, envisage, excogitate, hypothesize, intuit, mediate, mull, ponder, postulate, recall, reflect, resolve, theorize, think about, understand

## CONTEMPORARY

**a:** coetaneous, coeternal, *coeval,* coincident, coincidental, concomitant, concurrent, conjugate, contemporaneous, existing, extant, isochronous, simultaneous, synchronous

**n:** coetaneity, coevality, contemporaneity, contemporariness, simultaneity, symbiosis, synchroneity *person:* associate, *coeval,* fellow

## CONTEMPT

**a:** contemptible, contemptuous, contumelious, denigrating, derisible, derisive, despicable, despiteous, disdainful, haughty, hubristic, pitiable, scurrile, scurrilous, scurvy, toplofty

**n:** contumacy, contumely, denigration, depreciation, derision, despiciency, disdain, disparagement, *hauteur, hubris, misprision,* odium, pilgarlic, scorn

**v:** decry, denigrate, depreciate, deride, disdain, disparage, disrespect, misprize

## CONTEND

**a:** belligerent, contentious, contradictious, disputable, disputatious, dissentious, factious, hostile, litigious, mutinous, seditious, tauraine, turbulent

**n:** altercation, competition, contention, contestation, controversy, dissidence, donnybrook, litigiosity, rivalry

**v:** antagonize, grapple, oppugn

## CONTENT

**a:** calm, contented, *sans souci,* unperturbed

**n:** complacency, contentment, eudaemonia, euphoria, felicity, repose, satisfaction, tranquility

## CONTEST

**a:** agonistic, agonistical, contesting

**n:** agon, competition, contest, grapple, lottery, race, skirmish, sweepstakes, tournament, vellitation

**v:** fight, oppose

## CONTINGENCY

**a:** adjuvant, beholden, conditional, contingent, empirical, iffy, liable, subject

**n:** accident, accidentality, case, casualty, eventuality, fortuitousness, fortuity, juncture, peril, proviso, risk, uncertainty

## CONTINUE

**a:** consecutive, constant, continual, continuous, incessant, inveterate, perdurant, perennial, perpetual, persistent, progressive, recurrent, sempiternal, successive, unceasing, uninterrupted

**n:** continuation, continuousness, continuum, incessancy, incessantness, inveterateness, perduration, perpetuality, perpetuation, perpetuity, perseveration, persistence, persistency, prolongation, sequel

**v:** perdure, perpetuate, persevere, persist, peseverate, resume, subsist

## CONTOUR

**n:** appearance, configuration, conformation, feature, figure, form, outline, physiognomy, shape, silhouette

## CONTRACT

**a:** articled, astrictive, binding, contracting, indentured, oral, verbal

**n:** agreement, amendment, astriction, astrictive, bond, clause, compact, contractility, covenant, endorsement, escrow, *force majeure*

**v:** stipulate

　　*make ineffective:* invalidate, nullify, vitiate, void

## CONTRADICT

**a:** adverse, ambivalent, antonymous, contradicting, contradictious, contradictory, froward, incompatible, inconsistent, paradoxical, perverse, repugnant, schizoid

**n:** anomaly, antilogy, antilogy, antinomy, antithesis, contradiction, contrariety, incompatibility, oxymoron, paradox

**v:** belie, call into question, dispute, negate, oppugn

## CONTRARY

**a:** absonant, adverse, ambivalent, antagonistic, antipodal, antithetical, cantankerous, contradictious, contrarient, contrarious, diametrical, discrepant, fractious, forward, opposite, stubborn

**n:** antipodes, antithesis, contrariety

## CONTRIBUTE

**a:** accessorial, accessory, adjuvant, aiding, anonymous, auxiliary, complemental, complementary, contributory, supplemental

**n:** aid, alms, benefit, charity, complementarity, gift, grant, *largesse,* tip, widow's mite

**v:** bequest, confer, give, grant, shell out, subscribe

## CONTROL

**a:** controllable, educable, educatable, manipulatory, pliant, tractable, vulnerable

**n:** ascendancy, continence, custody, dominance, dominion, hierarchization, jurisdiction, manipulation, power, preeminence, restraint, sovereignty, stranglehold, subjugation, suzerainty, tractability

**v:** dominate, govern, harness, hierarchize, influence, manage, manipulate, monopolize, preside, regulate, restrain, stage-manage, subdue, subjugate, subordinate, superintend

> *controller:* comptroller, governor, helm, manipulator, regulator, superintendent, supervisor, tiller

> *impossible to:* incoercible, incorrigible, irrepressible

## CONTROVERSY

**a:** argumentative, contentious, controversial, dialectic, discursory, disputatious, eristic, polemical

**n:** altercation, argument, argumentation, brannigan, *cause celebre,* contestation, disputation, dispute, dissention, polemics

## CONVENIENCE

**a:** advantageous, convenient, expedient, expeditional, opportune, seasonable

**n:** advantage, amenity, expedience, expediency, facilities, opportunity

## CONVENT

**a:** cenobitic, solitudinarian

**n:** cenobite, cloister, priory, retreat, seclusion, solitude, solitudinarian

> *head:* superior

## CONVENTIONAL

**a:** academic, accepted, artificial, *au fait, bourgeois,* ceremonial, ceremonious, conventionalized, decorous, formal, nomic, orthodoxical, pedantic, Philistine, stilted, stylized, traditional

**n:** academicism, allopathy, amenity, commonplaceness, conformity, conventionality, decorum, formalism, mores, orthodoxy, propriety, stereotype

**v:** conventionalize, mainstream, stereotype, style, stylize

> *defier:* beatnik, Bohemian, iconoclast, solecist, transgressor

> *person:* academician, Babbitt, *bourgeois,* orthodoxian, Philistine, proprietarian, stereotype

## CONVERGENCE

**a:** confluent, convergent

**n:** concurrency, confluence, conflux, convergency, joining, meeting

**v:** disembogue, meet

## CONVERSATION

**a:** colloquial, conversational, informal, interlocutory, phatic

**n:** aside, backchat, badinage, banter, *causerie,* colloquy, confabulation, *conversazione,* dialogue, digression, discourse, discussion, excursion, *excursus,* conversationalist, gabfest, interlocution, parenthesis, parlance, *pourparler,* repartee, *tete-a-tete*

> *writing:* causerie, journalese

## CONVERT

**n:** disciple, neophyte, novice, proselyte

**v:** apostatize, change, commute, persuade, proselyte, renege, sublimate, tergiversate, transform, transmute

> *math:* cambist, ready reckoner

## CONVINCING

**a:** authoritative, cogent, compelling, evident, luculent, persuasive, plausible, suasive, telling

**v:** brainwash, demonstrate, propagandize, prove

## CONVULSION

**a:** convulsionary, convulsive, eclamptic, orgasmic, paroxysmal, spasmic, spasmodic

**n:** eclampsia, *grand mal,* jacitation, orgasm, paroxysm, *petit mal,* seizure

## COOK

**a:** *al dente, au naturel, bien cuit,* cooked, *cordon bleu,* culinary

**n:** *aide de cuisine, chef de cuisine,* cuisinier, culinarian

**v:** blanch, boil, broil, coddle, devil, dredge, *flambe,* infuse, marinate, parboil, *puree, saute*

   *cooking:* cuisine, *cuisine bourgeoise, cuisine minceur,* epicurism, gastronomy, *haute cuisine, magirics,* menu

## COOL

**a:** calm, cold, composed, cooling, dispassionate, frigorific, imperturbable, indifferent, judicial, nonchalant, refrigerant, unperturbed, unruffled

**n:** coolness, equanimity, indifference, nonchalance, phlegm, *sangfroid,* self-possession

## COOPERATION

**a:** accommodating, amenable, associative, biddable, collaborative, compatible, complaisant, compliant, cooperative, docile, flexible, *in tandem,* malleable, obliging, pliable, symbiotic, synergetic, synergic, synergistic, tractable

**n:** altruism, coadjuvancy, collaboration, commensalism, kibbutz, lip service, mutualism, mutuality, nutricism, parasitism, reciprocality, reciprocity, symbiosis, synergism, synergy

**v:** collaborate, concur, connive, cooperate, gratify, pander to, unite

*cooperator:* collaborateur, collaborator, colleague, coworker, phalansterian

## COPPER

**a:** cupreous, cupriferous, cuprous

**n:** *aerugo,* patina, *verd antique, verdigris*

   *combining forms:* chalc-, chalco-, cupr-, cupri-, cupro-

## COPY

**a:** apographal, ectypal

**n:** apograph, clone, counterfeit, counterpart, derivative, duplicate, duplication, ectype, facsimile, miniature, replica, reproduction, transcript, transcription, transumption, xerography

**v:** counterfeit, duplicate, imitate, plagiarize, replicate, reproduce, transcribe, xerograph

   *machine:* cyclostyle, duplicator, memeograph, Xerox

   *person:* amanuensis, scribe, scrivener

## CORN

**n:** callosity, chiropody, *clavus, ecphyma, papilloma*

   *cut corn:* flail, glean

   *eating:* Indian, maize, mealie

## CORPSE

**a:** cachectic, cadaverous, corpselike

   *combining forms:* necr-, necro-

## CORRECT

**a:** accurate, *au fait,* conventional, decorous, legitimate, meticulous, orthodox, precise, rectitudinous, scrupulous

**n:** accuracy, amendment, chastening, chastenment, correction, correctness, *corrigenda,* corrigendum, emendation, *errata, erratum,* orthodoxy, rebuke, rectification, rectitude, reformation

**v:** castigate, chasten, discipline, expiate, rectify

   *beyond:* incorrigible, irreclaimable, irredeemable, irreformable, irremediable, irreparable *correctable:* amenable, corrigible, perfectible, tractable

*corrective:* amendatory, castigatory, penal

## CORRESPONDING

**a:** accompanying, analogous, coincident, coinciding, commensurable, commensurate, equivalent, homologous, isonomous, proportionate

**n:** commensurability, commensuration, congruity, consonance, correlation, correspondence, counterpart, equiponderance, equivalence, homogeneity, homologue, mapping, reciprocation, symmetry, *vis-a-vis*

**v:** agree, coincide, commensurate, comport, conform, correlate, correspond, equate, match, reciprocate, tally

*combining form:* counter-

## CORROBORATIVE

**a:** adminicular, authenticative, confirmatory, corroboratory, justificatory, vindicatory

## CORRUPT

**a:** cankerous, contaminated, contaminating, corruptive, decadent, degenerate, demoralizing, immoral, infectious, mercenary, noxious, peccant, pernicious, pestiferous, pestilent, putrescent, putrid, scrofulous, tainted, venal

**n:** canker, contamination, debasement, debauchery, debauchment, decay, defilement, degeneracy, demoralization, depravity, evil, graft, jobbery, putrefaction, scrofulosis, squalor, venality

**v:** adulterate, debase, debauch, defile, demoralize, deprave, inquinate, pervert, pollute, putrefy, suborn, subvert, vitiate

## COST

**a:** costly, dispendious, exorbitant, extortionate, extravagant, inestimable, invaluable, lavish, prodigal

**n:** Pyrrhic victory, surcharge

**v:** defray, economize, meet, pay, retrench

## COUNCIL

**a:** conciliar

**n:** assembly, privy council, quorum

*person:* alderman

## COUNTENANCE

**n:** appearance, comportment, lineament, mien, physiognomy, sanction, visage

**v:** encourage, sanction, support

## COUNTERACT

**n:** complement, counterpart, obverse, opposition, *riposte*

**v:** antagonize, contrapose, neutralize, nullify, parry

*counterattack:* counteroffensive, repartee, *riposte*

*countercharge:* recrimination, retaliation

*countermove:* counteraction, *demarche*

## COUNTERFEIT

**a:** affected, apocryphal, artificial, delusive, ersatz, factitious, fake, false, fraudulent, imitative, inauthentic, pretended, pseudo, simulated, spurious, supposititious, synthetic, uncanonical

**n:** imitation

**v:** feign, imitate, pretend, simulate

*counterfeiter:* adulterator, imitant, impostor, imposture, mountebank, pretender

## COUNTLESS

**a:** incalculable, infinite, innumerable, legion, multitudinous, myriad

**n:** infinitude, infinity

## COUNTRY

**a:** agrestic, autochthonous, bucolic, campestral, countryfied, enchorial, idyllic, indigenous, pastoral, patrial, provincial, rural, rurigenous, rustic, Theocritean, unsophisticated, villatic

**n:** boondocks, bundu, enclave, fatherland, hinterland, idyll, outback, peninsularity, provincialism, provinciality, rustication, rusticity, villa

**v:** rusticate

*person:* agrestian, bucolic, compatriot, provincial, rustic

## COUPLE

**a:** coadunate, coadunative, conjugate, coupled, dyadic

**n:** accouplement, articulation, conjugation, copulation, coupling, dyad, junction, juncture, symphysis

**v:** conjugate, unite

## COURAGE

**a:** audacious, bold, brave, chivalrous, courageous, fortitudinous, Herculean, intrepid, resolute, Spartan

**n:** audacity, bravado, bravery, dauntlessness, derring-do, doughtiness, fortitude, gallantry, intrepidity, mettle, prowess, resolution, tenacity

**v:** muster

## COURSE

**n:** curriculum, *demarche*, entree, journey, maneuver, module, procedure, scenario, schedule, syllabus, tenor

**v:** pulsate, surge, transverse

## COURT

**a:** adjective, aulic, forensic, *in camera*, judicial, judiciary, juridical, juristic, justiciable, *sub judice*, substantive

**n:** *cause celebre*, docket, judicature, judiciary, jurisdiction, litigation, recourse, session, testimony, trial

## COURTESY

**a:** affable, attentive, chivalric, chivalrous, complimentary, courteous, debonaire, deferential, *gratis*, hospitable, ingratiating, obeisant, obsequious, parliamentary, servile, suave, urbane

**n:** address, amenity, civility, comity, deference, deferentiality, *devoir*, gentility, gratuity, homage, indulgence, obsequence, obsequiousness, obsequity, pleasantry, *politesse*, propriety, protocol, servility, urbanity

## COURTLY

**a:** aulic, courteous, obsequious, polite, stately, suave, unctuous

## COVER

**a:** a *couvert*

**n:** canopy, cloisters, cortex, covering, envelope, integument, mantle, *marquee*, operculum, pall, pallium, superimposition

**v:** laminate, obnubilate, superimpose, whitewash

## COVETOUS

**a:** acquisitive, *alieni appetens*, avaracious, extortionate, greedy, miserly, parsimonious, penurious, prehensile, rapacious

**n:** avarice, covetousness, cupidity, desire, greed, longing, lust, pining, pleonexia, venality

## COW

**a:** bovine

**n:** bovidae, bovine, heifer, ruminant, springer, stirk

## COWARD

**a:** caitiff, cowardly, craven, dastardly, irresolute, lily-livered, pusillanimous, recreant, timorous, tremulous

**n:** caitiff, craven, dastard, poltroon, recreant

*cowardice:* cowardliness, dastardliness, poltroonery, pusillanimity, recreancy, timidity

## COY

**a:** clever, coquettish, cunning, sly

**n:** coquetry, coyness, dalliance, minauderie, reluctance, reserve

## COZY

**a:** cheerful, congenial, friendly, *gemultlich*, informal, intimate, private

**n:** homeliness, intimacy, security, snuggery, snugness

**CRABBY**

**a:** acerbic, acidulent, acidulous, choleric, churlish, cranky, rebarbative, splenetic, vinegary

**n:** acerbity, asperity, crabbiness

**CRACK**

**a:** rimose, rimulose

**n:** break, chasm, cleft, crackling, *craquelure, crevasse,* crevice, fissure, gap, split

**CRADLE**

**a:** *ab incunabulis*

**n:** *creche, incunabula,* infancy, matrix

**CRAFTSMAN**

**n:** artificer, artisan, journeyman

**CRAFTY**

**a:** artful, astucious, astute, calculating, conniving, cunning, ingenious, insidious, insinuating, Machiavellian, politic, scheming, sophisticated, subtle, vulpine

**n:** astucity, astuteness, callidity, craftiness, *diablerie,* ingeniosity

**CRAMPED**

**a:** incapacious, incommodious

**n:** crick, rigor, strain

**CRANKY**

**a:** cantankerous, choleric, crabby, crochety, irascible, peevish, petulant, querulous, splenetic, vinegary

**n:** acerbity, angularity, asperity, crankiness, crotchiness, distemper, irascibility, peevishness, querulousness

**CRAVING**

**a:** appetant, appetitious, appetizing, desiderative

**n:** appetence, appetency, appetition, desideration, desideratum, hunger, itch, need, pica, thirst, yearning

**v:** crave, desire, hunger, long, lust, seek, solicit, thirst, want, yearn

**CRAWLING**

**a:** creeping, inching, sidling, sliding, slithering, snaking, subreptary

**CRAZED**

**a:** berserk, crazy, distraught, frantic, frenetic, harassed, insane, maniacal, monomaniac

**n:** craze, fad, mania, monomania, monomaniac, obsession

**CREATE**

**a:** constructive, creating, demiurgic, Dionysiac, Dionysian, formative, genetic, imaginative, ingenious, original, *poietic,* productive, Promethean, reproductive

**n:** afflatus, cosmos, creation, *elan vital,* genesis, inception, masterpiece, *poiesis,* procreation, universe

**v:** build, fabricate, generate, invent, reproduce

    *person:* Prometheus

**CREDIT**

**a:** attributive, commendable, creditable

**n:** acknowledg(e)ment, ascription, attribution, creditability, recognition

**v:** assign, redound

**CREDULOUS**

**a:** gullible, naive

**n:** credulity, gullibility, *naivete,* naivety

**CREED**

**n:** belief, confession, denomination, doctrine, dogma, philosophy, tenet

    *person without:* aporetic, apostasy, apostate, latitudinarian, nullifidian

    *without:* apostate, apostatic

**CREEPING**

**a:** crawling, procumbent, prostrate, reptant, reptatorial, reptilian, serpentine, serpiginous, subreptary, trailing, worming

**CREMATION**

n: burning ghat, cineration, pyre

**CRESCENT**

a: bicorn, bicuspid, lunate, lunular, lunulate, meniscoid

n: demilune, lunula, meniscus

**CREST**

a: crested, cristate, pileated

n: crown

　　*combining form:* lopho-

**CRIME**

a: blameworthy, *capax doli*, criminogenic, criminous, culpable, evil, extortionate, felonious, flagitious, fugitive, illicit, immoral, incriminatory, malefic, nefarious, nocent, unlawful

n: abduction, arson, barratry, bigamy, commission, contumacy, *crime passionnel*, defalcation, delict, delinquency, embezzlement, embracery, extortion, felony, incest, incrimination, infraction, iniquity, larceny, *lese majeste*, malefaction, malfeasance, *mens rea*, misdemeanor, offense, perjury, perpetration, polygamy, rape, transgression, treason, vagrancy, violation

v: connive, incriminate, inculpate, mastermind

　　*charge with:* criminate, incriminate, indict

　　*concealment: misprision,* subreption

　　*criminal:* accessory, convict, culprit, delinquent, felon, infractor, malfeasant, miscreant, sorcerer's apprentice

**CRINKLED**

a: bent, convoluted, corrugated, crispate, curled, folded, kinked

**CRISIS**

a: crisic, critical, dilemmatic, predicamental

n: apoplexy, climacteric, climacterium, conjecture, convulsion, criticality, cruciality, crux, dilemma, exigency, predicament, seizure

v: defuse

**CRITICIZE**

a: captious, censorial, censorious, climacteric, climactic, condemnatory, critical, crucial, cynical, dangerous, definitive, derisive, dilemmatic, exigent, imminent, resolute, scrupulous, squeamish

n: animadversion, censure, criticism, critique, derision, diatribe, evaluation, *exegesis*, impugnation, scarification, stricture

v: admonish, animadvert, castigate, censure, chastise, crucify, declaim, denounce, deplore, depreciate, derogate, disparage, evaluate, excoriate, execrate, fly, fulminate against, fustigate, impugn, insult, inveigh, moralize, pillory, reprehend, reprobate, revile, scarify, scold, sermonize, upbraid, vituperate

　　*critic:* Aristarch, carper, caviler, *cognoscente, connoisseur, exegete,* faultfinder, *feuilletonist,* momus, pundit

**CROOKED**

a: akimbo, askew, awry, bent, circuitous, devious, fraudulent, incurvate, insidious, perfidious, sinuous, stealthy, surreptitious, tortuous, twisted, unconscionable, vermiculate, winding, zigzag

n: circuitry, crookedness, deviousness, indirection, insidiousness, perfidy, surreption, tortuosity, unscrupulosity, villainy

**CROP**

n: agronomics, agronomy, commodity, plant, staple

v: glean, grow, harvest, rotate

**CROSS**

a: acidulous, allogamous, bilious, choleric, contentious, crucial, cruciate, cruciform, decussate, fractious, irascible, perverse, quadrivial, xenogamous

**n:** allogamy, *carrefour*, chiasma, crucifier, decussation, half-breed, hybrid, intersection, mongrel, pelican crossing, *quadrivium*, transom, xenogamy

**v:** decussate, delete

*types:* avellan, *botonee, clechee, fleuretee,* flyfot, gammadion, *hakenkreuz,* Maltese, moline, *patonce,* quadrate, swastika

**CROUCHING**

**a:** *couchant, crouchant*

**CROW**

**a:** corvine

**n:** carrion crow

**CROWD**

**a:** congested, crowded, gregarious, overcrowded, populous, serried, teeming

**n:** concourse, confluence, horde, mob, multitude, phalanx, ruck, stampede, throng, tumult

**v:** congregate

*fear:* demophobia, ochlophobia

**CROWN**

**n:** corona, coronet, culmination, diadem, laureate, pate, scepter, sovereignty, tiara

**v:** laureate

*crowning:* coronation

**CRUCIAL**

**a:** climacteric, climactic, critical, decisive, searching

**n:** crisis, criticality, cruciality, watershed

**CRUDE**

**a:** artless, basic, *gauche,* immature, inapt, incondite, inept, primitive, primordial, rude, rudimentary, rustic, uncouth, undeveloped, unpolished, unskillful. unsophisticated, vulgar

**n:** crudeness, crudity, *gaucherie,* grobianism, immaturity, impoliteness, ineptitude, ineptness, plebeianism, primitivity, rusticity

*person:* buffoon, grobian, rustic

**CRUEL**

**a:** barbarous, despiteful, diabolical, dispiteous, Draconian, ferocious, harsh, heartless, impiteous, implacable, indurate, inexorable, inhuman, insensitive, lupine, malicious, marblehearted, merciless, perverted, remorseless, sadistic, satanic, truculent, tyrannical, tyrannous, wicked

**n:** atrocity, barbarism, barbarity, callousness, cruelty, enormity, ferity, induration, inhumanity, persecution, sadism

*person:* harpy, ogre

**CRUMBLY**

**a:** frangible, friable, pulverent, pulverous

**v:** crumble, decay, molder

**CRUSADER**

**a:** crusading, evangelical, evangelistic, messianic, zealous

**n:** Messiah, messiahship

**CRY**

**a:** lachrymal, lachrymatory, lachrymose, lacrimal, lacrimatory, larmoyant

**n:** *cri de coeur,* deploration, lachrymation, lacrimation, lamentation, ululation

**v:** blubber, caterwaul, mewl, ululate, vociferate, yammer

**CULMINATION**

**a:** climacteric, culminant

**n:** acme, apex, apogee, climacteric, climacterium, climax, consummation, meridian, pinnacle, vertex, zenith

**CULTURE**

**a:** decadent, ethnic, ethnological

**n:** acculturation, enculturation, ethnology, heritage, humanities, melting pot, socialization, *zeitgeist*

**v:** acculturize

*cultured:* aesthetic, cultivated, esthetic, literate, polished, refined, urbane

*lacking:* *bourgeoise,* deracinated, *deracine,* philistine, Philistinic, uncouth *rebirh: renaissance, renascence*

## CUNNING

**a:** artful, artistic, astucious, astute, callid, crafty, daedalian, designing, dexterous, diplomatic, disingenuous, duplicitous, expedient, ingenious, insidious, parlous, sagacious, unscrupulous

**n:** artifice, astucity, callidity, craftiness, dexterity, guile, ingeniosity, ingenuity, insidiousness, Machiavellianism, wiles

## CURE

**a:** curable, curative, healing, medicable, remediable, remedial, sanable, sanative, sanatory, therapeutic, tractable, vulnerary

**n:** antidote, catholicon, elixir, nostrum, panacea, remediation, remedy, theriac

**v:** physic

## CURIO

**n:** antique, bibelot, *bric-a-brac*, curiosity, knickknack, *objet d'art*, trinket, *virtu*

## CURIOUS

**a:** agog, impatient, inquisitive, inquisitorial, nosy, piquant, provocative, provocatory, prurient, prying

**n:** *curiosa*, inquisitiveness, piquancy, prurience, pruriency, rarity

**v:** *pique*

    *person:* Pandora, *quidnunc*

## CURRENT

**a:** coetaneous, coeval, contemporaneous, contemporary, existing, extant, modern, popular, prevailing, prevalent, topical

**n:** contemporaneity, mainstream, modernity, prevalence, topicality

    *combining form:* rheo-

    *types:* AC, alternating, DC, direct, eddy, malestrom, race, undertow

## CURSE

**a:** accursed, anathematic, comminatory, cursed, cursing, detestable, execrable, imprecatory, maledictory, odious

**n:** anathema, anathematization, blasphemy, contamination, denunciation, execration, fulmination, imprecation, malediction, malison, scourge

**v:** anathematize, blaspheme, comminate, curse, execrate, imprecate, maledict, objurgate

## CURT

**a:** brief, brusque, condensed, crabby, cryptic, cutting, disagreeable, laconic, terse, unceremonious, unmannerly

## CURTAIL

**v:** abate, abbreviate, abridge, reduce, shorten, truncate

## CURVE

**a:** acinaciform, archiform, arcuate, circumflex, convoluted, crescentic, curvaceous, curved, curving, falciform, flexuous, helix, sinuous, spiral, undulating, volute, whorl

**n:** arcuation, asymptote, camber, catenary, circumflexion, convolution, cusp, flexure, French curve, hyperbola, meniscus, ogee, parabola, perimeter, sinuosity, spinose, trajectory

**v:** arcuate, circumflex, osculate

    *inward:* concave, incurved, involute

    *outward:* convex

## CUSTODIAN

**n:** caretaker, Cerberus, chaperone, claviger, concierge, *custos*, guardian, leader, master, protector, shepherd, superintendent, teacher, tutor

## CUSTOM

**a:** *ad amussim, ad us, ad usum,* censuetudinary, *comme il faut,* conventional, customary, *de regle, de rigueur, ex more,* nomic, prescriptive, prevalent, traditional

**n:** consuetude, convention, conventionality, methods, habit, habituation, habitude, mores, observance, patronage, *praxis,* precedent, prescription, protocol, rite of passage, rubric, usage, wont

    *combining form:* nomo-

**CUT**

**a:** acrimonious, caustic, cutting, incisive, keen, mordant, penetrating, piquant, poignant, sarcastic, trenchant

**n:** ablation, abscission, amputation, disjunction, dismemberment, dissolution, disunion, excision, extirpation, incision, mutilation, rescission, retrenchment, scission, sundering, vivisection

**v:** abbreviate, ablate, abscind, abscise, amputate, bevel, bowdlerize, crop, decapitate, decussate, dismember, emasculate, enucleate, excise, expurgate, extirpate, intercept, intersect, lacerate, poll, resect, scarify, syncopate, transect, whittle

> *combining forms:* -sect, tom-, -tome, -tomy

**CYCLE**

**a:** cyclic(al), ontogenetic, periodic(al), rhythmic(al)

**n:** biorhythm, change, circuit, course, epoch, era, interval, lap, loop, ontogenesis, ontogeny, oscillation, period, pursuit, round, sequence, series

**CYNICISM**

**a:** cynical, derisive, disabused, disenchanted, disillusioned, ironical, misanthropic(al), pessimistic, sarcastic, sardonic, satirical, unidealistic

**n:** Dadism, derision, irony, pantagruelism, pessimism, sarcasm, sardonicism, satire

> *cynic:* Anisthenes, Diogenes, misanthrope, skeptic, Timon

**DABBLER**

**n:** amateur, collector, *dilettante*, novice, sciolist, trifler

**v:** dabble, meddle, potter, tinker, trifle

**DAILY**

**a:** aday, circadian, diurnal, per diem, quotidian

**n:** per diem, quotidian

*twice:* semidiurnal

**DAINTY**

**a:** affected, airy, decorous, etherial, exquisite, fastidious, gossamery, mincing, overrefined, *recherce*

**n:** daintiness, delicacy, ethereality, *friandise*

**DALLY**

**a:** dallying, degage, desipient, relaxed

**n:** desipience, desipiency

**v:** dawdle, delay, loiter, philander, play, procrastinate, shilly-shally, tarry, toy, trifle, vacillate

**DAMAGING**

**a:** corrupting, deleterious, destructive, detrimental, harmful, hurtful, inimical, injurious, irreparable, malignant, nocent, nocuous, noxious, prejudicial, venomous

**n:** damages, detriment, devastation, dilapidation, disadvantage, disservice, havoc, vandalism

**v:** blight, damage, deface, devastate, disable, discredit, disfigure, impair, incapacitate, mar, mutilate, ravage, spoil, vandalize, vitiate, weaken

*repayment:* amercement, remuneration, reparation(s)

**DAMNATION**

**n:** hell, perdition, reprobate

**v:** curse, damn

**DANCE**

**a:** antiphonal, antiphonic, saltatorial, saltatory, *terpsichorean*

**n:** antiphony, ballet, ballroom, choreography, *danse macabre*, do-si-do, eurhythmics, feather, folk, *pas, pas de deux, poussette, prisiadka*, promenade, *terpsichore, the dansant*

**DANDRUFF**

**a:** furfuraceous, scurfy

**n:** furfures, scurf

**DANDY**

**n:** Beau Brummel, coxcomb, dandiprat, dandyism, fop, foppishness, jackanapes, macaroni, popinjay

**DANGER**

**a:** between a rock and a hard place, between Scylla and Charybdis, Circean, corrupt, critical, Damoclean, dangerous, evil, forbidding, formidible, hazardous, ignitable, imminent, insecure, insidious, jeopardous, menacing, *parlous*, perilous, perliculous, pernicious, pestiferous, pestilent(ial), precarious, risky, sematic, venturesome, venturous, vulnerable

**n:** difficulty, hazard, jeopardy, menace, pitfall, precipice, skull and crossbones, snake in the grass, temerity, venture, vulnerability

**v:** endanger, imperil, jeopardize, risk

**DARE**

**a:** adventurous, audacious, *aude sapere*, bold, courageous, dangerous, daring, fortitudinous, Icarian, intrepid, perilous, picaresque, unconventional, venturous

**n:** *bravura,* derring-do, *escapate, tour de force*

**v:** brave, gamble, hazard, risk, venture

## DARK

**a:** adiaphanous, adumbral, atramental, atramentous, caliginous, dim, drab, dull, fulginous, funereal, gloomy, ignorant, inexplicable, iniquitous, murky, mysterious, opaque, photochromic, sinister, somber, stygian, subfusc, swarthy, tenebrous, wicked

**n:** darkness, fuliginosity, night, nigrescence, nigritude, obscurity, penumbra, tenebrosity, umbra, umbrage

**v:** adumbrate, blur, darken, denigrate, obfuscate, obnubilate, obscure

> *combining forms:* melan-, melano-, nyct-, nycti-, nycto-

## DAUGHTER

**a:** filial, sibling

**n:** sibling

## DAWDLE

**n:** shilly-shally

**v:** dally, delay, dillydally, dream, idle, lag, loiter, mope, poke, procrastinate, tarry, toy, trifle, wait, waste

## DAWN

**a:** antelucan, auorean, auroral, eoan

**n:** aurora

**v:** work

## DAY

**a:** circadian, daily, diurnal, halcyon, hodiernal

**n:** equinox, solstice

> *sayings: carpe diem, dies faustus, dies infaustus,* dog days, halcyon days, *sine die*

## DAYDREAM

**a:** autistic, daydreaming, introspective, phantasmal

**n:** absentmindedness, autism, introspection, introspectiveness, phantasm, phantasy, reverie, stargazing, woolgathering

> *person:* Walter Mitty

## DAZZLING

**a:** foudroyant, fulgent, fulgurant, fulgurating, fulgurous, iridescent, meteoric, prismatic, pyrotechnic, radiant, resplendent, splendorous

**n:** dazzlement, radiance, resplendence, resplendency

## DEAD

**a:** *ad patres,* amort, anesthetic, barren, decease, defunct, demised, deserted, exanimate, extinct, inanimate, inert, inorganic, insensible, insentient, irrevocable, lifeless, manistic, monotonous, moribund, mortuary, necrolatrous, *post mortem,* unresponsive

**n:** annihilation, consummation, death, defunction, demise, *exitus,* extinction, fatality, mortality, necrophilism, netherworld, *quietus, rigor mortis*

**v:** anesthetize, benumb, deaden, hebetate, obscure, obtund, paralyze, stupefy

> *after:* posthumous, *post-mortem, post obitum*
>
> *before:* antemortem, premortal, premortem, preterminal
>
> *burial place:* cemetery, charnel house, ossuary, pantheon
>
> *combining forms:* mort-, necr-, necro-
>
> *dead-end:*    *cul-de-sac,*    deadlock, impasse
>
> *deadly:* baneful, cadaverous, devastating, fatal, feral, internecine, lethal, lethiferous, mortal, mortiferous, noxious, cachetic, charnal, ghastly, moribund, pernicious, pestilent, sepulchral, stygian, terminal, venomous, viperish
>
> *exam:* autopsy, necropsy, *post mortem*
>
> *fear:* necrophobia, thanatophobia
>
> *hymn:* requiem
>
> *mercy:* euthanasia
>
> *mourning:* elegy, monody, threnody

**DEAF**

n: deafness, surdity

*language:* dactylology

**DEBASE**

a: degrading

n: adulteration, debasement, degeneracy, deglamorization, depravation, depravity, dishonor, humiliation, squalidity, squalor

v: adulterate, bastardize, belittle, contaminate, corrupt, defame, deglamorize, degrade, demean, denigrate, deteriorate, discredit, dishonor, harm, heathenize, humble, minimize, paganize, pejorate, pervert, stigmatize, sully, vilify, vitiate, vulgarize

**DEBATE**

a: contentious, controversial, controvertible, debatable, dialectical, disputatious, dubious, dubitable, equivocal, forensic, polemical, questionable, *quodlibetic(al)*

n: argumentation, controversy, dialectic, disputation, dissension, forensics, moot court, polemics

v: argue, deliberate, discuss, negotiate, parley

*end:* closure, cloture

**DEBILITY**

a: adynamic, asthenic, cachectic, debilitated, impotent, weak

n: adynamia, asthenia, cachexia, cachexy, debilitation, decrepitude, enervation, impotence, impotency, languor, myasthenia, *myasthenia gravis,* weakness

**DEBRIS**

n: accumulation, detritus, dirt, fragments, garbage, lees, oddments, orts, refuse, remains, rubbish, scree, sediment, trash, trivia, waste

**DEBT**

a: bankrupt, beholden, indebted, insolvent, obliged

n: arrears, debenture, debit, insolvency, liability, lien, *post-obit*

v: amortize, commute, compound, contract, incur

*able to pay:* solvent

*settle:* extinquish, liquidate, quietus, quittance

*unable to pay:* insolvent

**DECAY**

a: broken down, consenescent, decrepit, dilapidated, rotting, saprophagous, saprophytic

n: canker, caries, consenescence, decadence, decadency, decomposition, decrepitude, deterioration, dilapidation, disintegration, dissolution, effluvium, gangrene, labefaction, mortification, necrosis, putrefaction, putrescence, putridity

v: crumble, decompose, disintegrate, fester, molder, putrefy, rot

*combining forms:* sapr-, sapro-

**DECEIVE**

a: alluring, cabalistic, clandestine, deceitful, deceptious, deceptive, dissimulative, duplicitous, fallacious, gnathonic, illusional, illusory, mendacious, misleading, obliquitous, perfidious, sirenic, specious, surreptitious, tricky

n: artifice, camouflage, chicanery, circumvention, cozenage, deceit, deceitfulness, deception, defraudation, desipience, disengenuity, dissimulation, duplicity, fabrication, *fourberie,* fraudulence, gambit, hocus-pocus, hyprocrisy, *ignis fatuus,* imposture, indirection, inveiglement, legerdemain, mendacity, obliquity, perfidy, prestidigitation, simulation, sinuosity, speciosity, subterfuge, trickery

v: bamboozle, beguile, blarney, cajole, camouflage, cheat, circumvent, cozen, defraud, dissemble, dissimulate, doublecross, ensnare, inveigle, masquerade, mislead, outwit, victimize

*deceiver:* charlatan, dissembler, dissimulator, imposter, mountebank, rogue

**DECENT**

**a:** acceptable, adequate, appropriate, chaste, decorous, demure, good, mannerly, modest, moral, noble, polite, satisfactory, suitable, virtuous

**n:** convention, conventionality, decency, decorum, modesty, propriety, pudency

**DECIDE**

**a:** absolute, adjudicative, Aerophagitic, apocalyptic(al), authoritative, categorical, clear-cut, conclusive, decisive, definitive, determinative, discretionary, final, implacable, indomitable, unalterable, unequivocal

**n:** *ad hoc* decision, adjudication, arbitrament, clincher, conclusion, definitude, determination, discretion, *fait accompli*, judgment, justiciability, mandate, *parti pris*, point of no return, precedent, *res judicata*, resolubility, resolution, settlement, sockdolager, trump card, umpirage, volition

**v:** determine, underwrite

*reverse:* disallow, invalidate, overrule, overturn, quash, rescind

**DECLAMATORY**

**a:** bombastic, Ciceronian, elocutionary, grandiloquent, oratorical, rhetorical, stilted

**n:** declamation, exposition, oration

**v:** advocate, declaim, elocute, exposit, expound, express, harangue, orate, profess, rant, rhetorize, spout, voice

**DECLARE**

**a:** affirmative, assertive, assertorial, asseverative, declaratory, enunciative, expository, proclamatory

**n:** asseveration, declaration, manifesto, white paper

**v:** annunciate, asseverate, claim, nuncupate, predicate, proclaim, promulgate

**DECLINE**

**a:** decadent, decaying, declining, involutional

**n:** decadence, decadency, declination, degeneration, degenerescence, degradation, degringolade, demotion, involution, lysis, retrocession, retrogression

**v:** decrease, degenerate, lessen, regress, relapse, renege, retrocede, retrograde, retrogress

**DECORATE**

**a:** attractive, decorative, gingerbread, ornamental

**n:** adornment, applique, atmosphere, bunting, caparison, citation, decor, decoration, embellishment, emblazonment, embroidery, festoon, filigree, garnish(ment), garniture, medallion, tinsel, trim

**v:** adorn, array, beautify, bedaub, bedeck, bedizen, chase, damascene, damask, embellish, emblazon, enchase, enrich, furnish, ornament, prettify, trim

**DECREASE**

**a:** declinatory, decreasing, decrescent, degressive, descrescendo, diminishing, reductionistic, reductive

**n:** abatement, attenuation, declension, declination, decrement, decrescence, decrescendo, degregation, degression, depreciation, deterioration, diminishing returns, diminuendo, diminution, lysis, retrenchment, retrogression

**v:** abate, diminish, dwindle, lessen

**DECREE**

**a:** nisi

**n:** command, decretum, fiat, judgment, mandate, ordinance, proclamation, pronouncement, *pronunciamento*

**DEDICATE**

**a:** consecratory, dedicatorial, dedicatory

**n:** consecration, dedication, devotement, devotion, enthusiasm, faithfulness, sanctification

**v:** consecrate, enshrine, hallow, honor, ordain, sanctify, vow

## DEDUCE

**a:** *a priori,* aprioristic, deducible, deductive, illative, inferential, syllogistic(al)

**n:** *a priori,* abatement, apriority, corollary, deductibility, deduction, hariolation, induction, inference, inferentiality, syllogism, synthesis

**v:** conclude, deduce, derive, estimate, extrapolate, guess, hariolate, infer, prove, work out

## DEED

**n:** achievement, *acta,* exploit, *gest, geste,* performance, transaction

## DEEP

**a:** abstruse, abysmal, bottomless, cavernous, endemic, fathomless, hermetic(al), ingrained, inveterate, mysterious, navigable, nethermost, penetrating, profound, recondite, subterranean, unfathomed

**n:** abstrusity, depth, nadir, profundity

*combining forms:* bath-, batho-, bathy-

## DEFAME

**a:** calumnious, defamatory, denigratory, libelous, slanderous

**n:** aspersion, defamation, denigration

**v:** asperse, calumniate, denigrate, disparage, libel, malign, revile, slander, sully, traduce, vilify

## DEFEAT

**n:** *bouleversement,* debacle, defeasance, discomfiture, downfall, failure, frustration, labefaction, overthrow, repulse, subjugation, Waterloo

**v:** annihilate, baffle, checkmate, conquer, crucify, crush, devastate, eclipse, excel, frustrate, nullify, outperform, outshine, overcome, overreach, overthrow, pulverize, route, subdue, subjugate, surmount, surpass, trounce, vanquish

## DEFECT

**a:** defective, deficient, dysgenic, impedimental, imperfect, incomplete, infelicitous, insufficient, lacunal, lacunar, mediocre, unsound

**n:** blemish, defectibility, defectiveness, deficiency, foible, handicap, impediment, lacuna, malfunction, shortcoming, weakness

**v:** apostatize, tergiversate

## DEFENSE

**a:** defensible, *en garde,* reasonable, tenable, territorial

**n:** aegis, apologetics, apologia, argument, armament, bastion, bulwark, defilade, deterent, extenuation, fortification, justification, materiel, munitions, outpost, protection, rampart, stronghold, weaponry

*defenseless:* exposed, impotent, indefensible, inexcusable, unjustifiable, untenable, vulnerable

*wall or shelter:* breastwork, bulwark, bunker, *cheval-de-frise, enceinte,* parados, parapet, redoubt, revetment, stockade, traverse, trenchment

## DEFER

**n:** continuance, prorogation

**v:** capitulate, comply, concede, continue, delay, hold, intermit, postpone, prolong, prorogue, protract, slow, submit, surrender, temporize

## DEFERENCE

**a:** complacent, considerate, courteous, deferential, fawning, loyal, meek, modest, regardful, respectful, reverential, sycophantic, unctuous, venerative, worshiping, yielding

**n:** agreement, allegiance, appreciation, capitulation, consideration, deferentiality, devoir, favor, fealty, groveling, homage, humility, obeisance, submission, veneration, worship, yielding

## DEFIANT

**a:** antagonistic, audacious, bold, challenging, insolent, recalcitrant, refractory

**n:** audacity, challenge, confrontation, defiance, effrontery, impudence, opposition, refractoriness, temerity

**v:** brave, break, challenge, confront, dare, defy, disobey, disregard, fight, front, impugn, infract, oppose, provoke, reject, repudiate, resist, revolt, rise, test, violate

**DEFICIENT**

**a:** crude, defective, dysgenic, immature, imperfect, incomplete, insufficient, lacking, mediocre, minus, rudimentary, underdeveloped

**n:** dearth, deficiency, *faiblesse,* foible, handicap, impediment, imperfection, inadequacy, lacuna, manque, ullage, weakness

**DEFILE**

**a:** contaminated, defiled, maculate, polluted, vitiated

**n:** adulteration, contamination, corruption, defilement, dirtiness, impurity, indecency, lewdness, licentiousness, pollution, putrescence, vitiation

**v:** befoul, contaminate, pollute, ravish, tarnish, violate, vitiate

**DEFINE**

**a:** defining, *ipso facto,* orismological

**n:** constraints, *defimens, definiendum, definiens,* definition, parameters

**v:** circumscribe, decipher, decode, delimit, delineate, demarcate, diagnose, diagnosticate, distinguish, explain, explicate, identify, interpret, outline, translate

**DEFINITE**

**a:** absolute, circumscribed, cogent, definitive, determinate, determinative, dogmatic, explicit, individual, material, mathematical, objective, particular, positive, specific, tangible, unqualified

**n:** definiteness, definitude, finality, finitude, inevitability, precision, tangibility

**DEFLATED**

**a:** burst, contracted, drained, empty, exhausted, kaput, punctured, reduced, sagging, shrunken

**DEFRAUD**

**n:** cozenage, defraudation, defraudment

**v:** bilk, cheat, cozen, deceive, dupe, fleece, fool, gyp, hoodwink, rob, swindle, trick, victimize, wrong

**DEGENERATE**

**a:** corrupt(ed), debased, debauched, decadent, deteriorated, devitalized, *effete,* retrograde

**n:** declination, degeneracy, degeneration, profligacy, retrogression

**DEGRADE**

**a:** degrading, dishonorable, disreputable, humbled, humiliating, humiliative, ignoble, ignominious, inglorious, menial, mortifying, shameful, sordid, squalid, unrespectable

**n:** debasement, declination, degradation, humiliation, pejoration, squalidity, squalor

**v:** belittle, censure, debase, demean, demote, denigrate, denounce, humble, humiliate, imbrute, pejorate, relegate, stigmatize

**DEGREE**

**a:** comparative, positive, superlative

**n:** coefficient, gradation, intensity, length, level, mark, measure, measurement, point, position, rate, standard

   *college:* aegrotat, baccalaureate, *cum laude,* honorary, *honoris causa,* licentiate, *magna cum laude, summa cum laude*

**DEHUMANIZE**

**v:** automate, automatize, barbarize, brutalize, imbrute, mechanize, robotize

**DEIFY**

**n:** apotheosis, canonization, deification, sanctification, transfiguration

**v:** apotheosize, canonize, enshrine, hallow, sanctify, spiritualize, transcend, transfigure

   *deity:* agathodaemon, divinity, god, godhead, numen, supreme being, tutelary

**DEJECT**

**a:** *a la mort,* abased, dejected, disconsolate, disheartened, dispirited, funereal, humbled, inconsolable, inconsolate, melancholic, melancholy, prostrate

**n:** dejection, depression, gloominess

**v:** discourage, dishearten, dispirit

**DELAY**

**a:** dawdling, delayed, dilatory, late, tardy

**n:** armistice, continuance, cunctation, deferment, detention, impediment, laches, moratorium, obstructionism, postponement, procrastination, protraction, reprieve, respite, retardation, suspension, temporization

**v:** continue, defer, detain, dilly-dally, dither, filibuster, impede, lag, loiter, postpone, procrastinate, protract, retard, shilly-shally, stonewall, tarry, temporize, vacillate

**DELEGATE**

**a:** delegated, deputed, substitutionary, vicarial, vicarious

**n:** commissioner, deputy, emissary, legate, representative, surrogate

**v:** commission, commit, depute

**DELIBERATE**

**a:** calculated, considered, intentional, planned, premeditated, studied

**n:** attention, deliberateness, deliberation, excogitation, ponderation, premeditation, reflection, volition

**v:** excogitate, meditate, ponder

**DELICATE**

**a:** dainty, epicene, ethereal, exquisite, fastidious, fragile, insubstantial, light, mincing, overnice, precarious, refined, sensitive, squeamish, subtle, superfine, uncertain

**n:** *bonne bouche*, confection, delicacy, *delicatesse*, ethereality, fastidiousness, finesse, fragility, *friandise*, kickshaw, meticulosity, nicety, overniceness, preciosity, sensitivity, squeamishness, tact, tidbit

**DELICIOUS**

**a:** ambrosiac, ambrosial, appetible, appetizing, choice, delectable, delightful, enchanting, esculent, flavorful, gustable, gustatory, luscious, nectarean, nectareous, palatable, piquant, pleasing, rich, savory, scrumptious, sweet, tempting, toothsome

**n:** ambrosia, nectar

**DELIGHT**

**a:** attractive, charming, delectable, delicious, delightful, Edenic, elysian, entrancing, felicitous, gratifying, idyllic, luscious, paradisiacal, scrumptious

**n:** charm, delectation, ecstasy, elation, exuberance, exultation, festivity, gloating, gratification, jubilation, merriment, oblectation, rapture, ravishment, Schadenfreude, transport

**v:** gloat, gratify, please

**DELIRIOUS**

**a:** agitated, crazed, excited, frantic, frenetic(al), mad, maniac(al), phrenetic(al), rabid, raging, raving

**n:** delirium, dementia, disorientation, frenzy, insanity, madness, mania, rabidity, restlessness

**DELIVERANCE**

**a:** emancipative, extricable, redemptive, redemptory, salvatory, salvific

**n:** atonement, emancipation, exoneration, extrication, liberation, manumission, reclamation, redemption, salvation, shot

**DELUDE**

**a:** beguiling, deceptive, delusional, delusive, delusory, fallacious, phantasmagoric, unrealistic

**n:** artifice, chimera, circumvention, cozenage, deception, delusion, delusions of grandeur, *folie de grandeur*, hallucination, *ignis fatuus*, illusion, mare's nest, paranoia, phantasm, phantasma, phantasmagoria, wile, will-o-the-wisp, wishful thinking

**v:** bamboozle, circumvent, cozen, deceive, delude, mislead, victimize

**DEMAGOGUE**

**a:** demagogic(al), rabblerousing

**n:** demagogery, demagogism, demagogy, ochlocrat, rabblerouser

**DEMAND**

**a:** arduous, clamorous, demanding, determined, exacting, exigent, importunate, niggling, onerous, painstaking, persistent, pressing, strident, taxing, tiring, urgent, vociferous

**n:** requisition, stickler

**v:** expostulate, hector, importune, lay down the law, necessitate, request, stipulate

**DEMOCRATIC**

**a:** egalitarian, equalitarian

**n:** democratization, egalitarianism, egalite, popularization

**DEMON**

**a:** demoniac(al), demonic(al), fiendish, frantic, frenzied, pandemoniac(al)

**n:** demoniac, devil, energumen, evil spirit, ghoul, *incubus, succubus*

**v:** conjure

   *rid:* exorcise

**DEMONSTRATE**

**a:** apodeictic, apodictic, deictic, demonstrative, effusive, epideictic, exhibitive, gushing, ostensive, overflowing, probative, showing, theatrical, unreserved, unrestrained

**n:** *apodeixis*, demonstration, effusion, effusiveness, exhibition, manifestation, picket, protest, rally

**v:** bespeak, betoken, demonstrate, evince, exhibit, indicate, manifest, promulgate, prove, reflect, signify

**DEMOTE**

**n:** demotion, denigration, pejoration, relegation

**v:** denigrate, depreciate, minify, minimize, pejorate

**DENIAL**

**a:** categorical, disclamatory, elenctic, renunciative, renunciatory

**n:** abnegation, denegration, disaffirmance, disaffirmation, disavowal, disclaimer, negation, renunciation, repudiation, traverse

**v:** abjure, abnegate, contradict, controvert, deny, disapprove, disavow, disclaim, disown, forswear, gainsay, negate, rebut, recant, refute, reject, renege, renounce, repudiate, retract

**DENOUNCE**

**a:** anathematic, comminatory, denunciative, denunciatory, fulminous, vituperative

**n:** accusation, anathema, commination, denunciation, diatribe, fulmination, invective, vituperation

**v:** abrade, censure, comminate, delate, denunciate, excoriate, fulminate, inveigh, lambaste, stigmatize

**DEPEND**

**a:** authentic, authoritative, calculable, contingent, dependable, inerrable, inerrant, inerratic, infallible, predictable, provisional, trustworthy, yeomanly

**n:** captivity, dependence, dependency, enslavement, leech, limpet, minion, relativity, reliability, reliance, succorance, symbiosis, thrall, thralldom

   *dependent:* adjectival, adjective, auxiliary, circumstantial, collateral, complementary, contingent, derivative, subsidiary, succursal, symbiotic(al)

**DEPLORABLE**

**a:** calamitous, contemptible, despicable, disreputable, execrable, grievous, lamentable, odious, shocking, unfortunate, wretched

**n:** bewailment, deploration, lamentation

**v:** bemoan, bewail, complain, cry, deplore, fret, lament, moan, protest, resent, wail

## DEPORTMENT

**n:** address, bearing, behavior, carriage, comportment, conduct, demeanor, manner, mien, posture

## DEPOSIT

**n:** alluvium, deposition, earnest, gage, sediment, silt, warp

## DEPRAVE

**a:** degenerate, depraved, dissolute, lewd

**n:** degeneracy, demoralization, depravity, iniquity, putridity, turpitude

**v:** corrupt, demoralize, depreciate, malign, pervert, pollute

## DEPRECIATE

**n:** denigration, depreciation, disparagement, pejoration

**v:** demote, denigrate, deprecate, disparage, minify, minimize, pejorate, revile, traduce, undervalue, vilify, vilipend

## DEPRESS

**a:** *a la mort,* dejected, depressed, depressing, dispirited, dispiriting, downcast, melancholic, melancholy, sad, *triste,* vaporish

**n:** boredom, dejection, depression, dispiritedness, doldrums, downswing, *ennui,* humiliation, inactivity, malaise, megrims, melancholia, melancholy, mortification, nadir, neurasthenia, slough of despond, *taedium vitae,* the vapors, *tristesse*

**v:** degrade, deject, depress, dishearten, dispirit, humble

## DEPRIVE

**a:** depriving, divestive, privative

**n:** deposition, deprivation, dispossession, divestation, divestiture

**v:** commandeer, confiscate, denude, despoil, divest, eviscerate, expropriate, strip

## DEPTH

**a:** asdic, echo, sonar

**n:** abstrusity, abyss, acumen, acuteness, deepness, depression, extent, gulf, ocean, penetration, perspective, perspicacity, profoundness, profundity, sagacity, sea

**v:** fathom, plumb, sound

*combining forms:* bath-, batho-, bathy-

## DEPUTY

**n:** agent, delegate, hatchet man, lieutenant, representative, stand-in, substitute, surrogate, vicar, vicegerent

## DERANGED

**a:** confused, crazed, demented, detraque, disordered, insane, irrational, mad, maniac, maniacal, nutty, obsessed, psychopathic, unbalanced, unsound

## DERISIVE

**a:** derisory, farcical, ironical, irrisory, mocking, sarcastic, sardonic, satiric(al), scurrilous, slurring, sneering, taunting

**n:** asteism, burlesk, burlesque, caricature, contumely, denigration, irrision, ridicule

## DERIVATIVE

**a:** derivational, epiphenomenal, etiological, secondary, supplemental

**n:** derivation, descent, epiphenomenon, etiology, etymology, genesis, lineage, pedigree, provenance, *stemma*

*combining forms:* ap-, apo-

## DESCENDANT

**a:** agnate, collateral, declinatory, declivitous, lineal, matrilineal, matrilinear, patrilineal, patrilinear, phyletic

**n:** ancestry, apparentation, declension, declination, decline, declivity, derivation, extraction, genealogy, issue, origination, pedigree, phylum, posterity, progeny, scion, *stemma*

## DESCRIPTION

**a:** delineative, descriptive, descriptory, illuminating, illuminative, picturesque

**n:** biography, delineation, depiction, hypotyposis, pen picture, portraiture, portrayal, portrayment, profile, sketch, specification

v: delineate, depict, describe, limn, portray

## DESECRATION

a: profanatory

n: corruption, debasement, defilement, profanation, violation, vitiation, vulgarization

v: debase, desecrate

## DESERT

a: deserted, desolate, uninhabited

n: abandonment, abdication, abrogation, abscondence, absentation, absquatulation, apostasy, defection, desertion, renunciation, tergiversation

v: abandon, abdicate, abscond, absquatulate, apostasize, decamp, defect, elope, forsake, renege, tergiversate

*area:* badlands, mirage, waste, wasteland

*deserter:* apostate, renegade, turncoat

*desertlike:* xeric

## DESERVED

a: appropriate, condign, merited, warranted

## DESIGN

a: conventionalized, crafty, designing, stylized, teleological

n: archetype, architectonics, arrangement, cipher, collage, decoration, delineation, device, emblem, format, intendment, monogram, montage, mosaic, motif, mural, pattern, prototype, purpose, scheme, teleology, tooling

v: inlay

## DESIGNATE

a: designated

n: assignment, circumscription, connotation, designation, name, nomination, specification, stipulation

v: circumscribe, identify, nominate, signify, specify, stigmatize, stipulate

## DESIRE

a: advantageous, advisable, appetible, appetitious, appetitive, aspirational, attractive, desiderative, desirable, epithumetic, expedient, gluttonous, insatiable, omnivorous, optative, optimal, orectic, orective, voracious

n: appetency, appetibility, appetite, appetition, aspiration, cacoethes, concupiscence, desiderata, desideration, Eros, gluttony, hankering, inclination, insatiability, insatiety, libido, *orexis*, passion, proclivity, propensity, yen

v: covet, crave, desiderate, gratify, indulge, relish, sate, satiate

*combining form:* -mania

## DESOLATE

a: abandoned, barren, dejected, desole, melancholy, ruined, run-down, stark, *triste*, used, wasted

## DESPAIR

a: appallingly, compelling, crucial, desperate, desperately, despondent, helpless, impetuously, indispensably, intensely, outrageous, overpowering

n: *accidie*, acedia, cruciality, *de profundis*, depression, desperation, doldrums, *fin-de-siecle*, futility, hopelessness, lethargy, megrims, *slough of despond*

## DESPISABLE

a: contemptible, contemptuous, contumelious, despicable, execrable, leprous

v: condemn, disdain, dislike, insult, scorn

## DESPONDENT

a: disconsolate, discouraged, disheartened, dispirited, forlorn, hypochondriacal, melancholy

n: apathetic inertia, dejection, despondency, dispiritment, doldrums, hypochondriasis, megrims, melancholia, melancholy

## DESPOT

a: absolute, absolutistic, anarchistic,

arbitrary, autarchic, authoritarian, auto-cratic, despotic, dictatorial, dogmatic, domineering, hierarchical, imperative, imperious

**n:** anarch, autarch, authoritarian, auto-crat, disciplinarian, martinet, rigorist, satrap, satrapy, totalitarian, tyrant

> *despotism:* absolutism, autocracy, totalitarianism, tyrrany

**DESTINY**

**a:** eschatological, manifest

**n:** bourn, destination, doom, eschatol-ogy, finishing point, fortune, goal, karma, moira, moirae, purpose, *terminus, termi-nus ad quem*

**v:** decree, *destine*, ordain

**DESTITUTE**

**a:** impecunious, impoverished, indigent, poor

**n:** destitution, impecuniosity, impecu-niousness, indigence, insolvency, mendi-cancy, pauperism, penury, poverty, squalor

**DESTROY**

**a:** annihilative, annihilatory, baneful, corrosive, deadly, decimated, deleterious, destroyed, destructive, devastated, dev-astating, devastative, eradicated, fordone, gratuitous, inimical, kaput, malignant, noxious, pernicious, ruinous, subversive, wanton

**n:** annihilation, cataclysm, catastrophe, corrosion, decimation, demolition, dera-cination, destruction, destructivity, dev-astation, dissolution, extinction, extirpa-tion, *Gotterdammerung*, havoc, hell, holo-caust, iconoclasm, immolation, invalida-tion, lysis, mayhem, perdition, pulveriza-tion, sabotage, subversion

**v:** abolish, annihilate, annul, corrode, decapitate, decimate, demolish, deraci-nate, devastate, dismantle, efface, eradi-cate, erode, exterminate, extinguish, extirpate, immolate, nullify, raze, scup-per, scuttle, spiflicate, vitiate, void

> *combining forms:* phag-, phago-, -phagous

*destroyer:* nemesis, predator

*mutually:* internecine

*life:* deadly, lethal, malignant, mortal, pernicious, pestiferous, pestilent

**DETACHED**

**a:** aloof, discrete, dissociated, disunited, enisled, fragmented, hermetic, insular, insulated, isolated, segregated, separate, unaffiliated, unbiased

**n:** abruption, detachment, dissociation, disunion, fragmentation, indifference, insularity, isolation, segregation, un-worldliness

**v:** detach, wean

**DETAIL**

**a:** chromatic, circumstantial, compre-hensive, definitive, explicit, finical, graphic, hairsplitting, meticulous, minu-tiose, minutious, nitpicking, overfussy, picayune, rabbinic, scrupulous

**n:** circumstance, circumstantiality, de-tails, dissection, meticulosity, *minutia*, *minutiae*, niggle, particular(s), particulari-ty, pedantry, *punctilio*, quibble, specifical-ity, specifications, specifics, specs, techni-cality, trivia, triviality

**v:** dilate, elaborate, embellish, embroi-der, enlarge, expatiate, particularize

**DETECT**

**a:** detective, discerning, revelative, reve-latory

**n:** ascertainment, detection, discern-ment, discovery, elicitation, revelation

**v:** apprehend, ascertain, descry, discern, elicit, unmask

> *person:* gumshoe, PI, private eye, shamus, sleuth

**DETERIORATION**

**a:** decadent, declensional, declinatory, degenerative, deteriorating, deteriora-tive, retrograde, retrogressive

**n:** decadence, declension, declination, degeneration, degenerescence, labefac-tion, retrocession, retrogression

## DETERMINE

**a:** decisive, definitive, determined, determining, diagnostic, dogged, dominative, foreordained, fussy, immovable, indomitable, insistent, pathognomonic(al), peremptory, predestined, resolute, resolved, stalwart, steadfast, tenacious, unalterable, unwavering

**n:** conclusion, decision, determination, impulsion, resoluteness, resolution

**v:** adjudicate, ascertain, diagnosticate, dijudicate, foreordain, regulate, resolve

## DETEST

**a:** abhorrent, abominable, anathematic, bad, contemptible, despicable, detestable, execrable, grievous, imprecatory, loathsome, odious

**n:** abhorrence, abomination, anathema, contempt, despicability, destestation, hate, loathsomeness, odium

**v:** hate, loathe

## DETRACT

**a:** denigratory, derogative, derogatory, detracting, disparaging

**n:** calumny, censure, denigration, derogation, detraction, disparagement, subtraction

**v:** calumniate, debase, defame, denigrate, derogate, disparage, minify, minimize

## DETRIMENTAL

**a:** adverse, baneful, damaging, deleterious, destructive, hurtful, inimical, injurious, malefic, malignant, nocuous, noisome, offensive, pernicious, prejudicial, toxic, unwholesome

## DEVELOP

**a:** aborning, burgeoning, culminant, developed, differentiated, exogenous, florescent, formative, matured, maturescent, morphotic, nascent, parturient, pubertal, pubescent, viable

**n:** advancement, consummation, development, differentiation, evolution, florescence, incubation, maturation, maturescence, maturity, morphosis, nutriment, ontogeny, phylogeny, puberty, pubescence, trajectory, viability

**v:** amplify, breed, burgeon, differentiate, effloresce, elaborate, enlarge, evolve, expand, expound, flourish, foment, foster, germinate, gestate, grow, incubate, maturate, mature, nurture, propagate, pullulate, reproduce

*combining forms:* -gen, -genesis, -geny, -plastic

*early:* embryonic, germinal, precocious, premature, prematurely, seminal

## DEVIATING

**a:** aberrant, aberrative, circuitous, devious, divaricative, divergent, excursional, excursionary, excursive, heteroclite, obliquitous, parenthetical, serpentine, straying, tangent, tangential, tortuous

**n:** aberrance, aberration, circuity, detour, deviate, deviation, divergence, divigation, eccentricity, heteroclite, intransigence, sinuosity, tangency, tortuosity

**v:** change, deviate, differ, divagate, divaricate, stray, turn, wander, yaw

## DEVICE

**n:** accouterment, artifice, contrivance, creation, expedient, *insigne*, insignia, invention, machination, machine, stratagem

## DEVIL

**a:** demoniac(al), demonic, devilish, diabolic, diabolical, diabolonian, fiendish, ghoulish, hellish, infernal, Luciferian, malicious, Mephistophelian, Satanic, Satanical, saturnine

**n:** demon, Satan

*study:* demonology, devilry, deviltry, *diablerie*, diabolism, diabology

*worshipper:* diabolist, diabolonian

## DEVIOUS

**a:** ambagious, anfractuous, circuitous, labyrinthian, labyrinthine, *louche*, oblique, perverse, roundabout, serpentine, sinister, sinuate, sinuous, tortuous, unscrupulous

**n:** anfractuosity, circuity, *circumbendibus*, deviation, deviousness, indirection, sinuosity, tortuosity

## DEVISE
**n:** machination

**v:** bequeath, contrive, create, fabricate, improvise, machinate, premeditate

## DEVITALIZE
**n:** devitalization, weakness

**v:** debilitate, desiccate, disembowel, emasculate, enervate, eviscerate, exenterate

## DEVOTION
**a:** devout, fetishistic, religiose, uxorious, zealous

**n:** allegiance, enthusiasm, fanaticism, fealty, fetishism, fidelity, hero worship, idolatry, loyalty, piety, religiosity, reverence, veneration, worship, zealotry

**v:** consecrate, dedicate, devote

*devotee:* adherent, *aficionado*, amateur, apostle, *energumen*, enthusiast, fanatic, follower, *liege man*, mercenary, minion, votary, zealot

## DEVOURING
**a:** annihilatory, consuming, corrosive, edacious, gluttonous, voracious

**v:** consume, cram, destroy, devour, down, eat, feast, glut, gorge, wolf

## DEVOUT
**a:** devoted, devotional, dutiful, pietistic(al), pious, *religiose*, sacrosanct, sanctimonious, uxorious

**n:** piosity, religiosity

## DEW
**a:** roric, roriferous

## DIAGNOSE
**a:** diagnostic, distinctive, pathognomonic, prodromal, symptomatic

**n:** diagnosis, stigma

**v:** diagnosticate, identify, trace

## DIAGRAM
**a:** diagrammatic(al), schematic

**n:** block diagram, blueprint, chart, cutaway, draft, exploded view, flow chart, graph, illustration, map, model, pie chart, plan, plot, *schema*, *schemata*

**v:** chart, design, draft, draw, graph, map, plan, plot, sketch, trace

## DIALECT
**a:** dialectal, dialectological

**n:** cant, colloquialism, dialoctology, jargon, *patois*, vernacular, vernacularity

## DIAMETRICALLY
**a:** antipodal, antipodic, antithetic(al), opposite

**n:** antipode, antithesis

## DIAMOND
**a:** adamantine, diamante, diamantine, diamondiferous

**n:** allotrope, bort, gemstone, lozenge, paragon, rhinestone, rhombus, solitaire, zircon

**v:** diamondize

## DICE
**n:** main, *quincunx*

**v:** main

*lowest:* ambsace, crabs

## DICTATOR
**a:** arbitrary, authoritarian, autocratic, cavalier, despotic, dictatorial, doctrinaire, dogmatic, domineering, hierarchical, imperative, imperious, magisterial, oracular, overbearing, peremptory, totalitarian

**n:** anarch, autarch, authoritarian, autocrat, benevolent despot, bully, *caudillo*, commissar, despot, duce, *fuhrer*, *junta*, martinet, oligarch, ruler, satrap, tyrant

*dictatorship:* absolutism, autocracy, Caesarism, monopolization, totalitarianism

**DICTION**

**n:** enunciation, expression, language, phraseology, speech, verbiage, vocabulary, wording, words

**DICTIONARY**

**a:** lexicographic(al), Websterian

**n:** *definiendum, definiens,* gazetteer, glossary, lexicography, lexicon, nomenclature, onomasticon, thesaurus, vocabulary

**v:** compile

　　*person:* lexicographer, lexicologist

**DIFFERENCE**

**a:** allogeneous, antagonistic, antipodal, antithetic(al), different, differential, differing, discordant, discrepant, disparate, dissenting, dissimilar, dissonant, divergent, diverse, heterogeneous, heterologous, heteromorphic, heteropathic, incongruent, incongruous, inharmonious, manifold, miscellaneous, motley, pied, sundry, unharmonious, variant, variegated

**n:** allogeneity, cleavage, controversy, *differentia,* differentiation, discrepancy, discrimination, disparity, dissention, dissimilarity, dissimilitude, dissonance, distinction, divergence, diversity, heterogeneity, heterology, heteromorphism, heteromorphosis, incongruity, inequality, mutation, *mutatis mutandis,* nuance, sport

**v:** differ

　　*combining forms:* all-, aniso-, dia-, heter-, hetero-, vari-, vario-, xeno-

**DIFFICULT**

**a:** abstruse, arcane, arduous, Byzantine, convoluted, delphic, devastating, elusive, esoteric, exacting, exigent, formidable, frenetic, hard, hectic, Herculean, impalpable, incorrigible, intractable, intricate, involved, laborious, labyrinthine, murderous, occult, onerous, opaque, operose, oracular, overwhelming, perplexing, perverse, recondite, scabrous, strenuous, toilsome, tortuous, unaccommodating, unintelligible, unmanageable, unyielding, vicissitudinous

**n:** difficulty, dilemma, embarrassment, embroilment, entanglement, Gordian knot, imbroglion, impediment, maelstrom, obstacle, ordeal, plight, predicament, problem, quagmire, quandary, riptide, snag, straights, strenuosity, tribulation, vicissitude, vortex

**v:** compound

　　*combining form:* dys-

**DIFFUSE**

**a:** osmotic, prolix, verbose, wordy

**n:** diffusion, dispersion, dissemination, osmosis, prolixity, promulgation

**DIG**

**n:** exhumation

**v:** disentomb, disinter, excavate, exhume, remove

**DIGESTION**

**a:** alimentary, eupeptic, peptic

**n:** assimilation, metabolism

**v:** assimilate, codify, comprehend, metabolize

**DIGNITY**

**a:** august, dignified, distingue, eminent, grandiose, hoity-toity, imperial, magisterial, noble, stately, statuesque, togated

**n:** courtliness, decorum, eminence, ennoblement, gentility, *grand seigneur,* grandeur, imperialism, lordliness, magistrality, majesty, nobility, pomposity, pompousness, pontification, solemnity, stateliness, sublimity

**v:** aggrandize, dignify, ennoble, exalt, nobilitate, pedestal

　　*below:* infra dig, *infra dignitatem*

**DIGRESS**

**a:** aberrant, apostrophic, changing, circuitous, devious, digressive, discursive, divaricative, divergent, excursional, excursive, parenthetical, sinuous, tangential, tortuous, vagrant

**n:** aberration, apostrophe, detour, digression, discursion, divagation, divarication, ecbole, excursion, excursus, irrelevancy, parenthesis, tangency, tangent

**v:** detour, deviate, divagate, divaricate, diverge, meander, parenthesize

## DILAPIDATED

**a:** beggarly, disreputable, retrogressive, tatterdemalian

**n:** decay, dilapidation

## DILEMMA

**a:** dilemmatic, nonplussed

**n:** crisis, difficulty, double bind, fix, jam, knot, nonplus, pickle, predicament, problem, puzzle, quagmire, quandary, scrape, trouble

## DILIGENT

**a:** assiduous, indefatigable, industrious, operose, painstaking, persevering, sedulous, solicitous, steadfast

**n:** assiduity, attention, business, consideration, diligence, operosity, perseverance, sedulity, steadfastness, zealotry

## DILUTED

**a:** adulterated, attenuated, homeopathic

## DIM

**a:** caliginous, crepuscular, faint, fuliginous, lackluster, opaque, wan, weak

**n:** crepuscle, dimness, fuliginosity, nebulosity, obscuration

**v:** becloud, befog, eclipse, efface, obfuscate, obnubilate, obscure, obscurify

## DIMINISHMENT

**a:** ablatitious, *decrescendo*, diminishing, *diminuendo*, extenuatory, regressive

**n:** attenuation, declination, depreciation, *diminuendo*, diminution, extenuation, regression, retrenchment

**v:** abate, attenuate, depreciate, diminish, dwindle, extenuate, lessen, palliate, recede, regress, retrench

## DINING HALL

**n:** cafeteria, frater, refectory

## DINNER

**a:** prandial

*after:* postcibal, postprandial

*before:* precibal, preprandial

## DIRE

**a:** awesome, bad, calamitous, catastrophic(al), cheerless, deadly, deplorable, desolate, desperate, disastrous, dispiriting, exigent, extreme, grievous, harrowing, horrendous, horrific, implacable, mortal, overpowering, woeful

## DIRECT

**a:** absolute, categorical, explicit, immediate, pertinent, positive, unconditional, undeviating, unequivocal

**n:** *aegis*, auspices, bearing, command, control, direction, directionality, directness, immediacy, inclination, mainstream, objective, orientation, presidence, superintendence, superscription, supervision, tenor, tropism, vector

**v:** administer, converge, focus, orientate, superintend, superscribe, supervise

*combining forms:* trop-, -tropic, tropo-, -ward, -wise

*director:* administrant, comptroller, conductor, curator, impresario, *regisseur*, superintendent

*opposite:* antipodal, diametrical, divergent

*reversal:* commutation

## DIRTY

**a:** bedaubed, bedraggled, befouled, despicable, dishonorable, disreputable, excrementitious, feculent, filthy, insanitary, ordurous, putrid, saprogenic, sleazy, sordid, squalid, stercoraceous, unsportsmanlike

**n:** Augean stable, cesspool, dirtiness, filthiness, hovel, immundity, putridity, sordidness, squalidity, squalor

**v:** adulterate, contaminate, defile, pollute, soil, spoil, sully, taint, tarnish

## DISABLE

**a:** disabled, incapacitated, kaput

**n:** disability, disadvantage, handicap, incapacitation, incapacity, invalidity

**v:** cripple, disqualify, founder, handicap, hobble, incapacitate, maim, weaken

**DISAGREE**

**a:** antagonistic, disagreeable, disagreeing, discordant, disputatious, dissentient, dissenting, dissentious, dissident, dissonant, incompatible, inconsistent, unharmonious, unpalatable

**n:** breach, contravention, disagreement, disharmony, disparity, disputation, dispute, dissent, dissentience, dissidence, dissonance, embroilment, entanglement, imbroglio, incompatibility, incongruity, inconsistency, inconsonance, irreconcilability, variance

**v:** contradict, contravene, dispute

**DISCERNMENT**

**a:** analytical, astucious, astute, clairvoyant, discerning, discriminating, discriminatory, judicious, knowledgeable, penetrating, penetrative, perspicacious, sagacious, trenchant

**n:** acumen, astucity, clairvoyance, clearsightedness, detection, discrimination, judgment, penetration, perception, perspicacity, profundity, sagacity, sapiency, telegnosis

　　*impaired:* astigmatic, astigmatical, myopic

**DISCHARGE**

**n:** acquittance, dismissal, elimination, flux, profluvium, quietus

　　*combining forms:* -rrhagia, -rrhea

**DISCIPLE**

**a:** apostolic, discipular

**n:** adherent, apostle, apprentice, chela, *epigone*, follower, learner, proselyte, satellite, sectary, sector, votary

**DISCIPLINE**

**a:** *aguerri*, ascetic, austere, castigatory, disciplinary, disciplinatory, penitentiary, punitive, Spartan

**n:** approach, ascesis, asceticism, castigation, chastenment, chastisement, method, punishment, self-mortification, self-restraint

**v:** castigate, chasten, chastise, hierarchize, mortify, regiment

　　*disciplinarian:* martinet, precisian, rigorist, sabbatarian, tyrant

**DISCLOSURE**

**a:** apocalyptic, apostolic, disclosing, expository, revelative, revelatory

**n:** apocalypse, divulgation, divulgence, exposition, exposure, manifestation, publication, revelation

**v:** demonstrate, disclose, unbosom

**DISCOLORATION**

**a:** black, discolored, ecchymotic, petechial, stained, tinged, ustulate

**n:** ecchymosis, *macula*, *petechia*, stain, tinge

**DISCOMFORT**

**n:** annoyance, chagrin, discomfiture, discomposure, disquietude, dysphoria, embarrassment, inquietude, malaise, unease

**DISCONNECTED**

**a:** abrupt, desultory, discrete, disjointed, disordered, dissociated, disunited, fractional, incoherent, jerky, rambling, staccato

**n:** disconnection, separation

**DISCONTENT**

**a:** alienated, disaffected, disappointed, discontented, disenchanted, disillusioned, dissatisfied, insubordinate, malcontent, rebellious, seditious, turbulent, unsatisfied

**n:** discomfiture, discontentment, dissatisfaction, dysphoria, frustration, insubordination, malaise, malcontent, sedition

**DISCONTINUE**

**a:** archaic, discontinuous, intermittent, irregular, obsolescent, obsolete

**n:** cessation, desistance, desuetude, discontinuance, intermission, interruption, obsolescence, prorogation, removal, *sine die*, surcease, termination

**v:** abandon, intermit, interrupt, obsolesce, pause, prorogue, sever, surcease, suspend, terminate

## DISCORD

**a:** absonant, cacophonous, contradictory, discordant, disputatious, dissociable, dissonant, gladiatorial, heterogeneous, incongruous, inconsonant, irreconcilable, quarrelsome, stubborn

**n:** anger, antagonism, *brouillerie*, cacophony, disharmony, disruption, dissension, dissonance, incongruity, inharmony, scission, variance

## DISCOURAGE

**n:** despondency, discouragement, dissuasion

**v:** daunt, demoralize, deprecate, deter, dishearten, dismay, dispirit, dissuade, intimidate, obstruct, prevent

## DISCOURSE

**n:** conversation, descant, disquisition, dissertation, expiation, lecture, narration, speech, thesis, treatise

**v:** discuss, expound, lecture, prelect, speak, talk

## DISCOURTESY

**a:** discourteous, disrespectful, fresh, ill-mannered, impolite, insolent, rude, vulgar

**n:** brusqueness, contumely, disrespect, impoliteness, incivility, insuavity, inurbanity, profanation

## DISCOVER

**a:** expiscatory, heuristic, serendipitous

**n:** ascertainment, detection, disclosure, discovery, eureka, expiscation, revelation, serendipity, *trouvaille*

**v:** ascertain, descry, detect, determine, disinter, episcate, exhume, ferret out, unearth

*discoverer:* Columbus, pathfinder, pioneer, trailblazer

## DISCRETION

**a:** cautious, choosing, circumspect, discretional, judicious, politic, prudent, reticent, silentious, Solomonic, taciturn

**n:** carefulness, circumspection, diplomacy, *finesse*, moderation, prudence, reserve, restraint, wisdom

## DISCUSSION

**a:** dialectic, dialectical, forensic, quodlibetic

**n:** argumentation, *causerie*, colloquium, colloquy, confabulation, conversation, dialectics, dialogue, disputation, disquisition, *excursus*, exposition, expostulation, forensics, forum, palaver, *pourparler*, powwow, *quodlibet*, seminar, symposium, *tete-a-tete*

**v:** broach, canvass, confabulate, confer, deliberate, descant, discourse, discuss, exchange, expostulate, moot, negotiate, parley

*avoid:* equivocate, evade, fence, prevaricate, temporize

*person:* collocuter, interlocutor

## DISEASE

**a:** contaminated, diagnostic, diseased, leprous, malignant, malingering, morbid, morbific, morbose, pathogenetic, pathogenic, pathognomonic, pathological, peccant, pestiferous, pestilent(ial), semeiotic, symptomatic, syndromic, unwholesome

**n:** affliction, ailment, distemper, indisposition, infirmity, malady, malignancy, morbus, pathogenicity, pathology, pathosis, syndrome, visitation

*classification:* diagnostics, nosography, nosology, pathogenesis, pathogeny, pathology

*combining forms:* dys-, nos-, noso-, -osis, -otic, -path, path-, patho-, -pathy

*contagious:* infectious, zymogenic, zymogenous, zymotic

*not causing:* apathogenic, nonpathogenic, physiological, sterile *origin:* nidus, situs

*shifting:* metastasis

*symptoms:* stigma, symptomatology, syndrome

## DISFAVOR

**a:** detrimental, disadvantageous, disreputable, odious

**n:** detriment, disadvantage, disesteem, disrepute, odium

## DISFIGURE

**n:** defacement, disfiguration, disfigurement, mayhem, scarification, uglification

**v:** maim, mutilate, scarify, uglify

## DISGRACE

**a:** criminal, disgraceful, dishonorable, disreputable, ignominious, *indign*, infamous, inglorious, notorious, obloquious, opprobrious, shameful, stigmatical, unbecoming

**n:** contempt, degradation, dishonor, disrepute, ignominy, infamy, obloquy, odium, opprobrium, stigma, turpitude

**v:** discredit, dishonor, ostracize, stigmatize

## DISGUISE

**a:** clandestine, covert, disguised, *incognito*, obscure, surreptitious

**v:** camouflage, counterfeit, dissemble, dissimulate, hide, impersonate, masquerade

## DISGUST

**a:** abhorrent, abominable, *ad nauseum*, disgusting, distasteful, foul, fulsome, loathsome, nauseating, noisome, odious, offensive, rebarbative, repugnant, repulsive, revolting, scrofulous, scurvy, sickening, unpalatable

**n:** abhorrence, abomination, antipathy, aversion, cesspool, nausea, *odium*, repugnance, revulsion

**v:** abominate, blench, make someone's stomach turn, nauseate, recoil

## DISH

**n:** cooking, *entree, entremets, piece de resistance, plat du jour*

## DISHARMONIOUS

**a:** allometric, cacophonic, cacophonous, discordant, disharmonic, disputatious, dissident, dissociable, dissonant, divisive, incongruous

**n:** antagonism, cacophony, disagreement, discord, discordance, disharmony, disonance, dissention, dissidence, incongruity, variance

## DISHONEST

**a:** deceitful, dishonorable, disingenuous, duplicitous, false, fraudulent, ignominious, knavish, lying, Machiavellian, mendacious, perfidious, roguish, sinister, sinuate, sinuous, surreptitious, treacherous, tricky, unscrupulous

**n:** dishonesty, dishonor, disingenuity, duplicity, improbity, indirection, indirectness, infamy, knavishness, perfidy, roguery, roguishness, sinuosity, unscrupulosity, villany

**v:** equivocate, prevaricate

## DISHONOR

**a:** base, despicable, disesteemed, disgraceful, dishonest, dishonorable, disreputable, ignoble, ignominious, infamous, inglorious, obloquious

**n:** cashiering, discharge, disrepute, ignominy, improbity, infamy, obloquy, opprobrium, stigma

## DISINTEGRATION

**a:** disintegrable, disintegrative, putrefactive

**n:** decentralization, decomposition, demoralization, dissolution, fragmentation, putrefaction

**v:** macerate, separate

## DISINTERESTED

**a:** candid, cool, disinclined, halfhearted, impassionate, impersonal, inertial, lazy, passive, reluctant n: disinterestedness, inertia, objectivity, passivity

**DISJOINT**

a: disconnected, disjointed, disordered, dissociated, inarticulate, incoherent

n: disarticulation, discerption, disjointing, disjointure, disjunction, dissociation, parting, separation, sundering

v: disarrange, disarticulate, discerp, dismember, luxate

**DISLIKE**

a: abhorrent, antipathetical, averse, dislikable, inimical, invidious, odious, repugnant

n: abhorrence, alienation, animosity, animus, antipathy, aversion, *bete noire*, detestation, disaffection, disapprobation, disfavor, disinclination, displeasure, distaste, estrangement, hate, hatred, hostility, *odium*, repugnance, revulsion

v: abominate, execrate

**DISLOCATION**

a: displaced

n: disarticulation, displacement, disruption, luxation

v: disarrange, disconnect, displace, misalign, part, remove, segregate, separate, uncouple, unjoin

**DISLOYAL**

a: disaffected, disobedient, faithless, mutinous, perfidious, recreant, renegade, seditious, traitorous, treacherous, unfaithful

n: anarchy, disloyalty, faithlessness, incivilism, infidelity, perfidy, recreancy, sedition, traitorousness, traitorship, treachery, villainy

*person:* apostate, conspirator, recreant, renegade, traitor, villain

**DISMAL**

a: calamitous, dispirited, dispiriting, funebrous, funerary, funereal, gloomy, lachrymose, lugubrious, melancholic, melancholy

n: dismality, lugubrosity, melancholia

**DISMAY**

n: amazement, consternation, disenchantment, disillusionment, fear, perturbation

**DISMISSAL**

n: cashiering, conge, deprivation, divestation, divestiture, heave-ho, manumission, *nunc dimittis*

**DISOBEDIENCE**

a: contrary, contumacious, defiant, disloyal, disobedient, dissenting, factious, froward, insubmissive, insubordinate, intractable, intransigent, mutinous, perverse, recalcitrant, recusant, refractory, restive, turbulent, unruly, wayward

n: insubjection, insubordination, intractableness, mutiny, perfidy, recusance, recusancy, refractoriness, treachery, unruliness

v: break law, confront, contravene, defy, disobey, flout, infringe, outface, transgress, violate

**DISORDER**

a: *a l'abandon*, chaotic, dishevelled, disordered, disorderly, disorganized, farraginous, immethodical, inchoate, inchoative, incoherent, inordinate, maniacal, pandemoniac, pandemoniacal, riotous, turbulent, unhinged

n: alarums and excursions, anarchism, anarchy, Babelism, Bedlam, *bouleversement*, brouhaha, chaos, confusion, disarrangement, discomposure, dishevelment, disorganization, distemper, embroilment, irregularity, mania, pandemonium, turbulence, turmoil

**DISORGANIZED**

a: confused, deranged, disarranged, disordered, fragmental, fragmentary, indecisive, inveterate, unhinged

n: disorder, disorganization

**DISOWN**

v: abjure, cast off, disclaim, repudiate

**DISPARAGING**

**a:** denigrating, depreciatory, derogative, epithetical, minimizing, pejorative, unfavorable

**n:** denigration, deprecation, disgrace, disparagement, epithet, indignity, meiosis, minimization, pejoration

**v:** belittle, disparage

**DISPARATE**

**a:** different, dissimilar, distinct, heterogeneous, separate, unequal

**n:** disparity, dissimilarity

**DISPLACED**

**a:** deranged, disturbed, ectopic, luxated, ousted, removed, uprooted

**n:** dislocation, displacement, luxation

**v:** dislocate

**DISPLAY**

**a:** showy, theatrical

**n:** blazon, blazonry, exhibition, fanfare, flourish, manifestation, ostentation, pageant, panoply, pomp, spectacle

**v:** brandish, disclose, manifest, ostentate

**DISPLEASURE**

**a:** annoying, displeasing, exasperated, frustrated, offended, unsatisfied

**n:** annoyance, disapproval, discomposure, indignation, *pique*, umbrage

**v:** bother, disgust, frustrate, irritate, madden, provoke, roil, trouble, vex

**DISPOSE**

**a:** disposable, expendable, inessential, unnecessary

**n:** liquidation

**v:** liquidate, obviate

**DISPOSITION**

**a:** amenable, congenial, disposed, favorable, inclinable, inclinatory, suasive, tractable

**n:** adminstration, arrangement, character, diathesis, idiosyncrasy, inclination, liquidation, management, mood, predisposition, proclivity, propensity

**DISPOSSESS**

**a:** displaced, dispossessed, lumpen, uprooted

**n:** abstraction, deprivation, dispossession, divestiture, divestment, expropriation, ouster, sequestration, usurpation

**v:** commandeer, confiscate, expropriate, oust, sequester, usurp

**DISPROOF**

**a:** disproved, disproving, incontrovertible, irrecusable, irrefutable, refutative, refutatory

**n:** confutation, refutation

**v:** confute, controvert, deny, disprove, invalidate, rebut, refute, reject, repudiate

**DISPUTE**

**a:** argumentative, contentious, controversial, controvertible, debatable, dialectic(al), disputatious, divisive, embroiled, polemic(al)

**n:** altercation, argument, argumentation, contravention, contretemps, controversy, debate, dialectics, disputation, dissension, internecine, invective, polemic, polemics, ruction, skirmish, variance, velitation

**v:** call into question, contend, contest, contradict, contravene, contravert, deny, gainsay, oppugn, polemize, repudiate

> *go-between:* arbitrator, honest broker, intermediary, mediator, moderator
>
> *person:* controversalist, disputant, polemic
>
> *settle:* arbitrate, compose, conciliate, determine, mediate, reconcile

**DISQUIETUDE**

**a:** annoying

**n:** agitation, anxiety, chemistry, disquiet, dyspathy, dysphoria, excitement, ferment, restlessness, uneasiness, unrest

## DISREPUTABLE

**a:** despicable, disgraceful, ignoble, ignominious, infamous, inglorious, *louche*, notorious, opprobrious, seedy, shifty, sleazy, sordid, squalid, unrespectable, unsavory

## DISRESPECTFUL

**a:** contemptuous, contumelious, derisive, despicable, discourteous, impertinent, impolite, infamous, opprobrious, profanatory, profane, sacrilegious, scurrilous, uncivil

**n:** contumely, discourtesy, disrespect, incivility, misesteem, profanation

**v:** trifle with

## DISRUPTION

**a:** cataclasmic, disruptive

**n:** bombshell, cataclasm, cataclysm, debacle, destruction, intrigue, rupture, stampede

## DISSATISFACTION

**a:** alienated, disaffected, disappointed, discontented, disenchanted, disgruntled, disillusioned, dissatisfied, dissentious, factious, mutinous, peeved

**n:** disapprobation, discontent, displeasure, dissidence

## DISSENT

**a:** dissentient, dissenting, dissentious, dissident, factious, heretical, nonconforming

**n:** cleavage, disagreement, dissension, dissidence, nonconcurrence, recusance, recusancy

**v:** disagree

*dissenter:* dissentient, dissident, recusant

## DISSIMILAR

**a:** anomalistic, anomalous, disparate, heterogeneous, incongruous

**n:** anomalism, anomaly, dissimilarity, divergence, divergency, heterogeneity, unlikeness

## DISSOLVE

**a:** deliquescent, dissolving, liquefactive, saturated, soluble

**n:** deliquescence, disintegration, liquefaction, solute, solvent

**v:** abrogate, decompose, deliquesce, disintegrate, leach, liquefy

*combining forms:* lys-, -lysis, lyso-

## DISTANCE

**a:** distant, forane, haughty, outlying, remote, shy, stiff, *tramontane*, *ultramontane*

**n:** fastness, *ultima*

*place:* backblocks, boondocks, bundu, bush, hinterland, outback, sticks

## DISTASTE

**a:** augean, disagreeable, distasteful, fastuous, fulsome, impalatable, insufferable, loathsome, nauseating, nauseous, noisome, obnoxious, offensive, repellant, repugnant, repulsive, revulsive, unpalatable

**n:** abhorrence, abomination, antipathy, disinclination, disrelish, *fastidium*, repugnance, revulsion

## DISTENDED

**a:** dilatative, dilated, gravid, inflated, patulous, swollen, tumescent, tumid, tympanic

**n:** dilatation, distention, tumescence, tumidity, turgescence, tympanites, tympany

## DISTINCT

**a:** articulate, characteristic, cogent, definitive, determinate, diacritic, diagnostic, discernible, discrete, discriminating, distingue, diverse, hairsplitting, illustrious, manifest, palpable, patent, peculiar, quodlibetic, separate, signal, transcendent

**n:** bouquet, cachet, *cordon blue*, differentiation, discrimination, disparity, dissimilarity, distinction, eminence, flamboyance, laureate, lineament, nicety, nuance, paladin, quiddity, savour, subtlety, tenuosity, timbre

**v:** differentiate

**DISTINGUISH**

**a:** celebrated, conspicuous, definitive, diacritical, diagnostic, differential, distingue, distinguished, distinguishing, eminent, honorific, illustrious, majestic, prominent, signal, transcendent

**n:** *cordon blue, differentia,* differentiation, laureate, paladin, stigma

**v:** differentiate, discriminate, distinguish, perceive, signalize, typify

**DISTORT**

**a:** circuitous, distorted, tortuous

**n:** caricature, distortion, tortuosity, tortuousness

**DISTRACTED**

**a:** absentminded, aloof, bemused, detached, disconcerted, distraught, perplexed, preoccupied

**n:** confusion, distraction, perplexity, perturbation

**DISTRESS**

**a:** affecting, agonizing, atrocious, calamitous, deplorable, distressed, distressing, flagrant, grievous, harrowed, harrowing, heinous, hurtful, lacerated, macabre, necessitous, poignant, tortured, vexatious

**n:** dysphoria, mayday, psychalgia

**DISTRUST**

**n:** apprehension, misdoubt, misgiving, suspicion

**v:** misdoubt

**DISTURB**

**a:** agitated, distressing, disturbed, disturbing, turbulent, vexatious

**n:** commotion, confusion, discomposure, disorder, disturbance, interruption, perturbation, rabblement, tumult, upheaval

**v:** agitate, annoy, boil, confuse, discomfit, discommode, discompose, disconcert, disquiet, embarrass, perturb, raise Cain

**DISUNITE**

**n:** alienation, dissension, dissociation, disunity, separation

**v:** alienate, disjoint, dissociate

**DISUSE**

**n:** *desuetude,* obsolescence

**DIVERGE**

**a:** deviant, deviating, digressive, divergent, parenthetical, tangential

**n:** bifurcation, detour, deviation, digression, dissimilarity, divagation, divarication, divergence, obliquity, parenthesis, tangency

**v:** bifurcate, detour, digress, divagate, divaricate, parenthesize

**DIVERSE**

**a:** distinct, heterogeneous, manifold, motley, multifarious, multiform, multiplex, multiplicious, multivarious, protean, variegated

**n:** diversification, diversity, heterogeneity, rotation, variegation, variety

**v:** diversify, intersperse, rotate, variegate

**DIVIDE**

**a:** *aliquot,* asunder, *bisulcate,* centrifugal, cleft, cloven, discerptible, discrete, disjunctive, dissociative, disunited, divaricate, divergent, divided, dividing, divisible, divisional, factional, fissiparous, multipartite, partite, phyletic, polychotomous, polytomous, schismatic, schizoid, sectile, segregated, separatist, stratified

**n:** alienation, *aliquot,* allocation, apportionment, boundary, category, classification, cleavage, compartmentalization, departmentalization, detachment, dichotomy, disjunction, dissolution, disunity, divarication, division, faction, fission, fissiparousness, meiosis, membrane, mitosis, partition, polarization, quotient, rupture, schism, scission, sectility, separation, septum, sundering

**v:** alienate, balkanize, bifurcate, compartmentalize, cut, departmentalize, disassociate, disjoint, dismember, disassoc ciate, disunite, divaricate, diverge, fractionalize, fractionate, fragment, graduate, partition, pigeonhole, polarize, segment, separate

*combining forms:* -kinesis, schiz-, schizo-, -sect, sect-

*three:* trichotomous, trichotomy, tripartite, tripartition, trisect

*two:* bifurcate, bifurcation, bipartient, bipartite, bisect, bisected, dichotomize, dichotomous, dichotomy, halve

## DIVINATION

**n:** astragalomancy, astromancy, catoptromancy, cleromancy, fortunetelling, haruspication, metagnomy, numerology, omoplastoscopy, oneiromancy, ornithomancy, rhabdomancy, scapulimancy, sortilege

*combining form:* -mancy

## DIVINE

**a:** ambrosiac, ambrosial, celestial, charismatic, deific, numinous, Olympian, sacred, Sophian, superhuman, supernal, theandric, theanthrophic, theopneustic

**n:** afflation, *afflatus, agathodaemon,* apotheosis, deification, divinity, epiphany, mysticism, Providence, Sophia, spiritualization, theanthrophy, theanthropism, *theologoumenon,* theophany, *theopneusty*

## DIZZY

**a:** confused, dazed, groggy, vertiginous, woozy

**n:** dizziness, giddiness, vertigo

## DOCTOR

**a:** Aesculapian, iatric(al)

**n:** attending physician, cardiologist, clinician, diplomate, general practitioner, gynecologist, intern, *locum, locum tenens,* pediatrician, physician, practitioner, psychiatrist, psychologist, resident

*causing disease:* iatrogenic, medicamentous

*related words: armamentarium,* beeper, caduceus, Hippocratic oath, malpractice, stethoscope

## DOCTRINE

**a:** cabalistic, doctrinaire, dogmatic(al)

**n:** cabala, cabalism, *credenda,* creed, dogma, occultism, organon, philosophy, precept, principle, tenet, theory

## DOER

**n:** executant, facient

*combining forms:* -tor, -tress, -trix

## DOG

**a:** canine, cynoid

**n:** caninity, *canis,* cur, cynology, dogginess, kennel, pack

*fear:* cynophobia

*love:* canophile, canophilist, cynolatrist, cynolatry

## DOGMATIC

**a:** arrogant, authoritative, dictatorial, doctrinaire, doctrinal, fussy, imperious, magisterial, opinionated, overbearing, pedantic, peremptory, precise, pronunciative, scholastic, self-assured, sophomoric, subtle

**n:** assertion, creed, *dicta, dictum, dixit,* doctrine, dogma, dogmatism, *ipse dixit, ipsedixitism*

**v:** dogmatize, pontificate

## DOMAIN

**n:** *arrondissment, demesne,* dominance, domination, dominion, estate, jurisdiction, power, principality, *seigniority,* sovereignty, supremacy, suzerainty, transcendency

## DOMESTIC

**a:** domesticated, enchorial, indigenous, internal, menial, tame, unskilled

**n:** domesticality, domesticity

## DOMINANT

**a:** autocratic, commanding, dominating, dominative, domineering, eminent, hegemonic, imperious, magisterial, overweening, powerful, preeminent, prepotent, prevalent, transcendent

**n:** ascendency, authority, bully, dictator, dominance, domination, hegemony, pre-eminence, sovereignty, superordination, supremacy, transcendency

**v:** bully, dominate, force, intimidate

**DONE**

**a:** consummate, consummated, unalterable, unchangeable

**n:** consummation, *fait accompli,* kaput

**DOOM**

**a:** apocalyptic(al), Damoclean, destined, doomed, fey

**n:** Cassandra, fate, handwriting on the wall, Jeremiah, sword of Damocles

**DOOR**

**n:** entrance, French door, gate, gateway, *louver,* portal, postern, threshold, *tympanum,* wicket

    *keeper:* caretaker, *concierge,* janitor, ostiary, porter, super, superintendent, tiler, tyler, usher

**DORMANT**

**a:** abeyant, comatose, cryptic, hibernant, inactive, latent, lethargic, potential, quiescent, quiet, sleepy, stationary, torpid

**n:** dormancy, hibernation, latency, latescence, quiescence

**DOT**

**a:** brindled, dotted, flecked, motley, piebald, pockmarked, punctate, punctated, punctiform, spotted, stippled, variegated

**n:** dieresis, ellipsis, polka dots, punctation, *punctum,* umlaut

**DOUBLE**

**a:** ambidextrous, bigeminal, binary, diploid, diplopic, dual, dualistic, duplex, duplicitous, equivocal, geminate, Janus-like, Machiavellian, twofold

**n:** alter ego, ambidexterity, counterpart, dichotomy, diphthong, diplopia, doppelganger, doubleness, duality, duplicate, duplicity, image, semblance, similitude, substitute, understudy

*combining forms:* amph-, amphi-, di-, dipl-, diplo-, zyg-, zygo-

*meaning:* ambiguity, ambiguousness, *double entendre, double entente,* equivoke, equivoque

**DOUBT**

**a:** agnostic, ambivalent, apocryphal, aporetic, doubtful, doubting, dubious, dubitable, dubitant, dubitative, equivocal, factious, improbable, incredible, incredulous, insecure, irresolute, legendary, niggling, perilous, precarious, problematic, questionable, skeptical, suspect, unlikely, vacillating, wavering

**n:** ambiguity, ambivalence, dilemma, distrust, dubiety, dubiosity, dubitation, incertitude, incredulity, indecision, miscreance, misgiving, qualification, qualm, quandary, reservation, scruples, skepsis, skepticism, suspicion, uncertainty, worry

**v:** demur, discredit

    *doubter:* aporetic, disbeliever, doubting

**DOUGH**

**a:** doughy, magmatic

**n:** leaven, *magma, torus*

**DOWN**

**a:** *a bas,* downy, floccose, flocculent, lanuginous, puberulent, pubescent, vilous, woolly

**n:** feather, *floccus, lanugo,* plumule, pubescence

**DOWNCAST**

**a:** cheerless, dejected, disheartened, dispirited, melancholic, melancholy, sad

**n:** blues, doldrums, lachrymals, megrims

**DOWNFALL**

**n:** debasement, degradation, labefaction, nemesis, retribution, ruin, undoing, Waterloo

**DOWNRIGHT**

**a:** absolute, arrant, certain, forthright, out-and-out, outright, plain, positive, unmitigated, utter

## DOWNWARD

**a:** declensional, declinatory, netherward

**n:** declension, declination, minim, slope

*combining form:* cata-

## DRAB

**a:** dark, dingy, dull, dusky, gray, grey, insipid, lifeless, monotonous, plain, sober, somber, subfusc(ous)

## DRAMA

**a:** artificial, compelling, declamatory, dramatic, dramaturgic(al), elocutionary, histrionic, operatic, showy, stagy, theatric(al), thespian

**n:** cliffhanger, ensemble, histrionics, melodrama, pyrotechnics, repertory, tetralogy

*dramatist:* dramaturge, playwright

*end:* catastrophe, climax, *denouement,* epilogue

*related words:* absurd, alienation, anagnorisis, black comedy, catharsis, corpse, curtain call, *deus ex machina,* dramatic irony, *dramatis personae,* dry, epitasis, extra, Grand Guignol, interlude, Kabuki, legitimate, masque, method, mime, *mise en scene,* monologue, morality play, *peripeteia,* prologue, protagonist, protasis, soliloquy, tableau, unities

## DRAW

**a:** ablatitious, delineative, evocative, graphic, retractile

**n:** cartoon, cross-hatching, cutaway, drawing, elevation, exploded view, graffiti, graphics, hatching, perspective, protraction

**v:** delineate, describe, limn

*away:* abduct, abstract

*back or in:* adduct, blench, cower, flinch, quail, recede, recoil, retract, retrench, shrink, wince

*combining forms:* -gram, -graph

*forth or out:* attenuate, elicit, evoke, extract, protract

## DREAD

**a:** awesome, dire, doughty, dreadful, fearful, formidable, horrendous, horrific, perilous, portentious, redoubtable, revolting

**n:** angst, anxiety, apprehension, trepidation, trepidity

## DREAM

**a:** absentminded, abstracted, chimerical, dreamy, fantasque, fantastic, impractical, langorous, languid, lost, moony, oneiric, preoccupied, surreal, utopian, veridical, visionary

**n:** chimera, cloud-cuckoo-land, daydream, fantasia, fantasy, hallucination, phantasm, phantasmagoria, REM, trance

**v:** fantasize

*combining forms:* oneir-, oneiro-

*dreamer:* fantasist, fantast, ideologist, ideologue, phantast, romancer, romanticist, utopian, visionary

## DREGS

**n:** debris, exuviate, feculence, grounds, grouts, lees, orts, residue, *residuum,* rubbish, sediment, sordor

## DRESS

**a:** accoutred, sartorial

**n:** accoutrement(s), apparel, array, attire, clothes, *couture,* drapery, haberdashery, habiliments, *haute couture,* outfit, panoply, regalia, toggery, toilette, trappings, uniform, vestments, vesture

**v:** accouter, *accoutre,* caparison, don, preen, primp, prink, tidy, titivate

*undressed or partly dressed:* deshabille, dishabille

## DRIFTER

**n:** flotsam and jetsam, *gaberlunzie,* homeless, itinerant, temporizer, vagabond, vagrant

## DRINK

**a:** bibacious, bibitory, bibulous, crapulous, drinkable, drunken, intemperate, nectarean, nectareous, potable n: alcoholism, bacchanalia, bender, beverage, bibation, carouse, chaser, compotation, drinking, imbibation, libation, nectar, potable, potation, stimulant

v: carouse, gulp, imbibe, ingurgitate, quaff, spike, swig, swill, wassail

*craving:* dipsomania, oenomania, potomania

*drinker:* alcoholic, bibber, lush, soak, sot, souse, tippler, toper

*sparing:* abstention, moderation

*vessel:* beaker, bumper, canteen, cask, costrel, cup, draft, goblet, mazer, pottle, rummer, stein, tumbler, blackjack, cannikin, glass, pot, schooner, tankard

## DRIVE

a: conational, conative, driving, dynamic

n: compulsion, conation, conatus, dynamism, impetus, incentive, momentum, propulsion, vector

v: coerce, flagellate, goad, impel, prod

*away:* aroint, banish, deport, dispel, disperse, dissipate, eject, evict, exile, exorcise, expatriate, oust, rebuff, repel, repulse, rout

*combining forms:* -fugal, -fuge

## DROLLERY

n: drolerie, foolishness, jest, raillery, whimsicality, whimsicalness, whimsy

## DROOPING

a: cernuous, enervated, flaccid, lackadaisical, languid, languorous, lethargic, nutant

n: flaccidity, lackadaisy, languour, lethargy

v: wilt

## DROP

a: guttate, stillatitious

n: driblet, droplet, globule

## DROWSY

a: comatose, hypnogenic, hypnogenous, hypnogogic, lethargic, oscitant, somnolent, torpid

n: drowsiness, latency, oscitancy, oscitation, somnolence, torpor

## DRUG

a: drugging, narcotic, pharmaceutical, pharmacological, potent, stupefacient

n: antagonist, hallucinogenic, medicine, narcotic, stimulant, synergism

*combining form:* pharmaco-

*science:* pharmaceutics, pharmacology

## DRUM

n: bongo, conga, percussion instrument, snare, tabla, tabor, tambour, timbal, tympan, vellum

*drummer:* tympanist

## DRUNK

a: alcoholic, bacchanalian, befuddled, besotted, bibacious, bibulous, buzzed, crapulent, crapulous, dipsomaniacal, drunken, heady, inebriate, inebrious, intoxicated, maudlin, mellow, pixilated, squiffy, tipsy

n: alcoholic, bacchanal, debauchee, dipsomaniac, drunkard, inebriate, libertine, oenophilist, winebibber

v: inebriate, intoxicate

*drunkenness:* alcoholism, dipsomania, inebriation, intoxication, potomania

*party:* bacchanal, bacchanalia, carousal, revel, wassail

## DRY

a: anhydrous, arenaceous, arid, brut, dehydrated, desiccated, desiccative, dull, *jejune,* monotonous, *sec, sere,* uninteresting, xeric, xerotic

n: aridity, dehydration, desiccation, dryness, xerosis

v: desiccate, parch, sear, shrivel, wither

*combining form:* xero-

## DUCT

n: channel, meatus, vas, vessel

**DUEL**

n: *affaire d'honneur,* joust, *rencontre,* rencounter, tilting match

**DULL**

a: anodyne, apathetic, arid, aseptic, banal, banausic, bland, bromidic, clinical, comatose, commonplace, conventional, faceless, hebetate, hebetudinous, humdrum, inactive, indistinct, insipid, *jejune,* lackadaisical, lackluster, languid, languorous, lethargic, lumbering, monotonous, moronic, mundane, nondescript, obtuse, opaque, oscitant, pallid, parochial, pedestrian, phlegmatic, pointless, prosaic, routine, soporific, stagnant, stereotyped, stereotypical, stolid, stylized, subfusc, tedious, unadventurous, unsensational, vacuous, vapid

n: apathy, bromide, commonplace, crassitude, drudgery, hebetude, inanity, insipidity, jejunity, lethargy, *longueurs,* monotony, obtuseness, platitude, ponderosity, prosaism, stereotypy, tepidity, *tristesse,* truism

v: hebetate, obtund, stagnate, vegetate

**DUNG**

a: coprophagous, fecal, fimicolour, merdivorous, ordurous, scatophagous, stercoraceous, stercoricolous

n: excrement, feces, guano, midden, ordure, *rejectamenta,* scats

*combining form:* copro-

**DUPLICATE**

n: copy, counterfeit, counterpart, double, facsimile, mimeograph

**DURATION**

n: endurance, infinitude, infinity, longanimity, perpetuality, perpetuity, perseverance, protension, *saeculum*

**DURESS**

n: coercion, constraint, durance, imprisonment, incarceration, restraint, stranglehold

**DUSKY**

a: cloudy, dark, dim, murky, obfusc, obfuscous, obscure, shadowy, somber

**DUST**

a: dusty, pulverous, pulverulent

n: mote

v: molder away

*fear:* amathophobia

**DUTY**

a: assiduous, conscientious, *de rigueur,* deferent, deferential, deontic, deontological, devoit, diligent, duteous, dutiful, filial, gung ho, imperative, incumbent, loyal, meticulous, obligatory, pastoral, preemptory, punctilious, sedulous

n: assignment, commitment, contract, deference, deferentiality, deontology, detail, devoir, dharma, fealty, honor, liability, *noblesse oblige,* obligation, onus, piety, promise, respect, responsibility, stint, trick, watch

v: delegate, depute, officiate

*beyond:* extracurricular, supererogatory, superogative

*failure:* delinquency, dereliction, goof off, irresponsibility, maladministration, malinger, misfeasance, misprision, negligence, shirk, skive

**DWARF**

a: diminutive, dwarfish, homuncular, lilliputian, microscopic, nanitic, nanous, sesquipedalian

n: diminutive, dwarfishness, dwarfism, gnome, homunculus, lilliputian, nanism, Pygmy, Rumpelstiltskin, sesquipedal

**DWELLING**

a: domiciliated, imminent, inherent, residentiary

n: abode, domicile, habitation, home, house, nest, quarters

**DYE**

a: substantive

n: batik, mordant, tracer, woad

**v:** imbue, tie-dye, tinge

### DYING

**a:** agonal, dead, expiring, fey, *in extremis*, moribund

**n:** moribund

*place:* hospice

### DYNAMIC

**a:** active, efficient, energetic, high-powered, kinetic, potent, powerful, strong, vigorous, virile, vital

## EAGER

**a:** agog, ardent, desirous, ecstatic, emotional, enthusiastic, expectant, fanatical, fervent, gluttonous, impetuous, importunate, insatiable, intent, obliging, obsequious, rapacious, rapturous, ravenous, servile, solicitous, voracious, zealous

**n:** ardor, captation, demonstrativeness, eagerness, *empressement*, enthusiasm, esurience, lust, solicitude, spirit, zest

**v:** salivate

## EAGLE

**a:** aquiline, eaglelike

*nest:* aerie, eyrie

## EAR

**a:** aural, auricular, auriculate, binaural, otic

**n:** auricle, tympanum

*combining forms:* -ot, ot-, oto-

*large:* macrotous

## EARLY

**a:** antecedent, anterior, archetypal, embryonic, germinal, inchoate, incipient, matinal, matutinal, nascent, preceding, precipitate, precocious, premature, premundane, previous, primal, primeval, primitive, primordial, pristine, punctual, rudimentary, seasonable, seminal, timely, ultimate, untimely

**n:** *deja vu,* flashback, *incunabulum,* infancy, precocity, *primordium*

**v:** antedate, anticipate

*combining forms:* eo-, pre-, proto-, ur-

*show:* matinee

*works: juvenilia*

## EARNEST

**a:** determined, eager, fervent, intense, intent, serious, zealous

## EARTH

**a:** cosmopolitan, earthen, earthly, factual, geocentric, global, human, mundane, planetary, realistic, sublunary, superterranean, superterraneous, telluric, temporal, terraceous, terranean, terraneous, terrene, terrestrial, terrigenous, worldly

**n:** ecumene, superterrene, *terra firma,* universe

*combining forms:* agr-, agri-, agro-, geo-

*goddess:* Ceres

*within:* chthonian, chthonic, nether, plutonic, subterranean

## EARTHQUAKE

**a:** seismic, seismical

**n:** aftershock, foreshock, seismology

*combining forms:* seism-, seismo-

*related words:* epicenter, magnitude, Richter scale, seismograph

## EARTHY

**a:** carnal, chthonian, chthonic, Falstaffian, gross, heathenish, Hogarthian, mortal, mundane, pagan, Rabelaisian, *risque,* terrestrial, visceral, vulgar, worldly

## EASE

**a:** accessible, alleviative, alleviatory, anesthetic, apathetic, cavalier, complaisant, conciliatory, consolatory, degage, docile, easy, effortless, extenuating, extenuative, facile, governable, indifferent, indulgent, jaunty, lenient, lenitive, lucid, manipulable, mitigating, nepenthean, palliative, perspicuous, placative, placatory, pliable, tractable, tranquilizing, transparent, unconcerned, unconstrained

**n:** alleviant, alleviation, assuagement, cinch, detachment, disengagement, docility, gravy train, leisure, lenitive, mitigation, naturalness, *nepenthe*, palliation, pushover, quietude, relaxation, repose, sinecure, tractability, tranquility

**v:** alleviate, assuage, compromise, extenuate, mitigate, moderate, placate, relax, tranquilize

**EAST**

**a:** gerontogeous, oriental, ortative

**n:** Levant

**v:** orientate

**EASTER**

**a:** lenten, paschal, quadragesimal

**n:** Lent, Passover

**EAT**

**a:** alimentary, carnivorous, cibarious, comestible, consuming, convivial, crapulent, devouring, eatable, edacious, edible, epicurean, esculent, gluttonous, herbivorous, ingestible, ingestive, intemperate, omnivorous, ravenous, voracious

**n:** comestible, cuisine, eating, edacity, edibility, edible, epicureanism, feeding, gastronomy, gluttony, ingestion, ingurgitation, manducation, voracity

**v:** consume, corrode, devour, gormandize, ingest, ingurgitate, manducate

> *after:* post-cibal, post-prandial
>
> *before:* ante-cibum
>
> *combining forms:* -phag, phag-, phago-, -phagous, -vorous
>
> *eater:* bon-vivant, cormorant, epicure, *gastronome*, glutton, gourmand, gourmet, sybarite, trencherman
>
> *not:* inedible, inesculent
>
> *sparing:* abstemious
>
> *together:* commensal

**ECCENTRIC**

**a:** aberrant, anomalous, atypical, bizarre, cantankerous, capricious, crotchety, fantastic, idiosyncratic, off-center, peculiar

**n:** aberrance, aberrancy, aberrant, aberration, Bohemian, deviant, eccentricity, idiosyncrasy, peculiarity, quiddity, quirk, whimsy

**ECHO**

**a:** echoic, polyphonic, polyphonous, reverborative, reverboratory

**n:** asdic, polyphony, repercussion, resonance, reverberation, sonar

**v:** reverberate

**ECONOMY**

**a:** cheeseparing, economic, economical, frugal, parsimonious, profitable, prudent, thrifty

**n:** austerity, conservation, economics, frugality, husbandry, macroeconomics, parsimony, plutology, plutonomy, prudence, retrenchment

**v:** curtail, cut back, economize, husband, retrench, retrench

> *related words:* arbitrage, blue chip, bull, collateral, common stock, conglomerate, consolidated stock, consolidation, deflation, Dow Jones Index, fiscal year, futures, gross national product, mutual fund, portfolio, preferred stock, recession, securities, stagflation, stock split, supply-side, treasury bill

**EDDY**

**a:** vortiginous

**n:** agitation, Charybdis, current, spiral, vortex, whirlpool

**EDICT**

**a:** edictal

**n:** command, decree, fiat, judgment, law, mandate, *mandatum*, manifesto, order, ordinance, proclamation, pronouncement, *pronunciamento*, rule, ukase, writ

**EDIT**

**n:** recension, redaction, *variorum*

**v:** blue-pencil, compile, correct, emend, redact, revise

*editor:* *diaskeuast,* redactor

*first:* *editio princeps, princeps*

**EDUCATION**

**a:** educated, enlightened, erudite, heuristic, learned, lettered, literate, philomathic, scholarly, tutored

**n:** background, breeding, curriculum, discipline, erudition, instruction, learning, pedagogics, pedagogy, pedaguese, pedantry, refinement, scholarship, scholasticism, Socratic method, tertiary education, tuition

**v:** educate, foster, nurture, teach, train

*educational:* academic, didactic, doctrinal, educative, instructive, pedagogic(al), propaedeutic, scholastic, tutorial

*educator:* pedagog(ue), teacher

*people:* clerisy, *cognoscenti, illuminati, intelligensia, literati, literatus, litterateur, savant*

*self:* autodidact, autodidactic

**EERIE**

**a:** bizarre, fantastic, frighful, ghostly, grotesque, haunting, mysterious, odd, phantasmal, phantasmic, spooky, uncanny, weird

**n:** *grotesquerie*

**EFFECT**

**a:** acceptable, aposterioristic, cogent, consequential, effective, effectual, efficacious, efficient, executive, incisive, penetrating, substantious, telling, trenchant, valid

**n:** *a posteriori,* appearance, augmentation, *causatum,* consequence, effectiveness, effectivity, efficacity, efficacy, encroachment, enhancement, impingement, infringement, manifestation, outcome, placebo effect, residuum, result, sequel

**v:** accomplish, augment, enhance, execute, potentiate, redound

**EFFEMINATE**

**a:** epicene, gynecoid, intersexual, muliebral, womanlike

**n:** androgyny, effeminacy, femineity, femininity, muliebrity

*person:* androgyne, androgynus, milksop

**EFFICIENT**

**a:** accomplished, adept, competent, consummate, dexterous, effective, efficacious, expeditious, ingenious, professional, proficient, virtuosic

**n:** accomplishment, competency, consummation, effectiveness, effectuality, efficacity, efficacy, efficiency, expedition, ingenuity

**v:** optimize, rationalize

**EFFIGY**

**a:** effigial

**n:** doll, dummy, effigiation, *envoutement,* facsimile, figure, image, manikin, model

**v:** effigiate

**EFFORT**

**a:** arduous, assiduous, conative, concerted, coordinated, Sisyphean, Sisyphian, strenuous

**n:** application, assiduity, assiduousness, *conatus,* diligence, endeavor, exertion, *nisus,* sedulousness, travail

*effortless:* facile, flowing, fluent, graceful

**EFFUSIVE**

**a:** demonstrative, ebullient, extravagant, exuberant, gushing, lavish, prodigal, scaturient, unreserved, unrestrained

**n:** ebullience, ebulliency, ebullition, effusiveness, exuberance, outpouring, unreserve, unrestraint

## EGG

**a:** gravid, ooid, ooidal, oologic(al), oval, ovate, ovicular, oviform, oviparous, ovoid, ovoidal, ovoviviparous

**n:** embryo, gamete, oolemma, oviparity, ovoviviparity, ovum, spawn, vitilline

**v:** brood, incubate, ovulate

*combining forms:* -oo, oo-, -ov, ov-, ovi-, ovo-

*eating:* oophagous

*making one:* uniparous

*study:* oology

*white:* albumen

*yolk:* parablast, vitellus

## EGYPT

**a:** Egyptian

*writing:* cuneiform, hieroglyphics

## EIGHT

**a:** octadic, octagonal, octennial

**n:** octad, octagon, octave, octet

*combining forms:* oct-, octo-

## EIGHTY

*to 89:* octogenarian

## EJECT

**n:** ejection, eviction

**v:** banish, chuck, disbar, dispossess, expel, oust, regurgitate, spew, throw out, toss

## ELABORATE

**a:** complex, complicated, decorated, diligent, garish, highfalutin, intricate, large, painstaking, rococo, showy, stupendous

**n:** elaboration, exegesis, expaciation, extravaganza, spectacular

**v:** decorate, develop, expaciate

## ELATED

**a:** buoyant, ecstatic, enraptured, eudamonic, euphoric, exhilarated, exultant, heady, intoxicated, rapturous

**n:** ecstasy, elation, euphoria, exultation, rapture, transport

**v:** animate, elate, enliven, exhilarate, lift, please, stir, support

## ELDER

**a:** aged, anile, antiquated, elderly, senile, venerated

**n:** anility, antiquity, doyen, doyenne, patriarch, primogeniture, senescence, senility, senior

## ELECTION

**a:** psephological

**n:** barnstorming, gerrymandering, hustings, manifesto, platform, primary, whistle-stop tour

**v:** appoint, canvass, co-opt, vote

*study:* psephology

## ELEGANCE

**a:** concinnous, elegant, elegantly, exquisite, genteel, lapidary, lavish, luxurious, mincing, modish, polished, *recherche*, refined, *soigne*, sophisticated, stately, statuesque, sumptuous, supernacular, supernal, urbane, well-groomed

**n:** comeliness, concinnity, courtliness, gentility, *luxe*, nicety, refinement, *savoir faire*, sumptuosity, urbanity

## ELEMENT

**a:** abecedary, elemental, elementary, fundamental, hypostatic, inchoate, incomplex, initiatory, integral, introductory, primitive, primordial, rudimental, rudimentary, ultimate

**n:** component, constituent, factor, ingredient, integral, integrant, trace

*study:* propaedeutics

*table:* periodic

## ELEPHANT

**n:** mastodon, pachyderm, tusker

## ELEVATE

**a:** edificatory

**n:** edification, elevation, enhancement, enlightenment, ennoblement, spiritualization, sublimation

**v:** edify, enhance, enlighten, ennoble,

escalate, exhilarate, pedestal, raise, refine, spiritualize, sublimate, transcend

## ELIMINATE

**n:** decimation, deletion, deracination, divestation, elimination, extirpation, ouster

**v:** abolish, decimate, delete, destroy, erase, exclude, expunge, exscind, extirpate, oust, resect, winnow out, wipe out

## ELITE

**a:** best, choice, cream, select, superior

**n:** aristocracy, aristocrat, aristocratism, bluestocking, *creme de la creme, magnifico, ne plus supra, ne plus ultra,* superior, *supernaculu*

## ELOPE

**n:** abscondence, absquatulation, elopement

**v:** abscond, absquatulate, depart, flee, marry

## ELOQUENT

**a:** Ciceronian, Demosthenic, facund, impassioned, oratorial, oratorical

**n:** eloquence, expressiveness, expressivity, facundity, oratory, speech

## ELUSIVE

**a:** baffling, cunning, ephemeral, equivocal, impalpable, insidious, intangible, lubricious, lubricous, saponaceous, subtle

## EMACIATED

**a:** attenuated, cadaverous, enfeebled, lean, macilent, malnourished, marasmic, narrow, skinny, tabescent, thin, wasted

**n:** atrophy, attenuation, emaciation, leanness, macies, *marasmus,* tabefaction, tabescence

## EMANATION

**n:** aura, cachet, effluence, effluvium, efflux, issue, outcome, radiation

## EMBARRASSMENT

**a:** ashamed, discountenanced, embarrassed, out of countenance

**n:** abashment, chagrin, *contretemps,* discomfiture, discomposure, disconcertion, discountenance, encumbrance, frustration, humiliation, impediment, mortification, perturbation

**v:** chagrin, daunt, deflate, demean, discomfit, discompose, disconcert, embarrass, humble, humiliate, mortify

## EMBEDDED

**a:** deep-seated, encapsulated, impacted, nested, nidulant

## EMBEZZLE

**n:** abstraction, appropriation, defalcation, embezzlement, malversation, misappropriate, peculation, substraction

**v:** appropriate, defalcate, misappropriate, misuse, peculate, purloin

*embezzler:* defalcator, peculator

## EMBITTER

**a:** embittered, rancorous

**n:** exacerbation, exacerbescence, rancor

**v:** aggravate, anger, exacerbate, ire, madden, sour

## EMBLEM

**a:** emblematic, representative, symbolic

**n:** badge, colophon, *insigne,* insignia, logo, symbol, trademark

## EMBODIMENT

**a:** embodied, incarnate

**n:** avatar, epiphany, incarnation, incorporation, personification, quintessence

**v:** personify

## EMBRACE

**a:** circumscriptive, comprehensive, embracing, encircling, enclosing, inclusive, incorporated, osculant

**n:** accolade, clinch, comprehension, embracement, incorporation

**v:** adopt, circumscribe, clinch, comprehend, comprise, embosom, encompass, enfold, incorporate, undertake

**EMERGE**

**n:** burgeoning, debouchment, debut, efflorescence, egression, emanation, emergence, evolution

**v:** burgeon, debouch, disembogue, effloresce, egress, emanate, evolve, materialize

**EMERGENCY**

**a:** critical

**n:** crisis, dilemma, exigency, flashpoint

*measure:* contingency, expedient, makeshift, stopgap

**EMIGRATION**

**n:** abandonment, departure, egression, exodus, flight, hegira

**EMINENT**

**a:** august, celebrated, conspicuous, distingue, distinguished, estimable, famous, honorific, illustrious, immortal, inimitable, leonine, magnific, magnificent, majestic, paramount, prestigious, prominent, resplendent, sovereign, superlative, transcendent

**n:** conspicuity, conspicuousness, *cordon blue,* eminence, esteem, magnificence, majesty, paramouncy, preeminence, prestige, principality, prominence, resplendency, salience, saliency, superiority, transcendence, transcendency

**EMOTION**

**a:** affective, dionysiac, dionysian, dithyrambic, dramatic, ecstatic, effusive, emotive, gushing, histrionic, hysterical, melodramatic, overwrought, passionate, poignant, rapturous, rhapsodic, theatrical, traumatic, vehement, vulnerable

**n:** affectivity, catharsis, delight, ecstasy, effusion, emotionality, emotivism, emotivity, empressement, feeling, fervor, histrionics, hysterics, melodramatics, nympholepsy, orgasm, paroxysm, rapport, rapture, rhapsody, Saturnalia, transport, vehemence

**v:** vent

*combining form:* -thymia

**EMPHASIZE**

**v:** accelerate, accent, accentuate, belabor, enhance, exacerbate, hammer home, highlight, intensify, stress, underscore

**EMPHATIC**

**a:** bold, coercive, cogent, compelling, conspicuous, dogmatic, forceful, glaring, imperative, intense, lexical, prominent, pronounced, salient, striking, vehement, vigorous

**n:** adjuration, asseveration

**v:** asseverate

**EMPTY**

**a:** barren, frivolous, fustian, inane, meaningless, pretentious, uninhabited, unoccupied, vacuous

**n:** barrenness, emptiness, inanition, inanity, nihility, nullibicity, nullibiety, senselessness, shallowness, vacuity, vacuum, void

**v:** clear out, disembogue, evacuate, remove, void

**ENABLING**

**a:** delegative, empowering, facultative, permissive, sanctioning

**ENCAMPMENT**

**n:** abode, bivouac, castramentation, etape, location, tent

**ENCHANT**

**a:** captivating, Circean, enchanting, fascinating, sirenic

**n:** bewitchment, captivation, conjuration, enchantment, ensorcelment, fascination, incantation, necromancy, sorcery, sortilege

**v:** allure, bewitch, captivate, ensorcel, enthrall, mesmerize, transport

*enchantress:* charmeuse, Circe, *femme fatale, lamia*

**ENCIRCLE**

**a:** circumambient, circumferential, coronary, encircling, encompassing, peripheral

**v:** circumnavigate, circumscribe, circumvallate, embosom, embrace, encompass, immure, impale, surround

**ENCLOSE**
**a:** enclosed

**n:** empalement, enclave, enclosure, precinct

**v:** circumscribe, embosom, encircle, environ, incarcerate, invaginate, sheathe

**ENCOMPASSING**
**a:** ambient, circumferential, encircling, enveloping, surrounding

**ENCOURAGE**
**a:** auspicious, encouraging, exhortative, exhortatory, hortative, hortatory, inspirational, inspiriting, persuasive, propitious, protreptic, psychagogic, sanctionative

**n:** approbation, championship, connivance, encouragement, excitation, exhortation, expostulation, fomentation, incentive, incitement, inducement, instigation, motivation, patronage, protreptic, sanction, sponsorship, stimulus

**v:** abet, advance, advocate, animate, buoy up, champion, connive, countenance, cultivate, embolden, endorse, exhort, expostulate, foment, foster, hearten, help, inspire, inspirit, instigate, invigorate, nurture, promote, reassure, sanction, stimulate

**ENCUMBRANCE**
**a:** impedimental

**n:** complication, debt, difficulty, embarrassment, handicap, hindrance, impediment, *incubus*, obstacle, perplexity, weight

**END**
**a:** autotelic, completed, conclusible, consummative, desinent, ended, ending, finished, moribund, telic, terminal, terminative, terminatory

**n:** abrogation, accomplishment, achievement, annihilation, *coda*, conclusion, consequence, consummation, culmination, demise, denouement, desinence, destina-

tion, dissolution, ending, epilogue, eventuality, exitus, expiration, extremity, finality, *finis*, goal, liquidation, omega, *sine die*, termination, *terminus*

**v:** abolish, abrogate, accomplish, consummate, crown, culminate, disassociate, discontinue, dissociate, expire, quash, resolve, scotch, squash, stop, terminate

*combining forms:* acro-, tel-, tele-

*endless:* ad infinitum, boundless, enduring, everlasting, illimitable, incessant, infinite, interminable, interminate, measureless, perpetual, protracted, sempiternal, unceasing

**ENDANGER**
**v:** imperil, jeopardize, put at risk

**ENDEARMENT**
**a:** endearing, hypocoristic, lovable

**n:** hypocorism

**ENDEAVOR**
**a:** conative, experimental, speculative, venturous

**n:** conatus, essay, experiment, go, *nisus*, speculation, try, undertaking, venture

**v:** essay, strive

**ENDOWMENT**
**n:** accomplishment, appanage, benefaction, benefit, capacity, gift, gratuity, *largesse*, perquisite, talent

**ENDURE**
**a:** abiding, chronic, classic, diuturnal, durable, enduring, established, immarcescible, long-suffering, monotonous, monumental, patient, perdurable, permanent, perseverant, persistent, protensive, sempiternal

**n:** continuance, continuity, diuturnity, endurance, fortitude, longanimity, longevity, marathon, momumentality, perdurability, perdurance, permanence, perseverance, perseveration, propensity, sempiternity, stamina, sufferance, tolerance, toleration

**v:** abide, brook, countenance, perdure,

survive, tolerate, undergo, weather, withstand

## ENEMY

**a:** inimical

**n:** adversary, antagonist, competitor, fifth column, opponent,

> *related words:* appeasement, beachhead, containment, decoy, diversion, fraternization, salient

## ENERGY

**a:** brisk, calorigenic, dionysiac, dionysian, dynamic, emotional, energetic, enthusiastic, forceful, hardworking, inspiring, resolute, sprightly, spry, strenuous, vibrant, vigorous, virile, vital

**n:** athleticism, *cathexis,* dynamics, dynamism, elan, energetics, fireball, firebrand, gusto, impetus, initiative, motivity, numen, potency, puissance, quantum, strenuosity, verve, vigor, vivacity, zest

**v:** harness, sublimate

## ENFORCE

**a:** coercive, compulsory, disciplinary, enforced, mandatory, obligatory, peremptory, tyrannical

**n:** coercion, compulsoriness, duress, enforcement, oppression

**v:** coerce, compel, drive, force, impose, invoke

> *enforcer:* disciplinarian, martinet, rigorist, tyrant

## ENGAGE

**a:** affianced, betrothed, engaged

**n:** assignation, betrothal, betrothment, engagement, espousal, involvement, plight, prepossession, rendezvous, tryst

**v:** betroth, participate, plight

## ENGLAND

**a:** *anglice*

> *combining form: baseadjs*
> *hate:* anglophobe, anglophobia, anglophobic
> *language:* pidgin

*love:* anglomania, anglomaniac, anglomaniacal, anglophile, anglophilia, anglophilic

*study:* anglistics

## ENJOY

**a:** apolaustic, delectable, delightful, enjoyable, entertaining, gratifying, hedonic, hedonistic, pleasing, pleasurable, satisfying, sensuous, sybaritic, voluptuous, zestful

**n:** *carpe diem,* delectation, desipience, desipiency, ecstasy, enjoyment, exultation, gusto, hilarity, *joie de vivre,* merrymaking, pleasure, vitality, zest

**v:** relish, savor

## ENLARGE

**a:** amplificatory, augmentative, augmented, enhanced, enlarged, enlarging, hypertrophic, intumescent, tumefactive, tumescent, turgescent, turgid

**n:** accession, aggrandizement, augmentation, enhancement, enlargement, expansion, expatiation, intumescence, majoration, tumefaction, tumescence, tumidity, turgescence

**v:** aggrandize, amplify, dilate, elaborate, enhance, exacerbate, expatiate, hypertrophy, increase, intumesce, magnify, omnify, protuberate, tumefy

## ENLIGHTENMENT

**a:** edificatory, enlightening, illuminant, illuminating, illuminative

**n:** edification, illumination, nirvana, revelation

**v:** edify, educate, elucidate, enlighten, illuminate, irradiate, teach

> *people: cognoscenti, illuminati, intelligensia*

## ENLIVEN

**v:** animate, exhilarate, give life, inspirit, invigorate, quicken, vivify

## ENMITY

**a:** antagonistic(al), antipathetic, malevolent, provocative, rancorous

**n:** animosity, animus, antagonism, antipathy, disgust, dislike, hate, ill will, malevolence, pique, rancor, unfriendliness

## ENORMOUS
**a:** colossal, cyclopean, cyclopic, gargantuan, gigantic, huge, inordinate, large, magnitudinous, monumental, ponderous, prodigious, titanic, vast

**n:** amplitude, colossality, enormity, hugeness, magnitude

## ENOUGH
**a:** adequate, ample, competent, copious, satisfactory, sufficient

## ENRICH
**v:** adorn, diamondize, expand, fertilize, fortify, garnish, improve, lard

## ENROLL
**n:** matriculation

**v:** enlist, enter, impanel, list, matriculate, recruit, register, serve, subscribe

## ENSNARE
**n:** circumvention, entrapment

**v:** circumvent, deceive, dupe, entice, entrap, fool, inveigle, lure, mousetrap, seduce, trick

## ENTANGLE
**n:** complexity, complication, embranglement, embroilment, entanglement, imbroglio, intricacy, involution, labyrinth, maelstrom, morass

**v:** catch, confuse, embrangle, embroil, ensnare, entrap, intertwine, perplex

## ENTER
**n:** access, entering, *entree*, entry, incursion, ingress, ingression, invasion, penetration

**v:** encroach, impinge, infiltrate, infringe, ingress, intrude, invade, irrupt, penetrate, permeate, trespass

    *not allowed:* impenetrable, impermeable, imperviable, impervious

## ENTERTAINMENT
**a:** amusing, distracting, diverting, divertive, entertaining, festive, recreative

**n:** amusement, diversion, *divertissement*, extravaganza, recreation

**v:** regale

    *entertainer:* comedian, contortionist, geek, troupe, ventriloquist

## ENTHUSIASM
**a:** ardent, avid, dithyrambic, ebullient, ecstatic, enthusiastic, euphoric, exuberant, fervent, fervid, flamboyant, glowing, gung ho, impassioned, intense, lyrical, perfervid, profuse, rapturous, rhapsodic, unrestrained, vehement, zealous, zestful

**n:** ardor, dash, ebullience, ebulliency, ecstasy, elan, euphoria, exhilaration, exuberance, fanaticism, fervency, impetuosity, lyricism, transport, vehemence, vigor, zest

    *enthusiast:* buff, devotee, energumen, exalte, fanatic, zealot

## ENTICE
**a:** alluring, beguiling, bewitching, captivating, Circean, engaging, enticing, exotic, glamorous, orphic, picturesque, prepossessing, seducible, seductive, sirenic

**n:** allure, allurement, enticement, entrapment, inveiglement, seducement, seduction, temptation

**v:** allure, attract, cajole, captivate, charm, entrap, incite, inveigle, lure, solicit

## ENTIRE
**a:** completely, comprehensive, entirely, *in toto*, integral, *pur et simple, tout a fait*, undiminished, undivided, unexpurgated, unimpaired

**n:** aggregate, entirety, integral, integrality, integrity, totality

    *combining form:* pan-

## ENTITY
**n:** being, concrete, essence, existent, individual, monad, organism, soul, substantive, thing, unit

## ENTRAILS

**a:** enteral, enteric, haruspical, intestinal, splanchnic, visceral

**n:** digestion, giblets, innards, numbles, umbles, viscera

> *remove:* disembowel, eviscerate, exenterate
>
> *soothsayer: haruspex*

## ENTRANCE

**a:** entering, liminal

**n:** access, *aditus,* antechamber, anteroom, atrium, doorway, *entree,* entry, foyer, hall, ingress, ingression, introitus, intrusion, irruption, lobby, *marquee,* open sesame, *os, perron,* porch, portico, *propylaeum,* stairway, stoop, threshold, vestibule

## ENTRANCING

**a:** delightful, enticing, fascinating, orphic, pleasing, rapturous, winsome

## ENTREAT

**a:** adjuratory, entreating, precative, precatory, supplicative, supplicatory

**n:** adjuration, entreaty, imprecation, obsecration, petition, prayer, solicitation, supplication

**v:** adjure, beg, beseech, implore, invoke, pray, request, solicit, supplicate

## ENVELOP

**a:** ambient, circumferential, encompassing, enveloping, pervading, pervasive

**n:** container, envelope, integument, wrapper

**v:** envelope, surround, swathe, wrap

## ENVIRONMENT

**a:** behavioristic, bionomic, ecological, environmental, facultative, projicient, syntonic, syntonous, vicinal

**n:** acclimatization, ambiance, ambience, background, behavioristics, bionomics, ecology, entourage, environs, habitat, habitation, heredity, inurement, matrix, *milieu, mise en scene,* orientation, projicience, surroundings, vicinage, vicinity

**v:** nurture

*combining form:* eco-

## ENVY

**n:** jaundice, prejudice, resentment

**v:** begrudge, covet, desire, hanker, long

## EQUAL

**a:** adequative, coetaneous, coeval, coextensive, commensurable, commensurate, congruent, constituting, contemporaneous, contemporary, coordinate, corresponding, coterminous, democratic, egalitarian, equable, equalitarian, equipollent, equiponderant, equivalent, homeostatic, isometric, isonomic, isonomous, proportionate, reciprocal, Rouseauesque, synonymous, tantamount, uniform

**n:** adequation, balance, coetaneity, coeval, commensurability, compeer, contemporaneity, coordinate, counterpart, egalitarian, equality, equation, equilibrium, equiponderance, equivalence, equivalent, homeostasis, isonomy, libertarian, osmosis, parity, peer, proportion, *quid pro quo,* stability, symmetry, uniformity

**v:** adequate, equalize, equate, equiponderate, librate, neutralize, stabilize, unify

*combining forms:* equi-, is-, iso-

## EQUIP

**a:** equipped, furbished, furnished, well-appointed

**n:** accouterment, *accoutrement,* apparatus, appurtenance, *armamentaria,* caparison, equipage, equipment, facilities, habiliment, *impedimenta, instrumentaria,* materiel, panoply, paraphernalia, trappings

**v:** accouter, *accoutre,* capacitate, caparison, habilitate

## EQUIVOCAL

**a:** ambiguous, ambivalent, amphibologic, cryptic, doubtful, dubious, enigmatic, evasive, indefinite, indeterminate, indistinct, multivocal, problematic, questionable, vague

**ERADICATE**

**v:** annihilate, decimate, delete, deracinate, erase, exterminate, kill, remove, smother

**ERASE**

**n:** deletion, erasure, excision, expunction, extirpation, obliteration

**v:** dele, delete, efface, eliminate, expunge, obliterate, rub out, wipe out

*incapable of being:* imperishable, indelible, ineradicable, inexpungible, inextirpable, irradicable

**ERECT**

**a:** orthograde, orthostatic, perpendicular, right, standing, straight, upright, vertical

**n:** perpendicularity, verticality

**v:** construct

**EROSION**

**a:** ablative, terrigenous

**n:** ablation, badlands, cavitation, corrasion, corrosion, denudation, depletion, deterioration, detrition, detritus, groyne, ulceration

**v:** albate

**EROTIC**

**a:** arousing, carnal, lewd, provocative, sensual, sensuous, sexual

**n:** erotica, esoterica, *facetiae*, pornography

**ERRATIC**

**a:** aberrant, capricious, circuitous, desultory, devious, eccentric, errant, fallible, fluctuating, nomadic, tangential, unpredictable, vagarious, vagrant

**n:** aberrancy, caprice, deviation, eccentricity, erraticism, fallibility, peculiarity, vagary, whim

**ERROR**

**a:** apocryphal, blatant, erroneous, fallacious, fallible, inaccurate, incorrect, pseudodox

**n:** barbarism, blunder, corrigendum, deviation, discrepancy, erratum, fallacy, *faux pas,* gaffe, gremlin, impropriety, inaccuracy, indiscretion, miscalculation, misconception, misinformation, mistake, *pseudodox,* transgression, typo, typographical error

*correction:* amends, *apologia, corrigenda, corrigendum, errata, erratum*

*fond of finding:* captious

*grammatical:* catachresis, hypercorrection, *lapsus linguae, parapraxia,* solecism

**ESCAPADE**

**n:** adventure, antic, dare, frolic, gambit, *geste, harlequinade,* lark, *peccadillo,* ploy

**ESCORT**

**n:** attendant, *cavalier,* chaperone, *cicerone,* consort, convoy, *duenna,* entourage, gallant, gigolo, guide, lead, outrider, retinue, shepherd, *vis-a-vis*

**v:** accompany, chaperone, consort, convoy, shepherd, usher

**ESSAY**

**n:** *belles lettres,* discourse, disquisition, dissertation, endeavor, *exegesis, festschrift,* treatise

**v:** endeavor

*essayist:* polemicist, polemist

**ESSENCE**

**a:** *au fond,* basic, basically, cardinal, characteristic, coessential, componential, compulsory, constitutional, constitutive, consubstantial, *de rigueur,* essential, essentially, fundamental, fundamentally, hypostatic, idiopathic, indispensable, inherent, integral, intrinsic, mandatory, obligatory, quintessential, statutory, substantial, substantive, vital

**n:** alpha and omega, anlage, attribute, aura, bedrock, burden, cachet, component, concoction, constituent, consubstantiality, cornerstone, decoction, *desideratum, desiderium,* distillate, elixir, embodiment, epitome, essentiality, gravamen, hypostasis, integrality, linchpin, nitty-gritty, personification, pith, prerequisite, principle, quiddity, quintessence, requirement, *sine qua non,* substratum, tenor, virtuality

## ESTABLISH

**a:** chronic, conclusive, determinate, determinative, documented, ensconced, enshrined, entrenched, estabished, firm, fixed, ingrained, inherent, institutive, inveterate, ordained, settled, substantiated, substantive

**n:** establishment, fixture, installation, institution, *probata, probatum*

**v:** determine, endow, ensconce, inaugurate, institute, ordain, predicate

*opposed:* antiestablishmentarianism

## ESTATE

**n:** appanage, *demesne,* freehold, *hacienda,* hereditament, home, house, land, manor, patrimony, perpetuity, plantation, principality, property, tenure

*holder:* bailiff, steward, trustee

## ESTEEM

**a:** celebrated, commendatory, eminent, esteemed, estimable, illustrious, majestic, meritorious, praiseworthy, prestigious, venerated, worthy

**n:** deference, distinction, eminence, estimableness, estimation, hall of fame, illustriousness, majesty, pantheon, perihelion, popularity, prestige, prominence, reverence, veneration

**v:** appreciate, honor, venerate

## ETERNAL

**a:** *ab aeterno,* ceaseless, constant, diuturnal, everlasting, immarcescible, immortal, immutable, *in aeternum,* indefectible, infinite, permanent, perpetual, sempiternal, supertemporal

**n:** diuturnity, endlessness, eon, eternality, eternity, eviternity, immortability, immortality, infinitude, infinity, perdition, perpetuality, perpetuity, semipiternity

**v:** eternalize, perpetuate

## ETHEREAL

**a:** airy, celestial, diaphanous, empyreal, empyrean, exquisite, heavenly, insubstantial, spiritual, tenuous

**n:** diaphaneity, ethereality, insubstantiality, tenuity

## ETHICAL

**a:** accepted, deontic, good, honest, moral, right, virtuous

**n:** ethicality, ethics, rights

## ETIQUETTE

**n:** ceremony, conventiality, decorum, formality, protocol, *punctilio*

## EULOGY

**a:** commendatory, elegaic, encomiastic, eulogistic, laudatory, panegyrical, praiseworthy

**n:** commendation, encomium, eulogium, laudation, panegyric, praise

**v:** applaud, eulogize, laud, praise

## EVASION

**a:** circumlocutory, disingenuous, duplicitous, equivocal, evanescent, evasive, nebulous, noncommital, oblique, periphrastic

**n:** ambiguity, artifice, *circumbendibus,* circumlocution, circumvention, equivocation, periphrasis, prevarication, shiftiness, sophistry, strategem, subterfuge, temporizing, tergiversation

**v:** circumvent, equivocate, evade, finesse, maneuver, tergiversate

## EVEN

**a:** calm, equable, equal, impartial, serene, uniform, unruffled

**n:** equanimity, equilibrium, stability

## EVENING

**a:** crepuscular, vespertinal, vespertine

**n:** crepuscle, dusk, eve, eventide, PM, sunset, twilight

*event:* serenade, *soiree,* vespers, vigils

## EVENT

**n:** breakthrough, circumstance, circumstantiality, contingency, episode, experience, landmark, milestone, occurrence, phenomenon, scenario

## EVER

**a:** aeonian, amaranthine, continual, diuturnal, eternal, everlasting, forever, immarcescible, in perpetuity, incessant, indelible, perennial, perpetual, sempiternal, unceasing

**n:** diuturnity, eternity, everlastingness, perpetuity, sempiternity

## EVERYWHERE

**a:** boundless, infinite, omnipresent, peregrine, prevalent, ubiquitous, universal

**n:** omnipresence, ubiquity, universality

*combining form:* omni-

## EVIDENCE

**a:** apparent, cognizable, collateral, conspicuous, corroborative, demonstrable, discernible, evident, incontrovertible, luculent, manifest, palpable, patent, perceivable, perceptible, ponderable, rampant, recognizable, sensible, substantive, symptomatic, tangible

**n:** criteria, criterion, demonstration, deposition, document, exhibit, hearsay, indication, manifestation, sign, symptom, testament, testimony, token

**v:** attest, corroborate, substantiate, testify

## EVIL

**a:** anathematic, baleful, demoniacal, depraved, diabolical, flagitious, guileful, heinous, immoral, imprecatory, infamous, iniquitous, maleficent, malevolent, malicious, maliciously, malign, malignant, miscreant, noxious, pernicious, pestiferous, pestilent, serpentine, sinister, vicious, wicked

**n:** abomination, anathema, calamity, canker, depravity, diabolism, disaster, enormity, foreboding, imprecation, iniquity, malefaction, maleficence, malice aforethought, malum, misfortune, sinisterity, turpitude, wickedness

**v:** anathematize, imprecate

*person:* criminal, culprit, delinquent, demonaic, energumen, felon, *incubus,* malefactor, miscreant, *succubus*

## EVOLUTION

**n:** adaptive radiation, advancement, change, cladistics, development, Lamarckism, Lysenkoism, metamorphosis, ontogeny, phylogeny, transformation, unfoldment

*evolutionist:* developmentarian

## EXACT

**a:** aliquot, arduous, ceremonious, conscientious, definitive, demanding, determinate, exacting, exigent, fastidious, literal, literatim, mathematical, meticulous, onerous, precise, punctilious, scrupulous, slavish, undeviating, verbatim, word-for-word

**n:** accuracy, chapter and verse, definitude, determinacy, exactitude, exactness, fidelity, meticulosity, precision, scrupulosity, specification, specs

**v:** extort

## EXAGGERATE

**a:** amplificatory, bizarre, eccentric, exaggerated, exaggerative, extravagant, fustian, histrionic, hyperbolic, megalomaniac, melodramatic, mythomaniac, *outre,* overweening

**n:** aberration, aggrandizement, eccentricity, exaggeration, hyperbole, idiosyncrasy, mannerism, megalomania, Munchausenism, mythomania, phantasm

**v:** amplify, embellish, embroider, enhance, magnify, malinger

## EXALTATION

**a:** aggrandized, apotheosized, awe-inspiring, canonized, deified, ennobled, enshrined, euphoric, exalted, magnific, sublime, transfigured n: aggrandizement, apotheosis, canonization, deification, enhancement, ennoblement, euphoria, nobilitation, spiritualization, transcendence, transfiguration

v: aggrandize, apotheosize, canonize, deify, enhance, ennoble, enshrine, exalt, nobilitate, pedestal, spiritualize, transcend, transfigure

### EXAMINE

a: analytical, exploratory, inquisitive, inquisitorial

n: analysis, anatomy, critique, examination, exploration, inquest, inquiry, inquisition, investigation, perlustration, probe

v: analyze, anatomize, appraise, assess, audit, collate, cross-examine, dissect, explore, interrogate, investigate, palpate, perlustrate, peruse, plumb, scrutinize, study, text, traverse

### EXAMPLE

a: commendable, exemplary, exemplificative, monitory, paradigmatic, prototypal, prototypic, quintessential

n: archetype, avatar, byword, epitome, exemplar, exemplification, exemplum, incarnation, *locus classicus, ne plus supra,* paradigm, paragon, personification, precedent, prototype, quintessence, speciment, type, typification

v: adduce, embody, epitomize, exemplify, typify

*term introducing: videlicet,* viz

### EXCEED

a: exceeding, inordinate, parlous, transcendent

n: transcendency

v: excel, preponderate, surpass, transcend

*combining forms:* super-, trans-, ultra-

### EXCELLENCE

a: admirable, best, blue-chip, copybook, excellent, exemplary, finest, incomparable, marvelous, matchless, meritorious, *ne plus ultra, par excellence,* paramount, peerless, perfect, preeminent, prominent, sig-

nal, significant, stellar, stupendous, sublime, superlative, supernal, superordinary, surpassing, transcendent, unequaled, unparalleled, unprecedented, unrivaled, unsurpassed, valiant

n: humdinger, nonesuch, nonpareil, paragon, phoenix

v: exceed, excel

### EXEMPTION

a: excipient

n: deviation, exclusion, *non obstante,* omission

### EXCEPTIONAL

a: choice, extraordinary, nonpareil, novel, preternatural, remarkable, supernal, supernatural, superordinary, surpassing, unprecedented

### EXCERPT

n: abstract, analecta, analects, citation, cite, *collectanea,* essence, extract, fragment, *miscellanea,* paraphrase, quote, reference, *scrapiana,* selection, verse

### EXCESS

a: cloying, copious, disproportionate, excessive, exorbitant, extortionate, extravagant, extreme, fulsome, immoderate, inordinant, intemperate, lavish, neurotic, officious, overweening, pleonastic, plethoric, profuse, redundant, replete, superabundant, supererogatory, superfluous, superlative, supernumerary, unduly

n: copiosity, exorbitance, exorbitancy, extravagance, inordinateness, intemperance, *luxus,* nimiety, overkill, plethora, prodigality, prolixity, redundancy, satiety, superabundance, supererogation, superfluity, superflux, surfeit, verbiage, verbosity

### EXCHANGE

a: commutable

n: barter, cambristry, clearing house, commutation, forum, *quid pro quo,* reciprocity, *rialto*

**v:** barter, commute, interchange, reciprocate, substitute

## EXCITED

**a:** *agitato,* atwitter, berserk, delirious, ecstatic, effervescent, excitable, excitatory, exuberant, febrile, frantic, frenetic, frenzied, hectic, hysterical, ignitable, incitatory, orgasmic, orgiastic, provocative, rapturous, riotous, skittish, stimulatory

**n:** adrenaline, agitation, alarum, ecstasy, epinephrine, excitement, fanteeg, fantigue, fillip, fomentation, furore, ignitability, incitation, incitement, instigation, orgasm, rapture, raptus, razzle-dazzle, razzmatazz, transport

**v:** ecstasize, electrify, energize, excite, fillip, galvanize, inflame, invigorate, pique, salivate, stimulate, stir, suscitate, titillate

*combining form:* -mania

## EXCLAMATION

**a:** ejaculatory, exclamatory, expletive, expletory, vociferant, vociferous

**n:** ecphonesis, ejaculation, eureka, expletive, hallelujah, hosanna, interjection, interrobang, vociferation

## EXCLUDE

**n:** censorship, debarring, exclusion, excommunication, ostracism, purdah, rejection, repression, segregation, separation, sequestration, suppression, taboo

**v:** banish, blackball, blacklist, boycott, debar, disbar, eliminate, excommunicate, ostracize, preclude, prevent, prohibit, reject, relegate, segregate, winnow out

## EXCLUSIVE

**a:** esoteric, exclusivistic, fashionable, rarefied, segregated, select, stylish, undivided

**n:** cabal, charmed circle, clique, *coterie,* elitism, exclusivism, exclusivity, monopoly, perquisite

## EXCOMMUNICATE

**a:** anathematic(al)

**n:** anathema, anathematization, banishment, censure, excommunication, interdiction, ostracism

**v:** anathematize, interdict, ostracize

## EXCREMENT

**a:** coprophagous, depurant, egestive, excremental, excretious, excretory, feculent, scatological, scatophagous, stercoraceous

**n:** coprolite, defecation, dung, egesta, elimination, excreta, feces, feculence, frass, guano, meconium, ordure, scats

**v:** defecate, egest, eliminate, excrete

*combining forms:* copro-, scato-

*study:* coprology, scatology

## EXCUSE

**a:** apologetic, conciliatory, condonable, excusable, excusatory, justificatory, pardonable, placable, venial, vindicatory

**n:** absolution, alibi, amnesty, condonation, dispensation, extenuation, indulgence, justification, palliation, pardon, pretext, provocation, rationalization, remission, salvo

**v:** absolve, acquit, conciliate, concoct, condone, exempt, exonerate, extenuate, forgive, mitigate, overlook, palliate, pardon, rationalize, vindicate

## EXECUTION

**a:** carnificial

**n:** decapitation, electrocution, garrote, guillotine, lapidation, noyade, strangulation

## EXEMPTION

**n:** dispensation, extraterritoriality, freedom, immunity, impunity, release

## EXHALATION

**a:** effluvial

**n:** breath, effluvium, emanation, expiration, *flatus*

**v:** aspire, blow, breathe, expire, suspire

## EXHAUST

**a:** debilitated, depleted, deprived, drained, *effete,* enervated, enfeebled, exhausted, impoverished, weakened

**n:** depletion, effluvium, emission, exhaustion, inanition

**v:** depauperate, deplete, discharge, evacuate, impoverish, pauperize

**EXHIBITION**

**a:** ostentatious

**n:** diorama, expo, exposition, ostentation, pavilion, retrospective

**v:** air, demonstrate, exhibit, flaunt

**EXHILARATED**

**a:** animated, cheerful, ebullient, euphoric, exhilarative, happy, heady, intoxicated, rapturuous, zestful

**n:** cheer, exhilaration, gaiety, glee, happiness, headiness, zest

**v:** cheer, elevate, exhilarate, gladden, please, stir

**EXILE**

**a:** banished, exiled, expatriate

**n:** banishment, Diaspora, expatriation, fugitivity, ostracism, relegation

**v:** banish, deport, expatriate, forbid, ostracize, outlaw, proscribe, relegate

**EXISTENCE**

**a:** aborning, contemporary, corporeal, existential, existing, extant, nascent, noumenal, objective, ontic, ontological, parturient, substantive

**n:** actuality, being, corporality, corporeity, entity, existent, individuation, materiality, notion, reality, *status quo*, substantiality, substantivity

**v:** continue, exist, hypostatize, manage, obtain, prevail, reify, remain, subsist

　*combining form:* onto-
　*study:* ongology

**EXIT**

**n:** egress, egression, escape, *exeunt, exeunt omnes*, outlet, vent

**EXONERATE**

**a:** exculpable, exculpatory, exonerated

**n:** exculpation, exoneration

**v:** absolve, acquit, exculpate, excuse, forgive, free, pardon, release, remit, vindicate

**EXPAND**

**a:** expanded, expanding, patulous, proliferous, spread out, tumefactive, tumescent

**n:** amplification, development, exacerbation, expansion, proliferation, tumescence, tympany

**v:** amplify, augment, delate, dilate, diversify, elaborate, enhance, expatiate, increase, inflate, intumesce, tumefy

**EXPECTED**

**a:** anticipated, contemplated, contingent, inchoate, inchoative, incipient, potential, prospective

**n:** anticipation, assumption, chances, contemplation, devoir, expectancy, expectation, hopes, outlook, prospect, prospects, supposition

**v:** anticipate, expect, look forward to

　*expecting:* anticipant, anticipatory
　*more than:* supererogative, supererogatory

**EXPEDIENT**

**a:** advisable, astucious, astute, efficient, expediential, favorable, fit, opportune, opportunistic, politic, politically correct, practical, proper, suitable, useful

**n:** *dernier ressort*, expedience, expediency, fitness, makeshift, *pis aller*, temporization

**EXPEDITION**

**n:** acceleration, advance, anabasis, *entrada*, promptness, quest, reconnaissance, safari

**EXPENSE**

**a:** confiscatory, costly, dispenditious, exorbitant, expensive, extortionate, extravagant, *hors de prix*, incidental, lavish, prohibitive, sumptuary, sumptuous

**n:** disbursement, dispensation, expenditure, white elephant

## EXPERIENCE

**a:** adept, *au fait*, capable, competent, consummate, conversant, empirical, existential, experienced, experiential, knowledgeable, materialistic, practiced, pragmatic, seasoned, utilitarian, versant, versatile, vicarious, worldly, worldly-wise

**n:** background, empiricism, identification, knowledge, ordeal, *savoir faire*, versatility, vicariousness, vicissitudes

    *beyond:* fourth-dimension, intuitive, supernatural, transcendental

    *person:* trouper, veteran

## EXPERIMENTAL

**a:** *a posteriori*, contingent, empirical, incomplete, inductive, provisional, tentative

**n:** experiment, test, vivisection

## EXPERT

**a:** able, adept, ambidexterous, *au fait*, dexterous, esthetic, proficient, skillful, versatile, virtuosic

**n:** adept, artiste, authority, brain trust, *cognoscente*, *connoisseur*, consultant, *cordon bleu*, deftness, *doyen*, *doyenne*, esthete, expertise, expertness, gourmet, hability, *illuminato*, *maestro*, maven, past master, past mistress, skill, virtuosity, *virtuoso*

## EXPLAIN

**a:** analytical, discurvie, essayistic, exegetical, explanatory, explicable, explicative, explicatory, exponent, expository, hermeneutic, interpretative, paraphrastic, resolutive

**n:** construction, hypothesis, theory

**v:** amplify, dilate, elaborate, elucidate, expatiate, explicate, exposit, expound, interpret, justify, make clear, rationalize, resolve, translate

    *explainer:* elucidator, exegete, explanator, exponent, interpreter, translator

## EXPLODE

**a:** detonative, explosive, fulminous, pyrotechnic

**n:** detonation, explosion, fiasco, fulmination

**v:** break, detonate, erupt, fire, flash, fulminate, spring, torpedo

## EXPLOIT

**a:** exploiting, predaceous, predacious, predatory

**n:** achievement, deed, exploitation, *geste*, manipulation, predacity, publicity, utilization

**v:** cultivate, manipulate, utilize

## EXPLORE

**n:** examination, exploration, inquest, investigation, probe, prospection, *recce*, reconnaissance, reconnoiter, safari, survey

**v:** examine, investigate, probe, prospect, reconnoiter

    *explorer:* adventurer, adventuress, navigator, traveler

## EXPOSE

**a:** denudative, exposed, exposing

**n:** denudation, expose

**v:** attack, denudate, denude, reveal, unmask

## EXPOUND

**v:** comment, defend, elocute, explain, exposit, express, inform, instruct, present, recite, speak, state, teach, utter, vent, voice

    *expounder:* advocate, exegete, exponent

## EXPRESSION

**a:** articulate, demonstrative, eloquent, emotional, emphatic, euphemistic, evocative, expressive, indicative, meaningful, moving, sententious, significant, vaporing, vaporizing

**n:** atticism, circumlocution, colloquialism, diction, ecstasy, eloquence, emotion, euphemism, expressiveness, expressivity, figure of speech, gesture, locution, manifestation, mien, modulation, parlance, periphrasis, phraseology, physiognomy, plangency, remark, scholasm, transport, trope, utterance, vaporing

**v:** articulate, couch, enunciate, evince, express, manifest, vent, ventilate, verbalize

*combining form:* -logy

**EXPURGATE**

**v:** bowdlerize, castrate, censor, emasculate, expunge, purge, purify

**EXTEMPORARY**

**a:** autoschediastic, extemporaneous, extempore, impromptu, improvised, improviso, off-hand, spontaneous, unexpected, unpremeditative

**n:** extemporization, improvisation, improviso, spontaneity

**v:** ad lib, extemporize, improvise

**EXTENT**

**a:** comprehensive, encyclopedic, extensive, far-reaching, illimitable, latitudinal, latitudinous, magnitudinous, measureless, panoramic

**n:** ambit, amplitude, caliber, compass, comprehensiveness, latitude, purview, range, scope

**v:** diversify, extend, perpetuate, prolong, quantify, span

**EXTERMINATE**

**n:** abolishment, annihilation, decimation, eradication, extermination, extirpation, genocide

**v:** abolish, annihilate, decimate, demolish, deracinate, destroy, eradicate, execute, extirpate, fumigate

**EXTERNAL**

**a:** adventitious, ectal, exogenous, exoteric, exterior, extraneous, extrinsic, foreign, heteronomous, peripheral, superficial, ulterior

**n:** aspect, coign, exteriority, externality, extraneity, periphery, quoin

*combining form:* exo-

**EXTOL**

**a:** commendable, eulogistic, extolling, panegyric

**v:** applaud, approbate, commend, deify, enhance, enshrine, eulogize, exalt, glorify, laud, magnify, panegyrize, praise, spiritualize, worship

**EXTRA**

**a:** accessory, additional, adjunctive, *de trop*, redundant, supererogant, supererogatory, superfluous, superior, supernumerary, supervenient, supplementary

**n:** *addendum*, afterthought, annex, appendix, fringe benefit, perk, perquisite, postscript, redundance, redundancy, reinforcement, superabundance, supererogation, superfluity, supernumerary, supplement, surcharge

> *extraneous:* accidental, extrinsic, foreign, irrelevant, ulterior, unrelated

**EXTRACT**

**n:** abstract, concentrate, decoction, *decoctum*, elicitation, essence, excerpt, extraction, genealogy, gobbet, quintessence, recycling

**v:** cite, decoct, distill, gut, pry out, reflux

**EXTRAORDINARY**

**a:** bizarre, exceptional, extraordinaire, inordinate, melodramatic, phenomenal, prodigious, rare, remarkable, sensational, singular, surpassing, wonderful

**n:** anomaly, extravaganza, mutation, phenomenality, phenomenon, prodigality, prodigy, *rara avis*, spectacular, sport

**EXTRASENSORY**

**n:** clairvoyance, cryptesthesia, perception, telesthesia

**EXTRAVAGANCE**

**a:** dispendious, exorbitant, extravagant, generous, gothic, immoderate, inordinate, intemperate, lavish, luxuriant, luxurious, nimious, prodigal, profligate, rampant, redundant, sumptuary, superfluous, unrestrained, wanton, wasteful

**n:** enthusiasm, exorbitance, extravagancy, extravaganza, luxuriance, nimiety, opulence, prodigality, profligacy, profusion, rampancy, redundance, superabundance, superfluity, superflux, wantonness

## EXTREME

**a:** arrant, *avant-garde*, bizarre, conspicuous, consummate, eccentric, egregious, eminent, extravagant, fanatical, fantastic, immoderate, *in extremis*, inordinate, intransigent, maximum, notorious, odd, *outre*, overweening, rabid, radical, remarkable, signal, special, ultimate, ultraistic, uncompromising

**n:** *dernier ressort, ne plus ultra, outrance, pis aller*, ultraism

*combining form:* ultra-

*extremist:* anarchist, *avant-garde*, Jacobin, nihilist, radical, revolutionary, *sansculotte*, ultraist

## EXUDE

**a:** exudative, osmotic, transudative

**n:** extravasation, exudation, osmosis, transudate, transudation

**v:** bleed, discharge, emanate, emit, flow, issue, leak, ooze, osmose, percolate, perspire, spew, stream, transude

## EYE

**a:** ciliary, macroscopic, ocular, optical, palpebral, superciliary, visual

**n:** fixation, *oeillade*, peripheral vision

**v:** avert, dilate

*bulging:* exophthalmic

*combining forms:* ocul-, ophthalmo-, -opia, -opsia, -opsy, -opy

*crossed:* exotropic

*eyebrow:* supercilium

*eyelash:* cilium

*eyelid:* blepharon, palpebrum

*one:* monocular, monophthalmic

*specialist:* oculist, ophthalmologist, optometrist

*study:* ophthalmology

*two:* binocular

*watering:* epiphora

## FABLE

**a:** Aesopian, Aesopic, allegoric, allegorical, apocryphal, fabular, fabulous, fictitious, mythical, parabolical, Scheheradazian

**n:** allegory, apologue, bestiary, exemplum, fabrication, fabulosity, legend, myth, untruth

**v:** allegorize, fabulize, mythasize, mythologize, parabolize

> *fabler:* allegorist, fabulist, *improvisatore,* improvisor, mythmaker, mythologist, parabolist

## FABRICATE

**a:** improvisatorial, improvisatory

**v:** construct, fabulize, improvisate, improvise

## FACE

**a:** *affronte,* obverse, prone, prosopic, prostrate, *tete-a-tete, vis-a-vis*

**n:** assurance, audacity, confrontation, countenance, effrontery, facade, facet, impudence, obverse, physiognomy, visage

**v:** beard, brave, challenge, orient, orientate

> *combining forms:* -ward, -wards

## FACIAL

**a:** deadpan, enigmatic, inscrutable, physiognomic

**n:** countenance, deadpan, facade, facies, grimace, lineament, *maquillage,* mien, physiognomy, poker face, visage

> *combining form:* -hedron

## FACT

**a:** *de facto,* earthly, empirical, factual, *ipso facto,* objective, pragmatic

**n:** actuality, circumstance, data, *datum,* facticity, factuality, *fait accompli, ipso facto,* occurrence, *res gestae*

**v:** materialize, pragmatize, rationalize, regurgitate

> *factors:* characteristic, feature

## FAD

**n:** caprice, fancy, foible, megrim, monomania, rage, style, vagary, vogue, whim

## FADE

**a:** blanched, etiolated

**v:** decline, decrease, dull, enervate, etiolate, evanesce, languish, waste

## FAIL

**a:** abortive, catastrophic, manque, unfulfilled, unsuccessful, would-be

**n:** abstentation, abstention, bankruptcy, catastrophe, damp squib, defalcation, delinquency, demise, dereliction, deterioration, failure, fiasco, insolvency, laches, miscarriage, misfeasance, neglect, nonperformance, omission, pretermission

**v:** abort, decline, default, flag, founder, go wrong, languish, miscarry, retrogress, welsh

## FAINT

**a:** caliginous, dim, indistinct, irresolute, obscure, pusillanimous

**n:** pusillaniminity, swoon, syncope

**v:** falter, keel, suffocate, swoon

**FAIR**

**a:** comely, detached, dispassionate, equitable, evenhanded, honest, honorable, impartial, impersonal, judicial, just, moderate, reasonable, unbiased, unprejudiced

**n:** detachment, disinterestedness, equity, fairness, impartiality, judiciality, Queensberry Rules

*event:* amusement, bazaar, exhibition, exposition, fete

*haired:* blond(e), xanthochroid

*skinned:* Caucasian, xanthochroid

**FAITH**

**a:** accurate, faithful, implicit, incorruptible, loyal, pistic, reliable, resolute, staunch, steadfast, unswerving, unwavering

**n:** allegiance, assurance, belief, confidence, conviction, credence, creed, devotion, doctrine, faithfulness, fealty, fidelity, loyalty, obedience, pistology, religion, steadfastness

**v:** espouse, testify

*abandon:* apostasize

*faithless:* agnostic, disloyal, false, perfidious, treacherous

**FALL**

**a:** anticlimactic, deciduous, precipitant, precipitate, precipitous

**n:** anticlimax, cadence, prolapse, ptosis

**v:** cascade, devolve on, grabble, gravitate, grovel, lessen, plummet, precipitate, sink, sprawl, straggle, subside

**FALSE**

**a:** apocryphal, apostate, apostatic, arrant, artificial, barmecidal, counterfeit, delusional, dishonorable, duplicitous, faithless, fictitious, fictive, hypocritical, ignominious, illusional, illusive, illusory, inauthentic, infamous, mendacious, meretricious, mythical, paradoxical, perfidious, perjurious, *postiche*, pseudo, pseudological, renegade, specious, spectral, spurious, traitorous, treasonable, trumped-up, untrustworthy

**n:** *bathos*, canard, cretinism, delusion, dissemblance, duplicity, fabrication, fabulation, facade, fake, falsehood, falseness, falsity, fib, frame-up, guise, hallucination, hypocrisy, inaccuracy, invention, inveracity, lie, mendacity, misconception, misrepresentation, paradoxicality, paralogism, perfidy, perjury, pretense, pseudology, roorback, sham, simulation, speciosity, tarradiddle, treachery, Trojan horse, unfaithfulness, unveracity

**v:** abuse, belie, defame, dissemble, fake, feign, libel, lie, simulate, slander

*combining forms:* pseud-, pseudo-

**FALSIFIED**

**a:** apocryphal, *Munchausen*, pseudeipigraphic, pseudological

**n:** apocryph, apocrypha, aspersion, calumny, canard, defamation, fabrication, falsification, libel, pseudepigraph, pseudograph, slander

**FAME**

**a:** acclaimed, august, celebrated, celebrious, classic, distingue, distinguished, eminent, fabled, famous, illustratory, illustrious, infamous, leonine, notable, noted, notorious, prominent, renowned, reputable, storied, venerable

**n:** *cause celebre*, celebrity, distinction, *eclat*, eminence, kudos, luminary, luster, notability, notoriety, prestige, renown, reputation, repute, stature, status, success, VIP

**FAMILIARITY**

**a:** *au fait*, avuncular, confidential, conversant, customary, familiar, friendly, intimate, intrusive, proverbial, unceremonious, versed

**n:** confidentiality, informality, intimacy, topos

**v:** acclimatize, accustom, acquaint, adapt, adjust, familiarize, habituate, orient, orientate, popularize

**FAMILY**

**a:** collateral, *en famille*, familial, familistic, gentilitial, gentilitious

**n:** ancestry, cognomen, domesticity, dynasty, extended family, family tree, genealogy, kin, kinsmen, lineage, menage, nuclear family, paternity, pedigree, relatives

*father's:* patriarchal, patrilocal, spear side, paternal

*head: materfamilias,* matriarch, *paterfamilias,* patriarch

*mother's:* distaff side, maternal, matriarchal, matrilocal, spindle side

**FAN**

**n:** aficionado, apostle, buff, devotee, enthusiast, fanatic, follower, votary

*fanatic:* bigot, energumen, extremist, radical, zealot

*fanfare:* blazonry, fanfaron, flourish, tantara, tantatara, tantivy, tucket

*fan-shaped:* flabellate, rhipidate

**FANCY**

**a:** capricious, chimerical, ethereal, extravagant, fanciful, fantastic, imaginary, premium, quixotic, romantic, utopian, vaporous, whimsical

**n:** aprice, capriccio, chimera, daydream, ethereality, fad, fantasy, *fata morgana,* kickshaw, megrim, phantasm, phantasy, tidbit, vaporosity, whimsy

**FANTASY**

**a:** baroque, bizarre, capricious, eccentric, extravagant, fanciful, *fantasque,* fantastic(al), gothic, grotesque, irrational, odd, preposterous, preternatural, supernatural, unearthly, unrealistic, visionary

**n:** apparition, autism, Cockaigne, ethereality, extravaganza, fantasia, fantasticality, fantastication, figment, hallucination, notion, phantasm, reverie, vagary, Walter Mitty, whimsy

**v:** fantasticate

**FAR**

**a:** away, distal, distant, forane, inaccessible, outlying, remote, tramontane, ultramontane, ultramundane

**n:** extremity, Ultima Thule

*far-sighted:* hypermetropic, hyperopic, presbyopic, presbytic, prophetic, provident

*farthest:* deepest, extreme, farthermost, furthest, lowest, nethermost, remotest, ultimate

**FARCE**

**n:** buffonery, burlesque, extravaganza, forcemeat, *harlequinade,* harliquin, *opera bouffe,* ridiculosity

**FAREWELL**

**a:** apopemptic, valedictory

**n:** *adieu,* bidding, conge, *envoi,* goodbye, swan song, valediction

**FAR-FETCHED**

**a:** catachrestic, laborious, preposterous, *recherche,* ridiculous, silly, unbelieveable

**FARMING**

**a:** agrarian, agricultural, agronomical, arable, geoponic, pastoral

**n:** agrarianism, agriculture, agronomics, agronomy, cooperative, geoponics, grange, husbandry, subsistence

*combining forms:* agr-, agri-, agro-

*farmer:* agriculturist, agronomist, cotter, crofter, *fellahin,* granger, grazier, husbandman, Okie, pastoralist, rancher, ruralist, serf, sharecropper, squatter, *villein,* yeoman

**FASCINATING**

**a:** alluring, attractive, captivating, Circean, enchanting, enthralling, irresistible, mesmeric, sirenic, tempting

**n:** Circe, *femme fatale,* intrigue

**v:** allure, bewitch, captivate, enamor, enchant, ensorcel, enthrall, fascinate, mesmerize

**FASHION**

**a:** *a la mode,* chic, *chichi,* fashionable, jaunty, *le bon ton,* modish, mondaine, *recherche,* sartorial, *soigne,* sophisticated, tonnish

**n:** *beau monde, dernier cri, grand monde, haute monde, haute couture,* sophistication, trendsetter, vanguard, vogue

**FAST**

**a:** accelerated, *allegro,* celeritous, expeditious, expeditive, intemperate, meteoric, precipitate, precipitous, prompt, quick, velocious

　*combining forms:* tach-, tacheo-, tachy-

**FAT**

**a:** adipogenetic, adipose, bloated, bulky, buxom, corpulent, fattening, fatty, liparous, lipogenous, obese, oleaginous, pinguescent, pinguid, portly, rotund, sonsy, steatogenous, steatopygic, stout, unctious

**n:** adipogenesis, adiposis, adiposity, blubber, cellulite, corporation, corpulence, fattiness, lipid, lipomatosis, obesity, paunch, pinguidity

　*combining forms:* lipo-, sebi-, sebo-, steat-, steato-

　*hips:* cellulite, steatopygia, steatopygy

**FATAL**

**a:** calamitous, deadly, disastrous, feral, lethal, lethiferous, malicious, malignant, mortal, mortiferous, pernicious, pestilent

**n:** determinism, fatalism, necessarianism, predestination, predetermination

**FATE**

**a:** fated, foredoomed, foreordained, ineluctable, inescapable, predestined, predetermined, unavoidable

**n:** destiny, disaster, doom, handwriting on the wall, karma, kismet, lot, Moira, portion, predestination, predetermination, Providence, quirk, will of gods

**v:** intervene

　*three:* Atropos, Clotho, Decuma, Greece, Lachesis, Morta, Nona, Parcae

**FATHER**

**a:** agnatic, fatherly, filial, paternal, pater-

nalistic, patriarchal, patricentric, patriclinous, patrilineal, patripotestal, patroclinous, patronymic, putative

**n:** agnate, ancestor, angation, author, fatherhood, genitor, *padre, pater, paterfamilias,* paternalism, paternality, paternity, patriarch, patrilineage, patrimony, precursor, predecessor, procreator, prototype

　*combining forms:* patr-, patri-

　*Father Time:* grim reaper

　*killing:* patricide

**FATIGUE**

**a:** adynamic, dyspneic, enervated, fatigued, languescent, languorous, lassitudinous, lethargic

**n:** dyspnea, enervation, exhaustion, hypokinesia, hypokinesis, impuissance, lackadaisy, languor, lassitude, lethargy, listlessness, weariness

**FAULT**

**a:** amiss, catachrestic, dilapidated, faulty, imperfect, *mea culpa,* paralogistic, suboptimal, substandard, unsound

**n:** captiousness, catachresis, *culpa,* culpability, cynicism, delinquency, dereliction, dislocation, dysfunction, foible, glitch, imperfection, misdemeanor, neglect, negligence, paralogism, *peccadillo,* scrupulosity, veniality

　*combining form:* dys-

　*faultfinder:* carper, caviler, censor, critic, cynic, malcontent, Momus, pettifogger

　*faultfinding:* captious, carping, censorial, censorious, condemnatory, critical, cynical, hypercritical, niggling, querulous, scrupulous

　*faultless:* immaculate, impeccable, impeccant, indefectible, infallible, innocent, irreproachable, unblemished, undeviating, unerring, unimpeachable

**FAVOR**

**a:** complimentary, *ex gratia,* fawning, free, *gratis,* gratuitous, ingratiating, nepotal, nepotic, obsequious, servile, sycophantic, toadying, unctuous

**n:** approbation, condescension, indulgence, obligation, *omen faustum*, patronage, *quid pro quo*, sponsorship, window dressing

**v:** abet, countenance, encourage, fawn, hector, importune, ingratiate, kowtow, truckle

> *combining form:* pro-
>
> *favorable:* advantageous, approbative, auspicious, beneficial, benign, benignant, commendatory, disposed, gracious, inclinable, optimal, preferential, propitious, salutary, strategic, tendentious, wholesome
>
> *favorite:* cosset, haunt, mignon, minion, nepotist, optimum, partisan, *persona grata*, toady
>
> *favoritism:* bias, cordiality, encouragement, nepotism, partiality, patronage, predilection, sanction

## FAWN

**a:** deferential, fawning, gnathonic, obsequious, oleaginous, parasitical, servile, sycophantic, toadying, unctuous

**n:** deference, groveling, kowtow, obsequiousness, obsequity, servility, sycophancy, toadying, unctuosity, unctuousness

**v:** grovel, kowtow

## FEAR

**n:** apprehension, bogey, bugaboo, bugbear, chimera, consternation, disquietude, *frisson*, funk, hobgoblin, misgiving, phobia, qualm, timidity, trepidation

**v:** apprehend, blench, cower, cringe, eschew, flinch, quail, recoil, shy, suspect, wince

> *aloneness:* autophobia, monophobia
>
> *animal:* zoophobia
>
> *being touched:* aichmophobia
>
> *bird:* ornithophobia
>
> *bridge:* gephyrophobia
>
> *buried alive:* taphephobia
>
> *cat:* ail(e)urophobia, galeophobia, gatophobia

> *children:* pedophobia
>
> *closed places:* claustrophobia
>
> *combining forms:* -phobe, -phobia, -phobic
>
> *crowd:* ochlophobia
>
> *dark:* nyctophobia
>
> *death:* necrophobia, thantophobia
>
> *depths:* bathophobia
>
> *dirt:* mysophobia, rhypophobia, rupophobia
>
> *disease:* hypochondria, pathophobia
>
> *dog:* cynophobia
>
> *dust:* amathophobia
>
> *fire:* pyrophobia
>
> *fish:* ichthyophobia
>
> *flying:* aerophobia
>
> *foreign:* xenophobia
>
> *germs:* microbiophobia
>
> *God's wrath:* theophobia
>
> *heights:* acrophobia, hypsophobia
>
> *horse:* hippophobia
>
> *idea:* ideophobia
>
> *illness:* nosophobia, pathophobia
>
> *injury:* traumatophobia
>
> *insanity:* lysophobia
>
> *insect:* entomophobia
>
> *men:* androphobia, apandria
>
> *mice:* musophobia
>
> *number 13:* triskaidekaphobia
>
> *old age:* gerascophobia
>
> *pain:* algophobia
>
> *particular place:* topophobia
>
> *poisoning:* toxiphobia
>
> *public place:* agoraphobia
>
> *public speaking:* glossophobia, lalophobia
>
> *punishment:* rhabdophobia
>
> *sea:* thalassophobia
>
> *sharp object:* aichmophobia
>
> *sleep:* hypnophobia
>
> *snake:* ophidiophobia

*society:* apanthropophobia

*sound:* phonophobia

*speed:* tacophobia

*spider:* arachnaphobia

*storm:* astraphobia

*streets:* dromophobia

*thunder and lightning:* astraphobia, brontophobia, tonitruphobia, tontitrophobia

*travel:* hodophobia

*uncleanliness:* mysophobia

*water:* aquaphobia, hydrophobia, hygrophobia

*wind:* aerophobia, anemophobia

*women:* gynephobia

*work:* ergasiophobia, ergophobia

## FEARFUL

**a:** appalling, apprehensive, awe-inspiring, doughty, fearsome, formidable, horrendous, horrific, pavid, redoubtable, timorous

    *fearless:* audacious, brave, chivalrous, courageous, dauntless, impavid, indomitable, intrepid, *sans peur*, temerarious, undaunted

## FEAST

**a:** Barmecidal, convivial, epulary, festal, festive, Lucullan

**n:** carnival, celebration, *Chanukah,* conviviality, *convivium,* epulation, feasting, fiesta, *Hanukkah,* holiday, Last Supper

## FEAT

**n:** exploit, gest, gymnastics, gyration, *passe-passe, tour de force*

## FEATHER

**a:** pinnate, winged

**n:** *aigrette,* auriculars, barba, barbula, cockade, covert, frill, hackles, mantle, osprey, *panache,* pinion, pinna, plumage, *rectrix, remex,* ruff, *tectrix,* vane, *vexillum, vibrissae,* web

**v:** preen, ruffle

    *combining form:* ptero-

*without:* callow, deplumate, molted, unfledged

## FEATURE

**a:** lineamental, physiognomic, physiognomonic

**n:** aspect, characteristic, countenance, eccentricity, facet, facies, *habitus,* landmark, lineament, mitigating factor, oddity, peculiarity, physiognomy, physique, redeeming feature, singularity, topography, visage

## FEBRUARY 29

**n:** bissextile, intercalary, Leap Day

## FECES

**a:** excremental, excrementious, fecal, scatological, steracoraceous, stercoral

**n:** dung, egesta, ejecta, ejectamenta, excrement, excreta, feculence, ordure

    *interest:* coprophilia

## FEE

**n:** commission, cost, emolument, honorarium, pay, percentage, tuition, wage

## FEEBLE

**a:** adynamic, asthenic, debilitated, decrepit, flaccid, impotent, *impuissant,* insipid, insubstantial, languid, languorous, pointless, unsubstantial

**n:** *adynamia, amentia,* cretinism, decrepitude, fatigue, feebleness, idiocy, imbecility, impotence, impotency, *impuissance,* moronity, *oligophrenia,* tenuity, weakness

## FEEL

**a:** altruistic, ardent, conscious, demonstrative, esthetic, felt, impassionate, impassioned, palpable, passible, pathetic, sensible, sentient, susceptible, tactual, tangible

**n:** affect, affectation, affection, altropathy, altruism, atmosphere, consciousness, *deja entendu, deja pense, deja raconte, deja vecu, deja vu,* ecstasy, enthusiasm, esthesia, experience, feeling, foreboding, impression, misgiving, opinion, palpation, parmnesia, *pathos,* perception, qualm, rapture, responsiveness, scruple, sensation, sensibility, sentience, sentiency, sentiment, stereognosis, transport, vibes

**v:** arouse, entertain, felt, grabble, harbor, impassion, nourish, palpate, reciprocate, return, sense

> *combining forms:* path-, -pathy
>
> *drug:* analgesic, anesthesia, anesthetic, anodyne
>
> *unfeeling:* anesthetic, apathetic, expressionless, impassible, impassive, impiteous, inanimate, incompassionate, indurate, insensate, insensitive, phlegmatic, stoical

**FEET**

**a:** pedal, pedigerous, podal, podalic

**n:** extremities

> *combining forms:* -pede, pedi-, -pod, -pode
>
> *four:* quadrupedal, tetrapod, tetrapodous
>
> *hanging by:* adhamant
>
> *large:* macropod, sciapodopous
>
> *many:* multiped, polyped
>
> *small:* micropodal, micropodous
>
> *two:* biped, bipedal

**FEIGN**

**a:** artificial, feigned, fictitious

**n:** malingering, pathomimesis

**v:** allege, fabricate, malinger, pretend

**FELLOW**

**a:** consociate, consociative

**n:** adjutant, associate, *bon ami, bon enfant,* brother, coadjutor, coeval, cohort, collaborator, colleague, compatriot, comrade, *confrere,* worker

> *fellowship:* alliance, association, *bon camaraderie,* brotherhood, *camaraderie,* comity, communion, community, conviviality, esprit de corps, foundation, fraternity, freemasonry, geniality, sociality, sodality

**FEMALE**

**a:** distaff, effeminate, feminal, feminine, gynecian, gynecic, gynecocentric, gynecological, maidenly, matrilineal, muliebral, spindle, uterine, womanish, womanlike, womanly

**n:** *doyenne,* enchantress, *succubus,* woman

> *combining forms:* -ess, gyn-, gyno-, partheno-, -tress, -trix
>
> *femininity:* effeminacy, feminality, femineity, muliebriety

**FENCE**

**a:** fenced

**n:** bulwark, circumscription, corral, hoarding, impalement, *kraal,* paddock, paling, palisade, perimeter, picket fence, *septum,* stockade, windbreak

**v:** circumscribe, equivocate, impale

**FENCING**

> *fencer:* foilsman, *sabreur,* swordsman
>
> *sword:* epee, foil, saber

**FERMENTATION**

**a:** fermentative, zymotic

**n:** must, stum, zymology, zymurgy

> *combining form:* zymo-

**FEROCITY**

**a:** barbaric, feral, ferocious, sanguinary, tartarly, vandalic

**n:** acharnement, barbarity, ferity, impetuosity, savagery, truculency

**FERTILE**

**a:** abounding, abundant, exuberant, fecund, fructuous, fruitful, *in vitro,* productive, profuse, progenitive, prolific, proligerous, uberous

**n:** autogamy, enrichment, fecundation, fecundity, fertility, fertilization, fruitfulness, impregnation, pollination, prolification, prolificity, xenogamy

**v:** enrich, fecundate, fecundify, fertilize, fructify, generate, impregnate, pollinate, prolificate, spermatize *cell:* gamete, ovum, sperm, zygote

**FESTER**

**a:** putrefactive, suppurative

**n:** maturation, putrefaction, suppuration

**v:** abscess, corrupt, inflame, maturate, putrefy, rot, suppurate, ulcerate

**FESTIVE**

**a:** carnivalesque, celebrious, convivial, festivous, Mardi Gras, sportive

**n:** cavalcade, conviviality, epulation, festival, festivity, fiesta, gaiety, holiday, jamboree, jollification, jollity, Mardi Gras, merrymaking, pageant, symposium

*combining form:* -mas

**FEVER**

**a:** bustling, febrile, feverish, fiery, hectic, hyperpyrectic, inflammatory, phlogistic, pyretic, pyrexial, pyrexic

**n:** agitation, ague, calenture, delirium, febricity, febrility, feverishness, hyperpyrexia, hyperthermia, impetuosity, pyrexia

*combining forms:* febri-, pyr-

*reducing:* antipyretic, febrifugal

**FEW**

**n:** brevity, dearth, exigency, exiguity, fewness, minority, paucity, scantiness, sparcity, sparsity

*combining form:* oligo-

*government:* oligarchy

**FIB**

**n:** falsehood, prevarication, taradiddle, white lie

**FICKLE**

**a:** capricious, chameleonic, erratic, flighty, inconstant, labile, mercurial, quicksilver, unpredictable, whimsical

**n:** fickleness, inconstancy, levity, mercurality, quicksilver, unsteadiness

**FIDGETY**

**a:** agitated, anxious, fretful, nervous, restive, restless, uneasy

**FIELD**

**a:** agrarian, agrestial, agrestic, campestral, fallow

**n:** ambit, bailiwick, compass, croft, discipline, domain, glebe, jurisdiction, lea, *metier*, *milieu*, orbit, preserve, province, sphere, study, subject

*combining forms:* agr-, agri-, agro-, -drome

**FIEND**

**a:** avernal, demoniac(al), demonic(al), diabolical, fiendish, frantic, frenzied, infernal, malevolent, Mephistophelian, sardonic, satanic, saturnine

**n:** demon, energumen, fanatic, Mephistopheles

**FIERCE**

**a:** angry, barbaric, cruel, feral, ferine, ferocious, inhuman, leonine, lupine, merciless, pugnacious, savage, taurine, truculent, untrained, violent, wild

**n:** ferocity

**FIERY**

**a:** angry, animated, ardent, blazing, choleric, combustible, evangelistic, fervent, fervid, feverish, flammable, hot, igneous, impassioned, impetuous, inflamed, irascible, mettlesome, passionate, rash, red-hot, spirited, vehement, vivacious

**FIFTEEN**

**a:** quattrocento, quindecennial

**n:** quattrocento, quindecennial

**FIFTH**

**a:** quinary, quinquennial, quintan

**n:** quinquennial

**FIFTY**

**a:** quinquagenarian

**n:** quinquagenarian

**FIGHT**

**a:** agonostic, antagonistic, at loggerheads, bellicose, belligerent, disputatious, embroiled, fighting, fractious, hostile, internecine, militant, oppugnant, pugnacious, taurine, truculent

**n:** affray, altercation, bellicosity, belligerency, broil, confrontation, contention, contest, *contretemps,* controversy, crossfire, crusade, dissension, donnybrook, engagement, feud, fracas, fray, friction, joust, melee, pugnacity, sciamachy, skirmish, strife, tilting match, tussle, vendetta

**v:** attack, contest, dispute, impugn, militate, retaliate, tilt at

*fighter:* boxer, pugilist

## FIGMENT

**n:** apparition, ghost, image, phantasm, phantasmagoria, phantom, specter

## FIGURATIVE

**a:** allegorical, anagogical, metaphoric, parabolic, synecdochical, tralatitious, tropological

**n:** alliteration, anacoluthon, anadiplosis, anastrophe, antiphrasis, antithesis, antonomasia, apostrophe, assonance, asyndeton, conceit, ellipsis, erotema, euphemism, hendiadys, hypallage, hyperbole, irony, litotes, malapropism, meiosis, metaphor, metonymy, onomatopoeia, oxymoron, pathetic fallacy, personification, pleonasm, polysyndeton, prospopoeia, rhetorical question, simile, syllepsis, synecdoche, tautology, tmesis, trope, tropology, zeugma

**v:** metaphorize

## FIGURE

**a:** curvaceous, hourglass, pneumatic

**n:** digit, numeral

**v:** calculate, cipher, compute, count, reckon, solve, sum, think, total

## FILE

**n:** *dossier,* following, record, ring binder

## FILLED

**a:** congested, engorged, full, glutted, gorged, gravid, overcrowded, overfilled, replete, sated, satiated

**n:** amalgam, filler, filling, size

**v:** imbue, impregnate, inculcate, infuse, instill, permeate, pervade, replenish, saturate, suffuse

## FILMY

**a:** diaphanous, ethereal, hazy, insubstantial, membranous, misty, obscure, opaque, pellicular, pelliculate, pellucid, shadowy, tenuous, vaporous

## FILTH

**a:** augean, excremental, feculent, filthy, immund, impetiginous, noxious, obscene, ordurous, putrid, pythogenic, scatological, sordid, squalid, stercoraceous, verminous

**n:** contamination, corruption, defilement, excrement, *excreta, fecula,* feculence, filthiness, immundity, offal, ordure, pollution, putrefaction, putrescence, putridity, recrement, sordidness, squalidity, squalor

*attraction:* aischrolatreia, coprophilia, mysophilia, scatology

## FINAL

**a:** *ad extremum,* conclusive, consummative, consummatory, decisive, definitive, dernier, *en fin,* eventually, finally, finitive, last-ditch, peremptory, telic, terminal, terminative, ultimate, ultimately

**n:** climax, *coda, coup de grace,* culmination, definitude, *denouement,* destiny, epilogue, eschatology, finality, finitude, inevitability, omega, perfection, peroration, swan song, teleology, ultimateness, ultimatum

**v:** clinch, complete, finish

*combining forms:* epi-, tel-, teleo-, term-

## FINANCES

**a:** cameralistic, financial, fiscal, money, sumptuary

**n:** cameralistics, economics, exchequer, subvention, Wall Street

**v:** finance, guarantee, subsidize, underwrite

*office:* bursar, bursary, comptroller, responsible, treasury

*supporter:* angel, patron, promoter, sponsor

**FIND**

**a:** serendipitous

**n:** bonanza, *decouverte*, El Dorado, eureka, serendipity

**v:** bring to light, comprehend, descry, dig up, discover, fathom, pry out, root out, understand, unearth

**FINE**

**a:** attenuated, belletristic, comminuted, excellent, exquisite, homeopathic, impalpable, tenuous

**n:** adornment, *beaux arts*, *belles lettres*, *creme de la creme*, elite, finest, *ne plus supra*, *ne plus ultra*, nicety, nonesuch, nonpareil, ornamentation, *rara avis*, regalia

**FINGER**

**a:** dactyloid, digitate, digitiform, pentadactyl(ate), spatulate

**n:** dactyl, digit, pentadactylism, phalanges

**v:** interdigitate

*combining forms:* dactyl-, dactylo-

*finger hole:* ventage

*fingernail:* cuticle, lunula

*little:* minimus, pinkie, pinky

*print:* arch, dab, dactylogram, dactylography, loop, whorl

*ring:* annulary

*sign language:* dactylolgy

*thumb:* pollux

**FINISH**

**a:** accomplished, *au fait*, complete(d), consummated, consummatory, culminated, ending, finished, finishing, kaput, perfected, proficient, *soigne*, terminated

**n:** *coup de grace*, *terminus ad quem*, veneer

**v:** complete, dispatch, dispose, end, stop

**FIRE**

**a:** conflagratory, flammable, igneous, ignescent, incendiary, inflammable, pyrogenic, pyrophoric

**n:** combustion, conflagration, embers, holocaust, inferno, phlogiston, pyre, spontaneous combustion

**v:** conflagrate, gut, ignite

*combining form:* pyro-

*divination:* pyromancy

*fear:* pyrophobia

*fireplace:* hearth, hob, mantel

*love:* arson, firebug, incendiary, pyromania

**FIREWORKS**

**a:** pyrotechnical

**n:** *cartouche*, *feux d'artifice*, firecracker, fizgig, *girandole*, petard, punk, pyrotechnics, Roman candle, squib, *tourbillion*

**FIRM**

**a:** adamantine, determined, essential, established, ineradicable, inexpugnable, inflexible, inherent, insoluble, preemptory, resolute, staunch, steady, substantive, sustained, tenacious, unassailable, unflatering, unwavering, unyielding

**n:** adhesiveness, consistency, determination, persistence, resolution, solidarity, solidity, tenacity, vertebration

**FIRST**

**a:** *ab ovo*, aboriginal, elementary, embryonic, germinal, inaugural, inceptive, inchoate, incipient, indigenous, initial, initiatory, introductory, maiden, nascent, original, preeminent, *prima facie*, primeval, primitive, primordial, pristine, rudimental, rudimentary, seminal

**n:** aborigine, alpha, archetype, baptism of fire, beachhead, *cordon bleu*, debut, freshman, *grand prix*, precedence, preeminence, premier, premiere, primacy, *princeps*, priority, prototype, rudiment, salient, supremacy, unveiling

*born rights:* primogeniture

*combining forms:* fore-, proto-, ur-

**FISH**

**a:** halieutic, ichthyic, ichthyoid, ichthyological, ichthyomorphic, ichthyophagous, piscatorial, piscatory, piscine, piscivorous

**n:** fingerling, fry, nekton, piscifauna, piscinity, run, shoal, spawn, tiddler

> *chowder: bouillabaisse*
>
> *combining forms:* ichthy-, ichthyo-, pisc-, pisci-
>
> *fisherman:* angler, piscator
>
> *fishing:* halieutics, open season, piscation
>
> *science:* halieutics, ichthyology, piscatology

**FISSURE**

**a:** sulcate

**n:** breach, break, chasm, cleavage, flaw, gap, groove, opening, rift, split, *sulcus*

**FIT**

**a:** appropriate, *apropos, comme il faut,* condign, congruent, congruous, consonant, decorous, expedient, felicitous, fitting, ideal, idoneous, kosher, legitimate, pertinent, prudent, relevant, seemly

**n:** accessory, adaptability, adjunct, appropriateness, aproposity, aptitude, coaptation, competency, decorum, eligibility, expediency, fitness, fixture, idoneity, paroxysm, propriety, seemliness, seizure, soundness, suitability, tantrum

**v:** behoove, connect, dovetail, join, mesh

> *combining form:* -lepsy
>
> *physical:* apoplexy, convulsion, ictus, nympholepsy, paroxysm, pique, seizure

**FIVE**

**a:** pentagonal, pentamerous, quinary, quinate, quinquarticular, quinquennial, quintuple

**n:** *cinque,* cinquefoil, limerick, *lustrum,* pentacle, pentad, pentagon, pentagram, pentangle, quincunx, quinquennial, quinquennium, quintuplet

**v:** quintuple

> *combining forms:* pent-, penta-, quin-, quinqu-
>
> *events:* pentathlon
>
> *five-hundred:* quincentenary

**FIX**

**a:** dilemmatical, predicamental

**n:** cruciality, dilemma, implantation, plight, predicament

**v:** arrange, attach, concentrate, determine, implant, install, join, radicate, repair, stabilize

> *fixed:* embedded, engraved, entrenched, firm, immobile, immotile, immovable, immutable, ineradicable, inflexible, irreversible, irrevocable, sedentary, sessile, stabile, stubborn, unswerving, unyielding
>
> *fixed idea: idee fixe,* obsession
>
> *fixed price meal: prix fixe, table d'hote*

**FLABBY**

**a:** drooping, ductile, flaccid, languid, limp, plastic, supple

**n:** dewlap, jowl

**FLAG**

**a:** vexillary

**n:** ancient, *banderole,* banner, bannerol, *bougee,* bunting, burgee, colors, ensign, gonfalon, guidon, hoist, jack, *oriflamme,* pencel, pennant, pennon, pennoncel, standard, streamer, *vexillum,* waft, waif

**v:** flaunt, furl, hoist, strike, unfurl

> *study:* vexillology

**FLAGRANT**

**a:** ardent, egregious, evil, execrable, flagitious, glaring, heinous, infamous, malicious, nefarious, raging, rampant, vicious, wanton, wicked

**FLAKE**

**a:** desquamatory, exfoliative, flaking desquamative, lamellar, lamelliform, laminar

**n:** desquamation, exfoliation, lamina

**v:** chip, chisel, desquamate, exfoliate, peel, scale, strip

## FLAME

**a:** fulgurating, ignescent, inflammatory, lambent, volatile

**n:** fire, *flambeau, ignis fatuus,* jack-o'-lantern, luminescence, will-o'-the-wisp

## FLASH

**a:** flashy, fulgurant, fulgurating, fulgurous, garish, gaudy, iridescent, lancinating, meretricious, ostentatious, pyrotechnic(al), showy, tawdry

**n:** fulguration, iridescence

**v:** coruscate, fulgurate, glitter, scintillate, sparkle

## FLAT

**a:** bland, even, flush, horizontal, immature, insipid, jejune, juvenile, level, monotonous, palnate, parallel, planar, prone, prostrate, recumbent, splayfoot, spread-eagled, supine, tabular, uninteresting

**n:** esplanade, horizontality, insipidity, jejunity, mesa, monotony, plateau, prostration

    *combining forms:* plan-, plano-, platy-

## FLATTER

**a:** adulatory, effusive, flattering, gnathonic, ingratiating, ingratiatory, obsequious, panegyric, servile, sycophantic, toadying, unctuous

**n:** adulation, allurement, banishment, blandishment, blarney, cajolement, cajolery, flattery, obsequiousness, sycophancy, unction, unctuosity

**v:** beguile, blandish, cajole, fawn, ingratiate, kowtow, lionize, panegyrize, praise, sycophantize, truckle, wheedle

    *flatterer: adulateur, adulatrice,* apple-polisher, claque, *courtier,* eulogist, flunky, lackey, lickspittle, minion, myrmidon, *proneur,* sycophant

## FLAVOR

**a:** agreeable, flavorful, flavorsome, palatable, tasty

**n:** *haut gout,* tang, taste

**v:** relish, savor, taste

## FLAWLESS

**a:** faultless, immaculate, impeccable, impeccant, indefectible, irreproachable, perfect

**n:** flawlessness, immaculacy, impeccability, indefectibility, perfection

## FLEE

**n:** flight

**v:** abscond, absquatulate, decamp, depart, elope, evade, fugitate, hightail, run away, scarper, skedaddle, vamoose

    *person:* emigrant, *emigre,* fugitive, refugee

## FLEECY

**a:** fluffy, lanate, laniferous, woolly

**n:** *flocculus*

## FLEETING

**a:** deciduous, diaphanous, ephemeral, ephemerous, ethereal, evanescent, fugacious, gossamer, impermanent, instantaneous, momentary, perishable, preterient, semelfactive, shadowy, temporal, transient, transitory, unenduring, unsubstantial, vanishing, vaporous, volatile

**n:** caudicity, diaphaneity, ephemerality, ethereality, fugacity, impermanence, volatility

    *fleet of ships:* argosy, armada, flotilla

## FLESH

**a:** *incarnadine,* incarnate, sarcous

**n:** carrion, corpulence, fleshniness, obesity

**v:** humanize, incarnate

    *combining forms:* carn-, carni-, sarc-, sarco-

    *eating:* carnivorous, creophagous, sarcophagic, sarcophagous, sarcophilous

**FLEXIBLE**

**a:** compliant, ductile, limber, lissom, lithe, manageable, pliable, resilient, supple, tractable, willowy

**n:** amenability, elasticity, flexibility, lissomeness, maneuverability, mobility, plasticity, tractability

**FLICKERING**

**a:** fulgurating, lambent, lancinating, meteoric, uncertain

**v:** blink, flair, flame, flicker, flit, flutter, glint, gutter, oscillate, shimmer, wave, wink

**FLIGHT**

**a:** Gaderine, volitant

**n:** elopement, exoaus, fugitation, hegira, holding pattern, long haul, migration, trajectory, volitation

*flightless:* ratite, struthious

**FLIGHTY**

**a:** anile, capricious, fickle, foolish, frivolous, giddy, helter-skelter, hoity-toity, imaginative, mercurial, pompous, quicksilver, quixotic, scatterbrained, utopian, volatile

**FLIMSY**

**a:** diaphanous, enfeebled, ethereal, fragile, gossamer, implausible, ineffective, insignificant, insubstantial, nebulous, poor, superficial, tenuous, trifling, unsubstantial

**n:** diaphaneity, ethereality, flimsiness, tenuity, tenuousness, unsubstantiality

**FLIPPANT**

**a:** bold, brassy, brazen, forward, fresh, sassy, saucy, smart-alecky

**n:** flipness, persiflage, *persifleur*, sassiness, sauciness

**v:** persiflate

**FLIRT**

**a:** amorous, flirtatious, vampirish

**n:** coquetry, dalliance, flirtation, loveplay, *passade*, philander, toying

**v:** *coquet*, dally, gad about, gallivant, philander, tease, toy, trifle

*female:* amourette, amoureuse, coquette, intrigante, nymph, nymphet

*male:* coquet, philanderer

**FLOAT**

**a:** floating, natant, supernatant

**n:** buoyancy, *caisson*, camel, flotsam, jetsam, levitation, outrigger, pontoon

**v:** hover, levitate, waft

**FLOCK**

**a:** flocking, gregarious

**n:** drove, herd, skein

**FLOG**

**v:** chastise, flagellate, lambaste, scourge, whip

**FLOOD**

**a:** cataclysmic, deluginous, diluvial, flooded, flooding, inundatory, postdiluvian

**n:** alluvion, avalanche, cataclysm, cataract, debacle, deluge, downpour, flash flood, freshet, inundation, spate, torrent

**v:** deluge, inundate, overflow, overwhelm

**FLORID**

**a:** erubescent, flourishing, flowery, melismatic, ornate, rubescent, rubicund, rufous, showy

**n:** erubescence, floridity, rubescence, rubicundity

**FLOUR**

**a:** farinaceous, floury, starchy

**n:** farina

**v:** dredge

**FLOURISH**

**a:** affluent, efflorescent, flourishing, lush, luxuriant, palmy, prosperous, rampant, verdant, verdurous

**n:** affluence, circumgyration, efflorescence, fanfare, quirk, *tanatara*

**v:** blossom, brandish, burgeon, effloresce, flaunt, prosper

## FLOWER

**a:** anthophorous, bombastic, efflorescent, embellished, euphuistic, floral, florescent, florid, floriferous, florulent, flowering, grandiloquent, inflated, reefflorescent, remontant, rhapsodic, rubescent, sessile

**n:** amaranth, ament, angiosperm, annual, anthesis, bouquet, catkin, corsage, cultivar, efflorescence, florescence, glomerule, heliotrope, horticulture, hybrid, inflorescence, nosegay, perennial, posy, truss

    *arranging:* ikebana

    *combining forms:* antho-, -anthous, flor-

    *description:* anthography

    *feeding on:* anthophagous, anthophilous

    *flowerless:* agamous, cryptogamous

    *living among:* anthophilous

## FLOWING

**a:** canorous, cantable, confluent, coursing, cursive, derivative, deriving, effluent, emanant, mellifluent, mellifluous, mellisonant, perfluent, profluent, sonorous

**n:** confluence, effluence, efflux, emanation, liquidity, *profluvium*

    *back:* refluent, reflux, regurgitating

    *combining forms:* -rrhagia, -rrhea

## FLUCTUATE

**a:** ambivalent, mercurial

**n:** ambivalence, fluctuation, oscillation, vacillation

**v:** alter, change, deviate, oscillate, sway, undulate, vacillate, vary, wander, waver

## FLUENCY

**a:** effortless, euphonious, facile, fluent, glib, insincere, liquid, loquacious, mellifluous, unembarrassed, verbose

**n:** *copia verboru,* eloquence, facundity,

grandiloquence, liquidity, loquaciousness, loquacity, mellifluence, verbosity

## FLUTTER

**a:** fluttering, palpitant, volitant

**n:** confusion, palpitation, vibration, volitation

**v:** fan, flap, flit, fluctuate, palpitate, quiver, throb, tremble, twitter, vibrate, volitate, wave

## FLY

**a:** volant, volitant, volitorial

**n:** aviation

**v:** barnstorm, circumnavigate, hedgehop, hover, skirr, volitate

## FOCAL

**n:** *centrum,* cynosure, epicenter, focus, *nidus,* nucleus, *omphalos,* point, *umbilicus*

## FOE

**n:** adversary, antagonist, combatant, competitor, enemy, opponent

## FOG

**a:** brumous, caliginous, confused, foggy, nubilous, tenuous, vague, vaporous

**n:** bewilderment, brume, perplexity, uncertainty, vapor, whiteout

**v:** blur, cloud, haze, vaporize

## FOLD

**a:** corrugated, folded

**n:** congregation, convolution, *gyri, plica, sulci,* volution

**v:** concertina, crease, crimp, curl, embosom, envelop, intertwine, plicate, pucker, quill, replicate, wrinkle

## FOLIAGE

**a:** foliaceous, umbrageous

**n:** boscage, leafage, leaves, shade, spray, umbrage, verdure

## FOLLOW

**a:** consecutive, consequential, ensuant, ensuing, *et sequens,* following, sequent, sequential, serial, seriatim, subsequent

**n:** abettor, acolyte, adherent, aficionado, apostle, attendant, audience, *claque, clique,* cohort, devotee, disciple, enthusiast, entourage, escort, fanatic, follower, henchman, minion, partisan, retinue, sequacity, *sequitur,* tractability, votary

**v:** drag, ensue, hound, persist, succeed, supervene

> *does not: lucus a non lucendo, nonsequitur*

**FOLLY**

**n:** absurdity, asininity, *betise,* desipience, fatuity, idiocy, imprudence, inanity, indiscretion, indulgence, infatuation, lunacy, whim

**FOND**

**a:** affectionate, amatory, amorous, ardent, devoted, enamored, loving, uxorious

**n:** affection, appetite, attachment, diathesis, fondness, partiality, penchant, predilection, propensity, tendresse

> *combining forms:* phil-, -phile

**FOOD**

**a:** alimental, alimentary, alimentative, cibarian, cibarous, culinary, gastronomic, nutrimental, nutritious, nutritive, omnivorous, pantophagic, pantophagous, polyphagous, trophic

**n:** aliment, comestible, cooking, cuisine, edible, fast food, grist, *ingesta,* menu, nourishment, nurture, nutrient, nutriment, nutrition, nutritive, *pabulum,* provender, refection, subsistence, sustenance, sustentation, swill, viand, victual

**v:** cook, garnish, gourmandize, ingest

> *conversion to energy:* metabolism
>
> *craving:* allotriophagy, geophagy, *parorexia,* pica
>
> *eating living:* biophagous
>
> *full of:* glutted, gorged, replete, sated, satiated
>
> *leftover: rechauffe*
>
> *lover: bon-vivant, connoisseur, epicure, gastronome(r),* gourmet

> *picky:* monophagous, oligophagous
>
> *preparation:* cuisine, gastronomy, *haute cuisine*
>
> *science:* cuisine, dietetics, gastronomy, nutrition, sitology, trophology
>
> *uncooked: au naturel*

**FOOL**

**a:** adventurous, fatuous, fooled, foolhardy, foolish, Icarian, inane, incautious, inept, infatuated, preposterous, puerile, reckless, silly, stupid, temerarious

**n:** addlepate, blatherskite, blunderer, booby, cretin, duffer, dunderhead, fop, idiot, imbecile, mooncalf, morosoph, nincompoop, ninny, nudnick, numskull, *radoteur, schlemiel,* simpleton, zombie

**v:** cheat, clown, victim

> *foolishness:* absurdity, buffoonery, fatuity, gaffe, ineptitude, insipidity, irrationality, ridiculosity, solecism, temerity
>
> *fool's gold:* iron pyrites, pyrite

**FOOT**

**a:** *a pied,* pedestrian, plantar, volar

**n:** feet, pedal extremity, trotter

> *combining forms:* -pede, pedi-, -pod, -pode
>
> *footprint:* moulage, spoor, vestige, vestigia
>
> *misshapen:* clubfoot, splayfoot, talipes
>
> *specialist:* chiropodist, pedicure, podiatrist

**FOR**

> *and against: pro et contra*
>
> *combining form.* pro-
>
> *example:* e.g., *exempli gratia*
>
> *now: pro tunc*
>
> *the present: pro nunc*
>
> *this purpose: ad hoc*

**FORBEARANCE**

**a:** compassionate, forbearing, forgiving, indulgent, lenient, longanimous, patient, soft, sympathetic, tolerant n: clemency, compassion, fortitude, leniency, lenity, longanimity, mercy, patience, resignation, toleration

## FORBIDDEN

a: inhibitory, prohibited, taboo, *tabu, tref, verboten*

v: ban, enjoin, forbid, inhibit, interdict, prevent, prohibit

> *forbiding:* dangerous, disagreeable, formidable, hazardous, menacing, repellant

## FORCE

a: agonistic, artificial, centrifugal, centripetal, coercive, constraint, contrived, dynamic, emphatic, forced, Herculean, impactful, intrusive, involuntary, mannered, *recherche*, resounding, stiff, stilted, tantamount, titanic, vigorous, *voulu*

n: act of god, coercion, cogency, compulsion, constraint, duress, dynamism, equilibrium, *force majeure*, impetus, import, impulsion, inertia, juggernaut, momentum, penal servitude, potency, propulsion, restraint, *torque*, validity, vector, *vis*

v: actuate, bludgeon, bulldoze, coerce, constrain, countervail, depose, dislodge, dragoon, eject, evict, exact, extort, extrude, foist, impel, oblige, obtrude, oust, railroad, repress, shanghai, strong-arm, subdue, subjugate, suction, supplant, suppress, usurp, wrest

## FOREBODING

a: adumbrated, apocalyptic, apprehensive, Delphian, Delphic, divinatory, fatidic, foretelling, oracular, portentous, premonitory, presageful, presentient, prophetic, pythonic

n: adumbration, apocalypse, apprehension, augury, clairvoyance, divination, ESP, foreshadowing, handwriting on the wall, portent, precognition, premonition, presage, presentiment, prognostication, soothsaying

v: adumbrate, augur, auspicate, bespeak, betoken, bode, forecast, foreshadow, foretell, portend, predict, prefigure, presage, presignify, prognosticate, prophesy, vaticinate

## FORECAST

a: divinatory, oracular, orphic, precognitive, prescient, prognostic, prophetic, visionary

n: foretune-telling, horoscope, meteorology, prognosis, prognostication

v: foretell, prognosticate, prophesy

> *foreknowledge:* foresight, intuition, precognition, precognitum, prescience, prospection, prudence
>
> *foresee:* adumbrate, anticipate, divine, envisage, envision, foretell
>
> *foretaste:* prelibation

## FOREFATHER

a: ancestorial, ancestral, primogenitive, primogenitorial

n: ancestor, antecedent, ascendant, forebear, forerunner, precursor, primogenitor, procreator, progenitor, prototype

## FOREFRONT

n: *avant-garde*, beachhead, firing line, van, vanguard

## FOREGO

a: antecedent, foregoing, preceding

v: eschew, neglect, pass, precede, renounce, sacrifice

## FOREHEAD

a: frontal, metopic, sinciputal

n: *frons*, frontlet, metopion, sinciput

v: recede

## FOREIGN

a: adventitious, adventive, alien, exotic, extraneous, extrinsic, forane, heterochthnous, heterogeneous, irrelevant, peregrinate, peregrine, tramontane, ultramontane, untramundane

n: extraneity, foreignness, heterogeneity, ultima Thule

> *combining form:* xeno-
>
> *fear:* xenophobia
>
> *foreigner:* alien, auslander, denizen, exoteric, outlander, peregrine, Philistine, tramontane

*lover:* xenophile

## FORERUNNER

**n:** ancestor, antecedent, antecessor, *avant-garde*, forebear, harbinger, herald, pioneer, precursor, predecessor, premonitor, presager, trailblazer, vanguard

## FOREST

**a:** nemoral, sylvan, sylvatic, sylvestrian

**n:** glade, *purlieu,* silviculture

## FOREVER

**a:** *ad infinitum,* everlasting, *in adfinitum, in perpetuity, in perpetuum,* incessantly, permanent

## FORFEIT

**a:** confiscatory

**n:** amercement, confiscation, forfeiture

**v:** amerce, confiscate, lose, surrender

## FORGED

**a:** counterfeit, spurious, supposititious

**n:** counterfeit, fabrication, forgery, invention, pseudograph, supposition, utter

**v:** counterfeit, forge

## FORGET

**a:** absentminded, abstracted, careless, forgetful, Lethean, nepenthean, oblivious, preoccupied, unaware, unmindful

**n:** amnesia, forgetfulness, *lethe,* limbo, oblivescence, oblivion, obliviscence

**v:** obliviate

*cause: nepenthe*

## FORGIVING

**a:** absolutory, clement, compassionate, conciliatory, indulgent, magnanimous, merciful, placable, venial

**n:** absolution, amnesty, clemency, conciliation, condonation, forgiveness, indulgence, leniency, remission

**v:** condone, excuse, forgive, pardon

## FORK

**a:** bidigitate, bifid, bifurcate, branching, dichotomous, divided, forcipate, forficulate, forked, furcate, furciform

**n:** bifurcation, dichotomization, dichotomy, divarication, forking, *fourchette, furcula,* tine, trident

**v:** bifurcate, bisect, branch, dichotomize, divaricate

## FORM

**a:** constructive, conventional, creative, *de rigueur,* developmental, fictile, formal, formative, nascent, perfunctory, plastic, *pro forma,* ritualistic

**n:** ceremony, configuration, conformation, contour, conventionality, echelon, formation, hierarchization, linearity, liturgy, manifestation, nascency, outline, perspective, phalanx, ritual, rule, shape, silhouette, stratification

**v:** crystallize, make

*beginning to:* aborning, nascent, parturient

*combining forms:* -fy, -gen, -genic, -genous, -morph, morph-, -morphic, morpho-

*formless:* amorphous, aplastic, chaotic, heterogeneous, immaterial, inchoate, incorporeal, nebulous, spiritual

*having various:* allotrophic, allotropic, polymorphic, polymorphous

*human and animal:* therianthropic

*identical:* isomorphic

*single:* monomorphic, monomorphous

*study of word:* morphology

## FORMAL

**a:** academic, ceremonial, ceremonious, conventional, decorous, dogmatic, formalistic, liturgical, mechanical, old-fashioned, pedantic, pharisaic, punctilious, ritualistic, scholastic, stiff, stylized, syntactical, traditional

**n:** academicism, academism, ceremonialism, ceremony, convenance, conventionality, etiquette, formality, liturgy, pedantry, protocol, *punctilio*, ratification, regularity, ritualism, rituality, sanction, solemnity, validation

## FORMER

**a:** anamnestic, ancient, antecedent, anterior, bygone, cidevant, elapsed, erewhile, erstwhile, one-time, *quondam*, whilom

**n:** antecedent, cidevant, *emeritus*

   *combining form:* ex-
   *life: anamnesis*

## FORMULA

**a:** *doctrinaire*, doctrinal, formulaic

**n:** alkahest, doctrine, *nostrum*, philosophy, prescription, recipe

**v:** concretize, confect, fabricate, forge, formulate, materialize, synthesize

## FORTIFY

**a:** castellated

**n:** bastion, blockhouse, bulwark, bunker, castle, defilade, enceinte, fastness, fortification, *lunette*, palisade, *parados*, rampart, *redan*, redoubt, retrenchment, stockade, stronghold, traverse

**v:** lace, munify

## FORTUNE

**a:** auspicious, beneficial, benign, benignant, *dexter*, fortunate, opportune, propitious, prosperous, reasonable, rich, serendipitous, timely, vicissitudinous

**n:** destiny, fate, fortuity, luck, prosperity, serendipity, success, vicissitude

   *by cards:* cartomancy, tarot
   *by crystal ball:* catoptromancy, scrying
   *by dreams:* oneiromancy
   *by fire:* pyromancy
   *by ghosts:* necromancy, sciomancy
   *by palm:* chiromancy, palmistry
   *by planet position:* horoscope
   *fortune-teller:* necromancer, Nostradamus, physiognomist, prognosticator, soothsayer

*fortune-telling:* augury, clairvoyance, divination, prognostication, prophesy, soothsaying

*goddess:* Tyche

*random book passages:* bibliomancy

## FORTY

**a:** quadragenarian, quadragenarious, quadragesimal

**n:** quadragenarian

   *forty-five degree arc:* octant

## FOUL

**a:** carious, disagreeable, entangled, feculent, fetid, leprous, loathsome, mephitic, noisome, noxious, pestilent(ial), polluted, putrescent, putrid, treacherous

**n:** *colluvies*, feculence, fetidness, foulness, loathsomeness, mephitis, noisomeness, pestilence, pollution, putrefaction, putrescence, putridity, stench

**v:** stink

   *foul-smelling:* fetid, malodorous, rancid, stinking

## FOUNDATION

**n:** base, basis, endowment, fundament, pile, *pilotis*, *principum*, raft, stereobate, substratum

## FOUR

**a:** quadrigeminal, quadripartite, quadrivial, quadruple, quadruplicate, quaternary, quaternate, tetrad

**n:** quadrigeminal, quadripartition, quadrivium, quadrumvirate, quadruple, quartet, quaternary, quaternity, tetrad, tetralogy

**v:** quadrisect

   *children:* quadruplets
   *combining forms:* quadr-, quadri-, quadru-, tetr-, tetra-
   *dimensional:* hyperspace, tesseract
   *every four years:* Olympiad, quadrennial, quadrennium
   *four-hundredth:* quadricentennial, quatercentenary

*legged animal:* quadruped, tetrapod

*letter word:* tetragram

*liberal arts:* quadrivium

*lines:* quatrain

*multiply by:* quadruple

*sided:* quadrangle, quadrilateral, tetragon

## FOX

a: alopecoid, foxlike, vulpine

n: Reynard

*female:* vixen

## FRACTION

a: aliquot, decimal, fractional, fragmental, fragmentary, improper, inconsiderable, insignificant, proper, reciprocal, segmental, vulgar

n: fragment, modicum, moiety, *quanta, quantum,* segment

  *number above:* dividend, numerator

  *number below:* denominator, divisor

## FRAGILE

a: diaphanous, ephemeral, ethereal, evanescent, fleeting, frangible, nebulous, tenuous, unsubstantial

n: diaphaneity, ephemerality, ethereality, evanescence, fragility, nebulosity, tenuity

## FRAGMENT

a: fractional

n: *analecta,* chrestomathy, *collectanea,* debris, detritus, fraction, *morceau,* morsel, residue, rubble, *scrapiana,* segment, shard, shrapnel, smithereens, spall, splinter

  *assemblage:* collage, montage

## FRAGRANT

a: ambrosiac, ambrosial, aromatic, balmy, odoriferous, odorous, redolent, refreshing, savory, smelly

n: aroma, aromaticity, bouquet, *effluvium,* emanation, fragrance, redolence

v: aromatize

## FRAILTY

a: brittle, fragile, frail, frangible, infirm, sickly, valetudinarian

n: defect, flaw, foible, imperfection, infirmity, insubstantiality, susceptibility, tenuity, tenuousness, vice, weakness

## FRAMEWORK

n: anatomy, cadre, constraints, fabric, gantry, husk, lattice, macrostructure, parameters, *parenchyma,* pattern, skeleton tenter, stanchion, superstructure, support, trellis

## FRANK

a: artless, bluff, blunt, brusque, candid, communicative, curt, demonstrative, explicit, forthcoming, forthright, foursquare, gruff, guileless, informative, ingenu(e), ingenuous, manifest, *naive,* nononsense, open, outspoken, simple, straightforward, unconstrained, unreserved, unvarnished, up-front

## FRANTIC

a: berserk, delirious, demoniac(al), demonic(al), frenzied, intense, maniac(al), obsessed, phrenetic, rabid, raging, raving, wild, zealous

n: frenzy

## FRAUD

a: clandestine, counterfeit, duplicitous, fraudulent, perfidious, sinister, spurious, surreptitious

n: adventurer, artifice, charlatan, circumvention, conjurer, deception, delusion, dissimulation, duplicity, empiric, fraudulence, humbug, hypocrite, imposition, imposter, imposture, mountebank, prestidigitator, pretender, stratagem, trickster

v: embezzle, salt, trick

## FREAK

a: bizarre, capricious, crochety, eccentric, fanciful, freakish, notional, uncertain, vagarious, whimsical

n: *capriccio,* caprice, crochet, *lusus, lusus naturae,* monstrosity, mutation, sport, vagary, whimsicality

**FRECKLE**

**a:** lentiginous

**n:** ephelides, *ephelis*, lentigo, liver spot, *macula*

**FREE**

**a:** *ad lib*, apathetic, autonomic, autonomous, cavalier, complimentary, degage, emancipated, exempt, frank, generous, *gratis*, gratuitous, independent, indifferent, ingenuous, jaunty, latitudinal, latitudinous, lenient, prodigal, *sans souci*, sovereign, spontaneous, unburdened, unconcerned, unencumbered, unlimited, unrestrained, unrestricted, vagile, voluntary

**n:** authority, autonomy, *carte blanche*, civil liberty, disengagement, dispensation, emancipation, freedom, immunity, impunity, independence, *laissez-aller*, latitude, leeway, liberation, liberty, license, manumission, parole

**v:** absolve, detach, disburden, disencumber, disentangle, emancipate, enfranchise, exculpate, exonerate, extricate, manumit, unfetter, unshackle, vindicate

*gift:* gratuity, *lagniappe, largesse*

**FREEZING**

**a:** cold, congealative, frozen, gelid, hyperborean, immobile, petrified, refrigerated, solidified

**n:** congealation, cryonics, gelation, gelidity, permafrost, solidification, tundra

**v:** coagulate, congeal, freeze, jell, solidify

*combining form:* cryo-

**FRENCH**

**a:** Gallic

*combining forms:* Franco-, Gallic-, Gallo-

*hate:* Francophobe, gallophobe

*love:* Francophile, gallomania, gallophile

**FRENZY**

**a:** berserk, corybantic, frantic, frenzied, furibund, hectic, nympholeptic, on the rampage, orgasmic, orgiastic, rampaging

**n:** deliration, delirium, fanaticism, mania, nympholepsy, orgasm, rabidity, *raptus*

**FREQUENCY**

**a:** common, continuous, frequent, habitual, normal, persistent, predominant, prevailing, prevalent, recurrent, repeated

**n:** commonality, incidence, *ogive*, perpetuality, prevalence

*visitor: habitue*

**FRESH**

**a:** blooming, bright, healthy, inexperienced, invigorating, lively, neoteric, original, striking, succulent, unspoiled, verdure, vernal, vibrant, vigorous, vivid, youthful

**n:** crispness, freshening, freshness, innovation, invigoration, newness, novelty, refurbishment, renovation, spontaneity, succulency, *tabula rasa*, vernalization, vividity, youthfulness

**v:** freshen, modernize, refurbish, renovate, vernalize

**FRETFUL**

**a:** fractious, ill-humored, impatient, irascible, irritable, peevish, petulant, querulous, restive, restless, waspish

**n:** irritability

**FRICTION**

**n:** attrition, erosion, traction

*combining form:* tribo-

**FRIEND**

**a:** accessible, affable, affectionate, amiable, amicable, *bonhomous*, compatible, congenial, convivial, cordial, courteous, *debonair*, expansive, favorable, fraternal, friendly, genial, gregarious, jovial, propitious, sociable, sympathetic

**n:** adherent, *alter ego*, benefactor, *bon ami*, boon companion, catercousin, colleague, companion, compeer, confidant, *confidante, confrere*, crony, devotee, familiar, follower, intimate, partisan, patron, protege, sectary, sidekick _friendship:_ affinity, amicability, amity, _camaraderie, esprit de corps,_ friendliness, graciousness, gregariousness, hospitality, intimacy, rapprochement, sociability

## FRIGHTEN

**a:** appalling, cowardly, daunting, discouraging, forbidding, formidable, frightening, frightful, ghastly, grotesque, hideous, horrendous, horrific, perilous, portentous, prodigious, rebarbative, redoubtable, repelling, scared

**v:** cow, discomfit, gorgonize, intimidate, petrify, terrorize, unnerve

## FRIGID

**a:** cold, gelid, glacial, hyperborean, passionless

**n:** frigidity, gelidity

## FRILL

**n:** affectation, bauble, decoration, extravagance, jabot, lace, _papillote, ruche,_ ruff, ruffle, superfluity, tucker

## FRINGED

**a:** circumferential, lacinate, laciniose

**n:** border, boundary, edge, fringe, periphery, selvage

## FRIVOLOUS

**a:** frolicsome, gay, hoity-toity, inconsequential, irrelevant, playful, superficial

**n:** absurdity, frivolity, irrationality, levity, nugacity, superficiality

   _person:_ futilitarian, _soubrette_

## FROG

**a:** anuran, batrachian, batrachoid, ranine, salientian

**n:** amphibian

   _eating:_ batrachophagous

## FROLIC

**a:** antic, frolicsome, larkish, mirthful, playful, prankish

**n:** _boutade,_ caper, caprice, carousal, festivity, frolicsomeness, gambol, marlock, roguery, vagary

## FROM

   _combining forms:_ ab-, de-, ex-
   _the beginning:_ ab initio, ab ovo
   _within:_ endogenous
   _without:_ exogenous

## FRONT

**a:** anterior, _avant-garde_

**n:** anterior, anteriority, _anticus, avant-garde,_ countenance, facade, frontispiece, obverse, physiognomy, recto, vanguard

   _combining form:_ fore-

## FROST

**a:** boreal, frosty, gelid, pruinose, pruinous, unfriendly

**n:** frostness, gelidity, hoarfrost, rime

   _combining form:_ cryo-

## FROTH

**a:** effervescent, frothy, spumescent

**n:** despumation, effervescence, foam, spume

## FRUGALITY

**a:** austere, frugal, parsimonious, simple, spartan, thrifty

**n:** exiguity, parcity, parsimony, paucity, thrift

## FRUIT

**a:** abounding, citrus, exuberant, fecund, feracious, fertile, fructiferous, fructificative, fructuous, fruitful, fruitive, gravid, procreant, prolific, proligerous, uberous

**n:** clingstone, drupe, fecundity, freestone, fruitfulness, fruition, frutescence, gravidity, pome, productiveness, prolificacy

**v:** fructify

   _combining forms:_ carp-, -carpy, -fruct, fruct-, fructi-, -frug, frug-, frugi-

   _eating:_ carpophagous, frugivorous

   _study:_ pomology

   _unbearing:_ acarpous, barren, fruitless, futile, infertile, infructuous, sterile

**FRUSTRATE**

**a:** frustrating, self-defeating, stultifying

**n:** circumvention, disappointment, frustration, impediment, nympholepsy, stultification

**v:** baffle, circumvent, exasperate, impede, outwit, stultify, tantalize, torment

**FULFILL**

**a:** consummative, fulfilling, implementary

**n:** accomplishment, consummation, end, execution, fruition, fulfillment, implementation

**v:** accomplish, consummate, execute, fructify, implement, redeem

**FULL**

**a:** abounding, abundant, brimming, comprehensive, copious, fraught, gorged, gutted, orotund, plenary, plentitudinous, plethoric, replete, resonant, rotund, sated, satiated, sonorous, surfeited, teeming, torrential, unabridged, unexpurgated

**n:** abundance, amplitude, complement, congestion, copiosity, copiousness, fullness, plentitude, plenum, plethora, repletion, satiation, satiety, surfeit

*combining form:* -ulent

**FUNCTION**

**a:** attributive, functional, occupational, operational, operative, physiological, psychogenetic, psychological, psychosomatic, utilitarian

**n:** attribute, attribution, functioning, mapping, metabolism, occupation, perquisite, psychogenesis, psychosomatics, purpose

*impaired:* afunction, dysfunction, malfunction

*lack of:* abiotrophy, hysteria

*various:* polymorphic, polymorphous

**FUNDAMENTAL**

**a:** basic, constitutional, essential, indispensable, inherent, primal, primary, primitive, substratal, substrate, substrative, ultimate, underlying

**n:** basic, essential, essentiality, fundamentality, intrinsicality, primality, primitivity, *quintessence*, ultimacy

**FUNERAL**

**a:** elegaic, epicedial, epicedian, exequial, funebrial, funebrous, funerary, funereal, monodic, mortuary, sepulchral, threnodial, threnodic

**n:** *cortege, exequy,* inhumation, interment, last post, obsequy, sepulcher, sepulchre, sepulture, solemnities, taps, wake

*words or song:* coronach, dirge, elegy, eloge, *encomium,* epicede, epicedium, epitaph, monody, obituary, requiem, threnody

*worker:* mortician, pallbearer, undertaker

**FUNNY**

**a:** bawdy, comical, diverting, facetious, farcical, gelastic, harlequin, hilarious, humorous, jocose, jocular, laughable, ludicrous, riotous, risible, uproarious, waggish, zany

**n:** facetiosity, flippancy, frivolity, levity, ridiculosity

*bone:* humerus, olecranon

*yet serious:* ludicropathetic, ludicroserious

**FURNITURE**

**a:** mobiliary, well-appointed

**n:** appointments, bric-a-brac, fitment, fixture, upholstery

**FURROW**

**a:** sulcate

**n:** chamfer, groove, *sulcus*

**FURTHER**

**a:** additional, ulterior

*furthest:* farthest, *ne plus ultra*

**FURY**

**a:** energetic, frenzied, furibund, furious, impetuous, maniacal, turbulent n: agitation, anger, frenzy, impetuosity, ire, madness, rabidity, rage, truculence, truculency, vehemence, wrath

**FUSE**

n: amalgamation, ankylosis, conflation, connation, synchronism, syncretism

v: amalgamate, ankylose, anneal, blend, coalesce, conflate, connate, grow together, join, meld, merge, synchronize, syncretize, weld

**FUSS**

a: choosy, discerning, discriminating, exquisite, fastidious, finical, finicky, fussy, grandmotherly, meticulous, overnice, persnickety, picky, precious, prissy, punctilious, quibbling, scrupulous

n: hubbub, pedantry, precisian, stickler

**FUTILE**

a: abortive, frivolous, fruitless, futilitarian, inadequate, ineffective, ineffectual, otiose, sterile, unrewarding

n: frivolity, fruitlessness, futility, inadequacy, ineffectuality, otiosity, uselessness

**FUTURE**

a: imminent, impending, prospective, subsequent

n: contingency, eventuality, futurity, millennium, posterity, prospect, vista

v: envisage, envision

*combining form:* -mancy

**GAIETY**

**a:** affable, amiable, blithe, buoyant, *cavalier*, convivial, *debonaire*, ecstatic, effervescent, euphoric, gay, genial, jaunty, joyous, phrenetic, rhapsodic, *sans-souci*, spirited

**n:** animation, buoyancy, ebullience, exhilaration, exuberance, festivity, geniality, jocularity, jocundity, jollification, jollity, joviality, jubilation, merrymaking, *nepenthe*, nonchalance, revelry, sprightliness, vivacity

**GAIN**

**a:** commercial, compensatory, gainful, mercenary, profitable, remunerative, remuneratory, venal

**n:** acquirement, acquisition, augmentation, compensation, emolument, enhancement, fiscality, increment

**v:** accomplish, achieve, acquire, obtain, outflank

**GALL**

**a:** annoying

**n:** acerbity, anger, assurance, audacity, bitterness, effrontery, impudence, presumption, rancor, temerity, wormwood

**GALLANT**

**a:** brave, *cavalier*, chivalresque, chivalric, chivalrous, magnanimous, stately, urbane

**n:** bravery, gallantry

**GAMBLING**

**a:** aleatory

**n:** bet, casino, poker, racing, roulette, tombola

**v:** brave, hazard, risk, venture

*dealer:* croupier

*gambler:* bettor, pone, punter

**GANG**

**n:** *Camorra, camorrista, canaille, carbonari,* mob

**GAP**

**a:** hiatal, lacunal, lacunar, parenthetical

**n:** abyss, adjournment, aperture, *caesura*, canyon, chasm, cleavage, cleft, *couloir*, cranny, crevice, *diastema*, discontinuity, fissure, gulch, gully, hiatus, hole, interim, intermission, *interregnum*, interruption, interspace, interstice, interval, lacuna, loophole, parenthesis, ravine, recess, respite, rift, synapse, vacuity, void

**GAPE**

**a:** cavernous, gaping, oscitant, patulous

**n:** dehiscence, oscitance, oscitation

**v:** dehisce, oscitate

**GARBAGE**

**n:** offal, recrement, refuse, rubbish, scrap, sewage, *sordes*, trash, waste

**GARDEN**

**a:** hortensial, landscaped

**n:** *parterre, potagerie*

*party: fete champetre*

**GARMENT**

**n:** habiliment, vestment

*religious:* cassock, *chasuble, soutane*

**GARNISH**

**n:** adornment, embellishment, garnishment, *jardiniere*, ostentation, panoply v: adorn, decorate, diamondize, embellish, furbish, lard

## GATHER

n: agglutination, assemblage, assembly, collection, *colluvies*, concourse, congregation, *coterie*, crowd, gathering, meeting, parliament

v: accumulate, agglutinate, aggregate, amass, assemble, coagulate, collate, compile, concentrate, conclude, conglomerate, convene, convoke, cull, enlist, forgather, garner, glean, infer, marshal, mobilize, muster, rally, store

## GAUDY

a: baronial, baroque, bedizened, blatant, *brummagem*, cheap, chintzy, extravagant, flamboyant, garish, grotesque, meretricious, ornate, rococo, showy, tasteless, tawdry, vulgar

n: bedizenment, blatancy, flamboyance, gaudiness, ostentation, panoply, showiness

## GEAR

n: *accoutrements*, apparatus, appointments, equipment, paraphernalia, toggery, trappings

## GEM

a: glyptic

n: agate, amber, amethyst, aquamarine, bezel, birthstone, cabochon, cameo, *chatoyant*, citrine, diamond, emerald, facet, garnet, gemstone, jade, *lapis lazuli*, opal, pearl, peridot, rhinestone, ruby, sapphire, solitaire, topaz, turquoise, zircon

   *art:* glyptography
   *maker:* lapidary

## GENERAL

a: catholic, cosmic, cosmopolitan, customary, ecumenical, *en masse*, encyclic, encyclopedic, endemic, epidemic, generic, macroscopic, pandemic, panoramic, prevalent, sweeping, synoptic, universal, unrestricted, versatile

n: abstraction, catholicity, consensus, conspectus, ecumenicity, *factotum*, gener-

ality, generalness, overview, plenum, tenor, *tout ensemble*, universality

v: subsume

## GENERATION

n: development, procreation, production

## GENEROUS

a: altruistic, beneficent, benevolent, bountiful, charitable, chivalrous, copious, indulgent, lavish, liberal, munificent, philanthropic, prodigal, profuse, ungrudging, unstinted

n: beneficence, benevolence, generosity, *largesse*, magnanimity, munificence, *noblesse oblige*, openhandedness, philanthropy, prodigality

## GENIAL

a: affable, amiable, benignant, *debonaire*, friendly, genteel

n: *camaraderie*, conviviality, *esprit de corps*, geniality, gentility, joviality

## GENIUS

n: aptitude, brainwizard, disposition, *genius loci*, gift, intellect, propensity, talent

## GENTLE

a: chivalresque, chivalric, chivalrous, conciliatory, considerate, courteous, courtly, docile, genteel, lenient, pacific, placid, tractable, tranquil

n: chivalry, docility, gentility, gentleness, leniency, lenity, mansuetude, mildness, refinement

   *gentleman:* caballero, cavalier, seigneur, seignior

## GENUINE

a: apostolic, authentic, authoritative, *bona fide*, canonical, documented, *echt*, ingenuous, kosher, legitimate, official, orthodox, *pukka*, real, sincere, straightforward, substantive, unadulterated, unaffected, unfeigned, veridical, veritable

n: genuineness, ingenuousness, legitimacy, sincerity

**GESTURE**

**a:** gesticulatory, paralinguistic

**n:** *beau geste*, body language, deportment, genuflection, gesticulation, kowtow, obeisance, *salaam*, salutation, tokenism

**v:** gesticulate

*study:* kinesics, pasimology

**GET**

**n:** acquirement, acquisition, comprehension, obtainment, obtention, procurement, securement

**v:** acquire, comprehend, gain, garner, obtain, procure, receive, secure

**GHASTLY**

**a:** awesome, cadaverous, corpselike, disagreeable, frightful, grisly, gruesome, hideous, horrible, horrid, horrific, livid, macabre, morbid, repellent, repulsive, spectral, terrifying

**n:** ghastliness, grisliness, lividity, morbidity, repulsiveness

**GHOST**

**a:** chthonian, delusive, ghostly, illusory, shadowy, spectral, spiritual, supermundane, supernatural

**n:** alter ego, *animus*, apparition, chimera, delusion, demon, *doppelganger*, ectoplasm, eidolon, phantasm, phantom, poltergeist, presence, revenant, shade, shadow, specter, spirit, visitation, wraith, zombie

**v:** materialize

**GIANT**

**a:** behemothian, brobdingnagian, Bunyanesque, cyclopean, cyclopic, elephantine, gigantic, huge, polyphemian, prodigious

**n:** behemoth, brobdingnagian, colossus, Gargantua, giantism, gigantism, goliath, macrosomia, monster, ogre, Paul Bunyan, Polypheme, titan, troll

**GIDDY**

**a:** capricious, changeable, exuberant, flighty, frivolous, gyratory, harebrained, heady, heedless, silly, vertiginous, volatile, wild

**n:** vertigo

**GIFT**

**a:** beneficent, benevolent, complimentary, *gratis*

**n:** aptitude, benefaction, benefice, beneficence, benevolence, bequest, consideration, contribution, devise, donation, faculty, favor, gratuity, keepsake, *lagniappe*, *largesse*, memento, perk, perquisite, recompense, sop, tribute, white elephant

*gifted:* prodigality, prodigy

*of Magi:* frankincense, myrrh

**GILDED**

**a:** aureate, festooned, gaudy, luxurious, meretricious, ornate, prosperous, tessellated, tawdry

**n:** *vermeil*

**v:** adorn, gild

**GIRL**

**n:** *belle*, colleen, damsel, *demoiselle*, *mademoiselle*, maid, maiden, nymph, sylph

*bold:* gamine, *hoyden*, minx, tomboy

*country:* amaryllis, urchin, waif

*group:* bevy

*immature:* backfische, ingenue, *jeune fille*, junior miss, *soubrette*

**GIST**

**n:** bottom line, core, essence, meaning, point, quintessence, significance, sum and substance, upshot

**GIVE**

**v:** accord, administer, afford, allocate, allot, apportion, bestow, cede, confer, consign, disburse, dispense, dispose, distribute, donate, emanate, emit, exhale, extend, exude, furnish, impart, invest with, lavish, ply, render

*and take:* compromise, *quid pro quo*, reciprocate

*giver:* benefactor, donor, eleemosyner, grantor, philanthropist, testator

*up:* abjure, abnegate, capitulate, disclaim, divest, forgo, forsake, relinquish, resign, submit, surrender, waive

## GLANCE

**n:** adumbration, *apercu, clin d'oeil, coup d'oeil*, glimpse, inkling, rebound

**v:** effleuer, ricochet

## GLARING

**a:** audacious, egregious, flagrant, garish, gaudy, glowering, impudent, lurid

## GLASS

**a:** crystal, crystalline, glassy, hyaline, obsidian, sanidinic, vitreous, vitric

**n:** goblet, jigger, prism, tankard, tumbler

*combining forms:* hyal-, hyalo-, vitr-, vitro-

*glasses:* bifocals, horn-rimmed, *lorgnette, lorgnon*, monocle, *pince-nez*

## GLEAM

**a:** clinquant, corsucant, coruscating, fulgent, fulgurant, gleaming, lambent, luminous, lustrous, phosphorescent, rutilant

**n:** clinquant, coruscation, fluorescence, fulguration, lambency, luminosity, phosphorescence

**v:** coruscate, fulgurate, phosphoresce, radiate, rutilate, scintillate

## GLOOM

**a:** dejected, disconsolate, disheartened, dolorous, dyspeptic, funebrial, funereal, inconsolable, melancholic, melancholy, morose, peevish, pessimistic, plutonian, plutonic, saturnine, sepulchral, splenetic, tenebrific, tomblike, unsociable

**n:** dejection, depression, despondency, disconsolation, doldrums, gloominess, lachrymals, megrims, melancholia, melancholy, morbidity, morosity, murkishness, pessimism, saturninity, unsociability

*causing:* luctiferous, tenebrific

*person:* atrabilarian, hypochondriac, melancholiac, pessimist

## GLORY

**n:** apotheosis, deification, effulgence, eminence, exaltation, glamorization, glorification, grandiloquence, illustriousness, kudos, laurels, luminosity, magnificence, repute, resplendence, resplendency, sanctification, splendor, sublimity

**v:** apotheosize, deify, exalt, glamorize, glorify, idealize, romanticize, stellify, transfigure

*to the Father:* ascription, *Gloria in Excelsis, Gloria Patri*

## GLOSS

**a:** glace, glossy, lustrous, *nitid*, polished, shiny, sleek

**n:** glossiness, luster, *nitidity*, sheen, veneer

## GLOW

**a:** ardent, candent, enthusiastic, fervent, glowing, impassioned, incandescent, intense, lambent, luminous, opalescent, perfervid, phosphorescent, refulgent

**n:** bioluminescence, cinder, embers, fire, fluorescence, incandescence, luminescence, phosphorescence, refulgence, refulgency

*sun:* alpenglow

## GLUE

**a:** gluey, glutinous, gummy, sticky, tenacious, viscid, viscous

**n:** adhesive, epoxy, mucilage, paste

*combining form:* collo-

## GLUTTON

**a:** cormorant, crapulent, crapulous, edacious, epicurean, gluttonous, polyphagous, rapacious, ventripotent, voracious

**n:** apician, appetite, cormorant, epicure, gormand, gormandizer, gourmand, gourmandism, gourmet

**v:** gormandize, gourmandize

## GO

**v:** depart, diminish, elapse, move, proceed, walk, wane, wend

*before:* precede, transcend

*-between:* arbitrator, broker, diplomat, emissary, intercessor, intermediary, *internuncio,* mediator, moderator, panderer, procurer, propitiator

*going before:* antecedent, anticipating, anticipatory, expectant, introductory, precedent, preceding, precursory, prefatorial, preliminary, premonitory, prevenient

## GOAL

**n:** aim, ambition, bourn, consummation, destination, ideal, intent, intention, Mecca, objective, telic, terminus, *terminus ad quem,* Thule, Zion

## GOAT

**a:** capric, caprid, caprine, hircine

*female:* nanny

*hair:* angora, mohair

*male:* billy

*young:* kid, yeanling

## GOD

**a:** deiform, divine, godlike, godly, religious, theological, theomorphic

**n:** *agathodaemon,* Almighty, deity, divinity, Jehovah, lord, pantheon, Prime Mover, Providence

**v:** apotheosize, deify, exalt, revere, translate, venerate

*appearance:* avatar, epiphany

*belief in many:* polytheism

*belief in one:* monotheism

*combining forms:* de-, deo-, the(o)-

*disbelief:* agnosticism, atheism

*fear of:* theophobia

*festival:* panegyris

*food and drink:* ambrosia, nectar

*hatred of:* theophobia

*hymn to:* doxology, theody

*narrative about:* aretalogy

*rule by:* theocracy, theonomy

*study:* theology

*subordinate:* demigod, demiurge, subdeity

*worship of:* henotheism, monolatry, monotheism, theolatry

*worship of all:* pantheism, polytheism

## GOLD

**a:** aureate, aurelian, aureous, auric, auriferous, aurous, aurulent, gilded, gilt, halcyon

**n:** aureity, bullion, filigree, ingot, noble metal, nugget

**v:** fossick, pan, prospect

*age:* millennium

*combining forms:* auri-, chrys-, chryso-

## GOOD

**a:** adequate, admirable, advantageous, angelic, beatific, beneficent, beneficial, benevolent, blissful, cardinal, commendable, crackerjack, creditable, decorous, delicious, estimable, excellent, laudable, meretorious, nutritious, perfect, prime, profitable, propitious, reputable, saintly, salubrious, salutary, seraphic, sterling, superlative, top-notch, vintage, worthy

**n:** altruism, benefaction, benefice, beneficence, benevolence, bonhomie, goodwill, intangible, integrity, mitzvah, philanthropy, probity, rectitude, uprightness, virtue

*and evil:* agathocacological, Jekyll-and-Hyde

*appearing to be:* hypocritical, religiose, sanctimonious

*combining forms:* bon-, eu-

*faith:* bona fides

*-for-nothing:* fustian

*highest:* summum bonum

*natured:* affable, amiable, congenial, cordial, gracious

*taste:* decorum

*ultimate:* agathism, agathology

**GOODBYE**

**a:** apopemtic, valedictory

**n:** *a bientot, adeus, adieu, adios, aloha, arrivederci, au revoir, auf wiedersehen, bene vale, bon voyage, ciao, conge,* farewell, *hasta la vista,* leave-taking, *sayonara,* valediction

**GOOSE**

**a:** anserine

  *bumps:* horripilation, piloerection

  *liver paste: pate de foie gras*

**GORGEOUS**

**a:** dazzling, flamboyant, grand, magnificent, resplendent, splendaceous, splendacious

**GOSSIP**

**n:** blatherskite, magpie, *quidnunc,* rumormonger, scuttlebutt

  *piece of:* bandy, gabfest, hearsay, on-dit

**GOURMET**

**n:** *bon-vivant,* epicure, *gastronome(r),* glutton, *gourmand,* trencherman

**GOVERNMENT**

**a:** federal, governmental, gubernatorial, statal

**n:** administration, bureaucracy, cabinet, dominion, jurisdiction, polity, regime, sovereignty, statecraft, supremacy

  *by few:* oligarchy

  *by fools:* foolocracy

  *by many:* polyarchy

  *by middle class:* mesocracy

  *by military:* junta, stratocracy

  *by one:* autocracy, dictatorship, monarchy, monocracy

  *by people:* pantarchy, pantisocracy

  *by rich:* aristocracy, plutocracy

  *by two:* diarchy

  *by woman:* gynarchy, matriarchy

  *combining forms:* -archy, -cracy, -nomy, -ocracy

  *old: ancien regime*

  *power over another:* hegemony, heteronomy, suzerainty

  *suspension of: interregnum*

  *without:* acephalous

**GRAB**

**n:** appropriation, arrogation, capture, confiscation, sequestration

**v:** appropriate, arrogate, capture, confiscate, sequester

**GRACE**

**a:** eloquent, fluent, graceful, gracile, limber, lissome, lithe, nymphean, nymphlike, sleek, slinky, soigne, *spirituelle,* svelte, sylphic, symmetrical, willowy

**n:** attractiveness, benefaction, clemency, consideration, dispensation, elegance, felicity, gracefulness, lenity, polish, thoughtfulness

  *gracious:* affable, auspicious, benignant, courteous, courtly, genteel, lenient, merciful, polished, refined, *suave,* urbane

  *note: acciaccatura, appoggiatura*

  *prayer:* benedicite, benediction, invocation

**GRADE**

**a:** graded

**n:** cline, *continuum,* curve, echelon, gradation, graduality, hierarchy, rank, standing, station

  *gradual:* fractional, fragmentary, incremental, piecemeal, progressive, subtle

**GRAIN**

**a:** farinaceous, frumentaceous, grainy, granular

**n:** granule, grist, grits, groats

**v:** flail, garner, glean, thresh, winnow

  *combining form:* grani-

  *eating:* graminivorous, granivorous

**GRAMMAR**

**a:** grammatical, syntactic

**n:** conjugation, purism, syntax

*error:* hypercorrection, solecism

## GRAND

**a:** apocalyptic, august, baronial, bombastic, cosmic, exalted, expansive, famous, flamboyant, flowery, grandiloquent, grandiose, great, highfalutin, illustrious, imposing, impressive, large, lavish, lofty, magisterial, magnificent, magniloquent, majestic, ostentatious, preeminent, prominent, rarefied, rubescent, stately, statuesque, sublime, sumptuous, transcendent, turgid, venerable

**n:** flamboyancy, grandeur, grandiloquence, grandiosity, impressiveness, magnificence, majesty, megalomania, regality, sublimity

## GRANT

**n:** accordance, concession, contribution, donation, gift, gratuity, subsidy

**v:** award, concede, give, vouchsafe

*for granted:* self-evident, *sub silento*

## GRAPE

**a:** aciniform, botryose, botyroid(al), racemose

**n:** vintage

*cultivation:* viniculture, viticulture

## GRASS

**a:** gramineal, gramineous, graminoid

**n:** divot, hassock, herbage, lawn, meadow, pasturage, pasture, prairie, sedge, steppe, sward, swath, tuffet, tussock

**v:** crop, cut, graze

*feeding on:* graminivorous

*study:* agrostology

*whitened:* etiolated

## GRATIFICATION

**a:** beholden, congratulatory, grateful, gratulant, indebted, obliged

**n:** appreciation, delectation, satiation, satiety, testimonial, tribute

**v:** delectate, gratify, indulge, please, satiate

*agent:* emollient, placebo, tranquilizer, unction

## GRATING

**a:** strident, stridulous

**n:** crepitus, grate, rasp, stridor, stridulation

## GRATUITY

**n:** benefaction, benefice, beneficence, benevolence, *douceur*, *honorarium*, *lagniappe*, *largesse*, perquisite, *pourboire*

## GRAVE

**a:** funereal, melancholy, mortuary, saturnine, sepulchral, sombrous, tumulary

**n:** barrow, burial, catacomb, columbarium, graveyard, hypogeum, mausoleum, ossuary, repository, sepulcher, terminus, tumulus

*inscription:* epitaph, *hic jacet*, ledger

## GREASY

**a:** adipose, butyraceous, fatty, lardaceous, oily, oleaginous, pinguid, saponaceous, sebaceous, slippery, unctuous

**n:** greasiness, lubricant, lubricity, oil, unctuousness

## GREAT

**a:** distinguished, estimable, famous, grand, huge, incalculable, incomputable, large, magnanimous, monumental, predominant, preeminent, prominent, renowned, supereminent, transcendent

**n:** abundance, eminence, grandeur, grandiosity, greatness, magnanimity, magnitude, nobleness, optimum, plethora, plurality, preeminence, preponderance, prominence, renown, stature, sublimity, transcendence

*combining form:* supra-

*deed:* magnalia, magnality

*greater:* preponderant

*greatest:* maximal, maximum, *ne plus supra*, *ne plus ultra*, optimal, paramount, preeminent, sovereign, utmost

*work:* *magnum opus*, *piece de resistance*

## GREECE
**a:** classical, Greek, Hellenic, philhellene, philhellenic

**n:** Grecism, Hellenist

*combining forms:* Graeco-, Greco-, Hellen-

*love:* Hellenism, philhellenism

## GREEN
**a:** aeruginous, greenish, ultramarine, verdant, verdigrisy, verdurous, virescent, virid, viridescent

**n:** chlorophyll, greenness, verdancy, verdure, virescence, viridity

*combining forms:* chlor-, chloro-, verd-

## GREETING
**a:** salutational, salutatory

**n:** compliments, *devoirs*, respects, *salaam*, salutation, salute

**v:** accost, address, salute, welcome

## GRIEF
**a:** disconsolate, dolorific, dolorous, funereal, grieved, grievous, inconsolable, lamentable, lamented, melancholy

**n:** affliction, desolation, dolor, heartache, lamentation, melancholy, misadventure, misfortune, mortification, sorrow, tribulation, *tristesse*

**v:** founder, pine

*reduce:* allay, alleviate, assuage

## GRIEVANCE
**n:** annoyance, displeasure, gravamen, lament, lamentation, oppression

## GRIM
**a:** ferocious, forbidding, ghastly, grisly, gruesome, inexorable, macabre, morbid, moribund, obdurate, plutonian, plutonic, relentless, ruthless, uncompromising

## GRIMACE
**n:** contortion, distortion, frown, *moue*, scowl, simagree

## GRIMY
**a:** dirty, scabrous, squalid, sullied

**n:** soil, soot, squalidity, squalor, uncleanness

## GRIND
**v:** abrade, bray, comminute, crush, gnash, harass, masticate, pound, pulverize, rub, triturate

## GROOVED
**a:** caniculate, cannellated, castellated, chamfered, channeled, ridged, scorbiculate, streaked, striate, strigose, sulcate

**n:** cannelure, chamfer, crenellations, flute, fluting, furrow, gain, glyph, groove, indentation, kerf, milling, mortise, notch, philtrum, rabbet, ridge, serration, slot, spline, *sulcus*

## GROSS
**a:** barbarous, crass, indecent, scurrilous, vulgar

**n:** barbarity, crassitude, crassness, grossness, indecency, scurrility, vulgarity

## GROTESQUE
**a:** bizarre, odd

**n:** bizarrerie, fantasia, gargoyle, grotesquery, *ignis fatuus*, phantasmagoria, will-ó-the-wisp

## GROUNDS
**n:** foundation, justification, rationale, reason, terrain

*groundless:* baseless, unfounded

*of the ground:* terrestrial, terricolous

*underground:* submundane, subterranean, subterrestrial

## GROUP
**a:** agglutinative, aggregatory, cumulative, *en masse*, generic, gregarious, hierarchical, plenary, sociable

**n:** alignment, alliance, assemblage, battery, bloc, caucus, class, classification, collection, commonality, consortium, convoy, corps, coterie, enclave, faction, fraternity, hierarchy, league, pattern, plenum, posse, retinue, sect, syndicate

**v:** agglutinate, assemble, catalog, categorize, classify, coagulate, codify, collate, colligate, collocate, conglomerate, congregate, coordinate, muster, tabulate

*doctrine:* ideology

*exclusive:* cabal, *claque, clique,* coterie, *creme de la creme*

*habits of:* mores

*large:* hecatomb, legion, multitude

*list:* matricula, roster, rota

*living together:* commune, phalanstery

*member:* congregant

*of miscellaneous:* menagerie

*of three: menage a trois,* ternion, triad, trio, triumvirate

*scientific or literary:* athenaeum, cenacle

## GROVE

**a:** nemoral

**n:** boscage, copse, spinney, thicket

## GROVELING

**a:** creeping, prostrating, reptilian, servile

## GROW

**a:** cumulative, embryonic, germinal, growing, nascent, rank, seminal

**n:** accrescence, accretion, augmentation, concrescence, development, differentiation, evolution, excrescence, growth, increment, maturation, maturescence, *naissance,* neoplasm, phylogeny, proliferation

**v:** augment, burgeon, enhance, flourish, foster, germinate, gestate, incubate, maturate, mature, nurture, proliferate, propagate, pullulate, rotate, sprout, vegetate

*combining forms:* -blast, blast-, blasto-, cresc-, nasc-, -plasia, -plastic, -plasy, -trope, troph-, -trophic, tropho-, -trophy, -tropic

*on living tissue:* biogenous

*overgrowth:* hypertrophy

*together:* accrete, amalgamate, ankylose, coalesce, conglomerate

*undergrowth:* atrophy, degeneration, hypotrophy

*up high:* alpestrine

*wild:* agrestial

## GRUDGE

**n:** animosity, *animus,* hatred, malice, *pique,* resentment

**v:** bear, harbor

## GRUESOME

**a:** appalling, cadaverous, frightful, ghastly, grisly, macabre, morbid, morbific, morbose, sinister, ugly

## GUARANTEE

**n:** covenant, earnestassurance, palladium, pledge, promise, surety, token, undertaking, warrant, warranty

**v:** underwrite, vouch for

*guarantor:* adpromissor, protector, warrantor

## GUARDIAN

**a:** tutelary

**n:** *alter ego,* Argus, Cerberus, chaperone, *daemon,* genius, *genius loci,* sentinel, tutor, vigil, watch

*guardianship:* care, custody, paternalism, tutelage, tutorship

## GUESS

**a:** academic, conjectural, divinatory, guessing, hypothetical, postulatory, presumptive, prophetic, suppositional, suppositious, theoretical

**n:** augury, conjecture, deduction, divination, estimation, guesswork, hariolation, haruspication, hypothesis, postulation, prognosis, prognostication, prophesy, speculation, supposition, surmise

**v:** anticipate, conjecture, deduce, divine, estimate, extrapolate, hariolate, hypothesize, infer, postulate, presage, prognosticate, surmise

**GUEST**

**n:** bludger, cadger, freeloader, frequenter, habitue, invitee, scrounger, sponger, visitor

**GUIDE**

**a:** didactic, heuristic, normative, prescriptive

**n:** attendant, beacon, chaperonage, ciceronage, cicerone, cynosure, dragoman, escort, gospel, guardianship, guidance, guru, lodestar, maxim, measure, mentor, motto, outrider, paternalism, polestar, precedent, sign, supervisor, warning

**v:** vector

> *book:* Baedeker, handbook, itinerary, *vade mecum*

> *by hand:* manuducative, manuducatory

**GUILE**

**a:** artless, credulous, guileless, gullible, ingenuous, naive

**n:** artifice, deceit, dissimulation, duplicity, rascality, stratagem, subtlety, treachery

> *guilelessness:* credulity, gullibility, naivete

**GUILT**

**a:** blameworthy, compunctious, contrite, culpable, demeritorious, guilty, hangdog, indictable, intropunitive, nocent, peccant, penitent, remorseful, reprehensible, reprehensive, shamefaced, sorry

**n:** compunction, contrition, criminality, culpability, delinquency, dereliction, penitence, remorse, repentance, reprehensibility, reprehension

> *admittance: mea culpa, peccavi*

> *forgiveness:* absolution, amnesty, atonement, exculpation, exoneration, expiation, purgation, redemption

> *person:* criminal, culprit, felon, misfeasor, tort-feasor

**GULLIBLE**

**a:** credulous, naive

**n:** credulity, cullibility, dupe, greenhorn, gull, gullibility, naivete, sucker

**GUSH**

**a:** demonstrative, effusive, emotive, gooey, gushing, scaturient

**n:** flow, regurgitation

**v:** flow, regurgitate

**GYPSIES**

**a:** *tzigane*

**n:** *gitano,* Gorgio, rom, Romany, rye, Tzigane, *zingaro*

**HABIT**

**a:** adamant, chronic, confirmed, consuetudinal, customary, habitual, inveterate, persistent, regular, routine

**n:** aberration, addiction, assuetude, constitution, consuetude, custom, demeanor, disposition, eccentricity, habituation, habitude, idiosyncrasy, mannerism, pattern, physique, *praxis*, *rota*, rote, routine, usage, wont

**v:** accustom, habituate

*bad: cacoethes*, pathological

*group's:* mores

*person with:* habitue, routineer

**HAIR**

**a:** capillaceous, capilliform, ciliate, comose, comous, crinate, criniferous, crinitory, hairy, hirsutal, hirsute, hoary, piliferous, pilose, pilous, polytrichous, villous, *xanthous*

**n:** *byssus, capillus, chevelure,* cilia, coif, coiffure, crinosity, escutcheon, feather, frill, hackles, hirsutism, pelage, pilosis, pilosism, pilosity, *pilus,* ringlet, ruff, shag, thatch, tresses, trichosis, *vibrissae, villus*

*blonde:* aurocephalous

*brunette:* melanocomous, melanous

*covered with fine:* lanate, laniferous, lanuginose, lanuginous, pubescent, velutinous, villoid

*curly:* ulotrichous

*erect:* horripilation, piloerection

*false:* postiche, toupee

*gray:* canities, poliosis

*hairless:* depilous, glabrous, study

*red:* hirsutorufous, phrrhotic, rufous, xanthous

*removal:* depilate, depilation, depilatory

*straight:* leiotrichous, lissotrichous

*wavy:* cymotrichous, encomic

*clip:* barrette, bobby pin

*combining forms:* pil-, pili-, pilo-, trich-, tricho-, -trichous

*hairdressing:* tonsorial

*hair loss:* alopecia

*untidy:* disheveled, rumpled, tousled, uncombed, ungroomed, unkempt

**HAIR-RAISING**

**a:** horripilant

**n:** goose-flesh, horripilation, piloerection

*hair-splitting:* casuistic, dialectic, sophistical, specious

**HALF**

**a:** bifid, bipartite, bisected, cloven, dichotomous, dimidiate, halved, imperfect, intermediate, mid, middle, midpoint, partial

**n:** bifurcation, dichotomy, dimidiation, hemisphere, mediety, moiety

*-baked:* immature

*-breed:* hybrid, mestizo, metis, mongrel

*combining forms:* bi-, bis-, demi-, dich-, dicho-, hemi-, semi-

**HALLOWED**

**a:** blessed, consecrated, holy, revered, sacred, sanctified

**n:** bethel, bethesda, halidom, sanctuary, *sanctum sanctorum*

**HALLUCINATION**

**n:** *delirium tremens*, dt's

　　*producing:* hallucinogen, psychedelic

**HALO**

**n:** anthelion, aura, aureola, aureole, aurora, corona, gloria, gloriole, glory, mandorla, *nimbus, vesica piscis*

**HAND**

**a:** ambidextrous, bimanous, bimanual, gesticulatory, manual, manuductive, manuductory, palmate

**n:** claw, extremity, hoof, *manus*, paw

**v:** gesticulate

　　*combining forms:* chiro-, manu-

　　*enlarged:* chiromegaly

　　*having 4:* quadrumanous

　　*having no:* amanous

　　*left:* sinistral

　　*right:* dextral

　　*sign language:* dactylology

　　*skill using:* dexterity, legerdemain, prestidigitation, sleight of hand

　　*using one:* unidextral

**HANDBOOK**

**n:** Baedeker, enchiridion, manual, prom-ptuary, *vade mecum*

**HAND DOWN**

**a:** traditional, tralatitious

**n:** bequest, legacy

**v:** bequeath, pass on

**HANDICAP**

**n:** disability, encumbrance, impediment, impost, *incubus*, liability

**v:** encumber, penalize

**HANDSOME**

**a:** adonic, beautiful, comely, fine, good-looking, personable, prepossessing, presentable, stunning

**n:** Adonis, Apollo, demigod

**HANDWRITING**

**a:** chirographic, holographic, onomastic, scriptorial, scriptory

**n:** autograph, chirography, longhand, manuscript, manuscription, script

　　*bad:* cacography, crabbed, griffonage, hieroglyphic, scrawl

　　*beautiful:* calligraphy, chirography, legible

　　*capital:* majuscule, uncial

　　*decoration:* flourish, quirk

　　*large:* macrography

　　*lower-case:* minuscule

　　*not block:* cursive

　　*on the wall: mene, tekel, upharsin*

　　*own:* autograph, autography

　　*study:* bibliotics, graphology

**HANDY**

**a:** adroit, convenient, dexterous, dextrous, facile, habile, ingenious, resourceful

**n:** adeptness, dexterity, expertise, handiness, virtuosity

　　*handyman: factotum, genius loci*

**HANG**

**a:** abeyant, appendicular, dangling, flaccid, hanging, impending, pendent, pendulant, pendular, pendulous, pensile, suspended

**n:** pendency, pendulation, pendulosity, pendulousness

**v:** impend, pend, pendulate, suspend

**HAPPENING**

**a:** concurrent, spasmodic, synchronized

**n:** contingency, incident

**v:** befall, betide, come to pass, ensue, eventuate, happen, materialize, occur, supervene, synchronize, take place, transpire

**HAPPINESS**

**a:** beatific, blithe, buoyant, carefree, cheerful, delighted, delirious, ecstatic, enchanted, enraptured, euphoric, exhilarated, exuberant, exultant, felicific, gratified, jaunty, jubilant, rapturous, satisfied, transported

**n:** beatitude, bliss, ecstasy, eudaemonia, eudemonia, felicity, *joie de vivre,* joy, seventh heaven, transport, well-being

**v:** beatify

*incapable of:* anhedonic

*place:* Eden, Elysium, paradise, utopia

## HARASS

**v:** badger, bedevil, bully, dragoon, exhaust, heckle, hector, importune, jeer

## HARD

**a:** adamant, arduous, difficult, exacting, grievous, impenetrable, incorrigible, inflexible, intractable, laborious, ruthless, stern, strenuous, unrelenting, unsparing

**n:** hardness, impetinence, induration, petrification, sclerosis, strenuosity

**v:** concretize, fortify, habituate, harden, indurate, inure, ossify, petrify

*combining forms:* dur-, scler-, sclero-

*hardened:* adamantine, concretive, confirmed, congelative, flinty, granite, impenitent, indurated, insensate, insusceptible, inured, inveterate, marmoreal, obdurate, ossified, petrous, unrepentant

*hardening of arteries:* arteriosclerosis

## HARE

**a:** leporid, leporine

**n:** coney, lagomorph, leveret

*lip:* cheilognathus, cheiloschisis

## HARM

**a:** bad, baleful, deleterious, detrimental, harmful, inimical, malefic, malevolent, malicious, malign, malignant, nocent, nocuous, noxious, pernicious, prejudicial, sinister, venomous, virulent

**n:** damage, detriment, disservice, injury, maleficence, malevolence, malignancy, molestation, ravages, toxicity, trauma, wound

*harmless:* beneficent, benign, impotent, innocent, innocuous, innoxious, inoffensive, insipid, salutary

## HARMONIOUS

**a:** affable, assonant, companionable, compatible, conciliatory, concinnous, concordant, conformable, congruent, congruous, conorous, euphonic, eurhythmic, henotic, in unison, irenic, mellifluent, mellifluous, melodic, melodious, pacific, pacificatory, reconciliatory, rhythmic, sociable, sonorous, symphonic, synchronous, syncretic, syncretistic, tranquilizing, unisonant

**n:** affability, amity, assonance, compatibility, concordance, concurrence, congruence, congruity, consonance, coordination, euphony, harmony, mutuality, rapport, symmetry, symphony, synchronicity, unanimity

**v:** agree, coordinate, correlate, harmonize, mediate, orchestrate, reconcile, synchronize, syncretize, synphonize, tranquilize

## HARSH

**a:** acerbic, acidulent, acidulous, antagonistic, asperous, astringent, austere, brusque, cacophonous, cruel, curt, desolate, discordant, disharmonious, dissonant, draconian, ferocious, gruff, inclement, inexorable, raucous, relentless, rigorous, ruthless, severe, spartan, stark, strict, strident, stringent, truculent, uncharitable, unremitting, vinegary

**n:** acerbity, asperity, cacophony, discordance, harshness, inclemency, mordacity, rigor

## HASTE

**a:** accelerated, celeritous, cursory, desultory, festinate, hasty, impatient, impetuous, impulsive, incautious, indiscreet, precipitate, rash, superficial

**n:** abruptness, acceleration, alacrity, celerity, dispatch, expediency, expedition, facility, impetuosity, impulsivity, precipitateness, precipitation, rapidity *hastener:* accelerant, catalyst, gadfly, precipitator, stimulant, stimulator, stimulus

## HATE

**a:** abhorrent, abominable, anathematic, defamatory, despicable, detestable, excreable, fastuous, flagitious, hateful, heinous, invidious, loathsome, nauseous, objectionable, obnoxious, odious, opprobrious, outrageous, repellant, repugnant, repulsive, vile

**n:** abhorrence, anathema, animosity, animus, antagonism, antipathy, aversion, detestation, enmity, hatred, malevolence, malice, malignity, misandry, misanthropy, misogyny, odium, phobia, rancor, repugnance, revulsion, vitriol

**v:** abhor, abominate, anathematize, execrate, loathe

*combining forms:* mis-, miso-, -phobe, -phobia, -phobic

*hater:* antipathist

*object of:* anathema, *bete noir*

## HAUGHTY

**a:** arrogant, *cavalier,* condescending, contemptuous, contumelious, despiteful, disdainful, egotistical, fastuous, grandiose, hubristic, patronizing, peremptory, petulant, pompous, portentous, prideful, proud, supercilious

**n:** arrogance, contempt, contumacy, disdain, fastuosity, haughtiness, *hauteur,* hubris, morgue, vainglory

## HAUNT

**n:** environ(s), habitat, haven, *milieu,* oasis, *purlieu,* rendezvous

## HAWK

**a:** accipitral, accipitrine

**n:** accipter, cast, eyas, haggard

*female:* formel

*male:* tercel

## HAZY

**a:** cloudy, ethereal, indefinite, indistinct, misty, nebular, nebulose, nebulous, obscure, tenuous, vague

**n:** cloudiness, ethereality, haziness, nebulosity, tenuosity, vaporosity

## HEAD

**a:** capital, capitate, cephalic, cephalous, cranial

**n:** capitulum, caput, cranium, crown, pate, poll, skull

*affecting both sides:* amphicranial, bicranial

*affecting one side:* hemicranial

*back:* occipital

*bald:* pilgarlic, tonsure

*cold:* coryza

*combining forms:* cap-, capit-, caput-, cephal-, cephalo-

*front:* sinciput

*large:* megacephalic, megacephalous

*many:* hydra-headed

*remove:* decapitate, guillotine, obtruncate

*small:* microcephalic, microcephalous

*to-foot:* cap-a-pie

*top:* corona, vertex

*two:* bicephalous

*without:* acephalic, acephalous

## HEADACHE

**n:** amphicrania, bicrania, cephalalgia, cephalodynia, hemicrania, *mal de tete,* megrim, migraine

## HEADLONG

**a:** heedless, impetuous, precipitant, precipitate, precipitous, rash, sudden

## HEALING

**a:** Aesculapian, assuasive, balsamic, curative, lenitive, medicamental, medicamentous, medicative, medicinable, medicinal, remedial, resoluble, restorative, sanative, therapeutic, vulnerary

**n:** granulation, salve

**v:** cicatrize, cure, heal, treat

*science:* iatrics, iatrology, therapeusis, therapeutics

*slow:* indolent

## HEALTH

**a:** beneficial, curative, fresh, hale, healing, healthful, hygienic, invigorating, nutritious, restorative, salubrious, salutary, salutiferous, sanitary, sprightly, spry, vigorous, wholesome

**n:** constitution, healthfulness, prosperity, robusticity, salubrity, salutariness, tonicity, verdure, vigor, vitality, wholesomeness

**v:** convalesce, rally, recuperate, rehabilitate

*anxiety:* hypochondria

*normal:* eucrasic, eudaemonia, euphoria, normality

*poor:* dyscrasia

*recovery:* convalescence, recuperation

## HEAP

**a:** acervuline, cumulative, pyramidal

**n:** accumulation, acervation, agglomeration, aggregation, barrow, congeries, mound, tumulus

## HEARING

**a:** acousmatic

*combining forms:* audi-, audio-, auscult-

## HEARSAY

**n:** dirt, gossip, *on dit,* rumor, scuttlebutt, talk

## HEART

**a:** cardiac, cardiological, cordate, cordial, cordiform, pectoral

**n:** affection, cardia, core, disposition, gist, interior

**v:** palpitate, pulsate, pulse

*combining forms:* cardi-, cor-, cord-

*fast-beat:* palpitation, tachycardia

*heartburn:* pyrosis

*instrument:* defibrillator, ECG, EKG, electrocardiograph, pacemaker

*slow-beat:* bradycardia

*study:* cardiology

## HEAT

**a:** calefacient, calefactory, calescent, caloric, calorific, calorigenic, geothermal, hot, igneous, ignescent, pyrogenic, pyrogenous, thermal, thermic

**n:** calefaction, calescence, candescence, greenhouse effect, temperature

**v:** insulate

*combining forms:* cale-, calor-, pyro-, therm-, thermo-, -thermy

*heater:* convector, furnace, radiator

*transfer:* conduction, convection, radiation

*treatment:* thermotherapy

## HEATHEN

**a:** foreign, heathenish, irreligious, pagan, uncircumcised, unenlightened, unfamiliar

**n:** idolater, pagan

## HEAVEN

**a:** angelic, beatific, blissful, celestial, edenic, elysian, empyreal, empyrean, ethereal, firmamental, heavenly, Olympian, paradisiac, paradisial, paradisian, rapturous, sublime, supercelestial, supernal

**n:** celestial sphere, Eden, Elysium, empyrean, firmament, Limbo, Olympus, paradise, sky, Utopia, Valhalla, welkin, Zion

**v:** ascend, translate

*combining forms:* celest-, uran-, urano-

*of heaven and earth:* cosmotellurian

*study:* astronomy, eschatology, uranology

## HEAVY

**a:** burdensome, consequential, cumbersome, elephantine, fat, grievous, huge, labored, massive, onerous, oppressive, ponderous, saturnine, stodgy, substantious, weighty

## HEDGE

**n:** maze, plash, pleach, quickset, septum, topiary, windbreak v: encircle, equivocate, obstruct

**HEED**

a: advertent, calculating, cautious, circumspect, heedful, mindful, vigilant, wary

n: apprehension, attention, attentiveness, circumspection, cognizance, perception

> *heedless:* neglectful, oblivious, precipitate, reckless, remiss

**HEIGHT**

a: altitudinous, culminant

n: acme, altitude, dimension, elevation, eminence, pinnacle, stature

v: accent, aggravate, augment, enhance, exacerbate, exaggerate, exalt, heighten, intensify

> *combining forms:* acro-, alt-, hyps-, hypso-
>
> *fear:* acrophobia, cremnophobia, hypsophobia
>
> *instrument:* altimeter, orometer

**HEIR**

a: ancestral, congenital, familial, genetic, hereditable, hereditary, inborn, innate, lineal, linear, paternal, patriarchal, patrimonial

n: atheling, coparcener, crown price, dauphin, heir apparent, heir presumptive, offspring, parcener, primogeniture, scion

> *disposition:* diathesis
>
> *heritable property:* hereditament, patrimony

**HELL**

a: chthonia, chthonic, demoniac(al), devilish, hellish, infernal, pandemoniac(al), sheolic, stygian, sulfurous, sulphurous

n: Abaddon, Acheron, Avernus, barathrum, Gehenna, Hades, holocaust, inferno, limbo, Orcus, Pandemonium, perdition, purgatory, Sheol, Tartarus

**HELP**

a: accessory, adminicular, advantageous, alleviatory, auspicious, auxiliary, beneficial, constructive, convenient, cooperative, corroborative, curative, helpful, helping, helpless, obliging, opportune, participative, promoting, propitious, remedial, salutary, subsidiary, therapeutic

n: adminicle, administeration, assistance, coadjuvancy, cooperation, encouragement, ministrations, recourse, subsidy, subvention, succor

v: abet, alleviate, avail, collaborate, connive, expedite, facilitate, participate, subsidize, succor

> *helper:* accessory, adjutant, adjuvant, adminicle, *aide, aide-de-camp,* ancillary, auxiliary, benefactor, coadjutor, collaborator, colleague, confederate, *confrere,* participant, participator

**HENCHMAN**

n: fall guy, goat, hatchet man, mercenary, minion, myrmidon, participant, satrap

**HERALD**

n: forerunner, harbinger, messenger, page, precursor, usher

**HERBS**

a: herbivorous, simple

n: allspice, aniseed, asafetida, balm, basil, bay leaf, borage, caraway, cardamom, cayenne, chervil, chili, chives, cinnamon, cloves, coriander, cumin, dill, fennel, mace, marjoram, nutmeg, oregano, paprika, rosemary, saffron, sage, tarragon, thyme, turmeric

> *study:* phytology
>
> *worker:* botanist, phytologist

**HERETIC**

a: heretical, heterodox, unorthodox

n: apostate, heresiarch, nonconformist, schismatic, unbeliever

> *heresy:* Albigensianism, Arianism, Catharism, Gnosticism, Jansenism, Pelagianism

**HERITAGE**

a: patrimonial

n: hereditament, inheritance, legacy, patrimony

**HERMIT**

a: anchoritic, cenobitic, eremitic, hermitic, troglodytic

n: anchoress, anchorite, cenobite, eremite, isolate, recluse, solitudinarian, stylite, troglodyte

**HERO**

a: chivalrous, courageous, dauntless, eponymous, extreme, heroic, Homerian, Homeric, illustrious, intrepid, knightly, powerful, radical, resolute, Samsonian, undaunted, unsung

n: Argonaut, demigod, demigoddess, paladin, pantheon, protagonist

*deed:* exploit, gest

**HESITATE**

a: dubitant, dubitative, halting, hesitant, indisposed, irresolute, jerky, shilly-shally, vacillating, vacillatory, wavering

n: demur, dubitation, hesitation, indisposition, pausation, vacillation

v: demur, falter, fluctuate, haver, hover, linger, procrastinate, pussyfoot, scruple, shilly-shally, vacillate, waver

**HICCUP**

n: hiccough, *singultus*

**HIDE**

a: abeyant, abstruse, arcane, cabalistic, clandestine, cloistered, covert, cryptic, cryptogenic, delitescent, dormant, enigmatic, esoteric, furtive, hidden, imperceptible, inapparent, inherent, larvate, latent, occult, potential, quiescent, recessed, recondite, secret, subterranean, surreptitious, ulterior, undercurrent, undisclosed, unexplained, veiled

n: abscondence, abstrusity, arcanum, clandestinity, fugitation, obscuration, occultation, sequestration, stowaway

v: abscond, cache, camouflage, closet, conceal, dissemble, ensconce, enshroud, fugitate, mantle, obscure, secrete, sequester, veil

*combining forms:* crypt-, crypto-

*hideaway:* hermitage, nidus, redoubt, refuge, retreat

**HIGH**

a: altitudinous, classic, elevated, eminent, extravagant, imposing, *in excelsis,* lofty, meridional, paramount, preeminent, soaring, stratospheric, sublime, supereminent, supernal, superordinate, supreme, top-echelon, towering

n: acme, aerie, apex, apogee, apotheosis, climax, culmination, exosphere, inosphere, meridian, mesosphere, *ne plus supra, ne plus ultra,* pinnacle, stratosphere, summit, vertex, zenith

*combining forms:* acro-, alti-

*higher combining forms:* super-, supra-

*highest combining forms:* arch-, ultim-

*spirits:* ebullience, ecstasy, euphoria, exuberance

*status:* aristocrat, cachet, *cordon bleu, grand prix,* luminary, *magnifico, mahatma,* minion, nonesuch, paladin, panjandrum, paradigm, paragon, patrician

**HILL**

a: hilly, tumular, tumulose, tumulous

n: butte, drumlin, elevation, eminence, esker, hillock, hogback, holt, hummock, inselberg, kame, knoll, kopje, mesa, monticule, monticulus, mound, namelon, os, scree, talus, tor, tuffet

**HINDER**

a: counterproductive, hindering, impedimental, obstructive

n: barnacle, barrier, encumbrance, hindrance, impediment, obstruction, perplexity, stultification

v: baffle, block, burden, encumber, filibuster, foil, foreclose, frustrate, hamper, hamstring, handicap, impede, limit, prevent, prohibit, retard, stifle, stonewall, straightjacket, stymie, trammel

**HINT**

a: insinuative, insinuatory

**n:** allusion, aspersion, forewarning, illusion, imputation, inkling, innuendo, insinuation, insinuendo, intimation, smack, soupcon, straw in the wind, suggestion

**v:** adumbrate, allude, imply, insinuate, intimate, outline, suggest

## HIRED

**a:** commercial, mercantile, mercenary, venal

**n:** hireling, mercenary, myrmidon, pensionary

## HISS

**a:** hissing, sibilant

**n:** sibilance, sibilant, sibilation

**v:** sibilate

## HISTORY

**a:** annalistic, diachronic, historic, historical, phylogenic

**n:** ancestry, annals, antiquity, archives, biography, chronicle, chronology, epoch, historicity, historiography, landmark, phylogenesis, phylogeny

**v:** historicize, historify, reconstruct

*historian:* analyst, annalist, chronicler, griot, historiographer

*study:* cliometrics, historiology

## HOARSE

**a:** husky, raucous, strident, stridulent, stridulous

**n:** hoarseness, phonasthenia, raucity, stridency, stridor, stridulation, stridulence

## HOAX

**n:** canard, fraud, imposture, mare's nest, rumor

## HOCUS-POCUS

**n:** abracadabra, legerdemain, nonsense, prestidigitation, thaumaturgy

## HODGE-PODGE

**n:** *colluvies, gallimaufry,* hash, miscellany, mixture, *pasticcio, pastiche,* potpourri, ragout, *salmagundi,* smorgasbord

## HOG

**a:** porcine, suoid, swinish

## HOLE

**n:** alveolus, aperture, cavity, concavity, excavation, fistula, foramen, gap, *lacuna, meatus,* mortise, orifice, *os, osculum,* perforation, punctulum, puncture, slit, spiracle, trepan, trephine, vent

**v:** broach, dig, excavate, hollow, perforate, pierce, ream, riddle, tunnel

## HOLLOW

**a:** concave, insincere, lacunal, lacunar, treacherous, tympanic

**n:** alcove, concavity, recess, sinus, slough

**v:** excavate

*combining forms:* -cele, coel-, coelo-

## HOLY

**a:** devout, hallowed, immaculate, inviolable, pietistic, religiose, reverent, sacred, sacrosanct, saintly, sanctified, sanctimonious, unctuous

**n:** adytum, godliness, holiness, religiosity, sacredness, saintliness, sanctification, sanctimoniousness, sanctitude, sanctity

**v:** consecrate, hallow, ordain, revere, sanctify, venerate

*combining forms:* hier-, hiero-, sacr-

*place:* bethesda, halidome, sanctuary, shrine

## HOMAGE

**n:** adoration, allegiance, deference, deferentiality, fealty, fidelity, latria, obeisance, reverence, sacredness, veneration

## HOME

**n:** abode, domicile, habitation, headquarters, hearthstone, ingleside, *pied-a-terre*

## HOMELAND

**a:** compatristic, patrial

**n:** chauvinism

**v:** repatriate

*from same:* compatriot

*homesickness:* nostalgia

**HONEST**

**a:** candid, conscientious, equitable, frank, honorable, impartial, incorrupted, ingenuous, judicial, legitimate, meticulous, rectitudinous, reputable, scrupulous, uncorrupt, upright, veracious

**n:** candor, fidelity, honesty, integrity, judiciality, probity, propriety, rectitude, scrupulosity, sincerity, truthfulness, uprightness, veracity

**HONEY**

**a:** alveolate, faveolate, faviform, melichrous, melleous, melliferous, nectariferous, nectarous

**n:** alveolus, halvah, nectar

**HONOR**

**a:** belaureled, chivalric, chivalrous, commendatory, commending, *cum laude,* estimable, eulogistic, honorable, honored, honorific, *honoris causa,* illustrious, laudatory, laureate, *magna cum laude,* praiseworthy, prestigious, reputable, respectable, revered, *summa cum laude,* venerable, venerated

**n:** accolade, approbation, bays, deference, deferentiality, eminence, ennoblement, esteem, homage, integrity, izzat, kudos, laurels, obeisance, praise, prestige, revere, reverence, testimonial, tribute, veneration

**v:** beatify, canonize, commemorate, confer, deify, dignify, elevate, enhalo, ennoble, exalt, fete, hallow, laureate, lionize, revere, reverence, worship

**HOODED**

**a:** cowled, cucullate, hood-shaped

**HOOF**

**a:** bisulcate, cleft, cloven, ungular, ungulate

**n:** frog, unguis, ungulate

**HOOK**

**a:** aduncous, ancistroid, ankyroid, aquiline, falciform, unciform

**n:** aduncity, crochet, gaff, grapnel, grappling iron, tenterhook

**HOOT**

**a:** ululant

**n:** ululation

**v:** ululate

**HOPE**

**a:** auspicious, bullish, buoyant, confident, enthusiastic, euphoric, expectant, hopeful, optimistic, promising, sanguine, utopian

**n:** anticipation, buoyancy, confidence, enthusiasm, euphoria, expectancy, hopefulness, optimism, reliance, sanguinity

*faint:* pipe dream, velleity

*hopeless:* immitigable, in chancery, incorrigible, irreclaimable, irredeemable

**HORIZONTAL**

**a:** decumbant, prone, prostrate, recumbent, supine

**n:** decumbency, horizontality, lintel, reclination, recumbancy, stringer, summer, transom

**HORN**

**a:** corneous, corniculate, hornlike, horny

*combining forms:* kerat-, kerato-

*of plenty:* cornucopia

*two:* bicorn, bicorned, bicornous, bicornuate

*without:* aceratophorous, polled

**HORRIBLE**

**a:** abhorrent, abominable, appalling, blood-curdling, excruciating, execrable, formidable, ghastly, grisly, gruesome, harrowing, horrendous, horrific, macrabe, unspeakable

**n:** *danse macabe,* horror

**v:** recoil

**HORSE**

**a:** equestrian, equinal, equine, hippoid

n: bronco, dam, entire, equestrianism, *equidae,* equitation, hack, horsemanship, jade, manege, mustang, nag, palomino, roan, sorrel, stallion, ungulate

*combining forms:* equin-, hippo-

*-eating:* hippophagous

*horseman: cavalier, chevalier,* dragoon, equestrian, *equestrienne*

*horseshoe-shaped:* hippocrepiform

*loving:* philhippic

*on horseback: a cheval*

*rearing on hind legs:* pesade

*study:* hippology

## HOSPITAL

n: dispensary, hospice, infirmary, *lazaretto*

## HOSPITALITY

a: amicable, *bonhomous,* companionable, congenial, convivial, cordial, gracious, gregarious, hospitable, neighborly, receptive, sociable

n: amicability, *bonhommie,* camaraderie, congeniality, conviviality, cordiality, friendliness, geniality, graciousness, welcome, xenodochy

## HOST

n: amphitryon, entertainer, innkeeper, landlord, publican, server

## HOSTELRY

n: caravansary, hostel, hotel, xenodochium

## HOSTILE

a: adverse, aggressive, antagonistic, antipathetic, averse, bellicose, belligerent, contentious, disaffected, discordant, feral, glacial, inimicable, inimical, irreconcilable, malevolent, martial, mutinous, provocative, pugilistic, pugnacious, rancorous, rebellious, repugnant, truculent, umbrageous, unfriendly, vehement, venomous, virulent, warlike

n: animosity, *animus,* antagonism, antipathy, backlash, bellicosity, cleavage, combativeness, disaffection, discordance, fifth column, friction, hostility, irreconcilability, pugnacity, rancor, *rencontre,* truculence, umbrage, vehemence

v: incur, polarize

## HOT

a: ardent, candent, choleric, fervent, humid, impetuous, incalescent, incandescent, muggy, pungent, sulfurous, sulphurous, sultry, sweltering, thermal, thermic, torrid, vehement

n: hotness

*combining forms:* cald-, pyro-, therm-, thermo-

## HOTEL

n: caravansary, hostel, hostelry, imaret, inn, parador, pension, spa, xenodocheum

## HOUSE

n: abode, *chateau,* domicile, habitation, mansion, tenement

v: contain, shelter

*gods: lares, penates*

*household:* menage, menagerie

*master:* chatelain, paterfamilias

*mistress:* chatelaine, materfamilias, matron

*valued effects: lares* and *penates*

## HOVER

v: cower, librate, linger

## HOWL

a: roborant

n: ululation, wail

v: ululate, wail

## HUBBUB

n: ado, agitation, brouhaha, coil, hullabaloo, turmoil

## HUE

n: aspect, complexion, shade, tincture, tint

## HUGE

**a:** amplitudinous, astronomical, behemoth, colossal, cyclopean, dinosauric, elephantine, gargantuan, giant, gigantic, Herculean, heroic, imposing, leviathan, macroscopic, magnitudinous, mammoth, monstrous, monumental, Olympian, polyphemic, prodigious, pyramidal, pythonic, stratospheric, titanic, tremendous

**n:** amplitude, behemoth, colossality, colossus, enormity, hugeness, immensity, leviathan, magnitude, prodigality, prominence, titan

*combining forms:* macro-, mega-, megalo-

## HUM

**n:** bombination, murmur, susurration

**v:** bombinate, murmur, susurrate

## HUMAN

**a:** anthropical, anthropogenic, anthropoid(al), anthropomorphic, anthropomorphous, anthropopathic, earthborn, finite, humane, humanoid, incarnate, mortal, mundane, personified, sympathetic

**n:** anthropoid, anthropomorphism, anthropopathite, avatar, clone, earthling, embodiment, hominid, *homo sapiens*, humanity, incarnation, individual, man, mankind, mortal, personification, primate

**v:** anthropomorphize, civilize, embody, humanize, incarnate, personify, refine

*action:* artifact

*and animal:* therianthropic

*below:* infrahuman, subhuman

*combining forms:* anthrop-, anthropo-

*-eating:* cannibalism

*feelings ascribed to inhuman:* anthropopathic

*figure:* antic, caryatid, manikin, telamon

*-like inanimate:* humanization, pathetic fallacy, personification

*study:* anthropogenesis, anthropology, anthropomony, anthroposophy, ecology, eugenics

## HUMBLE

**a:** abject, asking, begging, chastened, genuflectory, meek, modest, respectful, self-effacing, servile, subdued, submissive, suppliant, supplicant, unpretentious

**n:** humbleness, humility

**v:** bow and scrape, cringe, debase, degrade, demean, denigrate, efface, flatter, grovel, humiliate, minify, truckle

## HUMBUG

**a:** pietistic, sanctimonious

**n:** blague, flummery, hypocrisy, hypocrite, imposter, pretension

## HUMILIATE

**a:** chastened, debased, deflated, degraded, degrading, humiliating, ignominious, mortified, mortifying

**n:** abasement, abashment, chagrin, chastenment, debasement, humiliation, mortification

**v:** belittle, denigrate, derogate, disgrace, disparage, insult

*humility:* abjection, abnegation, humbleness, self-denial, self-effacement

## HUMOR

**a:** deadpan, facetious, farcical, funny, humorous, jocose, jocular, jovial, laughable, ludicrous, risible, sardonic, tongue-in-cheek, waggish, whimsical, wry

**n:** baboonery, badinage, caprice, comicality, disposition, *double entendre*, farcicality, humorousness, inclination, irony, jocosity, jocularity, joviality, ludicrousness, placebo, pleasantry, risibles, temperament, waggishness

**v:** indulge

*humorist: farceur*

*humorless:* serious, unmirthful

## HUMPBACK

**a:** gibbous, hunchbacked, kyphotic

n: deformity, gibbosity, hunchback, kyphosis

**HUNDRED**

a: centennary, centennial, centisimal, centuplicate, hundredth

n: centenarian

*combining forms:* cent-, centi-, hect-, hecto-

**HUNGER**

a: esurient, famished, gluttonous, hungry, insatiable, rapacious, ravenous, voracious

n: appetite, edacity, gulosity, pangs, voracity

v: appease, assuage, satisfy

*abnormal:* bulimia, hyperorexia

**HUNTING**

a: cynegetic, venatic

n: chase, coursing, cynegetics, safari, shikar, venation, venery

*hunter: chasseur,* huntsman, jaeger, master of foxhounds, Nimrod, whipper-in

**HURRY**

a: hurriedly, impetuously

v: chivy, decamp, expedite, harass, hightail, nag, precipitate, skedaddle, vamoose

**HURT**

a: aggrieved, atrocious, baneful, delete-

rious, distressed, flagrant, grievous, heinous, hurtful, inimical, injurious, malignant, nocent, nocuous, noxious, offended, pernicious, traumatic, venomous

v: alienate, antagonize, estrange, scarify

**HUSBAND**

a: patrilocal

n: consort, cuckold, spouse

*combining form:* andr-

*one:* monandry, monogamy

*two:* bigamy, polyandry, polygamy

**HYMN**

n: antiphon, canticle, chorale, dithyramb, doxology, introit, laud, magnificat, prayer, processional, recessional, requiem, Sanctus, *te deum,* theody

**HYPOCRISY**

a: disingenuous, dissimulative, hypocritical, insincere, Pecksniffian, pharisaical, pietistic, pretentious, religiose, sanctimonious, specious

n: cant, dissimulation, duplicity, piosity, pretense, religiosity, sanctimoniousness, self-righteousness, speciosity

*hypocrite:* dissembler, dissimulator, pretender

**HYPOTHESIS**

a: conjectural, hypothetical, notional, suppositious, theoretical

n: premise, thesis

## IDEA

**a:** conceptual, conceptualistic, hypothetical, ideational, ideative, ideogenetic, ideological, innate, notional, tumefacient

**n:** abstraction, archetype, axiom, brainstorming, concept, conception, conceptus, conjecture, construct, fixation, generalization, hunch, *idee fixe*, *idee recue*, impression, inkling, intuition, notion, obsession, percept, perception, postulate, preoccupation, sacred cow, supposition, surmise, vehicle

**v:** articulate, conceptualize, crystallize, formulate, gestate, ideate, reify, synonymize

> *advanced:* avant-garde, fin-de-siecle, visionary
> *combining form:* ideo-
> *fear:* ideophobia
> *one accepting new:* neoteric
> *one hating new:* misoneist

## IDEAL

**a:** aerial, altitudinarian, chimerical, doctrinaire, idealistic, messianic, paradisaical, paradisical, platonic, poetic, quixotic, romantic, sentimental, utopian, visionary

**n:** apotheosis, archetype, canonization, deification, embodiment, exemplar, idealization, idealogy, *imago*, incarnation, maxim, messianism, model, motto, original, personification, principle, prototype, spiritualization, stellification

**v:** apotheosize, canonize, deify, exalt, idealize, spiritualize, stellify

> *idealist:* altitudinarian, Don Quixote, utopian, visionary

## IDENTICAL

**a:** congruent, equal, equivalent, indistinguishable, isonomous, same, synonymous, tantamount

**n:** clone, equivalence, identicality, ringer, selfsameness, synonymity

> *combining forms:* homo-, synon-, taut-, tauto-

## IDENTIFICATION

**a:** identificatory

**n:** diagnosis, empathy, homoousia, identity, individuality, ipseity, persona, stigma, synonymity

**v:** diagnosticate, identify, recognize

## IDIOM

**n:** argot, cant, colloquialism, jargon, parlance, *patois*, vernacular

## IDLE

**a:** *faineant*, indolent, lackadaisical, otiose, slothful, superfluous, trivial, vacuous

**n:** aimlessness, disoccupation, flanerie, idleness, idling, inaction, inactivity, indolence, leisure, otiosity, sedentation, triviality

> *people:* badaud, dawdler, *faineant*, *flaneur*, flotsam and jetsam, loiterer, sluggard, vagrant
> *talk:* caquet, vaporing

## IDOL

**n:** demigod(dess), effigy, image
> *worship:* iconolatry, idolatry

## IGNORANCE

**a:** abysmal, agnostic, analphabetic, artless, benighted, ignorant, illiterate, incognoscible, inscient, nescient, ultracrepidarian, uncultured, unlearned, unlettered, unschooled, unsophisticated, unwitting

n: agnosticism, betise, ignoration, illiteracy, incognoscibility, inscience, nescience, rusticity, sciolism

v: bypass, circumvent, discount, disregard, elide, ignore, neglect, omit, overlook, pretermit, rebuff

## ILL

a: ailing, cachectic, cadaverous, hurtful, inauspicious, indisposed, infirm, invalid, maladive, morbid, morbose, pernicious, sick, under the weather, unpropitious, untoward, unwell, valetudinarian

n: affliction, ailment, cachexia, complaint, disease, ictus, illness, infirmity, invalid, malady, *malaise*, relapse

v: convalesce, malinger, recuperate

-*humored*: bilious, cantankerous, captious, churlish, contentious, disputatious, ill-natured, irascible, pettish, petulant, perverse, pugnacious, querulous, surly, waspish

*person imagining*: hypochondriac, valetudinarian

-*will*: animosity, animus, antagonism, enmity, hostility, malice

## ILLEGAL

a: contraband, criminal, illegitimate, illicit, misbegotten, nugatory, unauthorized, unconstitutional, unlawful

n: crime, malfeasance, malversation, misfeasance

## ILLEGITIMATE

a: counterfeit, debased, erratic, illogical, irregular, misbegotten, spurious, supposititious, supposititious, unwarranted

n: bar sinister, bastard, *filius populi*, mongrel

## ILLOGICAL

a: acategorical, equivocal, fallacious, incoherent, incongruous, inconsequent, inconsistent, irrational, parabolical, paralogical, paralogistic, rambling, unreasonable

n: fallacy, illogicality, incoherence, incoherency, *non sequitur*, paralogism, sophism, unreasonableness, unsoundness

## ILLUMINATING

a: enlightening, fluorescent, illuminated, incandescent, luminescent, luminferous

n: illumination, miniature, rubric

## ILLUSION

a: barmecidal, chimerical, deceptive, fatuitous, fictitious, ghostly, illusionistic, illusive, illusory, imaginary, phantasmagoric(al), phantasmal, phantasmic, phantom, prestidigitatory, spectral

n: aberration, anamorphosis, apparition, chimera, *deja vu*, *fata morgana*, hallucination, *ignis fatuuis*, mirage, misapprehension, misconception, paramnesia, phantasm, phenomenon, pipe dream, revenant, specter, spectrum

## ILLUSTRATIVE

a: delineative, demonstrative, descriptive, descriptory, illustrational, pictorial, picturesque, representative

n: cutaway, frontispiece, graphics, illustration, picture

## ILLUSTRIOUS

a: august, celebrated, distinguished, eminent, formidable, honorific, immortal, luscent, magnific, magnificent, majestic, prestigious, redoubtable, regal, resplendent, signal, transcendent

## IMAGE

a: conceptual, concipient, eidetic, imaginary

n: alter ego, conception, counterpart, effigy, icon, likeness, motif, opinion, portrait, replica, representation, resemblance, sculpture, semblance, similitude, simulacrum, stereotype, topos

*worship*: fetishism, iconolatry, idolatry

## IMAGINARY

a: apocryphal, apparitional, chimerical, fanciful, fictitious, fictive, hypothetical thing, idealistic, ideational, illusive, imaginational, insubstantial, legendary, mythical, notional, quixotic, simulated, supposititious, unrealistic, utopian, veritable, visionary

n: delusion, *fata morgana*, figment, genius, hallucination, hallucinosis, ideaphoria, imagination, ingenuity, phantasy, resourcefulness, reverie, unreality, visionary, whimsy

v: conceive, conjure up, envisage, fabricate, fantasize, fictionalize, ideate, imagine, meditate, mythologize, surmise, visualize

## IMITATION

a: counterfeit, derivative, echoic, emulatory, emulous, epigonic, epigonous, ersatz, fake, imitative, mimetic, mimical, sequacious, slavish, spurious, substitute, synthetic

n: burlesque, caricature, counterfeit, emulation, fake, imitancy, imitant, lampoon, mimesis, mimicry, mockery, parody, *pastiche*, *postiche*, pretense, sequacity, simulacrum, simulation, spoof, substitute

v: counterfeit, emulate, feign, imitate, pretend, reproduce, simulate

*imitator:* epigone, impostor

## IMMATERIAL

a: apparitional, asomatous, diaphanous, ethereal, illusionary, incorporeal, insubstantial, irrelevant, spiritual, transcendent, unimportant

n: diaphaneity, ethereality, immateriality, incorporeality, incorporeity, insubstantiality, irrelevancy

## IMMATURE

a: adolescent, basic, callow, fledgling, impubic, inchoate, infantile, jejune, juvenile, *nouveau*, puerile, rudimentary, underdeveloped, unripe, verdant

n: greenhorn, immaturity, incunabulum, infancy, infantility, juniority, juvenility, nonage, puerilism, puerility, verdancy

## IMMEASURABLE

a: abysmal, imponderable, incommensurable, infinite, unfathomable, vast

## IMMEDIATE

a: direct, forthwith, immediately, instantaneously, instanter, presto, proximate, straightaway, *tout de suite*

n: directness, immediacy, instantaneity

## IMMENSE

a: big, huge, humongous, large

n: colossality, immeasurability, immensity, indefinitude, magnitude, vastitude, vastity

## IMMODERATE

a: bizarre, eccentric, exaggerated, exorbitant, extravagant, inordinate, intemperate, *outre*, unreasonable

n: extravagance, gulosity, immoderation, inordinancy, intemperance

## IMMORAL

a: debauched, degenerate, dissolute, idssolute, lewd, libertine, licentious, orgiastic, pornographic, profligate, reprobate, Saturnalian, unedifying, unprincipled, unsavory, wanton

n: debauchery, depravity, dissipation, immorality, intemperance, lewdness, obliquity, orgy, Saturnalia, turpitude

## IMMOVABLE

a: fixed, implanted, monolithic, obdurate, sessile

## IMPARTIAL

a: candid, dispassionate, equitable, fair, impersonal, judicial, judicious, nonpartisan, objective, unbiased, unprejudiced

n: detachment, disinterestedness, fairness, impartiality

## IMPASSABLE

a: impenetrable, imperforate, impermeable, impervious, insurmountable, unconquerable

## IMPASSE

**n:** blind alley, block, crisis, *cul-de-sac*, deadlock, fix, obstruction, pickle, predicament, stalemate

## IMPASSIONED

**a:** (per)fervid, delirious, dithyrambic, enthusiastic, evangelistic, fanatical, hysterical, impetuous, maniac(al), vehement, wild, zealous

## IMPASSIVE

**a:** apathetic, calm, comatose, expressionless, hermetic, icy, imperturbable, inanimate, indifferent, insensate, invertebrate, motionless, nonchalant, phlegmatic, serene, spineless, stolid, torpid, torporific, unperturbed

## IMPATIENT

**a:** anxious, apprehensive, choleric, fidgety, footloose, impetuous, intolerant, on edge, pettish, petulant, precipitate, previous, restive, restless, waspish

## IMPEDIMENT

**n:** barricade, block, check, *cul-de-sac*, embarrassment, encumbrance, hindrance, hitch, *impedimentia*, inhibition, obstacle, obstruction, snag

## IMPENDING

**a:** apocalyptic, approaching, close, Damoclean, emergent, imminent, impendent, incumbent, inevitable, near, nigh, pressing, threatening

**n:** handwriting on the wall, sword of Damocles

## IMPERATIVE

**a:** cogent, compulsatory, compulsory, *de regle*, *de rigueur*, demanding, important, necessary, obligatory, peremptory, prerequisite, required, requisite

**n:** command, injunction, mandate, *mandatum*, prerequisite

## IMPERCEPTIBLE

**a:** gradual, hidden, impalpable, indiscernible, secret, slight, subliminal, subtle, unnoticed

**n:** graduality, imperceptibility

## IMPERFECT

**a:** atelic, contingent, defective, dilapidated, imperfective, inadequate, inchoate, inchoative, incipient, lacking, potential, rudimentary, short, suboptimal, substandard, unsatisfactory, wanting

**n:** blemish, discard, fault, imperfection, reject

## IMPERISHABLE

**a:** eternal, forever, immarcescible, immarcessible, immortal, indestructable, permanent, perpetual

**n:** eternality, imperishableness, perpetuality, perpetuity, subtility

## IMPERSONAL

**a:** detached, impartial, infrahuman, inhuman, mechanical, monolithic

**n:** dehumanization, depersonalization, personation

**v:** dehumanize, depersonalize, robotize

## IMPETUOUS

**a:** (per)fervid, *a corps perdu*, abrupt, bold, foolhardy, hasty, headlong, impassioned, impulsive, intractable, passionate, precipitate, rash, restive, temperamental, vehement

**n:** impetuosity, impulsivity

## IMPISH

**a:** elvish, frolicsome, pestiferous, playful, puckish, whimsical

**n:** impishness, puckishness, whimsicality

## IMPLICATION

**a:** connotated, connotative, hinted, implied, implying, indicated, inferred, insinuated, signified, subintelligential, tacit, unwritten

**n:** connotation, deduction, entanglement, inference, insinuation, insinuendo, significance, signification

**v:** allude, connote, entail, imply, infer, insinuate, intimate, involve, purport

*affirmative:* negative pregnant

## IMPOLITE

**a:** dedecorous, discourteous, disrespectful, indecorous, insolent, inurbane, rude, uncivil, uncourtly, uncouth, ungracious, unmannerly, unpolished, unrefined

**n:** discourteousy, impoliteness, incivility, inurbanity

## IMPORTANCE

**a:** acute, basic, basilic(al), cardinal, consequential, considerable, crucial, determinative, earthshaking, exalted, fateful, formidable, fundamental, impactful, impactive, imperative, influential, momentous, monumental, overriding, paramount, pivotal, pompous, portentous, predominant, preponderant, prominent, redoubtable, salient, seminal, signal, significant, strategic, substantive

**n:** aggrandizement, alpha and omega, celebrity, colossus, concernment, consequence, cruciality, eminence, flatulence, luminary, *magnifico*, magnitude, memorabilia, mogul, moment, panjandrum, *piece de resistance*, pomposity, potentate, precedence, prestige, sachem, signality, significance, staple, VIP, worthy

> *thing of little:* *bagatelle,* bauble, geegaw, gewgaw, gimcrack, inconsequence, *minutia, minutiae,* nihility, nonentity, nullity, trifle

## IMPOSING

**a:** august, commanding, exalted, grand, grandiloquent, grandiose, handsome, haughty, imperial, impressive, magnific, magnificent, majestic, pretentious, regal, sonorous, striking, superlative, tall, towering

**n:** grandiosity, imposture, majesty, regality

**v:** impose, levy

## IMPOSSIBLE

**a:** chimerical, fantastic, hopeless, impracticable, insuperable, insurmountable, invincible, unacceptable, unrealistic, unsurpassable

**n:** impossibilism, impossibility, impracticability, insuperability, invincibility

## IMPOSTOR

**n:** charlatan, cheat, epigone, humbug, hypocrite, imposter, mountebank, Pharisee, pretender, quacksalver

> *imposture:* charlatanry, hoax, hocuspocus, mountebankery, pretense, sham, simulacrum

## IMPOTENCE

**a:** deficient, impotent, incapable, powerless, sterile, unable, weak

**n:** anaphrodisia, fecklessness, feebleness, helplessness, impotency, sterility, weakness

## IMPRACTICABLE

**a:** impossible, imprudent, infeasible, insuperable, unrealistic, unwise

## IMPRACTICAL

**a:** academic, daydreaming, doctrinaire, dogmatic, escapist, feckless, idealistic, implausible, inexecutable, irresponsible, otherworldly, pedantic, poetic(al), quixotic, romantic, speculative, theoretical, unfeasible, utopian, visionary

## IMPREGNATION

**n:** fecundation, fertilization, indoctrination, spermatization

**v:** fecundate, fertilize, impregnate, inseminate

## IMPRESSION

**a:** baronial, commanding, dignified, elegant, formidable, grand, impactful, imposing, impressive, indelible, lofty, penetrative, redoubtable, stately

**n:** *apercu,* grandeur, grandiloquence, grandiosity, hunch, impact, impressiveness, imprint, indentation, influence, inkling, intimation, intuition, magnificence, opulency, panoply, tout ensemble, vista

## IMPRISON

**n:** confinement, durance, immuration, immurement, imprisonment, incarceration, limbo, restraint v: confine, detain, immure, incarcerate, intern, jail, restrain, shut up

## IMPROMPTU

a: *ad lib, ad libitum,* ad-libbed, autoschediastic, casual, extemporaneous, extemporary, extempore, improvisational, improvisatorial, improvisatory, improvised, improviso, impulsive, informal, off-hand, spontaneous, unpremeditated, unstudied

n: *ad lib,* autoschediasm, improvisation

v: improvise

## IMPROPER

a: errant, illicit, immodest, impertinent, inaccurate, inappropriate, incongruous, indecent, indecorous, indelicate, inexpedient, insubordinate, insurgent, irrelevant, malodorous, rebellious, scabrous, solecistic, unacceptable, unbecoming, unethical, unseemly, untoward, unwise

n: barbarism, *faux pas, gaffe,* impropriety, insubordination, insurgence, insurgency, insurrection, solecism

## IMPROVE

a: ameliorative, beneficial, improving, salutary

n: amelioration, enhancement, improvement, perfectionment, refinement, reformation

v: ameliorate, amend, augment, embellish, embroider, enhance, garnish, gild, gloss, make amends, meliorate, optimize, reclaim, rectify, redress, refine, refurbish, regenerate, rehabilitate, renovate, revamp, transfigure, transform

## IMPROVISE

a: extemporaneous, extempore, impromptu, improvised, makeshift, off-the-cuff, temporary, unrehearsed

n: *ad lib,* autoschediasm, improvisation

v: *ad lib,* extemporize, improvisate

## IMPRUDENT

a: audacious, ill-advised, impolitic, impracticable, improvident, incautious,

indiscreet, injudicious, procacious, rash, unwise

## IMPUDENT

a: audacious, cheeky, contemptuous, contumelious, disrespectful, forward, insolent, malapert, sassy, shameless, supercilious, toplofty, unmannerly

n: cheekiness, impudence, impudency, incivility, procacity, sassiness

## IMPULSE

a: ballistic, capricious, impetuous, impulsive, rash, reckless, spontaneous, unpremeditated

n: impetuosity, impetus, impulsiveness, impulsivity, incentive, incitement, instigation, nisus, spontaneity

## IMPURE

a: adulterated, blemished, contaminated, defiled, lewd, macular, maculate, polluted, unchaste, unrectified, unwholesome

n: adulteration, contamination, corruption, defilement, impurity, pollution, putrescence

v: adulterate, debauch, defile, impurify

## IN

*combining forms:* end-, endo-, ento-, intra-, intro-

*fact: de facto,* the place cited or quoted

*the same place: ibid, ibidem*

*the work cited: op cit, opere citato*

## INACCURATE

a: apocryphal, careless, discrepant, erroneous, fallacious, incorrect, inexact, misleading

n: discrepancy, erratum, fallacy, imprecision, inaccuracy, inexactitude, inexactness, misconception

## INACTION

a: anergic, comatose, deliquescent, dormant, faineant, feckless, inactive, inanimate, indolent, inoperative, latent, lethargic, otiose, quiescent, sedentary, slothful, supine, torpid, withdrawn n: *acedia,* deliquescence, depression, doldrums, dormancy, *ennui, faienance,* fecklessness, idleness, inactivity, indolence, inertia, inertness, lassitude, lethargy, otiosity, passivity, quiescence, quietude, sedentation, slothfulness, stasis, supinity, torpidity, torpor

## INADEQUATE

a: deficient, disabled, disproportionate, exiguous, futile, impotent, ineffective, inefficacious, insufficient, *jejune,* meager, mediocre, perfunctory, scanty, skimpy, sparse

n: dearth, deficiency, inadequacy, incapacitation, inefficacy, insufficiency

## INADVISABLE

a: contraindicative, disadvantageous, impolitic, impracticable, inappropriate, inexpedient, inopportune

n: contraindication, inadvisability

## INANE

a: empty, fatuitous, feckless, imbecile, insubstantial, *jejune,* pointless, puerile, shallow, stratospheric, stupid, vacant, vacuous, void

n: emptiness, hollowness, inanition, inanity, lethargy, *marasmus,* shallowness, vacuity

## INAPPROPRIATE

a: impertinent, inapposite, inapt, incongruous, inconvenient, indecorous, inexpedient, infelicitous, inopportune, *malapropos,* unbecoming, unseasonable, unsuitable, untimely, untoward

## INATTENTIVE

a: absent-minded, abstracted, astigmatic, bemused, distant, distracted, distrait, distraught, harum-scarum, heedless, incogitable, incogitant, incurious, negligent, oscitant, preoccupied, remiss

n: abstraction, heedlessness, ignoration, inadvertency, inattention, incogitancy, incuriosity, misfeasance, neglect, oscitancy, oscitation, preoccupation, remission

## INAUGURATE

a: auspicatory, inaugurative, initiatory, introductory

n: accession, inauguration, induction, installation, institution, investiture

v: auspicate, begin, found, induct, initiate, install, institute, introduce, invest, open, originate, start

## INBORN

a: ancestral, cognate, congenital, connate, constitutional, endogamous, endogenous, familial, hereditary, idiopathic, inbred, indigenous, ingrained, inherent, inherited, innate, institutional, intrinsic, intuitive, native, natural

n: diathesis, predisposition

## INCAPABLE

a: disabled, feckless, helpless, impotent, incapacitated, insufficient, powerless, sterile, unable, unqualified

n: helplessness

## INCENTIVE

n: allurement, attraction, catalyst, fillip, incitation, incitement, inducement, instigation, motivation, provocation, reason, stimulant, stimulation, stimulus, temptation

## INCEPTION

n: beginning, inauguration, initiation, origin, principium

## INCIDENTAL

a: accessory, added, adjunct, adscititious, adventitious, ancillary, apropos, auxiliary, casual, circumstantial, collateral, concurrent, consomitant, contingent, digressive, *en passant,* episodic, extraneous, fortuitous, helping, incidentally, interlocutory, intervenient, obiter, parenthetical, secondary, subordinate, subsidiary, supplementary, tangential

n: circumstance, circumstantiality, concomitant, contingency, digression, episode, event, incident, interlocution, *obiter dictum,* phenomenon

**INCITE**

**a:** animative, catalytic, hortative, hortatory, inciting, incitory, provocative, stimulatory

**n:** *agent provocateur*, concitation, fomentation, incitation, incitement, instigation, provocation

**v:** actuate, animate, entice, flagellate, foment, instigate, lure, seduce, solicit, stimulate, suborn, suscitate

**INCLINATION**

**a:** acclivitous, disposed, inclinable, inclinatory, inclining, predisposed, suasible, tendentious

**n:** acclivity, affectation, diathesis, disposition, gradient, partiality, penchant, predilection, predisposition, prejudice, proclivity, propensity, tendency, tropism, velleity, versant

**INCLUSIVE**

**a:** capacious, compendious, comprehensive, cyclopedic, encompassing

**n:** comprehensibility, inclusiveness

**v:** comprehend, comprise, consist of, contain, embed, embody, embrace, encompass, include, incorporate, subsume, take in

**INCOMPATIBLE**

**a:** disagreeing, discordant, dissonant, immiscible, incongruous, inconsistent, irreconcilable, repugnant, uncongenial

**INCOMPETENT**

**a:** impertinent, inadmissible, inapt, incapacitated, inept, *non compos*, unqualified

**n:** inaptitude, incapacitation, incapacity, incompetence, Peter principle

**INCOMPLETE**

**a:** contingent, defective, deficient, elementary, fractional, fractionary, fragmental, fragmentary, imperfect, inchoate, inchoative, incipient, insufficient, partial, potential, rudimentary, truncated, unperfected

**INCOMPREHENSIBLE**

**a:** ambiguous, enigmatic, impenetrable, indefinite, inscrutable, nebulous, numinous, undecipherable, unfathomable, unintelligible

**n:** ambiguity, enigma, incomprehensibility, indefinitude, nebulosity

**INCONSISTENT**

**a:** antagonistic, contradictuous, discordant, discrepant, immiscible, incompatible, incongruous, inharmonious, irreconcilable, paradoxical, repugnant

**n:** contrariety, disagreement, discrepancy, disparity, incompatibility, incongruity, inconsistency, misalliance, *non sequitur*, paradox, variance

**INCONSTANT**

**a:** alternating, ambivalent, capricious, chameleonic, changeable, fickle, fluctuating, mercurial, mutable, quicksilver, random, spasmodic, unstable, vacillating, vagrant, variable, vertiginous

**INCONTROVERTIBLE**

**a:** certain, immutable, incontestable, indisputable, irrecusable, irrefrangible, irrefutable, unmistakable, unquestionable

**INCONVENIENT**

**a:** disadvantageous, discommodious, embarrassing, inappropriate, incommodious, inexpedient, inopportune, unseasonable

**n:** disadvantage, handicap, impediment, inconvenience

**v:** annoy, *discommode*, embarrass, *incommode*, plague, vex

**INCORPORATION**

**n:** amalgamation, embodiment, incarnation, inclusion, synthesis, union

**INCORRECT**

**a:** adrift, amiss, awry, erroneous, fallacious, imprecise, improper, inaccurate, solecistic, sophistic, specious, unbecoming, unseemly

**n:** fallacy, imprecision, impropriety, inaccuracy, misapprehension, misconception, misconstruction, misnomer, mistake, paralogism

 *combining forms:* caco-, mal-, mis-

 *words:* cacography, catachresis, malapropism, pseudography, solecism

## INCREASE

**a:** accessorial, accumulable, accumulative, augmentative, cumulative, escalating, exacerbative, incremental, multiplicative, pyramiding

**n:** accretion, accruement, accumulation, additament, advancement, agglutination, aggrandizement, augmentation, concrescence, crescendo, enhancement, exacerbation, groundswell, increment, intensification, multiplication, progress, progression, propagation, tumescence

**v:** accrue, aggrandize, aggravate, amplify, augment, burgeon, dilate, distend, elevate, enhance, escalate, exacerbate, exalt, flare up, hypertrophy, inflame, inflate, irrupt, maximalize, multiply, proliferate, propagate, protract, spiral, surge, tumesce, wax, whet

 *gradual:* accrescence, accretion, agglutination

## INCURABLE

**a:** immedicable, incorrigible, insanable, intractable, irredeemable, irremediable, irreparable

 *optimist:* Micawber, Pollyanna

## INDECENCY

**a:** cloacal, coprophilous, *grivois,* immodest, improper, indecent, indelicate, lewd, ribald, rude, scabbrous, scatological, scurrilous, unseemly

**n:** grossness, immodesty, impudicity, indelicacy, obscenity, ribaldry, scurrility

## INDECISION

**a:** ambivalent, capricious, faltering, hesitant, inconclusive, indecisive, indefinite, indistinct, invertebrate, irresolute, vacillating, vague, wavering

**n:** ambivalence, doubt, fluctuation, *folie de doute,* incertitude, indecisiveness, irresolution

## INDEFINITE

**a:** ambiguous, amorphous, aoristic, equivocal, ethereal, general, heterogeneous, imprecise, inconclusive, indefinitive, indeterminable, indeterminate, nebular, nebulous, random, *sine die,* uncertain, unformalized, unmathematical, vague, vaporous

**n:** ambiguity, indefiniteness, indefinitude, nebulosity, uncertainty

## INDELICATE

**a:** coarse, immodest, lewd, salacious, scabrous, tactless, uncouth, unrefined, vulgar

**n:** immodesty, indelicacy, salaciousness, salacity, scabrousness

## INDEPENDENT

**a:** autonomic, autonomous, commutative, free, individualistic, objective, self-governing, sovereign, substantive, unconstrained, undoctrinaire, unregimented

**n:** autarchy, autonomy, emancipation, independence, objectification, sovereignty, unconstraint

 *person:* maverick, mugwump

## INDESCRIBABLE

**a:** awful, ineffable, inenarrable, unspeakable, unutterable, vague

## INDESTRUCTIBLE

**a:** adamantine, everlasting, immarcescible, inviolable, irrefragable, strong, tough

**n:** everlastingness

## INDETERMINATE

**a:** aoristic, capricious, dubious, imprecise, indefinite, indefinitive, irresolute, unstable, vague

## INDEX

**n:** concordance, indication, keyword-in-context, KWIC, repertory, token

**INDIA**

**a:** Bharati, Indian, Indic

*study:* Indology

**INDICATION**

**a:** emblematic, indicative, pathognomonic, prodromal, significant, significative, significatory, suggestive, symbolic, symptomatic

**n:** criterion, evidence, gesticulation, hallmark, index, indicator, insigne, insignia, measure, patent, sign, symbol, symptom, token

**v:** bespeak, betoken, denote, designate, disclose, evidence, evince, exhibit, harbinger, herald, indicate, manifest, particularize, presage, reveal, show, signal, signify, specify

**INDIFFERENCE**

**a:** adiaphorous, agnostic, aloof, anapodictic, apathetic, careless, cursory, detached, disinterested, imperturbable, incurious, indifferent, insipid, insouciant, insusceptible, languid, Laodicean, lethargic, lukewarm, mechanical, nonchalant, phlegmatic, *pococurante,* stolid, unconcerned, unenthusiastic, unexcitable

**n:** *acedia, adiaphoria,* agnosticism, apathy, detachment, inappetency, inertia, insouciance, lackadaisy, languor, listlessness, minauderie, nonchalance, phlegm, pococurantism, sangfroid, stoicism, stolidity, supineness, supinity

**INDIGNITY**

**n:** affront, dishonor, disrespect, humiliation, hurt, ignominy, infamy, injury, *lese majeste,* offense, unpleasantry, wrong

*indignation:* anger, contempt, fury, wrath

**INDIRECT**

**a:** abstruse, ambagious, circuitous, circumlocutious, circumlocutory, circumstantial, collateral, consequential, deceitful, devious, mediate, oblique, roundabout, secondhand, serpentine, vicarious

**n:** ambage, ambiguity, circuitry, circumbendibus, circumlocution, circumstan-

tiality, deceitfulness, detour, deviousness, duplicity, indirection, periphrasis, sinuosity, tortuosity

**INDISCREET**

**a:** heedless, imprudent, incautious, inconsiderate, injudicious, rash, untactful

**n:** foolishness, heedlessness, imprudence, incaution, indiscretion, injudiciousness, untactfulness

**INDISCRIMINATE**

**a:** desultory, haphazard, heterogeneous, hit-or-miss, indistinguishable, promiscuous, random

**n:** heterogeneity, indiscrimination, promiscuity, unrestraint

**INDISPENSABLE**

**a:** *de rigueur,* essential, fundamental, obligatory, prerequisite, requisite, *sine qua non*

**n:** condition precedent, essentiality, indispensability, prerequisite, requisite, *sine qua non*

**INDISPOSED**

**a:** adverse, aeger, averse, disinclined, hesitant, indolent, loath, reluctant, unfriendly, unwilling

**INDISPUTABLE**

**a:** apodictic, certain, incontestable, incontrovertible, indubitable, irrefrangible, irrefutable, undeniable, unquestionable

**INDISTINCT**

**a:** amorphous, ethereal, hazy, nebular, nebulous, vague, vaporous

**n:** penumbra, twilight zone

**INDIVIDUAL**

**a:** definite, discrete, diverse, explicit, idiomatic, ontogenetic, particular, personal, specific, subjective

**n:** individuality, individuum, ipseity, person, singleton

*combining form:* idio-

*individually:* respectively
*language:* idiolect
*mark:* haecceity, idiograph, individuality

**INDUCTIVE**

**a:** *a posteriori,* aposterioristic, empirical, inductive

**n:** empiricism, epagoge

**INDUSTRIAL**

**a:** assiduous, attentive, busy, diligent, indefatigable, industrious, operose, painstaking, persevering, proletarian, sedulous, zealous

**n:** assiduity, diligence, industriousness, industry, laboriousness, operosity, perseverance, sedulity, steadfastness

**v:** nationalize

*worker:* boilermaker, businessman, proletariat

**INEFFECTIVE**

**a:** abortive, feckless, flaccid, impotent, incapable, ineffectual, inefficacious, neutralized, powerless

**n:** flaccidity, impotency, ineffectiveness, ineffectuality

**v:** invalidate, nullify, vitiate, void

**INEFFICIENT**

**a:** clumsy, fumbling, inept, inexpert

**n:** inefficiency, maladministration

**v:** maladminister

**INEQUALITY**

**a:** unequal

**n:** anomalism, anomaly, disparity, disproportion, dissimilarity, divergence, diversity, imparity, inequity, injustice

*combining form:* aniso-

**INERTIA**

**n:** indisposition, inertness, laziness, neutality, sleep, sluggishness, stillness, torpidity, *vis inertiae*

**INESCAPABLE**

**a:** certain, doomed, imminent, ineluctable, ineludible, inevitable, unavoidable, unescapable

**n:** doom, fate, ineluctability, inescapability, inevitability, inevitableness

**INEXACT**

**a:** acategorical, desultory, equivocal, erroneous, imponderable, imprecise, incorrect, loose, uncertain, unclear

**n:** equivocality, imponderability, imprecision, inevitability, inexactitude

**INEXCUSABLE**

**a:** excuseless, inexpiable, irremissible, unforgivable, unjustifiable, unpardonable, unprovoked

**INEXISTENCE**

**n:** nihilism, nonentity, nonexistence, nullibicity, nullity

**INEXPERIENCED**

**a:** amateurish, callow, fledgling, immature, incompetent, inconversant, inexpert, maladroit, unfledged, uninitiated, unseasoned, unskilled, untrained, verdant

**n:** amateur, beginner, fledgling, greenhorn, neophyte, newcomer, novice, rookie, tenderfoot, tyro

**INEXPLICABLE**

**a:** enigmatic, mysterious, preternatural, strange, supermundane, supernatural

**INFAMOUS**

**a:** abhorrent, arrant, atrocious, dedecorous, despicable, execrable, heinous, ignominious, inglorious, nefarious, notorious, obloquial, opprobrious, wellknown

**n:** abasement, ignominy, infamy, obloquy, odium, opprobrium

**INFANCY**

**n:** *bas age,* childhood, incunabulum, minority, nonage

**INFECTION**

**a:** communicable, demoralizing, infectious, infective, pathological, pestiferous, pestilent, septic, transmissible, transmitted, virulent

**n:** contagion, contagiosity, corruption, infectivity, pathology, septicity, zymosis

   *source:* focus, *nidus*

**INFER**

**a:** denotative, illative, inferential, putative

**n:** conclusion, corollary, deduction, extrapolation, illation, inference

**v:** conclude, conjecture, deduce, educe, extrapolate, guess, surmise, work out

**INFERIOR**

**a:** *declasse*, mediocre, nether, subaltern, subnormal, suboptimal, subordinate, substandard

**n:** inferiority, mediocrity, subalternant, subalternation, subnormality, subordination

   *combining forms:* infra-, sub-

**INFERNAL**

**a:** avernal, bad, chthonian, chthonic, damned, demoniac, diabolical, fiendish, flagitous, hellish, horrible, horrific, malevolent, Mephistophelian, pandemoniac, stygian, tartarean, wicked

**INFERTILE**

**a:** barren, infecund, sterile, unfruitful, unproductive

**n:** barrenness, fruitlessness, infecundity, infertility, sterility

**INFINITE**

**a:** boundless, cosmic, eternal, illimitable, immeasurable, inexhaustible, infinitesimal, limitless, unlimited

**n:** eternity, inconsequentiality, infinitesimality, iota, negligibility, scintilla

**INFLAMMATION**

**a:** ignescent, incendiary, inflammatory, phlogenetic, phlogenic, phlogistic, provocative, seditious, suppurative

**n:** congestion, phlegmasia, phlogosis, suppuration

   *drug:* antiphlogistic, calmative

**INFLATED**

**a:** bombastic, exaggerated, flatulent, incrassate, magniloquent, pompous, portentous, swollen, tumescent, turgescent, turgid, tympanic, tympanitic

**n:** distention, flatulence, hedge, inflation, intumescence, pomposity, tumescence, tumidity, turgidity, turgidness, tympany

**v:** exaggerate, expand, inflate, swell, tumefy, tumesce

**INFLEXIBLE**

**a:** immutable, implacable, implastic, impliable, indocile, inductile, indurate, indurative, inexorable, intransigent, irreconcilable, obstinant, refractory, relentless, retractable, stubborn, unalterable, uncompromising, unrelenting, unyielding

**n:** immutability, implacableness, implasticity, induration, inexorability, inflexibility, intransigence, obstinacy, perseveration, relentlessness, rigidification, rigidity, unadaptability, unalterability

**INFLICT**

**v:** afflict, impose, lay, perpetrate, trouble

**INFLUENCE**

**a:** actuated, effective, guided, hierarchical, impelled, influential, instigated, miasmal, miasmatic, miasmic, potent, powerful, prominent

**n:** afflation, afflatus, ascendency, authority, charisma, clout, dominance, drive, force, impulsion, incentive, incitement, leverage, manipulation, miasma, patronage, predomination, preeminence, prestige, *puissance*, sanction, stimulus, vector

**v:** actuate, affect, brainwash, impel, impregnate, indoctrinate, infuse, lobby, militate, modify, predominate

   *easily:* docile, ductile, flexible, malleable, pliable, susceptible, tractile

   *impervious to:* hermetic, impassive, unperturbed

influential person: eminence grise, kitchen cabinet, luminary, magnate, Svengali, tycoon

## INFORM

**a:** *au courant, au fait,* cognizant, conscious, conversant, informed, up-to-date

**n:** afterthought, appendix, database, disclosure, *dossier,* feedback, hearsay, information, intelligence, *pabulum,* propaganda, revelation, tidings

**v:** acquaint, alert, apprise, brief, delate, denounce, divulge, enlighten, familiarize, impart, instruct, notify, prime

*informer:* decoy, delator, *quidnunc,* spy, stoolie, stool pigeon

## INFORMAL

**a:** casual, colloquial, *en famille,* irregular, natural, relaxed, simple, unceremonious, unconventional, unofficial, unorthodox

## INFRINGE

**n:** breach, contravention, encroachment, infraction, infringement, intrusion, nonfulfillment, piracy, plagiarism, transgression, trespass

**v:** contravene, encroach, infract, intrude, invade, poach, transgress, trespass, violate

## INGREDIENT

**a:** componential

**n:** component, constituent, detail, element, essence, factor, item, part, substance

## INHERENT

**a:** basic, connatal, connate, essential, immanent, inalienable, inborn, indwelling, ingrained, inseparable, intrinsic, latent, native, potential, structural, subjective

**n:** essentiality, intrinsicality

*not:* adventitious, extraneous, foreign, peripheral

## INHERITANCE

**a:** congenital, descendible, diathetic, genetic, hereditable, hereditary, inborn, inheritable, inherited, innate, transmissible

**n:** benefaction, bequest, diathesis, heirloom, hereditament, heritage, legacy, mutation, primogeniture, reversion, succession, tropism

*from father:* patrimony, patroclinic, patroclinical

*from mother:* matroclinic, matroclinical, matroclinous

*scientific:* Lamarckism, Lysenkoism, Mendel's laws

*shared:* coparcenary, parcenary

## INHUMAN

**a:** barbarous, cruel, diabolical, dispiteous, Draconian, impersonal, infrahuman, inhumane, insensate, insensible, mechanical, rough, ruthless, satanic, savage, subhuman, superhuman, truculent

**v:** dehumanize, mechanize, robotize

## INITIAL

**a:** *ab initio, ab ovo,* aborigine, beginning, inchoative, incipient, initially, initiatory, rudimental

**n:** beginning

*initials:* monogram

*repeated first letter:* alliteration

## INITIATED

**a:** epoptic, esoteric

**n:** actuator, bellwether, catalyst, inceptor, initiator, originator

*initiation:* baptism of fire, ceremony, experience, induction, introduction, rite of passage

*one who has been:* epopt, initiate

## INITIATIVE

**n:** *demarche,* enterprise, gumption, pluck, step

## INJURY

**a:** contagious, deleterious, harmful, incapacitated, inimical, injurious, invidious, malignant, nocent, nocuous, noisome, noxious, pernicious, traumatic, venomous

n: detriment, impairment, lesion, mayhem, mutilation, trauma

v: injure, maim, mutilate, traumatize, wound

　　*enduring:* forbearing, longanimous, long-suffering

　　*following:* post-traumatic, residual

　　*result:* disability, disablement, grievance, handicap, impairment, incapacitation, *residuum, sequala*

**INKY**

a: atramental, atramentous, colored, dark, murky, stained

**INN**

n: auberge, caravansary, hospice, hostel, hostelry, khan, lodge, poseda, pub, shelter, xenodochium

　　*worker:* hostler, innkeeper, ostler, servant, victualler

**INNATE**

a: congenital, endogenous, hereditary, idiopathic, inborn, inherited, intrinsic, intuitive, natural

n: *conatus, largesse*

　　*intelligence: elan vital,* entelechy

**INNER**

a: endogenous, inmost, innermost, interior, internal

n: interiority, penetrale, *penetralia,* sanctuary, *sanctum sanctorum*

**INNOCENT**

a: Arcadian, artless, blameless, candid, cherubic, faultless, guileless, immaculate, impeccable, impeccant, inculpable, ingenuous, innocuous, inoffensive, irreproachable, naive, pastoral, seraphic, unaware, undefiled, unsuspecting, virtuous

n: artlessness, blamelessness, immaculacy, impeccability, inculpability, ingenuousness, innocence, innocuity, innocuousness, *naivete,* simplicity, verdancy

v: exculpate, exonerate

　　*person:* bystander, ingenue

**INNUENDO**

n: allusion, aspersion, connotation, *double entendre,* hint, insinuation, intimation, suggestion

**INOFFENSIVE**

a: harmless, inobnoxious, peaceful, unobnoxious

**INOPPORTUNE**

a: impracticable, inappropriate, inconvenient, inexpedient, intempestive, *malapropos,* unseasonable, unsuitable, untimely

**INQUIRY**

a: disquisitive, inquisitive, inquisitorial

n: disquisition, examination, inquest, inquisition, investigation, query, reconnaissance, research, survey

　　*person:* busybody, gossip, *quidnunc*

**INSANE**

a: berserk, chaotic, compulsive, delirious, dithyrambic, frantic, frenzied, incompetent, irrational, lunatic, mad, maniacal, *non compos mentis,* psychotic

n: insanity, madness

**INSCRIPTION**

n: epigraph, epigraphy, etching, graffiti, *graffito,* label, legend, signature, title

**INSECURITY**

a: insecure, precarious, risky, susceptible, unstable, vulnerable

n: apprehension, apprehensiveness, incertitude, instability, jeopardy, peril

**INSENSITIVE**

a: analgesic, anesthetic, apathetic, comatose, impassive, inanimate, insensate, insentient, lethargic, lost, oblivious, obtuse, pachydermatous, philistine, philistinic, soporific, thick-skinned, torpid, unfeeling, unimpressionable

**n:** analgesia, apathy, *carus*, coma, insensibility, insensitivity, insentience, lethargy, obtuseness, obtusity, stupor, torpor, trance

*person:* pachyderm

**INSERT**

**a:** inserted, inserting, intercalary, interlarded, interpolated

**n:** inlay, inset, intercalation, interjection, interplantation, interpolation

**v:** intercalate, interlard, interpolate, interpose, intersperse, intromit

*between two: entredeux*

**INSIGHT**

**a:** prehensile, prescient, *spirituelle*

**n:** acumen, *apercu*, clairvoyance, discernment, discrimination, empathy, intuition, penetration, perception, perspicacity, perspicuity, prescience, shrewdness, understanding, wisdom

**INSIGNIFICANT**

**a:** commonplace, contemptible, immaterial, infinitesimal, irrelevant, minuscule, nugatory, paltry, small, trivial, worthless

**n:** infinitesimality, insignificance, minitude, nonentity, triviality

**INSINCERE**

**a:** artificial, counterfeit, deceitful, disingenuous, duplicitous, facile, fulsome, glib, hypocritical, ingratiating, meretricious, pat, specious, theatrical, tongue-in-cheek, unctuous

**n:** artificiality, *bathos*, cant, dissimulation, duplicity, hypocrisy, insincerity, sentimentalism, sentimentality, theatricality

*person:* charlatan, mountebank, opportunist, *posseur*, pretender, temporizer, timeserver

**INSIPID**

**a:** bland, cloying, commonplace, flavorless, inane, *jejune*, lackluster, mawkish, prosaic, savorless, trite, uninteresting, unsavory, vapid

**n:** insipidity, *jejunity*, vapidity

**INSISTENT**

**a:** conspicuous, exigent, importunate, persevering, persistent, pressing, prominent, strident, urgent

**INSOLENT**

**a:** arrant, arrogant, audacious, cocky, contemptuous, contumelious, hubristic, impudent, insulting, overbearing, sassy, shameless

**n:** arrogance, audacity, cheekiness, contempt, contemptuousness, contumacy, contumely, effrontery, flippery, haughtiness, *hubris*, impertinence, impudence, insolence, protervity, sauciness

*person:* jackanapes

**INSPECTION**

**a:** inspectorial

**n:** examination, probe, reconnaissance, reconnoiter, scrutiny, surveillance, survey

*person:* inspectorate, surveillant

**INSPIRATION**

**a:** afflated, clarion, infusive, inspiring, stimulating

**n:** afflation, *afflatus*, charisma, enthusiasm, inhalation, stimulant, stimulation, *trouvaille*

**v:** animate, encourage, exhilarate, imbue, infuse, inhale, inspire, invade, motivate, permeate, pervade, prompt

**INSTABILITY**

**n:** apprehensiveness, change, *disequilibrium*, flux, incertitude, inconstancy, insecurity, unbalance

**INSTALLMENT**

**n:** feuilleton

**v:** amortize

**INSTANCE**

**a:** e.g., *exempli gratia*

**n:** circumstance, exception, happening, illustration, suggestion

## INSTANT

**a:** instantaneous, momentary, semelfactive, simultaneous

**n:** *clin d'oeil,* instantaneity, moment, simultaneity, trice

## INSTILL

**v:** implant, impregnate, indoctrinate, infiltrate, infuse, inject, innoculate, insinuate, instil, introduce

## INSTINCT

**a:** gut, instinctive, intuitive, visceral

**n:** appetency, Eros, intuition, libido, motivation, propensity

## INSTRUCTION

**a:** catechetic, catechistic, didactic, edificatory, educational, expository, instructive, moralistic, preceptive, propaedeutic

**n:** catechesis, catechism, discipline, edification, education, enlightenment, improvement, indoctrination, information, order, precept, propaedeutics, teaching, tuition

**v:** catechize, discipline, edify, educate, indoctrinate, instruct

　*theory:* didactics, pedagogy, propaedeutics

## INSTRUMENT

**n:** armamentaria, equipment, instrumentaria, tool

　*types:* brass, electronic, keyboard, laboratory, measuring, medical, musical, percussion, string, wind

## INSUFFICIENCY

**a:** deficient, incomplete, insufficient

**n:** dearth, deficiency, inability, inadequacy, incompetency, paucity

## INTANGIBLE

**a:** aeriform, amorphous, diaphanous, ephemeral, immaterial, impalpable, imperceptible, incorporeal, insubstantial, invisible, nebular, nebulous, unknowable, vague, vaporous

**n:** aeriality, chemistry, ephemera, ephemerality, incorporeality, insubstantiality, intangibility, mystery, mystique, nebulosity

## INTEGRATIVE

**a:** centralizing, centripetal, combining, integrable, unifying

**v:** blend, combine, integrate

## INTEGRITY

**n:** candor, completeness, entireness, honor, sincerity, soundness

　*challenge:* discredit, impeach

## INTELLECT

**a:** Apollonian, cerebral, cognitive, dianoetic, epistemic, epistemological, gnostic, highbrow, intelligential, noetic, odyssean, rational, sagacious, sophic, sophical

**n:** acquaintance, acumen, cognition, comprehension, *elan vital,* entelechy, information, intellectuality, intelligence, luminosity, mentality, noesis, perspicacity, perspicuity, profundity, rationality, reason, sagacity, sapience

**v:** intellectualize, rationalize

　*food:* pabulum

　*hostility:* anti-intellectualism

　*lack: amentia,* insipience, moronity, nescience

　*person: academe, cognoscenti, illuminati,* intellectual, *intelligentsia, literati, literatus,* luminary, mandarin, pedant, salon, savant, sophist

　*quest for:* odyssey

## INTEMPERATE

**a:** excessive, extravagant, immoderate, inclement, incontinent, inordinate, violent, wild

**n:** acrasia, acrasy, immoderation, inclemency, incontinence, insobriety, intemperance

　*eating/drinking:* alcoholic, crapulent, crapulous, drunk, glutton

**INTENSE**

**a:** burning, comprehensive, consuming, consummatory, emphatic, inspissated, intensive, passionate, vehement, zealous

**n:** concentration, enhancement, enthusiasm, exacerbation, intensification, intensity, potency, profundity, saturation, strenuosity, temperature, vehemency

**v:** accentuate, augment, deepen, emphasize, enhance, exacerbate, exaggerate, intensify, sharpen, strengthen

**INTENT**

**a:** calculated, deliberate, designed, intentional, intentionally, permissive, premeditated, purposeful, *sic*, voluntary

**n:** aim, ambition, *animus*, *arriere-pensee*, consummation, contemplation, design, designedness, determination, goal, hidden agenda, import, impulsion, intendment, intention, motive, objective, purport, resolve, significance, ulterior motive

    *criminal:* malice aforethought, malice prepense, premeditation

    *without:* accidental, unmotivated, unpremeditated

**INTERCHANGE**

**a:** alternating, commutable, interchangeable, mutual, reciprocal, reciprocative

**n:** alternation, give-and-take, mutuality, *quid pro quo*, reciprocation, reciprocity

**v:** alternate, exchange, reciprocate

**INTERCONNECTING**

**a:** anastomotic, interrelated, intimate, syndetic

**INTEREST**

**a:** absorbed, catholic, concerned, engrossed, immersed, intent, interested, preoccupied, rapt, topical, usurious, versant

**n:** affinity, attraction, concern, consciousness, curiosity, cynosure, fixation, *idee fixe*, inquisitiveness, Mecca, polestar, topicality, vested interest

**v:** dabble, fascinate, haunt, intrigue, obsess, preoccupy, rivet

    *in others:* allocentric

    *in self:* egocentric

    *interesting:* absorbing, arresting, attractive, challenging, compelling, divertive, engaging, engrossing, enthralling, intriguing, mesmerizing, piquant, provocative, riveting, rousing, spellbinding, succulent, tantalizing, thought-provoking

    *lack:* acedia, ennui, lackadaisy, melancholia, otiosity, tepidity, torpor, unconcern

    *one with diverse:* Proteus

**INTERFERE**

**a:** adventitious, interfering, officious, overattentive, solicitous, supervenient

**n:** ingerence, intercession, interference, interposition, intervention, intrusion, maintenance, static

**v:** intercede, interlope, intermeddle, interpose, interrupt, intervene, intrude, meddle, obtrude, participate, supervene

    *person:* interloper

**INTERIOR**

**a:** central, domestic, inland, inner, inside, internal

**n:** domesticality, interiority, internality, internalization

**INTERLOCK**

**n:** interdigitation

**v:** engage, interdigitate, interlace, interlink, intertwine

**INTERLUDE**

**n:** armistic, break, gap, hiatus, hold, *intermezzio*, intermission, *interregnum*, interruption, parenthesis, pause, recess, respite, rest, space, *stasimon*, suspension

**INTERMEDIATE**

**a:** average, between, equidistant, inbetween, mean, medial, median, medium, mesothetic, middle, middling, midway, neutral

**n:** limbo, *quid*, *tertium*

## INTERMISSION

n: armistice, interlude, interruption, pause, recess, rest, stop, wait

## INTERNAL

a: domestic, endogenous, immanent, implicit, inherent, inside, internecine, intestinal, intramural, intraneous, intrinsic, municipal

n: domesticality, interiority, internality, internalization

v: interiorize, internalize

## INTERPOSE

n: arbitration, interpolation, interposition, mediation

v: arbitrate, insert, interfere, interject, interpolate, interrupt, intervene, medialize, mediate, sandwich

## INTERPRETATION

a: divinatory, exegetic, explanatory, expository, hermeneutic, interpretative, interpretive, prophetic, revelatory, significative

n: anagogue, anagogy, elucidation, exegesis, explanation, explication, exposition, gloss

v: clarify, construe, decipher, decrypt, elucidate, explicate, expound, illustrate, interpret, rationalize, translate

> *extra: eisegesis, epexegesis*

> *interpreter:* annotator, dragoman, exegete, exponent, expositor, expounder, hierophant, oneirocritic, scholiast

> *open:* ambiguous, susceptible

> *science:* exegetics, hermeneutics

## INTERRUPT

a: interruptive

n: armistice, arrest, disruption, distraction, hiatus, hindrance, interlocution, intermission, interpolation, interruption, pause, pretermission, suspension

v: arrest, disrupt, heckle, hinder, intercept, interfere, interject, intermit, interpose, intervene, pretermit, punctuate, supervene, violate

## INTERSECT

n: anastomosis, chiasma, collision, decussation, intersection

v: anastomose, bisect, collide, crisscross, cut, decussate, overlap, transect

## INTERVAL

n: armistice, *caesura,* gap, hiatus, interim, interlude, *intermezzo,* intermission, *interregnum,* interstice, lull, parenthesis, pause, respite, rupture

## INTERVENE

a: interjacent, interjaculatory, interjectional, interpolated, intervenient, intervening, mediatorial, mediatory, parenthetical

n: arbitration, conciliation, intercession, intermediation, interposition, intervenience, intervention, mediation, theurgy

v: arbitrate, interfere, interject, interpose, mediate

> *person:* intercessor, intermediary, intervenient, mediator

## INTESTINE

a: alvine, splanchnic, visceral

n: entrails, viscera

> *combining forms:* enter-, entero-

> *pains:* colic, gripes

> *rumbling sound:* crepitation, flatus

## INTIMATE

a: *a deux,* affectionate, confidential, contubernal, familiar, personal, private

## INTIMIDATE

v: browbeat, bulldoze, bully, cow, daunt, denounce, dishearten, dragoon, hector, scare, terrorize

## INTOXICATED

a: alcoholic, boozy, drunk, heady, inebriated, sotted, stewed, tipsy

n: alcoholic

> *that which:* inebriant, intoxicant

## INTRICATE

a: abstruse, complex, complicated, convoluted, *daedalian, daedalic,* entangled, Gordian, inexplicable, inextricable, involuted, labyrinthian, obscure, tangled

n: abstrusity, complexity, intricacy, labyrinth

### INTRIGUE

a: attractive, Byzantine, complicated, intriguing, labyrinthine

n: artifice, cabal, chicanery, collusion, conspiracy, *coup,* machination, plot, subtlety

> *female intriguer:* Circe, *femme fatale,* siren

### INTRODUCTION

a: antecedent, elementary, inductive, initiatory, innovatory, introductory, isagogic, liminary, manductive, manductory, precursory, prefatorial, prefatory, preliminary, preludial, preludious, prelusive, premonitory, preparatory, presaging, prolegomenous, prolusory, propaedeutic, rudimentary

n: debut, exordium, exposition, foreword, induction, innovation, isagoge, lemma, manduction, orientation, preamble, preface, prelude, prelusion, preparation, prodromus, proem, prolegomenon, prologue, prolusion, propaedeutic, protasis, rubric, unveiling

v: begin, harbinger, herald, inaugurate, induct, initiate, innovate, insinuate, install, intercalate, interpolate, interpose, introduce, invest, open, presage, usher in

> *combining forms:* fore-, pre-, pro-
>
> *study:* isagogics

### INTROSPECTIVE

a: autistic

n: autism, introspection, introspectiveness, introspectivity, recollection, reverie, self-examination

### INTUITION

a: aprioristic, clairvoyant, inborn, intuitive, percipient, prescient

n: *a priori, anschauung,* apprehension, apriority, clairvoyance, conception, cryptesthesia, *eidos,* ESP, extrasensory perception, foreknowledge, percipience, precognition, prescience

v: intuit

### INVALID

a: false, inauthentic, inoperative, nugatory, null and void, powerless, unlawful, unsound, valetudinarian

n: valetudinarian

v: invalidate, nullify, repeal, stultify, vitiate, weaken

### INVALUABLE

a: incalculable, inestimable, priceless

### INVASION

a: incursionary, invasive

n: aggression, assault, encroachment, incursion, influx, inroad, transgression

### INVENT

a: creative, ingenious, innovational, inventive

n: creativity, ingeniosity, ingenuity, inventiveness

v: concoct, contrive, create, develop, devise, evolve, excogitate, fabricate, improvise, machinate, make up, originate, pioneer, plan, produce

> *invention:* innovation, patent
>
> *payment:* royalty

### INVENTORY

n: catalog, catalogue, compendium, schedule, summary, survey, syllabus, tariff

### INVESTIGATION

a: disquisitive, exploratory, investigational, investigative, probative, zetetic

n: catechesis, catechism, disquisition, inquest, inquiry, inquisition, interrogation, perscrutation, reconnaissance, scrutiny, survey

v: inquisit, investigate, probe, sound

> *investigator:* inquisitor, questioner, searcher

## INVIGORATING

a: animating, bracing, exhilarative, roborant, spurring, stimulating, stimulatory, tonic, zestful

## INVINCIBLE

a: Achillean, formidable, unavoidable, unconquerable, unswerving

## INVOCATION

n: *absit omen, bismillah,* call, enforcement, incantation, litany, plea, prayer, supplication

## INVOLUNTARY

a: accidental, automatic, autonomic, inexorable, instinctive, irreparable, mechanical, spontaneous, uncontrollable, unmotivated, unrehearsed, unstudied, unwilling

n: automaticity, mechanicality, reflex

## INVOLVE

a: abstruse, complicated, confused, embroiled, enmeshed, entangled, implicated, inextricable, intricate, involuted, involved, labyrinthian, labyrinthine

n: complexity, confusion, embroilment, entanglement, involution, involvement

v: complicate, embarrass, embroil, entail, entangle, implicate, interpenetrate, permeate

## INWARD

a: centripetal, domestic, endogenous, immanent, intrinsic

n: immanence, intrinsicality, intrinsicalness, inwardness

*combining form:* intro-

## IRIDESCENT

a: kaleidoscopic, lustrous, margaritaceous, nacereous, opalescent, pavonine, pearly, pellucid

## IRON

a: chalybeate, ferric, ferriferous, ferrous, ferruginous, pig, wrought

n: fagot, hematite, limonite, magnetite, pyrite

v: galvanize

*combining forms:* ferr-, ferri-, ferro-, sider-, sidero-

## IRONIC

a: biting, caustic, facetious, ironical, mordant, Pantagruelian, sarcastic, satirical, tongue-in-cheek, wry

n: antiphrasis, asteism, buffoonery, contempt, disapprobation, dissimultation, irony, sarcasm, satire

## IRRATIONAL

a: absurd, addlepated, alogical, asinine, Dionysian, fatuous, grotesque, illogical, imbecilic, pathological, psychotic, surreal, transcendental, unbounded

n: absurdity, alogism, deliration, delirium, fanaticism, fatuity, foolishness, imbecility, irrationality, phobia, psychosis, unreasonableness

## IRREGULAR

a: aberrant, abnormal, anomalous, arrhythmic, asymmetrical, atypical, baroque, clandestine, corrugated, deviant, distorted, diverse, eccentric, episodic, erratic, fitful, heteroclite, heteromorphic, inconsistent, inordinate, intermittent, promiscuous, rambling, serrated, spasmodic, sporadic, straggly, tumultuary, unbalanced

n: aberration, abnormality, anomaly, arrythmia, asymmetry, caprice, delinquency, deviation, eccentricity, irregularity, promiscuity, sporadicity, unevenness

## IRRELEVANT

a: extraneous, extrinsic, heterogeneous, immaterial, impertinent, inapplicable, inapposite, incidental, inconsequential, marginal, peripheral, tangential, unrelated

n: extraneity, impertinence, inappositeness, inconsequentiality, irrelevance, irrelevancy

## IRREPARABLE

a: intractable, irremediable, irretrievable, irreversible, unfixable

**IRRESISTIBLE**

**a:** alluring, charming, fascinating, mesmeric

**IRRESPONSIBLE**

**a:** arbitrary, feckless, harum-scarum, impetuous, impractical, impulsive, irrational, reckless, scatterbrained, unthinking, visionary

**IRREVERENCE**

**a:** atheistic, blasphemous, impious, irreligious, irreverent, irreverential, sacrilegious, undutiful, worldly

**n:** agnosticism, atheism, blasphemy, impiety, irreligiosity, *lese majeste*, profanation, sacrilege, undutifulness, ungodliness

**IRRITABILITY**

**a:** acrimonious, atrabilious, bilious, cankered, cantankerous, caustic, choleric, churlish, crotchety, dyspeptic, fractious, fretful, iracund, irascible, irritable, peevish, perverse, pettish, petulant, splenetic, surly, testy, touchy, waspish

**n:** animosity, fantod, fretfulness, iracundity, irascibility, petulance, querulousness, waspishness

**v:** abrade, aggravate, anger, annoy, bait, bother, chafe, exacerbate, exasperate, fester, gall, harass, harry, hector, incense, intensify, irritate, nettle, provoke, rankle, stimulate

> *irritant:* abradant, gadfly, provocative

**ISLAND**

**a:** enisled, insular, nesiote

**n:** archipelago, atoll, cay, insularity, isle, islet, key, skerry

**ISOLATE**

**a:** discrete, isolated, ivory-towered, quarantined, segmental, segmentary, segregated, sporadic

**n:** ascesis, decentralization, immurement, incarceration, insularity, insulation, isolation, quarantine, segregation, sequestration, solitude

**v:** detach, enisle, ghettoize, immure, maroon, quarantine, seclude, segregate

**ISSUE**

**n:** child, *debouchment*, eggress, emanation, emergence, extravasation, issuance, outflow

**v:** circulate, *debouch, disembogue,* egress, emanate, evacuate, extravasate

**ITCH**

**n:** agitation, *cacoethes,* ferment, formication, prurience, *pruritus,* restlessness, urtication

## JACK-OF-ALL-TRADES
**n:** *factotem*, handyman, pantologist, Proteus

## JAGGED
**a:** indented, lancinate, lancinose, serrated, uneven

## JARGON
**n:** abracadabra, argot, balderdash, *baragouin*, cant, dialect, gibberish, lingo, *patois*, slang

## JAUNTY
**a:** affable, affected, *debonaire*, fashionable, genial, nonchalant, raffish, rakish, *soigne(e)*, sprightly, stylish
**n:** geniality, nonchalance, sprightliness

## JAW
**a:** mandibular, mental, orthognathous
**n:** chap, jowls, mandible, maw
  *combining forms:* gnath-, -gnathous
  *large:* pachygnathous
  *long:* longirostrine
  *lower projecting:* underhung, undershot
  *projecting:* prognathous
  *receding:* opistognathous
  *upper projecting:* overshot

## JEALOUSY
**a:** defensive, invidious, jealous, possessive, territorial
**n:** doubt, envy

## JERKY
**a:** episodic, fitful, halting, hesitant, intermittent, saccadic, spasmodic, sporadic

**n:** convulsion, episode, fit, paroxysm, seizure
**v:** jiggle, jounce, lurch

## JEST
**n:** banter, drollery, gag, humor, joke, pleasantry
  *jester:* *farceur*, idiot, merry-Andrew, *railleur*

## JEW
**a:** Hebraic, Judaic, Judaical
**n:** Hebraica, Hebraism, Judaica, Judaism
  *boy's rite:* bar mitzvah, bar mitzvoth
  *combining form:* Judeo-
  *girl's rite:* bas mitzvah, bath mitzvah, bat mitzvah

## JEWEL
**a:** *Brummagem*
**n:** bijou, *Brummagem*, gem, stone

## JOINED
**a:** affined, articulate, associated, concatenate, contiguous, convergent, coupled, intercatenated, joining, jointed
**n:** articulation, colligation, commisure, communication, concatenation, conjugation, copulation, joint, juncture, synchondrosis
**v:** agglutinate, amalgamate, articulate, associate, coagment, coalesce, colligate, communicate, concatenate, conjugate, consolidate, copulate, harness, interconnect, interlock, join, matriculate
  *combining forms:* arthr-, arthro-, artic-, co-, com-

## JOKE

**a:** facetious, jocose, jocular, jocund, joking, jolly, jovial

**n:** badinage, banter, facetiosity, farcicality, gag, gibe, jape, jest, jocosity, jocularity, jocundity, pleasantry, prank, repartee, wisecrack, witticism

> *joker: farceur,* humorist, *railleur*

## JOLLY

**a:** convivial, friendly, genial, happy, jocular, jocund, jovial, sportive

**n:** conviviality, jocosity, jocularity, jocundity, joviality

## JOURNEY

**a:** itinerant, Odyssean, peripatetic, viatic

**n:** bourn, entrada, excursion, expedition, hegira, itinerary, itineration, mecca, odyssey, peregrination, pilgrimmage, safari

**v:** itinerate, peregrinate, safari

## JOY

**a:** blithe, buoyant, ecstatic, elated, exuberant, exultant, gay, gratulant, jovial, joyful, joyous, jubilant, jubilean, rapturous, triumphant, zestful

**n:** beatitude, delight, ecstasy, exaltation, exuberance, felicity, festivity, gaiety, gratification, *joie de vivre,* joviality, joyfulness, jubilation, jubilee, merriment, transport, zest

**v:** jubilate

## JUDGE

**a:** accusatorial, analytical, circumspect, discerning, discretionary, discriminatory, inquisitorial, judged, judging, judgmatic, judgmental, judicable, judicative, judicial, judicious, justiciable, rational, sagacious

**n:** adjudicator, arbiter, arbitrator, bench, *cognoscente, connoisseur,* critic, judicator, judicature, judiciary, mediator, moderator, ordinary, *puisne,* Solomon

**v:** adjudicate, analyze, arbitrate, discriminate, recuse

> *judgment:* acumen, charge, circum-

spection, criticism, discernment, discretion, discrimination, injunction, insight, instruction, intuition, judicality, judicium, penetration, perception, precedent, prudence, rationality, sagacity, wisdom

## JUGGLING

**n:** legerdemain, *passe-passe,* prestidigitation, *tour de force*

## JUICY

**a:** dripping, luscious, lush, piquant, racy, succulent

**n:** piquancy, succulence, succulency

## JUMBLE

**a:** confused, disarranged, farraginous, indiscriminate, jumbled, macaronic

**n:** capharnaum, *colluvies,* confusion, disarrangement, *farrago, fatras,* gallimaufry, heterogeneity, hodge-podge, mare's nest, medley, mess, miscellany, mixture, *olla podrida,* potpourri, *salmagundi*

## JUMP

**a:** capering, desultory, salient, saltant, saltatorial

**n:** *entrechat, jete,* saltation, *saltus*

**v:** caper, cavort, gambol, prance, rebound, *saltate*

## JUNIOR

**a:** juvenile, *puisne,* subalternate, subordinate, youthful

**n:** juniority, minion, *puisne,* subalternate, subordinate

## JURISDICTION

**a:** justiciable, plenipotential, plenipotentiary, plentary

**n:** authority, bailiwick, bounds, cognizance, compass, control, domain, field, gamut, leeway, limits, plenipotentiary, province, sovereignty, sphere, territory, venue

## JUST

**a:** accurate, conscientious, deserved,

equitable, forensic, impartial, incorrupt-ible, judicatory, juridical, juristic, justicia-ry, merited, rectitudinous, righteous, unbiased

n: *dharma*, equity, impartiality, integrity, *justa causa*, justice, rectitude, righteous-ness, rightfulness

## JUSTIFY

a: justifiable, justificative, justificatory, justified, legal, legitimate, vindicatory, warrantable

n: *apologia*, apology, exoneration, extenu-ation, *justificandum, justificans*, justifica-tion, rationale, vindication

v: accept, authorize, excuse, justify, legit-imate, permit, rationalize, uphold, vindi-cate

## JUTTING

a: bulbous, protuberant, salient

n: protuberance, protuberancy, salience, saliency

v: beetle, extrude, overhang, project, protrude

## JUVENILE

a: ephebic, immature, puerile, young, youthful

n: adolescent, boy, child, girl, juniority, juvenility, minor, puisne, teen, youngster, youth

## KEEN

a: acrimonious, acuminous, analytical, appercipient, astucious, astute, caustic, discerning, eager, enthusiastic, incisive, moradacious, mordant, penetrating, per-spicacious, piquant, poignant, pungent, sagacious, solicitous, trenchant

n: acuity, acumen, asperity, astucity, astuteness, keenness, perspicacity, piquancy, pungency, sagacity, sharpness

## KEEPSAKE

n: *bibelot*, curio, gift, knickknack, memen-to, *objet d'art*, reminder, *souvenir, virtu*

## KERNEL

n: center, chromosome, gist, grain, meat, morsel, niblet, *nidus*, nucleus, nut, pith, quintessence, seed

## KILL

a: femicidal, fratricidal, infanticidal, matricidal, parricidal, patricidal, regici-dal, sorocidal, uxoricidal

n: homicide, killing, manslaughter

v: annihilate, asphyxiate, assassinate, cull, decapitate, dispatch, execute, extir-pate, immolate, lynch, suppress

   *by cutting throat:* jugulate

   *by stoning:* lapidate

   *combining form:* -cide

   *mercy:* euthanasia

   *of brother:* fratricide

   *of father:* patricide

   *of group:* genocide, pogrom

   *of infant:* infanticide

   *of king:* regicide

   *of mother:* matricide

   *of oneself:* suicide

   *of parent:* parricide

   *of sister:* sorocide

   *of wife:* uxoricide

   *of woman:* femicide

## KIND

a: altruistic, amiable, auspicious, avun-cular, beneficent, benevolent, benign(ant), charitable, clement, compassionate, cor-dial, eleemosynary, gracious, humane, indulgent, omnifarious, philanthropic, propitious, *simpatico*, sympathetic

n: amiability, benevolence, benignancy, clemency, complaisance, congeniality, cordiality, indulgence, kindness, lenity, magnanimity, philanthropy, prevenance

## KINDRED

a: cognate, congeneric, congenerous, congenital, consanguineous, sympathetic

n: affinity, agnation, birth, blood, clan, congener, consanguinity, genus, kinfolk, kinship, propinquity, race, relationship, relatives, species, tribe, variety

**KING**

**a:**, august, basilic, imperial, kingly, leonine, majestic, monarchial, palatine, regal, royal, sovereign

**n:** dynast, emperor, ermine, imperator, monarch, regent, regulus, rex, sovereign

**v:** accede

*privileges of:* regalia, regality

**KINGDOM**

**n:** demesne, domain, dominion, dukedom, jurisdiction, principality, realm, sultonate, vizierate

**KISS**

**a:** kissing, osculant, oscular, osculatory

**n:** osculation, *pax*, salutation

**v:** buss, caress, osculate, peck, smack

*science:* philematology

**KITCHEN**

**a:** culinary

**n:** caboose, cooking, cuisine, galley, scullery

**KNAVISH**

**a:** arrant, deceitful, dishonest, fraudulent, frolicsome, unscrupulous

**n:** dishonesty, knavishness, unscrupulosity

*knave:* betrayer, cheat, rogue, scoundrel, villain

**KNEE**

**a:** geniculate, patellar

**n:** patella, popliteal

**v:** geniculate, genuflex, kow-tow

*jerk:* automatism, dandling, reflex

*kneeling:* genuflection, genuflexion

**KNIGHT**

**a:** chivalresque, chivalric, chivalrous, equestrian

**n:** banneret, *chevalier*, companion, Galahad, knight errant, paladin, protagonist, templar

*helper:* armiger, esquire, varlet

*knighthood:* accolade, chivalry

**KNOCKDOWN**

**n:** *recumbentibus*

**KNOLL**

**n:** hillock, hummock, *tumulus*

**KNOT**

**a:** difficult, gnarled, knotty, twisted

**n:** burl, excrescence, exostosis, gibbosity, Gordian knot, knob, knur, knurl, node, nodule, projection, protuberance, swelling

**KNOWLEDGE**

**a:** apprehensive, astute, au fat, bibliognostic, chrestomathic, cognitative, cognitional, cognitional, cognitive, cognoscible, cognoscitive, conversant, discerning, encyclopedic, enlightened, epistemonic, gnostic, knowing, knowledgeable, omniscient, pansophical, penetrating, perceptive, percipient, proficient, sagacious, sciental, sciolistic, sciolous, sophisticated, versed, well-versed

**n:** Anschauung, apperception, clairvoyance, cognition, cognizance, comprehension, encyclopedism, episteme, erudition, ESP extrasensory perception, expertise, humanism, information, intuition, knowhow, learning, lore, omniscience, pansophism, pedantry, perception, profundity, rationalism, sagacity, savoir faire, savoir-faire, scholarship, science, scientia, technique, virtuosity

*body of:* hierology

*combining forms:* -gnosis, -nomy, -sophy

*denial of basis for:* acatelepsy, nihilism

*depreciation of:* antiintellectualism, obscurantism

*imparting:* informative, instructive, teaching, tutorial

*interested person:* cognoscente, illuminato, savant, virtuoso

*lack:* ignoration, nescience

*love:* epistemophilia, philomathy

*person:* polyhistor, polymath

*previous:* precognition

*secret:* arcanum, privity

*show of:* didacticism, pedantry, sciolism

*study of:* epistemology, gnoseology

*superficial:* sciolism

*universal:* pansophism, pansophy

## LABOR

**a:** arduous, Herculean, industrious, laborious, onerous, operose, slavish, toilsome, yeoman

**n:** laboriousness, lucubration, operosity, peonage, task, toil, travail, undertaking, work

**v:** lucubrate, struggle, toil, work

## LACKING

**a:** deficient, desiderative, destitute, devoid, devoid of, exigous, fictional, incomplete, insufficient, mythologic

**n:** dearth, default, deficiency, desideration, *desideratum, desiderium,* destitution, exigency, exiguity, famine, inadequacy, insufficiency, lack, paucity, penury, privation, requirement, sparsity

    *combining forms:* ap-, apo-, dis-, mis-, un-

## LADY

**n:** *belle dame,* damsel, *demoiselle, domina, donna, grande dame, ingenue, jeune fille,* mistress, queen, wife, woman

## LAKE

**a:** interlacustrine, lacustral, lacustrine

**n:** loch, mere, oxbow, pond, tarn

    *study:* limnology

## LAME

**a:** claudicant, halting, limping, maimed, spavined

**n:** claudication

## LAMENT

**a:** deplorable, despicable, doleful, grievous, lachrymose, lamentable, mournful, plaintive, plangorous, sorrowful

**n:** complaint, dirge, elegy, epicede, epicedium, jeremiad, keen, lachrymation, lamentation, languishment, monody, poem, threnody

**v:** bewail, deplore, elegize

## LAND

**a:** agrarian, compatriotic, patrial, terrcolous, terrene, terrestrial

**n:** demesne, domain, dominion, earth, estate, property, real estate, realty, terrain, terrene, topography

    *and water:* amphibian, terraqueous

    *for public:* eminent domain, expropriation, sequestration

    *landholding:* barony

    *landmark:* cairn

    *landscape:* panorama, paysage, scenery

    *promised:* Canaan

## LANGUAGE

**a:** articulate, colloquial, dialectal, dialectic, glottogonic, glottological, idiomatic, lingual, lingualistic, linguistic, phonetic, provincial, semantic, vernacular

**n:** argot, cant, dialect, dialectalism, diction, discourse, glottology, grammar, idiolect, idiom, jargon, *koine, lingua franca,* linguistics, linguistry, oracy, parlance, *patois,* philology, phraseology, register, rhetoric, *sprachgefuhl,* style, tongue, vernacular, villagism, vocabulary, vulgate

    *abusive:* invective, vituperation

    *affected:* ephuism, preciosity

    *ambiguous:* circumlocution

*clear:* explicit, limpid, stylistic, unambiguous, unequivocal

*combining forms:* gloss-, -glot, lingu-, lingua-

*confused:* Babelism, polyglot

*deceptive:* flummery

*English study:* anglistics

*expert:* anglicist, linguist

*figurative:* tropology

*foolish:* balderdash, flatulence, flummery, gasconade, gibberish, lallation

*incorrect:* abusage

*international:* Esperanto, Ido, Interglossa, Interlingua, Novial, pasigraphy, Volapuk

*obscene:* coprolalia

*of criminals:* argot

*several:* macaronic, multilingual, polyglot, polylingual

*study:* linguistics, philology, phonemics, phonetics, phonology, pragmatics, syntax

*substandard:* barbarism, vulgarism

*unit:* glosseme, morpheme, phoneme

*using one:* monoglot, monolingual

*using two or more:* polyglot, polylingual

*using unknown:* glossolalia

**LAPEL**

n: revers

*flower:* boutinniere

**LAPSE**

n: aberration, apostasy, backslide, brainstorm, caudicity, declination, decline, parapraxia, parapraxis, pause

**LARGE**

a: abundant, ample, baronial, Bunyanesque, capacious, commodious, comprehensive, copious, fat, formidable, generous, grandiose, huge, immeasurable, imposing, lavish, magnificent, magnitudinous, monstrous, palatial, ponderous, portentous, prodigal, rambling, spacious, substantial, wholesale

n: colossality, comprehensiveness, grandiosity, hecatomb, immensity, largeness, legion, magnitude, massivity, multitude, spate, vastity, voluminosity

*body:* macrosomatic

*combining forms:* macro-, maxi-, mega-, megalo-, super-

**LASSITUDE**

a: adynamic, comatose, hypokinesic, lackadaisical, languorous, lassitudinous, lethargic

n: *adynamia,* apathy, enervation, *ennui,* hypokinesia, lackadaisy, languor, laziness, lethargy, listlessness, weariness

**LAST**

a: concluding, conclusive, definitive, *dernier,* eventual, extreme, final, terminal, ultimate

n: *dernier cri, dernier ressort, omega, pis aller,* trump card, ultimate

v: abide, endure, perdure

*next to:* penult, penultimate

*two from:* antepenult, antepenultimate

**LASTING**

a: abiding, aeonian, boundless, diuturnal, eternal, in perpetuity, indelible, indissoluble, inefaceable, interminable, perseverant, pertinacious, protracted, unceasing

n: diuturnity, indissolubility, perpetuality, perpetuity, pertinacity

for year: perennial

*short time:* ephemeral, transitory

**LATE**

a: advanced, after, belated, dilatory, in arrears, later, neoteric, overdue, posterior, procrastinating, procrastinative, procrastinatory, recent, subsequent, subsequently, succedent, tardy

n: eleventh hour, Indian summer, lateness

v: delay, procrastinate, tarry

*combining forms:* meta-, post-

*latest fashion: dernier cri*

**LATENT**

**a:** abeyant, delitescent, dormant, hidden, inactive, invisible, potential, quiescent, secret, sessile, suppressed, unseen, veiled

**n:** deliquescence, dormancy, incubation, latency, possibility, potentiality, quiescence, quietude

**LATIN**

**a:** Latinian, Latinic, macaronic

**n:** classics, Latinism, Latinity, latinization

**LAUD**

**a:** commendatory, encomiastic, eulogistic, laudable, laudatory, panegyrical, praiseworthy

**n:** approbation, commendation, deification, encomium, eulogy, extolment, laudation, panegyric

**v:** acclaim, applaud, approbate, commend, deify, extol, felicitate, macarize, panegyrize

**LAUGH**

**a:** Abderian, cachinnatory, contagious, gelastic, gelogenic, infectious, risible

**n:** belly laugh, cachinnation, convulsions, glee, hilarity, horse laugh, laughter, mirth, risibility

**v:** cachinnate, chortle, giggle, guffaw, mock, ridicule, simper, smile, snicker, snigger, titter

*laughable:* cachinnatory, derisory, farcical, funny, ludicropathetic, ludicroserious, ludicrous, mirthful, riant, ridiculous, risible

*sarcastic:* derision, irrision

**LAVISH**

**a:** abundant, affluent, Babylonian, Babylonic, exorbitant, extravagant, exuberant, improvident, inordinate, luxurious, magnificent, opulent, prodigal, profuse, sumptuous, superabundant, unstinted

**n:** affluence, affluency, extravagance, exuberance, improvidence, lavishness, magnificence, opulence, opulency, prodigality, sumptuosity, waste

**v:** dissipate, overdo, squander

**LAW**

**a:** advocatory, authorized, barristerial, canonical, constitutional, *de jure*, forensic, judicatory, juridical, juristic, lawful, legal, legitimate, licit, litigious, nomological, nomothetic, permitted, rightful, sumptuary

**n:** canon, code, commandment, constitution, covenant, decalogue, Dharma, edict, enactment, fiat, formula, jurisprudence, lawmaking, legality, legislation, Magna Carta, mandate, nomography, nomology, ordinance, pandects, precept, procedure, proclamation, regulation, rescript, statute, ukase

**v:** ratify, sanction

*combining forms:* jur-, nom-, nomo-, -nomy

*conformity to: dharma,* legitimation

*government:* nomocracy

*lawless:* anarchic, anomalous, contumacious, Dionysian, disobedient, illegal, illegitimate, illicit, insubordinate, insurgent, mutinous, recalcitrant, recusant, refractory, riotous, seditious, transgressive, unbounded, unrestrained

*lawyer:* advocate, attorney, barrister, counselor, esquire

**LAX**

**a:** careless, easygoing, immoral, lethargic, loose, remiss, undutiful, unobservant, unprincipled, weak

**LAYER**

**a:** laminal, laminar, laminated, layered, stratal, stratified, superimposed, tunicate

**n:** aerugo, cortex, hierarchization, lamella, lamina, patina, stratification, stratum, *verdigris*

**v:** laminate

*combining form:* -foliate

**LAYMAN**

**n:** amateur, esoteric, laic, laity

**LAZY**

**a:** bovine, comatose, costive, dilatory, *faineant,* hebetudinous, hypnotic, idle, indolent, inertial, insouciant, lackadaisical, languid, lax, lethargic, listless, lymphatic, oscitant, otiose, phlegmatic, remiss, shiftless, slothful, sluggish, somniferous, spiritless, torpid, truant

**n:** dog days, faineancy, inanition, indolence, inertia, lackadaisy, lassitude, laziness, lethargy, oscitancy, otiosity, remission, sluggishness, supinity, torpidity

**v:** avoid, malinger, shirk

> *person:* couch potato, dawdler, *faineant, flaneur,* laggard, sloth, slouch, sluggard, sybarite, voluptuary, wastrel

**LEACH**

**a:** lixivious

**n:** lixiviation

**v:** lixiviate

**LEAD**

**a:** plumbeous, plumbiferous

**n:** graphite, plumb, plumbago

> *combining forms:* plumb-, plumbo-

**LEADER**

**a:** chief, enlightened, foremost, hierarchical, leading, manuductive, manuductory, messianic, principal, salient, signal, stellar

**n:** archimandrite, *avant-garde,* bellwether, *caudillo,* chairman, conductor, dean, *doyen, doyenne,* executive, figurehead, front man, governor, groundbreaker, guide, guru, hierophant, innovator, *maestro,* mentor, mogul, pacemaker, patron saint, pioneer, premier, president, primate, protagonist, speaker, spokesman, trailblazer, trendsetter, tycoon, vanguard

> *combining forms:* -arch, -gogue
>
> *following:* sequacious
>
> *leadership:* aegis, authority, chieftainry, command, manuduction

> *of chorus:* choragus
>
> *of politics:* sachem
>
> *of sect:* corypheus, hierarch
>
> *without:* acephalic, acephalous

**LEAF**

**a:** acerose, cordate, digitate, elliptic, falcate, foliaceous, foliate, hastate, lanceolate, linear, lyrate, obovate, orbicular, ovate, palmate, peltate, pinnate, pinnatifid, reniform, runcinate, sagitate, spatulate, subulate, ternate, trifoliate

**n:** fascicle, fascicule, foliage

> *combining forms:* foli-, folio-, -phyll, phyllo-
>
> *-eating:* phyllophagic, phyllophagous
>
> *-shedding:* deciduous
>
> *-stripping:* defoliate

**LEAGUE**

**n:** alliance, amalgamation, association, bloc, coalition, confederation, *entente,* group, union

**LEAN**

**a:** angular, attenuated, barren, deficient, emaciated, infertile, macilent, meager, scrawny, skinny, slender, slim, tabescent, unproductive, unremunerative

**n:** angularity, emaciation, leanness, macilency, tabescence

**LEANING**

**a:** inclinatory, recumbent, tendentious

**n:** conatus, disposition, flair, partiality, penchant, predilection, predisposition, prejudice, propensity, susceptibility, tendency

**v:** careen, heel over, keel over, lean, list, recline, tip

**LEAP**

**a:** capering, leaping, saltant, saltatorial, saltatorian, saltatory, subsultive, subsultory

**n:** catapult, *gambade, gambado,* gambol, saltation

**v:** bound, jump, lunge, rebound, rise, spring, vault

*year:* bisextile, intercalary

**LEARN**

**a:** academic, Aristotelian, bookish, chrestomathic(al), educated, enlightened, erudite, heuristic, inkhorn, learned, lettered, literate, omniscient, palladian, pansophic, pansophical, pedantic, philomatic, polymathic, profound, scholarly

**n:** apprenticeship, catecumnenate, conditioning, culture, enlightenment, erudition, humanism, hypnopedia, imprinting, knowledge, learning, omniscience, pansophism, pansophy, pedantry, philology, reinforcement, rote, sapience, scholarship

**v:** acquire, apprehend, ascertain, assimilate, determine, digest, discover, glean, intuit, memorialize, memorize

*encyclopedic:* polyhistoric, polymathical

*excess:* didactic, pedantic, sciolistic, sciolous

*helping:* heuristic

*hostility:* anti-intellectualism

*learner:* abecedarian, alphabetarian, apprentice, beginner, catechumen, inceptor, novice, novitiate, opsimath, probationer, trainee, understudy

*love:* intellectualism, intellectualist, philologist, philology, philomath, philomathy

**LEATHER**

**a:** coriaceous, distressed

**n:** cat-o'-nine-tails, goatskin, parchment, sheepskin, strop, taws, thong, tooling

**v:** crimp, curry, dub, pink, taw, tool

**LEAVE**

**a:** sabbatical, valedictory

**n:** *adieu*, AWOL, *conge*, *devoir*, *exeat*, farewell, French leave, furlough, goodbye, leave-taking, sabbatical, *shemittah*, valediction

**v:** abandon, depart, desert, forsake, relinquish

**LECTURE**

**a:** admonitory, castigatory, disquisitional, dissertative, homiletic

**n:** castigation, colloquium, colloquy, discourse, discussion, disquisition, dissertation, *excursus*, homily, reprimand, reproof, symposium, treatise

**v:** castigate, reprimand, reprove, sermonnize

*lecturer:* docent, lector, speaker

**LEFT**

**a:** *gauche*, larboard, levogyrate, levogyre, levorotary, levorotatory, port, sinister, sinistrad, sinistral, sinistromanual

**n:** larboard, port, southpaw, verso

*combining forms:* lev-, levo-

*hand:* minor hand

*-handed but right also:* ambidextrous, dextrosinistral

*left-handedness:* maneinism, sinistrality

**LEG**

**a:** crural, femoral

**n:** *cabriole*, crus, shank

*front:* antecnemion

*long-legged:* macropod, macropodal

*lower:* cnemis, tibia

*short-legged:* brachyskelic, brachyskelous

*upper:* femur

**LEGAL**

**a:** admissible, authorized, canonical, constitutional, *de jure*, eligible, juridical, juristic, justifiable, lawful, legitimate, liable, licit, official, permissive, permitted, statutory, valid, warrantable

**n:** lawfulness, legality, legitimacy

*competent:* compos mentis, sui juris

*incompetent:* incompetent, *non compos mentis*

**LEGENDARY**

**a:** apocryphal, epict, fabulous, fictional, fictitious, mythical, mythological, traditional, tralatitious, unwritten

**LEGIBLE**

**a:** comprehensible, decipherable, distinct, recognizable, scrutable, understandable

**LEISURE**

**a:** otiose

**n:** avocation, ease, hobby, holiday, otiosity, *otium*, relaxation, rest, vacation

**LENGTH**

**a:** lengthwise, longitudinal, protractive

**n:** cubit, dimension, duration, lengthening, protraction

**v:** elongate, expand, extend, lengthen, prolong, protract

**LEOPARD**

**a:** pardine

*spot:* maculation

**LESSEN**

**a:** ablatitious, alleviatory, decrescent, denigratory, derogative, derogatory, extenuative, less, palliative, palliatory, submarginal, subminimal, subnormal, suboptional, substandard, subtractive

**n:** abatement, attenuation, *decrescendo*, demotion, *diminuendo*, diminution, extenuation, lessening, mitigation, mollification, palliation, reduction

**v:** abate, abbreviate, adulterate, allay, alleviate, assuage, attenuate, belittle, compress, condense, constrict, contract, curtail, decrease, degrade, demote, deplete, depreciate, dilute, diminish, disparage, dwindle, ebb, extenuate, minify, mitigate, mollify, palliate, pare, pejorate, plummet, recede, retrench, slump, taper off, temper, truncate, wane, whittle

**LETHARGY**

**a:** dull, inert, lethargic, passive, slow, sluggish, soporific

**n:** apathy, lassitude, laziness

**LETTER**

**a:** epistolary, formal, literally, literatim, pharisaic, ritualistic, verbatim

**n:** epistle, epistolary, epistolography, grammatolatry, literality, missive, testimonial

*ending:* postscript, signature

*opening:* salutation, superscription

*transposition:* metathesis, strephosymbolia

*-writer:* epistolarian

**LEVEL**

**a:** balanced, equipotential, flat, flush, horizontal, planate, tabular, unexcited, uniform

**n:** echelon, *esplanade,* gradation, horizontality, plateau, stratum, terrace, tier

**LEWD**

**a:** aphrodisiac, carnal, concupiscent, cyprian, debauched, depraved, dissolute, ithyphallic, lascivious, lecherous, libidinous, licentious, lubricious, lustful, obliquitous, obscene, pornographic, profligate, prurient, salacious, sensual

**n:** debauchery, depravity, lewdness, lubricity, obliquity, obscenity, profligacy, salacity, wantonness

*person:* libertine

**LIABILITY**

**n:** debt, drawback, indebtedness, likelihood, obligation, obnoxiety, responsibility

**LIBEL**

**a:** calumnious, defamatory, libelous, slanderous

**n:** aspersion, calumny, defamation, lampoon, satire, slander

**v:** abuse, defame, denigrate, slander, smear, vilify

**LIBERAL**

**a:** abundant, bounteous, bountiful, copious, generous, hospitable, knowledgeable, latitudinarian, lavish, magnanimous, messianic, munificent, philanthropic, prodigal

n: copiosity, generosity, hospitality, latitudinarian, liberality, munificence, philanthropist, philanthropy, Young Turk

   *arts:* humanities, quadrivium, trivium

   *liberator:* emancipator, manumitter, Messiah, redeemer, redemptor, redemptrix

## LIBERTINE

n: cyprian, debauchee, debauchery, lecher, lechery, *paillard*, profligacy, profligate, satyr, sensualist, sensuality, thelemite, voluptuary

## LIBRARY

n: *athenaeum, atheneum, bibliotheca, bibliotheque*, carrel, Dewey decimal system, Library of Congress classification, stack

   *addition:* accession

   *librarian: bibliothecaire*, bibliothecarian

## LICE

a: pedicular, pediculous, verminous

n: pediculosis, phthiriasis

## LIE

a: abject, blatant, equivocative, lying, mendacious, prevaricative, tergiversatory

n: canard, concealment, equivocation, exaggeration, fabrication, fabulation, falsehood, hyperbole, inveracity, mendacity, misrepresentation, prevarication, pseudology, roorback, subreption, tergiversation

v: equivocate, fabricate, fabulate, fudge, palter, prevaricate, temporize, tergiversate

   *down: couchant*, decubital, decumbent, incumbent, recumbent, supine

   *face down:* procumbent, prone, prostrate

   *liar:* fabricator, fabulist, prevaricator, pseudologist, pseudologue

   *on back:* decubital, supine

## LIEN

n: encumbrance, hypothecation, mortgage

## LIFE

a: anabolic, biocentric, biogenic, biogenous, biological, Dionysian, lively, naturalistic, ontological, Promethean

n: anabolism, animation, biogenesis, biography, *elan vital*, Eros, genesis, longevity, macrobiosis, mana, metabolism, ontogeny, protozoan, spirit, vitality, vivaciousness, vivacity

v: enliven, revivify, vivify

   *absence of:* abiosis, death

   *combining forms:* bio-, vit-, viv-

   *giving long:* macrobiotic

   *necessity for:* aliment, sustenance

   *philosophy of:* ideology, *weltanschauung*

   *return to:* anabiosis, resurrection, resuscitation

   *science:* biology, physiology

   *way of: modus vivendi*

## LIFELESS

a: adenoidal, amort, apathetic, colorless, comatose, defunct, exanimate, inanimate, inert, insensible, insentient, insipid, lethargic, quiescent, spiritless, torpid, unconscious, unresponsive, vapid

n: coma, defunction, dormancy, immobility, insentience, insipidity, latency, lethargy, lifelessness, passivity, quiescence, quietude, torpidity, vapidity

## LIGHT

a: catoptrical, diaphanous, easy, ethereal, imponderous, incandescent, inconsiderable, lambent, lucific, luminary, luminescent, luminiferous, luminous, phosphorescent, photic, photogenic, scintillating, scintillescent, weightless

n: bioluminescence, fluorescence, illumination, incandescence, luminary, luminescence, luminosity, phosphorescence, scintillation

v: scintillate

*avoiding:* lucifugal, lucifugous, photophobic

*combining forms:* lumin-, -phos, phos-, -phot, phot-, photo-

*fear:* photophobia, photophobic

*impervious:* opacity, opaque

*lacking:* aphotic

*love:* photophilic, photophilous

*response:* photokinesis, tropism

*science:* actinology, catoptrics, optics, photics

*treatment with:* actinotherapy, heliotherapy

## LIGHTHEARTEDNESS

**n:** blitheness, buoyancy, ebullience, euphoria, jauntiness, *jeu d'esprit,* nonchalance, sprightliness

## LIGHTNING

**a:** fulgurant, fulgurous, fulmineous, fulminous, sheet, streak

**n:** fireball, levin

**v:** fulgurate

*fear:* astraphobia

## LIKABLE

**a:** appealing, attractive, comely, congenial, contential, personable, *simpatico,* sympathetic

**n:** diathesis, fancy, gusto, inclination, likability, likableness, liking, penchant, predilection, predisposition, preference, prejudice, propensity, relish, want

**v:** affect, bask in, cherish, dote on, esteem, fancy, favor, relish, revel in

*combining forms:* phil-, -phile

## LIKE

**a:** akin, *quasi,* similar

**n:** analogy, assonance, caricature, counterpart, equivalence, facsimile, image, likeness, parity, resemblance, semblance, similarity, similitude, *simulacrum*

*combining forms:* -esque, homeo-, homo-, -oid, -ose, para-

## LIKELY

**a:** apparent, believeable, conjectural, credible, feasible, ostensible, plausible, possible, presumable, presumptive, prima facie, probable, promising, prospective, specious, verisimilar

**n:** liability, likelihood, probability, speciosity, verisimilitude, verisimility

## LIMB

**a:** cursorial, prehensile

## LIMBER

**a:** acrobatic, agile, flaccid, flexible, graceful, gracile, lissome, lithe, loose, pliable, pliant, rubbery, supple

**n:** flacidity, lissomeness, lithesomeness

## LIMIT

**a:** adjectival, adjective, circumscribed, cloistral, confined, confining, demarcative, denominational, esoteric, exclusive, finite, inflexible, limited, limiting, parochial, prescribed, qualificatory, restrictive, sectarian, select, stunted

**n:** boundary, circumscription, closure, cloture, confines, constraints, curfew, delimitation, demarcation, finitude, horizons, limitation, parameters, perimeter, periphery, proviso, *purlieus,* quota, ration, restriction, Rubicon, solstice, statute of limitations, stint, straightjacket, stricture, terminus, tether, threshold

**v:** chasten, circumscribe, confine, delimit, demarcate, discriminate, localize, qualify, regulate, temper

*without: ad infinitum,* boundless, inexhaustible, infinite, limitless, uncircumscribed, unrestrained

## LIMP

**a:** claudicant, drooping, flabby, flaccid, halting, lame, limping, spiritless

**n:** claudication, flaccidity, lameness

**v:** hobble

## LINE

**a:** coaxial, collinear, lineal, linear, lineate, rectilinear

**n:** axis, collineation, cordon, crosshair, echelon, hairline, hatching, linearity, lineation, meridian, parallel, regimentation, reticule, tangent

**v:** align, intersect

   *combining forms:* -stich, -stichous

   *inbetween:* interlineal, interlinear, interlineate

**LINEAGE**

**n:** ancestry, background, blood, derivation, descent, family, genealogy, heredity, pedigree, stemma, succession, tree

**LINGUIST**

**a:** glottological, linguistic(al), philologic(al)

**n:** glottologist, linguistician, philologist

**LINK**

**a:** concatenate, intercatenated, joined, linked

**n:** bond, catena, concatenation, juncture, liaison, nexus, spline, suture, tie, vinculum

**v:** catenate, concatenate, interlock, join

**LION**

**a:** leonine

**n:** Leo, Simba

   *group:* pride

**LIP**

**a:** labial

**n:** labia, labium, philtrum, pout

**v:** labialize, phonate, pucker, purse

   *biting:* cheilophagia

   *combining forms:* labi-, labio-

   *large:* macrocheilous

**LIQUID**

**a:** liquescent

**n:** colloid, emulsion, magma, marinade, ullage

**v:** liquefy

   *combining forms:* hydr-, hydro-

**LIST**

**a:** catalogical

**n:** agenda, agendum, canon, catalog, catalogue, directory, enumeration, guide, inventory, muster, repertoire, repertory, rigmarole, roll call, roster, *rota*, specifications, specs, tariff

**v:** codify, detail, enroll, enumerate, itemize, particularize, register, specify, tabulate, tally

**LISTENING**

**a:** acousmatic, audient

**n:** auscultation

**v:** eavesdrop, hearken

**LISTLESS**

**a:** comatose, degage, dilatory, dispirited, dull, enervated, inactive, inattentive, lackluster, languid, languorous, lazy, lethargic, spiritless, supine, vacuous

**n:** abiotrophy, apathy, languor, lassitude, lethargy, listlessness, otiosity

**LITANY**

**n:** chant, recital, rite, rogation, service, supplication

**LITERAL**

**a:** categorical, exact, explicitly, literally, obvious, pedantic, prosaic, textual, unimaginative, virtually, word-for-word

**n:** exactitude, grammatolatry, literality, prosaism

   *opposite:* figurative, metaphorical

**LITERARY**

**a:** anthologized, Augustan, belletristic, bookish, erudite, inkhorn, scholary

**n:** *ana, analecta,* analects, anthology, *belles lettres,* cameo, chrestomathy, classics, collectanea, digest, drama, excerpt, *feuilleton,* journalese, literature, *miscellanea, scrapiana*

**v:** anthologize

   *adaptation: rifacimento*

   *category:* genre

*characters:* personae

*child to adulthood: entwicklungsroman*

*commentary:* annotation, apparatus, gloss

*group: cenacle, clique, coterie,* salon

*introduction:* prodromus, prologue

*person: bellelettrist, belletrist, intelligentsia,* literarian, *literati, literato, literatus, litterateur,* philologist

*real people disguised:* roman a clef

*sensational:* kitsch

*study:* philology

*theft:* piracy, plagiarism

*two-part:* diptych

## LITTLE

**a:** diminutive, exiguous, inconsiderable, lilliputian, mediocre, microscopic, miniature, paltry, petty, small, trifling, trivial

**n:** modicum, moiety, *soupcon,* triviality, *un peu*

    *-by-little:* inchmeal, piecemeal

    *man:* homunculus

## LIVE

**a:** alacritous, animated, biogenous, blithe, boisterous, ebullient, effervescent, exhilarating, extrovert, exuberant, fervent, fervid, impassioned, intense, invigorating, lighthearted, lively, parturient, piquant, proligerous, rambunctious, spirited, spiritous, sprightly, spry, vigorous, vital, vivacious, viviparous

**n:** animation, ebullience, effervescence, exhilaration, intoxication, invigoration, life, liveliness, living, *modus vivendi, savoir vivre,* sprightliness, viability, vivacity

**v:** dwell, manage, reside, subsist

    *again: redivivus,* reincarnated, resurgent, resurrected

    *dissimilar organisms:* symbionticism, symbiosis

    *for the day: carpe diem*

    *together:* cohabiting, contubernal

## LOAD

**n:** burden, encumbrance, hindrance, impedient, incubus, pack, ponderosity, quantity, resistance, stress

## LOAFER

**n:** chairwarmer, drifter, *flaneur,* idler, loiterer, lounger, slouch, sluggard, vagabond, vagrant

## LOATHE

**a:** abhorrent, abominable, anathematic, cloying, detestable, disgusting, hateful, loathing, loathsome, odious, offensive, repugnant, unprincipled

**n:** abhorrence, abomination, antipathy, aversion, detestation, execration, odium, repugnance, repugnancy

**v:** abhor, abominate, anathematize, detest, dislike, execrate, hate, scorn

## LOCAL

**a:** aboriginal, autochthonous, edaphic, enchorial, endemic, indigenous, native, parochial, peninsular, provincial, regional, restricted, sectional, topical, vernacular, vicinal

**n:** locality, loci, locus, *milieu, purlieu,* vicinage, vicinity

    *ideas:* parochialism, peninsularity, provincialism

## LODGING

**n:** abode, accommodation, cabin, camp, cottage, dorm, encampment, hotel, inn, motel, *pied-a-terre,* resort, shelter

## LOFTY

**a:** Alpine, altitudinarian, altitudinous, Andean, celestial, divine, eminent, ethereal, grand, grandiloquent, heavenly, high, magniloquent, Olympian, spiritual, *spirituelle,* stately, supernal, supreme, towering

## LOGIC

**a:** *a priori,* analytic, apodictic, Aristotelian, cogent, coherent, consistent, dialectical, dianoetic, legitimate, rational, reasonable, tautologous

**n:** affirmation, argument, *ars artium,* assertion, consistency, construct, deduction, dialectics, disjunction, induction, lemma, predicate, premise, ratiocination, reasoning, sorties, syllogism, syntactics, synthesis

   *beyond:* metaphysical

   *illogical:* alogical, dereistic, dilemmatic, incompatible, invalid, lateral, paralogistic, sophistical

   *poor:* sophism, sophistry

   *result:* consequence, logicality

## LONG

**a:** centenarian, chronic, circuitous, diuturnal, elongated, enduring, eternal, interminable, inveterate, longanimous, longevous, macrobian, marathon, persistent, prolonged, protracted, repetitious, sempiternal, seven-league, sustained, verbose

**n:** aeon, diuturnity, iliad, longanimity, longevity, macrobiosis, sempiternity

## LONGING

**a:** appetent, appetitious, desiderative

**n:** appetency, appetite, appetition, craving, *desiderata,* desideration, *desideria, desiderium*

**v:** desiderate, hanker, languish, pine, yearn

## LOOK

**n:** air, appearance, aspect, carriage, cast, countenance, expression, mien, patina, physiognomy, semblance, visage

## LOOP

**a:** ansiform, looping

**n:** coil, festoon, hank, lobe, picots, swag

## LOOSE

**a:** desultory, detached, disengaged, dissolute, flabby, flaccid, licentious, limber, lissom, lithe, rampant, unconnected, wanton

**n:** laxation, loosening, lysis, relaxation

**v:** pay, slacken, surge

   *combining forms:* -lys, lys-, -lysis, lyso-

## LOPSIDED

**a:** alop, asymmetric(al), disproportionate, unbalanced, uneven, unsymmetric(al)

## LORD

**a:** archidiaconal, arrogant, baronial, dignified, honorable, honored, imperial, imperious, lordly, majestic, overbearing, stately

**n:** *kurios, kyrios,* liege, *magnifico*

   *lordship:* domain, dominion, *seigneury, seigniory,* sovereignty

## LOSS

**a:** amissible, astray, disoriented, lost, missing

**n:** amissibility, bereavement, casualty, depreciation, deprivation, destruction, detriment, diminution, disintegration, divestation, elimination, eradication, forfeiture, misfortune, perdition, privation, ullage

**v:** default, falter, forfeit, mislay, misplace, succumb, waver

## LOTION

**n:** embrocation, emollient, liniment

## LOTS

**n:** legions, loads, many, oodles, plenty, reams, slathers, slew, slews, tons

   *casting:* cleromancy, sortilege, sortition

## LOUD

**a:** blaring, blatant, calliopean, clamorous, clangorous, *crescendo,* deep, ear-piercing, *forte, fortissimo,* multivocal, noisy, ostentatious, plangent, resonant, scurrilous, sonorous, stentorian, stentorious, stentorophonic, stertorous, strident, thersitical, tumultous, vociferous

**n:** amplitude, blatancy, *crescendo,* decibel, *diminuendo,* loudness, magnitude, volume

   *speaker:* PA, public address, tweeter, woofer

## LOUSY

**a:** abominable, pedicular, pediculous, repulsive, verminous, vile

**n:** pediculosis

## LOUT

**n:** boor, bumpkin, grobian, lummox, oaf, yokel

## LOVE

**a:** affectionate, amative, amatory, amorous, autotheistic, egocentric, enamored, erotic, infatuated, loving, narcissan, narcississtic, narcistic, painstaking, smitten, unrequited

**n:** affection, amorosity, amorousness, *amour*, benevolence, courtship, devotion, endearment, *grande passion*, infatuation, passion, reverence, storge, tenderness, *tendresse*, torch song, veneration

  *combining forms:* -phil, phil-, philo-

  *devotee:* amorist, amourist, gallant

  *goddess:* Aphrodite, Venus

  *letter: billet d'amour, billet doux*

  *lover: amour*, amourist, beau, Casanova, cavalier, concubine, devotee, gallant, *inamorata, inamorato*, Lothario, *paramour*, Romeo, *servente*, swain

  *non-sensual:* Platonic

  *of friends: philia*

  *of married person: cicisbeo, paramour*

  *of money:* plutolatry

  *of self:* autophilia, autotheism, egocentricity, egoism, egotism, iotacism, narcissism

  *passing: amourette, passade*

  *secret: amour*, intrigue, liaison, rendezvous, tryst

  *self-lover:* autophiliac, egocentrist, narcissist

  *writings about:* amoristics

## LOW

**a:** *chthonian*, contemptible, *declasse*, declensional, declinatory, despicable, despondent, dishonorable, groveling, ignoble, ignominious, inferior, leprous, nether, plebeian, plutonian, plutonic, reptilian, subterranean, vulgar, vulgarian

**n:** contemptibility, debasement, declension, degradation, demotion, denigration, despicability, ignobility, ignominy, minimization, pejoration, traduction, vulgarity

**v:** animalize, bastardize, debase, debauch, deglamorize, degrade, dehumanize, demean, demoralize, denigrate, derogate, devaluate, disparage, humble, mediatize, minify, minimize, pejorate, traduce

  *combining form:* basi-, cata-, hypo-, infra-

  *lowest:* bathetic, *bathos*, nadir, nethermost, perigee

  *lowing of cow:* mugient

## LOYAL

**a:** abiding, adhering, allegiant, faithful, obedient, slavish, staunch, tenacious, unswerving, yeomanly

**n:** adherence, *aficionado*, allegiance, *bonhommie*, camaraderie, constancy, devotee, devotion, *esprit de corps*, faithfulness, fealty, fidelity, homage, janisary, liege, liegeman, loyalty, mercenary, minion, partisan, *philia*, piety

  *pretended:* lip service

## LUCK

**a:** aleatory, auspicious, favorable, fortuitous, fortunate, lucky, miraculous, propitious, providential, serendipitous

**n:** amulet, bonanza, fate, fluke, godsend, mascot, periapt, serendipity, talisman, vicissitudes, windfall

  *bad:* ambsace, misfortune, unlucky

## LUKEWARM

**a:** Laodicean, tepid

**n:** Laodicean, tepidity

## LULLABY

**n:** berceuse, cradle song

**LUMP**

**a:** *en masse, en toto, holusbolus*

**n:** bolus, bulge, bump, chunk, gobbet, knob, lump, node, nodule, nugget, protrusion, protuberance, slub, swelling

**LUNCH**

**n:** *dejeuner,* luncheon, tiffin

**LUNG**

**a:** pectoral, pneumonic, pulmonary, pulmonic, respiratory, thoracic

**n:** alveolus, bronchi, pleura

   *combining forms:* pneum-, pneumo-

**LURE**

**n:** decoy, inveiglement

**v:** attract, entice, incite, inveigle, solicit, tempt

**LUST**

**a:** concupiscent, hircine, insatiable, lecherous, lewd, libertine, libidinous, lubricious, lustful, paphian, prurient, randy, salacious

**n:** carnality, concupiscence, eagerness, enthusiasm, leer, lewdness, sex

**LUXURY**

**a:** affluent, Babylonian, exuberant, fertile, florid, flourishing, inventive, lavish, luxuriant, luxurious, opulent, palatial, plenteous, prodigal, profuse, proliferous, sumptuous, superabundant, sybaritic, uberous

**n:** affluence, Babylon, extravagance, *luxe,* luxuriousness, luxury, sensuality, voluptuosity, voluptuousness

**v:** indulge, luxuriate, revel, voluptuate, wallow

   *lover: bon vivant,* epicurean, hedonist, prodigal, profligate, sybarite, voluptuary

## MACHINE

**a:** automatous, mechanical, mechanomorphic

**n:** appartus, appliance, automaton, contraption, engine, instrument, Luddite, mechanicality, robot, simulator, zombie

**v:** automae, automatize, dehumanize, mechanize, robotize

## MAD

**a:** angry, bedlamite, berserk, certifiable, crazy, demented, distracted, distraught, eccentric, fey, furious, idiosyncratic, impetuous, insane, loco, lunatic, maniac, maniacal, *non compos mentis,* obsessed, possessed, psychotic, senseless

**n:** aberration, acharnement, deliration, delirium, *dementia,* derangement, ecstasy, fanaticism, frenzy, hallucination, insanity, lunacy, madness, mania, paranoia, psychosis, rashness, schizophrenia

> *madman:* bedlamite, maniac, *noncompos,* psychopath

## MAGAZINE

**a:** journalese

**n:** digest, fanzine, glossy, journal, periodical, pulp, subscription

## MAGIC

**a:** alchemical, alchemistic, cabalistic, hermetical, incantatory, magical, mystic, necromantic, numinous, phylacteric, recondite, sorcerous, talismanic

**n:** abracadabra, alchemy, conjuration, conjury, *diablerie,* enchantment, gramary, hocus-pocus, incantation, legerdemain, necromancy, occult, prestidigitation, sorcery, sortilege, thaumaturgy, theurgy, witchcraft, witchery, wizardry

> *formula:* alkahest, philter

> *symbol:* charm, pentacle, pentagram, rune, talisman

> *word:* abracadabra, abraxis, open sesame, presto

## MAGNANIMITY

**a:** chivalric, chivalrous, generous, handsome, liberal, magnanimous, philanthropic, unselfish

**n:** chivalry, generosity, philanthropy

## MAGNATE

**n:** bigwig, mogul, nobleman, panjandrum, peer, titan, tycoon

## MAGNIFICENT

**a:** dazzling, grand, imperial, leonine, majestic, palatial, regal, resplendent, spectacular, sumptuous

**n:** grandeur

## MAID

**a:** daphnean, maidenish, maidenly, modest, virginal

**n:** Abigail, ayah, *soubrette*

> *maiden name:* nee

## MAIMED

**a:** battered, hurt, injured, lame, mangled, mutilated, truncated

**n:** mayhem

## MAINTENANCE

**a:** sustentative

**n:** aid, alimentation, board, keep, subsistence, support, sustenance, sustentation

**MAJESTIC**

**a:** dignified, grand, grandiose, imperial, kingly, princely, queenly, regal, royal, statuesque, sublime

**n:** grandeur

**MAJORITY**

**n:** adulthood, arithmocracy, generality, maturity, plurality, predominance, predominancy

**MAKE UP**

**a:** improvisatorial, improvisatory

**n:** aggregate, arrangement, chemistry, composition, disposition, improvisation, morphology, recoupment

**v:** compose, concoct, confect, contrive, fabricate, fashion, improvisate, improvise, invent, manufacture, recoup, synthesize

> *for:* requite
>
> *maker:* artificier, author, craftsman, fabricator, manufacturer, producer

**MAKESHIFT**

**a:** emergency, extemporaneous, extemporary, impromptu, improvisatorial, improvised, temporary

**n:** expediency, expedient, improvisation, *pis aller*, stopgap, substitute

**MALE**

**a:** androcentric, androcratic, androgenous, android, andromorphous, androphilic, anthropic, anthropogenic, anthropoidal, anthropomorphic, anthropophilic, anthropophilous, masculine, patrilineal, virile

**n:** androgyneity, androgynism, androgyny, android, animus, anthropoid, cavalier, earthling, hermaphroditism, hominian, hominid, hominois, *homo sapiens*, homunculus, mankind, masculinity, mortal, mortality, terrene

**v:** manhood

> *and female:* ambisexual, ambosexual, bisexual, epicene
>
> *combining forms:* andr-, andro-, -anthrop, anthrop-, anthropo-, vir-

*disease:* andrology

*distribution:* anthropogenography, ethnogeography

*fear:* androphobia, apandria

*group:* fraternity, patriarchy

*hate:* misandry, misanthropy, timonism

*homosexual:* uranism, uranist, urning

*newly-married:* benedict

*organ:* penis, phallus, priapium

*wise:* Nestor, Solomon

*worship of organ:* phallicism

*young:* ephebe

**MALIGN**

**a:** baleful, baneful, cancerous, dangerous, deadly, harmful, injurious, lethal, malevolent, malignant, pernicious, sinister, virulent

**v:** calumniate, censure

**MALNUTRITION**

**n:** beriberi, *cachexia*, cacotrophy, *kwashiorkor*, malnourishment, scurvy, tabescence

**MANAGE**

**a:** administrative, executive, governable, manageable, managerial, plastic, pliant, politic, supervisory, tactical, tractable

**n:** administration, cultivation, direction, dispensation, disposition, economy, eutaxy, government, husbandry, management, manipulation, negotiation, superintendence, supervision

**v:** administer, contrive, control, cultivate, direct, dispense with, engineer, forgo, govern, husband, manipulate, negotiate, regulate, superintend, supervise

> *manageability:* docility, manipulability, tractability
>
> *manager:* administrant, administrator, comptroller, *concierge,* director, executive, *gerent, impresario,* manipulator, steward, superintendent, supervisor, tactician

## MANDATORY

**a:** coercive, compelling, compulsory, enforced, exigent, impelling, imperative, obligatory, prerequisite

**n:** compulsoriness, exigency

## MANIA

**a:** delirious, hysterical, maniac(al)

**n:** *cacoethes*, delirium, frenzy, hysteria

**v:** alcohol

*cleanliness:* ablutomania

*flowers:* anthomania

*horses:* hippomania

*lying:* mythomania

*one thing:* monomania

*oneself:* egomania

*pleasure:* hedonomania

*power:* megalomania

*religion:* entheomania, theomania

*riches:* chrematomania, plutomania

*sex:* erotomania, nymphomania, satyromania

*stealing:* kleptomania

*surgery:* tomomania

*talking:* logomania, verbomania

*traveling:* dromomania

*work:* ergomania

## MANIFOLD

**a:** abundant, complex, diverse, many, much, multifarious, multitudinous, numerous, replete, replicate

## MANNER

**n:** bearing, demeanor, deportment, mien, *modus operandi, modus vivendi,* ostent, posture, procedure, *quo modo*

*combining form:* -wise

*mannerism:* affectation, artificiality, eccentricity, foible, idiosyncrasy, preciosity, singularity, whimsicality

## MANNERS

**a:** punctilious

**n:** breeding, code, courtesy, decorum, demeanor, etiquette, finish, mores, protocol, *punctilio,* rubric, *savoir faire, savoir vivre,* suavity, urbanity

*bad:* solecism

*pretended:* artificiality, histrionics, theatrics

## MANUAL

**n:** consuetudinary, encheiridion, guidebook, handbook, reference, vade mecum

## MANURE

**n:** dung, ejecta, excrement, excrementa, excreta, feces, feculence, ordure

## MANY

**a:** diverse, excessive, innumerable, legion, manifold, multifarious, multifold, multiple, multiplex, multiplicitous, multipotent, multitudinous, myriad, numerous, sundry, umpteen

**n:** lots, multeity, multifariousness, multiplicity, multitude, plenty, plurality, versatility

*colored:* kaleidoscopic, multi-colored, prismatic

*combining forms:* multi-, pluri-, poly-

*-sided:* hydra-headed, multifaceted, multilateral, multiphasic, multivarious, versatile

*-valued:* multivalent, multivalued, polyvalent

## MARBLE

**a:** alabaster, marmoraceous, marmoreal

## MARGINAL

**a:** circumferential, limitrophe, peripheral

**n:** indentation, latitude, leeway, postil, range

**v:** postil

*note:* annotation, *apostille, marginalia, postil, scholia, scholium*

## MARK

**a:** stigmatiferous

**n:** aura, cachet, characteristic, defacement, *differentia*, disfiguration, earmark, flag, hallmark, *imprimatur*, indication, lineaments, scarification, stigma, stigmata, watermark

**v:** characterize, circumscribe, deface, delimit, disfigure, scarify, signalize, stigmatize, subtend, temporize, typify

## MARRIAGE

**a:** betrothed, conjugal, connubial, epithalmic, espoused, hymeneal, marital, matrimonial, monandrous, monogynous, nuptial, spliced, yoked

**n:** conjugality, connubiality, espousal, matrimony, monandry, monogyny, nuptiality, nuptials, wedlock

**v:** solemnize

    *after:* post-nuptial

    before: antenuptial, premarital
    *combining forms:* -gam, gam-

    *hate:* misogamy

    *marriageable:* nubile

    *outside race:* exogamy, miscegenation, outbreeding

    *plural:* bigamy, polyandry, polygamy, polygyny

    *related by:* affine

    *royal and commoner:* morganatic

    *second:* deuterogamy, digamy

    *song:* epithalamion, epithalamium, hymenal

    *with other race:* miscegenation

    *within race:* endogamy, inmarriage

    *wrong:* misalliance

## MARSH

**a:** fenny, paludal, paludous, palustral, palustrine, uliginose

**n:** bog, fen, miasma, mire, muskeg, quagmire, sedge, slough

## MARVEL

**a:** marvelous, meritorious, mirific, transcendent

**n:** humdinger, *mirabilia*, miracle, phenomena, phenomenon, portent, prodigy

## MASKED

**a:** cabalistic, cryptic, disguised, *incognito*, larvate, latent

**n:** domino, mask, masquerade, visor

## MASS

**a:** concretionary

**n:** agglutination, aggregate, concretion, conglomeration, magnitude, ponderosity, shock, spissitude

**v:** agglomerate, agglutinate, aggregate, assemble, concentrate, concretize, conglomerate, join, lump, muster, pile

    *combining forms:* -oma, -ome

## MASSIVE

**a:** bulky, elephantine, heavy, huge, imposing, monumental, ponderous, substantial, weighty

## MASTER

**a:** arrogant, commanding, domineering, imperative, imperious, masterful, preemptory, skillful, sovereign

**n:** ascendency, command, dominion, *maestro*, mastery, sahib, subjugation, *sui juris*, superiority, *virtuoso*

**v:** conquer, dominate, overawe, overcome, overpower, subdue, subjugate, vanquish

    *masterpiece: chef d'oeuvre, magnus opus, meisterwerk, piece de resistance, tour de force*

    *of ceremonies: ceremoniarius, compere,* MC, officiator, toastmaster

## MASTURBATION

**n:** autoeroticism, malthusianism, manustupration, onanism

## MATCH

**a:** matching

**n:** coordinate, counterpart, pendant

**v:** agree, correspond, harmonize, tally

    *matchless:* consummate, incomparable, inimitable, *ne plus supra, ne plus ultra*, peerless, superlative, transcendent, unparalleled

**MATERIAL**

**a:** banausic, *bourgeois*, corporeal, democritean, essential, faustian, important, materialistic, mechanical, palpable, pertinent, philistine, philistinic, physical, ponderable, pragmatic, relevant, sensible, substantial, tangible, utilitarian

**n:** armamentarium, composite, corporeality, corporeity, instrumentaria, materiality, materialization, materiel, physicality, reification, substantiality, tangibility

**v:** hypostatize, materialize, reify

*materialism:* barbarism, evolution, heterodoxy, physicism, pragmatism, ultilitarianism

*materialist:* corporealist, evolutionist, heterodox, physicist, pragmatist, utilitarian

**MATHEMATICS**

**n:** algebra, arithmetic, geometry

*love:* philomathy

**MATTER**

**n:** corporality, material, materiality, substance, substantiality

*combining forms:* hyl-, hylo-, plasm-

*of-fact:* literal, pragmatic, prosaic, utilitarian

**MATURE**

**a:** adult, mellow, precocious

**n:** adult, adultness, maturation, maturity

**v:** develop, maturate

**MAXIM**

**a:** aphoristic, apothegmatic, gnomic, sentential

**n:** adage, aphorism, apothegm, axiom, byword, dictum, epigram, gnome, *logion,* motto, pearl, *sententia,* witticism

**MAZE**

**a:** daedalian, daedalic, labyrinthine

**n:** conglomeration, convolution, intricacy, labyrinth, maelstrom, perplexity, sinuosity, warren

**MEAGER**

**a:** exigous, infinitesimal

**n:** dearth, exiguity, famine, lack, meagerness, need, parcity, paucity, squalor, stringency, want

**MEAL**

**n:** breakfast, brunch, buffet, collation, dinner, lunch, repast, snack, supper, tiffin

*after:* postcibal, postprandial

*before:* precibal, preprandial

*complete: table d'hote*

*main dish: entree*

*outdoor: alfresco*

*separate: a la carte*

*side dish: entremet(s)*

**MEAN**

**a:** contemptible, despicable, duplicitous, intermediary, intermediate, parvanimitous, reptilian, stingy, wicked

**n:** despicability, duplicity, knavery, meanness, parvanimity, rascality, wickedness

*average:* center, intermediary, norm, par, rule

*meantime: ad hoc, ad interim,* interim, interval, meanwhile

*person:* caitiff, procrustean, sadist

**MEANING**

**a:** categorematic, definitive, expressive, knowledgeable, meaningful, notional, semantic, sententious, significant

**n:** acceptation, burden, connotation, context, denotation, drift, gist, gravamen, import, interpretation, nuance, profundity, purport, referent, significance, signification, subtext, tenor, understanding

*implied:* subaudition, *subintelligitur,* tacit

*many:* polysemous

*meaningless:* aimless, purposeless

*means:* channel, expedient, instrumentality, instrumentation, intermediary, medium, *modus operandi, quo modo,* resources, vehicle, wherewithal

*one:* univocal

*same:* synonymic, synonymous

*two or more:* ambiguous, amphibolic, amphibolous, *double entendre*, equivocal

*underlying: mythos*

**MEASURE**

**a:** calculated, commensurable, deliberate, finite, limited, measurable, measured, mensurable, mensural, mensurative, metrical, ponderable, quantitative, rhythmical

**n:** amplitude, barometer, capacity, coefficient, constant, criteria, criterion, dimension, fathom, girth, indication, magnitude, mensuration, sound, survey, thermometer, touchstone, weights

**v:** calibrate

*combining forms:* metr-, -metry

**MECHANICAL**

**a:** automatic, automatous, autonomic, indifferent, inhuman, involuntary, perfunctorious, perfunctory, reflex, routine, stereotyped, unconscious

**n:** automaticity, mechanicality, rote

**v:** automatize, dehumanize, mechanize, robotize

*man:* android, automaton, golem, robot

*mechanic:* artisan, engineer, mechanician

**MEDDLE**

**a:** impertinent, intrusive, meddlesome, meddling, officious, polypragmatic, pragmatic

**n:** impertinence, impudicity, intrusiveness, meddlesomeness, polypragmatism

**v:** butt in, interfere, interlope, interpose, interrupt, intervene, intrude, obtrude, pry, tamper

*meddler:* busybody, interloper, intervenient, *quidnunc*

**MEDIATE**

**n:** arbitrator, conciliator, go-between, intercessor, intermediary, intervenient, mediator, ombudsman, placator

**v:** arbitrate, intercede, interject, interpose, referee, settle, umpire

**MEDICAL**

**a:** Aesculapian, iatric, iatrical, medicative, medicinal, pharmaceutic(al), therapeutic(al), theriac(al)

**n:** iatrics, iatrology, medicament, medicant, medication, pharmaceutical, pharmaceutics, simple, specific, therapeusis, therapeutant, therapeutic, therapeutics, therapy, treatment

*combining forms:* -atrics, -iatr-, iatr-, iatro-, -iatry

*drug:* pharmaco-

*examination:* -opsy

*false:* placebo

*instruments:* armamentaria, instrumentaria

*medicinal:* medicative, medicinable, pharmaceutic, salutary, salutiferous, sanative, therapeutic

*practitioner:* Aescalapius, doctor, physician, therapist

*quack:* nostrum, panacea

*student:* intern, resident

*symbol:* caduceus

*treatment:* -path, path-, -pathy

**MEDITATE**

**a:** apollonian, apollonic, cogitable, cogitabund, cogitative, contemplative, deliberative, meditative, nomothetic, pensive, purposeful, reflective

**n:** cerebration, cogitation, contemplation, lucubration, mantra, meditation, mysticism, reflection, rumination

**v:** cogitate, consider, contemplate, deliberate, excogitate, lucubrate, ponder, reflect

**MEDLEY**

**n:** Babelism, brouhaha, *charivari*, diversity, *fantasia, farrago, fatras, gallimaufry,* heterogeneity, hodgepodge, melange, miscellany, mix, montage, *olio, olla podrida,* *pasticcio, pastiche,* potpourri, *salmagundi,* variety

**MEEK**

**a:** fawning, forbearing, humble, invertebrate, phlegmatic, placid, servile, submissive, sycophantic, unpretentious

**n:** abnegation, forbearance, humbleness, humility, mansuetude, meekness, submission, submissiveness

**v:** fawn, kowtow, truckle

**MEET**

**n:** amalgamation, assemblage, assembly, assignation, audience, brainstorming, caucus, clinic, collocation, *colloquium,* conclave, concourse, concursion, confluence, conflux, confrontation, congregation, congress, convention, convergence, *conversazione,* convocation, decussation, encounter, forum, intersection, junction, juncture, levee, meeting, plenum, powwow, rally, rendezvous, seminar, summit, symposium, synod, tryst, workshop

**v:** assemble, confront, congregate, convene, convoke, decussate, encounter, fulfill, intersect, rencounter, satisfy

*minimum for: quorum*

*place of:* concourse, rendezvous, reunion, tryst

**MELANCHOLY**

**a:** *atrabilarious, atrabiliar, atrabilious,* dispirited, hypochondriacal, sad

**n:** apanthropia, apanthropy, blues, dejection, depression, doldrums, gloom, hypochondria, lachrymals, megrims, melancholia, melancholy, sorrow, vapors

*person: atrabilarian,* hypochondriac, melancholiac, valetudinarian

**MELLOW**

**a:** classic, matured, mellowed, orotund, resonant, sonorous

**n:** orotundity, sonority

**v:** age, mature, ripen, season

**MELODY**

**a:** ariose, canorous, cantabile, dulcet, euphonious, lyric, lyrical, mellifluous, melodic, melodious, melopoetic, orphic, sirenic(al), sonorous, symphonizing, symphonous, unisonant

**n:** descant, diapason, euphony, harmonization, harmony, lyric, melopoeia, orchestration, sonority, symphony, syncopation

*single: leitmotif, leitmotiv,* monophonic, monophonous

*two or more:* contrapuntal, counterpoint, polyphonic, polyphonous, polyphony, polyrhythmic

**MELT**

**a:** deliquescent, liquescent, melting

**n:** deliquescence, liquefaction

**v:** ablate, deliquesce, disintegrate, dissipate, dissolve, liquefy, render, smelt

**MEMBER**

**a:** plenary

**n:** constituent, *plenum,* quorum

**v:** enlist, enroll, recruit

**MEMBRANE**

**n:** amnion, chorion, diaphragm, division, hymen, partition, peritoneum, septum, serosa

*pass through:* osmosis, transudation

*separate:* dialysis

**MEMORANDUM**

**n:** *aide-memoire,* letter, memento, *memoir,* note, protocol, reminder

**MEMORIAL**

**n:** cenotaph, commemoration, inscription, memento, monument, plaque, shrine, trophy, vestige

**MEMORY**

**a:** eidetic, engraved, inscribed, mnemonic, reminiscent, retentive, rote, tenacious

**n:** anamnesis, hypermnesia, recall, recollection, reminiscence, retention, retrieval, retrospection, rote

**v:** memorize

*aid:* aide-memoire, memoria, mnemonic device, mnemonics

*from:* ex capite

*gap:* amnesia, parapraxia, parapraxis

*loss:* amnesia, *fugue, lethe,* oblivion, paramnesia

*science:* mnemonics

## MENACE

**a:** dangerous, imminent, menacing, minacious, minatorial, ominous

**n:** anathema, Charybdis, commination, jeopardy, minacity, sword of Damocles

**v:** cow, frighten, intimidate, jeopardize, scare, terrify, threaten

## MENSTRUATION

**n:** catamenia, menorrhea, menses

*absence:* amenorrhea, menopause

*onset:* menarche

*painful:* dysmenorrhea

*profuse:* menorrhagia

*stoppage:* change of life, climacteric

## MENTAL

**a:** apperceptionistic, appercipient, cerebral, conceptual, concipient, ideological, intellectual, mentalistic, metaphysical, noological, phrenic, psychiatric, psychic, psychological, subjective

**n:** apperception, conception, impression, prehension

*competent: capax, compos mentis,* sane

*deficiency: amentia, aphronia,* cretinism, feeblemindedness, idiocy, imbecility, moronity, *oligophrenia*

*disorder:* aberration, alienation, deliration, delirium, delusion, *dementia,* hallucination, illusion, mania, psychosis

*distress:* dysphoria, psychalgia

*incompetent:* amental, cretinous, deficient, demented, incapacious, *non compos mentis,* psychotic, slow, obnubilation

*study:* noology, psychiatry, psycholo-

gy, psychostatics

## MENTOR

**n:** *cicerone,* coach, counsel, counselor, guide, preceptor, professor, teacher, tutor

## MENU

**n:** bill of fare, *carte du jour,* dietary, list, regimen, tariff

## MERCENARY

**a:** avaricious, commercial, mercantile venal

**n:** *condottiere,* extortioner, Hessian, hierling, janissary, Myrmidon, pensionary

## MERCY

**a:** clement, compassionate, forbearing, indulgent, lenient, merciful, sympathetic, tender, tolerant, warm-hearted

**n:** benignity, charity, clemency, commiseration, compassion, leniency, lenity, pity, toleration

*killing:* euthanasia

*merciless:* austere, barbarous, disputatious, imperative, implacable, inclement, inexorable, inquisitorial, intolerant, obdurate, pitiless, relentless, remorseless, *sans merci,* unfeeling, unsympathetic

## MERGER

**a:** amalgamative, coalescent, confluent, merging, osmotic

**n:** absorption, alliance, amalgamation, coadunation, coalescence, coalition, concursion, confluence, fusion, osmosis, union

**v:** absorb, amalgamate, blend, coalesce, connect, fuse, harmonize, incorporate, integrate, join, marry, merge, unify, unite

## MERIT

**a:** commendable, commendatory, condign, creditable, due, eminent, estimable, excellent, exemplary, fit, fitting, merited, meritorious, praiseworthy, prestigious, suitable, valuable, warranted, worthy

**n:** commendableness, eminence, estimableness, exemplarity, prestige

*having none:* adiaphorous

## MERRY

**a:** blithe, blithesome, carnivalesque, debonair, exuberant, exultant, festive, friendly, frolicsome, genial, happy, hilarious, jaunty, jocund, jovial, joyous, lively, mirthful, orgiastic, sportive

**n:** carousal, exuberance, exultation, festivity, geniality, hilarity, jocularity, jocundity, jollification, joviality, jubilation, merriment, merrymaking, orgy, revelry, sportiveness

## MESS

**n:** conglomeration, heterogeneity, hodgepodge, miscellany, mixture, potpourri

## MESSAGE

**a:** internuncial, internunciary

**n:** cryptogram, meaning, subtext

**v:** relay

*messenger:* agent, apostle, courier, emissary, envoy, forerunner, harbinger, herald, *internuncio*

## METAPHOR

**a:** figurative, metaphorical

**n:** allegory, anagoge, conceit, drift, imagery, meaning, metonymy, synecdoche, tenor, trope, vehicle

**v:** allegorize, metaphorize

*faulty:* catachresis

## METAPHYSICAL

**a:** clairvoyant, extraphysical, preternatural, stratospheric(al), supernatural, superphysical, telepathic, transcendent(al)

## METHOD

**a:** empirical, heuristic, methodical, orderly

**n:** approach, discipline, expertise, methodology, *metier*, modality, *modus operandi*, plan, procedure, regimen, strategy, tactics, technique, virtuosity

*lack:* disorder

*temporary: modus vivendi*

## MIDDAY

**a:** meridian

*meal:* lunch, tiffin

## MIDDLE

**a:** central, intermediate, medial, median, mediocre, mesothetic

**n:** center, centrist, golden mean, intermediate, limbo, mean, median, moderant, moderate, *tertium quid, via media*

**v:** mediatize

*ages:* medieval, *moyen-age*

*class: bourgeois(ie)*

*combining forms:* medi-, medio-, mes-, meso-

*man:* intermediary, intervenient, mediary

## MID-MORNING

**a:** antemeridian

## MIGHT

**a:** armipotent, efficacious, efficient, extraordinary, Herculean, invincible, mighty, momentous, omnipotent, potent, powerful, puissant

**n:** authority, capacity, force, potency, power, puissance, resources

## MIGRATION

**a:** migratory, moving, nomadic, roving, transient, unsettled, vagrant, wandering

**n:** *diaspora*, exodus, hegira, move, shift, transfer, trek

*non:* sedentary

## MILD

**a:** amiable, assuasive, clement, compassionate, complaisant, considerate, favonian, gentle, lenient, lenitive, mitigatory, palliative, palliatory, peaceful, placative, placatory, soft, temperate, tepid, tolerant, tranquil n: benignity, clemency, compassion, consideration, gentleness, lenity, mansuetude, mildness, tranquility

v: mitigate, mollify, palliate, placate, tranquilize

## MILITARY

a: martial

n: air force, army, battalion, cavalry, commando, detachment, infantry, *junta*, legion, marines, navy, outpost, paratroops, phalanx, rearguard, reinforcements, task force

*government:* stratocracy

## MILK

a: galactophorous, lacteal, lacteous, lactescent, lactic, lactiferous, milky, opalescent

n: lactescence, milkiness, opalescence

v: lactate

*combining forms:* galact-, galacto-, lact-, lacto-

*feeding on:* galactophagous, lactivorous

*secretion:* lactation, lactescent

## MIMICRY

a: echoic, mimetic, mimical, onomatopoeic

n: caricature, imitation, impersonation, mimesis, mimetism, parody, *pastiche*

## MIND

a: autopsychic, cerebral, endopsychic, intellectual, mental, noological, psychogenetic, psychological, psychosomatic

n: cerebration, cerebrum, consciousness, faculty, intellect, intelligence, *logos*, lucubration, mentality, mentation, *nous*, psyche, rationality, reason, sensorium, sentiment, thought, understanding

v: inculcate, indoctrinate

*combining forms:* cereb-, cogit-, cognit-, concept-, intell-, log-, noo-, -phren, phren-, phreno-, psych-, psycho-, ratio-

*confused:* dementia, escapism, obnubilation, psychosis

*keen:* acumen, discernment, discrimination, perspicacity, perspicuity, shrewdness

*reading:* clairvoyance, cryptesthesia, telepathy

*smallness:* parvanimity

*sound:* competency

*study:* noology, psychiatry, psychology

## MINERAL

n: lode, reef, seam, vein

*study:* mineralogy, oryctology

## MINGLE

v: amalgamate, associate, concoct, confuse, conglomerate, infiltrate, integrate, interpolate, intertwine, mix, unite

## MINIATURE

a: diminutive, lilliputian, microcosmic, small

n: diminutive, epitome, homunculus, lilliputian, manikin, microcosm, pygmy

## MIRACLE

a: miraculous, thaumaturgic

n: anomy, mirabilia

*study:* thaumatology

*worker:* magician, thaumaturgist

## MIRAGE

n: corposant, deception, *fata morgana*, illusion, St. Elmo's fire

## MIRROR

a: catoptric, specular

n: speculum

*study:* catoptrics

## MISAPPLY

n: malfeasance, peculation, subtraction, theft, trespass

v: defalcate, embezzle, misappropriate, misuse, steal

**MISBEHAVIOR**

n: delinquency, malbehavior, malconduct, misconduct, misdeed, offense

**MISBELIEF**

n: agnosticism, heresy, miscreance, skepticism, unorthodoxy

**MISCELLANEOUS**

a: assorted, diverse, heterogeneous, hodge-podge, indiscriminate, manifold, pied, promiscuous, sundry, varied, various

n: *adversaria*, bric-a-brac, *collectanea*, heterogeneity, hodge-podge, medley, *miscellanea*, miscellaneity, miscellany, *olla podrida*, *varia*

**MISCHANCE**

n: accident, calamity, catastrophe, *contretemps*, misadventure, miscalculation, misfortune, mishap

**MISCHIEF**

a: elflike, impish, injurious, malevolent, mischievous, puckish, roguish, venomous

n: adventure, caper, *diablerie*, escapade, hanky-panky, *harlequinade*, hocus-pocus, impishness, mischievousness, Pandora's box, ploy, prank, shenanigans

**MISCONCEPTION**

n: delusion, hallucination, illusion, misapprehension, misinterpretation, mistake, misunderstanding

**MISCONDUCT**

a: malfeasant

n: beastliness, bestiality, defaction, defalcation, delinquency, felony, malconduct, malfeasance, malversation, misbehavior, misdeed, misdemeanor, misfeasance, offense, sociopathy

   *person:* delinquent, malfeasor, misdemeanant, misfeasor

**MISERABLE**

a: abject, afflictive, contemptible, discreditable, shameful, worthless, wretched

n: agony, desolation, immiserization, misery, purgatory

   *place:* Gethsemane, hell, purgatory

**MISERLY**

a: acquisitive, avaricious, churlish, covetous, extortionate, frugal, penny-pinching, penurious, stingy

n: curmudgeon, miser, niggard, Scrooge, tightwad

**MISFORTUNE**

a: calamitous, catastrophic, unfortunate

n: accident, adversity, *ambsace*, bad luck, bereavement, calamity, catastrophe, *contretemps*, holocaust, misadventure, mishap, tribulation, visitation

**MISLEADING**

a: ambiguous, ambivalent, deceptive, delusional, delusionary, delusive, distorted, equivocal, factitious, garbled, illusive, illusory

n: *ignis fatuus*, will-o'-the-wisp

v: bamboozle, deceive, defraud, delude, equivocate, mislead, victimize, wrongfoot

**MIST**

a: *brumous*, *caliginous*, cloudy, crepuscular, hazy, misty, nebulous, nubilous, vaporific, vaporish, vaporous, volatile

n: *brume*, colloid, nebula, obscurity, whiteout

**MISTAKE**

a: adrift, amiss, awry, erroneous, fallible, mistaken, sophistic, specious

n: boner, catachresis, erratum, error, fallacy, fault, *faux pas*, Freudian slip, *gaffe*, inadvertence, inadvertency, *malapropism*, misapprehension, misconception, misperception, misunderstanding, oversight, paralogism, pratfall, solecism, typo

**MISTRESS**

n: *amour*, *chatelaine*, *demimondaine*, *inamorata*, *materfamilias*, matriarch, matron, *paramour*

## MISUNDERSTANDING

**a:** misunderstood

**n:** cross-purposes, disagreement, dissention, imbroglio, misapprehension, misinterpretation, misperception, *misprision*

**v:** misconstrue, misinterpret, misunderstand

## MISUSE

**v:** defalcate, embezzle, misapply, misappropriate, pervert

   *word:* malapropism

## MIXED

**a:** amalgamated, amalgamative, catachrestic, diffuse, diversified, farraginous, heterogeneous, hybrid, hyphenated, macaronic, miscible, mongrel, multifarious, omnifarious, promiscuous

**n:** amalgam, amalgamation, ambivalence, anthology, catachresis, commingling, compound, concoction, confection, conglomeration, *farrago, gallimaufry,* heterogeneity, hodgepodge, hyphenation, medley, *miscellanea,* miscellany, mixture, motley, *olio, olla podrida,* omnibus, *pastiche,* patchwork, potpourri, *salmagundi, smorgasbord*

**v:** amalgamate, assimilate, coalesce, commingle, confound, conglomerate, hybridize, integrate, interfuse, interlard, intermingle, levigate, mix, triturate

   *origin:* heterogeneity, hybrid, hybridization

## MOB

**n:** *canaille, claque, clique,* gang, *hoi polloi,* plebs, riffraff

   *rule:* mobocracy, ochlocracy

## MOCKERY

**n:** asteism, badinage, burlesque, caricature, counterfeit, derision, futility, imitation, lampoon, mimesis, mimicry, parody, persiflage, raillery, ridicule, sarcasm, satire

**v:** ape, catcall, deride, derogate, heckle, mimic, parody, ridicule, scoff, taunt

## MODEL

**a:** archetypal, archetypical, ectypal, example, exemplary, paradigmatic, prototypal

**n:** archetype, avatar, blueprint, ectype, example, exemplar, exemplarity, exemplum, lodestar, manikin, mannequin, matrix, microcosm, paradigm, paragon, prototype, replica

## MODERATE

**a:** abstemious, abstentious, calm, continent, mitigatory, modest, prudent, reasonable, temperate

**n:** abstention, abstinence, continence, discretion, golden mean, moderateness, moderation, prudence, restraint, temperance, *via media*

**v:** ease, mitigate, mollify, restrain, temper, tranquilize

   *person:* centrist, moderant, moderate

## MODERN

**a:** *au courant, avant-garde,* contemporary, *dernier cri,* futuristic, high-tech, latter-day, modernistic, neoteric, newfangled, progressive, recent, state-of-the-art, topical

**n:** modernity, modernness, neoteric, topicality

## MODESTY

**a:** chaste, decorous, demure, diffident, humble, moderate, modest, priggish, prudish, *pudibund,* self-effacing, shy, unassuming, unobtrusive, unpretentious, *verecund,* virginal, virtuous

**n:** demurity, diffidence, maidenliness, pudency, pudibundity, pudicity, sufficiency, verecundity

## MOISTURE

**a:** aqueous, bibitory, humectant, hydrogenous, moist, saturated

**n:** aquosity, humectation, humidity, moistness

   *combining form:* hygro-

## MOLT

**a:** deciduous, deplumate, exfoliative

**n:** deplumation, ecdysis

**v:** cast, deplumate, discard, exfoliate, exuviate, moult, shed, slough

## MOLTEN

*rock:* lava, magma

## MOMENT

**a:** ephemeral, evanescent, fleeting, instantaneous, momentary, semelfactive, short-lived, timely, transient, transitory

**n:** consequence, consideration, ephemerality

*momentous:* consequential, crucial, epochal, memorable, paramount, prominent, signal, weighty

## MONEY

**a:** commercial, commercialistic, financial, mercantile, mercenary, monetary, numismatic, nummary, pecuniary, quaestuary, sumptuary, venal

**n:** bequest, coin, currency, gratuity, income, legacy, legal tender, *lucre, mammon,* medium, proceeds, profit, property, purse, rebate, reimbursement, revenue, *specie,* wampum, wherewithal, windfall

*large sum:* king's ransom

*love:* fiscality, mammonism, plutolatry, plutomania

*small sum:* peanuts, pittance, token

*without:* impecunious, indigent, poor

## MONK

**a:** cenobitic, secular, solitudinarian

**n:** Benedictine, Capuchin, Carthusian, cenobite, Cistercian, Dominican, Franciscan, lama, monastic, neophyte, novice, postulant, votary

## MONKEY

**a:** anthropoidal, simian, simious

**n:** anthropoid, ape, primate, simian

## MONOTONOUS

**a:** banal, dull, stereotyped, stereotypical

**n:** dullness, monotony, prosaism, routine, treadmill

## MONSTER

**a:** atrocious, grotesque, heinous, hideous, huge, monstrous, prodigious

**n:** behemoth, chimera, dragon, enormity, fiend, Frankenstein, gorgon, leviathan, monstrosity, ogre, phoenix, sphinx

*combining forms:* terat-, terato-, theri-, thero-

## MONTH

**a:** mensual, *per mensem*

*current:* instant

*next: proximo*

*previous: ultimo*

*six:* semester, semestral

## MOOD

**a:** ambivalent, fastigial, hypochondriacal, irritable, melancholic, moody, temperamental

**n:** disposition, humor, inclination, proclivity, temper, temperament

*moodiness:* doldrums, hypochondriasis, megrims, melancholia, melancholy, sullenness

## MOON

**a:** lunar, selenian

*combining forms:* lun-, selen-, seleno-

*full:* plenilune

*study:* selenology

## MORAL

**a:** admonishing, allegorical, didactic, moralistic, puritanical, righteous, sabbatarian, sermonic, tropological, virtuous

**n:** allegory, apologue, *dharma,* ethics, moralities, mores, piosity, rigorism, sabbatarian, zeitgeist

**v:** admonish, lecture, moralize, sermonize

*immoral:* adiaphoristic, adiaphorous, amoral, dissolute, lecherous, lewd, libertine, licentious, maladive, profligate, scrofulous

*lower:* debauch

*study:* deontology

## MORBID
**a:** cachetic, cadaverous, diseased, grisly, gruesome, maladive, morbose, scrofulous

**n:** *cachexia,* gruesomeness, morbidity

## MORNING
**a:** *antemeridian, matinal, matutinal*

**n:** *ante meridiem,* dawn, daybreak, *matin,* sunrise

## MORTGAGE
**n:** encumbrance, hypothecation

**v:** amortize, hypothecate, impignorate

## MOTHER
**a:** maternal, maternalistic, matriarchal, matrilateral, matrilinean, matrilinear, matripotestal, matroclinal, matroclinic, matroclinous

**n:** ancestress, *genetrix, mater, materfamilias,* matriarch

*combining form:* matri-

*killing:* matricide

*motherhood:* maternity, *matrilineage*

## MOTION
**a:** kinetic, volitant

**n:** volitation

*loss of:* catalepsy, paralysis

*motionless:* impassive, inert, quiescent, static, still

*science:* dynamics, kinetics

## MOTIVE
**n:** consideration, design, determinant, *fillip,* impetus, impulse, incentive, incitement, inducement, intendment, intention, *motif,* motivation, provocation, stimulus

*hidden:* hypocrisy, ulterior motive

*without:* unmotivated, unpremeditated

## MOTTO
**n:** banner, epigram, epigraph, maxim, principle, quotation, slogan, watchword

## MOUND
**n:** barrow, hummock, *motte,* tuffet, tumulus

## MOUNTAIN
**a:** *alpestrine, montane,* mountainous

**n:** *cordillera, sierra*

*at foot:* subalpine, *submontane*

*between:* intermontane

*beyond:* tramontane, transalpine, *transmontane,* ultramontane

*climbing:* alpinism

*combining forms:* mont-, oro-

*formation:* orogeny

*near-side:* cismontane

*study:* orography, orology

*within:* intramontane

## MOURNFUL
**a:** deplorable, doleful, lamentable, luctiferous, sad, threnodic

**n:** lugubrosity, mournfulness, sadness, wake

*clothes:* crape, cypress, sackcloth, weeds

## MOUTH
**a:** buccal, circumoral, labial, oral, oscular, peroral

**n:** orifice, *os, stoma*

*combining forms:* bucc-, or-, oro-, -stom, stom-, stomato-, -stome

*large:* macrostomus, patulous

*small:* microstomatus, microstomus

## MOVE
**a:** ambulant, ambulatory, impressive, inconstant, kinetic, mobile, motile, motive, movable, moving, pathetic, poignant, tactic, touching

**n:** activity, advancement, automation, *demarche,* dynamism, emigration, flexibility, impetus, locomotion, maneuver, maneuverability, migration, mobility, momentum, motility, moveability, movement, procession, transition, transplantation, velocity

**v:** actuate, advance, affect, amble, bounce, coast, converge, emigrate, gravitate, impel, influence, lope, meander, migrate, mosey, proceed, relocate, romp, rove, saunter, scud, scurry, shift, traverse

> *combining forms:* -dromous, -grade, kin-, -kinesis, kinet-, kineto-, mot-, -tactic, -trop, trop-, -tropic, tropo-

## MUDDY

**a:** fuliginous, murky, obscure, roiled, roily, turbid

**n:** fulginosity, mud, murkiness, obscurity, sludge, turbidity

## MULTIPLY

**a:** burgeoning, commutative, multiplying, proliferous, reproductive, viviparous

**v:** augment, burgeon, increase, proliferate, propagate, pullulate, reproduce

> *by five:* quintuple
>
> *by four:* quadruple
>
> *combining forms:* multi-, pluri-, poly-
>
> *multitude:* aggregation, concourse, host, legion, manifold, multiety, multiplicity, myriad, ruck

## MURMUR

**a:** mormorando, purling, rustling, susurant, susurus, whispering

**n:** murmuration, susuration, susurus

**v:** susurate

## MUSCLE

**a:** kinesthetic, proprioceptive

**n:** biceps, constrictor, deltoid, gluteus, ligament, pectoral, pronator, sartorius, sinew, supinator, tendon, thews, trapezius, triceps

> *combining forms:* muscul-, my-, myo-
>
> *sense:* kinesthesia, proprioception
>
> *uncoordination:* abasia, astasia, astasis, ataxia

## MUSES

**a:** Pierian

**n:** Calliope, Clio, Erato, Euterpe, Melpomene, Polymnia, Terpsichore, Thalia, Urania

## MUSIC

**a:** aeolian, canorous, diapasonal, dulcet, euphonic, euphonious, Euterpean, harmonious, melic, melodious, melophonic, musical, orotund, philharmonic, sonorous, symphonic, symphonious

**n:** arabesque, diapason, *fantasia*, harmonization, harmony, medley, montage, *pastiche, phantasia*, revue, syncopation

> *closing: coda*, epilogue, postlude, postludium
>
> *love:* melomania
>
> *opening:* overture, *praeludium*, prelude
>
> *study:* musicology
>
> *writing:* composition, *melopoeia*, musicography

## MUTENESS

**n:** inarticulateness, *obmutescence, sordino*

## MUTUAL

**a:** alternate, alternating, coincident, common, complementary, correlative, homogeneous, interdependent, reciprocal, respective, symbiotic, synalgamatic, synchronous

**n:** interdependence, mutuality, reciprocality, synchroneity

> *combining forms:* inter-, reciproc-
>
> *destructive:* internecine

## MYSTERIOUS

**a:** anagogical, arcane, cabalistic, clandestine, cryptic, enigmatic, epoptic, esoteric, exotic, extraphysical, glamorous, hermetic, hidden, incomprehensible, inexplicable, inscrutable, mysterial, *mysterioso*, mystic, obscure, occult, oracular, orphic, paradoxic, picturesque, preternatural, recondite, sibylline, stratospheric, supernatural, surreptitious, symbolic, telestic, tenebrific, tenebrious, uncanny, unfathomed

**n:** *arcanum*, aura, *cabala*, cabalism, cachet, conundrum, enigma, halo, incomprehensibility, mystagogy, mysteriousness, mysticality, mystique, *nimbus*, oracularity, paradoxicality, perplexity

**v:** bewilder, mystify

   *person:* enigma, paradox, sphinx

**MYTH**

**a:** allegorical, apocryphal, arcane, fabricated, fabular, fabulous, fantastic, fictitious, legendary, mythical, mythopoetic, parabolical, visionary

**n:** anecdote, fabulosity, legend, saga

**v:** mythologize

# N

**NAIL**

**a:** unguiculate, unguiferate

**n:** claw, ungual, unguis

   *biting:* onychophagia, onychophagy, phaneromania

**NAIVE**

**a:** artless, candid, credulous, guileless, gullible, ingenuous, innocent, unfeigned, unphilosophic, unsophisticated

**n:** artlessness, credulity, gullibility, ingenue, ingenuosity, ingenuousness, naivete, Pollyanna, simplicity

   *pretending:* disingenuous, *faux-naif*

**NAKED**

**a:** *au naturel*, denudate, denuded, *dishabille*, divested, exposed, nude, obvious, unattired, unclad, unclothed

**n:** nakedness, starkness

   *practice:* gymnosophy, nudism

   *study by naked eye:* macrography, macroscopy

**NAME**

**a:** fictitious

**n:** agnomen, appellation, appellative, cognomen, denomination, designation, epithet, eponym, matronym, nomenclature, nomination, patronym, rubric, *sobriquet*

**v:** denominate, designate, entitle, identify, nominate, specify, stipulate, style

   *address by:* compellation

   *author's:* onomastic, onomatous, onymous

   *bad:* caconym, epithet

   *courtesy:* honorific

   *different:* heteronomy, heteronymous

   *false:* anonym, anonymity, pseudonym, pseudonymity

   *family:* cognomen, patronym

   *father's:* patronym

   *first:* Christian, forename, personal, *praenomen*

   *in name only:* nominal, titular

   *mother's:* matronym, metronym

   *nickname:* agnomen, alias, hypocoristic, sobriquet

   *no:* anonymous, innominate

   *wrong:* misnomer

**NAME**

**a:** suggestive, onomasiological

**n:** system

**v:** namely

**NARCOTIC**

**a:** anesthetic, somniferous, soporiferous, stupefactive

**n:** anesthetic, anodyne, dope, *nepenthe*, opiate, sedative, somniferant, soporific, stupefacient

**NARRATIVE**

**n:** account, iliad, narration, novel, odyssey, saga, tale

**NARROW**

**a:** bigoted, circumscribed, conservative, denominational, hidebound, illiberal, incapacious, incommodious, insular, jaundiced, limited, municipal, parochial, pedantic, petty, prejudiced, provincial, restricted, sectarian, stenotic

**n:** bigotry, exiguity, insularity, parvanimity, provincialism, sectarianism, tunnel vision

## NATIVE

**a:** aboriginal, autochthonal, autochthonic, autochthonous, demotic, domestic, edaphic, enchorial, endemial, endemic, indigenous, inherent, innate, local, natal, original, primitive

**n:** aboriginal, aboriginality, aborigine, authchthon, domestic, endemicity, endemism, inhabitant, vernacular

> *land:* compatriotic, habitat, habitation, *milieu,* natal, *patrial*
>
> *not:* foreign, heterochthonous

## NATURAL

**a:** *al fresco,* artless, *au naturel,* candid, congenital, endogenous, essential, hereditary, inborn, ingrained, inherent, innate, instinctive, *naturalesque,* physical, sincere, spontaneous, unaffected, unpremeditated, unsophisticated, unstudied

**n:** appetence, appetency, character, conatus, constitution, diathesis, essence, idiosyncrasy, inclination, naturality, nature, nurture, proclivity, propensity, quiddity, quintessence, texture, virtuality

**v:** commune

> *beyond:* paraphysical, parapsychological, preternatural, supermundane, supernatural
>
> *close to:* primitivistic
>
> *combining forms:* physi-, physio-
>
> *different:* heterogeneous, heterousian
>
> *force:* telesia, telesis
>
> *naturalized:* acclimated, adapted, heterochthonous
>
> *not:* artefactitious, artificial, foreign, illusive
>
> *same:* consubstantial
>
> *study:* cosmography, ontography, physiosophy
>
> *two:* amphibious
>
> *worship:* cosmotheism, pantheism, physiolatory, priaprism

## NAUSEOUS

**a:** abominable, bilious, disgusting, dizzy, fulsome, loathsome, nauseating, offensive, qualmish, repugnant, repulsive, revolting, sickening, squeamish

## NAVEL

**a:** omphalic, umbilical, umbilicate, umbilicated

**n:** omphalos, *omphalus,* umbilicus

> *meditation: omphaloskepsis*

## NAVIGATION

**a:** marine, maritime, nautical, naval, oceanic, sea-going

**n:** dead reckoning, sailing

**v:** boat, sail, ship

## NEAR

**a:** abutting, adjacent, adjoining, approaching, approximately, *circa,* contiguous, imminent, impending, nearby, nearly, neighboring, propinquant, propinquous, proximad, proximal, proximate, *quasi,* verging, virtually, within earshot

**n:** adjacency, appropropinquity, contiguity, environs, locality, nearness, propinquity, proximity, vicinity

**v:** appose, juxtapose

> *combining forms:* epi-, para-, peri-, pros-, prox-
>
> *in time: prochein,* propinquitous, propinquity
>
> *sighted:* myopic, purblind

## NEAT

**a:** concinnate, concinnous, dapper, fastidious, immaculate, modish, natty, proportional, shipshape, *soigne,* spruce, uncluttered, well-groomed

**n:** concinnity, fastidiousness, neatness

## NECESSARY

**a:** alimental, compulsory, contingent, *de rigueur,* essential, imperative, incumbent, indispensable, indispensible, inevitable, inexorable, inherent, integral, intrinsic, mandatory, needful, obligatory, perforce, prerequisite, requisite, statutory, unavoidable, unpreventable

**n:** aliment, *desideratum,* essential, essentiality, exigency, indispensability, necessity, need, obligation, prerequisite, requirement, requisite, *sine qua non,* subsistence

**v:** behove, entail

*needless:* gratuitous, unessential, unnecessary

*needy:* desiderative, destitute, insolvent, necessitous, poor, pressing

## NEEDLE

**a:** acerate, acerose, acerous, acicular, aciculate, aculeate, belonoid

**n:** acicula, aculeus, *aiguille,* stylus

## NEGATIVE

**a:** blank, negatory, neutral, privative

**n:** annihilation, contraindication, denial, disclaimer, negativism, negativity, negatory, nonentity, nullification, obliteration

## NEGLECT

**a:** careless, delinquent, improvident, inadvertent, inattentive, indifferent, neglectful, negligent, remiss, slack, unmindful

**n:** abandonment, delinquency, dereliction, disregard, failure, ignoration, inattention, indifference, indolence, laches, limbo, malfeasance, misfeasance, negligence, nonobservance, omission, pretermission, procrastination, remission

**v:** disregard, ignore, misprize, pigeonhole, pretermit

## NEIGHBORHOOD

**a:** adjacent, amicable, attingent, contiguous, friendly, gregarious, *limitrophe,* neighboring, neighborly, propinquant, tangential, vicinal

**n:** confines, environs, habitat, locality, *milieu,* precincts, propinquity, proximity, *purlieu,* suburb, vicinage, vicinity

## NEPHEW

**a:** nepotal, nepotic

## NERVE

**a:** afferent, deferent, efferent, neural, synaptic

**n:** audacity, effector, effrontery, fascicle, fasciculus, fortitude, funiculus, gall, ganglion, intrepidity, plexus, receptor, sinew, synapse, temerity

*combining forms:* neur-, neuro-

*nervous disorder:* chorea, neurasthenia, neurosis, neuroticism, psychoneurosis, psychosis, tic

## NEST

**a:** nidicolous, nidificat, nidifugous

**n:** abode, aerie, eyrie, nidification, nidus, retreat

**v:** nidificate, nidify

## NETWORK

**n:** complex, context, graticule, labyrinth, matrix, *nexus, plexus, reseau,* reticle, reticulation, reticule, reticulum

## NEUTRAL

**a:** adiaphorous, disinterested, dispassionate, epicene, impersonal, indifferent, nonaligned, nonpartisan, unbiased

**n:** adiaphoria, detachment, go-between, indifference, intermediate, neutrality

## NEW

**a:** immature, inexperienced, innovative, innovatory, modern, nascent, neoteric, newly, *nouveau,* novel, pristine, renovated, unaccustomed, unexampled, unfamiliar, unprecedented, vernal

**n:** debut, freshness, inauguration, innovation, neologism, neology, neoteric, neoterism, newness

*combining forms:* ana-, neo-

*hate:* misoneism, xenophobia

*newcomer:* fledgling, greenhorn, neophyte, *nouveau riche, parvenu,* rookie, tenderfoot, tyro, upstart

## NEWSPAPER

**n:** circulation, journalese, tabloid

## NEXT

**a:** abutting, adjacent, adjoining, contiguous, juxtaposed, penultimate, *prochein,* proximal, sequacious, tangential

## NICE

**a:** agreeable, decorous, demure, discriminating, fastidious, friendly, good, squeamish

**n:** fastidiousness, preciosity, scrupulosity

## NICKNAME

**n:** *agname,* agnomen, cognomen, epithet, hypocorism, hypocoristic, moniker, *petit nom, sobriquet*

**v:** designate, dub, nominate, style

## NIGHT

**a:** *noctivagous, noctivigant,* nocturnal

**n:** darkness, nocturnality

**v:** *pernoctate*

*blindness:* hemeralopia, nyctalopia

*combining forms:* noct-, nocti-, nyct-, nycti-, nycto-

*nightmare:* apprehension, *incubus, oneirodynia,* vexation, worry

*stick:* truncheon

## NIMBLE

**a:** agile, changing, dexterous, lissome, lithe, mercurial, quicksilver, supple

**n:** agility, dexterity, elasticity, flexibility, legerity, lissomeness, nimbleness, suppleness

## NINE

**a:** enneadic, ninth, nonagon, novenary

**n:** *ennead, nonagon*

*combining form:* nona-

*ninety:* nonagenarian, nonagesimal

## NOBLE

**a:** aristocratic, eminent, exalted, illustrious, lofty, magnanimous, magnificent, majestic, nobiliary, patrician, princely, *spirituelle,* stately, sterling, sublime, venerated

**n:** aristocracy, aristocrat, eminence, ermine, Galahad, gentility, gentry, grandee, grandeur, magnanimity, *magnifico,* nobility, nobleman, *noblesse,* patriciate, peer, peerage, ruler, sublimity

## NOISE

**a:** boisterous, cacophonous, clamorous, clangorous, effusive, noisy, obstreperous, raucous, riotous, roisterous, sonorous, strepitant, stridulous, termagant, thunderous, tumultuary, tumultuous, turbulent, undisciplined

**n:** acoustics, Bedlam, blatancy, brouhaha, cacophony, *charivari,* clamor, *crescendo,* detonation, discord, discordance, havoc, hubbub, pandemonium, phonics, reverberation, tintinnabulation, tumult, uproar

## NONCONFORMISM

**n:** *avant-gardism,* dissidence, heresy, individuality, nonconformity, recusance, recusancy

*nonconformist:* avant-garde, beatnik, Bohemian, disbeliever, dissident, heretic, recusant, renegade, schismatic, ultraconservative

## NONESSENTIAL

**a:** dispensable, gratuitous, supererogant, supererogative, supererogatory, unessential

**n:** luxury, *marginalia*

## NONPROFESSIONAL

**a:** amateur, dilettantish, lay

**n:** amateur, *dilettante,* laity, layperson

## NONSENSE

**a:** absurd, amphigoric, capricious, fanciful, imbecilic, ludicrous, macaronic, nonsensical, notional, preposterous, whimsical

**n:** abracadabra, absurdity, amphigory balderdash, bilge, bunk, drivel, folderol, gibberish, hocus-pocus, hokum, jabberwockey, malarkey, moonshine, nugacity rigmarole, stultiloquence, tomfoolery, tripe, trivia, trumpery

## NOON

**a:** meridian

*after:* postmeridian

*before:* antemeridian

**NORTHERN**

**a:** arctic, boreal, hyperborean, septentrional

   *star:* cynosure, lodestar, polestar

**NOSE**

**n:** *nasus, olfactus,* organon, proboscis

   *bleed:* epistaxis, rhinnorrhagia

   *combining forms:* nas-, naso-, rhin-, rhino-

   *hair:* vibrissa, vibrissae

   *hooked:* aduncous, aquiline

   *upturned:* pug, *retrousse,* snub

**NOTABLE**

**a:** celebrated, distinguished, eminent, illustrious, important, impressive, majestic, memorable, memorious, noted, noteworthy, observable, prominent, remarkable, renowned, salient, signal, significant, striking, supereminent

**n:** *aide-memoire,* anecdote, annotation, footnote, gloss, *marginalia,* memo, memorandum, minute, *miscellanea, personalia, scrapiana*

**NOTHING**

**n:** *bagatelle,* cipher, *nada,* naught, *nihil,* nihility, nil, nix, nonentity, nothingness, nullity, oblivion, trifle, trivia, triviality, vacuity, vacuum, zero, zilch

**NOTICE**

**a:** appreciable, arresting, conspicuous, discernible, evident, explicit, glaring, manifest, noticeable, observable, obvious, palpable, patent, perceptible, prominent, pronounced, salient, signal

**n:** advertence, announcement, attention, awareness, cognizance, conspicuity, conspicuousness, knowledge, observation, prominence

**v:** heed, recognize

**NOTION**

**a:** imaginary, notional, theoretical, unreal, visionary, whimsical

**n:** apprehension, *bibelot,* concept, conception, idea, impression, inclination, inkling, knickknack, knowledge, understanding, vagary, view, whimsicality

**NOTORIOUS**

**a:** arrant, celebrated, discreditable, disreputable, ignominious, inglorious, notable, renowned, unmitigated, villainous, well-known

**n:** notoriety

**NOTWITHSTANDING**

**a:** but, even, *howbeit,* mauger, *maugre,* nevertheless, nonetheless, still, though, yet

**NOUN**

**a:** ablative, abstract, accusative, common, concrete, count, countable, dative, genetive, mass, nominal, nominative, noncount, proper, vocative

**n:** gerund

**NOURISHMENT**

**a:** alible, alimental, alimentary, alimentative, invigorating, nourishing, nutritious, nutritive, nutritory, nutural

**n:** aliment, collation, eutrophy, food, forage, nurture, nutriment, nutrition, *pabulum,* sustenance

   *lacking:* atrophic, distrophic, inalimental, innutrious, oligotrophic

**NULL**

**a:** invalid, nonexistent, nugatory, void

**n:** invalidation, nihility, nullification, nullity, stultification, vitiation

**v:** abolish, abrogate, invalidate, negate, nullify, rescind, stultify

**NUMBER**

**a:** manifold, many, multifarious, multiplex, multitudinous, myriad, numerical, numerous, plentiful, plentious, populous

**n:** aggregate, cipher, factor, hecatomb, integer, legion, magnitude, manifold, many, multeity, multiplicity, multitude, myriad, numeral, numerousness, plurality, quantity *numberless:* innumerable, innumerous, unlimited

**NUN**

**a:** cenobitic

**n:** abbess, canoness, cenobite, neophyte, novice, postulant, prioress, recluse, religious, sanctimonial, votary

**NUT**

**a:** nuciferous, nucivorous

**NUTRITION**

**a:** nourishing, nutritious

**n:** diatetics, dietetics, eutrophy, food, nourishment, trophology

   *combining forms:* troph-, -trophic, tropho-, -trophy

## OATH

**a:** juratory, objurgative

**n:** adjuration, affidavit, affirmation, attestation, blasphemy, conjuration, curse, execration, expletive, fealty, Hippocratic, homage, imprecation, malediction, objurgation

**v:** testify

*breaking:* perjury

## OBEDIENT

**a:** acquiescent, amenable, biddable, compliant, conformable, deferential, docile, malleable, masochistic, obeisant, obsequious, pliable, submissive, sycophantic, tractable, unctuous

**n:** compliance, conformity, deference, docility, obedience, submission

**v:** abide, acquiesce, adhere, comply, defer, fawn, genuflect, humor, indulge, kowtow, obey

## OBESE

**a:** corpulent, fat, orbicular, overweight, portly, *pyknic*, rotund, stout, weighty

**n:** adiposis, adiposity, *avoirdupois*, corpulence, *embonpoint*, obesity, pinguidity, plumpness, portliness, pursiness, steatosis, stoutness, weight

## OBJECT

**a:** disagreeable, distasteful, inappropriate, inexpedient, loathsome, nauseous, noisome, objectionable, obnoxious, offensive, rebarbative, reprehensible, repugnant, repulsive, revolting, unpleasing

**n:** dissent, dissidence, exception, objection, protest, protestation, qualm, remonstrance, remonstration, scruple

**v:** cavil, complain, demur, dissent, expostulate, protest, quibble, remonstrate

*feel objective:* disinterested, dispassionate, impartial, material, postival, realistic, unbiased

*objective:* aim, artefact, artifact, aspiration, fetish, intention, materiality, numenon, phenomenon, talisman

## OBLIGATION

**a:** behooving, *de rigueur,* deontic, deontological, imperative, incumbent, mandatory, obligated, obligatory, pledged, prerequisite

**n:** debt, encumbrance, liability, *noblesse oblige,* onus, prevenance, responsibility

*obliging:* amiable, cooperative

*science:* deontology

## OBLIQUE

**a:** crooked, devious, duplicitous, evasive, indirect, *louche,* perverse, sideways, sinister, slanted, tangential, tilted

## OBLIVION

**a:** lethean, nirvanic, oblivial, oblivious, unaware

**n:** amnesty, forgetfulness, *lethe,* limbo, neglect, nirvana, obliviscence, silence

## OBSCENE

**a:** cloacal, coprophilous, ithyphallic, lascivious, lewd, pornographic, scatological

**n:** bawdry, coprolalia, coprology, pornography, scatology, vulgarism, vulgarity

*love:* coprophilia, scatology

*things:* erotica, esoterica, *facetiae,* pornography

## OBSCURE

**a:** abstruse, ambiguous, ambivalent, arcane, cabalistic, calignous, crepuscular, cryptic, Delphic, enigmatic, equivocal, esoteric, fuliginous, incomprehensible, inscrutable, obfuscatory, *recherche*, recondite, transcendent, unfathomable, vague

**n:** abstrusity, ambiguity, ambivalence, confusion, fulginosity, inconspicuousness, limbo, obfuscation, oblivion, obscuration, obscurity, opacity, *penumbra*, profundity, seclusion, turbidity, twilight zone

**v:** adumbrate, becloud, bedim, complicate, obfuscate, obnebulate, obnubilate

## OBSERVE

**a:** acuminous, alert, attentive, detectable, discernible, empirical, heedful, mindful, noticeable, objective, observable, observant, on the *qui vive*, overt, perceptive, percipient, perspicacious, regardful, surveillant, vigilant

**n:** acumen, descant, observance, observation, percipience, percipiency, perspicacity, perspicuity, reflection, surveillance, utterance

**v:** celebrate, commemorate, observe, scrutinize, see, solemnize, witness

*based on:* autoptic

*combining form:* -scopy

*observer:* bystander, kibitzer, onlooker, witness

*unable to:* astigmatic, myopic, purblind

## OBSESSION

**a:** fussy, neurotic, sensitive, worried

**n:** compulsion, fixation, *idee fixe*, impulse, *incubus*, mania, preoccupation

**v:** haunt

## OBSOLETE

**a:** antediluvian, antiquated, archaic, obsolescent, old-fashioned, outmoded, *passe*, rudimentary, timeworn, vestigal

**n:** depletion, obsolescence, supperannuation

**v:** obsolesce, superannuate, supersede

## OBSTINATE

**a:** dogmatic, firm, inflexible, opinionated, pertinacious, pervicacious, stubborn, tenacious, unpliable, unrepentant, untoward, unyielding

**n:** adamancy, asininity, contumely, inveteracy, obstinacy, persistence, pertinacity, pervicaciousness, pervicacity, stubbornness, tenacity

## OBSTRUCT

**a:** congested, impedimental, impedimentive, impeditive, obstructive, obstruent, occlusive, oppilative, stenotic

**n:** barrier, bottleneck, embolus, encumbrance, filibuster, impasse, impediment, *impedimenta*, logjam, obstacle, obstruction, occlusion, oppilation, sabotage, stenosis, strangulation, stricture, stumbling block, subversion

**v:** barricade, encumber, hinder, impede, incommode, occlude, oppilate, parry, prevent, retard, stonewall

## OBVIOUS

**a:** axiomatic, blatant, clearly, conspicuous, egregious, evident, flagrant, glaring, gross, literal, manifest, palpable, patent, patently, plainly, prominent, salient, self-evident, superficial, trivial, unambiguous, unequivocal

**n:** commonplace, conspicuity, conspicuousness, manifestness, obviousness, patency, platitude, truism

*below:* subintelligential, subliminal

## OCCASIONAL

**a:** episodic, incidental, infrequent, intermittent, irregular, periodic, sporadic

**n:** infrequency, occasionality, sporadicity

## OCCUPANCY

**a:** employmental, habitudinal, industrial, occupational, professional, vocational

**n:** habitation, incumbency, inhabitation, *metier*, occupation, profession, residency, tenancy, tenure, trade, vocation

**v:** disport, occupy

*occupant:* incumbent, inhabitant, tenant

*occupied:* abstracted, distracted, versant

## OCCURRENCE

**n:** accident, circumstance, contretemps, episode, incidence, incident

**v:** come to pass, ensue, eventuate, happen, materialize, occur, synchronize, take place, transpire

> *at same time:* coetaneous, coeval, coincidental, coinciding, coinstantaneous, concomitant, concurrent, contemporaneous, contemporary, coordinant, harmonious, synchronic, synchronistic, synchronous, unanimous

> *later:* subsequent, subsequential, supervenient

## OCEAN

**a:** abyssal, aphotic, bathyal, bathyalic, bathybic, bathypelagic, bathysmal, benthic, benthopelagic, hadal, marine, maritime, oceanic, pelagic, suboceanic, thalassic

**n:** brine, deep, main, sea

> *study:* oceanography, thalassography

## ODD

**a:** aberrant, anomalous, atypical, azygous, bizarre, capricious, curious, deviant, eccentric, eerie, erratic, esoteric, fantastic, grotesque, haphazard, idiosyncratic, incongruous, inexplicable, kooky, nondescript, occasional, outlandish, *outre,* perverse, pixilated, preternatural, quaint, quirky, singular, uncanny, unrealistic, vagarious, whimsical, zany

**n:** *bizarrerie,* caprice, curiosity, eccentricity, fantasticality, *foible, grotesquerie,* idiosyncrasy, oddity, particularity, peculiarity, quiddity, singularity, vagary, whim, whimsicality

## ODOR

**a:** aromatic, effluvial, fetid, malodorous, mephitic, nidorous, noisome, odiferous, odoriferous, *olent,* redolent, scented, smelly, stinking

**n:** aroma, aromaticity, cachet, effluvium, emanation, estimation, fragrance, mephitis, *nidor,* redolence, repute

> *odorless:* inodorous, scentless

## OFFENSE

**a:** blatant, condescending, defamatory, derogatory, displeasing, distasteful, execrable, fetid, gratuitous, invidious, loathsome, noisome, objectionable, obnoxious, obtrusive, odious, offensive, paternalistic, patronizing, reprehensible, repugnant, repulsive, ribald, ridiculous, unsavory, verminous

**n:** affront, crime, *culpa,* delictum, delinquency, dudgeon, felony, malfeasance, *malum,* misdemeanor, misfeasance, offensiveness, *peccadillo, pique,* resentment, transgression, trespass, veniality

**v:** affront, alienate, antagonize, estrange, hurt, offend, *pique,* take exception, transgress, trespass

> *caught: flagrante delicto,* red-handed

## OFFER

**n:** approach, bid, invitation, oblation, overture, propitiation, proposition

**v:** approach, proffer, tender

## OFFHAND

**a:** *ad lib,* autoschediastic, casual, extemporaneous, extempory, extempore, hasty, *impromptu,* improvisatorial, improvisatory, *improviso,* impulsive, informal, spontaneous, unceremonious, unconventional, unplanned, unpremeditated, unstudied

**n:** *autoschediasm,* improvisation

## OFFICE

**a:** administrative, clerical, *ex cathedra, ex officio,* functional, ministerial, perquisite

**n:** officialdom, preferment, tenure

> *extra:* attribution, perk, perquisite

> *out of: emeritus,* superannuated

> *rite:* inauguration, installation, investiture

## OFFICIAL

**a:** accredited, authoritative, authorized,

canonical, cathedral, legitimate, orthodox, sanctioned

**n:** *apparatchik,* bureaucrat, *functionaire,* functionary, incumbency, incumbent, inquisitor, mandarin, notary, officialdom, officiary, ombudsman, pedantocrat, tribune

> *speech:* federalese, gobbledygook, officialese

## OFFSET

**v:** checkmate, compensate, counteract, counterbalance, counterpoise, countervail, make up for, reimburse

## OFFSHOOT

**a:** tangential

**n:** consequence, digression, issue, outgrowth, ramification, *ramus,* result, tangent

## OFFSPRING

**a:** philoprogenitive, prolific

**n:** descendant, issue, posterity, progeniture, progeny, scion

**v:** procreate

> *bearing female:* thelygenic, *thelytokous*
>
> *bearing male:* androgenous
>
> *combining form:* -parous
>
> *hatch inside:* viviparous
>
> *hatch outside:* oviparous

## OILY

**a:** elusive, fatty, greasy, lardaceous, lubricious, oleaginous, oleiferous, pinguid, saponaceous, sebaceous, suave, unctuous

**n:** lubricant, lubricity, oiliness, plasticity, saponaceousness, unctuosity

> *combining forms:* chris-, ole-, oleo-

## OLD

**a:** aboriginal, ancestral, ancient, anile, antebellum, antediluvial, antediluvian, antemundane, antiquated, antique, archaic, archaistic, caducous, dated, decadent, decrepit, *demode,* doddering, former, geriatric, gerontal, gerontic, gerontogeous, hoary, immemorial, obsolescent, obso-

lete, ogygian, old hat, paleozoic, *passe,* patriarchal, paleolithic, prehistoric, primeval, primitive, *quondam,* senescent, senile, stale, troglodytic, *whilom,* wizened

**n:** antediluvian, antequarian, antiquation, antiquity, cidevant, dean, *dotard, doyen, doyenne, fogram, fogrum,* fogyism, graybeard, mossback, obsolescence, patriarch, veteran

**v:** senesce

> *age:* anecdotage, autumn of life, caducity, decrepitude, dotage, senectitude, senility
>
> *combining forms:* archeo-, geront-, geronto-, paleo-, senesc-
>
> *love:* archaeolatry, archaism
>
> *study:* geriatrics, gerontology, nostology

## OMEN

**a:** augural, augurous, auspicious, fateful, gravid, imminent, inauspicious, menacing, ominous, portentous, premonitory, sinister, unpropitious

**n:** augury, auspice, boding, divination, foretoken, handwriting on the wall, harbinger, portent, precursor, presage, presentiment, prophecy, sign

## OMISSION

**n:** aphaeresis, aphesis, apocope, backclipping, delinquency, elision, ellipsis, exclusion, failure, front-clipping, haplology, misfeasance, neglect, *paralipomena, paralipsis,* preterition, pretermission, syncope

**v:** elide, exclude, forbear, ignore, neglect, omit, overlook

## ONCE

**a:** annotinous, bygone, elapsed, erewhile, instantaneous, momentaneous, prompt, *quondam, tout de suite, whilom*

**n:** omneity, oneness, unanimity, unicity, uniquity, unity

> *1-1/2:* sesqialteral
>
> *150:* sesquicentennial
>
> *100:* centenarian, centenary, centennial, centuple, centuplicate, macrobian

*1000:* chiliad, millennium

*combining forms:* mon-, mono-, uni-

*one-sided:* excentric, *ex parte,* factionary, gratuitous, partisan, unilateral

*one-year-old:* annotinous

## OOZE

**a:** osmotic, transudative

**n:** extravasation, leakage, seepage, transudation

**v:** emerge, extravasate, exude, osmose, transudate, transude

## OPAQUE

**a:** adiaphorous, cloudy, dark, dim, fulginious, impervious, nubiferous, obscure, thick, unintelligible

## OPEN

**a:** accessible, ajar, dehiscent, exoteric, frank, free, gaping, inauguratory, initiatory, liable, manifest, notorious, openly, orificial, overt, patent, patulous, unconcealed, undisguised, undissembling, unfeigned, unobstructed, unrestricted

**n:** aperture, artlessness, breach, *debouche,* expanse, fenestration, foramen, gambit, hiatus, interstice, *naivete,* opening, openness, opportunity, orifice, *os,* outlet, patency

**v:** broach, extend, inaugurate, introduce, unfold, unveil

*combining forms:* stom-, stomato-, -stome

*of body:* aperture, fistula, foramen, meatus, orifice, *os,* sinus

*of event:* debut, inauguration, investiture

*of speech:* epigraph, exordium, prologue, salutation

## OPERATE

**a:** functional, manipulable, manipulatable, manipulatory, operational, physiologic

**n:** functioning, manipulation, operation, *processus*

**v:** manipulate

*not:* afunctional, quiescent

## OPINION

**a:** autotheistic, bigoted, conceited, doctrinaire, doctrinal, dogmatic, entrenched, officious, opinionated, philodoxical, pontifical, pragmatic, prejudiced, sophomoric, stubborn, vainglorious

**n:** belief, conclusion, conjecture, consensus, conviction, diagnosis, *dictum,* dogma, estimation, impression, judgment, *parti pris,* persuasion, sentiment, speculation, stereotype, surmise, unanimity

**v:** editorialize, opine, pontificate, render, sound

*differing:* controversy, dichotomy, divergence, heresy, heterodoxy

*love:* philodox

*person:* dogmatist, philodox

*unity:* consensus, consentience, solidarity, unanimity

## OPPONENT

**n:** adversary, antagonist, assailant, competitor, contender, defendant, disputant, dissident, Luddite, rival

## OPPORTUNITY

**a:** *a propos,* advantageous, auspicious, expedient, miraculous, opportune, pertinent, propitious, providential, seasonable, tempestive, timely

**n:** chance, conjuncture, occasion

**v:** capitalize on, *carpe diem,* exploit, utilize

## OPPOSE

**a:** adversative, adverse, alien, antagonistic, antipathetic, antipodal, antipodean, antonymous, argumentative, at variance, averse, contradictory, contralateral, contrariant, contrary, converse, diametrical, dilemmatic, double-dealing, duplicitous, hostile, incompatible, inverse, irreconcilable, militant, opposed, opposing, opposite, oppositional, oppositious, oppositive, perverse, pugnacious, *vis-a-vis*

**n:** ambitendency, ambivalence, antagonism, antinomy, antipod, antipodes, antithesis, antonym, complement, contraposition, contrareity, contrawise, contumacy, counterpart, dilemma, dissent, dissonance, impugnation, incongruity, opposition, oppugnation, polarity, polarization, recalcitration, resistance

**v:** antagonize, confront, contrapose, contravene, controvert, counteract, counterbalance, countervail, defy, gainsay, impugn, militate, oppugn, polarize, repudiate, thwart, withstand

> *combining forms:* a-, allo-, anti-, cata-, contra-, counter-, dia-, un-

## OPPRESS

**a:** exacting, grievous, onerous, oppressive, subordinate, tyrannical, tyrannous, underdog, unfortunate

**n:** oppression, tyranny

**v:** dragoon, overburden, persecute, tyrannize

> *person:* despot, tyrant

## OPTICAL ILLUSION

**a:** illusional, kaleidoscopic, phantasmagoric

**n:** *fata morgana, ignis fatuus,* mirage, *phantasmagoria,* phantasmagory

## OPTIMISTIC

**a:** confident, eupeptic, euphoric, expectant, happy, heartening, hopeful, Pollyannaish, promising, roseate, sanguine

**n:** euphoria, hopefulness, optimism, sanguinity

> *person:* Candide, Pollyanna

## OPTIONAL

**a:** alternative, contingent, discretional, discriminative, elective, facultative, preferential, voluntary

## ORAL

**a:** buccal, catechistic, declamatory, nuncupative, oratorical, phonetic, rhetorical, tacit, *viva voce,* vocal

**n:** declamation, oration

> *instruction: catachresis,* catechism
>
> *orator:* oratrix, rhetorician

## ORBIT

**a:** captured, eccentric, geostationary, synchronous

**n:** circle, cycle, epicycle, retrograde

> *farthest: apogee*
>
> *farthest from sun: aphelion*
>
> *nearest: perigee*
>
> *nearest to sun: perihelion*

## ORDER

**a:** alphabetical, calendric, categorical, chronological, concinnate, consecutive, consonant, harmonious, methodical, orderly, ordinal, pragmatic, programmatic, regimental, sequacious, sequential, seriatim, successional, systematic

**n:** adjuration, arrangement, *caveat,* chronology, command, concinnity, consecution, cosmos, curriculum, decretal, direction, discipline, disposition, *eutaxy, fiat,* formation, harmonization, harmony, husbandry, injunction, mandate, *mandatum,* ordinance, precedence, precept, protocol, regime, regimentation, requisition, sequence, sequent, seriality, symmetry, syntax, uniformity

**v:** coordinate

## ORDINARY

**a:** administrative, average, colloquial, commonplace, conventional, habitual, indifferent, inferior, lay, mediocre, middling, nominal, prosaic, quotidian, uneventful, unexceptional, vernacular, workaday

**n:** mediocrity

## ORGAN

**a:** splanchnic, visceral

**n:** entrails, innards, offal, viscera

## ORGANIC

**a:** constitutional, functional, fundamental, inherent, physiological, structural, systemic

**n:** animalcule, organism, organization, organonomy, protozoan, system

## ORGANIZATION

**n:** administration, *aegis,* arrangement, auspices, constitution, *cosmos,* establishment, hierarchization, logistics, regimentation, stratification, structure, systemization v: arrange, mobilize, orchestrate, organize

**ORGY**

a: bacchanal, bacchantic, orgiastic, saturnalian

n: bacchanal, bacchanalia, carousal, festivity, revelry, saturnalia

**ORIENTAL**

a: Asian, Asiatic, Byzantine, Chinese, Eastern, Japanese, Levantine, ortative, ortive

n: Orientalia

**ORIGIN**

a: aboriginal, aborning, autochthonous, embryonic, genetic, inaugural, inceptive, inchoate, indigenous, nascent, parturient, primordial, rudimental, rudimentary

n: ancestry, beginning, causation, derivation, etiology, genesis, inauguration, inchoation, incipience, nascency, parentage, primordia, primordium, provenance, provenience, source

v: begin, emanate, issue, originate

*common:* monogenetic

*externally:* exogenous

*internally:* endogenous

*more than one:* polygenetic

*spontaneous:* idiogenesis

*study:* etiology

*unknown:* cryptogenic, idiopathic

**ORIGINAL**

a: aboriginal, archetypal, authentic, autochthonous, causative, earliest, endemic, first, fontal, generative, genetic, germinal, germinative, inceptive, indigenous, inventive, *naissant*, native, neoteric, primary, primitive, primogenial, primogenital, primordial, pristine, Promethean, protogenic, prototypal, seminal, underivative

n: ectype, freshness, ingenuity, ingenuosity, inventiveness, *naissance*, native, neoteric, newness, novelty, originality

*combining forms:* arche-, incip-, init-, prim-, primo-, prot-, proto-, ur-

**ORNAMENT**

a: aureate, aurelian, *baroque*, bombastic, decorative, festooned, flamboyant, florid, grandiloquent, magniloquent, ornamental, ornate, orotund, ostentatious, resplendent, rococo, showy, spangled, sumptuous

n: adornment, bauble, bric-a-brac, *cloisonne*, embellishment, exornation, festoon, figurine, garniture, gimcrack, jabot, knickknack, novelty, ornamentation, swag, trim, trinket

v: adorn, embellish

**OSTRICH**

a: struthian, struthiform, struthious

n: emu, kiwi, ratite

**OUT-AND-OUT**

a: absolute, arrant, complete, confirmed, consummate, downright, notorious, shameless, sheer, thoroughgoing, unmitigated, unqualified, utter

**OUTBURST**

a: ebullient, paroxysmal

n: ebulition, eruption, fantod, fusillade, outpouring, paroxysm, rush, spate

**OUTCAST**

a: abject, expatriate, reprobative

n: abject, castaway, expatriate, Ishmael, leper, pariah, pariahdom, reprobate

**OUTCOME**

a: consequential, consummative, residual

n: conclusion, consequence, consummation, denouement, emanation, eventuality, *exitus*, possibility, probability, progeny, residual, residuum, result

**OUTCRY**

a: blatant, boisterous, clamorous, conclamant, vociferous

n: bruit, clamor, conclamation, outburst, uproar, vociferation, yell

**OUTDOOR**

**a:** *al fresco*, extraforaneous, *hypaethral*, hypoethial, open-air, *upaithric*

**n:** outdoors

**OUTFIT**

**n:** *accoutrements*, apparel, armamentarium, clothes, equipage, equipment, gear, paraphernalia, regalia, tackle, trappings

**v:** accouter, *accoutre*, caparison, endow, furnish, rig

**OUTGROWTH**

**n:** apophysis, consequence, offshoot, outcome, ramification, result

**OUTLET**

**a:** orificial

**n:** aperture, *debouche*, debouchment, egress, escape, exit, opening, orifice, *os*, vent

**OUTLINE**

**a:** diagrammatic, schematic

**n:** abridgement, adumbration, *apercu*, circumference, compendium, configuration, conformation, *conspectus*, contour, delineation, diagram, lineament, portrayal, prospectus, scenario, schema, *sciagram*, silhouette, summary, synopsis

**v:** adumbrate, delineate, describe, diagram, draw, sketch

**OUTLOOK**

**n:** chances, configuration, expectation, mentality, panorama, perspective, perspectivity, prognosis, prognostication, prospect, scope, view

    *limited:* cloistral, egocentric, parochial, provincial, sectarian

**OUTRAGE**

**a:** abhorrent, arrant, atrocious, egregious, extravagant, fantastic, flagrant, heinous, infamous, monstrous, notorious, outrageous, scabbrous, unconscionable

**n:** affront, dishonor, enormity, indecency, indignity, infamy

**OUTSET**

**a:** *ab initio, ab initium, ab ovo,* aboriginal, primordial

**n:** beginning, *primordium*

**OUTSIDE**

**a:** adventitious, exogenous, extracurricular, extraneous, extrinsic, supererogatory, transcendent

**n:** extraneity, invection

    *combining forms:* ab-, ecto-, exo-, extra-, super-

    *outsider:* auslander, exoteric, layman, *tramontane*

**OUTSTANDING**

**a:** conspicuous, eminent, excelling, noted, noticeable, paramount, pending, prominent, salient, signal, significant, significative, stellar, supereminent, superlative, supreme, unresolved

**n:** conspicuity, paragon, *piece de resistance*, predominance, predominancy, saliency, showpiece, signality

**OUTWEIGH**

**a:** precedental, preponderant

**n:** preponderance

**v:** preponderate, surpass

**OUTWIT**

**n:** circumvention

**v:** circumvent, deceive, frustrate, hoodwink, outfox, victimize

**OVAL**

**a:** almond, amygdaloid, curvilinear, elliptic, nummiform, nummular, ovate, ovoid, spherical, spheroidal

**OVERACTED**

**a:** histrionic, overacting, theatrical

**n:** histrionics, theatrics

**OVERBEARING**

**a:** arbitrary, arrogant, autocratic, *cavalier*, compelling, despotic, dictatorial, dogmatic, domineering, haughty, imperative, imperious, insupportable, lordly, masterful, overweening, peremptory, preponderating, supercilious

## OVERCOME

**v:** conquer, demolish, domineer, overpower, overwhelm, subdue, surmount, vanquish

> *impossible to:* insuperable, insurmountable, invincible, inviolable, unconquerable

## OVERCONFIDENT

**a:** cocksure, hubristic, overweening, presumptuous, proud

**n:** overconfidence, presumption

## OVERDO

**v:** cloy, exaggerate, overact, overplay, overreach, satiate, supererogate

## OVEREAT

**n:** anorexia, bulimia, gluttony

**v:** glut, gormandize, indulge, overindulge, satiate, wolf

## OVERFLOWING

**a:** abounding, abundant, copious, cornucopian, inundatory, redounding, scaturient, superabundant, swarming, teeming, torrential

**n:** cornucopia, deluge, freshet, inundation, profusion, redundance, redundancy, spate, spillway, superabundance

## OVERINDULGENCE

**a:** orgiastic

**n:** debauchery, depravity, dissipation, intemperance, orgy, satiation, satiety

## OVERLAPPING

**a:** imbricate, jugate, lapstrake

**v:** intersect, overlap

## OVERLOOK

**n:** condonation, pretermission, surveillance

**v:** command, condone, disregard, dominate, ignore, pretermit, superintend, tower above

## OVERNICE

**a:** euphemistic, fastidious, fastigial, meticulous, particular, persnickety, prudish, scrupulous, squeamish

**n:** correctitude, fastidiousness, fastidium, finicality, meticulosity, overnicety, persnicketiness, scrupulosity

## OVERSHADOW

**a:** adumbral

**n:** adumbration, eclipse

**v:** adumbrate, eclipse, reduce

## OVERSTATEMENT

**a:** hyperbolic

**n:** embellishment, exaggeration, hyperbole, ornamentation

## OVERTHROW

**n:** *coup d'etat*, debacle, defeasance, labefaction

**v:** demolish, dethrone, dislodge, exterminate, overturn, unhorse, vanquish

## OVERWHELM

**a:** copious, deluginous, devastating, ineffable, inundatory, murderous, overwhelming, torrential

**n:** flood tide, ineffability, inundation, vortex

**v:** confound, defeat, deluge, demolish, inundate, submerge, swamp, vanquish

## OWL

**a:** strigine

## OWNERSHIP

**a:** proprietary

**n:** domain, freehold, proprietary, proprietorship

**v:** acknowledge, concede

> *owner:* proprietor

## PACIFY

**a:** conciliatory, irenic, pacificatory, pacifistic, peaceful, placative, propitiative

**n:** amelioration, conciliation, mitigation, pacification, tranquilization

**v:** allay, alleviate, ameliorate, appease, assuage, calm, conciliate, mitigate, mollify, palliate, placate, propitiate, reconcile, tranquilize

## PAGE

**a:** paginal

**n:** foldout, *folio, octavo,* pagination, *quarto, verso*

**v:** paginate

## PAIN

**a:** afflictive, agonal, algedonic, algetic, algogenic, distressing, dolorific, excruciating, fulgurating, fulminant, hyperalgesic, hyperesthetic, hypersensitive, irksome, lancinating, painful, torminous, tortuous, troublesome, vexatious

**n:** affliction, agony, anguish, colic, distress, *dolor,* dysphoria, gripes, lancination, martyrdom, neuralgia, pangs, paroxysm, penance, psychalgesia, punishment, purgatory, suffering, throe, throes, torment, travail, wormwood

> *enduring:* forbearance, longanimity, sufferance, tolerance
>
> *fear:* algophobia
>
> *lessening:* assuasive, lenitive, mitigatory, palliative, palliatory
>
> *love of afflicting:* algophilia, masochism, sadism
>
> *relief:* analgesic, anesthetic, anodyne, hypnotic, opiate
>
> *sensitive:* hyperalgesia, hyperalgia

## PAIR

**a:** bigeminal, binary, didymous, duplex, dyadic, jugate, *jumelle,* paired

**n:** conjugation, counterpart, *doublet,* duality, dyad, partnership

**v:** conjugate, geminate
> *combining forms:* -jug, jug-, yoke-, zyg-, zygo-

## PALE

**a:** achromic, anemic, ashen, cadaverous, etiolated, ghastly, ischemic, livid, pallid, pasty, sallow, wan

**n:** etiolation, ghastliness, *ischemia,* lividity, pallidity

**v:** blanch, bleach

## PALMIST

**n:** chirognomist, chiromancer
> *palmistry:* chirognomy, chiromancy

## PAMPHLET

**n:** brochure, ephemera, handbill, handout, manual, monograph, treatise

## PANTING

**n:** anhelation, dyspnea, hyperpnea, palpitation

**v:** gasp, hyperventilate, puff

## PAR

**a:** average, inferior, suboptimal, substandard

**n:** average, balance, equality, level, norm, normality, parity

## PARADISE

**a:** Edenic, elysian, nirvanic, paradisiac, utopian

**n:** Arcadia, Avalon, Eden, elysian fields, elysium, Nirvana, oblivion, Shangri-la, utopia

**PARAGON**

**n:** ideal, masterpiece, *nonpareil*, paradigm, phoenix, standard

**PARALLEL**

**a:** analogous, collateral, companion, concurrent, correlative, correspondent, equidistant, paradromic

**n:** *alter ego*, analog, analogue, correlative, counterpart

**PARAPHRASE**

**n:** amplification, recapitulation, restatement, synopsis

**PARASITE**

**a:** parasitic, saphrophytic, sycophantic

**n:** leech, saphrophyte, sponger, sycophant, toady, trematode

**v:** infest, sycophantize

**PARDON**

**a:** excusable, pardonable, venial

**n:** absolution, acquittal, amnesty, condonation, indulgence, remission

**v:** absolve, acquit, condone, excuse, forgive, remit, shrive

**PARENT**

**a:** parental

**n:** ancestor, author, *genetrix*, genitor, originator, producer, progenitor

**v:** beget, sire

*love:* philoprogenitiveness, *storge*

**PARENTHETICAL**

**a:** ejaculatory, episodic, incidental, interjaculatory, interjectional, interjectural, interlocutory, tangential

**n:** *dictum*, digression, interlocution, *obiter dictum*, *scholium*, tangent

**PARODY**

**a:** parodistic, satirical

**n:** burlesque, caricature, lampoon, *pastiche*, satire, travesty

**PART**

**a:** bifid, bifurcated, cloven, componental, constituent, dichotomous, estranged, integral, multipartite, parted, partite, polychotomous, polytomous

**n:** component, constituent, element, essentiality, fragment, ingredient, integral, integrant, modicum, moiety, offshoot, particularity, quantum, sector, segment, snippet, subdivision

**v:** divide

    *combining forms:* hypo-, -mer, mer-, -mere, mero-, -ome, -tome

    *parting:* cleavage, disjunction, dismemberment, dissolution, disunion, estrangement, separation

    *three:* trichotomous, tripartite

    *two:* bifid, bifurcated, bipartite, dichotomous

**PARTIAL**

**a:** biased, fractionary, fragmental, fragmentary, incomplete, predisposed, prejudiced, segmented

**n:** bias, chauvinism, partiality, partisanship, predilection

**PARTICIPANT**

**n:** antagonist, combatant, competitor, entrant, entry, partaker, partner, party

**PARTICULAR**

**a:** captious, careful, definite, fastidious, finical, individual, scrupulous, specific

**n:** characteristic, particularity, scrupulosity

**PARTISAN**

**a:** denominational, dogmatic, factionary, sectarian

**n:** advocate, aficionado, ally, backer, factionary, follower, sectarian, sympathizer

**PARTNER**

**a:** collaborating, colluding, in cahoots

**n:** accessory, accomplice, associate, bedfellow, buddy, coadjutor, cohort, collaborator, colleague, compeer, confederate, *confrere*, consort, mate, partaker, participant, sidekick, sparring partner, teammate

    *combining form:* co-

**PARTY**

**n:** bacchanal, banquet, celebration, clambake, junket, levee, potlatch, reception, salon, shower, *soiree*

**PASS**

**a:** migratory, transient

**n:** col, crisis, intromission, *laissez-passer*, passport, permit, predicament, visa

**v:** admit, authorize, exceed, foist, intercept, intromit, ooze, percolate, relay, terminate, transcend, transit

**PASSION**

**a:** ardent, avid, bacchanalian, bacchic, besotted, Dionysian, ebullient, evangelistic, faustian, fervent, impassioned, impetuous, infatuated, inflammable, intense, orgiastic, passionate, perfervid, precipitate, sulfurous, sulphurous, sultry, tempestuous, torrid, tumultuous, turbulent, unrequited, vehement, voluptuous

**n:** ardor, *beguin*, enthusiasm, erogeneity, eroticism, erotomania, evangelism, fervor, infatuation, martyrdom, rapture, suffering, torridity, transport, zeal

    *person:* demagogue, firebrand, incendiary

**PASSIVE**

**a:** inactive, inert, inexcitable, invertebrate, negative, obedient, patient, quiescent, receptive, stoical, submissive, supine, unresisting, unresponsive

**n:** inactivity, passiveness, passivity, stoicism, submissiveness

**PASSOVER**

**a:** paschal

**n:** *Pesach, Seder*

**PASSWORD**

**n:** catch phrase, countersign, *mot de passe*, parole, sesame, *shibboleth*, slogan, watchword

**PAST**

**a:** nostalgic, retroactive, retrospective

**n:** antecedents, chronology, flashback, heritage, hindsight, legacy, *memoir*, *mortmain*, nostalgia, reflection, reminiscence, retrospection

    *person:* antediluvian, antequarian, *cidevant*, mossback, patriarch

**PASTORAL**

**a:** Arcadian, bucolic, geoponic, georgic, idyllic, innocent, picturesque, rural, rustic, simple, Theocritean

**PATIENCE**

**a:** bovine, calm, charitable, composed, dispassionate, enduring, forbearing, imperturbable, long-suffering, longanimous, patient, philosophical, resigned, sedate, stoical, temperate, tolerant, unimpassioned

**n:** composure, endurance, equanimity, forbearance, fortitude, imperturbability, indulgence, leniency, lenity, longanimity, perseverance, resignation, submission, sufferance, toleration

**PATRIOT**

**n:** chauvinist, flagwaver, jingo, jingoist, patrioteer, superpatriot, superzealot

    *patriotism:* chauvinism, ethnocentrism, jingoism, patriotics, superpatriotism

**PATRONIZING**

**n:** condescendence, condescension, paternalism

## PATTERN

**n:** archetype, *beau ideal,* blueprint, characteristic, configuration, conformation, design, device, exemplar, *exemplum,* modality, model, *modus operandi,* orthodoxy, paradigm, paragon, precedent, prototype, regimen, *schema,* stereotype, syndrome, template, texture, touchstone, yardstick

## PAUSE

**a:** cessative, hiatal

**n:** adjournment, armistice, *caesura,* cessation, hiatus, intermission, *interregnum,* moratorium, postponement, recess, respite, rest

**v:** intermit

## PAWN

**a:** in hock

**n:** hypothecation, impignoration, pledge

**v:** hypothecate, impignorate, pledge

## PAY

**n:** annuity, bonus, bribe, commission, compensation, consideration, defrayal, emolument, *guerdon, honorarium,* incentive, liquidation, maintenance, payment, rebate, recompense, remuneration, retainer, retribution, reward, salary, stipend, tribute

**v:** amortize, compensate, defray, disburse, indemnify, liquidate, recompense, reimburse, remunerate, render, satisfy

## PEA

**a:** *pisiform*

**n:** bean, caper, legume, *petit pois,* pod

## PEACE

**a:** affable, amiable, appeasing, calm, conciliatory, congenial, genial, halcyon, harmonious, *irenic,* neighborly, *nirvanic, oasitic,* pacific, pacifistic, pastoral, peaceable, peaceful, quiescent, serene, *tempean,* tranquil, unaggressive

**n:** amiability, amity, appeasement, armistice, calmness, conciliation, concord, *detente, fains, fen,* nirvana, olive branch, pacification, pact, *pax, pax vobiscum,* peaceability, placability, quiescence, *rapproachement,* repose, serenity, tranquility, tranquilization, treaty, vents

    ***peacemaker:*** conciliator, intercessor, mediator, placater

## PEACOCK

**a:** pavonian, *pavonine*

**n:** muster, ostentation, pride

## PEAK

**a:** apogeal, apogean, apogeic, maximum, supernal, zenithal

**n:** acme, apogee, climax, culmination, flood tide, high point, maximum, meridian, pinnacle, summit, ultimate, zenith

## PEARLY

**a:** cultured, iridescent, lustrous, *margaric,* margaritaceous, margaritiferous, nacreous, opalescent

**n:** mother-of-pearl, *nacre,* orient, paragon, seed

## PECULIAR

**a:** aberrant, anomalous, atypical, bizarre, characteristic, eccentric, grotesque, heterogeneous, idiocratic, idiomatic, idiopathic, idiosyncratic, inherent, innate, odd, *outre,* unconventional, whimsical

**n:** *bizarrerie,* caprice, characteristic, eccentricity, idiasm, idiocrasy, idiosyncrasy, individuality, oddity, particularity, peculiarity, quiddity, quirk, singularity, uniquity, vagary, whim, whimsicality

    ***combining form:*** idio-

## PEEL

**a:** deciduous, desquamative, desquamatory, exfoliative, exuviative, peeling

**n:** decortication, desquamation, ecdysis, excoriation, exfoliation, exuviation

**v:** bark, decorticate, desquamate, excoriate, exfoliate, exuviate, flake, flay, hull, husk, skin, strip, undress

## PEERLESS

**a:** eminent, immutable, incommensurable, incomparable, majestic, matchless, *ne plus ultra*, optimum, paramount, preeminent, sovereign, supereminent, superexcellent, superlative, unequaled, unsurpassable

**n:** *coeval*, contemporary, equal, nonesuch, *nonpareil*, paragon, phoenix

**PEEVISH**

**a:** atrabilarious, atrabiliar, atrabilious, caustic, choleric, fretful, gloomy, irascible, irritable, petulant, querulous, restive, splenetic, testy, waspish

**n:** crankiness, distemper, irascibility, peevishness, petulance, *pique, protervity*, querulousness

**PENAL**

**a:** castigatory, condign, corrective, disciplinary, expiatory, penitentiary, punitive, reformative, reformatory, retributive, retributory, subpoenal

**n:** amercement, chastisement, comeuppance, condignity, deserts, expiation, penalty, penance, punishment, retribution, sanction

**v:** amerce, penalize, punish

**PENDING**

**a:** abeyant, imminent, impending, pendant, pendent, pendular, pendulous, provisional, undecided, undetermined

**n:** abeyance, abeyancy, imminence, imminency, indecision, pendency, pendulation, pendulosity, suspension

**PENETRATE**

**a:** astute, caustic, discerning, incisive, keen, mordant, osmotic, penetrable, penetrated, penetrating, penetrative, perforating, permeable, permeated, pervious, piquant, poignant, sagacious, trenchant

**v:** diffuse, impenetrate, metastisize, permeate

**PENITENCE**

**a:** contrite, penitent, remorseful, repentant

**n:** attrition, compunction, contrition, regret, remorse, repentance, *satispassion*

**PENNILESS**

**a:** bankrupt, impecunious, indigent, poor

**n:** bankruptcy, impecuniosity, insolvency, mendicancy, pennilessness

**PENSIVE**

**a:** cogitable, *cogitabund*, cogitative, contemplative, engrossed, meditative, melancholic, occupied, reflective, thoughtful

**PEOPLE**

**a:** cosmopolitan, demotic, ethnic, gentilitial, gentilitious, lumpen, pandemic, plebeian, polyethnic, popular, proletarian, proletariat, universal

**n:** *canaille*, commonality, *demos, hoi polloi, homo sapiens,* mankind, masses, menagerie, multitude, nation, pandemia, person, plebeian, plebs, populace, population, proletariant, race, ragtag, riffraff, throng

> *combining forms:* dem-, demo-, ethn-, ethno-
>
> *high class:* nobility
>
> *lower class:* rabble
>
> *middle class: bourgeoise(ie)*
>
> *study:* agriology, anthropology

**PERCEIVABLE**

**a:** appercipient, cognitive, cognizable, cognoscible, cognoscitative, comprehensible, corporeal, discernible, intelligible, knowing, observable, observant, palpable, patent, perceptible, percipient, perspicacious, recognizable, sensible, sensitive, tangible, translucent, trenchant

**n:** apprehension, cognition, cognizance, comprehension, consciousness, corporeality, corporeity, discernment, ESP, extrasensory perception, insight, knowledge, observation, percipience, percipiency, perspicacity, recognition, sensibility, tangibility, telegnosis

**v:** perceive

> *barely:* liminal
>
> *gifted:* clairsentient, clairvoyant, hyperesthetic, keen, percipient, prehensile, sagacious, telepathic

*imagination:* delusion, *fata morgana,* hallucination, *ignis fatuus,* illusion, *phantasmagoria*

*not:* subliminal

## PERFECT

**a:** accurate, consummate, excellent, exemplary, expert, flawless, immaculate, impeccable, inerrant, inerratic, infallible, integral, inviolate, plenary, proficient, saintly

**n:** accomplishment, archetype, *avatar, beau ideal,* completion, consummation, embodiment, *epitome,* excellence, exemplar, exemplarity, expertise, finality, *grand prix,* immaculacy, impeccability, inerrancy, infallibility, integrality, maturity, millennium, paragon, perfectibility, perfection, personification, proficiency, utopia, virtuosity

**v:** perfectivize

> *person:* more, perfectibilist, perfectionist, *precieuse,* precisian, precisionist, purist

## PERIL

**a:** destructive, explosive, hazardous, *icarian,* jeopardous, malignant, *parlous,* perilous, risky

**n:** Charybdis, danger, hazard, insecurity, instability, jeopardy

## PERIOD

**a:** cyclic, cyclical, etesian, intermittent, periodic, periodical, recurrent, rhythmical

**n:** cycle, duration, eon, epoch, era, gestation, periodization, siecle

> *inactive:* deliquescence, dormancy, hibernation, indefinite, latency, quiescence

> *prosperous:* fluorescence, golden age, heyday, millennium, prime

## PERIPHERAL

**a:** circumferential, distal, external, marginal, peripheric, surface

## PERISHABLE

**a:** caducous, deciduous, ephemeral, evanescent, fleeting, fugacious, mortal, spoilable, transitory, volatile

**n:** caducity, evanescence, fugacity, perishability, perishableness, transience, volatility

## PERMANENT

**a:** abiding, constant, eternal, everlasting, immarcescible, immutable, imperishable, indefaceable, indelible, indestructable, indossoluble, ineffaceable, inextirpate, invariable, irreversible, irrevocable, lasting, sempiternal, substantive

**n:** durability, fixture, indissolubility, ineffaceability, perdurance, permanence, permanency, persistence, tenure

**v:** perpetuate

## PERMISSION

**a:** allowed, authoritative, authorized, elective, empowering, enabling, facultative, indulgent, lawful, legitimate, licit, official, optional, permissible, permissive, permitted, sanctioned, susceptible, tolerant, undemanding

**n:** authorization, carnat, *conge,* franchise, *laissez-passer,* license, permittance, sanction, sufferance, tolerance, toleration

**v:** acquiesce, authorize, concede, countenance, empower, franchise, permit, ratify, sanction, tolerate, vouchsafe, warrant

## PERPETUAL

**a:** constant, immortal, incessant, permanent, persistent, sempiternal, unceasing, undying

**n:** eternalization, immortalization, perpetuality, perpetuation, perpetuity

**v:** endure, eternalize, immortalize, perpetuate, persevere

## PERPLEX

**a:** anxious, bewildered, bewildering, disconcerted, disconcerting, distracted, distraught, enigmatic, inexplicable, nonplused, perplexed, perplexing, puzzling

**n:** conglomeration, cruciality, *cul-de-sac,* dilemma, embarassment, embranglement, embroilment, entanglement, exigency, *imbroglio, impasse,* labyrinth, morass, perplexity, plight, predicament, puzzlement, quandary

**v:** bewilder, complicate, confuse, disconcert, embrangle, entangle, interweave

**PERSECUTE**

**n:** oppression, paranoia, persecution, torment, tyranny

**v:** afflict, dragoon, oppress, torment, tyrannize

*persecutor:* sadist, tyrant

**PERSIST**

**a:** demanding, determined, enduring, importunate, indefatigable, indomitable, lingering, obstinate, perpetual, persistent, pressing, solicitous, stubborn, tenacious

**n:** stubbornness

**v:** perpetuate, persevere, sustain

**PERSON**

**a:** intimate, personal, personally, subjective

**n:** *dramatis personae,* existent, man, people, personality, *propositus,* specimen, subject

**v:** anthropomorphize, apostrophize, embody, incarnate, personify, zoomorphize

*personality:* disposition, egoity, facet, humor, individuality, personeity, temperament, trait

**PERSONATION**

**a:** anthropomorphic, anthropomorphous, apostrophic, personificative

**n:** anthropomorphism, anthropomorphization, apostrophe, embodiment, impersonation, incarnation, personification, prosopopeia

*of animal:* anthropomorphize, zoomorphize

**PERSPIRATION**

**a:** diaphoretic, egestive, excrementious, sudoriferous, sudorific

**n:** diaphoresis, *egesta, excreta,* exudation, sudation, sudor, sweat, transpiration

**v:** egest, excrete, perspire, sweat, transpire

*absence:* adiaphoresis, anhidrosis, anhydrosis

*check:* anhidrotic, anhydrotic, antiperspirant

*excessive:* hidrosis, hyperhidrosis, polyhidrosis

*smelly:* bromidrosis, kakidrosis

**PERSUADE**

**a:** cogent, compelling, ductile, encouraging, exhortative, expostulatory, flexible, impressionable, malleable, persuasive, plausible, pointed, tenable, tractable, trenchant

**n:** patter, persuasion, spiel

**v:** allure, canvass, coax, coerce, entice, exhortate, expostulate, finagle, induce, inveigle, lobby, prevail upon, smoothtalk, soft-soap, suborn, tout, wangle

**PERTINENT**

**a:** *ad rem,* applicable, apposite, appropriate, *apropos,* categorical, commensurate, congruent, felicitous, germane, material, opportune, proportional, proportionate, relevant

**n:** aproposity, pertinence, pertinency, relevance, relevancy

**PESSIMISM**

**a:** gloomy, morose, pessimistic, satirical

**n:** melancholia, miserabilism, *weltschmerz*

*pessimist:* cynic

**PETITION**

**a:** beseeching, petitionary, supplicative, supplicatory

**n:** appeal, complaint, entreaty, obsecration, prayer, solicitation, supplication

*petitioner:* applicant, candidate, orator, postulant, supplicant

**PETTY**

**a:** childish, contemptible, frivolous, ignoble, insignificant, lilliputian, meager, nagging, niggling, paltry, parochial, pettifogging, picayune, shabby, subordinate, trifling, trivial, unimportant

n: carping, caviling, criticism, faultfinding, nitpicking, parochialism, parochiality, parvanimity, pettiness, triviality

## PHASE

n: angle, aspect, condition, facet, state, transition

*many:* multiphasic, polyphasic

## PHENOMENA

a: phenomenological

n: development, experience, phantasm, phenomenality, wonder

*science:* phenomenology

*secondary:* epiphenomena

## PHILOSOPHY

a: abstract, deontic, metaphysical, noetic, philosophical

n: *cogito,* credo, dialectic, dialogue, doctrine, entelechy, epistemology, *ergo sum, quodlibet, weltanschauung*

*philosopher:* physiologizer, physiologue

*pretend:* philosophastry, sciosophy

## PHRASE

a: phraseological

n: catch phrase, construction, diction, lexiphanicism, neologism, parenthesis, parlance, syntax, word

## PHYSICAL

a: carnal, corporeal, manual, material, materialistic, muscular, natural, objective, palpable, physical, physiological, ponderable, sensual, somatic, tangible

n: constitution, corporeality, corporeity, *habitus,* materiality, physicality, physique, substantiality

## PIANO

a: pianistic

n: clavier, concert grand, keyboard, Pianola, player piano

## PICTURE

a: curiologic, hieroglyphic

n: collage, configuration, cyclorama, delineation, *diorama,* hieroglyphics, iconography, illustration, *montage, photomontage,* pictograph, *portraiture,* rubbing, scene, similitude, *tableau, vignette*

v: delineate, depict, illustrate, limn, photograph, portray, represent

## PIECEMEAL

a: *aliquot,* fractional, fractionary, fragmentary, gradual, part, partly

## PIERCE

v: impale, lancinate, penetrate, perforate, puncture, riddle, transfix

## PIGEON

a: columbine, peristeronic

n: fantail, pouter, roller, squab, tumbler

## PILE

a: cumulative

n: accumulation, agglomeration, aggregation, bank, congeries, cumulus, drift, heap, mound

v: accumulate, agglomerate, cumulate, pyramid

## PILLAGE

n: brigandage, depredation, despoliation, rapine, spoliation

v: despoil, devastate, maraud, plunder, ransack, ravage, steal, strip

## PIMPLY

a: papuliferous, papulose

n: blackhead, horripilation, *papilla, papule,* piloerection, pustule, sty, tetter, *wen,* zit

## PINCH

n: exigency, impingement, juncture, predicament, vellication, vicissitude

v: compress, constrict, crimp, impinge, vellicate

## PIOUS

**a:** canting, consecrated, devotional, devout, holier-than-thou, hypocritical, *religiose*, religious, reverent, sanctified, sanctimonious, self-righteous

**n:** piosity, religiosity, sanctimoniousness

## PIRATE

**a:** piratical

**n:** buccaneer, corsair, filibuster, freebooter, *picaroon*, privateer

*flag:* Jolly Roger, skull-and-crossbones

## PIT

**a:** lacunal, lacunar, pitted

**n:** crater, foxhole, lacuna

## PITFALL

**n:** artifice, inveiglement, maelstrom, problem, snare, strategem, subterfuge, temptation, trap

## PITH

**a:** aphoristic, apothegmatic, cogent, concentrated, epigrammatic, gnomic, laconic, pithy, sententious, terse, vigorous

**n:** embodiment, heart, medulla

## PITY

**a:** abject, commiserable, contemptible, despicable, lamentable, pathetic, piteous, pitiable, pitiful, squalid, touching

**n:** charity, commiseration, compassion, condolence, empathy, mercy, remorse, sympathy

**v:** commiserate, sympathize

## PLACE

**a:** *in loco, in situ*

**n:** haunt, locale, locality, *loci, locus, milieu, purlieu,* repository, setting, *situ,* situation, station, status, stronghold, vicinity, whereabouts

**v:** locate, lodge, pinpoint, situate, station

　　*combining forms:* -arium, -orium, -ory, top-, topo-

　　*list:* gazetteer

*name:* toponym

*out of:* ill-timed, inappropriate, *malapropos*

## PLAGUE

**a:** calamitous, pestilential, pestilentious

**n:** abomination, affliction, calamity, harassment, infestation, outbreak, pestilence

## PLAIN

**a:** candid, clear, conspicuous, evident, ingenious, literal, manifest, nondescript, perspicacious, salient, simple, transparent, unadorned, unalluring, unattractive, uncosmetized, unembroidered, unequivocal

## PLAN

**a:** architectonic, calculatory, concerted, coordinated, deliberate, forumlaic, intended, planned, premeditated, premeditative, projected, schematic, syntactic

**n:** architectonics, blueprint, conspiracy, cosmos, draft, forethought, format, formula, intrigue, itinerary, logistics, plot, preconception, project, prototype, regimen, *schema, schemata,* syntax

**v:** calculate, cogitate, conspire, contemplate, contrive, design, destine, envisage, execute, formulate, ideate, implement, meditate, precogitate, preconceive, prefigure, premeditate, purpose, scheme

## PLANT

**a:** biological, botanical, herbaceous, herbal, phytologic, vegetal

**n:** annual, biology, biota, denizen, flora, hybrid, perennial, vegetation

**v:** cultivate, domesticate, grow

　　*combining forms:* antho-, photo-, -phyt-, -phyte

　　*cultivation:* aquiculture, horticulture, hydroponics

　　*-eating:* herbivorous, phytiverous, phytophagous, phytophilous, vegetarian

*-loving:* phytolatry, phytophilous

*specialist:* botanist, herbologist, phytologist

*study:* biogeography, botany, herbology, phytology

**PLASTIC**

**a:** adaptable, creative, ductile, fictile, formative, governable, impressionable, labile, malleable, manageable, mutable, pliant, pluripotent, sculptural

**n:** acrylic, Bakelite, creativity, ductility, elasticity, formica, impressionability, linoleum, malleability, plasticity, polymer, polystyrene, vinyl

**PLATFORM**

**n:** *dais, haut pas,* lectern, *lyceum,* pallet, *perron,* podium, rostrum, scaffold, skid, tribune

**PLAUSIBLE**

**a:** colorable, credible, creditable, probable, reasonable, specious

**n:** credibility, plausibility

**PLAY**

**a:** convivial, facetious, frivolous, frolicsome, impish, jocose, jocular, jovial, ludic, playful, roguish, sportive

**n:** artifice, banter, drama, *finesse,* jocosity, jocularity, maneuver, playfulness, roguery, sportiveness, *stratagem*

**v:** dabble, trifle

*player:* actor, *dramatis personae*

*playwright:* dramatist, *dramaturge*

**PLEA**

**n:** advocation, allegation, blandishment, contention, entreaty, pretext, supplication

**v:** beg, intercede, plead

*pleader:* advocate, intercessor, paraclete, supplicant

**PLEASANT**

**a:** agreeable, amiable, captivating, comely, complaisant, consonant, elysian, empyrean, enchanting, euphonic, eupho-

nious, harmonious, idyllic, palatable, pellucid, personable, pleasing, prepossessing, sonorous

**n:** amiability, amity, euphony, facetiosity, facetiousness, harmonization, harmony, pleasantness, pleasantry

**v:** delectate, edulcorate, exhilarate, gratify, please, satisfy, titillate

**PLEASURE**

**a:** amatory, apolaustic, delectable, epicurean, eudaemonic, hedonic, hedonistic, pleasing, pleasurable, sensual, sybaritic, vicarious

**n:** cakes and ale, *carpe diem,* delectation, diversion, ecstasy, fruition, gloating, gratification, hedonism, inclination, oblectation, sybaritism, titillation, titivation

**v:** disport

*combining forms:* -mania, -philia

**PLEAT**

**a:** pleated, plicate

**n:** flounce, flute, *ruche,* ruffle

**v:** goffer, plicate

**PLEDGE**

**a:** impignorative

**n:** betrothal, collateral, guarantee, hypothecation, impignoration, plight, recognizance, surety

**v:** guarantee, hypothecate, pignorate, plight, redeem

**PLENTY**

**a:** abounding, abundant, ample, bottomless, bounteous, copious, cornucopian, exuberant, flush, inexhaustible, infinite, lavish, opulent, plenteous, plentiful, plentitudinous, plethoric, prodigal, replete, superabundant, teeming, untold

**n:** abundance, affluence, amplitude, copiosity, copiousness, *foison,* galore, opulence, plentitude, plethora, profusion, repletion, spate

**PLIANT**

**a:** adaptable, amenable, ductile, fictile, flexible, governable, malleable, manageable, plastic, pliable, susceptible, tractable, yielding

## PLIGHT

**n:** dilemma, predicament, problem, quandary

## PLOT

**a:** cabalastic, conspirative, conspiratorial, nefarious

**n:** cabal, collution, complot, conspiracy, conspiration, covin, frameup, intrigue, *junta,* machination, *scenario, stratagem*

**v:** collaborate, collude, connive, conspire, intrigue, machinate, plan

## PLUG

**n:** adapter, *embolus,* occlusion, pledget, spigot, spile, stopper, stopple, tampion, tampon

**v:** occlude

## PLUMP

**a:** buxom, corpulent, distended, fat, full, portly, rotund

**n:** corpulency, fatness, portliness, rotundity

## PLUNDER

**a:** rapacious

**n:** depredation, plunderage, rapine, spoiliation

**v:** depredate, despoil, maraud, pillage, ransack, rob, spoliate

## POEM

**a:** bardic, idealized, lyric, melic, metrical, poematic, poetic, poetical

**n:** eclogue, idyll, imagery, madrigal, metrification, pastoral, pegasus, poetry, verse, versification

   *poet:* bard, laureate, troubadour

## POINT

**a:** alphabetical, apical, cacuminal, cacuminous, categoric, poignant, seriatim

**n:** characteristic, climax, concurrence, cusp, gist, locality, locus, node, nuance, perspective, proposition, quiddity, sty-

lus, subtlety, technicality, tenuosity, thesis, *touche*

   *combining forms:* acro-, styl-, -styl, -stylar, stylo-

   *highest:* apogee, solstice

   *lowest:* nadir, perigee

   *pointed:* acerate, acerose, aciculate, aculeate, acuminate, apicular, apiculated, epigrammatic, incisive, poignant, pungent, spicate, spicigerous, stimulating, stimulative, zestful

   *pointless:* hebetudinous, impertinent, incongruous, ineffectual, irrelevant, obtuse

## POISE

**a:** libratory

**n:** adroitness, aplomb, bearing, carriage, composure, dexterity, equilibrium, equipoise, imperturbability, libration, nonchalance, perpendicularity, posture, *sangfroid, savoir faire,* serenity, tranquility

**v:** balance, librate, stabilize

## POISON

**a:** baneful, deadly, deleterious, loathsome, malevolent, malignant, mortal, nauseating, noxious, obnoxious, pernicious, poisonous, potent, septic, toxiferous, venomous, viperous, virulent

**n:** antigen, arsenic, bane, *belladonna,* botulism, cyanide, hemlock, malignancy, pestilence, pestilency, pollution, *salmonella,* toxicity, toxin, venenation, venom, virulence

**v:** corrupt, pollute, toxify

   *antidote:* alexipharmic, mithridate, mithridatum, prophylaxis, serum

   *combining forms:* tox-, toxico-, toxo-

   *study:* toxicology

## POLISHED

**a:** cavalier, courteous, couth, cultivated, diplomatic, elegant, polite, politic, refined, *soignee,* suave, tactful, urbane, vernicose

**n:** artistry, consummation, courtliness, diplomacy, elegance, finesse, gloss, luster, polish, preciosity, refinement, suavity, urbanity, veneer

**v:** burnish, furbish, simonize

## POLITENESS

**a:** affable, *cavalier*, ceremonial, civil, complaisant, courteous, courtly, decorous, deferential, diplomatic, gracious, phatic, polished, polite, politic, proper, sophisticated, *suave*, tactful, urbane

**n:** affability, civility, comity, complaisance, convention, courtesy, courtliness, decorousness, decorum, deferentiality, diplomacy, etiquette, euphemism, pleasantry, polish, *politesse*, protocol, suaveness, suavity, urbanity

## POLITICAL

**n:** democracy, hustings, politicization, polity, populism, *realpolitik*, temporality

**v:** politicalize, politicize

   *favor:* nepotism, patronage

   *politician: courtier*, mugwump, statesman

## POLLUTION

**n:** adulteration, contamination, corruption, defilement, desecration, impurity, poison, profanation, taint, uncleanliness

## POMPOUS

**a:** affected, aloof, bombastic, bumptious, canting, condescending, consequential, fatuous, fustian, grandiloquent, grandiose, hoity-toity, huffy, imposing, lofty, magisterial, officious, orotund, ostentatious, patronizing, pious, pontifical, portentous, preachy, pretentious, pushy, rubescent, sanctimonious, sententious, smug, snooty, strutting, supercilious, theatrical, turgid

**n:** *grandeur*, magnificence, orotundity, ostentation, pageantry, panjandrum, pomp, pomposity, pretense, ritual, rubescence, vainglory

**v:** pontificate

## POND

**a:** tychopotamic

**n:** lake, mere

## PONDER

**a:** cogitative, meditative, ruminative

**n:** cogitation, rumination

**v:** cogitate, deliberate, excogitate, meditate, perpend, ruminate, think

## POOR

**a:** bankrupt, deprived, despicable, destitute, distressed, humble, impecunious, impoverished, inadequate, indigent, insolvent, meager, necessitous, penurious, poverty-stricken, resourceless, shoddy, squalid, undesirable, unfavorable

**n:** immiserization, impecuniosity, impecunity, impoverishment, indigence, indigency, mendicancy, pauperization, poverty

**v:** depauperate, impoverish, pauperize

## POPE

**a:** episcopal, papal, pontifical

**n:** papacy, pontiff, Vicar, vicegerent

## POPULAR

**a:** accepted, approved, demotic, *en vogue*, enchorial, exoteric, fashionable, in vogue, modish, plebeian, prevailing, prevalent, proletarian, vernacular, vulgar

**n:** fashion, popularity, vogue, *vox populi*

## POPULATION

**a:** aboriginal, autochthonous, indigenous

   *combining forms:* dem-, demo-

   *study:* demography, larithmics

## PORTEND

**a:** auspicatory, foreboding, presageful

**n:** omen, presentiment

**v:** augur, auspicate, foretell, presage

## PORTION

**n:** allocation, allotment, amount, inheritance, part, *quanta*, *quantum*, quota, share

## PORTRAY

**v:** delineate, depict, describe, limn, represent

**POSE**

**a:** homologous, kinesthetic, proprioceptive

**n:** affectation, aspect, attitude, attitudinization, bearings, coign, employment, exposure, kinesthesia, mannerism, masquerade, *metier*, niche, orientation, *poseur*, position, posture, proprioception, rating, staginess, theatricality, ubiety, vocation

**v:** align, attitudinize, baffle, locate, orient, orientate, pinpoint

*combining forms:* -tactic, -wise

**POSITIVE**

**a:** absolute, affirmative, arbitrary, categorical, concrete, decisive, definitive, dogmatic, emphatic, indisputable, opinionated, peremptory, philodoxic, self-assured, substantive, thetical, unconditional, unequivocal

**n:** absolute, concretum, unconditionality

**POSSIBILITY**

**a:** achievable, conceivable, contingent, executable, facultative, feasible, implicit, latent, peradventure, possible, potential, potentially, practicable, practical, promising, superable, surmountable, uncertain, undeveloped, viable

**n:** contingency, *dynamis,* eventuality, feasibility, *potentia*, potential, potentiality, practicability, scenario, virtuality

**v:** possibilitate

**POSTCARD**

*collector:* deltiologist

**POSTER**

**n:** *affiche,* broadside, bulletin, card, notice, picture, placard, sign

**POSTERIOR**

**a:** behind, cauded, dorsal, posteriad, posteriorly, rear, rearward, subsequent

**POSTPONE**

**n:** back burner, continuance, deferment, delay, moratorium, postponement, procrastination, prorogation, rain check, repreive, respite

**v:** adjourn, continue, defer, equivocate, forbear, mothball, prevaricate, procrastinate, prorogue, protract, respite, shelve, suspend, table, temporize, waive

**POSTURE**

**a:** orthostatic

**n:** attitude, attitudination, bearing, carriage, gait, orthograde, pose

**POTENT**

**a:** cogent, convincing, dynamic, *puissant,* strong

**n:** potency, virility

**POTENTIAL**

**a:** latent, possible, potentially, *prima facie*

**n:** *manque*

**POUCH**

**a:** bursiculate, bursiform, saccate, scrotiform

**n:** cecum, diverticulum, marsupium, sac, sporran

*mammal:* kangaroo

**POUR**

**n:** affusion, effusion, libation

**v:** debouch, decant, discharge, disembogue, disgorge, transfuse

**POVERTY**

**n:** dearth, destitution, dire straits, impecuniosity, impecuniousness, impoverishment, inadequacy, indigence, lack, mendicancy, paucity, pauperism, penury, privation, scarcity, squalor, tenuity

**POWDERY**

**a:** farinaceous, friable, pulverous, pulverulent

**n:** bloom, powder, talc, talcum

**v:** bray, comminute, malleate, pound, pulverize, triturate

**POWER**

**a:** almighty, authoritarian, charismatic, cogent, dominant, dynamic, forceful, Herculean, influential, jurisdictional, multipotent, omnipotent, plenary, plenipotentiary, plutocratic, potent, powerful, puissant, strong, substantious

n: aptitude, ascendency, attribution, authority, capacity, charisma, clout, cogency, control, demiurge, disposal, domain, dominance, dominion, dynamism, faculty, force, influence, jurisdiction, plenipotentiary, potency, potentiality, powerhouse, prerogative, *puissance*, regency, rule, superiority, supremacy, sway

v: augment, potentiate

*combining forms:* dynam-, dynamo-

*person:* autocrat, leviathan, megalomaniac, mogul, plutocrat, potentate, tycoon

*powerless:* dead-letter, helpless, impotent, impuissant, nugatory, sterile

*unlimited:* absolutism, autarchy, authoritarianism, autocracy, *carte blanche, diadem, imperium,* omnipotence, omnipotency, sovereignty

**PRACTICAL**

a: banausic, empirical, existential, feasible, functional, materialistic, practicable, pragmatic, proficient, realistic, unromantic, unsentimental, utile, utilitarian

*person:* Aristotelian, materialist, practician, pragmatist, utilitarian

**PRACTICE**

n: dry run, orthopraxy, ply, *praxis*

**PRAISE**

a: approbative, commendative, commendatory, complimentary, *cum laude,* encomiastic, eulogistic, fulsome, panegyric(al), praising

n: acclamation, accolade, adulation, approbation, ascription, blandishment, commendation, *dithyramb,* doxology, elegy, encomium, eulogy, hagiography, hallelujah, homage, *hosanna, kudos,* panegyric, plaudit, tribute

v: adulate, applaud, approbate, celebrate, commend, compliment, endorse, eulogize, exalt, extol, laud, laureate, lion-

ize, panegyrize, proclaim, revere, rhapsodize, venerate

*eager for:* esurient

*great: magna cum laude*

*greatest: summa cum laude*

*hymn:* canticle, doxology, magnificat, *paean,* theody

*praiseworthy:* approbatory, commendable, commendatory, complimentary, credible, creditable, eminent, encomiastic, estimable, eulogistic, exemplary, honorific, laudable, laudatory, meritorious, panegyric, supereminent

**PRANK**

n: antic, caper, *dido,* escapade, frolic, *harlequinade,* high jinks, horseplay, tomfoolery, vagary, whim

**PRAY**

a: invocative, invocatory, prayerful, praying, precative, precatory, supplicatory, votive

n: *absit omen,* adjuration, benediction, conjuration, devotions, entreaty, imploration, imprecation, introit, invitatory, invocation, litany, obsecration, orison, petition, prayer, rosary, solicitation, supplication

v: beseech, entreat, implore, importune, invocate, invoke, solicit, supplicate

**PRECIOUS**

a: alembicated, invaluable, valuable

**PRECISE**

a: academic, ceremonious, conscientious, definite, definitive, determinative, discriminating, exact, explicit, fastidious, immaculate, impeccable, implicit, mathematical, meticulous, minute, orthodox, painstaking, punctilious, rigorous, scholastic, scrupulous, slavish, sophistical, specific, unequivocal, verbatim

n: ceremony, correctitude, definitude, delicacy, exactitude, exactness, literality, minuteness, *minutiae,* nicety, precision, scrupulosity, subtlety, trivia, veracity

## PRECONCEPTION

**n:** ideation, mindset, *parti pris*, predilection, prejudgment, prejudication, prejudice

## PREDATORY

**a:** carnivorous, harpactophagous, plundering, predaceous, predacious, predative, rapacious

**n:** predacity, rapacity

## PREDESTINATION

**n:** destiny, determinism, fatalism, fate, foreknowledge, foreordination, necessarianism, preordination

## PREDICAMENT

**a:** dilemmatic, nonplussed, predicamental

**n:** box, corner, cruciality, dilemma, entanglement, fix, hole, imbroglio, *impasse*, maelstrom, perplexity, pickle, quandary, spot, state, strait, vortex

## PREDICT

**a:** automatic, calculable, foreboding, haruspical, knee-jerk, ominous, Pavlovian, predictable, predicting, predictive, prognostic, prognosticable, prophetic

**n:** forecast, fortune-telling, haruspication, prediction, prognosis, prophecy, triangulation, vaticination

**v:** adumbrate, forecast, foretell, predicate, presage, prognosticate, triangulate

## PREDISPOSITION

**n:** diathesis, inclination, leaning, predilection, proclivity, tendency

## PREFACE

**a:** prefacatory, prefactorial, preliminary, premonitory, prolegomenous

**n:** *exordium*, foreword, front, introduction, *isagoge*, opening, preamble, prelude, *proem*, *programma*, *prolegomenon*, prologue, prolusion, protasis

## PREFERENCE

**n:** alternative, antecedence, discrimination, favorite, inclination, like, precedence, predilection, predisposition, prejudice, priority, want, wish

## PREGNANCY

**a:** antenatal, *enceinte*, expectant, fecund, germinal, gravid, obstetric, *parous*, pregnant, prenatal

**n:** fecundity, fetation, gestation, gravidation, gravidity

## PREJUDICE

**a:** biased, bigoted, determined, doctrinaire, dogmatic, insular, insulated, jaundiced, myopic, narrow, narrow-minded, parochial, partial, partisan, prejudiced, prejudicial

**n:** bigotry, discrimination, insularism, insularity, jaundice, misandry, misanthropy, *parti pris*, partiality, preconception, predilection, predisposition, preference, prepossession, sectionalism, xenophobia

## PRELIMINARY

**a:** antecedent, imperative, indispensable, introductory, liminary, precedential, precursive, precursory, prefatorial, prefatory, premonitory, preparatory

**n:** preamble, prerequisite, protocol, *reconnaissance*

## PREMATURE

**a:** anticipatory, inopportune, precipitate, precocious, prevenient, unseasonable, untimely

## PREPARATORY

**a:** antecedent, braced, *en garde*, expugnatory, introductory, poised, preconditioned, prefatorial, preliminary, prepared, propaedeutic, ready

**n:** concoction, conditioning, confection, preparation, purveyance

**v:** admonish, caution, concoct, confect, counsel, facilitate, make, precondition, prepare

## PREREQUISITE

**n:** condition, essentiality, indispensability, need, postulate, precedent, *sine qua non*

## PRESCRIBED

**a:** arbitrary, ethical, magistral, prescriptive, recommended, thetic, thetical

**n:** prescription

## PRESENT

**a:** contemporary, immediate, instant

**n:** *nonce, status quo,* temporality

## PRESERVATION

**n:** conservation, guardianship, immortalization, maintenance, perpetuation

**v:** cure, embalm, keep, preserve, protect

## PRESSING

**a:** clamorous, critical, exigent, imminent, impending, imperative, important, insistent, poignant, threatening, urgent

**n:** constraint, constriction, exaction, exigency, imminency, insistence, ponderosity, pressure

*combining forms:* baro-, piezo-

## PRESTIGE

**a:** eminent, illustrious, influential, prestigious, reputable

**n:** ascendency, authority, cachet, distinction, eminence, glory, influence, *kudos,* reputation, repute, superiminence

## PRESUME

**a:** circumstantial, presumable, presumed, presumptive, probable

**n:** arrogance, audacity, circumstantiality, effrontery, expectation, postulate, postulation, presumption, presupposition, prolepsis

**v:** anticipate, assume, *posit,* postulate, presuppose

*presumptuous:* arrogant, audacious, imperious, impertinent, insolent, overweening, pretentious

## PRETEND

**a:** affected, affectional, barmecidal, beseeming, *bogus,* disingenuous, hypocritical, ostensible, ostensive, pretended, *quasi,* self-styled, sham, simulated, so-called

**n:** affectation, artifice, charade, deceit, dissimulation, dodge, fabrication, feint, *finesse,* guile, guise, hypocrisy, parody, persiflage, pomp, *postiche,* pretense, pretention, pretext, semblance, *simulacrum,* simulation, subterfuge, travesty

**v:** affect, assume, beseem, counterfeit, dissemble, dissimulate, fake, feign, impersonate, mimic, sham, simulate

*combining forms:* pseud-, pseudo-

*pretender:* affecter, charlatan, claimant, counterfeit, deceiver, hypocrite, imposter, mountebank, *poseur,* sciolist

*sickness:* malingering, *pathomimesis*

## PRETENTIOUS

**a:** affectational, ambitious, bombastic, faustian, genteel, ostentatious, *pharisaical,* pompous, self-important, showy, sonorous

**n:** blague, bombast, flummery, frippery, kitsch, ostentation, panjandrum, pomposity, pretentiousness

## PREVAIL

**a:** ascendant, current, demotic, dominant, enchorial, epidemic, indigenous, popular, predominant, prevailing, prevalent, regnal, regnant, victorious

**n:** ascendency, circulation, currency, predominance, predomination, prevalence, regnance, regnancy

**v:** actuate, conquer, dominate, predominate, preponderate

## PREVENT

**a:** circumventive, prevenient, preventative, preventing, preventive, prophylactic

**n:** *alexeteric,* circumvention, preventative, prevention, preventive, prophylactic, *prophylaxis*

**v:** abort, anticipate, arrest, censor, circumvent, deter, forbear, forestall, hinder, hold back, intercept, limit, obviate, paralyze, preclude, preempt, restrain, stifle, suppress, veto

**PREVIOUS**

**a:** antecedent, anterior, earlier, preceding, premature

**n:** *deja vu*, precedent, *ultimo*

   *combining forms:* ex-, supra-, ult-

**PREYING**

**a:** predaceous, predacious, predative, predatory, rapacious, raptorial, ravening

**n:** predacity, predation, predatism, predatoriness, rapaciousness, rapacity

**PRICELESS**

**a:** costly, impayable, incalculable, inestimable, invaluable, matchless, rare, valuable

**PRICKLY**

**a:** acanthoid, acanthous, echinate, horrent, muricate, spinous, spiny

**n:** bramble, briar, burr

   *prickly:* echino-

**PRIDE**

**a:** fastuous, haughty, pompous, prideful, proud

**n:** arrogance, conceit, ego, egoism, egotism, *esprit de corps*, exaltation, *grandeur*, haughtiness, *hauteur*, *hubris*, pomposity, self-esteem, self-exaltation, vainglory, vanity

**PRIEST**

**a:** ecclesiastic, hieratic, hieratical, hierophantic, levitical, priestly, *sacerdotal*

**n:** celebrant, clergyman, clergywoman, cleric, ecclesiastic, hierophant, lama, monk, priestess

**PRIM**

**a:** affected, finicky, mincing, prissy

**n:** decorousness, preciosity, priggishness, primness, sanctimony, squeamishness

**PRIMARY**

**a:** basic, constitutional, elementary, fundamental, idiopathic, primitive, simple

**n:** abecedarium, hornbook, primer

**PRIMITIVE**

**a:** aboriginal, antiquated, archaic, autochthonal, autochthonic, autochthonous, elemental, fundamental, indigenous, native, original, prehistoric, primal, primeval, primogenial, primordial, pristine, rudimentary

**n:** aboriginal, aborigine, primitivism

   *combining form:* ur-

**PRINCIPLE**

**a:** magnanimous, principled, rectitudinous, *religiose*, righteous, sanctimonious

**n:** alpha and omega, axiom, canon, constitution, *credo*, creed, *decalogue*, declaration, doctrine, dogma, *elan vital*, essence, foundation, fundament, gospel, methodology, motto, Murphy's law, organon, Peter principle, philosophy, postulate, *principium*, quintessence, *substratum*, tenet, theorem, theory

   *combining form:* -nomy

**PRIOR**

**a:** antecedaneous, antecedent, anterior, precedential, preceding, precursory, preferential, preliminary

**n:** antecedence, anteriority, precedence, preeminence, preference, preferment, prerogative, primacy, priority, seniority, superiority, supremacy

**PRISON**

**n:** *bastille*, big house, can, clink, cooler, custody, detention, dungeon, *gulag*, jail, limbo, lockup, *oubliette*, penitentiary, pokey, reformatory, slammer, stockade, workhouse

   *prisoner:* detenu, detenue, inmate

**PRIVACY**

**a:** auricular, backstage, confidential, covert, delitescent, esoteric, in camera, intimate, personal, private, privately, *pri-*

*vatim*, privily, privy, proprietary, restricted, secluded, secret, sequestered, solitary, *sub rosa*

**n:** *esoterica*, hermitage, insularity, interiority, isolation, penetralia, privity, *sanctorum*, sanctuary, *sanctum*, seclusion, secrecy, solitude

**v:** interiorize

**PRIVATION**

**a:** privative

**n:** deprivation, destitution, hardship, penury, poverty, squalor

**PRIVILEGE**

**a:** immune, prerogative, privileged

**n:** dispensation, franchise, immunity, license, patent, precedence, prerogative, right

**PRIZE**

**a:** laureate

**n:** accolade, award, *cordon bleu*, honor

**PROBABLE**

**a:** apparent, circumstantial, colorable, credible, evidently, feasible, ostensible, plausible, presumable, presumptive, *prima facie*, probably, promising, prospective, verisimilar

**n:** probability

**PROBATION**

**a:** probationary

**n:** novitiate, postulancy

*probationer:* acousmatic, greenhorn, novice, novitiate, recruit, rookie, trainee

**PROBLEM**

**n:** bugbear, conundrum, difficulty, dilemma, enigma, hitch, *hydra*, *imbroglio*, labyrinth, morass, perplexity, plight, predicament, proposition, quagmire, quandary, snag, syndrome

**PROCEDURE**

**n:** *accouterment*, approach, method, methodology, *modus operandi*, program, protocol, regimen, rigmarole, technique

**PROCEEDING**

**n:** affair, *demarche*, event, maneuver, negotiation, step, transaction

**PROCLAIM**

**n:** edict, proclamation

**v:** announce, annunciate, asseverate, manifest, *nuncupate*, predicate, promulgate

**PRODUCE**

**a:** aborning, causative, constructive, creative, feracious, fructiferous, fructuous, fruitful, generative, originative, parturient, procreant, procreative, producing, productive, uberous, viviparous

**n:** commodity, composition, consequence, creativity, crop, fecundity, manifestation, performance, product, productivity, progeny, staple

**v:** accomplish, beget, derive, engender, fabricate, generate, manufacture, originate, procreate, propagate

*by human:* artifact

*combining forms:* -facient, fer-, -fic, -gen, gen-, -genic, -genous, -gon, gon-, gono-, -poiesis, -poietic

**PROFANE**

**a:** blasphemous, impious, irreverent, mundane, sacrilegious, secular, sulfurous, sulphurous, temporal

**n:** blasphemy, desecration, profanation, profanity, sacrilege

**v:** blaspheme, desecrate, pollute

**PROFICIENCY**

**a:** accomplished, adept, *au fait*, consummate, dextrous, masterly, proficient, skillful

**n:** ability, accomplishment, adeptness, competence, competency, dexterity, expertise, expertness, mastery, perfection, virtuosity

**PROFILE**

n: configuration, outline, portrait, silhouette

**PROFIT**

a: expedient, fructiferous, fructuous, fruitful, lucrative, profitable, remunerative

n: bottom line, dividend, emolument, gain, gravy train, grist, gross, increment, net, payment, proceeds, share, sinecure

**PROFUSE**

a: abundant, bountiful, copious, exuberant, lavish, prodigal, rampant, replete, superabundant

n: abundance, affluence, copiosity, extravagance, lavishness, opulence, plethora, prodigality, profusion, sumptuosity

**PROGRAM**

n: agenda, *agendum*, catalog, catalogue, curriculum, exhibition, prospectus, regimen, relay, roster, schedule, syllabus

**PROGRESS**

a: categorical, consecutive, modern, progressive, sequential, serial, successive

n: evolution, headway, movement, progression, progressivism, tenor

v: graduate

*combining form:* -grade

**PROHIBIT**

a: inhibitory, interdictive, interdictory, prohibitive, proscriptive, *verboten*

n: embargo, forbiddance, inhibition, injunction, interdiction, *interdictum*, preclusion, prohibition, proscription, writ

v: ban, debar, enjoin, excommunicate, inhibit, interdict, outlaw, preclude, proscribe, restrain, taboo, veto

**PROJECTING**

a: beetling, conspicuous, extruding, gibbous, prognathous, prominent, protruding, protuberant, proud, salient

n: enterprise, extrapolation, flange, lobe, protuberance, *ramus*

v: extrapolate, project

**PROLIFIC**

a: fecund, fertile, fruitful, philoprogenitive, propagative, reproductive

n: fecundity, fertility, philoprogeneity, productivity, prolificity, reproductivity

v: prolificate

**PROLONG**

a: profuse, *prolix*, prolonged, protracted, protractive, repetitious, *sostenente*, *sostenuto, sostinente*, sustaining

n: austentation, austention, prolixity, prolongation, prorogation

v: extend, lengthen, perpetuate, postpone, *prorogue*, protract

**PROMINENCE**

a: aquiline, blatant, celebrated, conspicuous, eminent, leading, notable, notorious, prominent, protuberant, renowned, salient, stellar, well-known

n: celebrity, conspicuity, conspicuousness, eminence, prestige, protuberance, salience, saliency, superiority

**PROMISE**

a: auspicious, budding, developing, favorable, promising, propititious, up-and-coming

n: covenant, guarantee, iou, mutuality, pledge, plight, promissory note, *quid pro quo*, reciprocity, recognizance, token, undertaking

v: covenant, pledge, plight, redeem

*land:* Canaan, utopia, Zion

**PROMOTION**

n: advancement, advertising, brevet, enhancement, preferment

*demotion:* lowering, relegation

*promoter:* abettor, encourager, entrepreneur, impressario

**PROMPT**

a: celeritous, expeditious, mercurial, punctual, telegraphic

n: alacrity, celerity, expedition, promptitude, promptness, punctuality, speed

v: actuate, animate, encourage

**PRONG**

a: bidentate, bidigitate(d), pronged

n: tine

**PRONUNCIATION**

a: enunciative, incisive, orthoepic, orthoepical, orthoepistic, phonetic, syllabic

n: articulation, diction, elocution, enunciation, orthoepy, phonemics, phonetics, phonology, speech, syllabification

v: articulate, enunciate, syllabicate, syllabify

*correct:* incisiveness, orthoepy, phonology

*poor:* cacoepy, cacology

**PROOF**

a: apodictic, axiomatic, confirmative, confirmatory, deductive, demonstrable, demonstrative, established, incontrovertible, indisputable, proved, proven, proving, substantive, tangible

n: attestation, certification, corollary, corroboration, demonstrability, demonstration, documentation, evidence, onus, *probatum*, testament, verification, vindication

v: attest, circumstantiate, conform, corroborate, demonstrate, establish, manifest, prove, substantiate, testify, verify

**PROOFREAD**

n: authentication, collation

v: collate

**PROPAGANDA**

n: agitprop, tract, window dressing

v: brainwash, indoctrinate, propagandize

**PROPER**

a: *a propos,* accepted, appropriate, *au fait,* canonical, comely, *comme il faut,* condign, conventional, decorous, felicitous, kosher, lawful, legitimate, licit, opportune, orthodox, seemly, suitable

n: etiquette, protocol

v: befit, behoove

**PROPERTY**

a: propertied, proprietarian

n: appanage, assets, attribute, chattels, conveyance, deed, domain, equity, essence, estate, personalty, resources, substance, title

v: bequeath, convey, demise, devise

*from father:* patrimony

**PROPHECY**

a: anticipative, apocalyptic, cabalistic, clairvoyant, divinatory, fatidic, foretelling, incantatory, interpretive, mantic, ominous, oracular, phylacteric, portentious, presageful, prognosticative, prophetic, relevatory, talismatic

n: apocalypse, divination, foretelling, haruspication, omen, portent, prediction, prognostication, pythonism

v: augur, auspicate, foretell, hariolate, prognosticate, prophesy, vaticinate

*combining form:* -mancy

*prophet:* augur, Cassandra, Chaldean, *haruspex,* Jeremiah, mantic, Nostradamus, oracle, predictor, prognosticator, seer, sibyl, soothsayer, vaticinator

**PROPORTION**

a: *aliquot,* commensurable, commensurate, corresponding, proportionate

n: commensurability, commensuration, harmony, percentage, perspective, ration, symmetry

**PROPOSITION**

n: assumption, description, hypothesis, lemma, *philospheme,* postulate, *postulatum,* premise, proposal, specification, specs

v: nominate, propose, propound

**PROPRIETY**

**a:** *a propos,* appropriate, decorous, pertinent, relevant

**n:** amenity, appropriateness, aproposity, convenance, conventionality, correctitude, decorum, grace, pertinence, pertinency, relevance, relevancy, rigorism, scrupulosity, suitability, urbanity

　　*person:* proprietarian, rigorist

**PROSAIC**

**a:** commonplace, down-to-earth, humdrum, *jejune,* literal, matter-of-fact, monotonous, *prolix,* tedious, terrestrial, unexciting, unimaginative, unleavened

**n:** prosaism

**PROSPECT**

**n:** anticipation, expectation, foresight, future, futurity, outlook, panorama, perspective, prognosis, purview, view, vision, vista

**PROSPERITY**

**a:** affluent, auspicious, flourishing, halcyon, propitious, prosperous

**n:** achievement, affluence, fortune, luck, riches, success, wealth

**PROSTITUTE**

**a:** meretricious

**n:** call girl, courtesan, *courtezan, debauchee, demimondaine, demimonde,* doxy, *grisette,* harlot, *hetria,* hooker, moll, quean, streetwalker, strumpet, trollop, whore, working girl

**v:** accost, hustle, importune, solicit

　　*boss:* pimp, procurer, whoremonger

　　*client:* john, trick

　　*love:* philopornist

　　*prostitution:* corruption, debasement, harlotry, promiscuity, venality

**PROSTRATION**

**n:** abashment, collapse, powerlessness, prosternation, stupefaction, submission, submissiveness, supinity

**PROTECTION**

**a:** custodial, maternal, patent, paternal, preservative, prophylactic, proprietary, protective, sheltering, territorial, tutelary, tutorial, vigilant

**n:** *aegis,* armament, asylum, auspices, bastion, bulwark, conservation, custody, fixative, guardianship, haven, hedge, indemnity, maintenance, muniment, *palladium,* patronage, preservation, rampart, refuge, sanctuary, tutelage, umbrella, upkeep

**v:** buffer, buttress, cocoon, harbor, indemnify, inoculate, insulate, safeguard, secure, vaccinate

　　*charm:* amulet, *palladium,* rabbit's foot, talisman

　　*coat:* armature, case, integument, shell

　　*protected: protege,* ward

　　*protector:* angel, *bastion,* benefactor, bulwark, champion, chaperone, custodian, *duenna,* guarantor, guardian, outpost, *paladin,* sponsor, stronghold

**PROTEST**

**a:** remonstrative, vociferous

**n:** civil disobedience, complaint, *demarche,* grievance, harangue, objection, protestation, remonstrance, remonstration

**v:** boycott, complain, criticize, demur, deprecate, dissent, expostulate, inveigh, lambaste, oppugn, picket, remonstrate

　　*person:* activist, complainant, militant, oppugner, protestant, remonstrator

**PROTUBERANCE**

**a:** bulbous, conspicuous, gibbose, gibbous, obtrusive, prominent, protuberant, salient

**n:** gibbosity, protrusion, protuberancy, salience, saliency

**PROUD**

**a:** aloof, arrogant, bloated, bombastic, conceited, contemptuous, disdainful, egocentric, egotistical, elated, exultant, grandiose, haughty, hubristic, imperious, inflated, insolent, lordly, narcissistic, overbearing, overweening, pompous, presumptuous, prideful, snooty, supercilious, vainglorious

n: pride

**PROVERB**

a: apothegmatic, gnomic, sententious

n: adage, aphorism, apothegm, gnome, homily, maxim, parable, precept, saw

*study:* paroemiology

**PROVISION**

n: allowance, *viatica, viaticum*

**PROVISIONAL**

a: *ad hoc,* circumstantial, conditional, contingent, experimental, interim, temporary, tentative

**PROVOKE**

a: hair-trigger, incendiary, inflammatory

v: aggravate, exacerbate, excite, foment, instigate, perturb, pique, quicken, stimulate

**PRUDENCE**

a: careful, circumspect, diplomatic, discreet, expedient, guarded, judicious, politic, prudent

n: calculation, canniness, cautiousness, circumspection, discretion, forethought, frugality, judiciousness, moderation, providence, restraint, *sophrosyne,* temperance, vigilance

**PRUDISH**

a: lily-white, priggish, prissy, puribund, rigid, squeamish

n: priggishness, prudery, puribundity, squeamishness

**PRYING**

a: curious, inquisitive, inquisitorial, nosy, voyeuristic

*person:* quidnunc, scopophiliac

**PUBERTY**

a: hebetic, pubertal, pubescent

**PUBLIC**

a: exoteric, lay, popular, secular

n: commonalty, community, populace, population

**PUBLICATION**

a: published

n: disclosure, divulgation, proclamation, promulgation

v: circulate, delate, disseminate, endorse, exploit, herald, *nuncupate,* proclaim, promote, promulgate, pronunciate, publicize, publish, ventilate

*publicity:* ballyhoo, dissemination, exploitation, promotion, promulgation, propaganda, *reclame*

**PULP**

a: macerated, magmatic, pulpy, pultaceous

n: cellulose, *magma, marc, pomace*

**PULSATE**

a: palpitant, pulsatile, pulsative, pulsatory, throbbing

n: ictus, oscillation, *palmus,* palpitation, pulsation, pulsing, undulation

v: oscillate, palpitate, pulse, vibrate

*combining forms:* sphygm-, syphygmo-

**PULVERIZE**

n: comminution, pulverization, trituration

v: annihilate, comminute, contriturate, crush, demolish, disintegrate, grind, levigate, triturate

**PUN**

n: admonimation, assonance, *calembour,* equivoke, paradigm, *paronomasia,* punning

**PUNISH**

a: castigatory, condemnatory, corrective, disciplinal, disciplinary, expiatory, flagellant, intropunitive, penal, penitential, penitentiary, punishing, punitive, punitory, retaliatory, retributive, retributory, vindicative, vindicatory

**n:** admonition, amercement, castigation, chastisement, correction, detention, discipline, expiation, just deserts, penalty, penance, peniality, punition, purgatory, retaliation, retribution

**v:** admonish, amerce, castigate, chasten, chastize, discipline, flagellate, penalize, retaliate

> *enforcer:* disciplinarian, martinet, rigorist
>
> *free of:* immunity, impunity, indiscipline
>
> *just:* comeuppance
>
> *lessening:* commutation, leniency, mitigation
>
> *study:* penology

## PUPIL

**a:** abecedarian, apostolic, *catechumenal*, scholarly, scholastic

**n:** abecedarian, alphabetarian, apostle, *catechumen, chela*, disciple, *dux*, neophyte, novice, probationer, *protege*, scholar

## PURE

**a:** absolute, archangelic, artless, chaste, cherubic, classic, crystalline, devout, guileless, hermetic, immaculate, impeccable, incorrupt, innocent, inviolable, inviolate, irreproachable, lustral, pristine, purificatory, puritanical, sanctimonious, simon-pure, spotless, sterile, unadulterated, unmitigated, vestal, virgin

**n:** ablution, abreaction, alembication, catharsis, chastity, cleanliness, continence, defecation, depuation, epuration, lustration, purgation, purification, puritanism, purity, sanctitude, sanctity, virtue

**v:** *alembicate*, chasten, consecrate, decontaminate, depurate, distill, *edulcorate*, epurate, exorcise, hallow, lustrate, purify, sanitize

## PURPLE

**a:** empurpled, porphyrous, porporate, purplish, purpureal, purpurean, purpureous, purpurescent, purpurine

**n:** lavendar, violet

**v:** empurple

## PURPOSE

**a:** directional, functional, intentional, multiphasic, multipurpose, multivious, purposeful, purposive, teleological, telic

**n:** ambition, *animus*, aspiration, design, destiny, determination, function, hidden agenda, impulsion, intendment, intention, philosophy, purport, resolution, significance, teleology, ulterior motive

> *purposeless:* aimless, amorphous, dysteleological, meaningless, purportless, random, undirected, unpremeditated

## PURSUIT

**a:** persequent

**n:** activity, *metier*, occupation, ploy, prosecution, quest

**v:** harass, hound, pursue

## PUS

**a:** *puriform*, purulent, suppurative

**n:** maturation, purulence, purulency, pustule, sinus, suppuration

**v:** fester, maturate, *suppurate*

## PUSHY

**a:** aggressive, arrogant, assertive, brash, bumptious, insistent, intrusive, obtrusive, officious, presumptuous, strident

## PUZZLE

**a:** ambiguous, ambivalent, bewildering, cabalistic, cryptic, enigmatic, equivocal, impenetrable, incomprehensible, inexplicable, inscrutable, mysterious, occult, paradoxical, perplexing, puzzling, sphinxlike, undecipherable, unfathomable

**n:** acrostic, conundrum, dilemma, enigma, mystery, plight, poser, predicament, quandary, *rebus*, sphinx

**v:** baffle, bamboozle, befuddle, bewilder, confound, flummox, nonplus, obfuscate, perplex, stump, stupefy, stymie

**PYRAMID**

a: pyramidal

n: ziggurat

**QUACK**

n: charlatan, empiric, humbug, imposter, medicaster, mountebank, pretender, quacksalver, snake-oil salesman

**QUAINT**

a: antique, bizarre, eccentric, ethnic, exotic, folksy, grotesque, odd, *outre*, picturesque, *rococo*, singular, whimsical

n: oddity, peculiarity, whimsy

**QUALIFY**

a: accomplished, capable, certified, competent, conditional, consummate, eligible, legitimate, licensed, qualified, registered, restricted

n: capacitation, capacity, credentials, expertise, expertness, habilitation, hability, qualification, virtuosity

v: capacitate, habilitate

*qualifying:* adjectival, adjective, limiting, parenthetical, qualificatory

**QUALITY**

n: accent, attribute, aura, *cachet*, caliber, character, characteristic, degree, *ethos*, hallmark, property, resonance, *timbre*, trait

*differing:* heterogeneous, *heterousian*

*superior: ne plus supra, ne plus ultra,* nonesuch, *nonpareil, supernaculum*

**QUANTITY**

a: quantitative

n: amplitude, extent, magnitude, proportion, *quanta, quantum,* size

*large:* hecatomb, legion, multitude, spate

*small:* diminutive, homeopathic, miniscular, miniscule, minuscule

**QUARREL**

a: argumentative, bellicose, belligerent, boisterous, cantankerous, choleric, combative, contentious, discordant, disputable, disputatious, dissentient, dissentious, dissident, divisive, fractious, gladiatorial, perverse, pugnacious, quarrelsome, querulous, refractory, ructious, *termagant,* turbulent

n: altercation, bellicosity, belligerency, breach, *caterwaul, contretemps,* dissention, donnybrook, *embroglio,* fracas, melee, pugnacity, ruction, variance, vendetta, wrangle

v: bicker, *caterwaul,* controvert, gainsay, oppugn, repudiate

**QUEST**

n: *desideratum,* emprise, expedition, grail, inquisition, odyssey, perlustration, perscrutation, pursuit, *reconnaissance,* reconnoiter, safari, venture

**QUESTION**

a: ambiguous, catechetic(al), catechistic, contentious, controversial, controvertible, cryptic, debatable, dialectical, disputable, disputatious, doubtful, dubious, dubitable, equivocal, hypothetical, impugnable, indeterminate, *maieutic,* obscure, paradoxical, polemical, problematic, provisional, questionable, shady, Socratic, suspicious, uncertain, unreliable, unsafe, vague

n: ambiguity, barrage, catechesis, catechism, catechization, dialectics, dubiosity, equivocality, equivocation, equivocity, impugnment, inquisition, *maieutics,* questioning, rhetorical question

v: catechize, cross-examine, debrief, impugn, *inquisit,* interrogate, pose

*questioner:* inquisitor

**QUIBBLE**

a: captious, carping, casuistic, causistic, quibbling, sophistic, sophistical, sophomoric, specious

n: chicanery, equivocation, scrupulosity, sophistry, speciosity

v: bicker, carp, cavil, equivocate

*quibbler:* carper, caviler, devil's advocate, equivocator

## QUICK

**a:** accelerated, animated, celeritous, cursory, curt, expeditious, facile, fleet, headlong, impetuous, instantaneous, mercurial, nimble, perfunctory, precipitate, summary, telegraphic, *tout de suite, volant,* volitant

**n:** acumen, alacrity, astucity, celerity, dispatch, expedition, facilitation, facility, instanteity, *nous,* perspicacity, quickness, sagacity

> *tempered:* choleric, contentious, fiery, *iracund,* irascible

> *witted:* astute, mercurial, perspicacious

## QUIET

**a:** calm, dormant, dumbstruck, inconspicuous, introspective, low-key, low-profile, mute, pacific, passive, pensive, quiescent, reflective, reposeful, reticent, secluded, serene, subdued, taciturn, tranquil, uncommunicative

**n:** backwater, dormancy, *nepenthe,* opiate, quiescence, quiet, quietness, quietude, repose, sedative, sedate, tranquilizer, tranquilty, undertone

**v:** allay, pacify, repress, tranquilize

## RABBIT

**n:** Angora, chinchilla, coney, *cuniculus*, hare, *lagomorph*

    *area:* warren

## RABBLE

**a:** lumpen, plebeian, proletarian, proletariat

**n:** *canaille*, commonalty, *demos*, dregs, *hoi polloi*, horde, masses, mob, multitude, populace, proletariat, riffraff, scum, varletry

    *rousing:* demagogic, incendiary, inciting, inflammatory, *ochlocratic*

## RACIAL

**a:** anthropological, cultural, ethnic, ethnocentric, ethnologic, ethnological, gentilic, phyletic, phylogenetic, phylogenic, tribal

**n:** genus, paternity, pedigree, people, phylum, *sept*

    *combining forms:* ethn-, ethno-

    *distribution:* anthropogeography, ethnogeography

    *history:* phylogensis, phylogeny

    *kill:* genocide

    *mixed:* hybrid, hybridization, mestization, mestizo, miscegenation

    *origin:* anthropogenesis

    *segregation:* apartheid

    *study:* anthropology, ethnology, raciology

## RADIANT

**a:** auroral, *aurorean*, blithe, brilliant, divergent, ecstatic, lambent, luminous, resplendent, scintillescent

**n:** effulgency, radiance, resplendency, scintillation

**v:** diffuse, disseminate, effulge, emit, give off, radiate

    *radiation:* infrared, ultraviolet

## RADICAL

**a:** drastic, extreme, heretical, heterodox, revolutionary, unconventional, unorthodox

**n:** anarchist, firebrand, Jacobin, maximalist, nihilist, rebel, revolutionary, *sansculotte*, septembrist, ultraist, Young Turk

    *radicalism:* heresy, heterodoxy, radicality, ultraism

## RAGE

**a:** berserk, blustering, cyclonic, frenzied, fulminating, fulminous, furibund, infuriated, livid, maniacal, paroxysmal, raging, rampant, violent

**n:** access, anger, conniptions, dudgeon, enthusiasm, fashion, fervor, fit, frenzy, paroxysm, *pique*

**v:** fulminate

## RAID

**a:** incursionary

**n:** foray, incursion, inroad, invasion, looting, predation, sally, sortie

**v:** attack, maraud, pillage, plunder, sack

## RAILLERY

**n:** *asteism*, *badinage*, fun, kidding, mockery, *persiflage*, play, pleasantry, ridicule, satire, sport

## RAIN

**a:** hyetal, pluvial, pluvian, pluvious, rainy, torrential

**n:** cataract, deluge, monsoon, precipitate, precipitation

**v:** precipitate

*abundant:* pluviosity

*combining forms:* hyet-, hyeto-, pluvi-, pluvio-

*gauge:* pluviometer, udometer

*love:* ombrophilous

*study:* ombrology

**RAINBOW**

**a:** iridescent, iridian, prismatic

**n:** spectrum

*colors:* blue, green, indigo, orange, red, violet, yellow

**RAISE**

**a:** elevatory, transcendent

**n:** advancement, elevation, enhancement, ennoblement, escalation, promotion, transcendency

**v:** aggrandize, elevate, enhance, ennoble, escalate, exalt, extol, intensify, leaven, levitate, prefer, promote, resuscitate, sublimate, transcend, trip, uprear, weigh, winch

**RAKE**

**a:** disreputable, libertine, profligate, raffish, rakehell, unconventional

**n:** *debauchee*, lecher, libertine, lothario, profligate, *roue*

**RAMBLE**

**a:** circuitous, circumambagious, desultory, devious, digressive, discursive, disorderly, excursive, meandering, parenthetical, perambulatory, *peregrine*, peripatetic, rambling

**n:** *circumbendibus*, circumlocution, meandering, perambulation, peregrination, ploy

**v:** meander, perambulate, peregrinate, wander

**RANDOM**

**a:** adventitious, aleatory, arbitrary, capricious, desultory, discretionary, fickle, fortuitous, gratuitous, haphazard, impulsive, indiscriminate, intermittent, purposeless, sporadic, stochastic, wanton

**n:** serendipity

**RANGE**

**a:** categoric(al), jurisdictional, latitudinal, latitudinous

**n:** ambit, bailiwick, catalog(ue), category, cognizance, compass, *diapason*, domain, excursion, gamut, gradation, incidence, jurisdiction, latitude, lexicon, orbit, outlook, panorama, preserve, prospect, province, purview, *repertoire*, spectrum

**RANK**

**a:** exuberant, flagrant, indecent, luxuriant, luxurious, rampant, rancid, serried

**n:** aristocratism, array, distinction, formation, grade, hierarchy, patriciate, precedence, prestige, rating

*lower:* *declasse*, declensional, declinitory, junior, *puisne*, subaltern, subordinate

*superior:* antecedent, precedent, senior, superordinate

**RAPID**

**a:** agile, cursory, desultory, expeditious, kaleidoscopic, meteoric, oscillatory, phantasmagoric, quick, superficial

*combining forms:* tach-, tacheo-, tachy-

*move:* tantivy

**RAPTURE**

**a:** delirious, ecstatic, elated, frenzied, orgiastic, paroxysmal, rapturous

**n:** delight, delirium, ecstasy, elation, enthusiasm, euphria, exaltation, love, orgasm, paroxysm, *raptus*, transport

**v:** ecstasiate, ecstasize

**RARE**

**a:** abstruse, arcane, estimable, exotic, incomparable, infrequent, novel, obscure, paranormal, *recherche*, supernacular, tenuous, uncommon, unexampled, unique, unknown, unparalleled, unprecedented

**n:** anomaly, attenuation, extravaganza, infrequency, phenomenality, prodigality, prodigy, *rara avis*, rarefaction, rareness, rarity, scarcity, subtilization, tenuity *meat: a point, au blue, saignant*

**RASCAL**

**a:** rascally, tricky, villainous

**n:** cad, dog, imp, miscreant, rapscallion, reprobate, ribald, rogue, scalawag, *scaramouche*, tough, varmit, villain

**RASH**

**a:** adventurous, audacious, devil-may-care, gung ho, headlong, headstrong, impetuous, improvident, imprudent, impulsive, inconsiderate, injudicious, madcap, precipitate, presumptuous, reckless, temerarious, trigger-happy, unadvised, venturous

**n:** assumption, audacity, effrontery, impetuosity, presumption, rashness, temerity

  *skin:* birthmark, *lupus, roseola,* scar, stigma

**RATE**

**n:** incidence, metabolism, pace, proportion, speed, tempo, velocity

**RATIONAL**

**a:** Apollonian, cognitive, consequential, defensible, deliberate, intellective, intellectual, intelligent, judicious, philosophical, reasonable, restrained, sapient, sensible, tenable

**RATTLE**

**a:** crepitant

**n:** crepitation

**v:** agitate, creak, crepitate, discomfit, discompose, disconcert, upset

**RAVAGE**

**n:** denudation, deplumation, depradation, deracination, despoilment, devastation, looting, plunder, rapine, robbing, sacking, spoliation

**v:** denudate, depauperate, deplumate, deracinate, despoil, devastate, extirpate, impoverish, pillage, spoliate

**RAVE**

**a:** beserk, delirious, frenzied, fulminating, maniacal, raving

**v:** blow, bluster, fulminate, fume, rampage

**RAVEN**

**a:** corvid, corvine

  *flock:* unkindness

**RAVENOUS**

**a:** gluttonous, greedy, hungry, insatiable, lupine, rapacious, voracious

**RAW**

**a:** *au naturel,* inclement, undigested, unevaluated, unprocessed, unseasoned

**n:** staple

  *eating flesh:* omophagia

**REACTIVATE**

**a:** recrudescent, revivescent

**n:** reactivation, recrudescence, resuscitation, revivification

**v:** recrudesce, restore, revive, revivify

**REACTOR**

**a:** catalytic

**n:** activator, catalyst, reagant

**READ**

**a:** comprehensible, decipherable, legible, literate, readable, scrutable, understandable

**n:** literacy

**v:** decipher, interpret, peruse, pore over

  *everything:* avid, omniligent, omnivorous, voracious

  *inability:* alexia, illiteracy

**READY**

**a:** available, braced, compliant, convenient, dextrous, *en garde,* expectant, expeditious, expungatory, facile, on standby, operational, opportune, poised, preconditioned, prepared, primed, resourceful, unhesitating

**n:** alacrity, aptitude, facility, promptitude, readiness

## REAL

**a:** actual, actually, authentic, *bona fide,* corporeal, *de facto,* definitive, demonstrable, disembodied, in fact, incorporeal, inherent, intrinsic, legitimate, naturalistic, objective, official, palpable, postival, practical, realistic, representational, substantial, substantive, tangible, unromantic, verisimilar, verisimilous, veritable, viable

**n:** actuality, entity, existent, objectivity, reality, verisimilitude, verity

**v:** hypostatise, hypostatize, reify

*none:* autism, escapism, nihilism

*science:* ontology

## REAR

**a:** astern, back, caudal, posterior

**n:** haunches, posterior, rump

**v:** construct, elevate, originate, produce

## REARRANGE

**n:** permutation, rearrangement, refurbishment, reordering

**v:** permutate, refurbish

## REASON

**a:** *a posteriori, a priori,* aposterioristic, aprioristic, cogent, compelling, deductive, empirical, inductive, intuitive, ratiocinative, rational, syllogistic

**n:** argument, argumentation, deduction, dialectic, dialectics, ergotism, induction, intellect, intuition, justification, logic, *logos,* motive, *noesis, nous,* pretext, *raison d'etre,* ratiocination, rationale, rationality, reasoning, syllogism, synthesis, understanding

**v:** adduce, derive, expostulate, intellectualize, ratiocinate, rationalize, think

*false:* alogistic, casuistic, paralogistic, sophistic, specious

*reasoner:* dialectitian, dialectologist, logician, ratiocinator, rationalist

## REBEL

**a:** anarchical, defiant, disaffected, fractious, insubordinate, insurgent, insurrectionary, malcontent, mutinous, perverse, rebellious, recalcitrant, refractory, restive, seditious, stubborn, unruly

**n:** agitator, anarchist, dissenter, dissident, firebrand, *frondeur,* heretic, incendiary, insurgent, mutineer, nonconformist, radical, recusant, *sansculotte,* subversive, Young Turk

**v:** oppose

*rebellion:* contumacy, *coup d'etat,* insurgence, insurrection, mutiny, putsch, sedition

## REBIRTH

**a:** reborn, *redivivus,* regenerated, reincarnated, renascent, revivified

**n:** metempsychosis, reincarnation, renaissance, renascence, revival, revivification, transmigration

*thing:* phoenix

## REBOUND

**a:** resilient, reverberative

**n:** carom, resilience, resiliency, ricochet

**v:** carom, leap, recoil, re-echo, repercuss, *resile,* reverberate, ricochet, spring

## REBUKE

**a:** admonishing, admonitory, castigatory, objurgatory, rebuking, reprehensive

**n:** admonishment, animadversion, castigation, comeuppance, deserts, just deserts, objurgation, reproff

**v:** admonish, animadvert, berate, castigate, objurgate, reprehend, reprimand, reprove, vituperate

## RECALL

**a:** reminiscent

**n:** recollection, reminiscence

**v:** recollect, remember, reminisce, revive, summon

## RECEDE

**n:** recession

**v:** back up, countermarch, depreciate, dwindle, fade, fall, regress, retreat, retrocede, retrograde, withdraw

**RECEIVE**

**a:** acceptant, receptive, recipient, susceptible, susceptive

**n:** acceptance, admittance, collation, intromission, introsusception, intussusception, reaction, reception, receptivity, recipience, recipiency, sentience, sentiency, *soiree*, susceptibility

**v:** acquire, admit, entertain, intromit

  *receiver:* bailee, conservator, donee, receptionist, receptor, recipient

**RECESS**

**n:** armistice, continuance, hiatus, interim, intermission, niche, respite

**RECESSION**

**n:** abatement, declension, decrescence, diminution, lull, pause, retreat, retrocession, withdrawal

**RECKLESS**

**a:** audacious, bold, foolhardy, heedless, improvident, imprudent, impulsive, incautious, irresponsible, negligent, precipitate, prodigal, rash, remiss, scatterbrained, slack, temerarious, thoughtless, unadvised

**n:** audacity, *bravado*, derring-do, improvidence, imprudence, prodigality, recklessness, temerity

**RECLINING**

**a:** decumbent, recumbent

**n:** accumbency, anaclysis, decubation, decubitus, decumbency, reclination, recumbency

**v:** incline, lean, lie, relax, repose, rest

**RECLUSE**

**a:** anchoristic, cloistered, eremitic

**n:** anchoress, anchoret, anchorite, ascetic, cenobite, eremite, hermit, solitudinarian, troglodyte

**RECOGNITION**

**a:** accredited, apperceptionistic, authorized, cognizable, cognoscible, cognoscitive, identificatory, received, recognitive, recognitory, recognizable, recognized

**n:** acknowledgment, apperception, discernment, identifiability, identification, recognizability, salutation

  *combining form:* -gnosis

**RECOIL**

**n:** boomerang, kickback, reaction, rebound, return, reverberation, ricochet

**v:** rebound, re-echo, reverberate, ricochet

**RECOLLECTION**

**a:** reminiscent

**n:** *anamensis*, *memoir*, remembrance, reminiscence

**v:** contemplate, meditate, recall, recollect, remember, reminsce, review

**RECOMPENSE**

**n:** amends, compensation, emolument, *guerdon*, indemnification, indemnity, quittance, reimbursement, remuneration, requital, retribution, salary, wage

**v:** compensate, reimburse, remunerate, requite

**RECONCILE**

**a:** conciliatory, henotic, irenic, reconcilable, reconciliatory, syncretistic

**n:** harmony, rapprochment, reconcilement, reconciliation, syncretism

**v:** appease, arbitrate, conciliate, harmonize, intercede, mediate, moderate, propitiate, reconciliate, synchronize, syncretize

**RECORD**

**n:** agenda, *agendum*, annal, archive, calendar, chronicle, compact disk, compendium, document, *dossier*, floppy disk, lexicon, minutes, proceedings, protocol, *resume*, tally, transcript, transcription, *vita*

**v:** enscroll, transcribe

*combining form:* -gram, -graph

*study:* phililogy

## RECOVER

**a:** convalescent, recuperative, valetudinarian

**n:** buoyancy, reacquisition, recoverance, recovery, recuperation, rehabilitation, resilience

**v:** rally, reclaim, *recoup*, recuperate, redeem, resuscitate, retrieve, revive, salvage

*unable:* irretrievable, irreversible, irrevocable

## RECUR

**a:** cyclical, iterative, perennial, periodic, recurrent, recurring, regular, reiterative, revenant

**n:** iteration, *leitmotif, motif,* motto, periodicity, perseveration, recurrance, recurrency, reiteration

**v:** iterate, perseverate, reappear, reiterate

## RED

**a:** erubescent, florid, flushed, hyperemic, incarmined, incarnadine, reddened, reddish, rosy, rubescent, rubicund, rubious, ruddy, rufescent, rutilant

**n:** blushing, erubescence, pyrrhotism, reddishness, rubescence, rubicundity, rufosity

**v:** empurple, miniate, rubify, rubricate

*combining forms:* erythr-, erythro-, rhod-, rhodo-, rub-

*haired:* hirsutorfous, rufous, xanthous

*skin:* erythema, hyperemia, rubefaction

## REDUCE

**n:** abridgement, conquest, declension, decrement, demotion, denigration, depreciation, diminution, lessening, minimization, mitigation, pejoration, reduction, subjugation

**v:** denigrate, lessen, minify, minimize

*by half:* bisect, dimidiate, halve

## REDUNDANCY

**a:** excessive, exuberant, immaterial, long-winded, *otiose, pleonastic, prolix,* redundant, superabundant, supererogative, supererogatory, superfluous, tautological, tautologous, verbose

**n:** attrition, circumlocution, copiosity, macrology, overabundance, *periphrasis, pleonasm,* profusion, prolixity, superabundance, supererogation, superfluity, tautology, verbiage, verboseness, verbosity

## REED

**a:** arundinaceous, reedlike

**n:** papyrus, sedge

## REESTABLISHMENT

**n:** *apocatastasis,* rapprochement, reacquisition, recuperation, resettlement, restoration

## REFERENCE

**a:** anent, *apropos of,* ascribable, assignable, attributable, imputable, *in re,* pertaining to, pertinent, referable, referential, referring

**n:** bibliography, citation, *compendia,* dictionary, footnote, index, lexicon, manual, testimonial, thesaurus, *vade mecum*

**v:** advert, allude, refer

*combining form:* -wise

## REFINE

**a:** alembic, alembicated, cultivated, dainty, elegant, ethereal, exquisite, fastidious, genteel, polished, *recherche,* refined, *spirituelle,* subtle

**n:** alembication, artistry, civilization, cultivation, discrimination, elegance, *finesse,* gentility, humanization, nicety, perfectionment, polish, preciosity, rarefaction, refinement, subtlety

**v:** alembicate, chasten, civilize, cultivate, debarbarize, depurate, educate, elevate, expurgate, rarefy, spiritualize, subtilize

## REFLECT

**a:** catoptrical, cogitative, deliberative, meditative, ratiocinative, reflective, reverberative, reverberatory, ruminant n: aspersion, cogitation, consideration, ideation, imputation, meditation, mirror, perpension, ratiocination, reflection, thought

v: cogitate, contemplate, deliberate, excogitate, ideate, mirror, perpend, philosophize, ponder, ratiocinate, re-echo, rebound, reverberate, ruminate

## REFORM

a: correctible, corrigible, docile, reformable, tractable

n: conversion, corrigibility, docility, emendation, redemption, reformation, renovation, tractability

v: chasten, convert, rectify, remodel

*reformer:* visionary, Young Turk

## REFRESHMENT

a: fragrant, heartening, oasitic, refreshing

n: collation, reanimation, recreation, regeneration, reinvigoration, revivification, stimulation

v: recreate, refocillate, reform, refresh, reinvigorate, replenish, revivify, vitalize

## REFUND

n: rebate, reimbursement, restitution

v: reimburse, restitute

## REFUSAL

a: declensional, declinatory

n: abnegation, declension, declination, disclaimer, rejection

v: balk, boycott, decline, defy, disdain, disoblige, dissent, ostracize, refuse, reject, renege, repel, repudiate, repulse, spurn, veto

*waste:* debris, *dejecta, detritus, ejecta,* offal, *rejecta*

## REFUTATION

a: anatreptic, elenchtic, refutative, refutatory, refuting

n: confutation, disproof, elenchus

v: deny, disprove, invalidate, rebut, repeal

## REGAL

a: imperial, imposing, kingly, majestic, noble, queenly, royal

## REGARD

a: *anent, apropos of,* pertaining to, regarding, *vis-a-vis*

n: admiration, compliments, deference, estimation, good wishes, reverence, salutations

v: adjudge, deem, pronounce

## REGION

a: native, polydemic

n: area, domain, dominion, environment, hemisphere, jurisdiction, kingdom, locale, *milieu,* precinct, *purlieu,* realm, terrain, topography

*combining forms:* top-, topo-

## REGRESS

a: recidivous, retrograde, retrogressive

n: recidivation, regression, retrogradation, retrogression

v: abate, ebb, recidivate, relapse, retrograde, retrogress, sink, withdraw

## REGRET

a: compunctious, contrite, deplorable, deprecative, lamentable, penitent, regretful, regrettable, remorseful, repentant, repining, rueful

n: attrition, compassion, compunction, contrition, lamentation, penitence, qualm, remorse, scruple

v: bewail, deplore, feel sorry, lament, repine, rue

## REGULAR

a: authorized, consistent, cyclical, equable, methodical, metronomic, monolithic, official, orderly, orthodox, predictable, recurrent, rhythmic, statutory, symmetrical, synchronous, typical, uniform

n: periodcity, production line, regularity, regulation, rubber stamp, rule, synchroneity, system

**v:** guide, regulate

**REHASH**

**v:** redo, refurbish, renovate, restate, summarize

**REJECT**

**a:** nihilistic, rejectable, rejectaneous, rejecting, rejectitious, renunciatory

**n:** abdication, anarchism, banishment, denigation, disavowal, disclaimer, disclamation, nihilism, ostracism, rebuff, rejection, relegation, renunciation, repudiation, snub

**v:** abjure, boycott, decline, defy, disavow, discard, discount, dismiss, disown, dissent, forsake, forswear, jettison, jilt, ostracize, renounce, repudiate, slight, veto

**REJOICING**

**a:** cheerful, exuberant, exultant, gleeful, happy, joyous, jubilant, mirthful

**n:** exuberation, exultation, festivity, jubilation

**RELAPSE**

**a:** palindromic, recidivant, recidivous, regressive, retrocessive

**n:** declination, palindromia, recidivation, recidivism, regression, retrocession

**v:** backslide, ebb, recidivate, retrocess, retrogress, sink, slip, subside, worsen

**RELATED**

**a:** affiliated, affinitive, agnate, agnatic, akin, analogous, ancillary, applicable, apposite, auxiliary, cognate, cognatic, congeneric, congenerous, consanguineous, correlate, correlative, germane, leagued, material, pertinent, satellite

**n:** affinity, agnate, agnation, bond, cogener, cognate, cognation, communion, connection, consanguinity, correlation, detente, footing, juxtaposition, kindred, kinship, kinsman, liaison, mutuality, narration, pertinence, rapport, relation, relationship, relativity, sib, sibling, standing, syngenesis

**v:** appertain, commune

*father's side:* patrilineal, patrilinear

*mother's side:* matrilateral, matrilineal, matrilinear

*relating to: anent, apropos,* pertaining, referring

**RELAXATION**

**a:** calm, cool, genial, mellow, soothing

**n:** abatement, cessation, detachment, *detente,* disengagement, dispensation, diversion, entertainment, laxation, meditation, rapprochement, recreation, remission, repose

**v:** ease, languish, loll, relax, thaw, unbend

*drug:* anodyne, narcotic, opiate, sedative, soporific

**RELEVANT**

**a:** *ad rem,* applicable, apposite, appropriate, *apropos,* apt, bearing, cognate, competent, congruous, germane, material, opportune, pertinent, seasonable, timely

**n:** applicability, homogeneity, materiality, relevance

**v:** pertain

**RELIABLE**

**a:** authoritative, credible, definitive, dependable, fail-safe, foolproof, infallible, reputable, steadfast

**n:** authenticity, credence, dependability, reliability, trustworthiness

**RELIEF**

**a:** relieved

**n:** alleviation, assuagement, deliverance, succor

**v:** alleviate, assuage, confess, deliver, diminish, ease, lessen, mitigate, relieve, spell, succor, unburden

*reliever:* alleviant, anesthetic, antidote, *nepenthe,* opiate, palliative

**RELIGION**

**a:** benedictional, devout, ecclesiastic(al), hierarchic, orthodox, pious, religious, sanctified, spiritual n: catechism, clericalism, creed, devoutness, doctrine, dogma, domination, faith, gospel, hierology, orthodoxy, orthopraxy, persuasion, sanctity, sect, tenets, theology

*disbeliever:* adiaphorist, agnostic, atheist, freethinker, latitudinarian

*not:* heathenish, impious, *laic*, pagan, secular, ungodly, worldly

*overly:* pietistic, *religiose*, sacrosanct, sanctimonious, theopathetic

## RELISH

n: appetite, *elan*, gratification, gusto, inclination, liking, pleasure, savor, zest

## RELUCTANT

a: averse, forced, grudging, indisposed, involuntary, recalcitrant, unwilling

## REMAINS

a: residual, residuary, vestigial

n: balance, debris, dregs, foots, grounds, lees, leftovers, *magma*, oddments, relic, remainder, remnant, residual, residue, *residuum*, rump, scraps, sediment, vestige

## REMARK

a: bromicid, parenthetical, platitudinal, platitudinous

n: *animadversion, apercu*, aside, expression, interjection, *non sequitur, obiter dictum*, parenthesis, Parthian shot

v: interject, interpose

*concluding:* envoi, farewell, valediction

*derogatory:* aspersion, barb, infelicitous, *innuendo*, insinuation

*rude:* causticity, mordacity, sagacity, spinosity, witticism

*trite:* bromide, *cliche*, incisive, platitude

## REMEDY

a: curative, efficacious, lenitive, medicamentive, *panacean*, polychrestic, remediable, remedial, reparable, restorative, salubrious, salutary, salutiferous, sanable, sanatory, sovereign, therapeutic

n: antidote, *arcanum, catholicon*, corrective, elixir, embrocation, medicament, *nostrum*, palliative, panacea, *pharmacon*, placebo, polychrest, prescription, remediation, reparation, restorative, specific, therapeutic, therapy

## REMEMBERING

a: anamnestic, commemorated, evocative, memoried, memorized, redolent, remembered, reminiscent

n: anamnesis, anamnestic, *feuilleton*, recall, recollection, reminiscence, reminiscent, rote

v: commemorate, memorize, recall, recollect, remember, reminisce, retain, retrace, retrieve

*aid:* mnemonic, mnemonic device

*remembrance:* aide-memoire, amulet, commendation, keepsake, memento, memorabilia, memorandum, memorial, phylactery, remembrancer, reminder, reminiscence, souvenir, token

## REMISSION

a: delinquent, derelict, dilatory, inattentive, misfeasant, neglectful, negligent, remiss

n: carelessness, delinquency, deliverance, dereliction, forgiveness, laxity, laziness, lysis, misfeasance, pardon, relaxation

## REMORSE

a: contrite, penitent, regretful, remorseful, repentant

n: compunction, contrition, grief, penitence, regret, repentance, rue, self-reproach, sorrow

## REMOTE

a: alien, antipodean, cloistered, distant, forane, inaccessible, isolated, outlying, secluded, segregated, separated, sequestered, solitary, *tramontane, transmontane*, ulterior, ultimate, ultramundane

n: boondocks, boonies, hinterland, outback, *Ultima Thule*

**REMOVE**

**a:** cloistered, lonely, remote, removed, secluded, sequestered, solitary

**n:** ablation, abstraction, deprivation, elimination, emasculation, eradication, expurgation, *purdah*, removal, separation, sequestration, supersedence, supersedure, supersession, transference

**v:** ablate, abstract, amputate, bowdlerize, cull, curtail, depose, disembarrass, dislodge, displace, divest, eliminate, enucleate, eradicate, excide, excise, expunge, expurgate, extirpate, extract, isolate, leach, obliterate, oust, prune, resect, segregate, sequester, supersede, supplant, transfer, truncate, uproot

*combining forms:* de-, dis-, -ectomy, ex-, un-

**RENEW**

**a:** renewed

**n:** renaissance, renascence, renewal, revival

**v:** reawaken, reestablish, refurbish, regenerate, rehabilitate, reinstate, reinvigorate, rejuvenate, renovate, repair, replenish, restore, resume, resuscitate, revitalize, start again

**RENOUNCE**

**a:** abjuratory, renunciatory

**n:** abjuration, abnegation, abrogation, apostasy, disclaimer, recantation, recission, renunciation, repudiation, sacrifice, waiver

**v:** abandon, abjure, abrogate, apostatize, disclaim, forswear, recant, repudiate, rescind, retract, waive

**REPAIR**

**a:** remedial

**n:** atonement, indemnification, propiation, recompense, reconditioning, redress, refurbishment, regeneration, remedy, renovation, reparation, repristination, requital, restitution, restoration, retribution

**v:** alter, ameliorate, amend, debug, fix, furbish, improve, overhaul, rebuild, recondition, reconstitute, reconstruct, refurbish, regenerate, remodel, renew, renovate, repristinate, restore, revamp, revive, tinker

*impossible:* irreparable

**REPAY**

**n:** amends, atonement, indemnification, quittance, recompense, redress, reparations, repayment, requital, restitution

**v:** compensate, indemnify, reciprocate, recompense, refund, reimburse, remunerate, requite, retaliate

**REPEAL**

**a:** recissory, revocatory

**n:** abrogation, recision, rescission, revocation

**v:** abandon, abrogate, cancel, rescind, revoke

**REPENTANCE**

**a:** contrite, penitent, remorseful, repentant

**n:** absolution, amends, attrition, contrition, expiation, penance, penitence, redemption, redress, remorse, restitution

*not:* impenitent

**REPETITION**

**a:** alliterational, alliterative, battological, echoic, frequentive, imitative, iterative, monotonous, perseverant, pleonastic, reduplicative, reiterative, repeating, repetitional, repetitious, repetitive, replicate, stereotypical, tautological

**n:** alliteration, anaphora, battology, burden, chorus, ingemination, *leitmotiv*, motif, perseverance, perseveration, reduplication, refrain, reiteration, replication, reprise, reproduction, rote, verbigeration

**v:** battologize, ingeminate, iterate, perseverate, recapitulate, redouble, reduplicate, reiterate, repeat, replicate, summarize, tautologize, verbigerate

*sound:* anaphora, tautophony

*words:* anadiplosis, battology, echolalia, motto, onomatomania, pleonasm, redundancy, tautology, verbigeration, verbomania

## REPLACE

**a:** substitutionary, substitutive

**n:** *locum,* removal, replacement, stand-in, substitute, surrogate

**v:** depose, deputize, displace, oust, regenerate, substitute, succeed, supersede, supplant

## REPLY

**a:** rescriptive

**n:** rejoinder, repartee, replication, rescription, retort, reverberation, *riposte,* RSVP

**v:** answer, rejoin, replicate, resound

*late: esprit d'escalier, treppenwitz*

## REPORT

**a:** reportorial

**n:** account, *cahier, charactes, communique,* dispatch, *expose,* fame, narration, reputation, repute

**v:** document, record

## REPOSE

**n:** calm, composure, peace, quiescence, relaxation, requiescence, respite, sleep, tranquility

## REPRESENTATIVE

**a:** emblematic, figurative, realistic, representational, symbolic, typical, typifying, vicarious

**n:** *alter ego,* ambassador, archetype, assignee, champion, commissary, delegate, deputy, diplomat, emissary, envoy, *epitome,* executor, executrix, exemplar, *factotum,* front person, incarnation, intermediary, legate, minister, personification, proctor, proxy, representant, specimen, substitute, surrogate, trustee, understudy

**v:** delineate, depict, depute, describe, emblematize, embody, epitomize, exemplify, incarnate, limn, personate, personify, portray, realize, render, represent, symbolize, typify

## REPROACH

**a:** admonitory, castigatory, chastening, reproaching, reproving

**n:** accusation, *bar sinister,* castigation, discredit, disgrace, ignominy, *opprobrium,* rebuke, reprehension, reproof

**v:** berate, blame, chasten, rebuke, reprimand, reprove, scold, taunt, vituperate

*above:* inviolable, inviolate, *sacrosanct,* unassailable

## REPRODUCTION

**a:** amphigonous, ectypal, gamogenetic, gestational, gestative, parturient, progenitive, reproductive, seminal, syngamic, syngamous, syngenetic, viviparous

**n:** amphigony, counterpart, duplicate, duplication, ectype, gamogenesis, gestation, parturition, procreation, reconstruction, regeneration, reproductivity, syngamy, syngenesis, viviparity

**v:** proliferate, propagate, reproduce

*budding:* gemmation, protogenesis

*combining forms:* -gen, gen-, -genesis, -gon, gono-

*cross:* allogamy, hybridization

*science:* genesiology

*sexless:* abiogenesis, accrementation, agamogenesis, autogenesis, fission, gemmation, parthenogenesis, protogenesis

## REPTILE

**a:** herpetological, ophidian, reptant, reptilian, reptiloid, serpentiform, serpentine

**n:** amphibian, groveling, ophidian, snake

*combining forms:* herpet-, herpeto-

*study:* herpetology, ophiology

## REPUDIATION

**a:** disclamatory, renunciative, repudiative

**n:** disaffirmance, disaffirmation, disclamation, renunciation

**v:** abjure, abrogate, deny, disaffirm, disavow, disclaim, renunciate, repudiate

## REPUGNANT

**a:** abominable, bitter, despicable, fulsome, hateful, incompatible, inconsistent, loathsome, nasty, objectionable, odious, offensive, repulsive, sordid, squalid, ugly, unfriendly, unsavory

**n:** despicability, repugnancy, repulsivity, squalidity, squalor

## REPUTATION

**a:** famous, prestigious, putative, reputable, reputed, respectable

**n:** *cachet*, character, distinction, estimation, fame, infamy, *kudos*, odor, prestige, regard, renown, repute, standing, stature, stock

  *injury:* aspersion, calumny, defamation, disrepute, libel, notoriety, slander, vilification

## REQUEST

**a:** at the behest of, requested, requisitorial, supplicatory

**n:** application, requisition, rogation, solicitation, supplication

**v:** ask, importune, pray

## REQUIRED

**a:** coercive, compelling, compulsory, *de rigueur*, deontic, essential, imperative, incumbent, indispensable, mandatory, obligatory, prerequisite, requisite

**n:** condition precedent, essentiality, indispensibility, precedent, precondition, prerequisite, *prius*, requirement, requisite, *sine qua non*, specifications, specs

**v:** demand, require, stipulate

  *more than:* supererogative, superogatory

## RESCUE

**n:** deliverance, emancipation, liberation, redemption, salvation

**v:** aid, emancipate, liberate, reclaim, redeem, retrieve, salvage, save

## RESEMBLANCE

**a:** analogical, analogous, bogus, ersatz, homologous, quasi-, resembling

**n:** affinity, analogy, approximation, assonance, counterpart, equivalence, facsimile, homology, image, parallelism, parity, representation, similarity, simile, similitude, *simulacrum*, uniformity, verisimility, versimilitude

**v:** mimic, resemble, simulate

  *combining forms:* -ine, -oid, -ose, para-, quasi-

## RESENTMENT

**a:** belligerent, invidious, offensive, resentful, umbrageous

**n:** anger, animosity, dudgeon, grudge, indignation, irascibility, jaundice, offense, *pique*, prejudice, temper, umbrage, vexation

## RESERVED

**a:** apathetic, detached, distant, egocentric, incommunicable, incommunicative, indrawn, phlegmatic, restrained, retarded, retentive, reticent, shy, silent, taciturn, unapproachable, uncommunicative, undemonstrative, unsociable, withdrawn

**n:** apathy, detachment, forbearance, reserve, restraint, retardation, reticence, self-control, self-restraint, taciturnity, unsociability

**v:** bespeak, reserve

## RESIDE

**a:** immanent, indwelling, native, residential, residentiary

**n:** domiciliation, inhabitance, inhabitancy, inhabitation, occupancy, residence

**v:** domicile, domiciliate

  *resident:* denizen, domicile, *habitue*, inhabitant, inhabitress, native, occupant, *sedens*

## RESIGNATION

**n:** abandonment, abdication, acquittance, defeatism, disaffiliation, disassociation, humility, obedience, obeisance, passivity, relinquishment, renunciation, retirement, submission

**v:** abdicate, disaffiliate, disassociate, resign

**RESIST**

**a:** immune, incompliant, involnerable, recalcitrant, resistant, stubborn, unassailable

**n:** resistance, resistivity, tolerance

**v:** fight

**RESONANT**

**a:** orotund, plangent, sonorant, sonoriferous, sonorous, tympanic, vibrant

**n:** orotundity, plangency, reconance, sonority

**RESOURCE**

**n:** expediency, expedient, makeshift, strategem, wherewithal

**RESPECT**

**a:** amenable, commendatory, complimentary, creditable, deferential, dutiful, estimable, honorable, honorific, praiseworthy, presentable, prestigious, reputable, respectable, respected, respectful, reverential, tractable, venerable, venerative

**n:** approbation, deference, deferentiality, *devoir*, devotion, esteem, estimability, fealty, genuflection, homage, obeisance, obsequiousness, obsequity, prestige, respectability, tribute, veneration

**v:** admire, esteem, honor

**RESPONSE**

**a:** amenable, antiphonal, hyperesthetic, reactive, responsive, sensible, tractable

**n:** answer, antiphon, feedback, hyperesthesia, reaction, retort, reverberation

**RESPONSIBLE**

**a:** accountable, amendable, answerable, culpable, liable, reliable, solvent, trustworthy

**n:** accountability, amenability, liability, obligation, *onus,* reliability, responsibility, solvency, trustworthiness

**REST**

**a:** diastolic, dormant, inactive, incumbent, latent, quiescent, resting, sabbatical, sessile, static

**n:** diastole, dormancy, immobility, immobilization, inertia, pause, repose, respite, sleep, tranquility

**v:** spell

    *place:* Canaan, nirvana

**RESTITUTION**

**n:** *apocatastasis*, indemnification, indemnity, reinstatement, reparation, restoration

**RESTLESS**

**a:** agitated, *agitato,* anxious, disobedient, erethic, fitful, footloose, impatient, obstinate, rebellious, restive, riotous, spasmodic, turbulent, unceasing

**n:** agitation, disquietude, dyspathy, dysphoria, fantods, fidgets, inquietude, restlessness, unease, uneasiness

**RESTORATION**

**a:** analeptic, curable, invigorating, reconditioned, *redivivus,* refurbished, reinvigorated, rejuvenated, reparable, restitutive, restored, restoring, resuscitative, roborant, tonic

**n:** cure, instauration, reanimation, reconstruction, redemption, reestablishment, refurbishment, rehabilitation, reimbursement, reinstitution, reinvigoration, rejuvenation, remedy, reparation, restitution, resurgency, revivification

**v:** reanimate, reawaken, reconstruct, redeem, rehabilitate, reinstate, reinstitute, reinvigorate, rejuvenate, renovate, repristinate, restitute, restore, resurrect, resuscitate, revamp, revivify

**RESTRAINT**

**a:** abstemious, Apollonian, circumscribed, disciplined, harmonious, inhibitory, rational, restrained, restrictive, retentive, retraining, sparing, temperate, unemancipated

**n:** circumspection, coertion, confinement, constraint, discipline, durance, duress, embargo, fetter, hindrance, inhibition, interdiction, limbo, manacle, monopoly, prudence, repression, restriction, retention, sanction, shackle, temperance

**v:** check, circumscribe, constrain, demarcate, discipline, enslave, fetter, hamper, inhibit, manacle, pinion, repress, restrain, restrict, shackle, stifle, suppress

## RESTRICT

**a:** abbreviated, abridged, arcane, circumscribed, circumscriptive, cloisteral, cloistered, esoteric, exclusive, hidebound, inflexible, insulated, parochial, peninsular, provincial, rarefied, restricted, select, truncated

**n:** circumspection, coercion, condition, curfew, delimitation, fetters, immanence, limitation, *proviso*, quota, regulation, restraint, restriction, sanction, shackles

**v:** circumscribe, delimit, delimitate, discipline, fetter, gag, hamper, hinder, hobble, limit, *pinion*, prevent, prohibit, restrain, straitjacket, tether

## RESULT

**n:** aftermath, backwash, conclusion, consequence, corollary, denouement, fallout, feedback, handiwork, ramification, repercussion, reverberation, sequel, side effect, spinoff, upshot

**v:** ensue, eventuate, redound, supervene

## RESUME

**n:** abridgement, abstract, compendium, *curriculum vita*, epitome, recapitulation, summary, syllabus, synopsis, *vita*

## RETAINER

**n:** adherents, *clique*, company, *cortege*, crew, entourage, followers, gang, minions, retinue, staff, train

## RETALIATION

**n:** comeuppance, *reparte*, retribution, reward, *riposte*, vengeance

## RETARDED

**a:** handcuffed, impeded, inhibited, primitive, repressed, slowed

## RETENTIVENESS

**n:** memory, retentivity, tenacity

## RETICENT

**a:** brachysyllabic, dumb, laconic, reserved, secret, silent, speechless, taciturn, uncommunicative

## RETIRED

**a:** cidevant, cloisteral, cloistered, discharged, *emeritus*, humble, immured, inactive, *otiose*, reserved, retiring, sequestered, shy, superannuated, withdrawn

**n:** insularity, invalidation, otiosity, retirement, sedentation, superannuation

**v:** retire, retreat, withdraw

## RETRACE

**v:** backtrack, perseverate, recall, recollect, reiterate, reminisce, repeat, retell

## RETRACTION

**n:** abandonment, disavowal, nullification, *palinode*, recantation, withdrawal

## RETREAT

**n:** asylum, harbor, haven, hermitage, privacy, recession, redoubt, retrocession, sanctuary, seclusion, solitude, withdrawal

## RETRIBUTION

**n:** correction, nemesis, penalty, punishment, vengeance

## RETURN

**a:** reciprocative, resurgent, retaliatory, retributory

**n:** atavism, rebate, reciprocation, reciprocity, recursion, requital, restoration, retribution

**v:** *quid pro quo*, rebound, reciprocate, recompense, reinstate, remand, requite, retaliate

## REVEAL

**a:** epiphanic, heuristic, revealing, revelative, revelatory

**n:** apocalypse, disclosure, divulgence, epiphany, expose, manifestation, numinous, revealment, relevation, theophany

**v:** confess, disburden, disclose, disinter, divulge, evince, manifest, uncover, unearth, unmask, unveil

## REVEL

**a:** gay, revelrous, roistering, roisterous

**n:** conviviality, ecstasy, revelry, *saturnalia*, wassail

**v:** carouse, celebrate, riot, roister, royster, wassail

## REVENGE

**a:** punitive, retaliative, retaliatory, retributive, retributory, revengeful, vindictive, viperish, vituperative

**n:** nemesis, redress, reprisals, requital, retaliation, retortion, retribution, revanchism, vendetta, vengeance, vindication, vindicativeness

**v:** requite, retaliate

## REVERE

**a:** religious, reverent, reverential, venerative, worshipful

**n:** reverence, veneration

**v:** esteem, honor, reverence, venerate, worship

## REVERSAL

**a:** anticlimactic, atavistic, backward, bathetic, conversely, recessive, regressive, retrograde, retrogressive, *vice versa*

**n:** about-face, anticlimax, *bathos*, inversion, *metathesis*, mutation, peripety, transposition, *volte-face*

**v:** invert, reverse, transpose

*reversion:* atavism, mutation

## REVISE

**a:** revisional, revisionary

**n:** recension, redaction, revision

**v:** rearrange, redact, renovate, revamp

*reviser: diaskeuast*, redactor

## REVIVE

**a:** redivivus, renascent, revivescent, reviving

**n:** anabiosis, recrudescence, renaissance, renascence, repristination, restoration, resurrection, revival, revivification, *riorgimento*

**v:** quicken, reanimate, reawaken, refresh, regenerate, reinspirit, reinvigorate, resurge, resurrect, resuscitate, revitalize, revivify, vivificate

## REVOKE

**n:** abrogation, counteraction, countermand, nullification, recantation, recision, repeal, reversal, revocation, vitiation, withdrawal

**v:** abrogate, countermand, nullify, recant, rescind, vitiate, withdraw

## REVOLTING

**a:** bilious, choleric, despicable, disgusting, fulsome, irascible, loathsome, nauseating, noisome, offensive, repugnant, repulsive, revellent, revulsive

**n:** anarchy, *coup d'etat*, insubordination, insurgency, insurrection, revolt, revolution, riot, sedition

## REVOLVE

**a:** vertiginous

**n:** circumduction, circumgyration, turnstile, volution

**v:** circumduct, circumgyrate, gyrate, vertiginate

## REWARD

**n:** bounty, guerdon, honorarium, indemnity, recompense, reinforcement, requital, retribution

**v:** guerdon, recompense, reimburse, remunderate, requite

## REWORD

**a:** paraphrastic

**n:** abstract, paraphrase, *precis*

**v:** paraphrase

**RHETORIC**

**a:** bombastic, declamatory, eloquent, *epideictic,* forensic, grandiloquent, rhetorical, rubescent

**n:** circumgyration, *trope*

  *teacher:* rhetorician

**RHINOCEROS**

**n:** pachyderm

  *herd:* crash

**RHYTHM**

**a:** cadenced, cadential, measured, rhythmic(al)

**n:** cadence, eurhythmics, *ictus,* lilt, melody, meter, oscillation, periodicity, *rubato,* syncopation, tempo

  *abnormal:* arrhythmia, asynchronism, cacophony, *dysrhythmia*

**RICE**

**a:** oryzivorous

**RICH**

**a:** abundant, affluent, daedalian, daedalic, flush, lavish, lucullian, luxuriant, luxurious, opulent, plentiful, prosperous, redolent, resourceful, substantial, sumptuous

**n:** abundance, affluence, bonanza, money, fortune, luxuriance, *mammon,* opulence, riches, sumptuosity, wealth

  *love:* plutolatry, plutomania

  *person:* Croesus, magnate, Midas, mogul, *nabob, nouveau riche, parvenu,* tycoon

**RICKETY**

**a:** feeble, flimsy, frail, rachitic, ramshackle, tenuous, tremulous, unsound, wobbly

**RID**

**v:** delete, disabuse, disencumber, eradicate, extricate, free, liberate, purge, relinquish, unburden, unload

**RIDDLE**

**a:** enigmatic

**n:** ambiguity, brainteaser, charade, conundrum, enigma, intricacy, *koan,* labyrinth, paradox, perplexity, quandary, *rebus,* sphinx

**RIDGE**

**a:** corrugated, grooved, ridged, rugose, serrated, striate, strigose

**n:** anticline, corrugation, crest, fluting, groove, hummock, knoll, levee, milling, ness, promontory, ruga, rugae, rugosity, serration, wale

**RIDICULE**

**a:** asinine, bizarre, derisible, derisive, derisory, eccentric, extravagant, farcical, fatuous, grotesque, inane, ludicrous, outlandish, *outre,* preposterous, ridiculous, risible, satirical

**n:** asteism, *badinage,* banter, burlesque, chaff, derision, farce, irony, lampoon, *pasquinade, persiflage,* pillory, *raillery,* ridiculosity, satire, skit, spoof, stultification, travesty

**v:** ape, caricature, debunk, deflate, deride, lampoon, mimic, parody, *pastiche,* satirize, stultify

**RIGHT**

**a:** advantageous, appropriate, deontic, dextral, equitable, inalienable, kosher, legitimate, opportune, orthodox, timely

**n:** appanage, constitution, eminent domain, faculty, franchise, *habeas corpus,* immunity, option, perquisite, power, prerogative, reservation, seniority, title

  *combining forms:* dext-, dextro-, ortho-, rect-

  *handed:* dexter, dextrad, dextral, droite

**RIGHTEOUS**

**a:** magnanimous, principled, rectitudinous, *religiose,* sanctimonious, equitable, upright n: dharma, probity, rectitude, religiosity, righteousness, sanctimoniousness, sanctimony, scrupulosity, uprightness

**RIGID**

a: austere, immalleable, inclement, inelastic, inexorable, inflexible, rigorous, scrupulous, strict, stringent, unshakable, unyielding

n: austerity, inclemency, inflexibility, insensitivity, rigidification, rigidity, rigor, rigorism, severity, strenuosity

**RIGOR**

a: accurate, asperous, austere, drastic, harsh, inclement, inexorable, peremptory, precise, Procrustean, rigorous, strenuous, uncompromising

n: ardor, austerity, inclemency, rigidity, scrupulosity, severity, strenuosity

**RIND**

n: bark, cortex, husk, integument, layer, skin

**RING**

a: annular, annulate, annulose, armillary, cingular, circinate, circular, circumferential, ringed, toroid

n: annulation, *annulus*, aureole, corona, encirclement, sonority

v: circumnavigate, encircle, surround

*combining forms:* circ-, gyro-

**RIOT**

a: abundant, agitated, bacchanalian, bacchic, exuberant, incendiary, inflammatory, mutinous, pandemoniac, profuse, riotous, seditious, tumultary, tumultuous, turbulent, ungovernable, unmanageable, unrestrained

n: donnybrook, insurrection, melee, pandemonium, revolution, riotry, tumult, turmoil, welter

v: foment

**RISE**

a: ascensive, ascentional, assurgent, meteoric, ortive, resurgent, rising

n: advance, ascension, assurgency, escalation, increase, levitation, upsurge

v: ascend, climb, heave, increase, increment, levitate, overcome, skyrocket, soar, spiral, surge, surmount, swell, transcend

**RISK**

a: dangerous, explosive, hazardous, jeopardous, ominous, *parlous*, precarious, risky, shaky, venturesome

n: jeopardy, peril, perilousness, precariousness, riskiness, speculation, temerity

v: brave, endanger, gamble, hazard, imperil, jeopardize, venture

*risque:* off-color, salacious, scabrous

**RITUAL**

a: ceremonial, ceremonious, ritualistic

n: ceremonialism, ceremony, formality, liturgy, procedure, protocol, rite, rite of passage

v: ritualize

**RIVAL**

a: antagonistic, competing, competitive, contesting, rivalrous

n: antagonist, competitor, enemy, foe, match, opponent, peer

v: emulate

**RIVER**

a: fluvial, potamic, riparian, riparious

n: effluent, rivulet, tributary

*between:* interamnian, mesopotamian

*spawning:* anadromous

*study:* potamology

**ROAD**

a: viatic, viatical

n: access road, back road, beltway, boulevard, bypass, byroad, causeway, concourse, detour, expressway, feeder, freeway, highway, interstate, parkway, portage, thoroughfare, thruway, turnpike

**ROAMING**

a: ambulatory, discursive, itinerant,

meandering, migratory, nomadic, perambulatory, peripatetic, prodigal, roving, vagarious, vagrant, wandering

## ROB

**a:** larcenous, predaceous, predacious, predatory, robbing

**n:** burglary, conversion, depredation, despoliation, embezzlement, larceny, malversation, peculation, pillage, piracy, predacity, robbery, spoliation

**v:** burglarize, depredate, despoil, plunder, rifle, spoliate

*robber:* bandit, brigand, highwayman

## ROBUST

**a:** athletic, brawny, lusty, muscular, *Rabelaisian*, robustious, robustuous, stalwart, virile

**n:** lustihood, lustiness, robusticity, robustness

## ROCK

**a:** geologic, geological, *petricolous*, petrologic, *petrous*, rupestral, rupestrian, rupicoline, *rupicolous, saxicolous, saxigenous*

**n:** bedrock, cobble, debris, geode, lamina, lode, monolith, nodule, scree, stalactite, stalagmite, *stratum*, talus

*combining forms:* -lite, -lith, lith-, litho-, petro-

*study:* geology, petrology

## ROD

**a:** bacillary, bacilliform, baculiform, baculin, penicillary, virgate, virgulate

**n:** fasces, spindle, staff

## ROGUE

**a:** arch, mischievous, picaresque, puckish, roguish, unprincipled, waggish

**n:** adventurer, caitiff, gamin, knave, malefactor, miscreant, *picaro, picaroon,* rapscallion, renegade, reprobate, ribald, scalawag, *scaramouche,* scoundrel, vagabond

## ROLLING

**a:** convolute, convoluted, involuted, lurching, resounding, reverberating, undulant, undulate, undulating

**n:** bolt, involution, scrolling, volution

**v:** furl, roll, trundle

## ROMANTIC

**a:** *cavalier,* chimerical, enticing, exotic, fanciful, glamorous, Gothic, idealistic, imaginative, melodramatic, picturesque, quixotic, Romanesque, sentimental, unrealistic, utopian, visionary

**n:** classicism, gest, idyll, romance, romanticism

## ROOF

**a:** tectiform

**n:** cupola, gable, parapet, rafter, truss

*roofless: alfresco,* homeless, hypaethral, upaithric

## ROOMY

**a:** ample, baggy, baronial, bulky, capacious, cavernous, commodious, large, spacious, voluminous

## ROOT

**a:** chronic, confirmed, fixed, immobile, ineradicable, ingrained, inveterate, radical, radicated, rooted, sessile

**n:** radicle, rhizome, tuber

**v:** deracinate, eradicate, exterminate, extirpate

*combining forms:* -rac, rac-, radic-, rhiz-, rhizo-

## ROSTER

**n:** agenda, *agendum,* catalog(ue), directory, inventory, list, register, roll, *rota,* slate

## ROSY

**a:** auroral, aurorean, blooming, optimistic, radiant, reddish, rosaceous, roseate, rubicund, ruddy, sanguine

## ROT

**a:** abominable, *carious,* decomposed,

dying, festering, fetid, high, maturating, necrotic, off, perished, purulent, pustulating, putrefactive, putrefied, putrescent, putrifid, rancid, rank, rotten, rotting, *saprogeneous*, saprogenic, suppurating, termitic, ulcerous

n: *caries*, corruption, degeneration, *effluvium*, gangrene, mortification, *necrosis*, putrescence

v: corrupt, decay, decompose, degenerate, deteriorate, fester, maturate, perish, pustulate, putrefy, *putresce*, suppurate

*combining forms:* sapr-, sapro-

**ROTATE**

a: gyrating, rotary, rotating, vertiginous

n: circumduction, circumgyration, *torque*, vortex

v: alternate, circulate, circumduct, circumgyrate, circumvolve, gyrate, oscillate, *pirouette*, revolve, vertiginate

*combining form:* gyro-

**ROUGH**

a: abrasive, asperate, asperous, boisterous, choppy, crusty, harageous, hispid, hispidulate, hispidulous, inclement, keyed, rasping, robustious, scabrous, tartarly, turbulent, unpolished

n: asperity, burr, harshness, hispidity, inclemency, robusticity, roughness, scabrousness, snag, texture

**ROUND**

a: annular, circular, convex, cylindrical, gibbose, gibbous, globular, *helix*, orbicular, protuberant, rotund, spherical, spheriform, spheroid, spheroidal, spiral, volute, whorl

n: ball, circularity, globe, globosity, orb, orbicularity, rotundity, roundness, sphere, spheroidicity

*combining forms:* cycl-, cyclo-, glob-, spher-

**ROUNDABOUT**

a: ambagious, ambient, anfractuous, circuitous, circumlocutious, circumlocutory, devious, indirect, labyrinthian, labyrinthine, periphrastic, serpentine

n: anfractuosity, circuity, circularity, *circumbendibus*, circumlocution, indirection, periphrasis

**ROUT**

n: debacle, defeat, retreat, vanquishment

**ROUTINE**

a: administrative, customary, formal, functional, mechanical, ordinary, perfunctory, periodic, *pro forma*, stultifying, usual

n: habit, MO, *modus operandi*, pattern, regimen, repetition, rote, treadmill, way

**ROVING**

a: ambulatory, arrant, desultory, digressive, discursive, itinerant, migratory, mobile, nomadic, *peregrine*, peripatetic, roaming, vagrant, wandering

n: ambulation, nomadism, peregrination, peregrinism, peregrinity, vagrancy

**ROYAL**

a: basilic, dignified, gracious, kingly, palatine, regal

n: royalty

*symbol: diadem, regalia,* scepter

**RUBBISH**

n: debris, detritus, *ejectamenta*, nonsense, offal, offscouring, remains, rubble, scoria, trash, trumpery

**RUDE**

a: abrupt, abusive, awkward, barbarous, bawdy, bold, brusque, contumelious, crusty, curt, dedecorous, discourteous, disrespectful, earthy, impudent, indecorous, insolent, inurbane, irreverent, prurient, racy, *risque*, salty, scatological, smutty, suggestive, terse, unceremonious, uncivil, uncourtly, uncouth, ungracious, unmannered, unmannerly, unsavory

n: barbarism, contumely, disrespect, expletive, impudence, incivility, insult, profanity, rudeness

**RUDIMENTARY**

a: abecedarian, abecedary, abortive,

beginning, contingent, elementary, embryonic, fragmental, fundamental, germinal, imperfected, inchoate, inchoative, incipient, incomplete, initial, nascent, potential, primary, undeveloped, vestigal

**RUIN**

**a:** baneful, cataclysmic, catastrophic, damnatory, destructive, disastrous, *flambe*, hopeless, kaput, malignant, perdue, pernicious, ruined, ruinous

**n:** annihilation, bankruptcy, blight, cataclysm, catastrophe, collapse, debris, decay, desolation, despoliation, detritus, devastation, dilapidation, downfall, excavation, havoc, holocaust, perdition, rubbish, ruins, undoing

**v:** desolate, destroy, devastate, ravage, scuttle, vandalize, vitiate, wrack

**RULE**

**a:** administrative, consuetudinary, conventional, *de rigueur*, executive, exemplary, ironclad, normative, orthodox, precedential, prescriptive, programmatic, reglementary, regnal, regnant, regulatory, reigning, ritualistic, ruling, stringent

**n:** administration, authority, axiom, canon, code, covenant, creed, criteria, criterion, decree, *dictum*, discipline, dominion, imperative, maxim, method, methodology, ordinance, precedent, precept, predomination, principle, protocol, regency, regime, regimen, regnancy, reign, rubric, technique, tenet, theorem, touchstone, yardstick

**v:** administer, determine, govern, predominate, preponderate

*absolute:* tyrannis, tyranny

*combining forms:* -arch, -archy, -cracy, -ocracy

*equal:* pantisocracy

*individual:* autocracy, monarchy, monocracy

*joint:* condominium, synarchy

*ruler:* dictator, *dynast*, *pantocrator*, potentate, protector, regent

*set:* constitution, *decalogue*, discipline, *magna carta*, *organon*

**RUMINANT**

**a:** bovid, bovine, meditative

**n:** bovine

**RUMOR**

**n:** canard, gossip, grapevine, hearsay, notoriety, prattle, roorback, scuttlebutt

**RUNDOWN**

**a:** debilitated, depleted, dilapidated, enervated, exhausted, squalid, tatterdemalian, worn out

**RUNNING**

**a:** continuous, cursive, cursorial, linear

*opposite:* countercourant, countercurrent

**RURAL**

**a:** agrarian, agrestic, agricultural, Arcadian, backwoodsy, bucolic, campestral, churlish, countrified, geoponic, georgic, idyllic, pastoral, peasant, provincial, rustic, sylvan, villatic

**n:** pastorality, peasantry, provincialism, rurality, rusticism, rusticity

*person:* bumpkin, clodhopper, hayseed, hick, mossback, peasant, rustic, simpleton, yokel

**RUSH**

**a:** Gaderine, impetuous, irrupt, precipitate, precipitous, torrential

**n:** avalanche, exigency, impetuosity, precipitation, rampage, spate, stampede

**RUST**

**a:** aeruginous, ferruginous, rubiginous

**n:** *aerugo*, *patina*, *verdigris*

**RUTHLESS**

**a:** barbaric, pitiless, *procrustean*, relentless, revengeful, savage, tough, unsparing, wild

## SACRED

**a:** consecrated, dedicated, divine, hallowed, ineffable, inviolable, inviolate, numinous, profane, sacramental, sacramentary, sacrosanct, sainted, sanctified, secular, taboo, venerated

**n:** sacramentality, sacredness, sacrosanctity, sanctification, sanctitude, sanctity

**v:** consecrate, enshrine, sanctify

> *combining forms:* hier-, hiero-
>
> *thing: halidome, palladium, sacramentalia,* sanctuary, shrine

## SACRIFICE

**a:** *piacular,* sacrificatory, sacrificial

**n:** deprivation, *hecatomb,* immolation, libation, *moloch,* oblation, offering, sacrification

**v:** immolate

## SACRILEGE

**a:** blasphemous, hypocritical, impious, irreverent, profane, sacrilegious

**n:** blasphemy, desecration, impiety, profanation

## SAD

**a:** atrabiliar, atrabilious, baleful, bleak, cheerless, crestfallen, dejected, desolate, despondent, disconsolate, dismal, distressing, doleful, dolent, dolorific, dolorous, downcast, elegiac, forlorn, funereal, inconsolable, lachrymal, lamentable, lovelorn, lugubrious, melancholic, melancholy, morbid, mournful, pathetic, pensive, plaintive, sepulchral, somber, sorrowful, sullen, woebegone, wretched

**n:** dejection, depression, doldrums, dreariment, forlornity, gloominess, languishment, lugubrosity, *megrims, melancholia,* melancholy, sadness, *weltschmerz*

## SAFE

**a:** certain, impregnable, invulnerable, reliable, unassailable, unconquerable

**n:** asylum, *palladium,* protection, refuge, safeguard, safety, safety net, sanctuary, stronghold

**v:** safeguard

## SAGE

**a:** acuminous, discerning, intellectual, judicious, Nestorian, perspicacious, profound, prudent, sagacious, *sapient,* smart, wise

**n:** Nestor, philosopher, pundit, *savant,* Solomon

## SAINTLY

**a:** angelic, beatific, holy, joyful, pietistic, sacred, seraphic

**n:** angel, saint

**v:** beatify, canonize

> *combining forms:* hagi-, hagio-
>
> *worship: dulia,* hagiolatry, hagiology, hierolatry

## SALARY

**a:** remunerative, stipendiary

**n:** allowance, compensation, emolument, *honorarium,* payment, profit, recompense, remuneration, stipend, wages

## SALE

**a:** marketable, mercenary, merchantable, salable, venal, vendible

**n:** spiel, vendition

## SALIVA

**n:** ptyalism, salivation, spit, spittle, sputum

**v:** drool, slaver, slobber

**SALT**
**a:** saliferous, saline
**n:** condiment, Epsom, salinity
**v:** salify

**SALUTE**
**a:** salutatory
**n:** allocution, compliment, praise, salutation, toast
**v:** congratulate

**SALVATION**
**a:** soterial, soteriological
**n:** absolution, atonement, deliverance, extrication, liberation, manumission, *nirvana*, preservation, redemption, regeneration, reprieve, soteriology
**v:** elect

**SALVE**
**n:** cerate, cream, goo, inunction, ointment, remedy, unction, unguent

**SAME**
**a:** adequate, alike, coeval, cognate, commensurate, congeneric, congenerous, congruent, consubstantial, contemporary, equiponderant, equipotent, equipotential, equivalent, homogeneous, identical, isonomous, symmetrical, synonymous, tantamount
**n:** analogy, clone, concurrency, congruency, consubstantiality, contemporaneity, coordinate, duplicate, equality, equiponderation, equivalence, homogeneity, identicality, parity, sameness, simultaneity, *status quo*, synchronicity, unanimity
**v:** constitute, equate
   *combining forms:* aut-, auto-, hom-, homo-, is-, iso-, sym-, syn-, taut-, tauto-

**SAMPLE**
**n:** archetype, cross section, exemplar, exemplification, microcosm, pattern, prototype, replica, specimen, swatch

**SANCTION**
**a:** authorized, conventional, institutive,

legitimate, official, orthodox, sanctioned
**n:** approbation, countenance, credit, dispensation, imprimatur, indulgence, license, permit, ratification, sufferance, suffrage
**v:** approbate, countenance, encourage, ratify, vouchsafe
   *sign: cachet*, hallmark, *imprimatur*

**SANCTITY**
**a:** holier-than-thou, *pharisaic*, pietistic, *religiose*, sanctimonious, self-righteous
**n:** beatification, godliness, holiness, inviolability, piosity, purity, religiosity, sacredness, saintliness, sanctimoniousness, sanctimony

**SANCTUARY**
**a:** oasitic
**n:** adytum, asylum, haven, hospice, oasis, penetral, *sacrarium, sanctum, sanctum sanctorum*
**v:** sanctuarize

**SAND**
**a:** *acervulus, ammophilous, arenaceous, arenicolous, sabulous*, sandy
**n:** silica, silt, warp

**SANE**
**a:** coherent, competent, *compos mentis*, conscious, logical, lucid, rational
**n:** competence, lucidity, rationality, sanity

**SANITARY**
**a:** clean, clinical, hygienic, sterile, surgical
**n:** sanification, sterilization
**v:** autoclave, sanify, sanitize, sterilize

**SARCASM**
**a:** abusive, acidulous, acrimonious, belittling, caustic, cynical, facetious, incisive, ironical, mocking, mordacious, mordant, sarcastic, sardonic, satirical, scornful, snide, sulfurous, sulphurous, trenchant, virulent, vitriolic, withering

n: aspersion, cynicism, derision, invective, irony, satire

**SASSY**

a: abusive, contemptuous, contumelious, despicable, disdainful, impertinent, impudent, insolent, irreverent, malapert, officious, saucy

n: abuse, arrogance, boldness, contemptibility, contumely, impertinence, impudence, insolence, procacity, protervity, sassiness, sauciness

**SATIRE**

a: *hudibrastic*, ironic, ironical, *pantagruelian*, sarcastic, sardonic, sardonical, satiric, satirical

n: burlesque, cynicism, diatribe, irony, lampoon, mock-heroic, parody, *pasquinade, pastiche, philippic*, raillery, sarcasm, sardonicism, skit, spoof, squib, travesty

v: ape, mimic

   *satirist: farceur, Pantagruelist, railleur,* sillographer

**SATISFACTION**

a: complacent, resting on laurels, satisfactory, satisfied, vicarious

n: atonement, complacency, contentment, gratification, indemnification, oblectation, reconciliation, repletion, restitution, satiability, satiation, satiety

v: appease, atone, convince, fulfill, gratify, indemnify, indulge, pander to, please, quench, reconcile, sate, satiate, satisfy, slake

   *hard to:* implacable, inexorable, insatiable, unappeasable

**SATURATION**

n: concentration, imbibition, impregnation, intensity, interpenetration, permeation, satiation, satiety, surfeit

v: imbue, impregnate, infuse, interpenetrate, permeate, pervade, saturate

**SAVAGE**

a: barbarous, feral, ferocious, heathen-

ish, inhuman, pagan, relentless, uncivilized, untamed, wild

n: barbarian, ferity, primitive

**SAVIOUR**

a: messianic

n: benefactor, deliverer, emancipator, liberator, messiah, preserver, redeemer, savior

**SAVORY**

a: ambrosial, appetizing, delectable, delicious, edifying, flavorous, fragrant, gustable, gustatory, nectareous, palatable, *piquant*, savorous, sweet, tasteful, toothsome, wholesome

**SAYING**

a: apothegmatic, gnomic, sentient

n: adage, aphorism, apophthegm, apothegm, *bon mot, dictum*, epigram, gnome, maxim, *mot*, motto, *obiter dictum*, precept, saw, slogan, witticism

   *trite:* banality, bromide, byword, cliche, platitude, *shibboleth*, stereotype, truism

**SCABBY**

a: desquamative, scabrous

n: eschar, scabrousness

**SCALE**

a: mailed, paleiform, scabrous, scaly, scutate, scutellate, squamous

n: desquamation, diapason, exfoliation, furfuration, gamut, gradationdespumation, incrustation, *lamella*, lamina, proportion, *ramentum*, scaliness, squama, squamosity

v: desquamate, exfoliate

   *combining forms:* lepid-, lepido-

**SCAMP**

n: black sheep, knave, rapscallion, rogue, scalawag, *scaramouche*, scoundrel, trickster

**SCANDAL**

**a:** atrocious, disreputable, flagitious, flagrant, heinous, infamous, malodorous, notorious, outrageous, scandalous, villainous

**n:** aspersion, *cause celebre*, defamation, *expose*, infamy, obloquy

**SCANTY**

**a:** bare, exiguous, inadequate, infinitesimal, lean, parsimonious, shy, slight, thin

**n:** barrenness, exiguity, frugality, parcity, paucity, scantiness, scarcity, stringency

**SCAR**

**n:** *cicatrice, cicatrix,* cicatrization, *keloid,* stigma, suture, *ulosis*

**v:** cicatrize, disfigure, scarify

**SCARCITY**

**n:** dearth, deficiency, exiguity, famine, inadequacy, insufficiency, lack, parcity, paucity, rareness, rarity, stringency, uncommonness

**SCARE**

**a:** apprehensive, cowardly, craven, fretful, intimidated, jittery, lily-livered, panic-stricken, paranoid, petrified, scared, timorous, tremulous, unnerved

**n:** fear

**v:** affright, agrise, cow, frighten, intimidate, panic, petrify, terrorize

> *scarecrow:* bugaboo, ragamuffin, tatterdemalian

**SCATHING**

**a:** caustic, corrosive, harsh, hateful, hurtful, mordant, sarcastic, severe, sulfurous, sulphurous, truculent, virulent, vitriolic, vituperative

**n:** causticity, corrosiveness, mordancy, vituperation

**SCATTER**

**a:** broadcast, discrete, disunited, infrequent, interspersed, isolated, scattered, sporadic, straggly, vagrant

**n:** *diaspora,* diffusion, disbursion, dispersion, dissemination, distribution, promulgation, scatteration, scattering, sporadicity

**v:** decentralize, derange, disband, dispel, disperse, disseminate, dissipate, diverge, diversify, intersperse, promulgate, rout, spread, strew

**SCENE**

**a:** kaleidoscopic, panoramic, phantasmagoric

**n:** *mise-en-scene,* panorama, *phantasmagoria,* phantasmagory, prospect, *tableau, tableau vivant,* venue, vista

> *combining form:* -scape

**SCENT**

**a:** aromatic, fragrant, odiferous, odorous, perfumed, pungent, redolent, scented

**n:** aroma, aura, bouquet, *cachet,* cologne, *eau de cologne,* effluvia, *effluvium,* essence, fragrance, perfume, potpourri, redolence, *sachet*

**SCHEDULE**

**n:** agenda, agendum, appointments, curriculum, inventory, list, menu, plan, program, *programme,* prospectus, regime, tariff, timetable

**SCHEME**

**a:** calculating, conniving, crafty, schematic, scheming, shrewd, stratagematic

**n:** architectronics, cabal, *cadre,* hypothesis, machination, stratagem, strategy

**v:** contemplate, contrive, machinate, plot, premeditate

**SCHOLAR**

**a:** academic, erudite, learned, philomathic, scholarly, scholastic

**n:** academician, academist, *intelligentsia, literati, literato, litterateur,* pandit, pedant, person of letters, philomath, polyhistor, polymath, pundit, *savant*

> *scholarliness:* erudition, scholarship

**SCHOOL**

**a:** academic, collegiate, scholastic, scholastical

**n:** academia, academy, *alma mater*, college, conservatory, gymnasium, *lycee*, prep school, scholasticism, university, *yeshiva*

   *fellow:* condisciple

   *graduate:* alumna, alumnae, alumni, alumnus

**SCIENTIFIC**

**a:** clinical, empirical

**n:** science

   *club:* athenaeum

   *combining forms:* -graphy, -logy, -nomy, -sophy

**SCOLD**

**a:** castigatory, scolding, termagant, vituperative

**v:** admonish, berate, castigate, censure, chastize, chide, criticize, excoriate, lambaste, objurgate, reprimand, reproach, reprove, upbraid, vilify, vituperate

**SCOPE**

**a:** comprehensive, jurisdictional, latitudinal, latitudinous, panoramic, scopic

**n:** ambit, bailiwick, cognizance, compass, comprehensiveness, diapason, domain, extent, gamut, jurisdiction, latitude, leeway, lexicon, orbit, panorama, preserve, province, purview, radius, range, spectrum

**SCORN**

**a:** contemptible, contemptuous, derisible, derisive, despicable, disdainful, disparaging, haughty, opprobrious, overweening, sardonic, scornful, supercilious

**n:** arrogance, asteism, condescension, contempt, contumely, derision, despicability, disdain, *hauteur, opprobrium*

**SCOTTISH**

**a:** Caledonian

**n:** Caledonian, Gael, Scotsman

**SCOUT**

**n:** exploration, reconnaissance, *reconnoiter, vedette*

**v:** explore, *recce, reconnoiter*

**SCRATCH**

**n:** abradant, *cicatrix,* cicatrization

**v:** abrade, cicatrize, grabble, lacerate, obliterate, scarify, score, scuff

**SCREAM**

**a:** clamorous, screaming, stentorian, vociferous

**n:** caterwaul, clamor, protestation, vociferation

**v:** caterwaul, cry, protest, screech, ululate, vociferate

**SCRIBBLING**

**a:** scribbled

**n:** cacography, *graffiti, graffito,* griffonage, hieroglyphics

   *scribe:* amanuensis, copyist, scrivener

**SCRUPLE**

**a:** compunctious, conscientious, fastidious, meticulous, painstaking, precise, punctilious, rabbinical, scrupulous

**n:** compunction, doubt, hesitation, meticulosity, peculiarity, penitence, punctiliousness, qualm, scrupulosity, suspicion, wait, wavering

**SEA**

**a:** bahypelagic, bathybic, bathysmal, benthopelagic, littoral, maricolous, marine, maritime, nautical, naval, oceanic, pelagic, thalassic

**n:** brine, briny, briny deep, gulf, main, mare, ocean, spume

   *beyond:* transmarine, ultramarine

   *combining forms:* hal-, halo-, mar-, naut-, pellag-, thallas-

   *plane:* hydroplane, pontoon

   *seaman:* matelot

   *sickness: mal de mer, naupathia, nausea marina,* woozy

*study:* oceanography, thalassography

*weed:* kelp, varec

**SEAL**

**n:** *bulla, cachet,* great seal, *imprimatur,* privy seal

   *study:* sigillography, sphragistics

**SEAM**

**n:** cicatrix, cicatrization, commisure, crease, fold, groove, hem, juncture, layer, *raphe,* ridge, stratum, suture, synchrondrosis, union

**SEARCH**

**a:** expiscatory, inquisitive, inquisitorial, inquisitory, scrutinous, searching

**n:** expiscation, exploration, foray, inquiry, inquisition, perlustration, perusal, *reconnaissance,* safari, scrutiny

**v:** cast about, delve, drag, expiscate, explore, forage, fossick, frisk, investigate, perlustrate, probe, reconnoiter, rummage, scavenge, scrutinize, winnow

   *document:* warrant

   *searcher:* disquisitor, inquisitor, investigator, querist, researcher

**SEASON**

**a:** auspicious, convenient, expedient, opportune, propitious, seasonable, timely

**n:** autumn, fall, spring, summer, winter

**v:** accustom

**SECLUDE**

**a:** ascetic, cloisteral, cloistered, deserted, desolate, enisled, hermitic, isolated, monastic, out-of-the-way, removed, secluded, seclusive, secreted, sequestered, unfrequented, withdrawn

**n:** detachment, isolation, retirement, seclusion, sequestration, solitude

**v:** cache, hide, isolate, protect, secrete, sequester

**SECOND**

**a:** accessorial, accessory, ancillary, attendant, auxiliary, *beta,* collateral, consequential, derivational, derivative, epiphenomenal, incidental, secondary, subaltern, subordinate, subservient, subsidiary, substandard, tangential, tributary

**n:** afterthought, footnote, postscript, tuism

   *combining forms:* by-, sub-

**SECRET**

**a:** abstruse, acroamatic, apocryphal, arcane, auricular, cabalistic, clandestine, classified, collusive, collusory, concealed, confidential, confidentially, conspiratorial, covert, cryptic, cryptogenic, enigmatic, epoptic, esoteric, furtive, hidden, hushhush, *in camera, incognito,* intimate, mysterious, occult, privy, recondite, secretly, stealthy, *sub rosa,* surreptitious, topdrawer, veiled

**n:** *ambage, apocrypha, arcana, arcanum, arcanum arcanorum,* cabal, cabalism, *cache,* clandestinity, collusion, confidentiality, connivance, conspiracy, *esoterica,* intelligence, intrigue, *junto,* machination, *penetrale,* privity, secrecy, stash

   *affair: amour,* assignation, conclave, intrigue, liaison, rendezvous, tryst

   *combining forms:* crypt-, crypto-

   *name:* cryptonym

   *place: adytum, penetrale,* rendezvous, *sanctum sanctorum,* tryst

   *teaching:* acousmatics, *acroamata,* acroamatics, *arcana, cabalas, esoterica*

**SECTION**

**a:** disjunctive, multipartite, provincial, provisional, sectional

**n:** clause, component, division, part, piece, portion, segment

**SECULAR**

**a:** civil, laic, lay, mundane, nonclerical, profane, temporal

**n:** secularity

**v:** secularize, temporalize

## SECURE

**a:** *a couvert*, dependable, impregnable, inalienable, inviolable, invulnerable, restricted, safe, tight, trustworthy

**n:** collateral, confidence, guarantee, guaranty, mooring, pledge, protection, security, stability, surety

sedentary

**a:** fixed, immobile, sedent, sessile, stationary

## SEDIMENT

**n:** *alluvium*, deposit, dregs, hypostasis, lees, precipitate, recrement, remains, *residuum*, scoria, scoriae, sedimentation, silt

## SEDUCE

**a:** alluring, seductive

**n:** debauchery, debauchment, seducement, seduction

**v:** allure, corrupt, debauch, entice

    *seducer:* Circe, Don Juan, ladykiller, Lothario, rake, seductress, *succubus*, vampire

## SEE

**v:** apprehend, ascertain, comprehend, descry, detect, discern, distinguish, envision, espy, look, penetrate, perceive, remark, understand, visualize, witness

## SEED

**a:** granivorous, seminal, seminivorous, viviparous

**n:** *acinus*, boll, legume, ovule

**v:** germinate

    *combining forms:* -gon, gon-, gono-, grani-, -sperm

## SEEKING

**a:** appealing, appetent, exploring, pursuing

**n:** appetency, desideration

## SEEMING

**a:** apparent, nominally, ostensible, ostensive, professed, purported, quasi, reputedly, seemingly, semblable, specious, verisimilar, virtual

**n:** parallax, versimilitude, versimility

## SEGREGATE

**a:** isolated, segregable, segregated, segregative

**n:** isolation, segregation

**v:** ghettoize, isolate, separate, sequester

## SEIZE

**a:** confiscatory, seizing

**n:** confiscaton, eminent domain, impressment, manucapture, orgasm, paroxysm, preemption, seizure, sequestration, spoliation

**v:** afflict, annex, appropriate, arrogate, commandeer, confiscate, embargo, impound, intercept, levy, pillage, preempt, rapine, sequester, take, usurp

## SELECTION

**a:** discriminative, eclectic, selected, selective

**n:** *analecta*, analects, anthology, chrestomathy, *collectanea*, discrimination, eclecticism, selectivity

**v:** choose, select

## SELF

**a:** ascetic, autogenic, autogenous, automatic, automatous, autonomic, autonomous, autotheistic, endogenous, narcissistic, narcistic, subjective

**n:** ego, egocentrism, individualization, ipseity, narcissism, personality, *proprium*, *psyche*, selfhood, substantive

**v:** -educated

    *-assured:* confident, sophomoric

    *-centered:* autotheistic, conceited, egocentric, egotistic(al), individualistic, introversive, selfish

    *combining forms:* aut-, auto-

    *-condemnatory:* apperceptionistic, com-punctious, intropunitive, penitent, remorseful, self-accusatory

    *-contained:* autonomous

*-contradicting:* antinomic, paradoxical

*-control:* abnegation, abstinence, aplomb, ascesis, asceticism, automaton, calmness, continence, poise, temperance

*-denial:* abnegation, abstinence, ascesis, humility

*-importance: amour,* arrogance, autophilia, conceit, consequentiality, egocentricity, flatulence, illuminism, introversion, narcissism, pomposity, pursiness

*other: alter ego,* alteregoism, *alter idem*

respect: *amour-propre*

*-righteous:* hypocritical, pharisaic, pietistic, rectitudinous, sanctimonious

*-satisfied:* complacent, vainglorious

*-sufficiency: aseitas,* aseity, confidence, perseity, resourcefulness, smugness

## SELFISH

**a:** asocial, egocentric, egotistic(al), expedient, gluttonous, intemperate, narcissan, narcissistic, narcistic, self-aggrandizing, self-centered, self-serving

**n:** asociality, autism, egocentricity, egoism, hedonism, introversion, iotacism, *outrecuidance,* self-love, self-satisfaction, selfhood, selfishness, solipism

> *person:* egocentric, egocentrist, egotist, hedonist, iotacist, misanthropist, narcissist, solipsist, sycophant

> *selfless:* altruistic

## SENILE

**a:** aged, anecdotal, *caducous,* decrepit, senescent, superannuated, venerable

**n:** Alzheimer's, anecdotage, anility, caducity, dotage, senescence, senility, superannuation

> *study:* geriatrics, nostology

## SENIOR

**n:** dean, *doyen, doyenne,* precedence, precedency, priority, seniority

## SENSATION

**a:** kinesthetic, perceptible, sensate, sensible, sensiferous, sensific, sensorial, sensory, sensual, sensuous, synesthetic

**n:** esthesia, kinesthesia, modalities, *noumenon,* perception, phenomenality, phenomenon, proprioception, receptor, sensibility

> *lacking:* anesthetic, hypalgesic, inanimate, insensate, insentient, paralgesic

> *more than one:* synesthetic

> *sensational:* arresting, extraordinary, melodramatic, phenomenal, sensationary, spectacular

> *transcending:* supersensory, supersensual

## SENSE

**n:** connotation, denotation, intendment, meaning, purport, signification

> *senseless:* fatuuous, insensate, irrational, irrelevant, nonsensical, pointless

## SENSIBLE

**a:** acute, aware, cognizant, conscious, judicious, material, perspicacious, philosophical, politic, prudent, rational, reasonable, sagacious, sapient

## SENSITIVE

**a:** allergic, fastidious, hyperalgesic, hyperesthetic, impressible, impressionable, leiodermatous, passible, sentient, subtle, susceptible, thin-skinned, vulnerable

## SENSUAL

**a:** anacreontic, carnal, concupiscent, concupiscible, epicurean, faustian, hedonic, hendonistic, irreligious, lurid, luxurious, orgiastic, scabrous, self-indulgent, sensualistic, sensuous, sultry, sybaritic, voluptuary, voluptuous

**n:** carnality, concupiscence, debauchery, dissolution, intemperance, sensualism, sensuality, sensuosity, sensuousness, sybaritism, worldliness

> *person:* epicure, hedonist, libertine, sybarite, voluptuary, *voluptueux*

**SENTENCE**

n: construction, syntax

*ambiguous:* amphibology

*backward and forward the same:* palindrome

*break thought:* antithesis, aposiopesis

*inverted:* anastrophe

*poor: anacoluthon*

*stop in middle:* abscission

**SENTIMENTAL**

a: bathetic, dramatic, maudlin, mawkish, melodramatic, nostalgic, poignant, romantic

n: *bathos,* hokum, *kitsch,* maudlinism, mawkishness, romanticism, schmaltz, sentimentalism

*weak:* cloying, conciliatory, insipid, maudlin, mawkish, nauseating, saccharine, wishy-washy

**SEPARATE**

a: asunder, centrifugal, cleft, cloven, compartmentalized, demarcative, departmentalized, detached, dialytic, discrete, disengaged, disjunctive, dissociative, distinct, distinguished, divisive, individual, schismatic, secluded, separated, separating, solitary, unaffiliated, unassociated

n: demarcation, deracination, detachment, dialysis, diremption, disarticulation, disjointure, disjunction, dissolution, distinction, distinctness, divarication, divergence, divorcement, divulsion, estrangement, individuality, parting, schism, seclusion, segregation, sejunction, separateness, separation, sequestration, severality

v: abstract, alienate, atomize, bifurcate, cleave, compartmentalize, cordon off, decollate, decompose, demarcate, departmentalize, deracinate, disaffiliate, disassociate, discriminate, disjoin, dislocate, dislodge, dismember, dissect, dissociate, distill, divaricate, diverge, divide, divorce, estrange, exclude, fractionalize, fragment, ghettoize, insulate, isolate, partition, quarantine, ramify, segment, segregate, sequester, subdivide, sunder, thresh, winnow

**SEQUENCE**

a: alphabetical, categorical chronological, consecutive, *en suite,* numerical, ordinal, sequacious, sequential

n: cascade, causality, concatenation, consecution, gamut, precedence, progression, sequacity, seriality, series, spectrum, succession

v: codify, collate, collocate, tabulate

*change:* permutation

*without:* aleatory, arbitrary, haphazard, random

**SERENE**

a: august, calm, easy, halcyon, limpid, placid, quiet, tranquil, undisturbed, unperturbed, unruffled

n: composure, equanimity, imperturbability, imperturbation, limpidity, *sangfroid,* serenity, tranquility

**SERF**

n: *colonus,* helot, *muzhik,* peasant, peon, *villein*

*serfdom:* bondage, helotism, helotry, peonage, servitude, subjection, thralldom

**SERIAL**

a: chronological, consecutive, ordered, sequential, seriatim, successive

n: alphabetization, cascade, categorization, catenation, chain reaction, cline, concatenation, continuum, *feuilleton,* gamut, gradation, hierarchization, hierarchy, iliad, medley, panorama, phantasmagoria, progression, sequence, seriality, series, spectrum, stratification, succession, suite

v: alphabetize, arrange, categorize, concatenate, hierarchize, serialize, stratify

*installment:* episode

**SERIOUSNESS**

a: acute, consequential, critical, deadpan, drastic, earnest, emphatic, fervent, formidable, grievous, heartfelt, humorless, intent, introspective, momentous, pensive, poker-faced, resolute, sedate, *serioso,* serious, significant, somber, staid, unmirthful

**n:** application, assiduity, conscientiousness, diligence, *gravitas*, gravity, sedateness, seriosity, sobriety, solemnity

**SERMON**

**a:** homiletic, sermonic

**n:** discourse, dissertation, exhortation, harangue, homily, lecture, lesson, message, moral, preachment, speech, tract

   *study:* homiletics, sermonology

**SERVANT**

**a:** ancillary, menial, servitorial

**n:** acolyte, amanuensis, *au pair*, bellhop, butler, chamberlain, chambermaid, domestic, *duenna*, esquire, *factotum, famulus*, flunky, Girl Friday, gofer, groom, lackey, Man Friday, menial, minion, page, *senechal*, serf, servitor, servitress, valet, varlet, vassal, yeoman

   *group:* retinue, suite, train

**SERVILE**

**a:** abject, compliant, cringing, deferential, fawning, imitative, menial, obsequious, parasitical, sequacious, servient, slavish, subordinate, subservient, sycophantic, toadyish, tractable

**n:** amenities, deference, facilities, ministrations, obsequiousness, obsequity, serfdom, service, servility, servitude, subservience, subserviency, sycophancy, toadyism

**SET**

**a:** *en suite*, ensconced, entrenched, fossilized, implacable, inflexible, intractable, inexorable, monolithic, ossified, rigid

**n:** battery, clique, ensemble, series

**v:** actuate, disabuse, *posit*

   *against:* contrapose

   *apart:* demarcate, discriminate, *enisle*, segregate, separate, sequester

**SETTING**

**n:** ambience, environment, locale, *milieu, mise-en-scene*, surroundings

**SETTLE**

**a:** ensconced, entrenched, immutable, inveterate, liquidated, resoluble, sedentary, sessile, settled, stable, steadfast, unswerving

**n:** accommodation, adaptation, colonization, compromise, disposition, habitation, harmonization, installation, liquidation, *quietus*, reckoning, reconciliation, sedentation, settlement, understanding

**v:** arbitrate, colonize, compose, conciliate, determine, establish, intercede, interpose, liquidate, mediate, moderate, reconcile, resolve, subside

**SEVEN**

**a:** septemviral, septenary, septennial, septennium, septuple

**n:** hebdomad, heptad, septenary, septuplicate

   *70-79:* septuagenarian, septuagenary

   *combining forms:* hebdo-, hept-, hepta-, sept-, septi-

   *days:* hebdomad, hebdomadal, hebdomatary

   *dwarfs:* Bashful, Doc, Dopey, Grumpy, Happy, Sleepy, Sneezy

   *group: septemvirate*

   *sins:* cardinal sins

   *years:* septennate, septennial, septennium

**SEVER**

**n:** disarticulation, disengagement, dissociation, dissolution, divorcement, severance

**v:** detach, disarticulate, disengage, disjoin, dissociate, divorce, separate

**SEVERAL**

**a:** divers, many, miscellaneous, myriad, sundry, various

**n:** polysynthesis

   *combining forms:* multi-, pluri-, poly-

**SEVERE**

**a:** arduous, ascetic, atrocious, austere, bluenosed, crucial, draconian, exacting, flagrant, grievous, harsh, heinous, inclement, inexorable, inflexible, ingravescent, ironclad, lamentable, moralistic, obdurate, Procrustean, Prustian, puritanical, rigorous, scathing, spartan, straitlaced, strict, stringent, Teutonic, tyrannical, uncharitable, unrelenting, vehement

**n:** austerity, harshness, inclemency, ingravescence, rigor, severity, stringency, vehemence

## SEX

**a:** ambisexual, ambosexual, androgynous, *dioecious*, epicene

**n:** dioecism, gender

*attraction to both:* amphigenous, bisexual

*attraction to opposite:* alleroticism, heterosexual, heterosexuality

*attraction to same:* homoerotic, homoeroticism, homosexual, homosexuality, uranism, uranist, urning

*development of interest:* altrigenderism

*double:* androgyneity, androgynous, androgyny, andrygyne, hermaphrodite, hermaphroditic, hermaphroditism, monoecious, monoecism, monoecy

*organs:* externalia, genitalia, naturalia, pudenda, vulva

## SEXUAL

**a:** amative, amatory, amorous, bawdy, erogenous, erotic, passionate, sexy, venereal, voluptuary

**n:** alleroticism, carnal knowledge, coition, coitus, concubitus, copulation, eroticism, heteroticism, libido, lustihood, *pareunia*, passion, potency, sexiness, venery

*abstinence:* chastity, continence, virginity

*arousing:* aphrodisiac

*craving:* aidiomantia, andromania, aphrodisia, *ardor veneris*, erogeneity, erogeny, eroticism, erotogenesis, erotomania, erotopathy, gynecomania, nymphomania, satyriasis

*inability:* impotence, impotency

*mistreatment:* algolagnia, masochism, paraphilia, sadism

*stimulating:* aphrodisiac, erogenous, erotic, erotogenic

*things:* erotica, pornography

*watching:* scopophilia, voyeurism

## SHABBY

**a:** abject, contemptible, despicable, deteriorated, dilapidated, dishonorable, dog-eared, dowdy, low, mangy, mean, paltry, poor, sordid, squalid, tacky, tatterdemalian, threadbare, unfair, untidy

**n:** shabbiness, squalidity

## SHADE

**a:** adumbral, bosky, macroscian, penumbral, sciophilous, shady, tenebrous, umbrageous, umbriferous

**n:** adumbration, aura, *frescade*, nuance, obscurity, penumbra, protection, shadow, skiagraphy, twilight zone, umbra, umbrage, umbrella

**v:** adumbrate, cross-hatch, inumbrate

*painting:* chiaroscuro, hatching, *sfumato*, tenebrism

*shadow-boxing:* sciamachy

*shady:* devious, disreputable, dubious, questionable, suspicious, uncertain, unreliable

## SHAGGY

**a:** bushy, comate, hairy, hirsutal, hirsute, unkempt, woolly

**n:** hirsutism

## SHAKESPEARE

**a:** Stratfordian

**n:** Stratfordian

*love:* bardolatry

## SHAKING

**a:** quavering, tremorous, tremulous

**n:** quaver, tremblement, tremor, tremulation

**v:** teeter, totter

**SHALLOW**

**a:** artificial, cosmetic, cursory, facile, frivolous, glib, inane, incondite, magazinish, sophomoric, specious, superficial, tenuous, token, trifling, trivial

**n:** emptiness, inanity, shallowness, shoal, sounding, speciosity, superficiality, tenuosity, triviality

**SHAM**

**a:** adulterated, apocryphal, artificial, bogus, *Brummagem,* dissimulative, factitious, *postiche,* pseudo, simulated, spurious

**n:** affectation, deceitfulness, deception, dissemblance, dissimulation, hyprocrisy, imposture, *legerdemain,* pretense, sciamachy, simulacrum, tokenism, travesty

**v:** counterfeit, simulate, travesty

**SHAME**

**a:** degrading, disgraceful, indecent, infamous, inglorious, ingnominious, outrageous, shameful

**n:** abashment, chagrin, degradation, discomfiture, disgrace, dishonor, embarrassment, humiliation, ignominy, infamy, modesty, mortification, opprobrium, prudishness, pudency, reproach, stigma

**v:** abash, discomfit, disconcert, discountenance, disgrace, dishonor

   *shameless:* arrant, brassy, brazen, immodest, impudent, outrageous, *sans pudeur,* unabashed, unblushing, unmitigated

**SHAPE**

**a:** curvaceous, determinative, formative, sculpturesque, shapely, shaping, statuesque, symmetrical

**n:** configuration, conformation, construction, contour, form, format, lineaments, outline, profile, silhouette

   *combining forms:* -form, -morph, morph-, -morphic, morpho-

   *shapeless:* amorphous, aplastic, heterogeneous, misshapen

   *similar:* homeomorphic, isomorphic

   *single:* momomorphous, monomorphic

**SHARE**

**a:** common, communal, joint, mutual

**n:** allocation, allotment, complicity, portion, quota, royalty

**v:** apportion, partake, participate

**SHARP**

**a:** acerbic, acrid, acuminate, angular, angulous, apiculate, caustic, hawkeyed, incisive, lyncean, mordant, *piquant,* poignant, pungent, sarcastic, trenchant

**n:** acuity, acutance, angularity, definition, keenness, mordacity, resolution, sarcasm, spinosity, tang

**v:** hone, sharpen, strop, whet

   *combining forms:* aichmo-, belone-, oxy-

**SHAVING**

**n:** pogonotomy, shave, tonsure

   *stick:* styptic pencil

**SHED**

**a:** deciduate, deciduous, desquamative, exfoliative, shedding

**n:** autotomy, desquamation, ecdysis, exfoliation, exuviation, sloughing

**v:** desquamate, exfoliate, exuviate, molt, slough

**SHEEN**

**n:** brightness, brilliance, fluorescence, fulguration, glossiness, illumination, luminosity, luster, nitidity, patina, phosphorescence, radiance, refulgence, refulgency, scintillation, water

**SHEER**

**a:** absolute, complete, diaphanous, downright, gross, out-and-out, precipitous, pure, quite, tenuous, transparent, unmitigated, unmixed, utter

**SHEET**

**n:** membrane, ply, shroud

**v:** laminate

**SHELL**

**a:** bivalve, conchiferous, univalve

**n:** armature, carapace, chitin, cowrie, *cuirass*, cuticle, test

   *combining forms:* conch-, concho-
   *remove:* enucleate

**SHELTER**

**a:** cloistered, secluded, sequestered, sheltered

**n:** asylum, bivouac, cove, covering, coverture, haven, hospice, protection, refuge, retreat, sanctuary, sanctum

**v:** embosom, harbor, protect

**SHEPHERD**

**a:** bucolic, pastoral

**n:** Amaryllis, guide, herder, herdsman, herdswoman, shepherdess, watch

**SHERIFF**

**n:** marshal

   *deputy(ies):* bailiff, posse

**SHIELD**

**a:** clypeate, clypeiform, peltate, scutate, scutellate

**n:** aegis, buckler, escutcheon, *pavis*, shelter, targe, target, *testudo*, tortoise

**SHIFT**

**a:** elusive, evasive, fickle, inefficient, lubricious, metastatic, oleaginous, shifting, shifty, unreliable, unstable, vagabond, vagrant

**n:** lubricity, metabasis, metastasis

**v:** change, drift, fluctuate, intermit, metastasize, shuffle, transfer, transpose, vary

   *person:* flotsam and jetsam, prodigal, vagabond

**SHIN**

**n:** *antecnemion, cnemis, crus,* shank, shinbone, tibia

**SHINING**

**a:** coruscating, effulgent, incandescent,

iridescent, lambent, lucent, lustrous, *nitid,* opalescent, phosphorescent, prefulgent, radiant, refulgent, relucent, resplendent, rutilant, scintillating, splendorous

**n:** burnish, luster, prefulgence, prefulgency, sheen, veneer

**v:** effulge, irradiate, phosphoresce, rutilate, scintillate, shine

**SHIP**

**a:** nautical, naval, navicular, navigable

**n:** boat, helm, steerage

   *wreckage:* flotsam, jetsam

**SHIRK**

**v:** avoid, evade, malinger, slack, sneak

   *shirker:* dodger, evader, goldbrick, malingerer, slacker

**SHOCKED**

**a:** aghast, appalling, dedecorous, degrading, deplorable, dismayed, frightened, humiliating, infra dig, jarred, offended, opprobrious, percussive, shocking, squeamish, ugly, vulgar

**n:** squeamishness

**SHORE**

**a:** littoral

**n:** bank, beach, land, littoral, sand, seacoast, seaside, strand, waterside

**SHORT**

**a:** abbreviated, abrupt, brief, compendious, concise, curtailed, deciduous, diminished, diminutive, ephemeral, expeditious, fugitive, gnomic, inadequate, insufficient, momentaneous, shortened, summary, terse, transient, transitory, truncated

**n:** abbreviation, abridgement, abstract, aphaeresis, apocopation, curtailment, digest, elision, ephemerid, ephemeron, epitome, *precis, resume,* retrenchment, syncopation, synopsis, transient, truncation

**v:** abbreviate, abridge, apocopate, condense, curtail, elide, shorten, syncopate, truncate *combining form:* brachy-

*in short:* basically, essentially, fundamentally

*piece: morceau,* cameo, vignette

*sighted:* astigmatic, myopic, purblind, strabismic

*winded:* dyspnoeic, pursy

## SHORTCOMING

n: blemish, defect, deficiency, dereliction, fault, foible, imperfection, remission, vice

## SHOUT

a: conclamant, conjubilant, fulminous, vociferous

n: conclamation, conjubilation, fulmination, hallelujah, *hosanna,* vociferation

v: bellow, conjubilate, cry, exclaim, fulminate, roar, scream, vociferate, yell

## SHOW

a: agonistic, baronial, baroque, blatant, *bravura, carnivalesque,* claptrap, deictic, demonstrative, dramatic, effusive, elenchtic, elenctic, flamboyant, garish, glitzy, grandiloquent, grandiose, *orgillous, orgulous,* ornate, ostensive, ostentatious, panoptic, pretentious, revelatory, *rococo,* showy, specious, splendorous, technicolor, theatrical

n: affectation, bric-a-brac, extravaganza, fanfare, floridity, flourish, furbelow, gaudiness, histrionism, orotundity, ostentation, pageantry, pomposity, pontificality, pretentiousness, showiness, theatricality, trumpery

v: attitudinize, demonstrate, evidence, evince, exhibit, flaunt, gaudify, glamorize, manifest, posture, prove, register, theatricalize

## SHREWD

a: acuminous, artful, astute, calculating, canny, careful, circumspect, diplomatic, discerning, heady, keen, knowing, *parlous,* penetrating, perspicacious, politic, prudent, reflective, sagacious, stratagematic, suave, wise

n: acumen, callidity, canniness, comprehension, craftiness, discrimination, perspicacity, sagacity, shrewdness

## SHRILL

a: calliopean, penetrating, strident, stridulous

n: chirp, shrillness, stridor, stridulation, treble

## SHRINE

n: *adytum,* mausoleum, reliquary, *sanctorium,* sanctuary, *sanctum sanctorum,* tabernacle

## SHRINK

a: abating, atrophic, atrophied, lessening, Sanforized, shrunk, shrunken, withdrawn, wizened

v: atrophy, contract, diminish, recoil, retract, telescope

## SHROUD

n: cerecloth, cerement, winding sheet

## SHRUB

a: arboresque, frutescent, topiary

n: arboret, boscage, brier, bush, foliage, topiary, tree

## SHUDDER

n: *frisson,* quake, tremor, tremulation, vibration

v: quake, quiver, shake, shiver, tremble

## SHUN

n: avoidance, eschewal, evasion, ostracism, *purdah*

v: avoid, disdain, eschew, evade

*person:* leper, pariah

## SHY

a: bashful, cautious, circumspect, constrained, demure, diffident, distrustful, hermetic, introverted, modest, pavid, reclusive, reserved, retiring, shamefaced, solitary, suspicious, tentative, timorous, unassuming, undemonstrative, verecund

n: bashfulness, coyness, diffidence, shyness, timidity, verecundity v: blench, demure, flinch, quail

**SICK**

a: *amort,* bilious, cachetic, chagrined, crapulent, crapulous, diseased, eager, indisposed, infirm, invalid, maladive, morbific, morbose, moribund, nauseous, queasy, sickly, unhealthy, unwholesome, valetudinarian, valetudinary, wretched

n: condition, crapulence, disease, paroxysm, qualm, seizure, sickness

v: deteriorate, nauseate, sicken

*pretend:* malinger

*sickening:* cloying, insipid, mawkish, nauseating, nauseous

**SICKLE**

a: falcate, falciform

**SIDE**

a: collateral, homolateral, homonymous, ipsilateral, juxtaposed, juxtapositional, lateral, paradromic, parallel, unilateral

n: broadside, profile

v: align, collocate, juxtapose

*both:* ambilateral, bilateral, bipartisan, bipartite, equilateral

*combining forms:* -gon, -gonal, -sided

*many:* multilateral, multiphasic, polygonal

*opposite:* contralateral, heteronymous, oppositional

**SIGH**

a: suspirous

n: sough, suspiration

v: breathe, suspirate

**SIGN**

a: augural, auspicious, emblematic, indicial, portentous, signific, symptomatic

n: adumbration, augury, criterion, divination, emblem, escutcheon, gesture, harbinger, hieroglyph, index, indication, *indicia, indicium,* logo, logogram, logograph, manifestation, monogram, portent, shingle, *signum,* symptom, vestige, warning

v: countersign, denote, endorse, gesticulate

*language:* dactylology

*of disease:* semiotics, stigma, symptom, syndrome

*signature:* autograph, curlicue, flourish, paraph, signum

*study:* semantics, semasiology, semiology, symptomatology

**SILENCE**

a: brachysyllabic, dumbstruck, inarticulate, inaudible, incommunicable, incommunicative, laconic, mute, passive, quiescent, reflective, reserved, retentive, reticent, silentious, speechless, *sub rosa,* tacit, taciturn, tranquil, uncommunicative

n: inarticulation, mussitation, muteness, obmutescence, quiescence, quietude, reticence, taciturnity, tranquility

*person:* pantomimist, Trappist

**SILKY**

a: diaphanous, sericeous

n: floss, *froufrou,* gossamer, silk

**SILVER**

a: argentiferous, argentine, argentous, silvery

n: filigree, luna, purl, sterling, tinsel

*combining form:* argent-

**SIMILAR**

a: akin, analogical, analogous, cognate, comparable, congruent, congruous, consonant, corresponding, duplicate, equivalent, homogeneous, homologous, homonymous, identical, indistinguishable, kindred, parallel, related, semblable, synonymous

n: affinity, analogue, analogy, community, counterpart, *doppelganger,* duplicate, homologue, kinship, metaphor, parallel, ringer, similarity, simile, symmetry

*combining forms:* homeo-, homo-, is-, iso-, -ose, para-, sym-, syn-

**SIMPLE**

a: accessible, artless, asinine, *au naturel,*

austere, bucolic, candid, clinical, conventionalized, credulous, easy, fatuous, guileless, homespun, humble, idyllic, ignorant, incomplex, incomplicate, inelaborate, ingenuous, intelligible, limpid, *naive*, pastoral, pellucid, perspicuous, primitive, rudimentary, rustic, simplified, translucent, transparent, person, uncomplicated

n: austerity, clarity, humility, intelligibility, *naivete*, simplicity, stereotype

v: clarify, generalize, informalize, paraphrase, reduce, simplify, streamline

*foolish:* answerine, asinine, fatuous

## SIMULATED

a: artificial, assumed, counterfeit, derivative, factitious, imitated

v: concoct, copy, counterfeit, fake, feign, mock, simulate

## SIN

a: culpable, depraved, flagitious, heinous, iniquitous, nefarious, peccable, piacular, sinful, unrepentant, venial, wicked

n: delict, depravity, immorality, iniquity, misdemeanor, peccability, *peccadillo*, peccancy, transgression, trespass, veniality, wickedness

v: transgress

*forgiveness:* absolution, remittance

*remorse:* contrition, penitence, repentance

*sinless:* impeccable, inculpable, innocent

## SINCERE

a: artless, bona fide, candid, devout, genuine, guileless, heartfelt, ingenuous, innocent, unaffected, unfeigned, unpretentious, wholehearted

n: candor, innocence, integrity, probity, sincerity, veracity

## SING

a: ariose, canorous, cantabile, cantatory, lyric, lyrical, melic, melodic, melodious, polyphonic, singing

n: *coloratura,* compass, descant, lyricism, melismatics, *obbligato,* register

v: cantillate, descant, intone, serenade, troll, warble, yodel

*singer:* cantor, chansonnier, chanteur, chanteuse, descanter, minstrel, precentor, *soubrette, troubadour,* vocalist

*song:* anthem, antiphony, *aria, canticle, chanson,* descant, doxology, hymn, lyric, *paen,* repertoire, rondo

*teacher: repititeur*

*voices: alto,* baritone, bass, *contralto,* countertenor, *mezzo-soprano,* tenor, treble

*without music: a capella*

*without music & solo:* monophonic, monophonous

*without sound:* mussitation

*writing: melopoeia*

## SINGLE

a: azygous, celibate, discrete, individual, particular, respectively, separate, singular, solitary, unique, unitary, unwedded

n: celibacy, individuality, particularity, peculiarity, singularity, specificity

v: particularize, specify

*combining forms:* mono-, uni-

## SISTER

a: sibling, sisterly, sororial

n: sibling

*group:* sisterhood, sorority

## SITTING

a: *in situ,* lotus, *sedent,* sedentary, situated

## SITUATION

a: predicamental, situational

n: conjuncture, dilemma, double bind, juncture, locality, plight, predicament, quandary, status

## SIX

a: hexadic, hexagonal, semestral, senary, sexagonal, sexangular, sextuple

**n:** hexad, hexagon, hexagram, semester, sextet, sextuplet

**v:** sextuple

*60-69:* sexagenarian, sexagenary, sexagesimal

*combining forms:* hex-, hexa-, sex-

*sense:* ESP, extrasensory perception

*sixteenth:* cinquecento

*years:* sexennial, sextennial

## SIZE

**n:** amplitude, caliber, dimension, dimensions, enormity, magnitude, proportions, volume

## SKELETON

**a:** cadaverous, skeletonic

**n:** armature, bones, *cadre*, cage, nucleus, phytotomy, support

## SKEPTICAL

**a:** aporetic, dissident, distrustful, dubious, dubitable, incredulous, negativistic, negatory, recusant

**n:** agnosticism, dogmatism, doubt, dubiety, dubiosity, dubitation, incredulity, negativism, negativity, *skepsis*, skepticism

*skeptic:* agnostic, *apikores, apikoros,* aporetic, disbeliever, doubting Thomas, freethinker, *giaour*, heretic, latitudinarian, nullifidian, pyrrhonist, zetetic

## SKETCH

**a:** adumbral, diagrammatic, sketchy, superficial

**n:** adumbration, *apercu*, cartoon, compendium, delineation, draft, outline, portrayal

**v:** adumbrate, draft, draw, *limn*, lineate, outline

*piece:* cameo, *feuilleton, vignette*

## SKILL

**a:** accomplished, adept, adroit, ambidexterous, *au fait*, competent, consummate, deft, dexterous, expert, *facile*, habile, ingenious, inventive, masterful, masterly, proficient, sciental, skilled, skillful, subtle, versatile, versed

**n:** adeptness, adroitness, ambidexterity, aptitude, art, artifice, competence, dexterity, efficiency, expertise, expertness, facility, faculty, finesse, *forte*, hability, ingeniosity, ingenuity, inventiveness, *metier, mystique,* prowess, repertoire, *savoir faire,* technique, virtuosity

## SKIM

**v:** *despumate,* glide, scud, skip, skitter

## SKIN

**a:** cutaneous, cuticular, dermal, epidermal, integumental

**n:** *cutis, dermis,* epidermis, fell, integument, *pelage,* pelt

*bumps:* horripilation, piloerection

*combining forms:* -derm, dermato-, dermo-

*dark:* melanochrous, melanous

*discoloration:* cyanosis, echymosis, jaundice, purpura

*red:* erythema

*sensitive:* hyperalgesic, hyperesthetic

*shedding:* desquamation, ecdysis, exfoliation, exuviation, molting, sloughing

*thick:* callous, pachydermatous, pachydermic

## SKINNY

**a:** cadaverous, emaciated, lean, malnourished, skeletonic, slender, tabescent, thin

**n:** malnutrition, skinniness

## SKIRMISH

**n:** battle, bout, clash, engagement, fight, fray, *recontre*, tilt, tournament, velitation

## SKULL

**a:** cephalic, pachycephalous

**n:** calvaria, cranium, skullcap, vertex

*combining forms:* -cephal, cephal-, cephalo-

*soft spot: fontanel(le)*

*thick:* pachycephalia, pachycephaly

**SKY**

**a:** *alfresco,* azure, celestial, cerulean, empyreal, firmamental, hypaethral, supernal, *upaithric*

**n:** atmosphere, empyrean, firmament, vault, welkin

> *combining forms:* uran-, urano-

**SLANDER**

**a:** calumnial, calumnious, defamatory, libelous, slanderous, vilifying

**n:** aspersion, calumniation, calumny, character assassination, defamation, execration, libel, malediction, traducement, traduction

**v:** calumniate, defame, denigrate, derogate, disparage, malign, revile, smear, traduce, vilify, vituperate

**SLANG**

**n:** argot, cant, colloquialism, dialect, jargon, *koine,* lingo, *lingua franca, patois,* pidgin, vulgarism

**SLAUGHTER**

**n:** *aceldama,* armageddon, carnage, hecatomb, holocaust, massacre

> *house: abattoir,* shambles

**SLAVE**

**a:** servile, slavelike

**n:** chattel, mameluke, mancipium, odalisk, odalisque, serf, servant

> *slavery:* bondage, helotism, helotry, peonage, servitude, subjection, thrall, thralldom, vassalage

**SLEEP**

**a:** comatose, dormant, dormitive, drowsy, hypnotic, latent, lethargic, oscitant, phlegmatic, quiescent, sleeping, sleepy, somnifacient, somniferous, somnolent, somnorific, soporiferous, soporific, yawning

**n:** dormancy, hibernation, hynosis, nap, quiescence, REM, repose, *siesta,* slumber, somnolence

**v:** estivate, hibernate, lull

> *abnormal:* somnipathy

> *combining forms:* hypn-, hypno-, morph-, narco-, somn-, somno-

> *daytime:* diurnation

> *deep:* coma, sopor, stupor

> *desire:* narcolepsy

> *drug:* hypnagogic, hypnotic, narcotic, opiate, somnolent, soporific

> *learning:* hypnopedia

> *sleeplessness:* insomnia, insomnolence

> *study:* hypnology

> *talk:* somniloquist

> *walk:* noctambulist, somnambulist

**SLENDER**

**a:** acicular, aciculate, gracile, lissome, lithe, lithesome, *soigne,* svelte, tenuous

**n:** gracility, slenderness, tenuity, thinness

**SLIGHT**

**a:** cursory, imperceptible, inconsiderable, insignificant, nominal, paltry, superficial, trivial

**n:** *bagatelle,* cut, denigration, detraction, disparagement, humiliation, *inconsequentia,* nihility, slur, snub, trivia, triviality

**v:** disparage, disregard, disrespect

**SLIMY**

**a:** glutinous, mucilaginous, offensive, oleaginous, saponaceous, unctuous, viscid, viscous

**n:** muck, ooze, slime, sludge

**SLIPPERY**

**a:** elusive, lubricious, slimy, smooth, treacherous, unreliable

**n:** lubricity, unctuosity

**SLOGAN**

**n:** catchword, logo, maxim, password, phrase, saying, *shibboleth,* watchword

**SLOPE**

**a:** acclivitous, declensional, declinatory, declivitous, inclined, oblique, perpendicular, precipitous, sloping n: acclivity, cant, declension, declination, decline, declivity, deviation, escarpment, *glacis*, gradient, inclination, perpendicularity, pitch, versant

v: bevel, slant, splay, traverse

　*combining forms:* -clin, clin-, clino-, plagi-, plagio-

**SLOPPY**

a: careless, dishevelled, effusive, gushing, haphazard, loose, messy, slovenly, tatterdemalian, unkempt

n: dishevelment, sloppiness

**SLOTH**

n: acedia, adynamia, inaction, inertia, lassitude, lethargy, otiosity, slothfulness, sluggishness, supinity, torpidity, *unau*

**SLOW**

a: *andante*, apathetic, bovine, comatose, costive, deliberate, dilatory, elephantine, lackadaisical, languescent, languid, languorous, leisurely, *lentago, lentissimo,* lethargic, listless, lumbering, phlegmatic, prolonged, protracted, purblind, sluggish, tardy, tedious, torpid, unenergetic, unprogressive

n: cunctation, inertia, lassitude, lethargy, osmosis, retardation, sloth, slowing, slowness, stasis, tediosity, torpidity

v: decelerate, procrastinate, recede, retard, slacken, subside, taper off, tarry

　*combining forms:* brady-, -stasis, -stat

　*witted:* adenoidal, cretinous, lumbering, moronic, stolid

**SLUGGISH**

a: adynamic, apathetic, indolent, inert, languescent, languorous, lethargic, listless, slothful, slow, stagnant, supine, torpid

n: inertia, lethargy, listlessness, logginess, slowness, sluggishness, torpidity

**SLUMP**

n: depression, dip, doldrums, drop, recession, repression, sag, slack

**SLUR**

n: aspersion, calumny, defamation, denigration, disparagement, elision, innuendo, insinuation, slight, vilification

v: asperse, denigrate, disparage, elide, slander

**SLY**

a: artful, astute, clandestine, cunning, diplomatic, disingenuous, duplicitous, furtive, guileful, ingenious, insidious, roguish, serpentine, sinuous, sneaky, stealthy, strategic, subtle, surreptitious, wily

v: insinuate

**SMALL**

a: atomic, diminutive, imperceptible, inappreciable, incommodious, infinitesimal, insignificant, lilliputian, little, microscopic, microsomatic, miniature, minikin, minimal, miniscular, miniscule, minute, petite, ultramicroscopic

n: dearth, diminutive, infinitesimality, insignificance, iota, lilliputian, midget, miniature, minitude, minnow, modicum, moiety, nihility, parvanimity, parvitude, paucity, pipsqueak, pittance, runt, semblance, smallness, *soupcon*

　*combining forms:* -cle, -cule, -ey, -ie, -kin, micro-, mini-, nano-, pico-, -ule, -y

　*letters:* lowercase, minuscule

　*smaller:* subliminal, subnominal, suboptimal

**SMART**

a: adroit, astute, dapper, intelligent, natty, rakish, *soigne,* spruce

v: smarten

**SMELL**

a: olfactory, osmagogue, osmatic, osphretic

n: aroma, atmosphere, aura, bouquet, effluvia, effluvium, fragrance, hyperosmia, incense, olfaction, osmesis, osphresis, redolence, scent

　*offensive:* fetid, frowsy, gamy, mephitic, musty, noisome, noxious, pestilential, rancid, rank, stale, stinking

*pleasant:* aromatic, fragrant, odoriferous, odorous, redolent

**SMILE**

**a:** beatific, smiling, subrident, subrisive

**n:** grin, rictus

**v:** grin, simper, smirk

**SMOOTH**

**a:** amiable, courteous, dolce, *dolcissimo,* easy, frictionless, glabrate, glabrescent, glabrous, glace, *legato, leiodermatous,* levigate, marmoreal, marmorean, mellifluous, oleaginous, saponaceous, sleek, unctuous, uninterrupted, velutinous

**n:** lubricity, polish, saponaceousness, smoothness, unctuosity

**v:** edulcorate, facilitate, palliate, polish, tranquilize

*sound:* fluent, glib, mellifluent, mellifluous, mellisonant, melodic, oleaginous, sonorous, unctuous

**SMUG**

**a:** affected, *bourgeoise,* complacent, contented, egocentric, pedantic, pretentious, priggish, self-satisfied

**n:** complacency, egocentricity, pedanticism, self-satisfaction, smugness

**SNAKE**

**a:** anguiform, anguinal, anguine, anguineous, colubrine, ophidian, reptilian, serpentiform, serpentine, sinuous

**n:** groveling, ophidian, reptile, reptilian, serpent

*love:* ophiolatry

*study:* herpetology, ophiology

**SNARE**

**n:** cajolement, enticement, inveiglement, lure, pitfall, subterfuge, trap, trick

**SNEAKY**

**a:** clandestine, cowardly, dishonest, duplicitous, furtive, low, mean, ophidian, perfidious, reptilian, serpentine, sinister,

sinuous, sly, stealthy, treacherous, two-faced

**SNEERING**

**a:** contemptible, cynical, derisive, ironical, sarcastic, sardonic, scoffing

**n:** cynicism, derision, irony, sarcasm, sardonism

**SNEEZE**

**a:** ptarmic, ptarmical, sternutative, sternutatory

**n:** *gesundheit,* sternutation

**SNOB**

**a:** chichi, haughty, hoity-toity, pedantic, pretentious, snobbish

**n:** *arriviste, nouveau riche, parvenu,* pedant

*snobbery:* arrogance, chichi, elitism, haughtiness, *hauteur,* pedantry, snobbishness

**SNORE**

**a:** rhonchial, stertorous

**n:** rale, rhonchus, roar, sniff, stertor

**SNOW**

**a:** nival, niveous, snowy, subnivean

**n:** blizzard, firn, graupel, *neve,* snowstorm

**SO-CALLED**

**a:** pretended, quasi, *soi-disant,* thus

*much the better: tant mieux*

*much the worse: tant pis*

**SOAK**

**a:** soaking

**n:** maceration

**v:** imbue, immerse, infuse, macerate, marinate, saturate, submerge

**SOAP**

**a:** saponaceous, soaplike, soapy

**v:** saponify

**SOBER**

**a:** abstemious, abstentious, ascetic, calm,

continent, dispassionate, moderate, self-controlled, temperate

**n:** ascesis, asceticism, continence, moderation, soberness, sobriety, temperance

## SOCIABLE

**a:** affable, amadelphous, companionable, convivial, festive, friendly, gregarious, hospitable, jolly, jovial

**n:** affability, conviviality, cordiality, extroversion, gregariousness, joviality, sociability, sociality

## SOCIAL

**a:** acculturational, acculturative, *comme il faut*, conventional, diplomatic, societal, sociogenic, suave

**n:** acculturation, association, companionship, conventionality, correctitude, *eclat, ethnos*, infrastructure, manners, *monde, savoir faire, savoir vivre*, scrupulosity, socialization, society, sodality, *stratum*, the establishment

**v:** consort, flirt, gallivant, hobnob, socialize

*charity:* confraternity, confraternization

*danger to:* pernicious, pestiferous, pestilent(ial)

*error:* blunder, *faux pas, gaffe*, impropriety, solecism

*fear:* anthropophobia, apanthropia, apanthropy

*group:* circle, clique, *coterie*, peers, set

## SOCRATES

**a:** maieutic, maieutical, Socratic

*method:* dialectic, maieutics, Socratic induction, Socraticism

## SOFTENING

**a:** crumbly, ductile, emollient, emulsive, flaccid, friable, lenitive, malleable, mitigatory, mollescent, *pianissimo*, pliable

**n:** maceration, mollescence, susurration, undertone

**v:** assuage, edulcorate, intenerate, macerate, mitigate, moderate, mollify, muffle, mute, palliate, soften, temper

*combining form:* malaco-

## SOIL

**a:** edaphic, pedologic(al), telluric, terrestrial

**n:** alluvium, loam, malm, silt

*combining forms:* agr-, agri-, agro-, ped-, pedo-

*study:* agrology, agronomics, agronomy, pedology

## SOLDIER

**a:** heroic, martial, military, soldierly

**n:** conscript, detail, guerrilla, mercenary, militia, orderly, partisan, recruit, volunteer

## SOLEMN

**a:** awe-inspiring, ceremonial, ceremonious, devout, dispassionate, formal, funereal, imposing, impressive, memorable, momentous, quiet, ritualistic, sedate, serious, sermonic, somber

**n:** ceremony, reverence, sedateness, solemnity

## SOLID

**a:** compact, concentrated, concretionary, massive, monolithic, ponderable, substantial, unanimous

**v:** clot, coagulate, congeal, curdle, solidify

*combining forms:* stere-, stereo-

*process:* calculus, concretion, concretization, gelation, solidification

## SOLITARY

**a:** desolate, hermitic, individual, isolated, ivory-towered, monophonic, monophonous, reclusive, secluded, sequestered, solitudinarian, solo

**n:** hermit, recluse

## SOLUTION

**a:** resoluble, soluble

**n:** *denouement, deux ex machina*, eureka, explanation, *nostrum*

**v:** decipher, fathom, solve, unravel

**SOMETIME**

**a:** erstwhile, formerly, intermittently, occasional, periodically, quondam

**SON**

**a:** filial, sibling

**n:** sibling

**SOOT**

**a:** fuliginous

**n:** fuliginosity, smut

**SOOTHING**

**a:** anodyne, anodynic, anodynous, assuasive, bland, calmative, conciliative, conciliatory, demulcent, dulcent, emollient, lenitive, mitigatory, nepenthean, palliative, placative, relaxing, sedative, tranquilizing

**n:** assuagement, conciliation, lenity, placation

**v:** allay, alleviate, appease, assuage, conciliate, mollify, pacify, palliate, placate, reconcile, soothe, tranquilize

> *agent:* antiphlogistic, calmative, demulcent, embrocation, emollient, liniment, *nepenthe*, opiate, placebo, salve, tranquilizer, unction, unguent

**SOOTHSAYER**

**a:** divinatory, haruspical, prognosticative

**n:** augur, auspex, diviner, haruspex, prognosticator, prophet, pythonist

**SOPHISTICATED**

**a:** alembicated, blase, chichi, cosmopolitan, cultivated, *debonair*, fashionable, highbrow, knowing, knowledgeable, precocious, *soigne*, suave, subtle, urbane, world-weary

**SORCERY**

**n:** black magic, conjuration, *diablerie*, diabolism, enchantment, exorcism, incantation, magic, necromancy, sortilege, thaumaturgy, theurgy, witchcraft

> *sorcerer:* alchemist, conjurer, conjuror, *haruspex*, necromancer, *sortileger*, thaumaturge, thaumaturgist, warlock, witch

**SORE**

**a:** purulent

**n:** abrasion, abscess, affliction, blain, blister, bunion, canker, carbuncle, excoriation, fester, furuncle, lesion, papule, trauma, ulcer, welt

**SORROW**

**a:** commiserable, compassionate, contemptible, contrite, doleful, dolent, dolorous, insignificant, lamentable, lamented, luctiferous, mournful, paltry, penitent, pitiable, plaintive, regretful, remorseful, rueful, sad, sorrowful, sorry

**n:** commiseration, compassion, compunction, dolor, lamentation, penitence, remorse, sympathy

**v:** commiserate, deplore, lament, regret, rue

**SORT**

**n:** character, class, disposition, grade, ilk, kind, nature, quality, thing, type, way

**v:** alphabetize, arrange, catalogue, categorize, classify, collate, compartmentalize, concinnate, dispose, distribute, orchestrate, segregate, systematize, tabulate

**SO-SO**

**a:** intermediate, mediocre, middling, ok, passable, tolerable

**n:** mediocrity

**SOUL**

**n:** anima, animism, *animus*, atman, pneuma, psyche, quintessence, spirit

> *damnation:* perdition, purgatory

> *migration theory:* metempsychosis, palingenesis, reincarnation, transmigration

**SOUND**

**a:** acoustic, articulate, aural, dulcet, echoic, euphonious, phonetic, polyphonic, polyphonous, resonant, sonant, sonic, soniferous, sonorant, sonorous, tintinnabular

**n:** articulation, audio, diapason, euphony, phonology, sonics, sonification, *timbre,* tintinnabulation

**v:** combining forms

*echo:* polyphony, reverberation

*fear:* phonophobia

*harsh:* cacophonic, cacophonous, calliopean, discordant, disharmonious, dissonant, immelodious, strident, unharmonious

*mind:* competent, *compos mentis*

*repeating:* echolalia, onomatomania, verbigeration

*science:* acoustics, phonetics, phonology, sonics

*similarity:* assonance, homeophony

*single:* homophonic, homophonous, monophonic, monophonous, monotonous, unisonous

*tricky:* ventriloquistic, ventriloquous

**SOUNDNESS**

**a:** acceptable, effective, valid

**n:** integrality, integrity, levelheadedness, solidarity, solidity, solvency

**SOUR**

**a:** acerbic, acetose, acetous, acid, acidulent, acidulous, austere, bitter, cynical, embittered, infestive, mirthless, morose, querulous, tart, vinegary

**n:** acerbity, acidification, infestivity, mirthlessness, sourness

**v:** acidify, ferment

**SOURCE**

**a:** seminal

**n:** bibliography, derivation, etiology, fountainhead, genesis, gravy train, headwaters, incipience, lode, origin, provenance, provenience, wellspring

*multiple:* eclectic, polygenetic, polyphyletic

**SOUTHERN**

**a:** austral, meridional, midi, southerly

**n:** meridionality

*Confederacy:* Dixie

*combining forms:* Austr-, Austro-, not-, noto-

*lights:* aurora australis

**SOUVENIR**

**n:** *bibelot,* gift, keepsake, memento, remembrance

**SOVEREIGNTY**

**n:** authority, autonomy, condonimium, dominion, dynasty, empery, independence, jurisdiction, kingship, supremacy, sway, throne

*emblem: regalia,* regality

**SPACE**

**a:** cosmic, extraterrestrial, hiatal, lacunal, lacunar, spacial, spatial

**n:** capacity, clearance, ether, expanse, firmament, hiatus, interstice, interval, lacuna, *lebensraum,* perspective, spatiality, ubiety

*creature:* alien, extraterrestrial

*filled:* gravid, plenum

*lacking:* incapacious

*spacious:* baggy, baronial, bulky, capacious, cavernous, commodious, comprehensive, copious, expansive, large, roomy, scopious, voluminous

*vacant:* vacuum

**SPANGLED**

**a:** adorned, bejeweled, caparisoned, clinquant, decorated, ornamented

**SPARK**

**a:** *cliquant, diamante,* rutilant, scintillescent

**n:** coruscation, iridescence, *lame,* luster, *scintilla,* scintillation, tinsel

**v:** coruscate, glisten, scintillate, shimmer, spangle, sparkle

**SPASM**

**a:** clonic, convulsive, intermittent, paroxysmal, spasmatic, spasmodic, spastic

**n:** agitation, cerebral palsy, clonicity, clonus, convulsion, orgasm, palsy, paroxysm, seizure, tetany, throe, tic, *tonus*, twitch

## SPEAK

**a:** colloquial, demegoric, elocutionary, enunciative, exophasic, glottological, idiomatic, labial, lexical, lingual, linguistic, oral, oratorical, peripatetic, phonetic, spoken, tropological, verbal, vernacular, *viva voce*, vocal

**n:** allocution, articulation, colloquialism, colloquy, confabulation, conversation, declamation, dialogue, diction, discourse, disquisition, elocution, enunciation, exophasia, facundity, fluency, glottology, grandiloquence, language, lexicality, linguistics, locution, loquacity, mellifluence, oration, parlance, *patois*, peroration, phonation, phraseology, pronunciation, recitation, recitative, speaking, speech, talk, tropology, vernacular, vocalization, vulgate

**v:** articulate, blabber, bluster, converse, dilate, dogmatize, drone, elaborate, enunciate, expatiate, expound, extemporize, filibuster, intonate, jabber, labialize, natter, perorate, phonate, pontificate, prate, pronounce, schmooze, sermonize, talk, utter, ventilate, verbalize, vocalize, yammer

   *affected or authoritative:* allocution, bombast, euphuism, exhortation, flatulence, grandiloquence, kompology, rhetoric, rodomontade

   *at length:* harangue, perorate

   *combining forms:* log-, logo-, -logue, phon-, -phone, phono-, -phony

   *concise:* brachylogy, incisiveness

   *defective:* idiolalia, idoglossia, lalopathy, pararthria, phoniatrics

   *disconnected:* maunder

   *figure of:* apostrophe, hyperbole, *litotes,* metaphor, metonymy, simile, *synecdoche,* tralatition, trope

   *internal:* endophasia

   *light:* levity

   *long:* macrology, monologue, pleonasm

   *not:* incommunicative, laconic, re-

served, retentive, reticent, taciturn

   *rhetorical:* perorate, rhapsodize

   *roundabout:* circuitousness, circumambage, circumlocution, periphrasis

   *short:* brachysyllabic, monosyllabic, telegraphic

   *speaker:* annunciator, collucator, conversationalist, orator, rhetorician

   *speech disorder:* -phasia

   *spokesman:* advocate, hierophant, prolocutor, protagonist

   *study:* glottology, linguistics, phonetics, phonology

   *thru nose:* nasality

   *thru teeth:* dentiloquy

   *to self:* endophasia

   *unable to:* aphonetic, aphonic, inarticulate

## SPEED

**a:** adept, alacritous, celeritous, expeditious, expeditive, fast, posthaste, precipitous, speedy, supersonic, velocious

**n:** acceleration, alacrity, celerity, deftness, dispatch, expedition, haste, promptitude, speediness, tempo, vector, velocity

**v:** accelerate, expedite

   *boat:* hydroplane

   *combining forms:* tach-, tacho-

   *reduce:* decelerate

## SPELL

**n:** chanting, charm, conjuration, enchantment, evocation, incantation, magic, sorcery, witchcraft

## SPELLING

**a:** phonetic

**n:** orthography

   *different:* heterography, metathesis, variant

   *other alphabet:* metagraphy, transliteration

**SPHERE**

**a:** cylindrical, discoid, globate, globose, globular, orbicular, orotund, rotund, spherical, spheriform, spheroidal, spheroidical

**n:** ambit, bailiwick, compass, domain, dominion, jurisdiction, *metier, milieu,* orbit, orrery, preserve, province, purview, sphericity, spheroid, spheroidicity, theater

**SPIKED**

**a:** spicate, spicigerous

**n:** piton, spike, stiletto

*combining forms:* acanth-, acantho-, echino-

*weapon:* caltrop, clamper, crampon, crowfoot, mace

**SPINE**

**a:** acanthaceous, acanthological, acanthous, acicular, aciculate, dorsal, juxtaspinal, neural, paraspinal, prickly, spicose, spicular, spiculate, spiculiferous, spiculose, spinose, spinous, spiny, spondylic, vertebral, vertebrate

**n:** acantha, axis, chine, quills, *rachis,* spicule, spinosity, vertebra

*combining forms:* echino-, myel-, myelo-

*spineless:* invertebrate

**SPIRAL**

**a:** cochleate, coiled, convoluted, helical, helicoidal, turbinate, volute, voluted, whorled

**n:** convolution, curl, helix, spirality, tendril, volute, vortex, whorl

**v:** gyrate

*combining forms:* gyro-, helic-, helico-

**SPIRIT**

**a:** animated, assiduous, brisk, *con brio, con spirito,* ebullient, energetic, enterprising, euphoric, exuberant, flamboyant, forceful, heady, intoxicated, plucky, spirited, spiritful, vigorous, vivacious, zealous, zestful

**n:** animation, animus, ardor, atman, *brio,* character, courage, ectoplasm, *elan,* enthusiasm, *esprit, esprit de corps,* exhilaration, *genie,* ghost, gumption, intoxication, invigoration, kelpie, lemures, mettle, morale, *mous,* muse, numen, optimism, peri, phantasm, pneuma, poltergeist, psyche, soul, sprite, sylph, vigor, visitation, vivacity, *zeitgeist*

**v:** manifest

*combining forms:* pneumat-, pneumato-

*evil:* cacodaemon, erlking, eudemon, incubus, succubus

*spiritless:* adenoidal, *amort,* apathetic, arenaceous, dejected, depressed, dispirited, exanimate, inanimate, lackluster, languorous, lethargic, listless, pusillanimous, unenthusiastic

**SPIRITUAL**

**a:** anagogic, anagogical, angelic, celestial, divine, ethereal, heavenly, immaterial, incorporeal, insubstantial, intellectual, pneumatic, psychic, religious, supermundane, supernatural, supersensible, supersensory, supersensual, unearthly, vital

**n:** apotheosis, deification, ethereality, incorporeality, incorporeity, interiority, mysticism, *raptus,* spirituality, spiritualization

**v:** apotheosize, canonize, celestialize, deify, etherealize, spiritualize

*apathy:* acedia, acidie, indifference, lethargy

*leader:* buddha, guru, maharishi

**SPITEFUL**

**a:** abusive, bitter, dispiteous, hateful, hostile, hurtful, malevolent, malicious, malignant, rancorous, splenetic, venomous, vicious, vindictive, viperous, virulent

**n:** malevolence, maliciousness, malignancy, spitefulness, venom, venosity

**SPLENDID**

**a:** aurelian, beautiful, *bravissimo,* effulgent, gorgeous, lustrous, magnificent, nice, opulent, refulgent, splendaceous, splendiferous, sublime, sumptuous, superb

**n:** *eclat*, effulgence, luster, magnificence, pomp, splendor, sublimity, sumptuosity, sumptuousness

**SPLIT**

**a:** *a cheval*, bifid, bifurcate, bipartisan, bipartite, bisected, cleft, cloven, dichotomous, dihiscent, dimidate, divided, schismatic, separated, spathic

**n:** bifurcation, cleavage, dichotomy, dihiscence, dissidence, disunion, divarication, diversity, fission, fracture, schism, scission, splitting

**v:** cleave, cut, dehise

*combining forms:* fissi-, schiz-, schizo-

*personality:* schizophrenia

**SPOIL**

**a:** blase, coddled, indulged, jaded, pampered, self-indulgent, spoiled

**n:** booty, loot, pillage, spoils, trophy

**v:** adulterate, alloy, barbarize, bastardize, blight, corrupt, debase, defile, degrade, devalue, foul, gratify, impair, indulge, mutilate, pamper, pander to, pervert, pollute, prostitute, putrefy, putresce, soil, sully, taint, tarnish, vitiate

**SPONGING**

**a:** parasitic, predatory, sycophantic

**n:** commensalism, loofah, parasitism, predation, symbiont, symbiosis, zoophyte

**SPONSORSHIP**

**n:** aegis, angel, auspice(s), benefactor, guardianship, patron, patronage, protection, protectorship, sponsor, tutelage

**SPONTANEOUS**

**a:** Apollonian, automatic, Dionysian, gratuitous, idiogenetic, idiopathic, impulsive, indigenous, intuitive, involuntary, knee-jerk, makeshift, natural, off-hand, reflex, spur-of-the-moment, stopgap, unpremeditated, unprompted, unthinking

**n:** automaticity, automatism, idiogenesis, impulsivity, spontaneity

*generation:* abiogenesis, autogenesis

**SPORT**

**a:** athletic, divertive, recreational, sportful, sportive

**n:** athletics, game, *bonvivant*, diversion, *divertissement*, mutation, recreation

**SPOT**

**a:** macular, maculate, maculose, mottled, *pardine*, piebald, punctated, puncticular, punctiform, spotted, sullied, tarnished, variegated

**n:** dot, drop, flaw, fleck, *macula*, maculation, macule, puncticulation, speck, stain, stigma, variegation

*spotless:* blameless, clean, immaculate, irreproachable, unblemished, unsullied, untarnished

**SPRAY**

**n:** atomizer

**v:** atomize, branch, mizzle, nebulize, scatter, spatter, spume

**SPREAD**

**a:** contagious, diffuse, dispersed, expanded, infectious, patulous, radial, radiate, radiating, rambling, rampant, serpiginous, splayed, sprawling, spreading, unfurled

**n:** circulation, decentralization, *diaspora*, diffusion, dispersion, dissemination, divarication, diversification, diversity, gamut, irradiation, metastasis, patulousness, proliferation, promulgation, propagation, ramification, spectrum

**v:** circulate, decentralize, diffuse, dilate, disperse, disseminate, divaricate, diversify, flare, imbue, infiltrate, infuse, irradiate, penetrate, permeate, proliferate, promulgate, propagate, publish, radiate, scatter, strew, suffuse

**SPREE**

**n:** antics, bacchanal, bender, brannigan, indulgence, orgy, party, splurge

**SPRIGHTLY**

**a:** animated, balletic, blithe, effervescent, exuberant, frolicsome, gay, jaunty, lively, perky, roguish, sharp, spirited, sportive, vivacious, zestful

n: *allegresse*, buoyancy, exuberance, gaiety, lightheartedness, sprightliness, vivacity, zest

## SPRINGTIME

a: primaveral, vernal

n: *le printemps, primavera*, prime, spring, vernal equinox

## SPROUT

a: burgeoning, pullulant

n: burgeoning, pullulation

v: burgeon, germinate, pullulate

*combining forms:* -blast, blast-

## SPUR

n: calcar, calcarium, goad, incentive, incitement, rowel, stimulus

v: galvanize, startle, stimulate

## SPURIOUS

a: adulterine, apocryphal, artificial, counterfeit, fake, feigned, forged, fraudulent, inauthentic, meretricious, pinchback, pseudepigraphic, pseudo, specious

*argument:* casuistry, philosophism, pilpul, sophism, sophistry, speciosity

## SQUALID

a: contemptible, crude, feculent, mangy, ordurous, sad, scabrous, shabby, sordid

n: scabrousness, squalidity

## SQUEAKY

a: *falsetto*, strident, stridulate, stridulous

## SQUEAMISH

a: fastidious, finicky, hypercritical, nauseated, overcareful, particular, prissy, sanctimonious, scrupulous

## SQUINT

a: *louche*, squinting, strabismic

n: cast, esotropia, exotropia, *strabismus*

## STAB

v: cut, gore, impale, knife, lancinate, pink, puncture, stick, strike

## STABILITY

a: immutable, inexpungable, irreversible, irrevocable, stable, steady

n: constancy, equilibrium, homeostasis, permanence, permanency, plateau, quo, status, steadfastness, steadiness

*combining form:* -stasis

## STAGE

a: contrived, dramatic, histrionic, manipulated, melodramatic, operated, showy, staged, theatric, theatrical

n: acrobatics, cabotinage, *dais*, drama, histrionics, histrionism, melodrama, melodramatics, *mise-en-scene*, podium, rostrum, setting, theater, theatre, theatricality, theatrics

*front: proscenium*

*manager: impresario, regisseur*

## STAGGER

a: titubant

n: titubation

v: alternate, hesitate, titubate, weave, welter

## STAGNATION

a: stagnant, unchanging

n: calm, dullness, quiescence, sluggishness, *stasis*, status, torpidity, torpor

## STALE

a: banal, cliche, commonplace, frowsy, hackneyed, *jejune*, musty, predictable, *rechauffe*, reworked, stereotyped, threadbare, trite, unoriginal, vapid

n: banality, bromide, chestnut, cliche, commonplace, jejunity, platitude, stereotype, superannuation, vapidity

v: obsolesce, supperannuate

## STAMP

a: philatelic

n: *cachet*, commemorative, hallmark, pane, platemark, *vignette*

*collecting:* philatelist, philately

**STANDARD**

**a:** canonical, classic, consuetudinary, conventional, *de rigueur*, emblematic, *en regle*, ethical, exemplary, orthodox, prime, proper, recognized, sanctioned, traditional, typical, uniform

**n:** *beau ideal*, benchmark, calibration, canon, civilities, control, convenances, conventions, criteria, criterion, differentia(e), differentiation, emblem, gauge, *gonfalon*, lodestar, modality, polestar, principle, touchstone, yardstick

**v:** calibrate, gauge, pass muster, standardize

*combining forms:* norm-, ortho-

*sub:* improper, subnormal, suboptimal

**STANDING**

**n:** antecedence, estimation, perpendicular, precedence, prestige, statant, stature, status, vertical

**STAR**

**a:** actinoid, asterial, asterismal, asteroid, astiferous, astral, constellational, constellatory, sidereal, starry, stellar, stellate, stelliform, visionary

**n:** alpha, asterisk, celestial body, cynosure, *etoile*, installation, lodestar, luminary, pentacle, pentagram, pentangle, stellification

**v:** stellify

*combining forms:* astr-, astro-, stell-

*group:* asterism, constellation, galaxy, nebula

*Jewish:* Magen (Morgan) David, Shield of David, Star of David

*love:* astrolatry, astrophile

*study:* astrology, astronomy, uranology

**START**

**n:** beginning, commencement

**v:** begin, jump-start

**STATE**

**a:** august, ceremonious, courtly, dignified, eminent, gubernatorial, imposing, majestic, marmoreal, palatial, pontifical, portentous, regal, stately, statuesque

**n:** body politic, *civitas*, commonalty, commonwealth, corridor, dilemma, enclave, plight, posture, predicament, situation, status, territory

**STATEMENT**

**a:** assertative, assertorial, assertoric

**n:** allegation, assertion, asseveration, *demarche*, *dictum*, generalization, presentation, profession, recital, recitation, verbality

**v:** asseverate, aver

**STATUE**

**a:** iconic, Junoesque, marmoreal, sculpturesque, statuesque

**n:** *colossus*, figurine, sculpture, statuette

**STATUS**

**a:** eminent, exalted, illustrious, prestigious

**n:** *cachet*, eminence, hierarchy, *kudos*, niche, pecking order, posture, prestige, recognition, situation, standing, stature

*lower:* decline, degrade, demote, denigrate, minimize, pejorate, plebify, vulgarize

**STEADY**

**a:** constant, continual, cool, dependable, disciplined, equable, firm, immutable, incessant, irreversible, irrevocable, persistent, reliable, resolute, stabile, stalwart, steadfast

**n:** equability, equanimity, stability

**v:** stabilize

**STEAL**

**a:** burglarious, kleptomaniac, larcenous, plagiaristic, thieving, thievish

**n:** abstraction, defalcation, embezzlement, extraction, kleptomania, larceny, misappropriation, peculation, piracy, plagiarism, stealing

**v:** abscond, abstract, appropriate, burglarize, convert, defalcate, embezzle, extort, extract, filch, liberate, misapply, misappropriate, peculate, pilfer, pirate, plagiarize, purloin, rifle, rustle, swipe, upsage

*stealer:* burglar, defalcator, embezzler, larcenist, peculator

**STEALTHY**

a: cabalastic, clandestine, duplicitous, furtive, insidious, Machiavellian, secretive, serpentine, sinuous, surreptitious, underhand

**STEEP**

a: abrupt, acclivitous, arduous, declivitous, exorbitant, inclined, perpendicular, precipitous, sheer, sloping

**STEM**

a: caulescent, cauline

n: bine, caulescence, corm, inflorescence, pedicel, peduncle, raceme, rachis, rhizome, rootstock, runner, stolon, tuber

**STEP**

a: plantigrade

n: *demarche*, echelon, flier, gradation, maneuver, plateau, progression, riser, winder

**STERN**

a: astringent, austere, exacting, harsh, inexorable, inflexible, inhospitable, resolute, rigorous, scrupulous, severe, strict, stringent, unbending, uncompromising, uninviting

**STEW**

n: *burgoo*, goulash, mixture, *olla podrida*, potpourri, *ragout, swivet*

**STICK**

a: adherent, adherescent, adhesive, agglutinant, clinging, gluey, glutinous, gummy, mucilaginous, sticking, sticky, tenacious, viscid, viscous

n: adherence, agglutination, conglutination, glutinosity, mucilage, resin, stickiness, tenacity, viscosity

v: adhere, agglutinate, cleave, cohere, conglutinate, glutinate, join

**STIFF**

a: ankylosed, ankylotic, inelastic, inflexible, monolithic, stiffened, stilted, unshakable, unwavering

n: ankylosis, arthritis, cramp, formalism, rigor, stiffness

**STILL**

a: becalmed, calm, dormant, halcyon, immobile, impassive, inactive, inarticulate, inert, inoperative, languishing, latent, obmutescent, quiescent, quiet, silentious, stagnant, static, stationary, tranquil, unmoving, unperturbed

n: immobility, languishment, lifelessness, quiescence, quietude, serenity, stillness, tranquility

v: languish

**STIMULATION**

a: accelerative, animating, aspirational, brisk, catalytic, galvanic, heartening, incisive, inspirational, inspiriting, *piquant*, poignant, promptive, provocative, psychogogic, pungent, stimulating, stimulative, stimulatory, stimulogenous

n: incentive, incitement, invigoration, piquancy, provocation, refreshment, stimulant, titillation, tittivation

v: activate, actuate, animate, egg on, foment, galvanize, goad, incite, innervate, inspirit, instigate, invigorate, kindle, motivate, provoke, stimulate, titillate, tittivate, vivify, whet

*stimulator:* accelerant, accentuator, agitator, catalyst, catalytic, fillip, flagellant, gadfly, incendiary, incentive, precipitator, propulsor, provocation, stimulus, synergist

**STINGING**

a: acrimonious, aculeate, cuastic, incisive, mordant, penetrating, *piquant*, poignant

n: hives, *uredo*, urtication

**STINGY**

**a:** avaricious, cheapskate, cheeseparing, curmudgeonly, extortionate, miserly, niggardly, parsimonious, penny-pinching, penurious, skimpy, thrifty, tight-fisted, tightwad, ungenerous

**n:** avarice, parsimony, penury, stinginess

**STINK**

**a:** effluvial, fetid, fulsome, graveolent, malodorant, malodorous, mephitic, nidorous, noisome, noxious, obnoxious, pestilent(ial), putrid, rank, reeking, stinking

**n:** *effluvium, fetor, mephitis, nidor,* putridity, stench

**STOIC**

**a:** dispassionate, impassive, imperturbable, indifferent, philosophical, phlegmatic, resolute, spartanic, Spartanic, stoical, stolid, undemonstrative, unmoved

**STOLID**

**a:** anserine, asinine, bovine, brutish, dull, stubborn, unexcited, wooden

**n:** asininity, bovinity, impassiveness, imperturbation, indifference, phlegm, stolidity

**STONE**

**a:** lapidary, lapideous, lithic, monolithic, petrefactive, petrescent, petrous

**n:** calcification, lapidification, megalith, menhir, monolith, petrification, rock

**v:** calcify, lapidate, lapidify, lithify, petrify

*ages:* Mesolithic, Neolithic, Paleolithic

*combining forms:* lapid-, -lite, -lith, lith-, litho-, petr-, petri-, petro-

**STOOPED**

**a:** bent, gibbose, gibbous, kyphotic, leaning, stoop-shouldered

**n:** gibbosity, gibbousness, *kyphosis*

**STOP**

**a:** cessative, in abeyance, oppilative, stopping

**n:** abscission, armistice, avast, cessation, *hiatus,* intermission, obstruction, obturation, occlusion, oppilation, quiescence, standstill, *stasis,* stoppage, surcease, termination

**v:** accost, adjourn, arrest, cease, checkmate, circumvent, desist, discontinue, end, forbear, intercept, intermit, obstruct, occlude, oppilate, pretermit, surcease, thwart, waylay

*combining forms:* para-, -stasis

**STORAGE**

**n:** ambry, arcade, argosy, arsenal, boutique, *cache,* commissary, depository, depot, emporium, *entrepot,* larder, magazine, mall, *repertorium,* repertory, repository, stash, stockpile, storehouse, thesaurization, trading post

**v:** garner, thesaurize

**STORK**

**a:** pelargic

**n:** adjutant bird, marabou

**STORM**

**a:** cyclonic, fulminous, inclement, passionate, procellous, stormy, tempestical, tempestuous, tumultuous, turbulent, wild

**n:** agitation, disturbance, inclemency, monsoon, stormines, tempest, turbulence, turbulency, vortex

**v:** besiege, bombard, fulminate

*center:* eye

**STORY**

**n:** anecdote, biography, chronicle, confabulation, conte, embellishment, epic, falsehood, lexicon, *memoirs,* narration, narrative, parable, romance, saga

**v:** concoct, confabulate, embellish, embroider, fantasticate, regale

*combined:* anthology, polymythy

*false:* canard, roorback

*installment: feuilleton*

*long:* epic, heroic, *iliad, spiel*

*sad:* jeremiad, lamentation

*teller: conteur,* narrator, *raconteur*

## STOUT

**a:** corpulent, courageous, forceful, hearty, implacable, liparous, lusty, obese, orbicular, plentitudinous, plethoric, portly, powerful, replete, resolute, robust, rotund

**n:** corpulence, fortitude, plethora, ponderosity, portliness, robusticity, stoutness, thickness

## STRAIGHT

**a:** arrowlike, direct, linear, perpendicular, rectilinear, *sagittal,* straightforward, undiluted, uninterrupted, unmixed, unmodified, vertical

**n:** perpendicularity, verticality

*combining form:* ortho-

## STRANGE

**a:** alien, anomalous, atypical, bizarre, eccentric, exceptional, exotic, extraordinary, fantastic, foreign, glamorous, grotesque, idiosyncratic, outlandish, *outre,* picturesque, preternatural, singular, *sui generis, tramontane,* uncanny, unfamiliar, unique, unusual

**n:** *bizzarerie, grotesquerie,* strangeness

*fear:* misoxeny, xenophobia

*stranger:* auslander, foreigner, *inconnu,* outlander, *tramontane*

## STRAW

**a:** stramineous, strawlike

**n:** litter, stem, *tatami*

## STRAYING

**a:** aberrant, aberrational, aberrative, errant, straying

**n:** aberrance, aberrancy, aberrant, aberration, deviation, divagation, divergence, maverick, straggler, waif

**v:** deviate, digress, divagate, divaricate, lag, meander, straggle, stray

## STREAKED

**a:** brindled, grooved, linear, line--aristic, lineate, marked, pied, ridged, striate, striated, strigose, variegated

**n:** lineation

## STREAM

**a:** autopotamic

**n:** brook, creek, effluent, flow, flume, freshet, influx, race, rivulet

*between:* interfluvial, mesopotamia

*combining form:* rheo-

## STRENGTH

**a:** adamantine, bracing, brawny, castellated, cogent, corroborative, emphatic, ensconced, fortified, Herculean, invincible, potent, *puissant,* resurgent, roborant, robustious, stalwart, strengthening, strong, vigorous

**n:** backbone, brawn, chastenment, concentration, durability, fortitude, intensity, lustihood, permanency, physique, potency, power, reinforcement, robusticity, sinew, spunk, stamina, *sthenia,* strenuosity, thews, valor, vigor, virility, vitality

**v:** anneal, augment, buttress, chasten, confirm, consolidate, corroborate, encourage, enhance, fortify, hearten, intensify, invigorate, lace, potentiate, reinforce, strengthen, substantiate, support, sustain, underpin, verify

*strenuous:* arduous, Herculean, onerous, rigorous, vigorous

*stronghold:* bastion, blockhouse, breastwork, citadel, fastness, Gibraltar, redoubt

## STRESS

**a:** traumatic

**n:** accent, *ictus,* pressure, trauma, traumatism

**v:** accent, accentuate, belabor, emphasize, highlight, intensify, traumatize, underscore

## STRICT

**a:** adamant, ascetic, austere, cenobitic, conscientious, Draconian, exacting, inclement, inexorable, inflexible, inquisitorial, intransigent, ironclad, obdurate, onerous, orthodox, pharisaical, precise, puritanical, rhadamanthine, rigoristic, rigorous, ruthless, sabbatarian, scrupulous, stern, stringent, tyrannical, uncompromising

**n:** austerity, correctitude, obduracy, preciseness, puritanism, rigidity, rigorism, scrupulosity, strictness, stringency, tyranny

> *person:* ascetic, authoritarian, disciplinarian, fundamentalist, martinet, Pharisee, precisian, purist, rigorist, ritualist, sabbatarian

**STRIFE**

**a:** internecine

**n:** *concours,* contention, dissension, fight, turmoil, warfare

> *person:* incendiary, mutineer, stormy petrel

**STRIKING**

**a:** conspicuous, eminent, extraordinary, impressive, noticeable, notorious, outstanding, percussive, prominent, remarkable, salient

**STRIP**

**a:** defoliative, denudative, stripping

**n:** decortication, defoliation, denudation, desquamation, dismantlement, divestiture, ecdysis, excoriation, exfoliation

**v:** decorticate, defoliate, denudate, denude, deplume, deprive, desquamate, disembellish, dismantle, divest, excoriate, ransack

> *teaser:* ecdysiast, stripteuse

**STRIVING**

**a:** conative, Dionysian

**n:** conation, conatus

**v:** attempt, contend, contest, crusade, endeavor, strive, try, vie, work

**STROKE**

**n:** brainstorm, *coup, coup d'etat, coup de grace,* fit, *ictus, tour de force*

> *illness:* apoplexy, cerebral hemorrhage, hemiplegia

**STRUCTURE**

**a:** architectonic, classified, constitutional, edifical, homologous, isomorphic, isomorphous, skeletonic, structural, structured, systematic

**n:** anatomy, architecture, *cadre,* configuration, conformation, edifice, fabric, fabrication, framework, lineament, morphology, organization, pattern, skeleton, texture

> *irregular:* heteromorphic, heteromorphous

**STRUGGLE**

**a:** agonistic, contending, contentious, infighting, internecine

**n:** *agon,* colluctation, contention, effort, endeavor, fight, infighting, throes, warfare

**v:** fight, grapple

**STUBBORN**

**a:** absonant, adamantine, calcitrant, cantankerous, contemptuous, contumacious, contumelious, defiant, determined, disdainful, disobedient, dogged, fractious, implacable, indurate, inexorable, inflexible, insubordinate, intractable, intransigent, inveterate, irreconcilable, monolithic, obstinate, oppositious, persistent, pertinacious, perverse, pigheaded, preemptory, rebellious, refractory, renitent, resistant, restive, tenacious, uncompromising, untoward, willful

**n:** adamancy, contumely, crotchiness, determination, incompliance, intractability, noncompliance, obduracy, obstinacy, persistency, pertinacity, pigheadedness, recalcitrance, stubbornness

**STUDENT**

**a:** disciplinary, interdisciplinary, scholastic

**n:** condisciple, disciple, freshman, graduand, junior, pupil, scholar, scholastic, senior, sophomore, undergraduate

**v:** abstract, analyze, anatomize, concentrate, contemplate, cram, examine, grind, investigate, lucubrate, meditate, peruse, ponder, reflect, scrutinize, study, traverse

> *combining forms:* -graphy, -ics, -istics, -logy, -ology
>
> *place: atelier, phrontistery, sanctum*

## STUFFED

**a:** copious, *farci,* replete, sated, satiated, surfeited

**n:** bombast, copiosity, flock, satiety, stuffing, upholstery

## STUN

**a:** confused, stunned, stupefied

**n:** stupefaction

**v:** amaze, astonish, daze, flabbergast, paralyze, perplex, stupefy

## STUNT

**n:** acrobatics, act, derring-do, feat, *forte,* performance, prestidigitation, *tour de force,* trick

## STUPID

**a:** anserine, asinine, bovine, brutish, crass, cretinous, doltish, fatuous, foolish, hebetate, idiotic, imbecilic, imperceptive, inane, insensate, loutish, moronic, oafish, obtuse, oscitant, purblind, silly, stultifying, vacuous

**n:** absurdity, fatuity, hebetation, hebetude, inanity, insipience, moronity, obtusity, stupidity, stupidness

**v:** stultify

## STUPOR

**a:** cataleptic, comatose, hypnotic, lethargic, stupefactive, stuporous

**n:** asphyxia, catalepsy, coma, daze, hypnosis, insensibility, lethargy, narcosis, sleepiness, stupefaction, torpor

## STURDY

**a:** hale, hardy, lusty, pyknic, roborant, robust, stalwart, strong, yeomanly

## STYLE

**a:** *a la mode, bon ton,* classic, fashionable, modish, pretentious, *recherche,* showy, *soigne,* stylish

**n:** *brio,* dash, *dernier cri, elan,* eloquence, fashion, fashionableness, flair, *panache,* register, stylishness, verve, vigor, vivacity

> *out of:* archaic, *demode,* obsolescent, obsolete, old-fashioned, outdated, *passe*

## SUAVITY

**a:** diplomatic, gracious, modish, oily, oleaginous, politic, suave, unctuous, urbane

**n:** amenity, diplomacy, mildness, polish, propriety, unctuosity, urbanity

## SUBDUE

**v:** conquer, defeat, lick, master, overwhelm, quash, reduce, repress, subjugate, subordinate, surmount, vanquish

## SUBJECT

**a:** accountable, emotional, psychic, psychological, psychosomatic, subjective, susceptible

**n:** *liege, propositus, protege,* subordinate

**v:** enthrall

> *multiple:* interdisciplinary, polygraphic
>
> *one:* monographic

## SUBLIME

**a:** eminent, empyreal, exalted, magnanimous, magnificent, majestic, supreme, transcendent

**n:** ecstasy, eminence, exaltation, happiness, heaven, magnanimity, magnificence, majesty, rapture, sublimity

## SUBMISSIVE

**a:** amenable, cringing, deferential, fawning, genuflectory, humble, menial, ministerial, obedient, obeisant, obsequious, penitent, servile, slavish, subalternate, subject, subservient, subsidiary, sycophantic, tractable, truckling, yielding n: acquiescence, amenability, deferentiality, genuflection, inertia, obsequiousness, obsequity, servility, submissiveness, tractability

**SUBORDINATE**

a: ancillary, auxiliary, derivative, satellite, satellitic, secondary, segmental, segmentary, servant, servile, subalternate, submissive, subordinated, subservient, succursal, supplemental, tangential, tributary

n: accessory, *ancilla*, ancillary, assistant, auxiliary, minion, parergon, protege, satellite, *satrap*, servant, *subaltern*, subordination, subserviency, subsidiary, tributary

*combining forms:* para-

**SUBSTANCE**

a: abundant, coessential, consubstantial, corporeal, essential, formidable, fundamental, hypostatic, material, plenteous, plentiful, ponderable, substantial, substantious

n: corporeality, corporeity, essence, materiality, physicality, resource, *substantia*, substantiality

v: prove, substantiate, substantify, validate, verify, vouch

**SUBSTITUTE**

a: substituted, substitutional, substitutionary, substitutive, *succedaneous*, vicarious

n: agent, commutation, *ersatz*, exchange, expedient, imitation, proxy, *quid pro quo*, substitution, surrogate, surrogation, understudy, vicar, vicariousness

v: commute, exchange

**SUBTLE**

a: *alembicated*, crafty, elusive, hairsplitting, imperceptible, ingenious, insidious, intangible, quibbling, scholastic, skillful, sophistical, sophisticated, wily

n: nuance

**SUBURB**

a: *suburbicarian*

n: bedroom community, *environs*, *faubourg*, outskirts, precincts, *purlieu*, suburbia

**SUCCESS**

a: efficacious, flourishing, fruitful, potent, successful

n: *eclat*, fruition, realization, *succes d'estime, succes fou*

**SUCCESSION**

a: alphabetical, categorical, consecutive, hereditary, ordered, repetitive, sequacious, sequential, seriate, subsequential, succedent, successive

n: alternance, alternation, consecution, progression, sequacity, sequence, subsequence

**SUCKING**

a: aspiratory, paratrophic, suctorial

n: lactation, suction

**SUDDEN**

a: abrupt, fast, headlong, imminent, impetuous, impulsive, meteoric, precipitate, rapid, spur-of-the-moment, subitaneous, uncontrolled

n: about-face, caprice, cataclysm, *deus ex machina*, ejaculation, epiphany, exclamation, interjection, pang, *peripeteia*, revelation, saltation, *saltus, volte-face*, windfall

v: catapult

**SUFFER**

a: downtrodden, maltreated, on the rack, oppressed, persecuted, suffering, tyrannized

n: adversity, affliction, agony, anguish, languishment, martyrdom, penance, resignation, satispassion, travail, tribulation

v: agonize, allow, brook, endure, experience, languish, permit, tolerate

*combining form:* -otic

*place of:* calvary, Gethsemane, hell, inferno, purgatory

## SUFFICIENT

**a:** adequate, commensurate, equipollent, equiponderant, resourceful

**n:** adequacy, competence, satisfaction, sufficiency, suitability

**v:** adequate

## SUFFOCATE

**n:** asphyxia, asphyxiation, suffocation

**v:** asphyxiate, smother, stifle

## SUGAR

**a:** glace, mawkish, *sacchariferous*, saccharine, *saccharogenic*

**n:** carbohydrate, dextrose, fructose, glucose, lactose, maltose, saccharose, sucrose, xylose

> *combining forms:* glyc-, glyco-, -ose, racchar-, saccharo-
>
> *deficiency:* hypoglycemia
>
> *excess:* hyperglycemia

## SUGGESTION

**a:** connotative, evocative, indelicate, insinuative, meaningful, provocative, reminiscent, *risque*, seminal, significant, suggestive

**n:** aspersion, connotation, *double entendre*, implication, imputation, *innuendo*, insinuation, *insinuendo*, overtone, *soupcon*, undercurrent

**v:** adumbrate, advance, advocate, allude, commend, connote, evidence, float, insinuate, intimate, predicate, prompt, propose, propound, suggest

## SUICIDE

**n:** *felo-de-se, hara-kiri, kamikaze,* parasuicide, Russian roulette, *seppuku, suttee*

## SUITABLE

**a:** adequate, appropriate, *apropos,* apt, befitting, condign, congruent, congruous, consonant, convenient, creditable, decorous, eligible, expedient, felicitous, fit, idoneous, meet, opportune, pertinent, plausible, proper, propitious, semblable

**n:** appropriateness, aproposity, creditability, expediency, fitness, idoneity, plausibility, propriety, suitability

**v:** appertain, bear upon, pertain

## SULLEN

**a:** *atrabiliar,* dour, grim, grouchy, grumpy, irascible, melancholy, morose, obstinate, peevish, saturnine, splenetic, stubborn, unsociable

**n:** irascibility, melancholy, moodiness, morosity, saturninity, sullenness

## SULTRY

**a:** humid, miasmic, sulfurous, sulphurous, sweltering, torrid, tropical, voluptuous

## SUM

**n:** aggregate, complement, *epitome,* nominal, quantity, recapitulation, result, substance, summation, total, whole

## SUMMARIZE

**a:** recapitulative, recapitulatory, summarizable, summative

**n:** abbreviation, abridgement, abstract, *aide-memoire, apercu,* breviary, breviate, compendium, condensation, conspectus, *curriculum vitae,* CV, digest, docket, encapsulation, *epitome,* outline, overview, pandect, paraphrase, potted bio, *precis,* profile, *prospectus,* recapitulation, *resume,* scenario, *schema,* summarization, summary, summation, syllabus, synopsis, truncation, *vita,* wrap-up

**v:** epitomize, recapitulate, synopsize

## SUMMER

**n:** dog days, estivation, Indian summer

**v:** estivate

## SUMMIT

**n:** acme, apex, *apogee, arete,* climax, consummation, crown, culmination, meridian, pinnacle, spire, top, zenith

## SUMMON

**n:** arraignment, citation, convocation, evocation, invocation, muster, *subpoena,* summoning

**v:** conjure, convene, convoke, invoke, muster

**SUN**

**a:** solar

**n:** *aubade,* flare, sunlight, sunrise

    *at equator:* equinox

    *bathe:* apricate

    *burn:* melanosis

    *combining forms:* heli-, helio-, sol-

    *farthest:* aphelion, solstice

    *fear:* heliphobia

    *highest:* zenith

    *nearest:* perihelion

    *therapy:* heliotherapy

    *worship:* heliolatry

**SUPERFICIAL**

**a:** casual, cursory, desultory, fake, incondite, meretricious, perfunctory, sciolistic, shallow, sophomoric, specious, tenuous

**n:** externality, gloss, inanity, sciolism, speciosity, superficiality, tenuosity, tokenism, triviality, veneer

**SUPERFLUOUS**

**a:** *de trop,* excessive, extravagant, nonessential, prodigal, profuse, recrementious, redundant, superabundant, supererogatory, supernumerary

**n:** extravagance, prodigality, superabundance, supererogation, superfluity, superflux

**SUPERIOR**

**a:** antecedent, excellent, haughty, magisterial, meritorious, palmy, paramount, perfect, predominant, preeminent, prepotent, supercilious, supereminent, supernal, supernatural, superordinary, superordinate, unsurpassed

**n:** antecedence, chauvinism, conspicuity, eminence, ethnocentrism, illuminism, *magnifico,* meliority, *ne plus supra, ne plus ultra,* precedence, predominance, preeminence, preponderance, seniority, sociocentrism, superciliousness, supereminence, superiority, *supernaculum,* transcendence, vantage point, worthiness

**v:** predominate, preponderate

**SUPERLATIVE**

**a:** choice, consummate, exaggerated, excessive, incomparable, peerless, perfect, pluperfect, prepotent, supreme, transcendent

**n:** acme, peak, supereminence, *supernaculum,* utmost

**SUPERNATURAL**

**a:** charismatic, clairvoyant, extraphysical, extrasensory, fey, hyperphysical, incorporeal, metaphysical, miracular, miraculous, numinous, paraphysical, parapsychological, phantasmagoric, preternatural, psychic, superhuman, supermundane, transcendent(al), visionary

**n:** charm, ESP, extraphysicality, extrasensory perception, fetish, incorporeality, incorporeity, *juju,* magic, *mana,* occult, phantasmagoria, supermundanity, transcendence, transcendentality

    *appearance:* epiphany, revelation, theophany, visitation

    *study:* metaphysics, parapsychology

**SUPERVISE**

**a:** supervisorial, supervisory, *surveillant*

**n:** *chaperonage,* invigilation, oversight, proctorship, superintendence, supervision, surveillance

**v:** chaperone, invigilate, proctor, scrutinize, survey

    *supervisor: chaperone,* director, overseer, proctor, superintendent

**SUPPLE**

**a:** complacent, compliant, gracile, limber, lissom, lissome, lithe, obsequious, submissive

**n:** gracility, lissomeness, suppleness

**SUPPLEMENT**

**a:** accessorial, accessory, additititious, adjunctive, adjuvant, adminicular, adscititious, ancillary, auxiliary, complemental, complementary, contributory, corollary, corroborative, succenturiate, supervenient, supplemental, supplementary, tangential n: addenda, *addendum*, *additament*, annex, *paralipomena*, pendant, postscript

**SUPPLICATION**

n: appeal, *ave*, entreaty, litany, obsecration, petition, prayer, request, rogation, solicitation

**SUPPLY**

n: affluence, *armamentaria*, copiosity, *impedimenta*, lode, *materiel*, reservoir, spate, stockpile, *viaticum*

v: furnish, give

**SUPPORT**

a: adminicular, alimentative, ancillary, auxiliary, corroborative, corroboratory, supporting, supportive, sustentacular, sustentative, tangential

n: abetment, adminicle, advocacy, alimentation, assistance, auxiliary, clientele, corroboration, espousal, patronage, sponsorship, stanchion, subsidy, subvention, sustentation, sustention, truss

v: abet, advocate, approve, bolster, brace, buttress, champion, corroborate, countenance, encourage, endorse, espouse, maintain, patronize, proselytize, reinforce, sanction, sponsor, substantiate, sustain, verify, vouch for

  *combining form:* pro-

  *supporter:* abettor, accessory, accomplice, adherent, advocate, *aficionado*, angel, apologist, apostle, cohort, colleague, confederate, constituency, constituent, devotee, follower, henchman, patron, proponent, stalwart, votary

**SUPPOSE**

a: academic, alleged, conjectural, deemed, hypothetical, presumptive, putative, reputed, supposed, suppositional, supposititious, suppositive, theoretical

n: assumption, conception, conjecturality, conjecture, divination, hypothesis, philosophy, postulation, *postulatum*, speculation, supposition, surmise, theory

v: conceive, conjecture, divine, postulate, presume, speculate, surmise, theorize

**SUPPRESS**

a: inhibitory, suppressive

n: abreaction, catharsis, inhibition, repression, suppression

v: annihilate, extinguish, gag, inhibit, muzzle, overpower, overwhelm, quash, quell, repress, stifle, subdue

**SUPREMACY**

a: celestial, crucial, eminent, incomparable, inimitable, matchless, *nonpareil*, outstanding, paramount, peerless, predominant, preeminent, preponderant, signal, significant, sovereign, stellar, sublime, supereminent, superlative, supreme, transcendent, vital

n: ascendancy, ascendency, domination, dominion, eminence, precedence, preeminence, preeminency, preponderance, primacy, priority, sovereignty, *suzerainty*

**SURE**

a: authentic, certain, confident, enduring, indubitable, ineluctable, inevitable, secure, unfaltering

n: certainty, indubitability, ineluctability, inevitability, sureness

  *surety:* *adpromissor*, assurance, certainty, guaranty, recognizance

**SURFACE**

n: burnish, exterior, exteriority, externality, facet, lineament, *mien, patina*, periphery, *superficies*, texture, topography, veneer

  *floating on:* supernatant
  *on or near:* superficial

**SURGERY**

a: medical, surgical

n: abscission, enucleation, incision, resection, section

v: ablate, abscise, enucleate, excise, resect

  *combining forms:* -ectomy, -otomy, -stomy, -tom, -tome, -tomy *removal:* ablation, amputation, excision, extirpation

## SURLY

**a:** acrimonious, boorish, churlish, crabbed, grumpy, haughty, morose, peevish, sullen, touchy, unkind

**n:** curmudgeon

## SURMISE

**n:** belief, conclusion, conjecture, deduction, extrapolation, hypothesis, inference, peradventure, presumption, suspicion

**v:** conjecture, deduce, extrapolate, hypothesize, imagine, infer, suppose, theorize

## SURNAME

**a:** patronymic, surnominal

**n:** agnomen, appellation, cognomen, cognomenation, eponym, family name, *nom de famille*, patronym, patronymic

## SURPASS

**a:** excelling, preponderating, surpassing, transcendent

**n:** preponderance

**v:** eclipse, exceed, outrank, outstrip, overstep, preponderate, surmount, transcend

## SURPRISE

**a:** agape, aghast, disbelieving, dumbfounded, flabbergasted, flustered, *in flagrante delicto*, incredulous, nonplussed, rattled, red-handed, stupefied, surprised, thunderstruck, unnerved

**n:** bombshell, *coup d'etat*, *coup de main*, *deus ex machina*, thunderclap, *trouvaille*

**v:** amaze, astonish, astound, baffle, caught unawares, confound, electrify, evince, perplex, perturb, stagger, waylay

## SURRENDER

**a:** capitulatory, unconditional

**n:** abandonment, capitulation, cessation, cession, compliance, resignation, waiver

**v:** abandon, abnegate, acquiesce, capitulate, cede, kowtow, relinquish, submit, succumb

## SURROUNDINGS

**a:** circumambient, circumferential, circumjacent, *circumvallate*, encapsulated, encompassing

**n:** *alentours*, ambient, ambit, circumfusion, circumvention, compass, confines, entourage, environment, *environs*, externality, *milieu*, *mise-en-scene*, orbit, periphery, precinct, *purlieus*

*combining forms:* amph-, amphi-, circum-, peri-

## SURVEY

**a:** panoramic

**n:** *conspectus*, examination, panorama, perlustration, prospectus, recension, *reconnaissance*, scrutiny, surveillance

**v:** appraise, estimate, evaluate, inspect, *perlustrate*, *recce*, *reconnoiter*

## SURVIVAL

**a:** extant, leftover, remaining, residual, surviving, vestigial, viable

**n:** continuation, natural selection, survivance

**v:** subsist, survive, weather

*object:* relic

*species:* relict

## SUSCEPTIBLE

**a:** easy, impressible, pliable, prone, responsive, sensitive, subject, tendentious, tender, weak

**n:** impressibility, impressionability, predilection, sensitivity, susceptibility, tendentiousness

## SUSPEND

**a:** *sine die*

**n:** abeyance, abeyancy, armistice, cessation, intermission, *moratorium*, pendulosity, pretermission, suspension

**v:** adjourn, discontinue, intermit, interrupt, postpone, pretermit, refrain, transfer, *waive*

## SUSPICIOUS

**a:** accusatory, askance, distrustful, doubtful, dubious, equivocal, furtive, incredulous, incriminatory, leery, paranoid, querulant, querulent, questionable, umbrageous

n: dubiety, incredulity, skepticism, suspicion

*person:* paranoiac, paranoid

**SUSTAIN**

a: sustaining, sustenacular, sustentative

n: aliment, alimentation, food, maintenance, nutriment, refreshments, sustenance, sustention

v: corroborate, endure, prolong, support, undergo

**SWAGGER**

a: jaunty, swaggering, swashbuckling

n: arrogance, bravado, cockiness, *fanfaronade,* flamboyance, *gasconade, panache, rodomontade*

v: bluster, brag, hector, strut, swashbuckle

*swaggerer: braggadocio,* bravado, *gasconade, rodomontade,* swashbuckler

**SWALLOWING**

a: *hirundine*

n: deglutition, ingurgitation

v: drink, ingest, swallow, swig, swill

*difficult: aphagia,* quinsy

**SWAMP**

a: deluginous, fenny, paludal, paludinal, paludine, paludious, palustral, palustrine, swampy, uliginose, uliginous

n: bayou, bog, everglades, fen, marsh, miasma, mire, morass, muskeg, quagmire, slough, swale, wash

v: deluge, engulf, inundate, overwhelm

*gas: effluvium,* methane

**SWAN**

a: cygneous

*female:* pen

*young:* cygnet

**SWASTIKA**

n: fylfot, gammadion, gammation, *hakenkreuz, tetraskelia, tetraskelion, tetraskelions*

**SWAY**

n: ascendency, dominance, dominion, influence, oscillation, *puissance,* sovereignty

v: fluctuate, hang, oscillate, swing, vacillate

**SWEAR**

n: adjuration, affirmation, asseveration, blasphemy, conjuration, deposition, epithet, expletive, perjury, profanity, swearing, testimony

v: adjure, affirm, anathematize, asseverate, curse, depone, depose, perjure, pledge, testify

**SWEET**

a: cherubic, cloying, *dolce, dolcissimo,* dulcet, engaging, honeyed, mellifluous, nectareous, personable, saccharine, sugary, treacly, winsome

n: amiability, candy, confection, marzipan, saccharinity, sweetness, truffle

*sweetheart: cherie, dulcinea, inamorato,* lover, valentine

**SWELL**

a: bulbous, distended, dropsical, edematous, gravid, hypertrophied, incrassate, intumescent, nodal, nodose, nodular, overweening, pompous, protuberant, swollen, tumefacient, tumefactive, tumescent, tumid, turgescent, turgid, undulatory, undulous

n: apophysis, bilge, bulge, *crescendo,* edema, inflation, intumescence, node, nodosity, nodule, protuberance, protuberation, swelling, tubercle, tumefaction, tumescence, tumidity, turgescence, turgor, undulation

v: dilate, distend, inflate, intumesce, protrude, tumefy

**SWIFT**

**a:** celeritous, expeditious, fast, mercurial, meteoric, precipitous, quicksilver, summary, telegraphic

**n:** acceleration, alacrity, celerity, expedition, swiftness

**SWIMMING**

**a:** floating, natant, natatorial, natatory

**n:** natation

*pool:* natatorium

*swimmer:* natator

**SWINDLE**

**n:** defalcation, embezzlement, peculation, scam, scheme

**v:** cheat

*swindler:* charlatan, cozener, embezzler, imposter, mountebank, quacksalver

**SWINE**

**a:** porcine, suoid, swinish

**SWING**

**a:** fluctuating, oscillating, pedant, pendular, pendulous, swinging, undulating

**n:** oscillation, pendulation, pendulosity, swinging, undulation

**v:** brachiate, fluctuate, oscillate, pendulate, suspend, undulate, vacillate

**SWORD**

**a:** ensiform, gladiate, xiphoid

**n:** backsword, bilbo, brand, broadsword, cutlass, estoc, falchion, foil, *glaive,* hanger, kris, *rapier,* saber, scimitar, smallsword, *yalaghan*

**v:** pink, port

*combining forms:* xiph-, xiphi-

**SYLLABLE**

**n:** syllabary, syllabification

**v:** syllabify

*contraction of two:* synecphonesis, syneresis, synizesis

*more than two:* polysyllabic(al)

*next to last:* penult(ima), penultimate

*no first:* aphaeresis, apheresis

*no last:* apocopation, apocope

*no middle:* syncope

*omission of unstressed:* elision

*one:* monosyllabic(al)

*stressed:* nuclear, tonic

*two from last:* antepenult(ima)

*word of many:* plurisyllable, polysyllable, sesquipedalian

**SYMBOL**

**a:** allegorical, emblematic, fetichistic, figurative, hieroglyphic, ideogrammatic, ideogrammic, *labrum,* logogrammatic, metaphoric(al), pathognomonic, representative, schematic, semantic, symbolic, symbolic(al)

**n:** archetype, attribute, colophon, device, emblem, ensign, glyph, hieroglyphic, icon, ideogram, logo, logogram, logograph, logotype, mark, notation, *oriflamme,* pentacle, pentagram, subscript, superscript, symbolization, totem, typification

**v:** allegorize, emblematize, embody, hypostatize, personify, reify, symbolize, typify

*science:* semiotics, symbolics, symbology

*worship:* symbololatry

**SYMPATHETIC**

**a:** altruistic, attuned, compassionate, condolatory, congenial, empathetic, empathic, *en rapport,* infectious, kind, Samaritan, *simpatico*

**n:** altropathy, altruism, benevolence, clemency, commiseration, compassion, condolence, empathy, fellow feeling, identification, mercy, *pathos,* pity, rapport, *simpatico, tendresse*

**v:** commiserate, condole, sympathize

*arousing:* pathetic

**SYMPTOM**

**a:** diagnostic, pathognomonic, prodromal, semeiotic, subclinical, symptomatic

**n:** clew, clue, criteria, criterion, indication, prodrome, sign, syndrome

> *disappearance:* crisis, delitescence
>
> *hysterical:* imesis
>
> *study:* semeiotics, semiotics, symptomatology

**SYNONYM**

**a:** synonymatic, synonymic, synonymous

**n:** synonymicon, synonymics, synonymization, synonymy

**v:** synonymize

> *book:* reverse dictionary, thesaurus

**SYNOPSIS**

**n:** abridgement, *apercu,* brief, compendium, digest, *epitome,* outline, *precis,* summary

**v:** abbreviate, epitomize, synopsize

**SYSTEM**

**a:** architectonic, cosmic, methodical, orderly, regular, symmetrical, taxonomic

**n:** arrangement, cosmos, economy, edifice, network, organism, organization, paradigm, regime, regimen, syntax

> *combining form:* -nomy

## TABLE

**a:** mensal, tabular

*companion:* commensal, deipnosophist

## TABOO

**a:** contraband, ineffable, inviolate, prohibited, proscribed, proscriptive

**n:** ban, bar, convention, embargo, exile, hindrance, interdiction, prohibition, proscription, restraint, superstition, *tabu*

## TACT

**a:** adroit, consummate, diplomatic, discreet, discriminating, fitting, judicious, perspicacious, politic, prudent, sensitive, *suave,* tactful

**n:** acumen, address, aptness, delicacy, *delicatesse,* diplomacy, discernment, discretion, discrimination, *finesse,* perspicacity, poise, prudence, refinement, *savoir faire,* sensitivity

> *tactless: gauche,* impolite, impolitic, inconsiderate, indiscreet, inept, maladroit, undiplomatic, untactful

## TAIL

**a:** caudal, caudate, caudiform, prehensile

**n:** brush, bush, *cauda,* caudal appendage, empennage, flag, scut

> *combining forms:* caud-, -ur, ur-, uro-, -urous
>
> *long:* macrurous
>
> *short:* brevicaudate
>
> *tailless:* acaudal, acaudate, anurous, ecaudate
>
> *toward the:* caudad

## TAILOR

**a:** sartorial

**n:** draper, *maestro-sastre, sartor*

## TAINT

**a:** bad, corrupt, decayed, fetid, polluted, putrid, rancid, rank, septic, sour, tainted, vitiated

**n:** blemish, cloud, contamination, corruption, defilement, maculation, pollution, reproach, vitiation

**v:** contaminate, corrupt, debase, defile, deprave, pollute, tarnish

## TAKE

**a:** confiscatory, preemptive, usurpative, usurpatory

**n:** appropriation, confiscation, eminent domain, preemption, sequestration, usurpation

**v:** accroach, appropriate, arrogate, assume, belittle, commandeer, confiscate, derogate, detract, embezzle, preempt, *purloin,* seize, sequester, spheterize, usurp

## TALE

**n:** *fabula, fabulae,* fiction, legend, myth, narrative, story, yarn

## TALENT

**a:** charismatic, versatile

**n:** accomplishment, adeptness, adroitness, aptitude, attribute, capacity, charisma, dexterity, endowment, expertise, facility, flair, *forte,* genius, hability, ingeniosity, inventiveness, *metier,* penchant, virtuosity

> *person:* prodigy

## TALK

**a:** articulate, colloquial, communicative, conversable, conversant, conversational, discursive, effusive, fluent, garrulous, loquacious, multiloquacious, multiloquent, profuse, talkative, verbose, vocative, vociferous, voluble, wordy

**n:** articulation, asetism, badinage, banter, *bravado*, *causerie*, colloquy, communication, confabulation, conversation, *descant*, discourse, discussion, *gasconade*, lecture, loquacity, palaver, parlance, persiflage, speech, *tete-a-tete*, witticism

**v:** articulate, communicate, confabulate, converse, *descant*, discourse, gesticulate, palaver, say, speak, state

> *abnormal:* logomania, logorrhea, verbomania
>
> *dull:* monosyllabism
>
> *in sleep:* somniloquy
>
> *inaudible:* endophasia
>
> *indirect:* ambage, circumlocution
>
> *meaningless: galimatias*, gibberish, stultiloquence, stultiloquy
>
> *not talkative:* laconic, reticent, taciturn, trenchant
>
> *sign:* dactylology, gesticulation
>
> *talker:* blabbermouth, *causeur*, colloquist, confabulator, conversationalist, flibbertigibbet, popinjay, *raconteur*, windbag
>
> *to oneself:* monologue, soliloquy

## TALL

**a:** altitudinous, gangling, statuesque, strapping, towering

## TAME

**a:** amenable, benign, cultivated, docile, domestic, domesticated, tractable

**n:** complaisance, docility, domesticality, domesticity, tameness, tractability, tractableness

**v:** domesticate, train

## TAMPER

**a:** manipulable, manipulatory

**v:** alter, machinate, manipulate, meddle

## TAPERING

**a:** acuminate, acuminous, fusiform, lanceolar, lanceolated, wedged

## TARDY

**a:** comatose, dilatory, indolent, late, lethargic, procrastinative, remiss, slow, sluggish

## TARNISH

**n:** *aerugo*, debasement, deterioration, *patina*, rust, stain, *verdigris*

**v:** darken

## TASK

**a:** Herculean, onerous, Sisyphean

**n:** assignment, *devoir*, enterprise, onus, project, undertaking

## TASTE

**a:** aesthetic, appetizing, artistic, discerning, discriminating, gustatory, palatable, savory, tasteful, tasty

**n:** appetite, degustation, flavor, gustation, inclination, penchant, predilection, preference, sapidity, sapor, savor

**v:** degustate

> *abnormal:* allotriogeustia, allotriophagia, allotriophagy, cacogeusia, geophagy, parageusia, pica
>
> *decreased:* hypogeusia
>
> *increased:* hypergeusia
>
> *tasteless:* banal, inartistic, insipid, uninteresting, unleavened, unsavory, vapid

## TEACH

**a:** didactic, disciplined, docible, docile, educable, educatable, educational, governable, instructible, instructional, instructorial, manipulable, pedagogic, preceptorial, professorial, propaedeutic, sermonic, teachable, tractable, tutelary

**n:** didacticism, didactics, docility, instruction, pedagogics, pedagogism, pedagogy, professordom, professoriate, propaedeutics, teaching, tractability, tuition, tutelage

**v:** brainwash, discipline, disseminate,

edify, educate, enlighten, exhort, exposit, expound, inculcate, indoctrinate, instill, tutor

*not teachable:* indocile, intractable, uneducable, unteachable

*teacher: archididascalos,* didact, didacticist, disciplinarian, docent, doctor, educator, guru, instructor, *maestro,* mentor, pedagogue, pedantocrat, preceptor, scholastic

**TEAR**

**a:** asunder

**n:** disarticulation, discerption, dismemberment, divulsion, laceration, rupture

**v:** dilacerate, disarticulate, discerp, disjoin, dismember, lacerate, lancinate, laniate, raze, rupture

**TEARFUL**

**a:** lachrymal, lachrymatory, lachrymose, maudlin, mawkish, weepy

**TEEM**

**a:** alive, bustling, fertile, replete, rife, teeming

**n:** burgeoning, pullulation

**v:** burgeon, pullulate

**TEETH**

**a:** dentate, denticular, denticulate(d), dentiform, dentulous, periodontal, serrate(d)

**n:** bridgework, dentition, denture

*combining forms:* dent-, denti-, -odon, -odont

*gap:* diastema

*large:* macrodont

*odd:* bruxomania, dentiloquy

*small:* denticulate

*without:* edentate, edentulate, edentulous

**TELL**

**v:** acquaint, annunciate, articulate, asseverate, communicate, differentiate, disclose, distinguish, divulge, enunciate, inform, narrate, recite, recount, regale, rehearse, relate, unbosom

**TEMPER**

**a:** acerbic, asperous, hair-trigger, inflammable, irascible, vinegary, volatile

**n:** acerbity, asperity, bile, irascibility, irritability, pique, spleen, tantrum

**TEMPERAMENT**

**a:** capricious, mercurial, quicksilver, temperamental, volatile

**n:** composure, constitution, crasis, disposition, equability, equanimity, humor, mood, personality, propensity, *sang froid*

*steady:* equable, equanimous, undemonstrative

**TEMPERANCE**

**a:** abstemious, Apollonian, calm, continent, moderate, self-controlled, sober, temperate

**n:** abnegation, abstention, abstinence, composure, consistency, measure, mediocrity, moderation, restraint, self-control, sobriety, sophrosyne

**TEMPERATURE**

**a:** ambient, isothermal, synthermal

**n:** Celsius, Centigrade, Fahrenheit, Kelvin, Rankine

*control:* thermostat

*high:* hyperpyrexia, hyperthermia

*low:* hypothermia

**TEMPORARY**

**a:** *ad hoc, ad interim,* conditional, deciduous, ephemeral, ephemerous, episodic, evanescent, expedient, extemporaneous, fleeting, impermanent, interim, intermistic, makeshift, mundane, *pro tem, pro tempore,* provisional, stopgap, temporal, tentative, topical, transient, transitional, transitory

**n:** ephemerality, impermanence, impermanency, temporality, temporariness, topicality

**TEMPTATION**

**a:** alluring, enticing, fascinating, gullible, peccable, provocative, seducible, seductive, sirenic, tempting n: allurement, enticement, seduction

v: allure, attract, entice, inveigle, lure, persuade, provoke, seduce, tempt

**TEN**

a: decagonal, decennial, decimal, decuple, denary, tenfold

n: decade, decagon, decapod, decemvir, decemvirate, decennary, decenniad, decennium

>*combining forms:* dec-, deca-, deci-, dek-

>*thousand:* millennium, myriad

>*10 years:* decennial

**TENACIOUS**

a: adhesive, cohesive, obstinate, retentive, stubborn, viscous

n: grit, guts, mettle, nerve, pluck, tenacity

**TENDENCY**

a: prejudiced, susceptible, tendential, tendentious

n: affinity, appetency, bent, *conatus*, diathesis, direction, disposition, entropy, inclination, innate, *nisus*, partiality, penchant, predilection, predisposition, proclivity, propensity, susceptibility, temperament, vocation

>*opposite:* ambitendency, ambivalence

**TENDER**

a: affectionate, benevolent, clement, compassionate, *con amore*, fragile, hyperalgesic, hyperesthetic, merciful, mild, solicitous, sympathetic, warm

n: empathy, hyperalgesia, hyperesthesia, sympathy, tenderness, *tendresse*

v: intenerate, soften, tenderize

**TENSE**

a: edgy, frenetic, hectic, high-strung, jittery, nervous, stiff, stressed, tight, tired, tonic, unrelaxed

n: fanteeg, fantigue, tautness, tension, tonicity

**TERM**

a: orismological, terminological

n: condition, duration, hypocorism, jargon, name, nomenclature, orismology, semester, tenure, terminology, trimester

>*defining:* orismology

>*idea without term:* anonym

**TERRIBLE**

a: apocalyptic, appalling, awesome, calamitous, formidable, frightening, ghastly, horrific, portentous, redoubtable, shocking, ugly

**TERRITORY**

n: *demesne*, dominion, empire, enclave, *imperium*, jurisdiction, *lebensraum*, mandate, terrain, *terrene*, topography

**TERROR**

a: fearful, *gorgonesque*, Gorgonian, hideous, scared, terrifying

n: apprehension, *bete noir*, bugbear, consternation, scourge

v: affright, agrise, appall, gorgonize, paralyze, petrify, terrify

**TERSE**

a: abbreviated, aphoristic, axiomatic, brachysyllabic, compact, compendious, concise, epigrammatic(al), exact, laconic, monosyllabic, poignant, pointed, postulational, sententious, short, succinct, telegrammatic, telegraphic, trenchant

n: monosyllabicity, monosyllabism

**TEST**

a: analytical, exploratory, probative, probatory, substantiating

n: analysis, audition, criteria, criterion, norm, sounding board, touchstone, yardstick

v: appraise, assay, examine

**TESTIFY**

n: allegation, attestation, declaration, deposition, evidence, testimony

v: affirm, depone, depose, profess, swear, vouch, witness

**THAW**

**a:** deliquescent

**n:** deliquescence

**v:** deliquesce, melt, unbend, unfreeze

**THEATRE**

**a:** artificial, dramatic, dramaturgic, histrionic, melodramatic, meretricious, operatic, pompous, showy, stagey, stagy, theatrical, thespian

**n:** cabotinage, drama, dramatics, dramaturgy, footlights, histrionics, histrionism, theatrical, theatricalities, theatricality, theatrics, *troupe*

**THEFT**

**a:** piratical, plagiaristic

**n:** conversion, defalcation, embezzlement, filching, larceny, misappropriation, peculation, pilferage, piracy, plagiarism, rustling, stealing

**v:** abscond, pilfer, plagiarize, steal, take

**THEME**

**a:** monothematic, thematic

**n:** burden, chorus, image, *leitmotif, leitmotiv, motif,* motto, *mythos,* refrain, subject, *topos*

**THEORETICAL**

**a:** academic, conjectural, contemplative, doctrinaire, fictitious, hypothetical, impractical, nominal, notional, platonic, postulatory, presumptive, putative, *quodlibetic,* received, speculative, suppositional, supposititious, theoretic

**n:** conjecture, creed, doctrine, dogma, explication, fundament, hypothesis, *philosopheme,* philosophy, postulate, presupposition, speculation, supposition, surmise, theorem, theoretics, theory, thesis, working hypothesis

**v:** adhere, subscribe

> *theorist:* doctrinaire, dogmatist, ideologist, theoretician, theorician, visionary

**THICK**

**a:** clavate, claviform, coagulated, consolidated, inspissate(d), viscid, viscous

**n:** diameter, thickness, width

**v:** clot, coagulate, condense, congeal, inspissate, solidify, thicken

> *skinned:* callous, insensate, insensitive, pachydermatous

**THICKET**

**n:** boscage, brush, bush, chaparral, coppice, copse, covert, grove, wood

**THIEF**

**a:** burglarious, furtive, larcenous, mercurial, stealthy, thievish

**n:** burglar, depredator, embezzler, felon, *ganef,* larcener, larcenist, peculator, *picaroon,* pilferer, rascal

> *language:* argot, cant

**THIGH**

**a:** crural

**n:** femur, flank, groin, loins

**THIN**

**a:** attenuated, cadaverous, chiffon, diaphanous, emaciated, gossamer, gracile, ichorous, lank, lean, macilent, malnourished, meager, scrawny, sheer, skeletal, skeletonic, slender, spare, stringy, svelte, tapering, tenuous, translucent, wiry

**n:** filament, macilency, malnourishment, malnutrition, tenuity, thinness

**THING**

**n:** entity, *noumenon,* phenomenon, *res gestae*

**v:** hypostatize, materialize, reify

**THINK**

**a:** abstracted, Aristotelian, bemused, cogitable, cogitabund, cogitative, conceptual, conceptualistic, contemplative, dianoetic, intellectual, meditative, mentiferous, pensive, ruminant, ruminative, telepathic, thinkable n: abstraction, science, cerebration, cogitation, conception, conceptualization, consideration, contemplation, daydream, excogitation, ideation, ideology, intellection, lucubration, meditation, mentation, perception, philosophy, ponderation, reverie, speculation, thinking, thought

v: assume, cerebrate, cogitate, conceive, conceptualize, conjecture, contemplate, deduce, deem, deliberate, entertain, estimate, excogitate, figure, hypothesize, ideate, intellectualize, introspect, intuit, lucubrate, meditate, mull over, muse, opine, ponder, presume, ratiocinate, rationalize, reflect, ruminate, speculate, theorize

*illogical:* alogical, dereistic

*thinker:* contemplater, philosopher, speculator, theorist

**THIRD**

a: tertian, tertiary, triennial

n: trimester

*combining form:* ter-

*fear of 13:* triadaidekaphobia

**THIRST**

a: parched, thirsty

n: anadipsia, dipsomania, polydipsia

v: quench, satisfy, slake

**THOROUGH**

a: arrant, complete, consummate, extreme, out-and-out, perscrutative, thoroughly

*combining form:* cata-

**THOUGHTFUL**

a: abstracted, calculative, circumspect, cogitative, considerate, contemplative, deliberative, discreet, engrossed, heedful, immersed, intent, introspective, judicious, meditative, mindful, penetrating, pensive, philosophical, politic, preoccupied, provident, prudent, reflective, sagacious, speculative, studious, wise

*thoughtless:* abstracted, frivolous, heedless, improprietary, improvident, imprudent, inattentive, incogitable, incogitant, incogitative, inconsiderate, insensate, unmindful

**THOUSAND**

a: chiliadal, chiliastic, millenarian, millenary, millennial, millesimal

n: chiliad, millenary, millennial, millenniary, millennium

*combining forms:* kilo-, milli-

*thousand-millionth:* billionth, giga-, nano-

**THRASH**

v: beat, drug, flog, flourish, lambaste, lick, paddle, thump, vanquish, whip

**THREAD**

a: capillaceous, capilliform, filamentous, filar, filipendulous

n: filament, floss, ligature, ravel, warp, weft, woof

*ball:* clew, cop, hank, skein

*combining forms:* nemat-, nemato-

*of story:* leitmotif, leitmotiv

*threadbare:* banal, barren, commonplace, deteriorated, hackneyed, *jejune*, shabby, stale, stereotyped, tatterdemalion, trite, vapid, worn

**THREAT**

a: apocalyptic, baleful, comminatory, denunciatory, fateful, foreboding, imminent, impending, inauspicious, menacing, minacious, minatorial, minatory, ominous, overhanging, portentous, pressing, prognostic, sinister, threatening

n: anathema, *caveat*, coercion, commination, constraint, danger, denunciation, duress, Four Horsemen, hazard, jeopardy, menace, minacity, omen, peril, portent, presage, risk, saber rattling, sword of Damocles, ultimatum

v: bluster, comminate, deter, fulminate, hazard, hector, imperil, intimidate, inveigh, jeopardize, lower, menace, portend, suborn, threaten

**THREE**

**a:** *a trois*, pyramidal, ternary, ternate, third, treble, triangular, trichotomic, trichotomous, trigonal, trigonous, trilateral, trinal, trinary, trinitarian, tripartite, triple

**n:** *menage a trois*, *ternion*, third, triad, trichotomy, trilogy, trinity, trio, tripartition, triplet, triplex, triplicate, triplication, triplicity, triumvirate, *trivium*, *troika*

**v:** triplicate, trisect

*300:* tercentenary, tercentennial

*cards or dice:* trey

*combining forms:* stere-, stereo-, ter-, tri-

*dimensional:* anaglyph, *diorama*, *grisaille*, hologram, perspective, *trompe l'oeil*

*in one:* triune

*leaved:* trefoil, trifoliate

*months:* trimester, trimestrial

*-part painting:* triptych

*stand:* teapoy, tripod, trivet

*wise men:* Magi

*years:* triennial, *triennium*

**THRESHOLD**

**a:** liminal

**n:** beginning, boundary, eve, gate, limen, outset, verge

*below:* subliminal

**THRIFT**

**a:** frugal, miserly, parsimonious, provident, prudent, scrimping, skimping, sparing, sumptuary, thrifty

**n:** conservation, economy, frugality, husbandry, parcity, providence, prudence

*unthrifty:* improvident, imprudent, lavish, prodigal, wasteful

**THRILL**

**n:** bang, enchantment, enthrallment, *frisson*, kick, shiver

**THROAT**

**a:** gular, guttural, jugular

**n:** gorge, gullet, thorax

**THROB**

**a:** palpitant, pulsatile, pulsating, pulsatory

**n:** *ictus*, oscillation, *palmus*, palpitation, pulsation, undulation

**v:** beat, oscillate, palpitate, pulsate, undulate, vibrate

**THROUGHOUT**

**a:** completely, *passim*

**THRUST**

**n:** abstrusion, assault, intrusion, punch, *repartee*, *riposte*, shove, stab, *touche*

**THUMB**

**n:** pollex

*lacking:* epollicate

*pad:* heel, thenar

**THUNDER**

**a:** foudroyant, fulminating, fulmineous, fulminous, sulfureous, sulphureous, thunderous, tonitruant, tonitruous

**n:** boom, fulmination, roar

*fear:* tonitruphobia

**THUS**

**a:** consequently, *ergo*, hence, *sic,* so, yet

**TICKET**

**n:** *carte d'entree*, coupon, docket, label, pass, slip, voucher

*reseller:* scalper

**TICKLE**

**n:** titilation, titivation

**v:** annoy, excite, provoke, stimulate, titillate, titivate, torment

**TIDBIT**

**n:** bit, bite, kickshaw, *morceau*, morsel

**TIDY**

**a:** careful, dapper, methodical, natty, neat, orderly, painstaking, shipshape, *soigne, soignee,* spruce, systematic, trim

**n:** nattiness

**v:** primp, spruce up

**TIE**

**n:** ligation, ligature, linchpin, *nexus*, stalemate, *vinculum*

**v:** attach, bond, link, truss

**TIME**

**a:** *ad hoc,* calendric, calendrical, chronological, *pro tempore,* temporal

**n:** chronology, duration, interim, interval, nonce, period, span

**v:** temporalize

> *combining forms:* chron-, chrono-, temp-, tempor-

> *duration: ad infinitum,* aeonial, aeonian, aeonic, infinity, longitudinal, perpetual, perpetuity, temporality, timelessness

> *happening at same:* coincident, contemporary, simultaneous

> *measuring:* chronometry, chrononomy, horology

> *out of order:* anachronism, anachronistic

> *timeless:* dateless, eternal, everlasting, in perpetuity, indefinite, infinite, intemporal, interminable, perpetual

> *timepiece:* chronometer, clock, horologue, sundial, watch

> *tree ring:* dentrochronology

**TIMELY**

**a:** abreast, advantageous, apposite, appropriate, auspicious, expedient, lucky, opportune, propitious, providential, relevant, seasonable, tempestive, topical, up-to-date

**TIMID**

**a:** cowardly, craven, effeminate, gentle, humble, irresolute, pavid, pusillanemous, shrinking, shy, timorous, tremulous

**n:** fear, inferiority complex, pusillanimity, timidity, weakness

**TIN**

**a:** metal, stannic, stanniferous, stannous

**TINGE**

**n:** cast, color, dye, hue, shade, stain, tint, tone

**v:** affect, imbue, impregnate, tincture

**TINGLE**

**n:** *frisson,* glow, stimulation

**v:** excite, glow, prick, stimulate, sting, tickle

**TIP**

**n:** *baksheesh,* bribe, buckshee, dash, *douceur,* gift, gratuity, insinuation, *lagniappe,* perquisite, *pourboire, terminus, trinkgeld*

> *combining form:* acro-

**TIRADE**

**n:** fulmination, harangue, invective, philippic, protest, rage

**TIRED**

**a:** *blase,* bushed, depleted, *effete,* enervated, fatigued, flagging, jaded, languid, lazy, lethargic, overextended, prostrate, somnolent, soporific, weary

**n:** apathy, *ennui,* hebetude, languor, lassitude, lethargy, listlessness, sluggishness, *taedium vitae*

> *tireless:* indefatigable, sustained, unflagging, untiring

> *tiresome:* bromidic, dull, exhausted, exhausting, irritating, monotonous, tedious, weary

**TITLE**

**a:** titular, titulary

**n:** appellation, appellative, denomination, designation, honorific, legend, *lemma,* name, ownership, rubric, style, titularity

**TOAST**

**n:** pledge, salute, wassail

**v:** pledge

> *master: arbiter bibendi,* emcee, officiator

**TOE**

**a:** digiform, digit, phalanx

**n:** dactyl, digit, phalanges, phalanx
*big: hallux*
*combining forms:* dactyl-, dactylo-
*hoofed animal:* artiodactyl

**TOGETHER**

**a:** companionate, concomitant, conjoined, conjoint, conjointly, corollary, *en masse*, integrated, jointly, mutually, reciprocally, *tete-a-tete*, unanimous, unisonous, *vis-a-vis*

**n:** concentricity, concourse, concursion, confluence, congress, cooperation, mutuality, omneity, oneness, rapprochement, simultaneity, solidarity, togetherness, unanimity
*combining forms:* co-, com-, sym-, syn-

**TOLERANT**

**a:** agnostic, benevolent, benign, benignant, broadminded, complaisant, enduring, forbearing, indulgent, latitudinarian, lenient, long-suffering, magnanimous, mild, peaceable, permissive, placable, submissive, tractable, undogmatic

**n:** allowance, benevolence, fortitude, habituation, indulgence, *laissez faire*, latitudinarianism, license, magnanimity, stamina, sufferance, tolerance, toleration

**v:** brook, condone, countenance, endure, forgive, overlook, sanction, stomach, tolerate, withstand

**TOMB**

**n:** grave, mausoleum, sarcophagus, sepulcher, vault
*inscription:* epitaph
*monument:* cenotaph

**TOMBOY**

**a:** gamine, hoydenish, tomboyish

**n:** gamine, *garcon manque*, hoyden

**TONE**

**n:** accent, nuance, pitch, resiliency, *timbre*, tonality, tonicity, *tonus*

**v:** modulate

**TONGUE**

**a:** glossal, lingual, linguiform, lingulate
*combining forms:* -gloss, gloss-, glosso-

**TONIC**

**a:** bracing, invigorating, refreshing, restorative, roborant

**n:** catalyst, fillip, roborant

**TOO MUCH**

**a:** *de trop*, excessive, redundant, replete, superabundant, supererogatory, supernumerary, too many

**TOOL**

**a:** chrestic

**n:** armamentaria, armentarium, implement, instrument, materiel, utensil

**TOOTH**

**a:** dentate, denticulate(d), dentiform, serrate(d)

**n:** bicuspid, canine, dent, dentation, denticle, eyetooth, fang, incisor, laniary, molar, premolar, serration, wisdom
*combining forms:* dent-, denti-, -odon, odon-

**TOP**

**a:** apical, cacuminal, cacuminous, climactic, consummate, meridian

**n:** acme, apex, apogee, climax, consummation, crest, crown, culmination, maximum, meridian, *ne plus ultra*, pinnacle, summit, zenith

**v:** superimpose, surmount
*combining form:* acro-

**TOPIC**

**a:** current, thematic, timely, topical

**n:** gambit, issue, item, matter, question, *themata*, theme, *theorum*, thesis

**TORMENT**

**n:** affliction, agony, calamity, distress, excruciation, persecution, plague, purgatory, scourge, visitation

**v:** afflict, agonize, dragoon, excruciate, harrow, lacerate, persecute, plague, tantalize, tease

**TORPID**

**a:** apathetic, comatose, dormant, dull, hypnotic, lackadaisical, lethargic, nonchalant, phlegmatic, pococurante, sleepy, somnolent, stagnant, stolid, toporific

**TORTOISE**

**a:** chelonian, testudinal, testudinarious

**n:** terrapin, turtle

*shell:* carapace

**TOTAL**

**a:** absolute, all, *in toto,* out-and-out, sum, summatory, thoroughgoing, totally, utter

**n:** aggregate, entirety, integrality, mutuality, omneity, recapitulation, summarization, summation, totality, unanimity, universality

*combining forms:* hol-, holo-, pan-, pano-, pant-, panto-

**TOUCH**

**a:** abut, abutting, adjacent, attingent, concerning, contiguous, coterminous, juxtaposed, lambent, osculant, palpable, poignant, tactic, tactile, tactual, tangent, tangential, tangible

**n:** contact, contingence, continuity, impingement, *modicum,* palpation, *scintilla,* smattering, *soupcon,* tactation, taction, tangency, tincture, touching, trace, vestige

**v:** caress, fondle, impinge, manipulate, osculate, palpate

*increased sense:* hyperesthesia

*loss of:* astereognosis

**TOUCHY**

**a:** choleric, irascible, precarious, umbrageous

**TOUGH**

**a:** adamant, adamantine, aggressive, bold, crustaceous, durable, enduring, feisty, fibrous, forceful, hard-nosed, hardy, impassive, inured, resilient, resistant, spartan, stoical, stubborn, tenacious, threatening

**n:** hardihood, tenacity, toughness

**TOUR**

**n:** circuit, excursion, expedition, itineration, peregrination, pilgrimage, promenade, safari, whistle-stop

**TOWN**

**a:** *bourgeois,* municipal, *oppidan,* urban, urbanistic, urbanistic

**n:** city, municipality

*citizen: burgess, burgher,* citizen, *oppidan,* townsman, urbanite

**TOY**

**n:** bauble, geegaw, kickshaw, knickknack, whirligig

**TRACE**

**a:** delineative, vestigial

**n:** iota, jot, *modicum, scintilla,* semblance, vestige, vestiges, *vestigium*

**v:** delineate

**TRADE**

**a:** commercial, mercantile

**n:** clientele, commerce, commutation, merchandise, *metier,* occupation, patronage, profession, transaction

**v:** barter, negotiate, ply, traffic

*center: entrepot,* market, *rialto*

*restrictions:* boycott, embargo, protectionism, sanctions

*trader:* chandler, chapman, peddler, supplier

**TRADITION**

**a:** ancestral, characteristic, conventional, customary, filiopietistic, legendary, orthodox, prescriptive, traditional, tralatitious, unwritten, venerated, veteran

**n:** acceptation, convention, custom, folklore, habit, habits, practice, usage

**TRAGEDY**

**a:** calamitous, cothurnal, deplorable, lamentable, tragic, tragical, woeful

**n:** anagnorisis, catharsis, drama, hamartia, hubris, nemesis, peripeteia

**v:** tragedize

**TRAIT**

n: characteristic, feature, hallmark, idiosyncrasy, mark, particularity, peculiarity, point, quality

**TRAITOR**

a: faithless, iscariotic(al), perfidious, traitorous, treacherous, treasonable

n: *agent provocateur*, apostate, collaborator, defector, double-crosser, Judas, mole, plant, quisling, recreant, renegade, sleeper, stool pigeon, stoolie, subversive, tergiversator, turncoat, Uncle Tom

**TRANCE**

n: absorption, abstraction, coma, daze, ecstasy, hypnosis, raptus, somnolence, stupor, transport

**TRANSFORM**

a: metamorphic, metamorphous, permutative, transformative, transmutative

n: change, conversion, metamorphosis, permutation, renovation, transfiguration, transformation, transmogrification, transmutation

v: change, convert, metamorphose, renovate, transfigure, transmogrify, transmutate, transmute, turn

**TRANSIENT**

a: brief, deciduous, ephemeral, ephemerous, evanescent, fleeting, flighty, fugitive, impermanent, momentary, moving, preterient, short-lived, temporal, temporary, transitory

n: ephemerality, evanescence, flotsam and jetsam, fugacity, temporality, transiency, transitoriness

**TRANSLATE**

a: literal, *verbatim*

n: conversion, gloss, metagraphy, rendition, surtitle, transformation, transition, translation, transliteration, transmutation

v: dub, paraphrase, transliterate

 *loose:* paraphrastic

**TRANSMIGRATION**

n: metempsychosis, reincarnation

**TRANSMISSION**

n: conductance, conduction, conveyance

v: bear, carry, impart, metastasize, propagate, send, transfer, transmit

**TRANSPARENT**

a: amorphous, crystalline, diaphanous, fine, gossamer, hyaline, hydrophanous, intelligible, limpid, luminous, pellucid, perspicacious, sheer, translucent, transpicuous, vitreous, vitrescent

n: clearness, crystallinity, diaphaneity, limpidity, perspicacity, translucence, translucency, transparency, transpicuity, vitrescence

**TRANSPLANT**

a: heterochthonous, transplanted

**TRANSPOSITION**

n: metathesis, strephosymbolia

**TRAP**

a: insidious

n: deadfall, incarceration, inveiglement, pitfall, snare

v: capture, ensnare, incarcerate, inveigle

**TRASH**

a: cheap, trashy

n: balderdash, debris, *dejecta*, *detritus*, *ejecta, fatras*, garbage, muck, refuse, scrap, scum, waste

**TRAVEL**

a: ambulatory, discursive, errant, *incognito*, itinerant, locomotive, migrant, nomadic, perambulatory, peripatetic, portable, traveling, *viatic*

n: commutation, excursion, expedition, itineration, peregrination, pilgrimage, safari, wanderlust

v: commute, itinerate, journey, peregrinate, post, safari, tour, traverse

 *combining forms:* -drom, drom-, viat-

*expenses: per diem, viaticum*

*musician: jongleur,* minstrel, *troubadour, trouvere*

*refuge:* caravansary, hospice, hostelry, xenodochium

## TREACHERY

**a:** arrant, duplicitous, faithless, infamous, insidious, iscariotic, malignant, perfidious, Punic, rascally, traitorous, treacherous, unscrupulous, venomous, viperish

**n:** breach, disloyalty, duplicity, perfidy, treason, triplicity

## TREASON

**n:** betrayal, duplicity, *lese majeste, lese majesty,* perfidy, prodition, treachery

**v:** impeach

## TREASURE

**n:** *cache,* repository, thesaurization

**v:** thesaurize

*ship:* argosy

## TREASURER

**a:** financial, fiscal

**n:** bursar, chamberlain, *exchequer, quaestor*

## TREAT

**a:** therapeutic

**n:** medicament, medication, remedy, therapeusis, therapeutics, therapy, treatment

**v:** administer, attend, medicate, negotiate, nurse, regale

*science:* dosage, iatreusiology, iatrics, medicine, therapeutics, therapy

## TREATISE

**a:** epexegetic, exegetic

**n:** abecedarium, account, catholicon, discourse, disquisition, dissertation, encyclopedia, epexegesis, essay, exegesis, exposition, hornbook, pandect, primer, thesis, tract

*single subject:* monograph

## TREE

**a:** arboraceous, arboreal, arborescent, arboresque, arboriform, arborous, bosky, dendriform, dendroid, dendrophagous, dendrophilous

**n:** arboretum, boscage, conifer, coppice, copse, deciduous, evergreen, silva, spinney

*combining forms:* arbor-, dendr-, dendri-, dendro-, silv-

*spirit:* dryad, hamadryad

*time:* dendrochronology

## TREMBLE

**a:** quavering, trembling, tremorous, tremulous

**n:** agitation, murmur, tremblement, tremor, tremulation

**v:** agitate, quake, quaver, quiver, shake, shiver, throb, tremulate, vibrate

## TRENCH

**n:** bank, *banquette,* channel, chase, groove, *parados, scorbicula*

## TRESPASS

**n:** encroachment, impingement, infringement, misfeasance, transgression

**v:** encroach, impinge, infringe, intrude, invade

*trespasser:* encroacher, misfeasor, transgressor

## TRIAL

**a:** accusatorial, empiric, inquisitorial, judiciary, justiciable

**n:** affliction, calvary, demonstration, endeavor, experiment, hearing, ordeal, probation, tribulation, visitation, wager of battle

*and-error:* empiric, experimental, factual, heuristic, observational, problem-solving

## TRIANGLE

**a:** deltoid, deltoidal, pyramidal, pyriform, triangular, trigonal

**n:** pyramid, set square

**TRIBE**

**a:** ethnocentric, phratric

**n:** clan, ethnocentrism, phratria, phratry, tribalism

> *combining forms:* ethn-, ethno-

**TRICK**

**a:** artful, captious, circuitous, devious, dishonest, disingenuous, duplicitous, foxy, ingenious, ingenuous, insidious, intricate, machiavellian, shifty, skillful, sly, stratagemic, subtle, tortuous, tricky, unreliable

**n:** artifice, confidence trick, deception, duplicity, evasion, expedient, *finesse*, gambit, hocus-pocus, maneuver, manipulation, ploy, prestidigitation, roguishness, shift, stratagem, subterfuge, subtlety, trickery, wile, wiles

**v:** cajole, cheat, cozen, defraud, dodge, finagle, inveigle, manipulate, stunt, victimize

> *trickster:* charlatan, mountebank
>
> *victim:* dupe, fall guy, mark, pawn

**TRIFLE**

**a:** banal, commonplace, contemptible, decipient, frivolous, hackneyed, inconsequential, insignificant, negligible, nugacious, nugatory, paltry, picayune, puerile, ridiculous, trifling, trivial

**n:** *bagatelle*, bauble, desipience, flotsam and jetsam, folderol, geegaw, inconsequence, *inconsequentia*, kickshaw, *minutiae*, negligibility, *nihility*, nothingness, particle, *quelque-chose*, quibble, quiddity, subtlety, triviality

**TRINKET**

**n:** *bagatelle*, bauble, *bibelot, bijou*, bric-a-brac, doodad, folderol, frippery, gaudery, geegaw, kickshaw, knickknack, novelty, *objet d'art, quelque-chose*

**TRIP**

**n:** excursion, expedition, jaunt, junket, outing, peregrination, safari, travel

**v:** gallivant

> *record:* itinerary, plan

**TRIPLE**

**a:** ternary, ternate, third, threefold, treble, trichotomous, trinal, trine, trinitarian

**v:** triplicate

**TRITE**

**a:** banal, bromidic, commonplace, hackneyed, pedestrian, platitudinous, stereotyped, stereotypical, threadbare

**n:** banality, *bathos*, bromide, cliche, pedestrianism, platitude, stereotype, triteness

**TRIUMPHANT**

**a:** conquering, elated, exultant, jubilant, triumphal, victorious

**TRIVIAL**

**a:** inconsequential, inconsiderable, mediocre, nugacious, petty, trifling

**n:** banality, *inconsequentia*, inconsequentiality, *marginalia, minutiae*, mouse, nugacity, trivia, triviality

**TROOP**

**a:** logistic(al)

**n:** detachment, garrison, picket, reinforcements, vanguard

**v:** deploy, marshal, mobilize, muster, rally

> *formation:* array, echelon, *enfilade*, phalanx

**TROUBLE**

**a:** agitated, arduous, belligerent, distressing, disturbing, fractious, inconvenient, laborious, lamentable, obstreperous, onerous, pestilent, refractory, solicitous, stormy, troubled, troublesome, troublous, turbulent, unruly, vexatious

**n:** adversity, annoyance, chagrin, encumbrance, hindrance, obstruction, perplexity, uneasiness, vexation

**v:** discommode, perplex, raise Cain

> *person:* enfant terrible, powder keg, stormy petrel

**TRUE**

**a:** a *posteriori, a priori,* accurate, alethic, analytic, apodictic, authentic, candid, *en verite,* gnomic, indisputable, inherent, intrinsic, kosher, legitimate, official, orthodox, *pukka,* sincere, trustworthy, truthful, unassailable, unfeigned, veracious, veridical, verisimilar, verisimilous

**n:** accuracy, actuality, axiom, certainty, certitude, dialectic, fideism, fidelity, maxim, platitude, postulate, precision, probity, truism, truth, truthfulness, veracity, verity, verisimilitude

**v:** attest, corroborate, substantiate, validate, verify

*denial:* nihilism

*lover:* philalethist

**TRUST**

**a:** dependable, fiduciary, trustworthy

**n:** assurance, confidence, credence, dependence, monopoly, reliance

*betrayal:* duplicity, perfidy, traitorism

**TRY**

**a:** annoying, arduous, exacting, irritating, rigorous, strenuous, trying

**n:** attempt, foray

**v:** assay, contend, endeavor, essay, vie

**TUBERCULOSIS**

**a:** *phthisic,* tubercular, tuberculous

**n:** consumption, *phthisis,* TB

**TUFTED**

**a:** cespitose, comose, feathered, wispy

**TUMULT**

**a:** noisy, termagant, tumultous, turbulent

**n:** agitation, Babelism, brouhaha, commotion, disturbance, paroxysm, Sturm and Drang, turmoil, welter

**TUNE**

**a:** assonant, *chantant, d'accord, en rapport,* harmonious, homophonous, melodious, rhythmic, symphonious, syntonic, syntonous, tuneful, unisonant

**n:** air, *aria,* chorus, *continuo, descant,* intonation, jingle, measure, medley, *melisma, quodlibet,* refrain, sonance, strain, syntonization

**v:** syntonize

**TURN**

**a:** alternating, anfractuous, contorted, flexuous, rotary, rotating, serpentine, tortuous, vertiginous

**n:** about-face, flexure, gyration, reversal, *torque,* torsion, turning, *volte-face*

**v:** eddy, evert, gyrate, introvert, metamorphose, permute, *pirouette,* pivot, revolve, rotate, slue, swivel, transfigure, transmogrify

*aside:* aversion, declination, deflection, deviation, divergence, diversion, ricochet, veering

*combining forms:* -trop, trop-, -trope, -tropic, tropo-

*point:* climax, crisis, fulcrum, juncture, Rubicon, watershed

*to bone:* ossify

*to salt:* salify, salinize

*to stone:* petrify

*up: retrousse*

**TURTLE**

**a:** chelonian, testudinal

**n:** chelonian, terrapin

*shell:* carapace, mail

**TWELVE**

**a:** duodecennial, duodecimal, duodenary, twelfth

*combining form:* dodeca-

*night:* Epiphany

**TWILIGHT**

**a:** crepuscular, dim, vespertilian, vespertine

**n:** crepuscule, dusk, gloaming

**TWIN**

**a:** bigeminal, binary, didymous, dioscuric, duplicate, dyadic, gemel, *jumelle,* parallel n: *alter ego*, counterpart, sibling

*combining forms:* zyg-, zygo-

*of one ovum:* enzymotic, identical, monovular, monozygotic

*of two ovum:* biovular, dizygotic, dyzygotic, fraternal, non-identical

## TWINKLING

a: chatoyant, scintillating, scintillescent

n: fire, scintillization

v: scintillate, twinkle

## TWIRL

a: convolute, intorted, meandering, serpentine, sinuous, tortile, tortuous, vertiginous, volute

n: convolution, sinuosity, tortuosity, twistification

v: circle, contort, gnarl, gyrate, intort, vertiginate

## TWITCH

n: fasciculation, spasm, tic, vellication

v: vellicate

## TWO

a: *a deux*, amphibian, amphibious, bicameral, bifurcate, bigeminal, bilateral, binal, binary, bipartient, bipartisan, bipartite, bisected, dichotomic, dichotomous, diploid, distichous, dual, dualistic, dyadic, syngalagamatic, twifold, twiformed

n: bifurcation, bilaterality, deuce, dichotomy, diremption, duality, duplexity, duplicity, dyad

v: bifurcate, bisect, dichotomize, divide, halve

*combining forms:* ambi-, bi-, di-, dich-, dicho-, duo-, zyg-, zygo-

*conversation:* duologue

*-faced:* double-dealing, duplicitous, Janus-faced

*-footed:* biped

*government:* diarchy, diumvirate, *duumvir, duumvirate,* dyarchy

*-headed:* bicephalous

*-hoofed:* bifid, bisulcate

*-sided:* bilateral, bipartisan

*years:* biennial

## TYPE

a: average, characteristic, classic, commonplace, emblematic, exemplary, paradigmatic, prefigurative, quintessential, representative, run-of-the-mill, statutory, stereotypical, stock, symbolic, symptomatic, textbook, typic, typical, uniform

n: archetype, description, embodiment, epitome, exemplar, exemplarity, exemplification, exemplum, ilk, kidney, model, nature, personification, quintessence, quintessentiality, representation, species, stripe, type, typicality, typification

v: exemplify, typify

## TYRANNY

a: oppressive, tyrannous

n: absolutism, autocracy, despotism, oppression

*tyrant: autarch*, autocrat, *commissar*, despot, dictator, martinet, monocrat, overlord, *satrap*, warlord

## UGLY
**a:** disfigured, dowdy, grisly, grotesque, gruesome, homely, inaesthetic, misshapen, mutilated, repellent, repulsive, unappealing, unbeauteous, uncomely, uncosmeticised, unesthetic, unsightly

**n:** abomination, eyesore, hideosity

## ULTERIOR
**a:** hidden, latent, obscure, obtruse, remote, unavowed

## UNABRIDGED
**a:** complete, comprehensive, cyclopedic, *in extenso*, uncensored, uncut, unexpurgated

## UNADULTERATED
**a:** genuine, pure, simon-pure, true, uncorrupted

## UNAFRAID
**a:** bold, brave, fearless, unapprehensive

## UNANIMOUS
**a:** concordant, consentient, harmonious, *nem con, nemine contradicente, una voce,* unanimously, unisonant, unisonous

**n:** concordance, consension, consentience, harmony, unanimity

## UNAPPEALING
**a:** banal, dreary, dull, impersonable, inaesthetic, insipid, somber, subfuscous, trite, ugly, unbeauteous

## UNATTACHED
**a:** alone, bachelor, celibate, discrete, isolated, lone, loose, single, stag, uncommitted

## UNATTEMPTED
**v:** unessayed, untested, untried

## UNAUTHORIZED
**a:** apocryphal, contraband, counterfeit, illegal, illicit, proscriptive, spurious, unapproved, unauthoritative, unofficial, unorthodox, unsanctioned

## UNAVOIDABLE
**a:** accidental, certain, indubitable, ineluctable, inescapable, inevitable, unpremeditated

**n:** act of God, *casus foritus, force majeure*

## UNAWARE
**a:** ignorant, incognizant, nescient, oblivious, unconscious, unwitting

**n:** incognizance, incognoscibility, unawareness

## UNBALANCE
**a:** asymmetric, imperfect, unbalanced

**n:** astasia, disequilibration, disequilibrium, imbalance, instability

## UNBEATABLE
**a:** invincible, unconquerable, unexcelled, unsurpassable

## UNBECOMING
**a:** demeritorious, dishonorable, disreputable, immodest, impertinent, improper, inappropriate, inapt, incongruous, indecent, indecorous, unseemly, unsuitable, untoward

## UNBELIEVABLE
**a:** *ab absurdo,* improbable, incredible, incredulous, preposterous, prodigious

n: incredibility

*unbeliever:* atheist, disbeliever, heretic, infidel, latitudinarian, miscreant, nihilist, skeptic

*unbelieving:* aporetic, heretical, heterodox, incredulous, skeptical, unorthodox

## UNBEND

v: condescend, relax, slacken, straighten, unflex, vouchsafe

## UNBREAKABLE

a: adamant, adamantine, immarcescible, immutable, imperishable, indestructible, indissoluble, infrangible, inviolable, inviolate, invulnerable, irrefragable, irrefrangible

n: contiguity, continuity, continuum, perseverance, steadfastness

*unbroken:* contiguous, continuous, intact, inviolate, uninterrupted, unsubsided, untamed

## UNBRIDLED

a: crapulous, incontinent, intemperate, rampageous, rampant, riotous, unchecked, ungoverned, unrestrained

## UNCALLED FOR

a: gratuitous, impertinent, inappropriate, indecorous, unbecoming, unjustified, unmerited, unnecessary, unseemly

n: impertinency, impropriety, indecorousness, indecorum, unseemliness

## UNCERTAIN

a: ambiguous, ambivalent, amphibolic, contingent, controversial, dubious, dubitable, enigmatical, equivocal, flickering, impredictable, improbable, incalculable, inconclusive, indecisive, indefinite, indefinitive, indeterminate, irregular, moot, nebulous, penumbral, precarious, problematic, questionable, tentative, unformalized, vacillary, vacillating, vague, variable, visionary, wavering

n: ambiguity, ambivalence, amphibologism, contingency, dilemma, doubt, dubiety, dubiosity, fluctuation, fortuitousness, fortuity, incertitude, indefinitude, indetermination, inexactitude, penumbra, precariousness, predicament, quandary, skepticism, uncertainty

## UNCHANGEABLE

a: absolute, adamant, adamantine, changeless, consistent, constant, dependent, eternal, fixed, immutable, immutable, implacable, inalienable, inconvertible, inexorable, intact, intractable, irreversible, monolithic, permanent, pristine, sedentary, sessile, stabile, static, stationary, steadfast, stubborn, unchanged, uncompromising, unfaltering

n: staticism, status quo

## UNCIVILIZED

a: barbarian, barbaric, barbarous, discourteous, feral, Gothic, haughty, inhuman, primitive, savage, uncultivated, uncultured

n: barbarity, ferity, inhumanity, primitivity

## UNCLASSIFIABLE

a: acategorical, amorphous, heterogeneous

## UNCLE

a: avuncular, avunculocal

n: avuncularity

## UNCLEANLINESS

a: dirty, excrementious, filthy, immund, impure, maculate, putrid, unclean

n: acatharsia, feculence, immundity, maculacy, squalor

*fear:* mysophobia

*love:* mysophilia

## UNCOMMON

a: exceptional, outstanding, rare, *recherche*, special, strange, unusual

## UNCOMMUNICATIVE

a: laconic, obmutescent, reserved, reticent, silent, speechless, taciturn n: obmutescence, reticence, taciturnity

## UNCOMPLIMENTARY

a: antagonistic, derogatory, disparaging, dyslogistic, ungracious

## UNCOMPROMISING

a: extreme, firm, inflexible, intractable, intransigent, recalcitrant, severe, strict, ultra, unyielding

n: intransigence, recalcitrance

## UNCONCERN

a: apathetic, calm, *debonair*, indifferent, insouciant, lackadaisical, nonchalant, phlegmatic, *pococurante*, uncolicitous, unconcerned

n: apathy, indifference, insouciance, nonchalance

## UNCONDITIONAL

a: absolute, infinite, plenary, raw

n: unconditionality

## UNCONGENIAL

a: asocial, discordant, discourteous, incompatible, incongruous, inharmonious, uncivil, ungregarious, unsociable

n: asocialism, asociality, incompatibility, uncongeniality, unsociability

## UNCONQUERABLE

a: Achillean, impregnable, indefeasible, indomitable, inexpugnable, insurmountable, intractable, invincible, invulnerable, irrepressible, unsurpassable, unyielding

n: impregnability, invincibility

## UNCONSCIOUS

a: comatose, insensible, unaware

n: catalepsy, catatonia, coma, insensibility, narcosis, unconsciousness

## UNCONTROLLED

a: disobedient, incontinent, irrepressible, rampant, stubborn, unbounded, unbridled, unchecked, uncontrollable, ungoverned, unrestrained

n: rampancy, unrestraint

## UNCONVENTIONAL

a: alternative, Bohemian, degage, disreputable, eccentric, heretical, heterodox, *outre*, raffish, uncultured, unorthodox

n: heresy, heterodoxy, solecism, transgression, unconventionality, unorthodoxy

## UNCOUTH

a: agrestic, barbarous, clownish, incondite, indecorous, plebeian, provincial, rude, rustic, uncultivated

n: babbittry, baboonery, *gaucherie*, *indecorum*, rudeness, rusticity

## UNCOVER

a: *al fresco*, hypaethral, naked, uncovered, upaithric

v: disinter, exhume, expose, reveal, unearth

## UNDAUNTED

a: bold, brave, fearless, intrepid, staunch, undiscouraged, undismayed

## UNDECIDED

a: abeyant, ambivalent, inconstant, irresolute, pendant, pendent, pending, *sub judice*, uncertain, under advisement, undetermined, unresolved, unsettled, vacillating, volatile, wavering

## UNDENIABLE

a: clear, *flagrante delicto*, incontestable, incontrovertible, indisputable, indubitable, red-handed, unquestionable

n: indisputability, indubitability

## UNDER

a: below, inferior, nether, subalternate, subjacent, subordinate, substrative

n: inferior, infraposition, subalternity, subordination

v: infrapose, infraposition

　　*combining forms:* hypo-, infra-, sub-

## UNDERGROUND

a: chthonian, submundane, subterranean, subterrestrial

*transportation:* bunker, catacombs, crypt, metro, subway, undercroft

## UNDERHAND

**a:** chicane, clandestine, deceitful, devious, disingenuous, duplicitous, furtive, Machiavellian, oblique, sinister, stealthy, surreptitious, wily

**n:** chicanery, duplicity, sinisterity, stealth, surreption, underhandedness

## UNDERLYING

**a:** basic, beneath, fundamental, implicit, innate, subjacent, substantive, substratal, substrative, subtending, underneath

## UNDERSTAND

**a:** accessible, apperceptive, appercipient, clear, connotative, empathetic, empathic, exoteric, implicit, implied, intelligible, intelligential, intuitive, limpid, perspicacious, sympathetic, tacit, translucent, understandable, understood

**n:** acumen, apperception, apprehension, comprehensibility, discernment, empathy, *entente*, impenetrability, implication, insight, intelligence, intuition, perception, perspicacity, rapport, reason, savvy, signification, understanding

**v:** apprehend, compass, comprehend, conceive, digest, discern, encompass, fathom, penetrate, perceive

*beyond normal:* abstruse, arcane, cabalistic, profound, recondite

*slow:* astigmatic, ignorant, pedestrian, purblind

*study:* noology

## UNDERWORLD

**a:** chthonian, infernal, plutonian, plutonic, subterranean

**n:** Dis, Hades

## UNDESIRABLE

**a:** bad, cancerous, egregious, evil, flagrant, inappropriate, inexpedient, inopportune, leprous, malignant, objectionable, rejected, sarcomatous, scabrous, unenviable

## UNDEVELOPED

**a:** crude, embryonic, immature, inchoate, incipient, latent, nascent, primitive, primordial, quiescent, rudimentary, vestigial

## UNDISCIPLINED

**a:** aimless, disaffected, haphazard, intractable, mutinous, recalcitrant, refractory, tumultuary, unrestrained, unruly

## UNDOING

**n:** defeasance, destruction, labefaction, reversal, ruin

*combining forms:* de-, dis-

## UNDRESSED

**a:** *deshabille, dishabille*

**v:** disrobe, doff

## UNDULY

**a:** all-out, excessively, overweening

## UNDYING

**a:** amaranthine, continuous, endless, everlasting, immarcescible, immarcessible, immortal, immutable, indestructible, lasting, permanent, perpetual

## UNEARTHLY

**a:** celestial, chthonian, fantastic, heavenly, miraculous, preternatural, supernatural, unworldly

## UNEASINESS

**a:** dysphoric, erethic, restless, uneasy

**n:** agitation, angst, anxiety, apprehension, compunction, constraint, disquiet, disquietude, dyspathy, dysphoria, inquietude, instability, malaise, penitence, queasiness, remorse, restlessness, scruple

## UNEQUAL

**a:** disparate, disproportionate, dissimilar, inadequate, incommensurate, inegalitarian, inequalitarian, inequitable, irregular, unjust, variable

**n:** inequality

*combining form:* aniso-

## UNEQUALED

**a:** incommensurable, incomparable, matchless, *ne plus ultra, nonpareil,* peerless, transcendent, unparagoned, unparalleled, unprecedented, unrivaled, unsurpassed

**n:** *ne plus ultra,* nonesuch, nonpareil, paragon

## UNEVEN

**a:** asperate, asperous, asymmetric, asymmetrical, disparate, dissymetric, dissymetrical, erratic, inadequate, inequitable, irregular, spasmodic, unproportionate, unsymmetric(al)

## UNEXPECTED

**a:** accidental, adventitious, aleatory, fortuitous, incongruous, sudden, supervenient, unannounced, unanticipated, unforeseen, unheralded, unsuspected

**n:** serendipity, *trouvaille,* unawares

## UNEXPLORED

**a:** uncharted, undetermined, unfathomed, uninvestigated, unplumbed

**n:** *terra incognita*

## UNEXPRESSED

**a:** implicit, implied, inarticulate, tacit, unspoken, unuttered

## UNFADING

**a:** amaranthine, immarcescible, immortal, permanent, undying

## UNFAIR

**a:** biased, disproportionate, excessive, inequitable, invidious, partial, prejudiced, unjustified, unwarranted

**n:** inequity

## UNFAITHFULNESS

**a:** errant, unfaithful, wayward

**n:** apostasy, disloyalty, improbity, infidelity, perfidy, treachery

*person:* cuckold, philanderer, philogynist

## UNFAMILIAR

**a:** exotic, foreign, inconversant, strange, unaccustomed, uncanny, unknown

## UNFATHOMED

**a:** ethereal, immense, infinite, undetermined, unsounded, vast, wide

## UNFAVORABLE

**a:** adverse, depreciatory, derogatory, detrimental, disadvantageous, disparaging, dyslogistic, inauspicious, inclement, inimical, ominous, pejorative, portentous, sinister, sinistrous, undesirable, unpropitious

*combining forms:* -dys, dys-

## UNFEELING

**a:** analgesic, apathetic, callous, impassible, impenitent, impervious, impiteous, implacable, incompassionate, indurate, insensitive, insentient, obdurate, stoical, uncaring, unemotional, unresponsive

**n:** callousness, insensibility

## UNFORGIVABLE

**a:** inexcusable, inexpiable, irremissible, unpardonable

*unforgiving:* impenitent, implacable, relentless

## UNFORTUNATE

**a:** calamitous, deplorable, hapless, inappropriate, infelicitous, inopportune, lamentable, unlucky, unpropitious, unsuitable, untoward

## UNFRIENDLY

**a:** alienated, aloof, asocial, clannish, cliquish, cold, disaffected, estranged, exclusive, forbidding, frosty, hostile, inhospitable, inimical, unapproachable, uncongenial, unfavorable, ungregarious, unsympathetic, xenophobic

## UNGODLY

**a:** blasphemous, desecrating, heathenish, impious, irreligious, pagan, profane, sacrilegious, sinful, terrible, unholy n: blasphemy, impiety, irreligiosity, ungodliness

v: heathenize, paganize, vulgarize

**UNGRATEFUL**
a: crude, repellant, thankless, ungracious

**UNHAPPINESS**
a: alienated, anhedonic, antagonized, disconsolate, disgruntled, dismayed, disquieted, dysphoric, estranged, inept, infelicific, infelicitous, melancholy, miserable, mournful, unfortunate, unhappy, wretched

n: anhedonia, dysphoria, infelicity, melancholy, misfortune, sadness, wretchedness

v: bemoan, lament, repine, rue

**UNHEALTHY**
a: inimical, insalubrious, insalutary, insanitary, morbid, noxious, pathological, pernicious, septic, unhealthful, unwholesome

n: insalubrity, malady, malaise, morbidity

**UNIFIED**
a: afferent, amalgamative, cementatory, centralizing, centripetal, coadunate, coadunative, conjugate, conjugative, consociate, consolidating, ecumenical, henotic, integrated, integrative, *irenic*, syncretic, syncretistic, unifying, united

n: accouplement, alliance, allness, anastomosis, *anschluss*, association, coalescence, concordance, concrescence, conjugation, fusion, *gestalt*, harmony, integral whole, integration, omneity, oneness, rapprochement, singleness, solidarity, suture, totality, unanimity, unification, union, unity

v: agglutinate, amalgamate, associate, centralize, coadunate, colligate, concatenate, concur, conglutinate, conjugate, consolidate, cooperate, federate, incorporate, join, syncretize, unify

   *unifier:* concatenator, integrationist, syncretist

**UNIFORM**
a: comparable, consistent, constant, equable, equiform, harmonious, homogenous, invariable, isogenous, monolithic, symmetrical, synonymous, unanimous, unchanging, undifferentiated

n: equability, equanimity, homogeneity, isogeny, monolithism, monotony, panoply, resemblance, semblance, similitude, unanimity, uniformity

**UNIMAGINATIVE**
a: frigid, insipid, *jejune*, monotonous, pedantic, pedestrian, pointless, practical, prosaic, spiritless, torpid, unleavened

**UNIMPORTANT**
a: dispensable, finical, frivolous, immaterial, incidental, inconsequential, insignificant, insubstantial, irrelevant, marginal, meticulous, minor-league, minutiose, minutious, nugatory, paltry, picayune, rabbinic(al), subordinate, trifling, trivial, unessential, unimpressive

n: *bagatelle*, insignificance, makeweight, *minutia*, *minutiae*, nonentity, nonevent, passenger, trivialities, unimportance

**UNINTENTIONAL**
a: accidental, inadvertent, involuntary, unintended, unpremeditated, unwitting

n: inadvertence, inadvertency

**UNIQUE**
a: eccentric, exceptional, idiographic, incomparable, matchless, *nonpareil*, peerless, preeminent, rare, *sui generis*, transcendent, uncommon, unequaled, unexampled, unparalleled, unprecedented, unrivaled

n: nonesuch, *nonpareil*, paragon, phoenix, phoenixity, *rara avis*, unicity, uniqueness, uniquity

   *combining form:* idio-

**UNIT**
a: integrative, monadic, monadological, monistic, unitary

**n:** denomination, entity, existent, grade, measure, monad, weight

**UNIVERSAL**

**a:** catholic, cosmic, cosmological, cosmopolitan, ecumenical, encyclopedic, epidemic, macrocosmic, pandemic, panharmonic, peregrine, transcendental

**n:** catholicity, cosmos, firmament, *logos*, macrocosm, universality, universe

  *combining forms:* cosm-, cosmo-

  *knowledge:* pansophism, pansophy

  *language:* Esperanto, pasigraphy

  *small scale:* microcosm

  *study:* cosmogeny, cosmogony, cosmography, cosmology, teleology, universology

**UNJUST**

**a:** aggrieved, inequal, inequitable, iniquitous, unequal, unwarranted, wrong, wrongful

**UNJUSTIFIED**

**a:** gratuitous, iniquitous, injudicious, insulting, needless, uncalled for, unwarranted

**UNKIND**

**a:** cruel, disgracious, disobliging, harsh, inconsiderate, inhumane, severe, ungracious, ungrateful

**n:** inconsideration, ingratitude, ungratefulness, unkindness

**UNKNOWN**

**a:** agnogenic, anonymous, cryptogenic, idiopathic, imponderable, incalculable, incogitable, incomprehensible, inconspicuous, inglorious, innominate, noumenal, obscure, phanterogenetic, uncharted, unhonored, unknowable, unsung

**n:** imponderables, *inconnu, noumenon, terra incognita*

**UNLAWFUL**

**a:** *bar sinister,* illegal, illegitimate, illicit, irregular, malfeasant

**n:** crime, malfeasance, misdemeanor

**UNLEAVENED**

**a:** azymous, banal, pedestrian, tedious, trite, unimaginative

**n:** *matzo*

**UNLIKE**

**a:** anomalous, antipathic, disparate, dissimilar, heterogeneous, incongruous

**n:** disparity, heterogeneity, incongruity, unlikeness

**UNLIKELY**

**a:** doubtful, dubious, dubitable, except, implausible, improbable, incredible, *nisi,* save

**n:** dubiety, dubiousness, implausibility, improbability, unlikelihood

**UNLIMITED**

**a:** boundless, endless, free, immeasurable, immeasurate, imponderable, infinite, innumerable, interminable, perpetual, plenipotent(ial), plenipotentiary, unconfined, unimpeded, untrammeled, vast

**n:** boundlessness, infinity, perpetuity

**UNLOAD**

**v:** disburden, discard, discharge, disencumber, disgorge, dump, eject, jettison

**UNLUCKY**

**a:** disastrous, foreboding, hapless, ill-starred, inauspicious, inopportune, ominous, portentous, star-crossed, unfortunate, unpromising, unpropitious, untoward

**n:** jinx

**UNMANAGEABLE**

**a:** disobedient, recalcitrant, reckless, stubborn, uncontrolled, undisciplined, wild

**n:** recalcitrance

**UNMARRIED**

**a:** celibate, common-law, parthenian, parthenic

**n:** celibacy, celibate, *posslq*
**v:** cohabit

**UNMINDFUL**
**a:** abstracted, careless, forgetful, inattentive, neglectful, oblivious, remiss, unaware

**UNMISTAKABLE**
**a:** clear, clear-cut, cut-and-dried, decisive, definite, definitive, manifest, obvious, patent

**UNNAMED**
**a:** anonymous, *incognito*, innominate, nameless, pseudonymous, undubbed, unidentified, unknown, unsigned, unspecified
**n:** anonymity, pseudonymity

**UNNECESSARY**
**a:** dispensable, expendable, gratuitous, inessential, needless, redundant, supererogatory, superfluous, supernumerary, uncalled for, undeserved, unjustified, unwarranted
**n:** inessentiality
**v:** forestall, obviate, preempt

**UNOBSERVANT**
**a:** astigmatic, impercipient, inattentive, incurious, unseeing

**UNOFFICIAL**
**a:** contraband, informal, officious, offstage, unauthorized, unorthodox, unsanctioned

**UNORIGINAL**
**a:** conventional, counterfeit, derivative, imitative, musty, predictable, shopworn, stereotype, timeworn, trite, unimaginative
**n:** bromide, cliche, commonplace, inanity, platitude

**UNORTHODOX**
**a:** heretical, heterodox, radical, unconventional

**n:** heresy, heterodoxy, unconventionality, unorthodoxy
*person:* maverick

**UNPAIRED**
**a:** azygous, odd, single, uncoupled, unmatched

**UNPARALLELED**
**a:** epochal, exceptional, *ne plus ultra*, *nonpareil*, supreme, unequaled, unsurpassed

**UNPARDONABLE**
**a:** inexcusable, inexpiable, unforgivable, wrong

**UNPLEASANT**
**a:** abhorrent, bilious, depreciatory, disagreeable, disgusting, disparaging, horrible, insufferable, pejorative, plutonian, plutonic, repugnant, rude, spiteful, unpalatable, unpleasing, unwholesome, vexatious
**n:** disagreement, disamenity, unpleasantness
*combining form:* caco-

**UNPOLISHED**
**a:** agrestic, boorish, coarse, gauche, ill-mannered, inurbane, rough, uncivilized, uncouth, unrefined

**UNPREDICTABLE**
**a:** ambivalent, capricious, chameleonic, erratic, fickle, incalculable, mercurial, quicksilver, volatile

**UNPREJUDICED**
**a:** amenable, cosmopolitan, detached, disinterested, dispassionate, equitable, impartial, objective, receptive, unbiased

**UNPREMEDITATED**
**a:** accidental, extemporaneous, hasty, headlong, impromptu, undesigned, unintentional

**UNPROFITABLE**
**a:** dry, frustaneous, idle, infructuous,

inutile, sterile, unremunerative, unrewarding, useless

n: inutility

**UNQUALIFIED**

a: disbarred, disqualified, incompetent, ineligible, plenary, unreserved, unrestricted, unworthy

**UNQUESTIONABLE**

a: certain, clear, implicit, indisputable, indubitable, positive, sure, undisputable, undoubted

**UNREALISTIC**

a: affected, artificial, barmecidal, *baroque*, chimerical, delusive, disembodied, dramatic, fantastic, fictitious, Gothic, histrionic, idealistic, illusional, illusive, illusory, imaginary, impalpable, imperceptible, impracticable, incorporeal, insubstantial, intangible, melodramatic, phantasmagoric, phantasmal, phantom, platonic, quixotic, romantic, staged, unreal, unsubstantial, utopian, visionary

n: aeriality, ideality, unrealism, unsubstantiality

**UNREASONABLE**

a: absonant, excessive, fatuous, illogical, inappropriate, incongruous, inordinate, irrational, paralogical, paralogistic, preposterous, stubborn, unconscionable

n: illogicality, incoherence, irrationality, unreasonableness, unsoundness

**UNREFINED**

a: barbaric, brutish, coarse, earthy, inelegant, primitive, troglodytic, uncultured, unsophisticated

**UNRELATED**

a: accidental, arbitrary, discrete, disjointed, dissociated, extraneous, extrinsic, heterogenous, impertinent, inapplicable, inapposite, incidental, intercalary, irrelevant, parenthetical, separate, tangential

**UNRELIABLE**

a: arbitrary, capricious, changeable, contradictuous, dangerous, disreputable,

duplicitous, erratic, feckless, fickle, fitful, flighty, fly-by-night, haphazard, impetuous, impulsive, mercurial, quicksilver, random, shiftless, skittish, tenuous, treacherous, tricky, unconscionable, undependable, unprincipled, unscrupulous, untenable, untrustworthy, villainous, volatile, whimsical

n: unreliability

**UNRESTRAINED**

a: bizarre, exaggerated, excessive, extravagant, flamboyant, free, immoderate, immoral, impertinent, indiscriminate, inordinate, lawless, limitless, open, *outre*, plenary, plenipotential, rampant, spontaneous, unchecked, uncontrolled, wanton

**UNRIVALED**

a: incomparable, *nonpareil*, peerless, supreme, unequaled, unparalleled

**UNRULY**

a: boisterous, disobedient, feral, headstrong, intractable, mutinous, obstinate, rampageous, rampant, recalcitrant, recusant, refractory, stubborn, turbulent, unbridled, undisciplined, ungovernable, wanton, willful

**UNSATISFIED**

a: insatiated, unfulfilled, unhappy, unsatisfiable

**UNSEASONABLE**

a: improper, inexpedient, inopportune, *malapropos*, untimely, unusual

**UNSEEMLY**

a: inappropriate, indecent, indecorous, solecistic, unbecoming, unseasonable

thing: barbarism, impropriety, solecism

**UNSELFISH**

a: altruistic, charitable, chivalrous, concerned, generous, magnanimous, philanthropic, selfless

n: altropathy, altruism, generosity, magnanimity, philanthropy, unselfishness

**UNSETTLED**

**a:** abeyant, aimless, deranged, erratic, itinerant, nomadic, pendant, pendent, unstable, vagrant

**n:** instability, itinerancy, vagrancy

*person:* drifter, vagabond, vagrant

**UNSHAKABLE**

**a:** adamant, firm, impregnable, inflexible

**UNSIGNED**

**a:** anonymous, blank, pseudonymous, unidentified

**UNSKILLFUL**

**a:** amateurish, awkward, gauche, inapt, inept, inexperienced, *maladroit*, menial, unartful, unskilled

**UNSOCIABLE**

**a:** antisocial, asocial, detached, discordant, incompatible, inharmonious, inhospitable, insociable, isolated, moronic, reserved, solitary, solitudinarian, troglodytic, uncompanionable, uncongenial, ungregarious, withdrawn

**n:** reserve

**UNSOLVABLE**

**a:** inextricable, inscrutable, insoluble, unexcogitable

**UNSPARING**

**a:** free, hard, inexorable, procrustean, profuse, profuse, relentless, ruthless

**UNSOPHISTICATED**

**a:** artless, crackerbarrel, guileless, homespun, ignorant, ingenuous, modest, *naive,* oafish, philistine, plebeian, simple, simpleminded, uncouth, unenlightened, uninformed, unpolished, unpretentious, unworldly

**n:** bumpkin, great unwashed, hayseed, hick, *hoi polloi,* lowest common denominator, riffraff, rustic, yokel

**UNSPEAKABLE**

**a:** execrable, *horrible dictu,* indescribable, ineffable, nefandous, unmentionable, unutterable

**UNSPOKEN**

**a:** implicit, implied, inarticulate, obmutescent, tacit, uncommunicated, understood, unexpressed, unsaid, unuttered

**UNSTABLE**

**a:** astatic, ataxic, fickle, fluctuating, in flux, inconstant, labile, mercurial, mutable, precarious, protean, teetering, titubant, tottering, unbalanced, unreliable, unsteady, vacillating, variable, vertiginious, volatile, voluable, wobbly

**n:** astasis, astaticism, ataxia, lability, volatility, volubility

**UNSUBSTANTIAL**

**a:** aerial, diaphanous, ethereal, filigree, imaginary, inane, *papier-mache,* shadowy, unreal, visionary

**n:** aeriality, ethereality

**UNSUITABLE**

**a:** discordant, inapplicable, inappropriate, inapt, incongruent, inept, infelicitous, inharmonious, inopportune, unseemly, unsuited, untimely

**UNTAMED**

**a:** barbarous, feral, ferocious, fierce, rambunctious, unsubdued, vicious, wild

**UNTHINKABLE**

**a:** extraordinary, incogitable, inconceivable, incredible, unimaginable, unspeakable

*unthinking:* careless, casual, glib, heedless, inattentive, incogitant, inconsiderate, mechanical, unmindful, unmotivated, uphilosophic

**UNTIDY**

**a:** bedraggled, careless, disheveled, dowdy, frowsy, haphazard, scraggly, slipshod, slovenly, tatterdemalian, unfastidious, ungroomed, unkempt

**n:** bedlam, dishevelment, mare's nest, untidiness

**UNTIMELY**

**a:** inappropriate, inauspicious, inconvenient, inexpedient, inopportune, intempestive, premature, unfavorable, unpropitious, unpunctual, unseasonable, unsuitable, unsuited

**UNTIRING**
**a:** endless, everlasting, indefatigable, sustained, tireless, unflagging, unwearying

**UNTOUCHABLE**
**a:** impalpable, imperceptible, intangible, inviolable, invulnerable, sacrosanct

**UNTRAINED**
**a:** illiterate, inexperienced, inexpert, nescient, uncultivated, uneducated, untaught, untutored

**UNTRIED**
**a:** callow, fledgling, green, immature, inexperienced, unattempted, unexpert, unfledged

**UNTRUE**
**a:** counterfeit, disloyal, fabulous, false, fictitious, mendacious, mythological, spurious, supposititious, unfaithful, untruthful, wrong
**n:** dishonesty, inaccuracy, inveracity, mendacity, untruthfulness

**UNUSUAL**
**a:** anomalistic, anomalous, bizarre, ectopic, exceptional, exotic, extraordinary, fantastic, grotesque, heteromorphous, heteromorphic, irregular, odd, *outre*, paranormal, peculiar, phenomenal, *recherche*, remarkable, singular, strange, unique, unorthodox, unwonted
**n:** *rara avis*, rarity, unusuality

**UNWANTED**
**a:** *de trop*, nonessential, redundant, superfluous, undesirable

**UNWELCOME**
**a:** *de trop, non grata,* redundant, superfluous, unacceptable

**UNWHOLESOME**
**a:** decayed, deleterious, immoral, inimical, insalubrious, malignant, morbid, pathological, pernicious, unhealthy

**UNWIELDY**
**a:** awkward, bulky, cumbersome, cumbrous, elephantine, hippotamian, involved, ponderous, ungainly

**UNWILLING**
**a:** adverse, averse, indisposed, involuntary, reluctant, stubborn
**n:** aversion, disinclination, nolition, reluctance, reluctancy, reluctation, repugnance, unwillingness

**UNWISE**
**a:** ill-advised, impolitic, impracticable, imprudent, indiscreet, inexpedient, injudicious, rash, senseless, untimely

**UNWORTHY**
**a:** base, derogatory, despicable, indign, ineligible, inglorious, undeserving, unmeet, unqualified, worthless

**UNYIELDING**
**a:** adamant, adamantine, inexorable, obstinate, perseverant, persistent, pertinacious, recalcitrant, remorseless, resolute, rigid, stubborn, tenacious, unbudging, unshakable

**UPHEAVAL**
**a:** cataclysmal, cataclysmic
**n:** agitation, cataclysm, change, convulsion, labefaction, orogeny, overthrow

**UPKEEP**
**a:** sustentative
**n:** care, conditioning, maintenance, support, sustentation

**UPLIFTING**
**a:** inspirational, inspirative, inspiriting, instigative

**UPRIGHT**
**a:** chivalrous, conscientious, honorable, perpendicular, plumb, punctilious, rectitudinous, scrupulous, vertical

n: integrity, mullion, perpendicularity, probity, rectitude, scrupulosity, stanchion, stile, uprightness, verticality

**UPRISING**

a: insurgescence, mutinous

n: *coup d'etat*, insurgence, insurgency, insurrection, mutiny, rebellion

**UPROAR**

a: pandemoniac

n: bedlam, brouhaha, *charivari*, clamor, confusion, furor, hubbub, pandemonium, tumult

**UPROOT**

a: deracinated, deracine, displaced, lumpen, rootless, uprooted

n: deracination, extirpation

v: deracinate, eradicate, exterminate, extirpate

**UPSET**

a: agitated, disconcerted, disquieted, distressing, flustered, harrowing, perturbed, worried

n: upheaval

v: capsize, discompose, disconcert, disparage, overthrow, overturn, subvert

**UPSIDE-DOWN**

a: inside-out, inverted, topsy-turvy

**UPSTART**

n: *arriviste*, johnny-come-lately, *nouveau riche, parvenu*

**UPWARD**

a: anabatic, ascensional, ascensive, assurgent

n: acclivity, assurgency, escalation

**URGENCY**

a: clamant, compelling, critical, exigent, imminent, impending, imperative, imperious, importunate, insentient, menacing, momentous, necessitous, peremptory, persistent, poignant, pressing, solicitous, straitened, urgent, vehement, vital

n: criticality, exigency, imminence, importunity, instancy

**URINE**

a: diuretic

n: miction, micturition

v: micturate, urinate, void

*part:* ureter, urethra

**USE**

a: advantageous, beneficial, chrestomathic, consuetudinal, customary, efficacious, expedient, feasible, functional, instrumental, opportune, practicable, practical, remunerative, traditional, usable, useful, utile, utilitarian, yeoman

n: applicability, application, consuetude, custom, deployment, disposition, efficacy, employment, exercitation, feasibility, functionality, mores, prescription, tradition, usage, utility, utilization

v: capitalize on, deplete, employ, exhaust, expend, exploit, impoverish, parlay, squander, utilize

*many:* polychresty

*useless:* afunctional, fruitless, futile, ineffectual, inefficient, inutile, nugatory, obsolete, otiose, outmoded, superannuated, unavailing, unprofitable, vain

*user:* beneficiary, consumer

**USUAL**

a: accustomed, common, commonplace, consuetudinary, conventional, current, customary, habitual, ordinary, predictable, prescribed, prevailing, prevalent, traditional, wonted

n: conventionality, prevalence, staple, tradition, usualness

**UTTER**

a: absolute, arrant, complete, consummate, effable, incarnate, peremptory, pluperfect, rank, sheer, unqualified, unspeakable, uttermost

n: arrant, articulation, descant, expression, observation, utterance

v: articulate, phonate, pronounce, speak

## VACANT

**a:** bare, barren, blank, empty, untenanted, vacuous, void, wanting

## VAGABOND

**a:** Bohemian, circumforaneous, homeless, itinerant, nomadic, *peregrine*, peripatetic, *picaresque*, roving, vagabondish, vagrant, wandering

**n:** Bohemian, flotsam and jetsam, gypsy, itinerant, nomad, *peregrine*, peripatetic, rogue, truant, wastral

## VAGUE

**a:** abstract, acategorical, aerial, ambiguous, ambivalent, amorphous, amphibolic, amphibological, cryptic, doubtful, dubious, dubitable, elusive, equivocal, illogical, imprecise, indecisive, indefinite, indeterminate, indistinct, intangible, obscure, undecided, vacillating, vague, vaporous

**n:** dubiety, dubiosity, insubstantiality, vagueness

   *suggestion:* hint, inkling, intimation, notion, nuance, *soupcon*, trace, umbrage

## VAIN

**a:** abortive, dogmatic, egoistical, egotistical, flatulent, fruitless, frustaneous, hollow, hopeless, hubristic, nugatory, officious, ostentatious, otiose, pedantic, pompous, pragmatic, pretentious, trifling, trivial, vainglorious, visionary

**n:** *amour-propre*, arrogance, egoism, egotism, flatulence, hollowness, *hubris*, ostentation, otiosity, pomposity, vainglory, vanity

## VALIANT

**a:** bold, brave, chivalric, chivalrous, intrepid, noteworthy, stalwart, stouthearted, valorous

**n:** *arete*, chivalry, gallantry, intrepidity, valor

## VALID

**a:** legitimate, reasonable

**n:** nostrification, validity

**v:** nostrificate, ratify

## VALUE

**a:** *ad valorem*, axiological, cherished, classic, coveted, esteemed, estimable, inestimable, irreplaceable, meritorious, priceless, treasured, valuable

**n:** asset, equity, heirloom, premium

   *little:* ambsace, anarchism, *bagatelle*, continental, nihility, triviality

   *rise:* accession, appreciation

   *study:* axiology

## VAMPIRE

**n:** Dracula, extortioner, *lamia*, sorceress, *succubus*, witch

## VANISHING

**a:** diaphanous, ephemeral, ethereal, evanescent, fleeting, unsubstantial

**n:** diaphaneity, ethereality, evanescence

**v:** disappear

## VAPOR

**a:** effluvial, miasmatic, miasmic, volatile

**n:** cloud, effluvium, exhalation, gas, miasma, smoke

**v:** sublimate

   *combining form:* atmo-

## VARIABLE

**a:** allotropic, alterable, ambivalent, bivalent, capricious, chameleonic, changeable, fickle, inconstant, irresolute, kaleidoscopic, manifold, mercurial, multiple, multiplex, multiplicitous, mutable, omnigenous, polymorphic, polymorphous, protean, quicksilver, vagrant

**n:** alternation, diversification, diversity, heterogeneity, latitude, *miscellanea*, miscellaneity, modification, multiformity, mutation, nuance, permutation, play, polymorph, saltation, tolerance, *varia*, variance, variation, versatility

**v:** diversify, vary

> *combining forms:* trop-, -trop, -tropic, tropo-
>
> *varied:* different, diverse, diversified, manifold, miscellaneous, mosaic, multifarious, multiform, multiple, myriad, sundry, variegated
>
> *variety:* assortment, genre, genus, medley, *melange*, stock, strain
>
> *various:* eclectic, *variorum*

## VARIEGATED

**a:** checked, checkered, chimeral, dappled, diversified, heterogeneous, iridescent, kaleidoscopic, mosaic, motley, multicolored, opalescent, parti-colored, piebald, pinto, prismatic, speckled, spotted, tessellated, varied

**n:** diversification, heterogeneity, iridescence, mosaic, tessellation, variegation

## VAST

**a:** boundless, colossal, comprehensive, cosmic, cyclopean, elephantine, gargantuan, grandiose, herculean, huge, immeasurable, imponderable, infinite, titanic, unlimited, worldwide

**n:** comprehensiveness, enormity, globality, immensity, infinitude, magnitude, vastitude, vastity, vastness

## VAULT

**a:** concamerated

**n:** concameration, crypt, *fornix*, groin, undercroft

## VEGETATION

**a:** herbivorous, phytophagous, vegetarian, verdant, verdurous

**n:** flora, herbage, verdancy, verdure

> *cultivation:* olericulture
>
> *eater:* fruitarian, *herbivora*, herbivore, vegan, vegetarian
>
> *garden: potagerie*

## VEILED

**a:** *chiaroscuro*, curtained, hidden, *incognito*, penumbral, *sfumato*, tenebrous

## VELVET

**a:** velutinous, velvety

**n:** nap, pile

## VENERABLE

**a:** ancient, patriarchal, respected, reverential

## VENGEANCE

**n:** fury, nemesis, reprisal, retaliation, retribution, revenge, scourge

**v:** exact, inflict, wreak

## VENTURE

**a:** adventurous, hazardous, venturesome

**n:** attempt, chance, endeavor, enterprise, gamble, jeopardy, risk, speculation, test, try, undertaking

## VENUS

**a:** Cytherean, Paphian, venereal, venerean, Venusian

**n:** Cytherean

## VERB

**a:** auxiliary, denominative, indicative, intransitive, irregular, modal, periphrastic, phrasal, prepositional, subjunctive, substantive, suppletive, transitive

**n:** deponent, gerund, infinitive, participle, verbification

**v:** verbify

**VERIFIED**

**a:** audited, confirmable, documented, established, seen, substantiated, verifiable, verificatory

**n:** verificability

**VERSATILE**

**a:** adept, ambidextrous, handy, inconstant, multiskilled, polygraphic, skilled

**n:** ambidexterity, versatility

**VERSE**

**n:** burden, chorus, doggerel, limerick, metrification, poem, poetry, posy, prosody, refrain, stanza, stave, strophe, versification

**VERTICAL**

**a:** erect, orthograde, orthostatic, perpendicular, plumb, upright

**n:** perpendicularity, verticality

**VETERAN**

**a:** seasoned, venerable

**n:** *grognard*, old hand, oldster, patriarch, patrician, pro, professional, stager

**VEX**

**a:** afflictive, annoying, choleric, disordered, impatient, pestilent, petulant, restive, vexatious

**n:** affliction, chagrin, displeasure, impatience, irritation, mortification, pique, vexation

**v:** afflict, annoy, bother, bug, harass, pique, roil, trouble, worry

**VIBRATE**

**a:** oscillant, tremulant, tremulous, undulant, undulatory, vibratory

**n:** quivering, shaking, tremor, vibration

**v:** oscillate, palpitate, quaver, resonate, tremulate, undulate

**VICIOUS**

**a:** cruel, egregious, feral, flagitious, flagrant, immoral, iniquitous, spiteful, villainous, wicked

**n:** barbarity, egregiousness, ferity, flagitiousness, flagrancy, iniquity, viciousness, villainy

**VICTORY**

**a:** epinician, resounding

**n:** achievement, ascendancy, bidigitation, Cadmean victory, conquest, mastery, ovation, prevailment, Pyrrhic victory, subjugation, supremacy, triumph, trophy, vee, walkover

**VIEW**

**a:** commanding, dominant, panoptic, panoramic, synoptic

**n:** *coup d'oeil*, diagram, frame of reference, illustration, opinion, outlook, overview, panorama, perspective, perspectivity, prospect, scope, scrutiny, survey, viewpoint, vista

    *combining forms:* -scape, -scopy

**VIGILANT**

**a:** aware, Cerberean, circumspect, heedful, observant, wary, watchful

**VIGOR**

**a:** animated, bracing, *con brio*, cyclonic, dynamic, energetic, flourishing, forceful, *puissant*, robustious, spirited, strenuous, torrential, vehement, vigorous, virile

**n:** ardor, *brio*, dynamism, *elan*, flair, gusto, impetuosity, lustiness, *panache*, robusticity, stamina, tonicity, verve, vitality, vivacity, zest

**VILE**

**a:** abhorrent, abominable, bad, contemptible, degenerate, despicable, egregious, flagitious, flagrant, infamous, ignominious, low, odious, profligate, putrid, shocking, sordid, vicious, vulturine, vulturous, wicked

**n:** abomination, abuse, despicability, putridity, vileness

**VILLAGE**

**a:** microcosmic, villageous, villagic

**n:** hamlet, microcosm, settlement, town

**VILLAIN**

**a:** miscreant, rapscallion, unconscionable, unprincipled, unscrupulous, villainous

**n:** blackguard, caitiff, charlatan, criminal, dastard, delinquent, miscreant, mountebank, ne'er-do-well, profligate, rapscallion, rascal, recreant, rogue, scalawag, scamp, traitor, varlet, wrongdoer

*villainy:* miscreancy, wickedness

**VINDICATION**

**a:** revengeful, vindictive, wrathful

**n:** compurgation, exoneration, justification, revenge, substantiation

**v:** absolve, exculpate, exonerate, justify, substantiate, vindicate

**VINEGAR**

**a:** acetic, acetous, acidulant, acidulous, vinegary

**n:** alegar

**VIOLATE**

**a:** transgressive, violational, violative

**n:** contravention, desecration, encroachment, impingement, infraction, infringement, misdeed, profanation, ravishment, transgression, trespass, violation

**v:** contravene, defile, desecrate, impinge, ravish, traduce, transgress

**VIOLENT**

**a:** amok, destructive, *Grand Guignol,* gratuitous, impetuous, maniacal, raging, rampant, tempestuous, torrential, turbulent, vehement

**n:** barbarity, cataclysm, convulsion, disturbance, ferocity, fervor, flashpoint, fury, impetuosity, impetuousness, mania, mayhem, outrage, passion, rampancy, tempestuousness, turbulency, upheaval, vehemence, violence

**VIOLIN**

**a:** pandurate, panduriform

**n:** Amati, fiddle, kit, *pochette,* Stradivarius

**VIRGIN**

**a:** parthenian, parthenic, undefiled, unspoiled, unsullied

**n:** *houri,* vestal virgin, virgination

*combining forms:* parthen-, parthenopartial: *demi-vierge*
*worship:* parthenolatry

**VIRTUE**

**a:** exemplary, holier-than-thou, meritorious, rectitudinous, righteous, sanctimonious, seraphic, virginal, virtuous

**n:** *arete,* chastity, *dharma,* fidelity, integrity, morality, probity, rectitude, sanctity, uprightness

*four:* fortitude, justice, prudence, temperance

**VISION**

**a:** apparent, discernible, macroscopic, manifest, obvious, patent, perceptible, visible

**n:** acuity, apparition, discernment, eyesight, foresight, hallucination, illusion, keenness, oxyblepsia, perception, percipience, perspicacity, prospect, vision

**v:** envision, foresee, imagine, perceive, visualize

*bad:* amblyopia, astigmatism
*double:* diplopia

**VISIONARY**

**a:** aerial, chimerical, doctrinaire, dogmatic, dreamy, idealistic, impractical, irresponsible, ivory-tower, laputan, notional, platonic, platonistic, poetic, quixotic, romantic, starry-eyed, theoretical, translunary, unsubstantial, utopian

**n:** doctrinaire, dogmatist, dreamer, enthusiast, fantast, ideologist, ideologue, philosopher, romancer, romanticist, theorist

**VISIT**

**n:** frequentation, sojourn, sojournment, visitation

**v:** frequent, habituate, haunt, sojourn

*visitor: habitue,* sojourner, visitant

**VITAL**

**a:** animated, energetic, essential, fundamental, important, indispensable, mortal, pivotal

**n:** *elan vital,* vigor, vitality

*lack:* abiotrophic, adynamic, desiccated, devitalized, enervated

*science:* demography

**VIVID**

**a:** eidetic, glowing, lively, picturesque, piquant, poignant, striking, trenchant, visual

**VOCALIZE**

**a:** articulated, enunciated, phonated, phonetic, sonant, sonic, sonorous, vocalized, voiced

**n:** articulation, cadence, *diapason,* enunciation, inflection, intonation, modulation, phonation, register, *timbre,* vocalization

**v:** articulate, enunciate, inflect, modulate, phonate, pronounce, voice

*clearness:* lamphrophonia

*combining forms:* -phon-, -phone, phono-, -phony

*high:* gynecophonous

*loss:* aphonia, obmutescence

*of people: vox populi*

**VOID**

**a:** nugatory, null, vacuous

**n:** vacuum

**v:** abrogate, delete, negate, nullify, quash, repeal, rescind, veto

**VOLUME**

**a:** bouffant, bulky, encyclopedic, huge, multitudinous, voluminous

**n:** amount, amplitude, capacity, cubage, extent, loudness, magnitude, mass, number

**VOMIT**

**a:** emetic, regurgitating, vomiting

**n:** disgorgement, emesis, hyperemesis, regurgitation

**v:** disgorge, heave, regurgitate, retch

*drug:* emetic

*illness:* bulimia, *bulimia nervosa,* bulmorexia, nausea

**VOTE**

**a:** plebiscitary, plebiscitic

**n:** franchise, plebiscite, referendum, suffrage, voting

**v:** canvass, solicit

*study:* psephology

*voter:* constituency, constituent

**VOW**

**a:** votary, votive

**n:** profession

**VOWEL**

*more than one:* plurivocalic

*preceding:* antevocalic, prevocalic

**VULGAR**

**a:** bathetic, boorish, common, earthy, ignoble, irreverent, lewd, maudlin, mawkish, meretricious, obscene, philistine, plebeian, *Rabelaisian,* ribald, scurrile, scurrilous, sordid, specious, tawdry, uncouth, unrefined, yahoo

**n:** commonness, plebeianism, profanity, ribaldry, scurrility, vulgarity, vulgarization

**v:** heathenize, paganize, plebeianize, vulgarize

**VULTURE**

**a:** vulturine, vulturous

**WAGE**

**a:** *bourgeois,* proletarian, stipendiary

**n:** compensation, emolument, fees, honorarium, remuneration, stipend

    *earner:* blue-collar, *bourgeois,* proletarian, proletariat

**WAIL**

**a:** plangorous, ululant, wailing

**n:** caterwaul, keen, lamentation, ululation

**v:** caterwaul, deplore, lament, mewl, pule, ululate, whimper, whine

**WAIST**

**n:** corsage, girth

    *slender:* waspish

**WAITER**

**n:** *garcon, maitre d'hotel*

**WALK**

**a:** *a pied,* ambulant, ambulatorial, ambulatory, circumnambulatory, deambulatory, gressorial, itinerant, orthograde, orthostatic, pedestrian, perambulatory, peripatetic, plantigrade

**n:** carriage, circumambulation, constitutional, deambulation, department, gait, peregrination, peripateticism, promenade

**v:** amble, ambulate, circumambulate, dally, deambulate, mosey, move, pace, pedestrianize, perambulate, peregrinate, promenade, ramble, roam, rove, sashay, saunter, sidle, stride, strut, swagger, toddle, traipse, traverse, trudge, waddle

    *alone:* solivagant

    *combining form:* -grade

*horizontal as animal:* pronograde

*inability:* astasis, ataxia

*with only toes:* digitigrade

**WALLOW**

**n:** degeneration, degradation, volutation

**v:** flounder, grovel, languish, welter

**WANDER**

**a:** circumforaneous, circumambulatory, desultory, digressive, discursive, errant, erring, itinerant, meandering, migratory, nomadic, Odysseyan, peregrinic, peripatetic, pleonastic, *solivagant,* straying, vagabond, vagarious, vagrant

**n:** circumambulation, divagation, dromomania, errantry, excursion, expatiation, fugivity, itinerancy, itineration, meandering, odyssey, perambulation, peregrination, peregrinism, peregrinity, vagabondage, wanderlust

**v:** circumambulate, deviate, divagate, expatiate, gad about, gallivant, itinerate, meander, perambulate, peregrinate, ramble, roam

    *wanderer: goliard,* itinerant, migrant, minstrel, Odysseus, peregrinator, *peregrine, solivagant, troubadour,* vagabond

**WANING**

**a:** declinatory, decrescent, ebbing, lessening

**n:** abatement, declension, declination, decrescence, diminution, flagging, recession

**WANT**

**a:** deficient, desiderative, destitute, lacking, necessitous, poor, short, wanting n: dearth, deficiency, *desiderata, desideratum, desideria,* destitution, exigency, indigence

v: desiderate, necessitate, need, require

## WAR

a: agonistic, amazonian, armigerous, bellicose, belligerent, disputatious, hawkish, hostile, internecine, martial, militant, oppugnant, Spartan, unpacific, warlike

n: armageddon, carnage, *casus belli,* holocaust, hostility, warfare

v: mobilize

*after:* postbellum

*before:* antebellum

*between:* interbella, interbellum

*combining forms:* -machia, -machy

*opposition:* mispolemical, pacifistic

*ship:* armada, *barbette,* flotilla, squadron

*weaponry: armamentarium,* armaments, materiel

## WARM

a: ardent, calefacient, calefactory, calescent, calid, enthusiastic, euthermic, incalescent, lukewarm, tepid, thalpotic, warming

n: ardency, ardor, calefaction, calescence, calor, cordiality, empressement, fervor, graciosity, graciousness, heat, hospitality, passion, temperature, thalposis, warmth

v: limber up

*-blooded:* endothermic, homeothermic, homoiothermic

*dish:* chafing dish

*extreme:* hyperpyrexia

*warmed-over: rechauffe*

*warmup:* prologue, prolusion

*wine: chambre*

## WARNING

a: admonitorial, admonitory, deterrent, exhortative, homiletic, monitorial, monitory, ominous, pathognomonic, premonitory, prodromal, salutary, sematic

n: admonition, augury, auspice, beacon, *caveat, caveat emptor,* denunciation, exhortation, homily, jeremiad, monition, omen, portent, premonition, presage, presentiment, prodrome, sign, tocsin

v: admonish, caution, counsel, exhort, precondition, sermonize, warn

## WART

a: verrucose, verrucous

n: ecphyma, excrescence, keratosis, papilloma, plantar, tubercule, *verruca, verruca vulgaris*

v: vegetate

## WASHING

a: ablutionary

n: ablution, *lavabo,* lavage, lavation, maundy, nipter

v: clean, deterge, douse, elutriate, eluviate, erode, irrigate, leach, mundify, wash

## WASTE

a: atrophic, atrophied, emaciated, tabescent

n: carrion, debris, decrement, detritus, dross, effluent, *egesta, ejecta,* excrement, *excreta,* feces, offal, offscourings, *ordure,* recrement, *rejecta, rejectamenta, scoria,* slag

v: denudate, depauperate, depredate, deracinate, despoil, devastate, dissipate, exhaust, pillage, squander

*giving off:* depurant, emunctory, excremental, excrementious, excretory

*land:* desolation, devastation

*time:* dally, dawdle, dilatory, fritter away, lollygag, procrastinating, tarry

*waste away:* atrophy, emaciate, macerate

*wasteful:* extravagant, immoderate, improvident, imprudent, lavish, prodigal, profligate, spendthrift, superfluous, thriftless, wanton

## WATCH

a: alert, Argus-eyed, aware, on the *qui vive,* surveillant, vigilant, watchful, wideawake

**n:** chaperonage, invigilation, scrutiny, surveillance, vigil

**v:** *chaperone*, invigilate, proctor, supervise, survey

*instrument:* analog, chronograph, chronometer, digital, fob, stem-winder

*watcher:* chaperone, custodian, surveillant, voyeur, watchdog

*watchmaking:* horology

**WATER**

**a:** aquatic, aquiferous, humid, hydrated, hydrous, ichorous, natant, natatory, serous, subaqueous, submarine, suboceanic, watery

**n:** *aqua pura*, aquosity, humectation, humidity, seven seas

**v:** therapy

*absorbing:* bibulous, deliquescent, hydrophilic, hygroscopic, osmotic

*flowing:* autopotamic, eupotamic

*hate:* hydrophobia

*land and water:* amphibious

*living in:* helolimnic, lotic

*needing:* anhydrous, desiccated

*needing little:* xerophilous

*plant:* aquiculture, hydroponics

*remove:* dehydrate, desiccate, distil, evaporate, inspissate, subliminate

*salt:* halophilic

*shallow:* adlittoral

*still:* eupotamic, lentic, stagnicolous, tychopotamic

**WAVY**

**a:** flexuating, flexuous, ondoyant, oundy, plangent, undulant, undulating, vermiculate, waving

**n:** billow, breaker, comber, roller, tsunami, undertow

**v:** brandish, flourish, gesticulate, heave, oscillate, surge, swell, undulate, wave

**WAVER**

**a:** ambivalent, desultory, fitful, inconclusive, indecisive, intermittent, irresolute, pendulous, spasmodic, vacillating, wavering

**n:** indecision, irresolution, oscillation, vacillation

**v:** fluctuate, hesitate, oscillate, vacillate

**WAX**

**a:** ceraceous, ceriferous, ceruminous, waxlike, waxy

**n:** ambergris, cerumen, spermaceti

**v:** simonize

*combining form:* cero-

**WAY**

**a:** multivious

**n:** *modus operandi, modus vivendi*

**v:** wend

*waylay:* ambush

**WEAK**

**a:** adynamic, anemic, anile, anodyne, asthenic, atonic, attenuated, bland, debilitated, debilitating, decrepit, degenerate, devitalized, devitalizing, *effete,* enervated, enervating, enfeebled, etiolated, feckless, fragile, impotent, *impuissant,* ineffective, ineffectual, infirm, insipid, invertebrate, irresolute, languid, lethargic, lily-livered, maladive, powerless, pregnable, rickety, spineless, supine, valetudinarian, vulnerable, weakened, weakening, wishy-washy

**n:** Achilles heel, adynamia, asthenia, atony, attenuation, attrition, cachexia, cowardice, debility, defect, enervation, erosion, flaw, foible, hypodynamia, hypokinesia, hypokinesis, imbecility, impotence, inanition, infirmity, labefaction, languor, lassitude, myasthenia, soft underbelly, tabes, tenuity, vulnerability, weakness

**v:** adulterate, atrophy, attenuate, debilitate, denudate, devitalize, dilute, disable, emasculate, enervate, enfeeble, exhaust, flag, incapacitate, languish, sag, stultify, subvert, undermine, unnerve, weaken, wilt

*combining form:* -asthen, asthen-

**WEALTH**

**a:** abundant, affluent, chrematistic, luxuriant, luxurious, mammonish, opulent, profuse, rich, wealthy

**n:** abundance, affluence, bonanza, El Dorado, Golconda, *lucre*, luxuriance, luxury, opulence, profusion, prosperity, substance

> *opposite:* illth, poverty
>
> *person:* Croesus, fat cat, leviathan, *nouveau riche*, plutocrat, plutogogue, rich, tycoon
>
> *study:* chrematistics
>
> *worship:* mammon, plutolatory, plutomania

**WEAR**

**n:** attrition, corrosion, detrition, erosion

**v:** corrade, erode

**WEARINESS**

**a:** *ad nauseum*, apathetic, *blase*, bored, burnt-out, flagged, spent, tuckered, weary

**n:** boredom, *ennui*, fatigue, languishment, lassitude, lethargy, monotony, tedium

**WEATHER**

**a:** meteorologic(al), synoptic(al)

**n:** depression, front, high, hurricane, jet stream, low, monsoon, rainstorm, snowstorm, storm, tornado

> *forecasting:* aeromancy, biometeorology, climatology, meteorology, prognostication
>
> *harsh:* asperity, inclemency

**WEDDING**

**a:** epithalmic, hymeneal, nuptial

**n:** *charivari*, marriage, nuptials, shivaree

**WEDGE-SHAPED**

**a:** cuneal, cuneate, cuneatic, cuneiform, sphenic

**n:** chock, coign, cuneiform, *quoin*

**WEEK**

**a:** hebdomadal, weekly

**n:** hebdomad

**WEIGHT**

**a:** burdensome, corpulent, cumbersome, cumbrous, gravid, grievous, important, influential, momentous, onerous, ponderable, ponderal, ponderous, significant, solemn, weighty

**n:** *avoirdupois*, barbell, consequence, dumbbell, gravity, importance, influence, plumb, ponderability, ponderance, ponderosity, prestige, tare

**v:** burden, encumber, hinder, weigh

> *combining form:* baro-
>
> *equal:* equiponderant, isonomous
>
> *great:* preponderant
>
> *little:* imponderable

**WEIRD**

**a:** bizarre, cabalistic, eerie, grotesque, incantatory, *Kafkaesque*, mysterious, odd, strange, supernatural, talismanic, uncanny, unearthly, unusual

**n:** *bizarrerie, grotesquerie*

**WELCOME**

**a:** delectable, felicitous, salutatory, salutiferous

**n:** *bienvenue*, greeting, open arms, *persona grata*, salutation

**WELL**

**a:** *bravissimo, bravo*, eudaemonic, euphoric, euphorious

**n:** *eudaemonia*, euphoria

> *known:* celebrated, classic, eminent, notorious, proverbial
>
> *water:* artesian, phreatic

**WESTERN**

**a:** American, European, Hesperian Occident, Occidental, west, westerly

**n:** Occident, sunset

> *westerner:* Hesperian, Occidental

**WET**

**a:** clammy, dank, humectant, humid, hydrophanous, muggy, paludal, paludian, paludinal, paludine, paludous, sodden, soggy

**n:** aquosity, humectation, humidity, wetness

**v:** douse, saturate, sluice, soak, swill

*combining form:* hygro-

**WHALE**

**a:** cetacean, cetaceous

**n:** baleen, beluga, cetacean, finback, grampus, narwhal, orc, porpoise, rorqual

*bone:* scrimshaw

*food:* krill

*herd:* gam, pod

*parts:* ambergris, blowhole, blubber, fluke, spermacei, spiracle

**WHEAT**

**a:** farinaceous, frumentaceous

**n:** cracked wheat, durum, gluten, semolina

**WHEEL**

**a:** rotal, rotary, trochal

**n:** castor, lathe, sheave, sprocket, wharl, whorl

**WHIM**

**a:** capricious, captious, crotchety, fanciful, fantastic, impish, notional, peculiar, puckish, roguish, vagarious, whimsical

**n:** *bizarrerie,* caprice, chimera, eccentricity, fancy, *fantasque,* idiosyncrasy, megrims, oddity, peculiarity, puckishness, quiddity, quirk, roguery, singularity, vagary, whimsicality

**WHIP**

**n:** crop, rod, scourge, switch, taws

**v:** castigate, chastise, flagellate, flay, flog, fustigate, scourge

**WHIRL**

**a:** revolving, vertiginous

**n:** bustle, commotion, dervish

**v:** *pirouette,* vertiginate

*whirlpool:* charybdis, eddy, gulf, gurge, helix, maelstrom, riptide, spiral, volute, vortex, whirlwind, whorl

*whirlwind:* cyclone, dust devil, hurricane, tornado, twister, typhoon, waterspout

**WHISPER**

**a:** murmuring, whispering

**n:** murmur, rustling, sough, susurration, susurrus

**v:** siffilate

**WHISTLE**

**n:** feedback, *siffleur*

**v:** siffle

**WHITE**

**a:** albescent, candent, candescent, canescent, etiolated, marmoreal

**n:** candescence, canescence, etiolation

**v:** blanch, whiten

**WHOLE**

**a:** *en bloc, en masse,* impartite, *in toto,* intact, maiden, panoramic, synoptic, unbroken, undivided, unimpaired, unitary, unmarred, unmotivated, wholly

**n:** aggregate, analysis, ensemble, gestalt, integer, integral, integrality, integrity, macrocosm, plenitude, plenum, *solidium,* sum, sum total, synthesis, totality, wholeness

**v:** consolidate, synthesize

*combining forms:* hol-, holo-

**WHOLESOME**

**a:** beneficial, curative, healthful, remedial, restorative, salubrious, salutary, salutiferous

**n:** salubrity, salutariness, wholesomeness

**WICKED**

**a:** abhorrent, abominable, atrocious, base, blasphemous, devilish, diabolic(al), dissolute, evil, execrable, flagitious, hateful, heinous, hellish, immoral, impious, iniquitous, intractable, irreligious, licentious, malignant, nefarious, notorious, odious, profane, sacrilegious, satanic, saturnine, scandalous, vicious, vile, villainous, viperish, viperous

**n:** abomination, *diablerie*, enormity, evil, infamy, iniquity, sinfulness, turpitude, wickedness

## WIDE

**a:** allopatric, broadcast, catholic, comprehensive, diffuse, dispersed, epidemic, expansive, extensive, far-reaching, illimitable, intensive, magnitudinous, pandemic, *peregrine*, predominant, prevalent, regnal, regnant, rife, universal, widespread

**n:** amplitude, catholicity, comprehension, diameter, dimension, ecumenicity, expansiveness, expansivity, fullness, liberality, magnitude, prevalence, regnancy, spaciousness, thickness, universality, width

> *knowledge:* bibliognostic, cyclopedic, omniscient, pansophic(al)

## WIDOW

**n:** dowager, relict

## WIFE

**a:** matrilocal, *uxor*ial, uxorious, wifely

**n:** consort, helpmate, helpmeet, spouse, *uxor*

> *murder:* uxoricide
>
> *one:* monogamy, monogyny
>
> *two or more:* polygamy, polygyny

## WILE

**n:** artifice, deception, feint, fraud, guile, machination, stratagem, trickery

## WILL

**a:** arbitrary, capricious, contrary, perverse, testate, volitional, willful

**n:** determination, disposition, inclination, intention, legacy, resolution, testament, velleity, volition

**v:** bequeath, demise, devise

> *without:* intestate

## WILLING

**a:** acceptant, acquiescent, amenable, complaisant, compliant, disposed, obliging, ungrudging, voluntary, willingly

**n:** alacrity, amenability, tractability, willingness

## WIND

**a:** aeolian, aeolic, anemophilous, blustery, eolian, wind-blown, winnowed

**n:** flatulence, *flatus*, jet stream, scud, sough, squall, susurration, zephyr

**v:** waft

> *away from:* upwind
>
> *combining forms:* anem-, anemo-, vent-, vento-
>
> *study:* anemography, anemology, anemometry
>
> *toward:* downwind, leeward

## WINDING

**a:** anfractuous, circuitous, contorted, devious, flexuous, meandering, meandrous, serpentine, sinuate, sinuous, tortuous, twisted

**n:** anfractuosity, flexuosity, intorsion, sinuation, sinuosity, torsion

**v:** intort, meander, undulate, wreathe

## WINDOW

**n:** aperture, casement, fenestra, fenestration, skylight

> *between:* interfenestral

## WINE

**a:** bacchant, oenopoetic, vinic, vinous

**n:** vintage

> *combining forms:* vin-, vini-, vino-
>
> *lover:* enologist, oenologist, oenophile, oenophilist
>
> *maker:* viniculturist, vintner, viticulturist
>
> *science:* oenology
>
> *steward: sommelier*

**WING**

**a:** aliferous, aliform, bipentate, dipterous, pteric

**n:** airfoil, *pinion*, pinna

*combining forms:* -pter, pter-, -ptero, ptero-

**WINK**

**n:** nictitation

**v:** nictate, nictitate, palpebrate

**WINTER**

**a:** boreal, brumal, heimal, hibernal

*dormancy in:* hibernation

**WISDOM**

**a:** acuminous, aphoristic, apothegmatic, circumspect, cognizant, discerning, discreet, discriminating, equitable, erudite, judicious, Nestorian, oracular, orphic, perspicacious, politic, profound, sagacious, sapient, Solomonian, sophistic, wise

**n:** acumen, discernment, discretion, discrimination, judgment, judicality, knowledge, perspicacity, prudence, rationality, sagacity, sageness, sanity, sapience, sapiency, subtlety

*combining forms:* prud-, sap-, -sophy

*hate:* misosophy

*human:* anthroposophy

*person:* guru, luminary, Nestor, patriarch, philosopher, sage, Solomon, *Solon*

**WISH**

**a:** benedictive, optative, precative

**n:** castle in the air, pipe dream, velleity

*bone: furcula*

**WIT**

**a:** Aristophanic, coruscating, epigrammatical, facetious, jocose, jocular, laconic, lambent, mercurial, pyrotechnic, scintillating, vivacious, wry

**n:** acumen, badinage, *bon mot, causerie,* coruscation, cuasticity, drollery, esprit, facetiousness, irony, jocosity, jocularity, liveliness, mordacity, persiflage, repartee, retort, sarcasm, spirit, whimsicality, witticism

**v:** coruscate, scintillate

*witticism:* aphorism, apothegm, *bijouterie, bon mot,* coruscation, epigram, *jeu de mots, jeu d'esprit,* jocosity, maxim, satire, truism

**WITCH**

**n:** Circe, enchantress, familiar, *lamia,* necromancer, pythoness, sibyl, sorcerer, sorceress, vampire, warlock, wizard

*group:* coven, *sabbat*

*witchcraft:* diabolism, enchantment, necromancy, occult, sorcery, *sortilege,* witchery

**WITHDRAW**

**a:** cloistered, isolated, secluded, sequestered, withdrawn

**n:** detachment, insularity, retraction, revocation, revulsion, subduction, withdrawal

**v:** abjure, countermand, disavow, dissociate, evacuate, recant, recede, relinquish, *renege,* repeal, rescind, retract, retreat, revoke, secede, subduct

*person:* hermit, recluse

**WITHER**

**a:** dry, *sere,* shriveled, withering

**n:** annihilation, devastation, senescence, tabescence, withering

**v:** atrophy, decline, paralyze, senesce, wizen

**WITHIN**

**a:** *ab intra,* autogenous, endogenous, esoteric, immanent, implicit, indwelling, inherent, internal, intrinsic

*combining forms:* end-, endo-, ento-, intra-, intro-

**WITHOUT**

**a:** advenient, adventitious, exogeneous, extraneous, extrinsic, inadvertently, irrespective of

*combining forms:* a-, an-

## WITHSTAND

**v:** bear, bide, brook, contest, endure, oppose, resist, take, wear

## WITNESS

**n:** deponent, deposition, obtestation, testimony

**v:** attest, obtest, testify

## WOE

**a:** crestfallen, forlorn, lamentable, melancholy, sorry, threnodic, woebegone, woeful

**n:** affliction, anguish, dolor, heartache, tribulation

    *tale:* jeremiad, lamentation, threnode, threnody

## WOLF

**a:** lupine

    *group:* pack, rout

    *turned into: loup-garou,* lycanthrope, lycanthropy, werewolf, wolfman

## WOMAN

**a:** distaff, feminine, muliebral, seductive

**n:** *charmeuse,* Circe, enchantress, feminality, femineity, femininity, *femme fatale, ingenue,* Mata Hari, siren, sorceress, vamp, womanhood, womankind

    *childless:* nullipara

    *club:* sorority, sorosis

    *distressed:* maenad

    *exclusion: purdah*

    *fashionable:* mondaine, sophisticate

    *fear:* gynephobia

    *government by:* gynarchy, gynecocracy, matriarchy

    *hate:* misogynism, misogyny

    *head of house: chatelaine, materfamilias,* matriarch

    *learned:* bluestocking

    *love:* philogyny

    *mean:* Delilah, shrew, termagant, *virago,* vixen

    *of age: bat(h)* or *(bas) mitzvah*

    *old:* beldame, dowager

    *silly: coquette,* flibbertigibbet, *soubrette*

## WONDERFUL

**a:** admirable, astonishing, astounding, extraordinary, ineffable, marvelous, miraculous, mirific, phenomenal, prodigious, stupendous, surprising, wondrous

**n:** *mirabile dictu*

    *year: annus mirabilis*

## WOOD

**a:** arboraceous, arboreal, arboreous, arborescent, ligneous, lignescent, nemoral, silvicolout, sylvan, sylvatic, sylvestran, wooded, wooden, woody, xyloid

**n:** driftwood, kindling, lumber, *marquetry, parquet,* pulp, timber, tinder

    *alcohol:* carbinol, methanol, methyl alcohol

    *combining forms:* lign-, ligni-, ligno-, xyl-, xylo-

    *eating:* xylophagous

## WOOLLY

**a:** flocculent, lanate, laniferous

**n:** alpaca, batting, cashmere, flock, shag, shetland

## WORD

**a:** lexical, semantic, semasiological, verbal, vocabular

**n:** *etymon, mot juste,* name, *semanteme*

    *adapt to English:* anglicise, anglicize

    *add letter:* prosthesis

    *agreeable:* euphemism

    *ambiguous:* amphibolism, amphibology, verbal fallacy

    *arbitrary coinage:* logodaedaly, nonce word

    *backward same as forward:* palindrome

    *catchword:* shibboleth

    *defining:* lexicography

    *degeneration:* bastardization, corruption, pejoration, verbicide *derived from foreign:* paronym

*derived from sound:* onomatopoeia, onomatope

*disparaging:* dysphemism

*drop first letter or syllable:* aphaeresis

*drop last letter or syllable:* apocopation, apocope, elision

*drop middle letter:* syncope

*expert:* etymologist, lexicography, morphologist, philologist, phonemicist, semanticist

*few syllables:* brachysyllabic

*for symbol:* ideogram, logogram

*for-word:* ad verbum, literal, literalistic, literatim, textual, *verbatim, verbatim et liberatim*

*four-letter:* tetragram

*game:* anagram, logomachy

*history:* etymology, lexicology, phylogeny, provenance, semantics

*idea with no:* anonym

*last syllable: ultima*

*long:* multisyllabic, polysyllabic, sesquipedalian

*many syllables:* polysyllabic, sesquipedalian

*misuse:* cacology, catachresis, impropriety, malapropism, solecism, spoonerism

*more than one meaning:* polysemantic, polysemous

*new:* neologism, neoterism

*next to last syllable:* penult, penultima

*of first letters:* acronym

*omission of sound:* apocopation, elision, haplology

*one meaning:* univocal

*parting: envoi,* farewell, valediction

*play on: equivoque*

*pronounced alike but spelled different:* homophone

*pronounced and spelled alike:* homograph, homonym

*repeat for effect:* alliteration, anadiplosis, battolology, cataphasia, iteration, ploce

*repeating:* echolalia, onomatomania, verbomania

*sentence expressed by:* holophrastic, polysyntheism

*spelled alike but different meaning and pronunciation:* heteronym

*study:* etymology, semantics, semasiology, semology, significs

*transposition of letters:* metathesis, strephosymbolia

*transposition of sounds:* spoonerism

*two syllables from last:* antepenult

*use other than intended:* antiphrasis, heterophemy, trope, tropology

*worship:* grammatolatry

*write in other alphabet:* transliterate

**WORDINESS**

**a:** circumlocutious, circumlocutory, copious, diffuse, garrulous, logorrheic, palaverous, pleonastic, profuse, prolix, protracted, redundant, repetitious, talkative, tautological, verbose, voluble, wordy

**n:** catalogic, circumlocution, diffusion, fecundity, garrulity, logorrhea, loquaciousness, loquacity, macrology, officialese, periphrasis, pleonasm, prolixity, redundancy, tautology, verbality, verbiage, verbigeration, verbomania, verbosity

**WORK**

**a:** assiduous, conscientious, diligent, employmental, industrial, occupational, sedulous, vocational, vocative

**n:** accomplishment, assignment, career, *chef d'oeuvre,* commission, corpus, drudgery, employment, exertion, *forte, magnus opus, metier, moil,* occupation, *oeuvre, opus, piece de resistance,* production, profession, quota, sedulity, task, vocation

*able to do any:* panurgic

*class:* proletarian, proletariat

*combining forms:* erg-, ergo-, oper-

*easy:* sinecure

*extra:* parergon, supererogation

*fear:* ergasiophobia, ergophobia

*love:* ergasiomania, ergomania, ergophilia

*minor:* opuscule, opusculum

*worked-over: rechauffe,* refurbished

*workmanship:* artisanship, artistry, craftsmanship, expertise, skill, virtuosity

*workshop: atelier*

## WORLD

**a:** cosmic, cosmopolitan, earthly, ecumenical, global, intramundane, macrocosmic, mundane, pandemic, peregrinic, planetary, secular, subastral, subcelestial, sublunary, temporal, *terrene,* terrestrial, universal, unspiritual, worldwide

**n:** creation, earth, ecumenicity, humanity, macrocosm, mankind, pandemia, secularism, secularity, sphere, temporality, universality

*ancient:* foreworld

*before creation:* antemundane, premundane

*belief in better:* meliorism

*end: gotterdammerung*

*little:* microcosm

*lower:* chthonian, plutonian, plutonic, subterranean, subterrestrial

*of dead:* netherworld

*outside:* extramundane, extraterrestrial, supermundane, supernatural, transmundane

*person: boulevardier,* cosmopolitan, cosmopolite

*private:* autocosm

*view: weltanschauung*

*-weariness: ennui*

## WORM

**a:** vermicular, vermiculate, vermiform

**n:** annelid, centipede, millipede, nematode, trematode

*combining forms:* helminth-, vermi-

*infested:* vermiculate, verminous, vermoulu

## WORN

**a:** debilitated, decrepit, degenerate, dilapidated, *effete,* enervated, etiolated, hackneyed, haggard, stereotyped, threadbare, trite, vapid

**n:** attrition, dilapidation, erosion

## WORRY

**a:** apprehensive, concerned, disconcerted, distressed, perplexed, worrying

**n:** angst, annoyance, anxiety, bugaboo, burden, complication, consternation, discomfiture, disquietude, *fantod,* harassment, nightmare, vexation

**v:** disconcert, harass, hector, importune, tantalize, torment

## WORSEN

**a:** denigrative, exacerbative, ingravescent, pejorative

**n:** declination, denigration, deterioration, disimprovement, exacerbation, ingravescence, pejoration, relapse, retrogression

**v:** aggravate bastardize, compound, debase, decline, degenerate, degrade, denigrate, deteriorate, disimprove, exacerbate, minify, pejorate, regress, relapse, retrograde, retrogress, tragedize

## WORSHIP

**a:** hierurgical, liturgical, monolatrous, monotheistic, religious, ritualistic, rubrical

**n:** adoration, adulation, devotion, *dulia,* henotheism, hierurgy, homage, *latria,* liturgy, monolatry, monotheism, observation, veneration

**v:** adore, adulate, observe, venerate

*of ancestors:* ancestor cult, filopietism, manism

*of Bible:* Biblioatry

*of books:* biblioatry, bibliomania

*of church:* ecclesiolatry

*of dead:* necrolatry

*of devil:* demonolatry, diabolism

*of dogs:* cynolatry

*of female clothing:* fetichism

*of foreign gods:* allotheism

*of government:* statolatry

*of idols:* iconolatry, idolatry

*of man:* anthropolatry

*of many gods:* polytheism

*of money:* mammonism, plutolatry, plutomania

*of nature:* pantheism, physiolatry, priapism

*of obscenity:* aischrolatreia

*of old things:* archaicism, archeolatry

*of religion:* ecclesiolatry, hierolatry

*of self:* autotheism

*of Shakespeare:* bardolatry

*of snakes:* ophiolatry

*of sun:* heliolatry

*of symbols:* symbololatry

*of virgin:* parthenolatry

*of women:* philogyny

*of words:* grammatolatry

*place of:* adoratory

**worshiper:** adulator, congregant, devotee

## WORTH

**a:** appropriate, chivalrous, commendable, condign, creditable, eligible, estimable, exemplary, heroic, honorable, laudable, meritorious, qualified, worthy

**n:** appreciation, estimation, excellence, importance, integrity, merit, morality, nobleness, rectitude, sincerity, stability, usefulness

## WORTHLESS

**a:** contemptible, despicable, fustian, impotent, incompetent, ineffectual, insignificant, inutile, nugatory, paltry, profligate, stramineous, trifling, unproductive, valueless

**n:** *ambsace, bagatelle,* dross, nihility, recrement, trifle, worthlessness

## WOUND

**a:** traumatic, vulnerary

**n:** contusion, laceration, lesion, sore, trauma, traumatization, *vulnus*

**v:** lacerate, maim, mutilate, scarify, traumatize

## WRATH

**a:** Achillean, angry, wrathful

**n:** anger, animosity, condemnation, exasperation, indignation, ire, irritation, resentment

**v:** incur

## WRETCHED

**a:** abominable, abysmal, calamitous, contemptible, damnable, deplorable, despicable, detestable, disgusting, execrable, lamentable, miserable, odious, paltry, squalid, unfortunate

## WRINKLE

**a:** corrugated, rugate, rugose, shriveled, wizened

**n:** corrugation, crow's feet, rugosity

**v:** crease, fold, pucker, purse, ruck, rumple

## WRITING

**a:** belletristic, contributorial, epistolary, graphic, literate, scriptorial, scriptory, scripturient, textual

**n:** *belles lettres,* canon, communication, corpus, dissertation, literature, lucubration, *ouevre,* scrivening, thesis, treatise

**v:** elaborate, enlarge, expatiate, explain, indite, inscribe, rhapsodize, scrawl, scribble, transcribe, transpose

*abstruse:* esoterica, esoterics, hermetics

*ancient: cuneiform,* hieroglyphics

*bearing name of:* onomatous, onymous

*collection:* collectanea, corpus, *miscellanea, syntagma, variorum*

*conversational:* causerie, journalese

*cramp:* chirospasm

*false: anagignoskomena,* apocrypha, pseudepigraph, pseudograph

*handwritten:* holographic, onomastic

*man using woman's name:* pseudogyny

*modern:* neoteric

*not bearing name:* anonymous, pseudonymous

*obscene:* erotica, esoterica, pornography

*on both sides of paper:* opisthographic

*on multiple subjects:* polygraph

*on one side of paper:* anopisthographic

*on one subject:* monograph

*on walls:* graffiti, *graffito*

*ornate:* gongorism, mandarinism, rubescence

*picture:* curiologics, hieroglyphics

*pompous:* fustian, *gasconade,* grandiloquence, grandiosity, lexiphanticism, pomposity

*praising:* dithyramb

*woman using man's name:* pseudandry

*writer:* author, bohemian, communicator, contributor, correspondent, epigrammatist, essayist, *litterateur,* novelist, prosaist, *prosateur,* satirist, sillographer

*written above:* antescript, superscription

*written after:* postscript

*written as: ad lit, ad literam, sic*

## WRONG

**a:** errant, erring, erroneous, false, immoral, inappropriate, incorrect, in-equitable, iniquitous, straying, unjust, venal, villainous, wrongful

**n:** delict, delinquency, grievance, iniquity, malefaction, malfeasance, malversation, misdemeanor, misfeasance, mistake, tort, transgression, turpitude, venality, villainy, violation, wrongdoing

**v:** confute, instigate, provoke, rebut, refute

*avenger:* nemesis, retributor

*combining forms:* caco-, cata-, dis-, dys-, mal-, mis-, para-

*wrongdoer:* criminal, delinquent, knave, malefactor, miscreant, reprobate, transgressor, villain

## YAWN

**a:** cavernous, drowsy, gaping, oscitant, patulous, yawning

**n:** dehiscence, drowsiness, oscitance, oscitation

**v:** dehisce, oscitate

## YEAR

**a:** annual, annually, per annum

*of origin:* vintage

*relief:* jubilee, sabbatical

## YELLOW

**a:** flavescent, flavous, fulvid, fulvous, luteous, lutescent, sallow, xanthic, xanthous, yellowish

**n:** icterus, jaundice

*combining forms:* flav-, xantho-

## YIELDING

**a:** adaptable, amenable, capitulatory, compliant, deferential, ductile, fawning, malleable, obsequious, plastic, pliant, servile, submissive, susceptible, tractable

**n:** capitulation, cession, complaisance, compliance, deference, resignation, submission, succumbence, succumbency, surrender, waiver

**v:** accede, acquiesce, capitulate, cede, concede, defer to, gratify, indulge, kowtow, relent, relinquish, submit, succumb, surrender, waive, yield

## YOUNG

**a:** adolescent, callow, hebetic, immature, inexperienced, junior, juvenile, maidenly, nealogic, neanic, puerile, *puisne*, vernal, virginal, youthful

**n:** adolescent, cadet, fledging, juvenile, minor, *puisne*, stripling, suckling, *wunderkind*

**v:** juvenesce, rejuvenate

*bearing:* aborning, parturient

*bearing eggs:* oviparous, ovoviparous

*bearing live:* parturient, proligerous, viviparous

*combining forms:* juv-, -ling

*make young again:* reinvigorate, rejuvenate, rejuvenesce, renaissance

*man: ephebe,* ephebus, *younker*

*things for: juvenilia*

*woman:* debutante, ingenue, *soubrette*

*youth:* adolescence, juniority, juvenescence, minority, nonage, puberty

## ZEAL

**a:** animated, ardent, assiduous, devoted, diligent, eager, evangelistic, fanatic(al), fervent, fervid, impassioned, intense, perfervid, rabid, sedulous, vehement, vivacious, zealous, zestful

**n:** animation, ardor, assiduity, calenture, devotion, diligence, eagerness, enthusiasm, fanaticism, fervidity, fervor, fidelity, gusto, intensity, loyalty, passion, rabidity, sedulity, vehemence, verve, vigor, zealotry, zest, zestfulness

# Index by Category

The list of categories used to group the entry words is:

1. *Actions and events:* Anything done, especially a deed, a happening.

2. *Business:* Any domain, discipline, work-related object, or happening.

3. *Feelings and communication:* Any mental state, condition, or emotion, or the conveying of feelings or information.

4. *Ideas, ideals, and values:* Any plan, thought, or suggestion for a possible action or series of actions; the conception of an idea, action, or thing; the qualities, features, or values of anything.

5. *Measurements:* Any dimension or measure of something; the passing of or periods of time for events or actions.

6. *People and the social world:* Any person or action performed only by persons, especially social actions and events.

7. *Space, form, and placement:* Anything measurable or defined by its shape and the positioning or arrangement of something.

8. *Structures, materials, and parts:* Something formed of parts and the pieces or divisions that make up a whole and which can be separated from or connected with it

9. *The living world:* Anything within the plant and animal kingdom, other than humans.

10. *Transport, movement, and transfer:* Any physical transfer or movement of something, especially active or guided movement or transport.

This small, manageable hierarchy divides the "world" into ten pieces. These broad categories appear in alphabetical order, as do the entry words under them. The index organizes the entry words in a way that mirrors the way we "classify" and "connect" vocabulary in our brains. It allows users to enhance their prose from another perspective and to think more about the relationships between the words and expressions.

# Actions and Events

abbreviate
abet
abolish
abrade
absorb
abuse
accept
accident
accumulate
act
action
active
adapt
add
addict
adhere
adjust
admit
adorn
adroit
advance
adventure
agile
aid/aide
align
allot
alter
amaze
annihilate
annul
anticlimax
appear
appease
appetite
applause
apportion
arduous
arouse
arrange
array
arrest
asleep
assail
assemble
assign
assist
associate
athletics
attack
attempt
augment
austere
automatic

avoid
awakening
awkward
backslide
baffle
balance
balk
ballet
ban
banish
barbaric
bask
bath
battle
beat
bedeck
beg
behead
bellow
bend
besiege
bet
bilk
bind
bleach
blend
blink
block
bloom
blow
blunder
boisterous
bold
bounce
bow
boxing
brass
bravado
brawl
brazen
breach
break
brew
being
bruise
brutal
bud
build
bulge
bungling
burden
burial
burn

burst
busy
buzz
bypass
calamity
call
cancel
caper
caress
carnival
carouse
carry
cast
castrate
catastrophe
cater
caught
cause
celebrate
ceremony
change
charge
cheat
check
chew
chivalry
chorus
clash
climax
cloaked
coincide
collapse
collect
combat
commotion
compensate
compete
compliance
composed
concentrate
conclusion
concurrence
condense
conduct
conflict
conquer
consequence
constriction
construct
consume
contaminate
contend
contest

continue
contribute
control
convert
cook
copy
corroborative
corrupt
counteract
course
create
crime
culmination
curtail
cut
dally
damaging
dance
dawdle
deed
defeat
defense
defer
defile
defraud
dehumanize
delay
delegate
deliberate
demonstrate
deprive
derivative
desecration
design
destroy
develop
devitalize
devouring
dice
digress
disable
discharge
discipline
discontinue
discover
discretion
disfigure
disguise
disintegration
dismissal
display
dispossess
dispute

**383**

# Business

acquittal
acting
actor/actress
advertise
agriculture
aim
alliance
allow
amateur
ambition
appointment
art(s)
attorney
auction
authority
bankrupt
bargain
barter
brothel
business
college
commercial
conference
contract
council
court
cure
demote
depreciate
designate
diligent
economy
edit
election

embezzle
expert
fee
field
file
finances
guarantee
guide
handbook
handwriting
hired
hospital
hostelry
hotel
incorporation
index
industrial
inn
inspection
installment
instruction
invent
inventory
judge
jurisdiction
labor
league
leave
legal
liability
library
lien
list
magazine

manage
manual
mediate
medical
memorandum
merger
military
money
mortgage
network
newspaper
nonprofessional
obligation
office
official
petition
political
poster
prize
privation
program
promotion
proofread
prosperity
provision
publication
refund
repeal
report
restitution
resume
retired
revise
reward

roster
salary
sale
sanction
schedule
school
scientific
seal
sovereignty
sponsorship
stamp
state
subordinate
substitute
success
survey
system
test
theater
ticket
tip
trade
trial
unauthorized
unclassifiable
underworld
unofficial
unprofitable
unqualified
unsigned
venture
vote
wage
work

# Feelings and Communication

abash
aberration
abhorrence
abject
abreast
abrupt
accent
accord
accuse
accustom
acquainted
acrimony
acute
adage
address
admire
adverse
advice
advocate
affable
affected
affirm
affliction
affront
afraid
aggravate
aggressive
agitated
agony
agree
agreement
airy
alarm
alert
allegory
allusion
aloof
aloud
alphabet
amative
ambiguity
amends
amiable
amuse
analogous
analysis
anger
anguish
animate
annotation
announcement
annoy
answer

antagonism
anticipation
anxiety
apathy
apology
apparent
appeal
appetizing
apprehension
approval
ardent
argue
arrogance
artless
ascetic
ascribe
assent
assertive
assume
assure
astonish
atone
attention
attitude
attract
audacity
augur
avarice
aversion
avowed
aware
awe-inspiring
awful
babble
banter
base
bearings
behavior
belittle
belligerent
berate
beseech
betray
bewail
bewilder
bewitch
bitter
blame
blue
blunt
boast
bombast
book

booklet
boon
boor
bore
bracing
brag
browbeat
callous
candid
captivate
care
careful
careless
carp
caustic
caution
censor
censure
charm
chat
cheer
cherish
choice
claim
clarification
clue
coarse
coax
code
coerce
comedown
command
commend
communication
compassion
compatible
compel
complain
comprehend
compromise
compunction
concede
conceit
conceive
conciliate
concord
condemn
condescending
condole
confession
confidence
confidential
confirm

confuse
congratulate
conjecture
conjunction
conscious
consent
consideration
contempt
content
contradict
conversation
convincing
cooperation
courage
courtesy
courtly
coy
crabby
cranky
craving
crazed
credulous
criticize
cruel
cunning
curious
curse
curt
cynicism
dare
debase
debate
deceive
declamatory
declare
decree
defame
deference
defiant
define
degrade
deject
delight
delirious
delude
demand
denial
denounce
depress
derisive
description
desire
despair

# Ideas, Ideals, and Values

ability
abnormal
abominable
absolute
abstract
abstruse
absurd
academic
acclaim
accomplish
according
accurate
accursed
actual
adequate
advantage
afresh
akin
almighty
alternative
anchor
angel
anointing
applicable
appropriate
apt
arbitrary
artificial
as
ascendency
aspect
assorted
attribute
auspices
authentic
available
award
axiom
bad
banal
basic
beauty
belief
benefit
best
better
bias
bigoted
bilateral
bizarre
bland
bless
bliss

*bogus*
bookish
borderline
brave
bugbear
calm
capable
capacity
casual
category
certain
chance
charity
chastity
chief
circumstance(s)
civil
clamor
class
classical
clean
clear
clever
comedy
comfort
commemorate
common
compare
competent
complete
complex
complicated
concern
concrete
condition
conform
conservative
consistent
conspire
constitution
contemplate
contingency
contrary
controversy
convenience
conventional
correct
covetous
crafty
credit
creed
crisis
crucial

custom
damnation
danger
dark
daydream
dazzling
debt
decent
decide
dedicate
deduce
defect
definite
degenerate
deify
delicious
deliverance
demagogue
democratic
demon
depend
deplorable
deprave
deranged
deserved
detail
detect
determine
detrimental
deviating
devil
devious
devise
devotion
devout
diagnose
diametrically
difference
difficult
dignity
dire
discernment
disharmonious
dishonor
disloyal
disobedience
disown
disproof
disreputable
distance
distinct
distinguish
diverse

divination
divine
doctrine
dogmatic
dominant
doom
doubt
downfall
downright
dream
duty
earthy
ease
eccentric
education
elaborate
elegance
elusive
eminent
endowment
enlightenment
enrich
equivocal
erratic
essence
esteem
ethereal
ethical
evil
example
excellence
exceptional
exclusive
exonerate
expedient
exploit
extraordinary
fact
fad
fair
faith
false
fame
familiarity
fantasy
far-fetched
fascinating
fate
fault
feature
figment
fine
fit

# Measurements

afternoon
age
all
almost
always
amount
ample
ancient
anew
annual
appreciable
approximation
around
auxiliary
before
begin
big
bond
brevity
brief
brisk
bulk
bygone
calculate
calendar
century
cheap
chill
chronic
chronological
cold
color
compact
concise
constant
contemporary
cool
corresponding
cost
countless
couple
current
cycle
daily
dawn
day
decline
decrease
deep
deficient
degree
depth
destitute

dim
diminishment
discoloration
disparate
dissimilar
double
drab
dry
dull
duration
dusky
dwarf
early
effusive
eight
eighty
empty
enlarge
enormous
enough
entire
equal
eternal
even
evening
ever
exact
excess
expense
extent
extra
extravagance
extreme
fast
fat
few
fifteen
fifth
fifty
figure
filled
final
first
five
flabby
fleeting
forever
forty
four
fraction
freezing
frequency
full

further
future
giant
grade
gratuity
green
group
half
heavy
height
high
hot
huge
hundred
identical
immeasurable
immediate
immense
imperishable
inclusive
incomplete
increase
infinite
inky
instant
intense
intermediate
iridescent
irregular
large
lasting
late
lean
length
lessen
little
lofty
long
lots
loud
low
lukewarm
majority
manifold
many
massive
mathematics
mature
meager
measure
mellow
midday
middle

mid-morning
mild
miniature
moderate
modern
moment
month
morning
neutral
new
night
nine
noon
nothing
null
number
obese
occasional
old
once
opaque
outweigh
overflowing
pair
pale
par
partial
past
peak
pending
penniless
period
permanent
perpetual
phase
piecemeal
pile
plenty
plump
poor
potent
precise
present
primitive
profit
profuse
prompt
proportion
purple
quantity
quick
range
rate

# People and the Social World

abandon
ado
adultery
adult/adulthood
adversary
agent
alcohol
alien
allure
anal
anatomy
ancestor
anemia
apostle
archery
aristocrat
Aristotle
arm
artery
attendant
audience
author
autobiography
baby
bachelor
background
backer
bald
banquet
baptism
bastard
beard
bearing
benefactor
betroth
biography
boil
boy
brother
buffoon
bully
bureaucrat
busybody
buyer
calf
cancer
candidate
cannibal
caretaker
carriage
caste
cemetery
*chaperon(e)*

chapter
character
cheek
chief
chest
child
childbirth
childhood
chin
Chinese
citizen
clergy
clerk
clown
club
colony
coma
commentator
community
companion
comrade
convent
convulsion
corn
corpse
countenance
coward
cradle
craftsman
cremation
crowd
crusader
cry
culture
custodian
dabbler
dandruff
dandy
daughter
deaf
debility
deportment
deputy
descendant
despot
dictator
dinner
disciple
disease
dish
dizzy
doctor
doer

domestic
dough
drifter
drunk
Easter
effeminate
effigy
Egypt
elder
elite
elope
enemy
engage
England
escort
facial
family
fan
father
fellow
fickle
fiend
finger
flavor
flesh
foe
fool
forefather
forehead
freckle
French
friend
funeral
gang
girl
glutton
gourmet
grave
Greece
grimace
guardian
guest
gypsies
hair
hair-raising
hand
handsome
haunt
headache
health
heir
henchman
herald

heretic
hermit
hero
hiccup
hoarse
home
homeland
host
human
humpback
husband
idol
ill
impostor
inborn
incurable
India
individual
infancy
infection
inheritance
insane
intestine
intoxicated
island
jack-of-all-trades
Jew
junior
juvenile
kindred
king
kingdom
knight
lady
layman
leader
lineage
linguist
loafer
lout
mad
magnate
maid
marriage
meal
member
menstruation
mentor
mercenary
mistress
mob
monk
mother

# Space, Form and Placement

about
above
absence
acme
adjacent
adjunct
after
ahead
alike
alone
alongside
altitude
altogether
among
and
angle(s)
another
area
back
backward
bare
behind
below
beneath
between
border
bound
boundless
capital
celestial
center
circle
clinging
close
cluster
cohere
coil
come between
connection
consecutive
contour
country
crooked
cross
crouching
curve
desolate
detached
direct
disconnected

disjoint
disorder
disorganized
displaced
distended
downward
drooping
east
embedded
erect
everywhere
external
far
firm
fissure
flat
follow
forefront
foreign
forerunner
fork
former
fringed
front
gap
grooved
hard
hole
hollow
hooded
hook
horizontal
image
impassable
initial
inner
interconnecting
interior
internal
introduction
inward
jagged
joined
jumble
jutting
last
leaning
left
level
local

loop
loose
lopsided
maimed
marginal
masked
mixed
mutual
naked
near
neat
next
northern
*oblique*
obscure
occupancy
outdoor
outline
outside
oval
overlapping
parallel
pattern
peripheral
pith
place
posterior
posture
preliminary
previous
prior
profile
projecting
random
reclining
remote
rigid
ring
rough
round
rundown
scabby
scale
separate
sequence
serial
set
setting
shade
shape

sickle
side
slope
solid
solitary
sort
southern
space
spiked
spiral
step
stiff
stooped
straight
suburb
succession
summit
supple
surroundings
tapering
territory
tidy
tie
together
top
triangle
tufted
type
unattached
unbalance
uncleanliness
under
underground
underlying
unearthly
uneven
unified
untidy
upright
upside-down
upward
vacant
vertical
wavy
wedge-shaped
western
winding
within
without

# Structures, Materials and Parts

abode
abundance
accessory
acid
air
aperture
apex
apparatus
appetizer
arch
architecture
arms
armor
arrow
ash
aspirin
atomic
attire
baggage
ball
banner
bark
barrel
bed
bell
belong
beverage
bit
black
blemish
blotch
blush
boat
bracelet
brandy
bread
bright
brink
bristles
brittle
broken
brown
bubbling
butter
camp
cane
caravan
card
catalog(ue)
chain
chair
chamber
channel

chink
church
city
clay
cleft
cloister
clothing
coating
cocktail
coffee
coffin
coin
*commodious*
*compendium*
conspicuous
copper
*counterfeit*
cozy
crack
cramped
crescent
crest
crinkled
crown
crude
crumbly
curio
dainty
debris
decay
decorate
deflated
delicate
deposit
deterioration
device
diagram
diamond
dictionary
dilapidated
diluted
dining hall
dirty
domain
door
dot
dregs
dress
drop
drug
drum
duct
dust

dwelling
dye
element
emblem
encampment
entity
entrance
estate
evidence
exit
fancy
fashion
fence
filmy
filth
flag
fleecy
flimsy
florid
flour
fog
forged
form
formula
foundation
fragile
fragment
framework
frill
froth
furniture
garbage
garment
gear
gem
gift
gilded
glass
glue
gold
greasy
grimy
heap
heritage
hodge-podge
house
impediment
impure
indestructible
inflated
inflexible
ingredient
instability

instrument
intricate
invincible
iron
jewel
kernel
kitchen
knot
lapel
layer
lead
line
liquid
load
lodging
look
lotion
lump
luxury
machine
makeshift
marble
material
matter
maze
mechanical
medley
memorial
mess
mirror
miscellaneous
muddy
narcotic
needle
oily
ornament
outfit
outlet
page
pamphlet
part
pearly
perishable
piano
pit
plastic
platform
pleat
portion
pouch
powdery
preface
prison

# The Living World

abdomen
alive
animal
ant(s)
ape
apple
arid
asexual
astronomy
atmosphere
bacteria
balmy
barren
bat
beak
bean
bear
beast
being
belly
biological
bird
birth
bisexual
blood
blind
body
bog
bone
born
bowels
brain
bran
branch
breast
breath
breed
butterfly
buttocks
cat
cave
cell
claw
climate
cloud
coast
coexist
contagious
cow
creeping
crop
crow
dead

dew
digestion
dog
down
drink
dung
dying
eagle
ear
earth
earthquake
eddy
egg
elephant
emaciated
embodiment
energy
entrails
environment
evolution
excrement
exhalation
existence
eye
farming
fatal
feast
feather
feces
feet
female
fertile
fish
flame
flock
flower
foliage
food
foot
forest
fox
frailty
frog
frost
fruit
furrow
garden
generation
goat
goose
grain
grape
grass

grove
hare
hawk
head
hearing
heart
heat
hedge
herbs
hill
hog
honey
hoof
horn
horse
hunger
inexistence
infertile
innate
jaw
juicy
knee
knoll
lake
land
leather
leaf
leg
leopard
lice
life
lifeless
light
lightning
limb
lion
lip
listening
live
lung
male
malnutrition
manure
marsh
membrane
menu
milk
mind
mineral
mist
moisture
molt
molten

monkey
monster
moon
mound
mountain
mouth
muscle
nail
native
natural
navel
nest
nose
nourishment
nut
nutrition
ocean
offshoot
offspring
optical illusion
orbit
organic
organ
origin
ostrich
owl
parasite
pea
peacock
pigeon
plant
poison
pollution
pond
predatory
preying
prickly
pulp
pus
rabbit
rain
rainbow
raven
reed
region
reptile
rhinoceros
rice
rind
river
rock
ruminant
rural

# Transport, Movement and Transfer

access
accompaniment
arising
clog
clot
clumsy
collision
combine
conceal
confine
contact
convergence
cover
crawling
desert
destiny
dig
dislocation
dispose
disunite
diverge
elevate
emerge
emigration
encircle
enclose
enter
envelop
exile
expedition
expurgate
extract
flee
flexible
flickering
flight
float
flood
flowing
fluctuate

flutter
fly
fold
friction
fuse
gather
grab
gush
immovable
insert
integrative
interchange
interlock
intersect
jerky
journey
juggling
jump
leap
limber
limp
link
migration
motion
move
navigation
nimble
open
penetrate
pliant
plug
prostration
pulsate
raise
ramble
rapid
rearrange
rebound
recede
receive

recoil
regress
relapse
remove
replace
retrace
retraction
retreat
rid
rise
road
roaming
rolling
root
rotate
roving
running
rush
scatter
scout
seclude
sedentary
segregate
seize
settle
sever
shaking
share
shed
shift
ship
shrink
sitting
skim
sponging
spray
spread
stagger
steady
still

straying
swagger
swell
swimming
swing
take
theft
thrash
throb
thrust
touch
tour
transient
transmission
transplant
transposition
travel
tremble
trespass
trip
turn
twinkling
twirl
unbend
uncover
unload
unshakable
unstable
uproot
vanishing
vibrate
visit
walk
wander
waver
whirl
withdraw
wither
wrinkle
yielding

# About the Reviser

Dr. Barbara Ann Kipfer is the author of 1990's bestselling *14,000 things to be happy about* (Workman) which has 660,000 copies in print and has been translated into Danish, Norwegian, Swedish, Finnish, Korean, and Japanese. She also compiled *Roger's 21st Century Thesaurus, 21st Century Spelling Dictionary, 21st Century Manual of Style,* and *21st Century Synonym and Antonym Finder* (Dell/Laurel). Dr. Kipfer recently compiled *Bartlett's Book of Business Quotations* and *Bartlett's Book of Love Quotations,* both published by Little, Brown, and Company in 1994.

Dr. Kipfer works full-time for Knowledge Adventure, Inc., a software company of La Crescenta, California, developing and writing "interactive" multimedia reference books for exploring information on-line.

Previously, she spent many years designing and assembling lexicographic references and conducting linguistic research for such companies as Reference Software, General Electric Research, Bellcore, IBM, and Wang. Her other clients have included Dorling Kindersley, Simon & Schuster/Paramount, Fitzhenry & Whiteside, Macmillan, Random House, Grolier, BellSouth Publishing, and Ameritech Publishing.

She holds a Ph.D. and M.Phil. in Linguistics from the University of Exeter. Her doctoral thesis, "Towards the Onomasiological Dictionary: The Use of the Computer in Providing Diversified Access" was an investigation of preparing dictionary material so that users may go from "meaning to word" rather than the traditional "word to meaning."